The European Rescue of the Nation-State

Review of the first edition:

'There is some irony in the fact that the country which has contributed least to European integration should have produced the historian who has illuminated it most. No other scholar within the Union approaches the combination of archival mastery and intellectual passion that Milward has brought to the question of its origins.'

Perry Anderson, *London Review of Books*

For the second edition of this classic economic and political account of the origins of the European Community Alan Milward has completely revised and updated the chapter on the United Kingdom. On one level the book is an original analysis of the forces which brought the EC together, on another it is an explanation based on historical analysis of the future relationship between nation-state and the European Union. Combining political with economic analysis, and based on extensive primary research in several countries, it offers a challenging interpretation of the history of the western European state and European integration.

Alan S. Milward is Professor of Contemporary History at the European University Institute, Florence, Official Historian, and Emeritus Professor of Economic History at the London School of Economics.

WITHDRAWN

The research for this book was carried out with the help of the Leverhulme Trust (Grant A/88/226, S/87/2646; F.4 AB) and the Economic and Social Research Council (Grant E 0023 2270).

The European Rescue of the Nation-State

Second edition

Alan S. Milward
with the assistance of
George Brennan and Federico Romero

London and New York

First published in Great Britain 1992 by Routledge
First published in paperback 1994

Second edition published 2000
by Routledge
11 New Fetter Lane, London EC4P 4EE

Simultaneously published in the USA and Canada
by Routledge
29 West 35th Street, New York, NY 10001

Routledge is an imprint of the Taylor & Francis Group

Typeset in 10/12 Times by Florence Production Ltd, Stoodleigh, Devon
Printed in Great Britain by T.J. International Ltd, Padstow, Cornwall

British Library Cataloguing in Publication Data
Milward, Alan S.
　European Rescue of the Nation-State
　I. Title
　341.24

Library of Congress Cataloguing in Publication Data
Millward, Alan S.
The European rescue of the nation-state / Alan S. Milward. – 2nd ed.
　　p.　　cm.
　Includes bibliographical references and index.
　1. European Economic Community　2. European Economic Community–
　Economic policy.　3. European Economic Community–Great Britain.
　4. Great Britain–Economic policy–1945–1964.　　　I. Title.
HC241.2.M487　1999
337.1′42–dc21　　　　　　　　　　　　　　　　　　　　99-44300

ISBN 0–415–21628–1 (hbk)
ISBN 0–415–21629–X (pbk)

Contents

List of tables

LIST OF FIGURES

Preface to the first edition

Now that this book is finished I can not perfectly understand the frenzy that kept on driving me back to it. Some explanation though is surely required of why the world should be assaulted by so many tables and footnotes.

One reason was exasperation at the shallowness of the debate in Britain about the European Community. The Community's supporters argue as though there were no history whose influence could not be set aside with no more cost than an effort of will. Its opponents confront this ahistorical stance with separate and irreconcilable histories of the nation and the Community. My first objective in writing was to put this debate in historical context by showing the development of the European Community for what it really is, one more stage in the long evolution of the European state. It would be wonderful if this could put an end to the hollow clanging of clichés hurled around the media by politicians and journalists.

A second reason was simply to tell people how the European Community came about. If anyone looks for a book in English which does this, they will not find one. There are innumerable accounts of how the Community is organized and what it does, but none of them really explains why. I have gone into some detail here in the hope that people do need a history book in English which explains how and why the Community happened.

I think there was a third motive, exasperation with British historiography. Most British historians write the history of Britain as if it were that of a wholly different society from other European countries. There are practically no studies of British history and politics after 1945 which take account of any other society except the United States, and that only because America became so dominant over British foreign policy. It is as though the United Kingdom's post-war development were as remote from that of France or Germany as from that of Thailand. There were so many common tendencies within western European countries after 1945 that the first approach to their history should surely be to write it as a whole. The whole includes the United Kingdom.

There may have been a fourth motive. If politicians and journalists miscomprehend the European Community, maybe this is the fault of the type of history which is written. Virtually every book that exists about the history of the European Community is to all intents and purposes a history of diplomacy. Small wonder that most commentators assume that the Community came into existence primarily for foreign policy reasons. There are many works that explain the process of European integration as a device to bind West Germany to the western political bloc, and there they stop. As an explanation it is hopelessly incomplete. To write about twentieth-century states as though they could adjust their foreign policies on such purely pragmatic grounds is to explain the process of European integration as a choice of tactics in a board game and no more. The European Community has self-evidently had other functions, as well as embodying other aspirations and ideas. This purely diplomatic approach to the history of the Community fits well with the erroneous elitist historiographical tradition that it is states and institutions which mould events. The reader of chapter seven will easily observe the consequences of that intellectual tradition in action in British diplomacy, with disastrous results. The true origins of the European Community are economic and social. There were other diplomatic arrangements by which an effort could have been made to bind West Germany to western Europe. The only ones with any chance of success were those which found the point of intersection with the successful pursuit of the national economic and social advantage of all parties.

It is the post-war economic and social forces which have shaped the European state which therefore need to be analysed if the origins and purpose of the Community are to be explained and questions about the past, present and future of European integration are to be answered. This does not reduce the great importance of the Community to the resolution of the problem of European security; it puts it in a truer perspective. Security for Europeans since 1945 has always been much more than military security. To explain what the forces were which brought the Community into existence I have analysed in detail three issues where national policy became Europeanized. These are: employment and welfare; foreign trade and its relationship to economic growth; the protection and development of agriculture and the maintenance of agricultural incomes. These detailed studies are set inside general essays about the nature of integration, the character of the post-war state, and the nature of security in the post-war world. Lastly, I have added a detailed exploratory essay on the relationship between the United Kingdom and the European Community in formation.

I was encouraged in my frenzy by the munificence of the Leverhulme Trust which funded the research for four years. The work is based on research in archives in eight different countries as well as on those of the European Community itself. Such an effort would have been unthinkable without the Trust's help, as would the effort in collecting and refining statistical data. I am most genuinely grateful for its confidence and generosity. I am grateful too to the Economic and Social Research Council which gave additional support. The Research Council of the European

xii   *The European Rescue of the Nation-State*

University Institute also helped by financing a small part of the work as a joint research project with one of their own teams. At the end, Norges Allmennvitenskapelige Forskningsråd gave me the opportunity to work on the manuscript while delivering a course of lectures in Oslo and seminars elsewhere in Norway on the history of the Community. The period coincided with the EFTA/EC negotiations, with Sweden's decision to apply for membership of the Community, and with the reawakening of memories of the earlier Norwegian referendum on membership. Nowhere else could there have been so cogent a reminder of the continuing power of national myth, of genuinely democratic national sentiment, and of the seriousness of the issues involved.

Two people worked with me almost throughout, making large contributions to the book. George Brennan, who worked so hard in the course of duty to discover acceptable statistical information and to make it more acceptable, went far beyond the call of duty in relentlessly turning my allusive thought and language into something clearer. I have argued long, hard and enjoyably with him at every stage and never failed to profit from it. Important parts of the book are as much his as mine. Federico Romero was my constant guide to the intricacies of the government of the United States, and its archives. The development of our ideas had been a joint one before we began the book and his contribution while it was in progress continued to be substantial.

Others – friends, colleagues and students – will recognize their help in different parts of the work. Especially I would like to thank for generous scholarly help at particular moments, Gösta Esping-Andersen, Patrick Fridenson, Carl Glatt, Richard Griffiths, Patrick Lefèvre, Frances Lynch, Thierry Mommens, Régine Perron, Anne-Sophie Perriaux (who does not even need to open the book to recognize one of her contributions), Pierre Pflimlin, Helge Pharo, Sidney Pollard, Ruggero Ranieri and Henry Stanhope.

The preparation of the seemingly innumerable drafts of the manuscript was an awful task. At one point it seemed to occupy three whole rooms of complete disorder. It would never have been beaten back between boards without the organizing abilities at first of Beatrijs de Hartogh and later of Tricia Hammond. The reader can thank them both that there is only one volume; I thank them for being so much more efficient than myself.

I have always thought that to dedicate books to others was hypocritical. It is for oneself that they are written and no activity is more selfish than writing. There is no shortening the time it takes to set so much down on paper and in that time love, friendship and duty are all postponed. One of the sufferers has asked me so often to dedicate this to her and has proved so courageous a companion, that I nevertheless bow to her wishes, hoping that she will eventually forgive both the hypocrisy and the sound of her father humming tunelessly for years over a piece of paper.

March 1992

Preface to the second edition

This thick and heavy work still being bought and used in 1999, the publishers asked me to prepare a new edition. I have done that by almost completely rewriting the chapter on the United Kingdom, chapter seven. From the start of that chapter to the end of the book the pagination and the numeration of the tables are all changed, as is the order of the text.

More importantly, the nature and conclusions of the argument are substantially different from earlier editions. Since the book was first written historians of Britain have written vigorously about the history of its relationship to the emerging European Communities and I have myself been busy with a government-commissioned history of the same subject. While, following their august tradition, British diplomatic historians have not, as far as I can tell, read a word of the earlier edition, historians in many other countries as well as political scientists, some in Britain, have taken the story beyond what I first wrote and raised many interesting questions about it. It is time for an up-to-date, more specific and more pertinent discussion of the issues that have been raised. Mainly, these are issues about post-war national strategies – diplomatic, security and economic – of the British state. Following my aim in the first edition of this book, I have tried to set those strategies in the wider, non-British context. Was there a European rescue of the British nation-state? If not, would it have been better had there been one? I am only too aware that this raises further questions, still to be more clearly answered, but that is the nature of a historian's trade and so long has the political debate over Britain's relationship to the European Union now lasted that I am sure nobody expects the answers to be simple.

It would obviously be preferable if future references to this book, where they concern the United Kingdom, should be to this new edition.

Florence, July 1999

List of abbreviations

BDL	Bank Deutscher Länder
BIS	Bank for International Settlements
CAP	Common Agricultural Policy of the European Community
CEA	Confédération Européenne de l'Agriculture
CGA	Confédération Générale d'Agriculture
CIA	Central Intelligence Agency of the United States of America
Cobéchar	Comptoir Belge des Charbons
Coldiretti	Confederazione Nazionale dei Coltivatori Diretti
DC	Democrazia Cristiana
DDF	*Documents Diplomatiques Français*
ECA	Economic Cooperation Agency
ECSC	European Coal, Iron and Steel Community
EDC	European Defence Community
EEC	European Economic Community
EPC	European Political Community
EPU	European Payments Union
FAO	United Nations: Food and Agriculture Organization
Fédéchar	Fédération Charbonnière Belge
FNSEA	Fédération Nationale des Syndicats d'Exploitants Agricoles
FRUS	*Documents on the Foreign Relations of the United States of America*
GATT	General Agreement on Trade and Tariffs
GDP	Gross Domestic Product
GNP	Gross National Product
IFAP	International Federation of Agricultural Producers
IMF	International Monetary Fund
MRP	Mouvement Républicain Populaire
MSA	Mutual Security Agency
NAC	National Advisory Council on International Monetary and Financial Problems
NFU	National Farmers Union of Great Britain
OECD	Organization for European Cooperation and Development
OEEC	Organization for European Economic Cooperation

ONIC	Office National Interprofessionel des Céréales
SFIO	Section Française de l'Internationale Ouvrière
SIBEV	Société Interprofessionelle du Bétail et des Viandes
SITC	Standard International Trade Classification
UN	United Nations
USDA	United States Department of Agriculture

Key to archival references

ACS	Archivio Centrale dello Stato, Rome
AN	Archives Nationales, Paris
AR	Algemeen Rijksarchief, The Hague
BA	Bundesarchiv, Koblenz
BOE, OV	Archives of the Bank of England, Overseas Division
ECSC	Historical Archives of the European Coal, Iron and Steel Community (Florence)
EL	Eisenhower Memorial Library (Abilene, Kansas)
FJM	Fondation Jean Monnet pour l'Europe (Lausanne)
FRC, ECA	Federal Records Center, Papers of the Economic Cooperation Agency and its Successor Agencies (Suitland, Maryland)
MAE	Ministère des Affaires Etrangères (Paris)
MAECE	Ministère des Affaires Etrangères et du Commerce Extérieur (Brussels)
MBZ	Ministerie van Buitenlandse Zaken (The Hague)
NA	National Archives of the United States (Washington DC)
NAC	Papers of the National Advisory Council on International Monetary and Financial Problems (Washington DC)
PRO BOT	Public Record Office, Kew. Archives of the Board of Trade
PRO CAB	Public Record Office, Kew. Cabinet Papers
PRO FO	Public Record Office, Kew. Archives of the Foreign Office
PRO MAF	Public Record Office, Kew. Archives of the Ministry of Agriculture and Fisheries
PRO PREM	Public Record Office, Kew. Prime Minister's Papers
PRO T	Public Record Office, Kew. Archives of the Treasury
SD	Archives of the United States Department of State (Washington DC)
US T	Archives of the US Treasury Department

1 History and theory

Our lives in western Europe* for almost two hundred years have been moulded by the nation-state. It is now commonly said and written that this organization has had its day. Indeed, for forty years some western European states, including those with the most celebrated historical traditions, have openly discussed the possibility of eventual political unification. This has not been merely the indulgence in abstract political debate and utopian speculation about European unity which at the level of political elites goes back more nearly four hundred than forty years. It has been accompanied by real changes in political structures, whose proclaimed purpose has been to bring that unity nearer. It is not merely that a long-running abstract political debate has been recently democratized, like so many other physical and intellectual pleasures. Changes have occurred since 1945 which give citizens of European countries real cause to ask whether national government, which has so long shaped the basic organizational framework within which they live, will continue to do so.

Since the agreement on the Treaty of Paris in 1950 when six western European governments, in agreeing to create the European Coal, Iron and Steel Community (ECSC), declared their intention ultimately to achieve some form of political union, there has grown an actual, rather than merely an abstract, political alternative to government from the national centre. The same six nations reaffirmed that intention in the Treaty of Rome in 1957. The number of adherents to that treaty has since grown to twelve. Several others now wish to adhere. The institution of the Common Agricultural Policy (CAP) of the European Economic Community in the 1960s, the election of the European Parliament, the Single European Act in February 1986, and the Treaty of European Union (Treaty of Maastricht) in 1992, pointing the way to monetary and then political union, have re-emphasized the existence of that alternative. From the moment of its creation, the political machinery of the successive European Communities

---

* 'Western Europe' has been used throughout to mean the member-states of OEEC; 'western Europe' the geographical concept.

has consistently maintained the ideological position that it is an embryonic supranational European government. Since becoming president of the European Commission M. Jacques Delors has publicly maintained that one consequence of the Single European Act will be that four-fifths of those decisions presently taken in national capitals will eventually be taken in Brussels.

That these nation-states, some of them of the most ancient lineage, with their distinctive histories and cherished myths, on which have been nurtured generations of citizens, should declare their intention of voluntarily achieving political unification is a political and historical change of the first magnitude. Yet it remains one of the most ill-understood aspects of recent history and present political life. For this lack of understanding much blame must lie with the absorption into popular discussion of an assumption which underlies most of the theoretical and scholarly writing about the European Community, the assumption that it is in antithesis to the nation-state.

The word which is commonly used to describe the evolution of the European Community, 'integration', is itself a reflection of that assumption. It implies that the economies, societies and administrations of these national entities become gradually merged into a larger identity. Defenders of the nation-state, those for whom it remains an indispensable form of organization, politically, economically, culturally or even psychologically, therefore clamour for a halt to the process of integration. The most ardent supporters of the European Community in return denounce the nation-state as an anachronistic barrier to the final achievement of a more advanced stage of government and society, the supranation. This antithesis between the concepts of nation-state and Community has frequently been emphasized by the European Community's interpretation of its own history. Homage has always been required to the idea that the Community represented the birth of a new historical epoch, in which the nation-state would wither away. Lord Cockfield, rumoured to have been originally appointed as a European Commissioner by the British government because of his alleged scepticism about the Community, summed up his views after his replacement by saying 'The gradual limitation of national sovereignty is part of a slow and painful forward march of humanity.'[1] Against such an argument only a similarly categorical statement is likely to serve. Thus opponents of the European Community demand that a finite limit be drawn now to the process of integration in order to save the nation.

But is there in fact an antithesis between the European Community and the nation-state? Does the evolution of the Community imply the replacement of the nation-state as an organizational framework and its eventual supersession? It is the argument of this book that there is no such antithesis and that the evolution of the European Community since 1945 has been an

---

[1] *The Guardian*, 11 November 1988.

integral part of the reassertion of the nation-state as an organizational concept. The argument goes, however, beyond this, because the historical evidence points to the further conclusion that without the process of integration the west European nation-state might well not have retained the allegiance and support of its citizens in the way that it has. The European Community has been its buttress, an indispensable part of the nation-state's post-war construction. Without it, the nation-state could not have offered to its citizens the same measure of security and prosperity which it has provided and which has justified its survival. After 1945 the European nation-state rescued itself from collapse, created a new political consensus as the basis of its legitimacy, and through changes in its response to its citizens which meant a sweeping extension of its functions and ambitions reasserted itself as the fundamental unit of political organiz-ation. The European Community only evolved as an aspect of that national reassertion and without it the reassertion might well have proved imposs-ible. To supersede the nation-state would be to destroy the Community. To put a finite limit to the process of integration would be to weaken the nation-state, to limit its scope and to curb its power.

The state became the dominant form of political, economic and social organization in western Europe from the sixteenth century, when the territorial limits of centres of political power became more sharply defined by rulers and their armies and courts. Its political dominance was rein-forced by its apotheosis into the representative of the nation and the people in the French Revolution, and by the subsequent identification of the nineteenth-century state with linguistic, ethnic and cultural nationa-lism. People, language and culture, nationalist movements argued, had a right to a separate organizational unity overriding the rationales of political expediency and local power which had first defined the frontiers of states. The concept of a central parliamentary representation of the people, the 'national assembly' as it has continued to be called in France, meant that the development of parliamentary democracy sanctified the nation-state as the legitimate basis of political organization, until in the Treaty of Versailles ethnic and linguistic unities were seen as the indispensable foundation of political stability on the European continent.

Nevertheless, while greatly strengthening the political claim of the nation-state to be the dominant form of organization, these nineteenth-century tendencies did not substantially add to the extent of its functions, its powers, and its obligation to its citizens. The rights and powers of the state apparatus to raise and control armed forces, to raise taxes, to mint money, and to enforce a national law remained not only the core but also the greater part of its organizational activity. It is only in the late nine-teenth century, and then only on a small scale, that any important addi-tions to these functions can be discerned. Together with the popularization and educational dissemination of a mixture of national history and myth designed to increase the sense of ethnic and cultural collectiveness, these limited functions and obligations still enabled the nation-state to exercise remarkable claims on the loyalties of its citizens. Under its banners men were to die in terrifyingly large numbers, many for causes that in retrospect appear far from just.

From this relatively simple mechanism of national governance, to which allegiance was obtained through a mixture of power, myth and the protection of property, can be seen emerging from the end of the nineteenth century a different conception of the nation-state as a more complex network of mutual political obligations of rulers and ruled. The world wars accelerated this tendency. In both, the nation-state was required to undertake feats of organization on a scale far greater than anything it had previously attempted. At the same time it was forced to call on the allegiance of its citizens to a degree which it had not previously attempted. To inflict on such huge numbers the experience of relentless war fought with murderous modern technology was not possible without an extension of the state's obligations to them, nor without the changes in the political system which that implied. Through these changes came other demands forcing the state to take a wider interest even in peace in the human condition. Few European nation-states found themselves able in the interwar period successfully to make the transition to a new form of governance securely founded on this larger pattern of obligations.

Between 1938 and the end of 1940 most of them proved incapable of fulfilling even their oldest and primary duty, the defence of the national territory and the protection of their citizens. Of the twenty-six European nation-states in 1938, by the close of 1940 three had been annexed, ten occupied by hostile powers, one occupied against its wishes by friendly powers, and four partially occupied and divided by hostile powers. Two others had been reduced to a satellite status which would eventually result in their occupation. The only one which had extended its power and triumphantly dominated the continent offered as little hope to mankind as any political organization which had existed.

The rescue of the nation-state from this collapse, which appeared to mark the end of its long domination of European history, is the most salient aspect of Europe's post-war history. The development of the European Community, the process of European integration, was, so runs the argument of this book, a part of that post-war rescue of the European nation-state, because the new political consensus on which this rescue was built required the process of integration, the surrender of limited areas of national sovereignty to the supranation. The history of that surrender is but a small part of the post-war history of the nation-state, though it may eventually seem to have been the most significant. What is described in the detailed studies in this book is the reassertion of the nation as illuminated by the history of the construction of the European Community. Ultimately this will have to take its part in the greater history of the post-war nation-state, a history whose beginnings are only now appearing. It seems essential, though, that this greater history should not start from the widespread theoretical assumption of an antithesis between nation and Community, for were it to do so it would be myth.

The assumption that there is a fundamental antithesis between the nation-state and the Community was set in circulation by academic discourse. It has lain at the heart of virtually all attempts to construct comprehensive theoretical explanations of the evolution of the European Community, as well as of the early attempts to write its history. Much of the theory which has sought to explain the process of European integration is in fact constructed on a historical foundation, deriving from conclusions about long-run historical trends which historians, perhaps by the default of silence, have allowed to become established.

Sometimes it is derived from very long-run historical trends indeed. It is not uncommon to find the argument in works about European integration that all of Europe is a common culture, formed at first by the influences of classical Greece and the Roman empire and reshaped by the common experience of christianity, so that national differentiation was never more than a temporary aberration imposed by the localization of secular power. It is not however with any such conservative conceit, whose usual purpose has been to uphold the political domination of governing elites, defined by an ability to master dead languages and to misinterpret past cultures, that the argument of this book deals, but with a much larger body of political analysis which relates the process of European integration to more recent historical trends.

One part of this analysis, which underlies much of the writing about European integration, links the whole process of modern economic development since the eighteenth century to a gradual weakening of the nation-state. It relies on the observation that national economies, as they develop economically, become more interdependent, so that the nation-state consequently loses much of its capacity for independent policy formulation and for control over its own destiny. Some argue that the same process actually renders the nation-state meaningless as an organizational entity, so that it will have to be replaced by some more effective form of political organization. Among the trends cited are the following: the dependence of modern economies on an ever-greater quantity of imports and exports of goods, capital, ideas and people; the immediate and severe impact of national economic policy decisions in large economies on smaller ones; the evolution of modern technology in transport, communications and warfare; the growing difficulty of controlling even the national physical environment. All these are used to illustrate and predict the growing inappropriateness of national frontiers as boundaries of organizational activity.

There has been a strong tendency to assume that the explanation for the process of European integration is to be found in these long-run economic trends. Because it is only in western Europe that the process of modern economic development has brought to a high level of per capita income a cluster of territorially small, contiguous nation-states, it is there that the nation-state first and most has had to come to terms with the problems of interdependence and there consequently that the increasing incapacity of national government should be first and best observed. Sometimes this assumption is taken even further and integration is explained as the end of an unavoidable linear continuum originating with the process of modern economic development. As the steam locomotive in the 1840s made the borders of a state such as Saxe-Coburg-Gotha meaningless, because it could travel through the whole territory in half an hour, so have successive stages of technological advance, it is argued, rendered the frontiers of larger states similarly pointless. A fast-flying aircraft traverses Belgium in less than the time it took the train one hundred and fifty years ago to traverse Saxe-Coburg-Gotha. A spy satellite traverses Belgium in even less time. Furthermore, even highly developed states, it is correctly pointed out, no longer have the resources to master technologies which might be regarded as fundamental to their survival as separate national entities. The production of nuclear armaments and effective methods of delivering them, for example, might take so disproportionate a share of national resources as to have to be renounced as national policy even by a country with a very high relative level of GNP per capita. Certain areas of industrial production of the kind which European nations have previously thought it in their own interests to foster in order to remain in the forefront of technological advance, the manufacture of large long-distance passenger jet aircraft for example, or equipment for exploring space, appear now to require technological cooperation between all but the largest economies before they can be achieved at a politically acceptable cost. Recently it has become the fashion to argue that reducing pollution and averting an ecological catastrophe is far beyond the financial, as well as organizational, capacities of national government.

The impact of technological innovation both on manufacturing and transport in the nineteenth century was the immediate cause of an increase in international trade in commodities which shows no signs of slowing. Exchanges of goods across frontiers have reached such proportions that the satisfaction of the consumption needs of national citizens depends on imports, which in turn depends on the facility with which the nation itself can sell goods and services abroad. The development of international commerce in manufactures on such a scale was only possible because of an increase in international flows of capital and the international provision of financial services. As manufacturing has been replaced in highly developed economies by the service sector as the main contributor to the growth of national income so, it is often argued, does the dependence of the national unit on the rest of the world in this most modern stage of development become even greater, because it has always been much more difficult for the state to regulate the movement of capital and services across its frontiers than that of commodities. Whereas the control and taxation of commodities on national frontiers is almost as old as the state itself and a universal attribute of it, the control of capital crossing national frontiers has proved an altogether more difficult task, rarely and only briefly done with any effectiveness. As the structure of large firms has become increasingly international, and as some of them achieve an annual turnover almost as great as the annual revenues and expenditures of smaller states, the organization of their markets and the disposition of their investments and profits escape the control of the nation under whose flag they are legally constituted and whose government seeks to levy revenue from them.

By the 1950s, the period with which this book is mainly concerned, more than 40 per cent of the national income of the Netherlands was earned outside the national frontier. The Netherlands does indeed emerge in this book as a good example of the constraints imposed on the liberty of national policy choice by the process of modern economic development. So, too, does Belgium, more than a third of whose national income in the same period also came from outside the country. The decision of both countries to enter a customs union, at first with each other under the terms of the wartime Benelux agreements and later the common market of the European Economic Community, although a great many other causes were more important, did reflect a background recognition that their sustained economic development required a larger market for their goods and services than that offered by the narrow confines of their national territories.

But observations of this kind are far too general to serve as explanations of the specific phenomenon which distinguishes the European Community, the voluntary surrender by the nation-state of specific areas of national sovereignty to the Community's own political structures. It is this surrender of national sovereignty which is the new and specific phenomenon with which the book deals and there is nothing in the observation of the general trend towards greater interdependence associated with the process of modern economic development to explain why the reaction of the state to it should be to make this surrender, unless it is assumed that interdependence does lead in a linear continuum to the supersession of the nation-state by more appropriate forms of political organization, and that the 1950s were the historical moment when the continuum had arrived at that point.

The tendency to argue that there is indeed such a continuum is greatly strengthened by the persistent hold of economic theory as a basic intellectual map for understanding the universe. It is an underlying principle of classical economic analysis that factors of production tend to flow to where their combination will produce the highest return. Although much economic theory has dealt with the impact of barriers, particularly national barriers, on this inherent tendency of factors to move, these barriers are seen as obstacles to perfect efficiency. The ideal of the perfect market within which the factors of production are free to be combined according to the respective comparative and competitive advantages of different areas and different products so as to produce the maximum increase of income remains the standard of logical reference. In this intellectual map the state is an imperfection. The tendency of economic reasoning is to advance the belief that the search for profit, the driving force behind the maximization of incomes and thus behind the process of economic development, will erode the state and its frontiers, and that this erosion will result in an increase in income and welfare. Customs unions and common markets are usually conceived, theoretically, as steps in that direction.

This progressivist simplification is ahistorical. The nineteenth and twentieth centuries are replete with histories of customs unions which did not survive. Where now is the Austro-Hungarian customs union? The great economic benefits which it brought to its constituent parts could not overcome the nationalist forces of political disintegration within it. Were we to rely solely on the history of previous customs unions we would be as likely to conclude that the Single European Act would lead to a disintegrative outburst of nationalist separatism as to a European government. A reasonable conclusion from the history of customs unions would surely be that only specific historical circumstances can explain why they have on occasions proved more durable.

That the process of economic development leads through interdependence progressively to integration is also far too simple a conclusion. Interdependence can be rejected by an act of national political will. So it was, even by a west European state whose economy was intimately dependent on the functioning of the international economic system. The case of Germany under the national-socialist regime would seem an irrefutable proof of this, that of Russia in 1917 another. The ultimate costs of such a rejection may have been very high, but it involved countries so important to the world capitalist economy and lasted so long as to make the assumption that interdependence leads relentlessly in a linear continuum into integration shallow and implausible. It is not even clear that interdependence has grown in consonance with the development of capitalist economies, even if we discount the case of Nazi Germany as a unique aberration.

In the early nineteenth century national government exercised little influence over the process of modern economic development. From the mid-nineteenth century that situation began to change. The adjustment of national tariffs to economic rather than merely revenue purposes, the interference of foreign policy objectives with the international flow of capital, national economic development policies in the more backward countries, all began to lead the state to attempt to impose barriers to interdependence. National economic policies, however, remained sporadic, haphazard and often ineffective. Nineteenth-century government did not have the financial resources, nor in many cases a sufficiently powerful executive, for its policy choices to be more than inconsistent interventions. Although the intention of the state apparatus was often to lessen the extent of interdependence, its capacity to do so may well have been too limited for it to succeed. One prime interest of the restricted social groups in whose interest the state was run was that the state should maintain the external value of the national currency. This pressure, together with the similarities between the few national economic policies in the major developed trading economies, meant that exchange rates between national currencies over the last two decades before the First World War stayed remarkably stable. This greatly facilitated international trade and capital movements and seems to have led to an increase in interdependence even as public belligerence between heavily armed nations grew. Some measurements of the extent of interdependence suggest that it was in fact greater between 1890 and 1914 than in the 1950s.

The difficulty, though, is how to measure it. The attempts which have been made do not carry historical conviction. The basis of most of them seems to be the idea that 'if the average level of prices of a set of products or factors of production converges between two countries, or if fluctuations in these prices move more closely in line, then the level of economic integration between these countries has increased at least over the set of markets looked at'.[2] Although a similar analysis has sometimes been used by historians to measure the degree of market integration within the nation, it is a more complicated and dubious technique to extend such a procedure to a set of economies, because of the different currencies and the many influences which determine the exchange rates between them. The assumption that the greater the convergence of prices and wages the more the separate economies are progressing towards interdependence appears a great exaggeration in the international context. By assuming that in a system of relatively free competition prices of similar goods will tend to fluctuate together, it distinguishes between the degree of competition in markets, but does little more. For what it is worth as an observation, a lower level of correlation is observed in the movement of retail and wholesale prices, wage rates and interest rates in major capitalist economies between 1950 and 1958 than under the gold standard before 1914. The level of correlation increases in the 1960s but in the 1970s falls once more.[3]

Once this type of measurement of correlations proceeds beyond prices, making normative use of all the technical definitions with which it must begin, and enters the realm of international comparison of wages and interest rates, the historian, faced with a mass of acquired knowledge of the specific government policies which affected all those entities, must regard such a procedure as an unacceptable simplification. In fact the

[2] D. Tollison and T.D. Willett, 'International Integration and the Interdependence of Economic Variables', in *International Organization*, vol. 27, 1973.

[3] R. Rosecrance *et al.*, 'Whither Interdependence?', *International Organization*, vol. 31, 1977.

attempt to make such measurements can only show that the barriers which the nation-state seeks to erect against excessive interdependence have increased as nation-states have embarked on a much greater range of domestic policies. Governments throughout the period 1945–68 manipulated interest rates, exchange rates, taxes and wages for their own domestic political purposes far more extensively than in earlier periods and it is obvious that these quantities did not move only in relation to the volume of international transactions and the facility with which they could be made. Have the differentials between national interest rates shrunk now that the capital markets of the advanced economies are much freer than in the 1950s? No, they have become wider as national governments have clung to distinctive national policy choices.

Interdependence is not, therefore, a phenomenon which has progressively and inexorably developed in twentieth-century western Europe. States, far from being its helpless prisoner, have actively sought to limit its consequences. Their will and capacity to do so grew together after 1945. The process of integration on the other hand was a particular reality in the 1950s when interdependence was probably a less noticeable phenomenon than earlier.

Most of the theoretical explanations of integration – the specific process of the surrender of national sovereignty – while they usually assume it to have been favourably encouraged by a persistently increasing trend towards interdependence, see it also as a response to particular historical circumstances in western Europe after 1945. When Deutsch, for example, offered a theoretical foundation for the growth of 'community' as an international phenomenon, the specific historical circumstances of postwar western Europe played a large part in it. His definition of 'community' depended on the sudden emergence of an American strategic interest in western Europe leading to military alliances with west European countries. It depended also on the active cooperation of the United States and Western Europe within new post-war international organizations. And it depended on the greater cultural familiarities between western societies which these new historical phenomena generated.[4] When Haas and Lindberg offered functionalist explanations of the process of integration those too depended on specific historical events in western Europe in the 1950s.[5] Starting from the theoretical position that the nation-state is ultimately shaped as an organization by the functions which it exists to fulfil, each argued that the fulfilment of these functions in the 1950s and 1960s increasingly required action in an international context. Specifically, they concentrated their attentions on the regulation of the markets for coal, iron and steel by the European Coal, Iron and Steel Community and on the

[4] K. Deutsch *et al.*, *Political Community and the North Atlantic Area* (Princeton, 1957).
[5] E. Haas, *The Uniting of Europe. Political, Social and Economic Forces, 1950–1957* (Stanford, 1958). L.N. Lindberg, *The Political Dynamics of European Economic Integration* (Stanford, 1963).

regulation of movements of intra-west-European commodity trade and labour by the European Economic Community. The border disputes relating to access to resources of coal and iron, and the long and unsuccessful struggle of private firms themselves to carry out a functional regulation of the markets in these resources, led, both argued, to their functional regulation by the first supranational authority, the High Authority of the ECSC. Theoretically, the implication was that there was a linear continuum from the functional origins of the state to the point where the continued pursuit of its functions would necessarily lead to integration.

While reinforcing the theoretical argument that the process of integration was explained by the growing incapacity of the state to carry out its functional tasks within its own borders and that the European Community was the vanguard of a more advanced stage of political organization, Haas gave somewhat more weight to accidental historical occurrence in explaining the origins of the ECSC. He did not see the High Authority in any way as an inevitable and necessary development in 1952, as the first historical moment when the functional incapacity of the state became so apparent that it had to be acknowledged. He saw it as an artificial political creation intended to give an idealistic supranational gloss to a traditional diplomatic agreement regulating traditional issues of high-level diplomacy between the countries concerned. The moment of its creation, the birth of the supranation, was therefore entirely the product of the interplay of historical events in which chance played its usual part. But once created, the High Authority, he argued, behaved in the way which the functional nature of the state required in regulating lower-level issues and became the advance guard of supranational functional governance. The problems which it was called upon to resolve were typical of those which states themselves increasingly, he and Lindberg suggested, had to resolve, issues more suitable to regulation by neutral technical expertise, as opposed to the grand issues of foreign policy and national security which had constituted the main activity of states in earlier periods. In the common pursuit of the resolution of these lower-level problems within a functional, non-political framework, irrespective of the purpose for which that framework had originally been created, the functional state first made the transition to the functional supranation.

As general observations about the period after 1945 the starting-points of the theoretical expositions of Deutsch on the one hand and Haas and Lindberg on the other are not without some validity, and the work of Haas displayed sufficient knowledge of and sensitivity to historical detail to serve as a substitute for the history books which had not then been written. There was indeed, as Deutsch propounded, a much more intricate and more frequent set of contacts between western nations at all levels, strategic, economic, cultural, touristic, and sporting than before 1939. This did reflect closer common political sympathies. And it was also true, as Haas and Lindberg argued, that the range of functions carried out by states did extend. There is no evidence, however, that there was any inevitability about this; these were trends which arose from a set of political choices.

The historical evidence linking these general trends to the specific choice of surrender of national sovereignty was left unexplored. As soon as historians set to work it became evident that the theoretical explanations of the rise of the European Community offered by Deutsch, Lindberg and Haas, although they relied on the historical particularities of the post-war period, simplified history unacceptably. Furthermore, they all did so in the same way, by greatly exaggerating the incapacity of the state. From the beginnings of detailed historical research into the origins of the European Community it became clear that nation-states had played the dominant role in its formation and retained firm control of their new creation. This in itself showed why these theories of integration proved after 1960 to have such poor predictive value. It would be fair to say that such comprehensive theories of integration are more frequently now regarded by political scientists as having been an academic dead-end. In their implication, that governance by the nation-state was a thing of the past and governance by the supranation the image of the future, such theories did however set the assumptions and the tone of political discourse about European integration and provide it with the erroneous assumptions on which so much of it now relies.

These theories of integration had two characteristics in common. Firstly, they depended on a deep belief in the rationality of mankind, or at least the more educated part of it. Increases in contacts were held to develop affinities; institutions and forms of international organization were of central importance because they could have an educative influence. People of rational goodwill and neutral expertise could be mutually involved, given the correct institutions, Deutsch, Lindberg and Haas all supposed, in a learning process which would elevate them from national citizens to international problem-solvers. For Haas, it was the creation of the institution, more than the nature of the problem with which it was supposed to deal, which was all-important. Provided there was a sound inter-governmental bargain whose premises remained unchallenged, the institutional framework which it created would, he argued, incrementally increase its powers through the spillover process that comes from cooperation in the rational solution of functional problems.

Secondly, like much of the theory of interdependence, the theory of integration supposed that integration is in some way a higher state of political organization to which humankind is carried on the ultimately irresistible tide of historical progress. It was the failure of this tide to flow in the 1960s as strongly as during the 1950s which, before the onset of historical criticism based on research, first brought disillusionment with the theory of integration and initiated the search for an explanation of European integration which relied less on such progressivist assumptions. These assumptions themselves seem to have been simply transposed on to

European history from the conventional and comforting liberal interpretation of America's own history, to which most American scholars felt it
necessary to conform during the Cold War. American political science
served American foreign policy, which throughout the period covered by
this book pursued unswervingly the goal of the integration of western
Europe and saw a future United States of Europe as a heavenly city
profiled on the horizon toward which it travelled. Far from being critical of
these simplicities of the American foreign policy establishment, American
political science reinforced them by clothing them in the garb of academic
theory and taking the United States as a model for the evolution of
Europe.

Deutsch was entirely correct to argue that there was so great an increase
in the frequency of personal and cultural contacts between western societies after 1945 as to denote a new historical phenomenon. However, by far
the greatest increase in the number of contacts between them was caused
by the remarkable increase in tourism. Even if not all persons registered as
tourists actually were such, this was the phenomenon which really constituted the new historical trend. Difficult though it is to reconstitute and give
precision to the data, the figures suggest that in the immense growth of
international tourist movements from 25 million in 1950 to 285 million in
1980, more than half were always within western Europe.[6] About 45 per
cent of world tourist movements across frontiers still in fact take place
within western Europe. Most of the tourists to western European countries
between 1945 and 1970 were from other western European countries. It is
by no means evident that this remarkable and new phenomenon produced
the emerging sense of 'community' on which Deutsch depended for an
explanation of the process of integration.

The greatest increase in numbers of visitors from other western
European countries throughout this period was recorded by Spain. What is
to be said about the impact on European integration, either in the sending
or receiving country, of those many millions stretched out on its sandy
beaches? The process of European integration scarcely concerned Spain in
those years, and the great increase in those who visited it has not, although
this may be an error, usually been described as representative of Europe's
finer cultural affinities. Their contribution to the development of common
cultural attitudes, like that of the great increase in the number of spectators
of sporting events, seems to have been mainly to an increase in popular
comparative international knowledge of riot police procedures, sentencing
traditions and prison conditions. Deutsch laid much emphasis on the
increase in cultural contacts, as they were officially defined in the 1950s;
academic conferences, research visits, tours by symphony orchestras and
so on. But this very argument reveals the development of a national
definition of culture after 1945 which was largely lacking earlier. It was

[6] World Tourism Organization, *Yearbooks of International Travel Statistics*, various issues.

precisely in those years that European states officially developed the concept of a distinctive national culture and for the first time spent public money on promoting and exporting this fabrication. The increase in cultural contacts was a symptom of the growing self-confidence of the nation-state, rather than one of the processes which was weakening it.

It would surely be wrong to say that there has been within western Europe no increase in familiarity with neighbouring societies. This greater familiarity has become a factor in national political life. Comparisons are frequently drawn with things done better elsewhere in western Europe, and this is a new development. But it is not the phenomenon on which Deutsch relies to explain integration. In fact there is no reason why either increasing contacts or increasing familiarity should explain integration in any way.

It is obvious that problems which do require functional regulation at an international level have been more numerous since 1945 than in earlier periods; the problems of noxious wastes, the control of air traffic, and so on. It is plausible to argue that these are indeed better regulated at the level of mutual technical functional expertise than by politicians. But firstly it must be asked whether these problems have required any fundamentally different form of international organization than did the successful regulation of international postal or railway traffic in the mid-nineteenth century. Secondly, it must be asked how many such problems, given the way that national government is structured, are genuinely capable of being resolved at this merely functional level without serious conflicts of interest in which national politicians will take sides. Thirdly, it must be asked whether there is any correspondence between the history of attempts at functional regulation of problems of this kind and the actual history of European integration since 1945.

The number of issues which could be regulated between states at the merely functional level after 1945 seems on the evidence of present historical research to have been very small. Most, no matter how apparently unthreatening, were elevated into matters of political principle and high-level diplomatic dispute. The regulation of air traffic would be a good example. It was at once raised to the level of a major issue of foreign policy and national security. Lindberg and Haas concentrated on the regulation of the European coal, iron and steel markets, but it is evident from recent research into the origins of the ECSC that it was not conceived by national diplomats as the transfer of a functional problem to the supranational level. It was the assertion by the states that on such an important question of national security merely functional regulation would have to cede place to the resolution of war and peace.[7] This would presumably be fully accepted by Haas, but the evidence in chapter three of this volume about

---

[7] A.S. Milward, *The Reconstruction of Western Europe, 1945–1952* (London, 1984). K. Schwabe (ed.), *Die Anfänge des Schuman Plans 1950/51* (Baden-Baden, 1988).

the functioning of the ECSC indicates that the High Authority did not subsequently operate as a neutral functional regulator as he claimed. It remained a forum where policies based entirely on the pursuit of national advantage were supported by its supposedly neutral members. Where issues could successfully be regulated internationally at the merely functional level after 1945 this was probably, as in the nineteenth century, because they were so unimportant. Integration, in the case of the ECSC, took place precisely because the issues involved could not be reduced to the merely functional level.

The assumption that the nation-state was withering away because it was becoming incapable was by no means confined to theorists of interdependence or integration. Federalists, and other politicians in western Europe who supported the political unification of the continent, often shared this assumption. For them, history had to show the evolution of the European Community as part of the progress of mankind to a higher state. They wished to interpret it as a profound shift in political consciousness, for a mere diplomatic arrangement would not have had the inherent political momentum to grow into the government of Europe. Many of them for this reason were deeply displeased by the functionalist explanation for the process of integration. It seemed to preclude the need for the transition to parliamentary democracy at the supranational level, which alone could acknowledge this new stage of political consciousness. This was the standpoint of the first scholar to attempt serious historical research into the process of integration and the origins of the Community, Walter Lipgens, whose work set the agenda for future research for some time after its publication.

His studies were aimed at showing why, how, and when this change in popular political consciousness had taken place. With a mass of historical detail Lipgens argued that the experience of resistance to national socialism in Germany and to German occupation elsewhere forced European political thought towards political constructions which superseded the nation-state. The concept of European unity, he argued, developed strongly in opposition to the Nazi 'world-outlook'. The realization of the extent of the weakness of the European nation-state in comparison with the two post-war superpowers then strengthened, he argued, the small separate movements in favour of European unity and fused them into a single movement by 1947. From that fusion a powerfully influential political force was born, leading to the beginnings of European political unity within four years.[8] The conclusions to which he

---

[8] W. Lipgens, *Europa-Föderationspläne der Widerstandsbewegungen, 1940–45*, (Munich, 1968); W. Lipgens (ed.), *Documents on the History of European Integration*, vol. 2, *Plans for European Union in Great Britain and in Exile, 1939–1945*, European University Institute Series B1.2 (Berlin, 1986); W. Lipgens, *A History of European Integration, 1945–1947*, vol. 1, *The Formation of the European Unity Movement* (Oxford, 1982); W. Lipgens and W. Loth (eds), *Documents on the History of European Integration*, vol. 3, *The Struggle for European Union by Political Parties and Pressure Groups in Western European Countries, 1945–1950*, European University Institute Series B1.3 (Berlin, 1988).

came thus tended to confirm the assumptions which underlay integration theory.

In spite of the accumulation of detailed knowledge of the many movements advocating European unity and the sheer weight of documentation which he adduced, Lipgens's work has serious defects. The extensive collections of statements in favour of European unity by wartime and post-war figures published in the volumes of documentary evidence are usually taken out of the immediate context of the speech or article in which they appeared as well as out of the context of the author's life and ideas. Anybody who mentioned any form of European unity as being desirable, albeit that it might have been the only occasion in a long and active life mostly devoted to different and sometimes opposed causes, was sure to be cited for the paragraph in which his thoughts strayed for whatever temporary motive in that direction. As a historical method this resembled beach-combing and the sheer volume of the findings was presumably supposed to prove that it could only have been washed up by a high historical tide. The detailed narrative history of the movements for European unity up to the year 1948, the main body of Lipgens's work, is no more convincing in its method. That almost all the 1,100 political figures who appear in the index of Lipgens's history of those ill-matched movements were of little importance or influence in the political life of their own countries, that they had the most seriously divisive disagreements, and that the European Unity Movement which they eventually formed in 1947 appears to have had practically no influence on the negotiations for the Treaty of Paris three years later, are facts which never appear for one moment to have troubled the author.

No one would reasonably dispute Lipgens's argument that, because there were universal implications in the ideas of national socialism and fascism, resistance to them could not be merely a reassertion of the past, but had to hold out the prospect of a universally better future. Nor would many dispute that among the numerous proposals for a better future after the defeat of national socialism and fascism the idea of a peacefully united Europe did make an appearance. But was it more prominent than the idea of resurrecting the conquered nations and restoring them to their former individuality? Surely the feelings most engendered by resistance were patriotism and even nationalism. And was it not the stimulation of these feelings which helped in the reassertion of the nation-state as the organizational foundation of European political life in the post-war reconstruction? Can we see, for example, the first French medium-term national plan, the Plan for Modernization and Equipment, which stands as the very symbol of post-war national resurrection in Europe and which led to a series of further plans for national development, as embodying any of these aspirations for a less nationalistic world after 1945?

Yet the architect of that plan, Jean Monnet, is also revered by European federalists as 'the father of Europe', and Robert Schuman, the architect of the Treaty of Paris, was a firm supporter of the Plan.[9] That was a paradox which Lipgens and those who followed and popularized his interpretation ignored, perhaps because it was too disconcerting. Some of the most revered figures in the early history of the European Community and of European federalism were also, like Monnet, central figures in the post-war reassertion of the nation-state. In the case of Jean Monnet this seeming paradox tended to be explained by some kind of conversion in 1947 or 1948 to the greater and nobler cause. With others this was less plausible. Early historical accounts of the Community divided politicians into those who still in the 1940s inhabited the benighted world of European nationalism and those around whom the great light had shone, the prophets of the new order.

It was only with the elapse of the thirty years during which government archives in most western European countries and the United States must remain secret that this view was seriously challenged. Historians working on the diplomatic records in the conventional mode of diplomatic history began to present European integration as an aspect of national diplomacy. Far from appearing as the response to powerful and inevitable economic changes, or to a large-scale popular conversion to belief in a united Europe, it appeared as a diplomatic manoeuvre. The first serious studies of French post-war diplomacy made it obvious that integration was an attempt to restore France as a major national force by creating an integrated area in western Europe which France would dominate politically and economically. The German Federal Republic began to be depicted as a country which espoused the cause of European integration precisely in order to establish itself as the future German nation-state. There was no room here for popular influence on diplomacy. The extreme political insignificance of the influence of the European federalist movement on the negotiations for the Treaty of Paris was curtly noted. Lipgens's massive study had been, after all, only the chronicle of fringe political groups. And as for the influence of popular will of a more direct kind, the implication of these diplomatic studies was that diplomats had done well to keep European integration away from it, for popular opinion if allowed to intrude too early might well have stopped the whole construction by a barrier of national sentiment. From long theoretical wrangles about the future of the nation-state, opinion passed within five years after 1984 to the acceptance of this narrow historical pragmatism. The formation of the European Community is now described even by political scientists as a set of specific historical events, highly interesting in themselves, but from whose study no long-run trends or predictions about the future of government or of countries could be safely deduced.[10]

---

[9] R. Poidevin, *Robert Schuman; Homme d'état* (Paris, 1986), *passim*.

[10] The latest summary of theoretical opinion about the development of the Community, W. Wallace, (ed.), *The Dynamics of European Integration* (London, 1990) plainly exposes this

This is how the matter now stands. History has conquered theory, but it has done so in an entirely negative way. No historian has tried to construct from the heap of historical fact which has been accumulated over the last seven years any alternative theoretical explanation for the formation and growth of the European Community and the persistence of European integration as idea and actuality. If all the long-run interpretations of the future of nations previously offered by economics and political science have to be judged with great scepticism once they are compared to the long run of real historical change, if there is no acceptable theoretical explanation of the specific case of European integration, historians can hardly leave the matter there. It is surely up to them to construct something in place of what they have eliminated.

Any new theoretical explanation of integration will have to start from a new set of basic assumptions in conformity with the facts which historical research has brought to light. Integration was not the supersession of the nation-state by another form of governance as the nation-state became incapable, but was the creation of the European nation-states themselves for their own purposes, an act of national will. This is not surprising, because in the long run of history there has surely never been a period when national government in Europe has exercised more effective power and more extensive control over its citizens than that since the Second World War, nor one in which its ambitions expanded so rapidly. Its laws, officials, policemen, spies, statisticians, revenue collectors, and social workers have penetrated into a far wider range of human activities than they were earlier able or encouraged to do. If the states' executive power is less arbitrarily exercised than in earlier periods, which some would also dispute, it is still exercised remorselessly, frequently, in finer detail and in more directions than it was. This must be reconciled in theory and in history with the surrender of national sovereignty.

The tentative beginnings of such a reconciliation can be found in the works of theorists who resisted the extreme positions taken up by exponents of integration theory. Gilpin, for example, argues strongly that while interdependence is an increasingly important reality, the state retains most of its capacity for national choice.[11] Keohane and Hoffmann, while accepting the political importance of integration, insist that 'The European Community political system rests on national political systems, especially that of the Federal Republic.'[12] Keohane and Nye take this further and suggest that there is a theoretical possibility that the choice of integration

retreat, for some of its contributors, once among the more ambitious theorists of integration, convey an air of baffled acceptance of the damage done by historians to their earlier efforts.

[11] R. Gilpin, *The Political Economy of International Relations* (Princeton, 1987).

[12] R.O. Keohane and S. Hoffmann, 'Conclusions: Community Politics and Institutional Change', in W. Wallace, *The Dynamics . . .*, op. cit., p. 279. S. Hoffman, 'Reflections on the Nation State in Western Europe Today', *Journal of Common Market Studies*, vol. xxxi, no. 1, 1982.

might be a choice to erect finite barriers to the process of interdependence. Accepting that the number of transactions at all levels between nations does increase with modern economic development, they argue for a distinction between such transactions to the mutual advantage or the mutual indifference of the transacting parties, which leads merely to an increase in international cooperation or interconnectedness, and the different case where the parties (or one party) accept that the transaction has costs. In this second case the transacting states (or state) in maximizing their (or its) national advantage must sacrifice some element of preferred policy. Transactions between states of equal power are of course rare. In unequal transactions the weaker party to any transaction is, Keohane and Nye suggest, 'vulnerable' to interdependence, whereas the greater partner is merely 'sensitive' to it. It is conceivable, they suggest, that a small power's vulnerability to interdependence might actually be reduced by extending the range and complexity of the transactions in which it engages, and conceivable also that the formalization of such transactions in international treaties and agreements would further reduce its vulnerability. Thus the serious costs of interdependence to a weaker state could be theoretically reduced by the formalization of rules of interdependence, of which one specific example could be the process of European integration.[13]

That the state by an act of national will might pursue integration as one way of formalizing, regulating and perhaps limiting the consequences of interdependence, without forfeiting the national allegiance on which its continued existence depends, appears to be confirmed by what we know of public opinion about the Community in the member-states. The conversion away from a primary national allegiance, for which European federalists hoped, has not taken place. National allegiance remains undiminished, but national citizens have developed a strong secondary allegiance during the Community's existence. In almost every member-state a majority of them believes that the extent to which national policy now has to coexist with other policies arising from membership of the Community, and the degree to which national law and power are moderated also by European Community membership, are desirable. The majority would not wish to see a withdrawal from the Community and the nation left standing on its own.[14] In general, the interests of citizens appear to be conjointly satisfied by both forms of governance. A theoretical explanation of integration would also need to show how this double allegiance has become so strong without weakening the primary allegiance.

These are only pointers towards an alternative theoretical framework, falling far short of the comprehensiveness of the work of Haas or Lindberg, and themselves open to serious question. The theory that integration is a

---

[13] R.O. Keohane and J.S. Nye, *Power and Interdependence; World Politics in Transition* (Boston, 1977), pp. 12 ff.

[14] M. Hewstone, *Understanding Attitudes to the European Community: A Socio-Psychological Study in Four Member States* (Cambridge, 1986).

policy choice designed to limit the costs of interdependence, while it is plausible for a small state, does not look so plausible for larger powers. Larger economies are likely, for example, to have a smaller share of their trade in any given market or in any particular commodity, and accordingly to be less in need of reducing the costs of a switch of direction by formalizing interdependence through the process of integration. Would the costs of a change of policy ever be so high for them as to warrant a sacrifice of national sovereignty? Historical exemplification is needed, and that is usually where political science falls down. Much of the theorizing about interdependence and integration tends to be a piquant but watery soup through which the historian hunts in vain for solid scraps of nutriment. The purpose of the substantial meal, hopefully not too indigestible, of historical fact which forms the core of this volume is to arrive at a better theoretical perception of the process of European integration. The task is to reconcile two dominant aspects of European history in the last half-century, on the one hand the reassertion of the nation-state as the fundamental organizational unit of political, economic and social existence, on the other hand the surrender of some of its powers to the European Community.

2 The post-war nation-state

Nothing in the history of western Europe resembles its experience between 1945 and 1968. By the end of this period the perpetual possibility of serious economic hardship which had earlier always hovered over the lives of three-quarters of the population now menaced only about one-fifth of it. Although absolute poverty still existed in even the richest countries, the material standard of living for most people improved uninterruptedly and often very rapidly for twenty-three years. Above all else, that marks the uniqueness of the experience.

The improvement is usually measured in a generalized way by calculating the increase in national income per capita. If we compare the period of 1948–68 with that of 1922–37 the rate of increase of GDP for most western European countries was more than twice that of the earlier period. The exceptions are on the one hand Norway and Sweden, because the rate of GDP growth was already high in the 1930s, and on the other hand Denmark and the United Kingdom, where the increase in the later period was not so dramatically greater. Even in these countries however the post-war period was uniquely prosperous. Since 1973 the rate of increase of GDP has fallen again to its earlier levels, except in Norway where it has maintained its historical trend. Taking Western Europe as a unit, therefore, the period is statistically distinct as an episode in income growth.

Despite unprecedented levels of peacetime taxation, the growth of per capita national income was closely correlated with the growth of personal disposable income. Even in the United Kingdom, which recorded only low rates of national income growth relative to other Western European countries, personal disposable income measured in 1975 prices grew at an annual average of 2.5 per cent over the period 1950–68, declining in only one year, 1951. The uniqueness of the period could be measured in a less abstract way by measuring the much higher rate of acquisition of cars, televisions, refrigerators, washing-machines, furniture, clothing and housing than in other periods. It was also the period when the increases in public expenditure on welfare, education and health were the greatest. The security and comfort for which Europeans had so ardently longed in 1945 was amply provided, not least because within western Europe itself the period was one of uninterrupted peace. More education, more comfort, more leisure, and more income altered the range of personal ambitions, increased the chances of their fulfilment, and led the western European population by the 1960s beyond the search for security. It was only when the gains in income began to be eroded after 1973 by lower rates of national income growth and the redistributive impact of higher inflation that this statistically and politically unique period ended.

As soon as any attempt is made to answer the question why growth rates were so exceptionally high, other unique characteristics of the period appear. It was a period of much less unemployment than the twenty years before or after, and this was an important reason for the great gains in income that were made. The unemployment rate in most countries was between a quarter and a third, sometimes even less, than its level of the 1930s. The sole exception is Italy, and there the figure for the 1930s means little because of the laws forbidding people to leave rural areas and agricultural employment. In the 1970s it began again to move up to its unhappy levels of the inter-war period and in several countries it has now exceeded them. It was a period of economic stability in which cyclical fluctuations were so limited in their impact that some economists claimed that they had been eliminated by economic policy and that a new and more humane form of regulated capitalism had emerged.[1] So much for human vanity; the cyclical movements since 1973 have been more marked than, and their social consequences every bit as serious as, those between 1890 and 1914, a period when some writers also thought a more regulated form of capitalism was emerging. The post-war period was also one of exceptionally high gains in productivity per worker. The rate of growth of GDP per hour worked was typically twice as high over the period 1950–73 as in 1913–50 or 1973–87.[2] It was, lastly, a period in which foreign trade grew explosively and the international trade and payments system functioned remarkably easily. Exchange rates between currencies were kept stable, fixed indeed for long periods, whereas the preceding and succeeding twenty-five years were characterized by wild gyrations in currency values on international markets.

Attempts to explain the uniqueness of this period usually lay heavy stress on the behaviour of the state as a crucial, often the single most important explanatory factor. 'The acceleration of growth in the West after the war cannot be ascribed solely to a catching-up process', writes van der Wee in his survey of the period. 'There was clearly more to it than that. The mixed economy itself, run on Keynesian economic principles, generated dynamic

---

[1] 'This is not to deny that the control over the business cycle, which owes so much to Keynes's work, has been one of the decisive factors in establishing the dynamic and prosperous capitalism of the post-war era. Indeed, it is probably the single most important factor in this change.' A. Shonfield, *Modern Capitalism. The Changing Balance of Public and Private Power* (London, 1965), p. 64.

[2] A. Maddison, *Dynamic Forces in Capitalist Development. A Long-Run Comparative View* (Oxford, 1991), p. 51, table 3.3.

growth.'[3] Writing in the middle of the experience Shonfield believed that successful institutional management of the economy, although by no means the sole reason for the high growth rates of income, was a major explanatory factor.[4] Maddison, looking back on it from 1991 agreed, specifying three areas where government policy was crucial to enhancing economic performance. These were, 'the successful reapplication of liberal policies in international transactions', the 'promotion of buoyant domestic demand' and policies 'that kept inflation relatively modest in conditions of very high demand'.[5] The most comprehensive survey of the problem is that of Abramovitz.[6] The idea that the actions of the state were themselves a potent cause of national income growth because of the desire of developed nations to compete with the Soviet Union (or America), and of under-developed nations to 'catch up', underlies his statistical analysis. The cumulative political will of the national entity determines state action to facilitate investment, to implant more advanced technologies, or to trans-fer labour from less productive sectors of the economy.

Yet in spite of this general acceptance that the state was and is important in explaining variations in the rate of growth of national income, both economists and historians have had difficulty in explaining the precise way in which changes in the state were connected to the unique characteristics of the period 1945–68. Growth accounting can show that in that period the ratio of capital investment to national product was uniformly higher than in the inter-war period and that this was a major cause of the extra growth achieved. The historian is disinclined to regard that as an explanation. He is inclined to want to know why investment was higher, seeing the answer to that further question as illuminating a cause of growth, and seeing the demonstration that investment ratios were exceptionally high as no more than an observation. It is at that point that the state often wanders into the explanation from outside in order to provide an answer. The desire to 'catch up', state aid to investment, state investment itself in a much larger public sector; all appear as possible answers. Likewise, when the same theoretical approach demonstrates that the much more rapid increase in the value and volume of foreign trade over the period 1945–68 may have resulted in great gains in productivity because of the increased specializ-ation of function which it permitted, the historian asks why there was such an increase. The state is often at that point brought in as one of its causes, because it pursued more liberal commercial policies. But this only pro-vokes the further question, 'Why?', which could only be answered if the state and its politics were integral to the explanation of economic growth rather than an exogenous actor waiting in the wings to move the plot along.

[3] H. van der Wee, *Prosperity and Upheaval. The World Economy 1945–1980* (London, 1986), p. 54.
[4] A. Shonfield, *Modern Capitalism . . .*, op. cit.
[5] A. Maddison, *Dynamic Forces . . .*, op. cit., p. 168.
[6] M. Abramovitz, *Thinking About Growth and Other Essays on Economic Growth and Welfare* (Cambridge, 1989).

If the state was an important influence on the higher rates of growth achieved after 1945, why were its actions different in that period? If we accept, as most writers about growth implicitly do, that integration was also favourable to growth because it furthered the process of market extension and productivity growth, the need for an answer becomes more pressing, and the intellectual confusion of using the state only as a *deus ex machina* even more evident. Both the nation-state and integration appear as fortunate accidents of the time, fundamentally contradictory tendencies, which nevertheless in promoting economic growth fortuitously complemented each other. This falls well short of a satisfactory explanation of the relationship of the state to economic growth and to integration and something better is clearly needed. If there was a more positive role by government which created favourable conditions for the realization of the growth potential existing in western European economies, whence did it come? By what precise political mechanism did the organizational unit of the state, so feebly incapable even of fulfilling its primary task of protection in 1940, come to play such a role in the vast improvement in human life which took place? At this point some concept of the historical tradition of the state is needed.

In spite of the widespread collapse of national government in 1940 the Allies never had any serious intention during the war of altering the national frontiers of western Europe or debasing the primacy of national government. Liberation always meant restoration of the national entity. No practical alternative presented itself, although many were discussed, and in the case of Germany the discussions were far from abstract. However, even for Germany, American and British policy, to which France eventually had to conform, was that after unconditional surrender some form of national government would be created as quickly as possible. Austria indeed was forced back into a separate national existence which much of its population had never wanted. In occupied countries either the wartime government, as in Denmark, was still recognized as legitimate or, more typically, a national government in exile was recognized as that which would take over on liberation. In spite of various territorial claims on Germany, its western frontiers, like other national frontiers in Europe, were left virtually unaltered.

Yet national government that was restored in name and which maintained the long historical tradition, in practice was to be a different form of political organization based on a new distribution of political power. Force was to remain as it always had been the core of the state. The cruel penalties imposed by its judges, the weapons of its police and armed forces were what, finally, commanded allegiance. Liberal advocates of the democratic, parliamentary nation-state have always hoped it would be otherwise, as also have many advocates of ethnic and linguistic community as the foundation of the state. But government which relies purely on force endures only with difficulty and one of the characteristics of the new power structure of the post-1945 state in western Europe was that it needed to have less recourse to force than did its precursors. The other was that it was based on a much more solid and extensive political consensus than in the inter-war period.

It was the organizational framework which early states imposed within their frontiers which first and foremost created the political consciousness of belonging to a nation and, as far as the mass of the population has been concerned, national consciousness has always been more the consequence than the cause of nation-states. National consciousness does, certainly, like nationalism, have other roots than those watered by the nation-state. Both have often grown up as a form of social and cultural differentiation as much as identification. Both have typically been bred from economic and social grievances and aspirations, more than from linguistic differences or instinctive awareness of cultural or racial separateness. Yet even in established nation-states it has been an inherently almost impossible task for national movements to impose on the diverse and local origins of national consciousness one universally acceptable image of the nation. They have always had to call on the central executive power of the state itself to reinforce that image as well as to command allegiance to it.

Creating allegiance has been an unremitting effort by the nation-state since its origins, but on the scale required one frequently beyond its powers. Flags, national anthems, the nationalistic rhetoric of politicians and state-servants, the hours devoted in schools to instruction in a carefully constructed myth of national history, the publicity which is built up around national sporting successes, leave a large part of the population sceptical or only spasmodically enthusiastic. All such propagandistic attempts to win allegiance by the creation and dissemination of national myth are filtered down through a thick and complex mesh of social class, regional, group, and family affinities and at every stage encounter a natural human resistance to demands for conformity and subservience. What, for example, the Norwegian language actually was, the teaching of which should be encouraged in schools in the process of nation-building was a question evoking so many particularities of region, class, and social attitude that the Norwegian state was obliged to insist on the teaching of two versions of it, and at one point was not far from propagating three. For some states it has been easier. But the homogeneity of Sweden in modern history is an unusual inheritance. More typical are the myriad petty tyrannies practised elsewhere, at times descending as they did in Germany or Turkey to systematic slaughters.

In that light the collapse of so many nation-states in 1939–40 is no matter for surprise. Their inherent fissile tendencies had been exacerbated by the economic collapse of 1929–32. The political allegiance of important groups was withdrawn, sometimes even given to rival states or to the new conceptions of the state which emerged in the Soviet Union, in Nazi Germany, or fascist Italy. The nerves, arteries and vital organs which surround the hard skeleton of state power are alone what give the national body life and creativity. They are infinitely responsive to the ideas, sights, sounds and other stimuli from outside. In the 1930s the many alternatives to liberal parliamentary democracy were close at hand, and democracy itself not a notably successful form of governance. Defeat and occupation were not merely a collapse in the face of overwhelming military superiority; in most cases they were also a collapse of internal morale.

Renan, trying to define the concept of a nation, suggested that it was a 'daily plebiscite' and in so doing offered a justification for nineteenth-century French republican democracy as a form of government well suited to winning allegiance.[7] This, even with the extensive suffrage rights which existed in the Third Republic, was a remarkably complacent view. A plebiscitary rejection of the government's will would have needed to be massive and repeated. Yet Renan did identify the only alternative mechanism to tyranny by which the nation-state could hope to win the allegiance formerly given to kings and churches and claim its place as the culmination of historical progress. Its claim to legitimacy could only be sustained were it able to respond to a greater range of demands from its citizens. The weakness of the European nation-state in the inter-war period was that it was unable to do that in such a way as to establish a durable governing consensus.

It was already the case even before 1918 that merely providing defence, a national law, and a small range of public services such as a post office, roads and railways was seen as insufficient by an increasing number of citizens. A plebiscitary democracy was already generating a range of new demands for state action from the new groups and classes produced by economic development. The sweeping extensions of the franchise between 1918 and 1920 marked a steep and sudden further increase in these demands. The Weimar Republic stands as the classic example of a state trying, and failing, to establish legitimacy through a comprehensive response. An important part of that response was the extension of material welfare by protecting wages and enforcing minimum hours of work and by extending welfare benefits. It only increased the opposition to democracy as a form of government from other interest groups and classes. Similar attempts can be discerned elsewhere. In the United Kingdom the long quarrel over the high level of unemployment and the fluctuating levels of financial relief to the unemployed was largely a quarrel over the extent of the duty of the state machinery to deal with the problem. Only in Norway and Sweden, with the formation of a tacit alliance in the 1930s between the agricultural sector and the social-democratic parties, was a broad enough political consensus constructed to attempt to respond to these new demands without endangering democracy, although outside Europe the New Deal offered another example.

[7] E. Renan, 'Qu'est ce que c'est une nation?', Lecture delivered at the Sorbonne, 1 March 1882.

The national-socialist state, the instrument which completed the collapse of democracy, never won majority support even in Germany and the great mass of Europe's population found it repulsive. But the dissatisfaction of large numbers with pre-1940 parliamentary democracies was no less plain. The scattered proposals during the war for the merging of the European states into a federation, which Lipgens and his associates discovered almost everywhere they looked, were but one small part of a tumult of wartime proposals for the post-war reconstruction of state and society. These had one predominating characteristic: the post-war state in western Europe had to be constructed on a broader political consensus and show itself more responsive to the needs of a greater range and number of its citizens if its legitimacy was to be accepted. This came to mean attempting a much greater range of tasks. It was in the attempt to reassert itself as the basic unit of political organization that the parliamentary democratic state came to be a force for higher rates of economic growth.

This experience was common to western Europe. It seems reasonable therefore to examine the post-war consequences in terms of their similarities. A cluster of features can be identified which made western European states resemble each other much more than they resembled those of other places or other times. No one state perfectly embodied all these features, nor was there one feature perfectly present in all these states without exception. Nevertheless it is possible to characterize the western European state of 1945–73 in terms of a common model.

The post-war state was reconstructed on a much wider political consensus than that which had shaped policy in the inter-war period. Into this consensus were brought three large, overlapping categories of voters whose demands on central government had been hitherto imperfectly met or even refused: labour, agricultural producers, and a diffuse alliance of lower and middle income beneficiaries of the welfare state. The further extensions of the franchise which took place after 1945 provided one of the impetuses to that political reconstruction, but were not the greatest of them. The more powerful impulses were the desire for security, the general sentiment that only the nation-state could offer it, and the need for national parliamentary government to restore its legitimacy by purchasing allegiance. A further component in the model of the reconstructed state was the transformation in the nature and role of political parties in response to these impulses. They became the sensitive measure of a much larger public opinion than had been taken into account by the pre-war state – hence the sudden rise to prominence of the public opinion poll – and the conduit by which demands for concessions were transmitted to the parliamentary centre. It was they who had to undertake the necessary brokerage at the centre to keep the new consensus together. The national parliaments became the arena in which they performed stylized rituals which ratified the policy choices already made from the assessment of information gathered deep in the roots of local society and government where they now began to function.

The Christian Democratic parties in Italy and Germany are paradigms of a successful adaptation by political parties to this larger and deeper framework of democratic politics. Their influence over appointments and general favours reached down to the most local level. A party like the Italian Christian Democracy or the Social Democratic Party in Sweden, could aspire to become a state-party, in almost permanent power providing it was able to continue to embrace all the elements out of which the new political consensus was formed. In other states, Austria being a good example, political parties shared out the power in systems which were basically non-adversarial because consensus was sufficiently close for them to share at local and national level the power which it gave to them. The difference between the post-war Christian Democratic Union in Germany (CDU) and the inter-war Zentrum encapsulates the way in which the role of political parties changed. The Zentrum was almost wholly a catholic party essentially under the political domination of the catholic hierarchy and taking its political positions in parliament according to that hierarchy's wishes. It was typical of most pre-war political parties in western Europe in that it more resembled a club of like-minded individuals associating to vote together at the parliamentary centre than a machine for discovering the demands coming from below in society and transmuting them into policies. The CDU by contrast quickly became a complicated and pervasive political machine, whose parliamentary positions were shaped by responses to pressures from below, rather than from above.

It was the broader post-war political consensus and the political machinery by which it was operated which led to the economic and social policies to which growth theorists point as part of their explanation for the high rates of growth of the period. The reassertion of the nation-state, because it required the satisfaction of so many demands if it were to succeed, was the start of the higher growth rates of the post-war world. This does not mean that government policy was the chief cause of those high growth rates. But as long as they were achieved they strengthened the reassertion of the nation-state, so that from its collapse in 1940 it had achieved in twenty years a degree of power and a legitimacy founded on an allegiance stronger than any in its previous history. It could not have done this so successfully without the process of integration, for that proved necessary to make some of its responses effective.

The incorporation of organized labour into the machinery of policy formulation of the post-war state has been frequently noted. It was, as Maier has cogently argued, a conscious post-war bid for political stability.[8] The way in which this covenant was encouraged by American aid during

---

[8] C.S. Maier, *In Search of Stability. Explorations in Historical Political Economy* (Cambridge, Mass., 1987).

the Marshall Plan has been illustrated by several authors.[9] But in most countries it could make little difference to establishing political power, because organized labour was so small a part of the total labour force. The acceptance of the political status of trade unions is better understood as one small part of the response to much more complex demands for welfare relating to the whole of the labour force and carried to the top of the political agenda by political parties dependent on the votes of wage labour. This response was announced in the sweeping wage increases granted as almost their first political act by the liberation governments in Belgium and France. In several countries, notably Sweden and the United Kingdom, this response took the form of a public commitment to full employment policy.

Keynes and others had provided the intellectual justification for the argument that governments could eliminate long-term mass unemployment by manipulating the level of aggregate demand. Writing when unemployment in the United Kingdom was the lot of 17 per cent of the labour force, Keynes variously estimated the equilibrium level of unemployment at between 3 and 6 per cent and his theoretical and empirical work was concerned with the shaping of policies which could return the economy to that equilibrium level and keep it there. The policies suggested by his work, deficit spending from government budgets at the bottom of cyclical troughs, regulation of the level of demand by changes in fiscal policy and by adjustments of the volume of money and credit, were used as regulators of the economy and the employment level. As table 2.1 shows, however, the level of unemployment in the period 1950–69 was not only dramatically lower than in the 1930s, it was also much lower than the levels at which Keynes had suggested his policies should be put into practice. The causes for these high levels of employment went far beyond government commitment to Keynesian policies, narrowly defined.[10] Indeed several major countries in the 1950s, Germany and Italy for example, ignored these policy ideas almost completely.

None the less, the motive that inspired Keynes was widespread; to rescue the capitalist economy by eliminating a waste of human resources and an economic injustice which had weakened allegiance to the state. Even in the Federal Republic when in the 1967 recession the economy first appeared unable to continue to increase the number of jobs available, the principles of Keynes's work were officially enshrined in a law to promote the stability of growth of the economy. The high levels of employment achieved everywhere were in fact in large measure a result of the way other economic policies emerging from the new consensus sustained the demand

[9] A. Carew, *Labour under the Marshall Plan: The Politics of Productivity and the Marketing of Management Science* (Manchester, 1987); F. Romero, *Gli Stati Uniti e il sindicalismo europeo, 1944–1951* (Rome, 1989).

[10] R.C.O. Matthews, 'Why Has Britain Had Full Employment Since the War?', *Economic Journal*, vol. lxxviii, 1968.

Table 2.1   Unemployment as a proportion of the labour force in western Europe, 1930–88 (average percentage over the period)

	1930–8	*1950–69*	*1970–88*
Austria	13.4	2.9	2.4
Belgium	8.7	3.1	7.9
Denmark	6.6	2.8	6.5
France	3.3	1.4	6.6
Germany	8.8	2.5	6.2
Italy	4.8	5.6	8.1
Sweden	5.6	1.7	2.4
Switzerland	3.0	0.1	0.5
United Kingdom	11.5	1.4	6.9

Source: A. Maddison, 'Economic Policy and Performance in Europe', in C.M. Cipolla (ed.), *The Fontana Economic History of Europe*, vol. 5 (London, 1976), pp. 452 and 479

for goods, and in so doing met more political encouragement on the grounds that they induced growth and employment than discouragement on the grounds that they were inflationary.

A second common feature of the post-war state is that support by the state for incomes in the agricultural sector became a universal practice on a large scale. The widening gap between incomes in manufacturing and agriculture had been one of the main causes of the fracture of the political base of democracy in the inter-war period, especially over the period 1929–32 when agricultural prices fell three times as steeply as those of manufactures. Support for authoritarian movements became a notable feature of the politics of agricultural regions even in highly industrialized states such as Germany. Voters there whose livelihoods depended on agriculture supported in turn almost the whole gamut of non-socialist parties before turning to the national socialists and giving them for the first time in 1930 a large parliamentary representation. It was the discontent of agriculture in northern Italy which first laid the power base of the *fascisti*. In Austria, a wide collection of anti-democratic movements relied on rural support. A priority of the post-war state everywhere in western Europe was to forestall any similar future developments.

Progress towards the inclusion of agriculture in a political consensus can be observed everywhere from the disasters of 1931 onwards. It was the basis of the reformulation of the politics of liberal democracy in Norway and Sweden in the 1930s. The Third Reich also brought agriculture under the protective state umbrella, albeit in a political framework where consensus was less needed. In the post-war world organized agriculture, farmers' own representative associations, became institutionalized inside the governmental system as the state's own agricultural executive. In many countries they achieved a more assured seat at the tables where policy was decided than organized labour. How this happened is described in detail below.[11] In effect, agriculture became a state-managed concern, one of whose central purposes was to support and raise incomes in the sector relative to those elsewhere in the economy. As a general estimate it seems fair to conclude that three-quarters of the farmers in Western Europe had a large supplement to their incomes as a result of state policy. This was a lot of votes in the 1950s, 6.8 million in Italy, if agricultural labour is also included amongst the beneficiaries, and 5 million in the Federal Republic.

The third common feature of the consensus is those sets of policies loosely referred to as the welfare state. National welfare regimes came in different political forms, because their earlier historical origins were different, because the state machinery varied, because they were animated by different political philosophies, and because the specific concessions which they offered were to different categories of voters. The sweeping reform of the German pensions system in 1955–7, a bid by the Christian Democratic Union for long-term middle-class electoral support, had little in common, for example, with the extension of public welfare in Sweden or Norway except an adherence to the view that the stability of the state required a positive response to the demand for welfare. The typology of welfare states has been set out on a historical basis in an interesting study whose differentiations are a valuable corrective to the assimilations made here.[12] The assimilations however are justified, both because the underlying political motivation was broadly similar, a bid for the electoral support of that large and rapidly growing income group, loosely defined as the lower middle class, whose propensity to switch votes had become a decisive factor in elections, and because in consequence the increase in magnitude of the provisions is general to countries but unique to the period.

Nowhere in the 1940s had private or corporate welfare schemes catered cheaply or efficiently enough to the needs of a sufficient number of citizens to bind them into a lasting allegiance. It was the use of state-supported insurance funds, offering a much more consistent pattern of security to a broader stratum of voters, which was adopted as the main way of remedying this defect after 1945. The commitment of the post-war state to this generalized form of welfare appeared as an extension of earlier middle-class demands for a vote and participation in the state; the right to the vote, once obtained, was followed with demands for the right to welfare. Scarcely a year passed in western European states after 1945 without the extension of these new rights to some group or other. Pension coverage, for example, was extended to additional groups in Italy in 1945, 1950, 1957, 1958, 1959, 1963 and 1966, health insurance coverage in 1945, 1953, 1954, 1955, 1956, 1959, 1963 and 1966.

The index of social insurance coverage for western European states compiled by Flora and Alber shows that the evolution of this type of welfare provision was not evenly spread over time. For almost every

[11] See pp. 237–53.
[12] G. Esping-Andersen, *The Three Worlds of Welfare Capitalism* (Cambridge, 1990).

western European country one particular period of exceptionally rapid increase is apparent, for Belgium the period 1944–6, for Switzerland 1947–8, for the Netherlands 1951–7, for Sweden 1955, for Norway 1956, and for Italy 1955–60.[13] Weighted indices of this kind could be constructed according to different principles and give different results. Flora and Alber do not, for instance, single out the period 1945–50 in the United Kingdom, because the weights they use mean that social insurance coverage already appears as very high there before 1945. But all historians agree that this was the period of decisive extension of British welfare provision. Although the extension of welfare provision continued throughout the 1960s everywhere in western Europe and on a financially much more ambitious level than before, it was the continuation of a process which had usually established itself in a political breakthrough before the mid-1950s.

Over the whole period 1945–68 social insurance played the key role both in extending welfare and using welfare extensions to build and sustain consensus. It created a robust national framework of personal claims on the state's finances, mediated through a rapidly expanding welfare bureaucracy. This huge extension of state welfare cannot be historically characterized in abstraction from the massive and vigorous exercise of political rights which gave rise to it. Bismarck, in pioneering the concept of state-supported social insurance in the 1880s had hoped that workers would find it a substitute for political rights. It became, on the contrary, part of the continuum of political rights for which citizens have extended their demands since the French Revolution. William Beveridge's dry actuarial report on the unification and extension of the existing social insurance schemes in Britain became a best-seller during the war, the symbol of national renewal, because in language and thought its one readable passage so unreservedly encapsulated the desire for personal security and the concept of all citizens as equally privileged members of one nation.[14] Lukewarm support and spasmodic opposition cost the country's great, uncomprehending wartime leader the first post-war election.

The extension of the social insurance principle was not the only aspect of general welfare provision by the post-war state. Welfare in the widest sense, embracing almost the whole range of economic and social policy, was probably the issue most susceptible to manipulation for electoral purposes. The real growth rate of all social expenditure at 1970 prices in pre-election and election years in the Federal Republic between 1950 and 1983, for example, was always 1 per cent higher than in other years.[15] The

---

[13] P. Flora and J. Alber, 'Modernization, Democratization, and the Development of Welfare States in Western Europe', in P. Flora and A. Heidenheimer (eds), *The Development of Welfare States in Europe and America* (New Brunswick, 1981) pp. 55 ff.

[14] Sir W. Beveridge, *Social Insurance and Allied Services, Parliamentary Papers*, Cmd. 6404, 1942.

[15] J. Alber, 'Germany', in P. Flora (ed.), *Growth to Limits. The Western European Welfare States since World War Two*, vol. 2 (Berlin, 1986), p. 113.

welfare state was also a commitment to the extension of public provision of housing, education, leisure and health.

Attempts to measure the increase of welfare provision in the widest sense have been made by Flora and his collaborators. In Western Europe as a whole social security expenditure, including all income maintenance and public health programmes, averaged about 9.3 per cent of GNP in 1950 and 13.4 per cent by 1965. If spending on education and housing is included expenditure on welfare rose from about 25 per cent of GNP in 1950 to about 45 per cent by the mid-1970s.[16] Dwellings completed by public authorities, usually local government with the help of the central state revenue, accounted for more than 70 per cent of the new dwellings completed in 1949 in France, Germany, the Netherlands, Norway, Sweden and the United Kingdom. Indeed in the Netherlands they made up 97 per cent of the total.[17] The allocation of public housing could also create a political core of supporters for certain political parties, as well as being a valuable instrument of political manipulation at local level.

It is to the economic consequences of the post-war political consensus that we must now turn. They were interlinked, so that the outcome of what was only political pragmatism came to have a surprisingly coherent economic appearance. Support for agricultural incomes was an essential support to the welfare state; poor farmers would otherwise have made bigger demands on social insurance systems. High levels of state expenditure on housing construction and other aspects of the economy, such as defence and social security, sustained employment levels by sustaining demand. Full employment gave social insurance a much sounder actuarial basis. Social insurance systems, in their turn, provided governments with a larger financial reserve with which to pursue counter-cyclical economic policies aimed at maintaining high employment. This apparent coherence was largely coincidental, both in thought and action.

The finer aspects of demand management, the use of fiscal policy and alterations in interest rates to stabilize demand and reduce economic fluctuations, have not always been judged a success. Reactions to reflationary or deflationary adjustments of this kind in Britain, for instance, usually occurred after a longer time-lag than foreseen and could thus exaggerate rather than diminish cyclical fluctuations. And the pressure to concede welfare increases before impending general elections usually overrode more abstract principles of demand management. It is not only in the United Kingdom that almost every pre-election budget since 1950 has been more than normally inflationary. If governments were not successful in fine tuning the economy according to Keynesian prescriptions, the trend line of income growth was nevertheless higher and steeper because of the increase in size of the national budgets, whether balanced or not, because of the

---

[16] P. Flora (ed.), *Growth to Limits*, op. cit., vol. 1 (Berlin, 1986), p. xxii.
[17] UN, ECE, *Economic Bulletin for Europe*, 4th qtr, vol. 4, no. 1, 1951.

massive and stabilizing impact of the states' other interventions, and because of the microeconomic activities of government in stimulating particular industries.

Government budgets, released from the alleged necessity of being balanced, were growth-inducing, because their role in maintaining the new political consensus made them so much larger than earlier. Hansen estimated that over the period 1955–65 the total effect of the government budget, including local authority budgets and investment by the state in public enterprise, accounted for 18 per cent of the actual growth rate of GNP in Italy and Sweden, and in France for 12.5 per cent.[18] The calculation is necessarily a rather narrowly based one. It cannot take into account for example the effect of high and predictable levels of government expenditure on mood and the climate for investment. This was particularly important where the state regularly published its expansionary investment intentions in advance, as it did in the case of the French plans or the Norwegian 'national budgets'. When government consumption and expenditure took up so much larger a share of national income, the psychological influence of the government's general stance towards the economy could be of great consequence. Since Keynes, the level of investment has been seen as basically determined by expectations in an uncertain market, and therefore not as something which can be safely left to the hidden hand.

Government consumption of goods and services as a share of national income sometimes fell in the immediate post-war period from its 1938 level, which was heavily influenced upwards by rearmament. This was the case in Germany (comparing the Federal Republic to the Third Reich) and Italy. Where some countries showed a significant increase in the share, notably Sweden, this too was mainly related to changed patterns of defence expenditure in the other direction. The return to high levels of defence expenditure after 1950 may well have been one of the sources of sustained high demand, although the sudden variations to which they were subjected hardly made them a stabilizing element. Even countries which had virtually no armed forces before 1939, such as Denmark and the Netherlands, adopted conscription and built up a complex of highly sophisticated armaments. Over the period 1949–68 military expenditure increased in the former by an annual average of 5.9 per cent and in the latter by 4.9 per cent.[19] In France and in Italy over the period 1949–68 the average annual rate of increase of military expenditure was 5 per cent. In fact in both Britain and France defence expenditure in the 1950s was almost the same share of GDP as it had been in that year of large-scale rearmament, 1938, when both countries were preparing to fight for their existence.

As soon, however, as we look at total government expenditure rather

[18] B. Hansen, *Fiscal Policy in Seven Countries 1955–1965* (OECD, Paris, 1969), p. 58.
[19] Stockholm International Peace Research Institute, *Yearbook of World Armaments and Disarmament 1968/9*, p. 23.

Table 2.2 Total government expenditure as a percentage of GDP, 1938–73 (current prices)

	1938	*1950*	*1973*
France	23.2	27.6	38.8
Germany	42.4	30.4*	42.0*
Netherlands	21.7	26.8	45.5
United Kingdom	28.8	34.2	41.5
* German Federal Republic			

Source: A. Maddison, *Dynamic Forces in Capitalist Development* (Oxford 1991); A. Maddison, 'Origins and Impact of the Welfare State, 1883–1983', in *Banca Nazionale del Lavoro Quarterly Review*, vol. 37, no. 184, 1984

than consumption the increased financial weight of the post-war state in the economy becomes more evident. Total government expenditure as a share of GDP at current prices moved upwards relentlessly in Western Europe as a whole, and this was a process which broadly coincided with the heyday of integration. For this upward movement the overwhelming reason was the transfer payments made to support the welfare state. In some countries in the 1950s, including France, Germany and Italy, these were larger than government spending on goods and services. The precise effect on demand of these massive transfers, the single most obvious consequence of the politics of the post-war state, has been the subject of incessant political argument. They were essentially transfers of the burden of taxation from the better-off to the less well-off citizens and so reduced the personal disposable income of some consumers below what it would otherwise have been. At higher levels of unemployment, such as still obtained in the 1950s in Belgium, Germany and Italy, they clearly did help maintain demand, because of the much higher level of unemployment benefits compared to before the war. It seems highly probable also that the redistribution of purchasing power which they brought about favoured the growth of the mass markets and standardized patterns of consumption on which so many of the productivity gains of manufacturing industry in that period depended. Full employment plus income redistribution created a large new body of consumers. The most striking example comes from the ageing of western Europe's population. With pre-war welfare provision this would have meant that a far greater proportion of it would have been past active working life and in that stage of the life cycle when its income and consumption were close to or below the poverty line. Transfers maintained the aged as active consumers, albeit at a low level. If a collapse of demand as catastrophic as in 1929–32 is unlikely to reoccur in 1992, even though governments seem to have left themselves with few fiscal or monetary weapons, that is largely because of the built-in stabilizers which now exist through the development of the welfare state.

Transfer payments helped to stabilize the economy even where governments did not vary them in a deliberate attempt at demand management. Only in the United Kingdom, which relied heavily after 1951 on abrupt changes in interest rates as well as experiments in demand management through fiscal policy, was the government budget destabilizing. Elsewhere in Europe, at least over the period 1955–65, a large fiscal presence stabilized the trend of GNP growth. This was most markedly the case in countries such as Belgium, Germany and Italy which had high levels of transfer payments and made no experiments with demand management policies of the kind Keynes had proposed.[20]

Beyond the impact of large government budgets on sustaining demand and possibly creating a more dynamic climate of expansion it is necessary to look at specific areas of government investment. Apart from the impact of defence expenditure on sustaining demand, two other areas appear of particular importance, housing and industrial modernization, with education joining them in the 1960s.

In most western European countries between 1945 and 1968 the majority of houses were built with government subsidy. Italy and Switzerland were the only exceptions. Elsewhere more than a half of the new housing stock was financed by central or local government budgets, two-thirds of it in Norway, and in some years in France, the Netherlands and Sweden virtually the whole of it. In addition rents of dwellings which remained in public ownership were often subsidized. The financial commitment to housing by government over Western Europe as a whole was as high as that to defence. Since buildings and other construction projects represented between one-half and two-thirds of total gross fixed capital formation in Europe as a whole over the period 1950–69 the preponderant influence of government policy on housing construction clearly was very important in determining the generally high levels of investment throughout the economy.

Over the period 1950–70 the rate of growth of output in the construction sector was between 4 and 7 per cent a year over Western Europe as a whole, and thus somewhat higher than the rate of growth of total output. In terms of added value it accounted for between 7 and 9 per cent of GDP in Western Europe in the 1960s. Its impact on the rest of the economy was larger than this figure might suggest, because usually about half of the value of its gross output was made up of purchases of goods and services from other sectors. In 1959 for example in the EEC countries, 10.2 per cent of the output of wood products and paper was bought by the construction industry, as was 9.3 per cent of the output of the mining and quarrying sector, 7.7 per cent of total metals output, and 61.2 per cent of the output of other non-metallic mineral products.[21] The high involvement of government with housing provision has been criticized as a misallocation of

[20] B. Hansen, *Fiscal Policy. . .*, op. cit., p. 69.
[21] UN, ECE, *Economic Survey of Europe in 1971*, Part 1, *The European Economy from the 1950s to the 1970s* (New York, 1972), p. 62.

resources which might otherwise have gone into more productive investment. We have only to look at the very high growth rates of industrial
output in the Federal Republic where housing investment was as high a
proportion of total investment as anywhere in Western Europe to cast
serious doubts on that argument.

Government involvement in attempts to modernize manufacturing
industry was also a distinctive aspect of the post-war period. Some government intervention in industry was not primarily for that purpose, but is
better seen as another aspect of employment policy. There were extensive
investments intended to avoid the political problems caused by industries
contracting too quickly. One such, government involvement in coal mining
in Belgium, is considered in the next chapter. But the counterpart of this
type of state policy was the neo-mercantilist effort of the post-war state to
shift the patterns of comparative advantage in its own favour in selected
manufacturing sectors. This was one of the outcomes of the reassertion of
national will.

From its outset post-war national reconstruction was not aimed solely at
repairing the physical damage of war and merely restoring the pre-war
economy. It was aimed at building a greater and richer national economy,
at industrialization, at modernization, and at the full utilization of hitherto
idle national resources. This was in striking contrast to the attitude after
1918, when the pre-war economic order had appeared as the normality to
which government should try to return. Now the pre-war period appeared
as one of fatal economic weakness and division. In France, for example, all
political parties combined in condemning the stagnation after 1933 as the
cause of the political and military collapse. The Plan for Modernization
and Equipment, the first of a series of medium-term plans for developing
the economy, was always able to draw on the consensus of opinion that a
large national effort was needed because France had in some way become a
backward country in the 1930s.[22] There was disagreement about the extent
of the state effort needed, but the reality was that up to 1953 state
expenditures dominated investment in the French economy. Public funds
financed 58 per cent of investment over the years 1947–52. The central
bank's balances were mainly made up of low interest bearing treasury
bonds; it was being treated, it complained, as the 'biggest bank on the
square'.[23]

France might be considered an exceptional case both because of this very
high share of public investment in the total and because of the existence of
official planning machinery, not, however, because of the insistence on
modernization and the rhetoric which accompanied it. What was called

[22] P. Mioche, 'Aux origines du Plan Monnet: les discours et les contenus dans les premiers
plans français (1941–1947)' in *Revue historique*, no. 538, 1981; P. Mioche, *Le Plan Monnet.
Genèse et élaboration 1941–1947* (Paris, 1987).
[23] C. Andrieu, 'La politique du crédit, frein ou moteur de la modernisation (1945–1950)?', in
P. Fridenson and A. Straus (eds), *Le capitalisme français* (Paris, 1987).

modernization in France was called industrialization elsewhere. The same assumption, that the state must change the balance of the economy towards a larger, more modern, more internationally competitive manufacturing sector was widespread. Industrialization as a state objective was proclaimed as public policy at various times in Austria, the Netherlands and Norway. The Norwegian government after their return to a liberated country began to publish an annual 'national budget' which was both a set of national accounts and a statement of the allocation of national resources for the coming year. Investment as a proportion of these national resources was to be higher for the next forty years than anywhere else in Western Europe, at the expense, it was assumed, of what had earlier gone to savings or consumption.[24]

The differences in the scale and pervasiveness of this economic nationalism reflected differences in the perceived need to reassert the nation-state, and also differences in its governmental machinery. It was only in the 1960s, after twenty years of comparatively low rates of national income growth, that the United Kingdom began to interest itself in the ideas of the French medium-term plans; in 1945 a programme of industrialization would have seemed too fanciful to be supported. In spite of the high proportion of industry in public ownership, the governmental machinery which in France coordinated high investment levels was lacking in Italy, which none the less makes an excellent case study of microeconomic intervention in industry by government for the same purpose, albeit of a less coherent type.[25] The main intellectual current after 1945 flowed towards state-guided capitalism. The extensive nationalizations in Britain and France, including in the French case Renault, one of Europe's largest car producers, had diverse origins, but all could be justified by the widespread argument that the capitalist economy now had to meet so many demands that it could not be safely or wisely left to the capitalists themselves. In countries where nationalization was eschewed, state guidance and indirect management of large areas of the manufacturing economy was still the norm.

Public enterprise as a whole accounted for 32 per cent of total gross fixed investment in the United Kingdom in 1957, in Austria, France and Italy for between 25 and 27 per cent, in the Netherlands, Norway and Sweden for between 13 and 15 per cent.[26] If we single out the modernizing sectors they were probably absorbing about a third of the investment and managerial effort, leaving aside the importance of modernization in the public infrastructural services such as gas, water and telephones which were more often

[24] A. Bourneuf, *Norway, The Planned Revival* (Cambridge, Mass., 1958).

[25] F. Bonelli (ed.), *Acciaio per l'industrializzazione: Contributi allo studio del problema siderurgico italiano* (Turin, 1982); M. Doria, *Ansaldo: L'impresa e lo stato* (Milan, 1989); V. Zamagni, 'Betting on the Future: The Reconstruction of Italian Industry, 1946–1952', in J. Becker and F. Knipping (eds), *Power in Europe? Great Britain, France, Italy and Germany in a Post-War World, 1945–1950* (Berlin, 1986).

[26] UN, ECE, *Economic Survey of Europe in 1959* (Geneva, 1960), chapter V, p. 3.

nationalized than not. The most significant modernizing industrial sectors which typically depended wholly or in part on state finance for modernization were steel, nuclear engineering, aircraft, and energy production. Outside this general picture, however, governments tried to pick other national champions. Volkswagen was such an example, kept in public ownership and receiving many favours from the state. Fiat and Renault were others. The aluminium industry in Austria, molybdenum in Norway, provide further examples of heavy state investment in sectors which it was hoped would bring valuable returns in the future. It was not merely of course a question of investment; the state could disburse numerous favours through commercial policy privileges. Quotas on imports stifled foreign competition against a wide range of Dutch infant industries as they did against the Italian car industry.

Where government involvement was so pervasive it is arbitrary to distinguish at the level of the enterprise between official planning, French-style, and management based on better and longer-term prediction, although of course the French plans had wider political implications. At the enterprise level the question becomes merely whether planning or state management provided a more vigorous and a more stable growth. Quantitative study of the French plans and the extent to which their publicly proclaimed targets were achieved suggests that the French economy was managed no more accurately than any other in western Europe and that to its general level of successful economic performance the official Plans made only a small contribution.[27] Nevertheless, planning and state management alike across western Europe, for all their failings and inaccuracies did contribute something lacking in the inter-war period. They envisaged the growth of industrial output in a wider national context, in a longer-term perspective, and in a world of much more information. They assumed also that short-term crises would be circumvented by the state in the interests of pursuing longer-term advantages.[28]

As the more traditional concern of the state with seizing economic advantage became transmuted in the course of the 1950s into the ideology of economic growth, various other ways in which it was thought the state could improve the long-term rate of growth of the economy were also adopted as policy. Of these the most persistently attempted was to steer expenditure towards education and towards research and development.

---

[27] V. Lutz, *Central Planning for the Market Economy. An Analysis of the French Theory and Experience* (London, 1969).

[28] 'We have given a good deal of attention to the role of national planning, and have concluded that it did indeed have an influence on growth. It is the most visible expression of a dynamic and somewhat original concept of the role of government in running the economy, and this concept also inspires economic management in the short-term, the regulation of prices and agreements, the management of major public enterprises etc. By attempting to clear away obstacles to economic expansion and to spread relevant information over a wide field, national planning assisted growth, diffusely but undeniably.' J.-J. Carré *et al.*, *French Economic Growth*, (Stanford, 1975), p. 499.

Expenditure on education as a share of GNP in Western Europe varied in 1955 between 2.8 per cent in the Federal Republic to 4.4 per cent in Sweden. By 1964 the lower and upper bounds were 3.4 per cent in the Federal Republic and 5.7 per cent in the Netherlands and Sweden. The amount spent on education was typically growing faster than national income itself.

The share of government expenditure on research and development in GNP was typically very small, about 0.5 per cent on average, except in Britain and France with their atomic weapons and large armed forces where it varied between 1.0 and 1.5 per cent. But everywhere it climbed and in many countries, Denmark, France, Ireland, Italy, Norway and the United Kingdom for example, it was larger than equivalent expenditure by private business. The industrial sectors with the fastest rates of growth of output in the period were generally those which also had the highest inputs of research and development and needed the most educated labour force. Chemicals, electronics, engineering and communications industries, all of which had especially high rates of growth, increasingly and inherently depended on government's role in supporting education and sometimes on the spin-off from military research sponsored by government.

It is not easy to make meaningful quantitative estimates of the contribution of government policy to the higher rates of growth of national income in the twenty-five years after the war. Two statements can be ventured as reasonable conclusions from the evidence. One is that government policy was successful for a long time in fostering growth and stabilizing the economy. The critique of it at the time and since, that the system was inherently unstable because of its inflationary propensities, had less force than its advocates believed. Between 1953 and 1959 the most inflationary country in Western Europe, France, saw an average annual increase in consumer prices of only 3.4 per cent.[29] More typically, rates of inflation over that period were less than 2.5 per cent. Over almost twenty years of anti-inflationary policy since 1973 rates of inflation have never been so low for so long. The higher rates of price inflation before 1953 were accepted as the cost of national reassertion. The second statement that can be made is that government policy made a much less important contribution to growth than the changes that occurred in western European economies independently of the state and its activities.

Historians looking back on the period will surely eventually see it as the culmination of the great wave of European industrialization which began in the seventeenth century. It was the period when manufacturing became the predominant sector in the Austrian, Dutch, Italian, Spanish and Norwegian economies and greatly increased its importance in Denmark, Ireland and Portugal. To this process of change government attempts at industrial modernization were only a marginal contribution. Many of the

---

[29] IMF, *International Financial Statistics*.

rest of the economic changes which made a large contribution to the higher growth rates of national income, the movement of large numbers of people out of agriculture for instance, were consequences of this culmination of the process of industrialization. To explore and explain that process, the real underlying cause of high growth rates which governments could encourage but not induce, would be to begin a book on another subject. Here, we can only be concerned with the way that these dynamic economic trends appeared to justify national reassertion, even where they were not wholly responsible for them.

Whereas most of the government policies to foster growth briefly considered here at first sprang directly from the effort to build and maintain political consensus, they were soon to acquire an intellectual justification as a desirable economic and social aim in themselves. By the mid-1950s the theory of economic growth was to become the ideology which justified the merely pragmatic policies which had emerged from the political realities of post-Second-World-War democracy. It was the one ideology which explained how the political consensus could permanently endure.

Keynes did not deal theoretically with the growth of national income but with the static case where a fixed quantity of resources was underused. It proved easy for his followers, observing what was happening after 1945, to dynamize his ideas by grafting them on to models in which factor productivity increased and investment was not only a source of additional demand but a cause of potential growth. National income, that entity which Keynes's theoretical work had done more than anyone else's to make measurable and controllable, became the new basis of national self-consciousness. Its growth came to occupy in the national collective psyche of western Europe the place formerly occupied by the growth of national territory. Soon economists had measured the relative success of all the world's states by estimating their per capita national incomes and their rates of growth, stringing them in diagonal order along the horizontal axis of a graph, up which they climbed or down which they were relegated according to the growth rate of GNP like teams in a football league, with the United States and Switzerland as first division champions whose playing systems were to be emulated by second division strugglers like Spain and even by non-league teams on the far periphery of Africa.

National policy was believed to be a critical element in success or failure in this league. The recipes for successful state action were many. The state, it was argued, could stimulate technological modernization, could accelerate the redistribution of the labour force away from the lower-productivity sectors, could steer investment towards projects which would generate long-term growth, could provide an encouraging framework for dynamic entrepreneurship, could direct the educational system to produce the managers and workers who were needed, and so on. It was but a short step from the dynamization of Keynesian models of the economy to establishing the concepts of productivity and national income growth as the intellectual basis of the post-war political consensus. If a permanently sustained increase of national income and personal disposable income was possible, the political economy of the post-war state was permanently viable. If productivity improvement was indefinitely possible national resources could grow so rapidly that the disputes of the inter-war period over how to share them out could be stilled.[30]

Politics was not, so ran the new orthodoxy, about redistributing the national wealth, but about devising economic strategies which made everyone's share greater. Those who put some other priority first, their wages perhaps, became 'extremists'. Providing no one probed the true origins of differences in rates of productivity growth in too determined a manner, the ideology of growth provided a comprehensive political theory for much of the government intervention in the productive economy.

National reassertion required a national ideology and no concept could have been more narrowly nationally based than national income accounting. Its founders, Simon Kuznets and Colin Clark, established national frontiers as the basic framework for measuring economic transactions as well as economic progress. In his intellectual crusade to rescue liberal capitalism Keynes never appears to have doubted that the nation was the correct object and unit of measurement and the correct field for action. His policy recommendations were an exaltation of the concept of the nation-state as an organizing principle. The resources which unemployment wasted were national resources. The instruments for its cure were the national budget and national taxes. The measure of the resources at the state's disposal, national accounting, became the primary statistical concept for policy formulation in the post-war state, in spite of its apparent and growing inappropriateness to an interdependent economic world. It is right that it should have been his name which has characterized the range of interventionist policies associated with the post-war state.

State expenditure on welfare, the support of agricultural incomes, attempts by the state to develop and industrialize the economy, would have followed the same post-war pattern had Keynes never written, and were logically independent of his ideas. Other economists discovered 'Keynesianism' earlier, and sometimes with greater clarity. The policies actually pursued were some way from his prescriptions. There is no reason to think he would have believed in fiscal fine tuning to the neglect of monetary measures in an economy with less than 3 per cent unemployment and with rising prices. But in placing the nation in the centre of his intellectual map he offered, firstly, an intellectual justification for some of the interventionist policies on which the rescue of the nation-state depended and, secondly, a way of representing the welfare state as an economic gain rather than a charitable burden. He created a mental world in which the political

---

[30] C.S. Maier, 'The Politics of Productivity: Foundations of American International Economic Policy after World War II', in P. Katzenstein (ed.), *Between Power and Plenty: The Foreign Economic Policies of Advanced Industrial States* (Madison, 1978).

machinery of the nation could be used to improve the lot of mankind and helped to give post-war national politicians the justificatory ideology they needed.

The nationalistic attitudes which underlay these developments showed in the way that welfare states were justified in terms of national efficiency and in the way, also, that they reasserted separate national traditions. Beveridge himself was a liberal thinker in the classic nineteenth-century British political mould, wherein 'social progress' was seen as a prime objective of political action. Beginning his career with the same fundamental concern as Keynes, that too high a level of unemployment, which he incorrectly labelled in his 1943 report as 'Idleness', was an unacceptable waste of national resources, he moved over a long life to the conviction that only the financial power of the state could provide a satisfactory level of personal income throughout the life cycle of most people. The British welfare state was conceived partly as a substitute for a more interventionist microeconomic policy. It would be left to Keynesian macroeconomics to return the economy to an equilibrium employment level at which a comprehensive national social security system would be financially viable.

This can be contrasted with the reiteration of a quite different state tradition in Sweden. There, a long history of centralization and rationalizing intervention by the state was taken over by the Social Democratic Party. It committed itself very heavily to social insurance with high benefits for almost the whole population, but at the same time it espoused detailed microeconomic employment policies and a much higher level of personal taxation. In both cases maximizing the number of people in employment enlarged the tax base for social welfare provision. The Federal Republic, to make a further contrast, acting within a catholic and patriarchal welfare tradition, left the welfare of women and children more to the family, while providing exceptionally generous benefits and security including high pensions, for those in employment. In Germany too, however, the readiness to finance such a programme in the long term through personal taxation and redistributive income transfers proved greater than in the United Kingdom. 'A revolutionary moment in the world's history is a time for revolutions, not for patching', Beveridge wrote at the beginning of his report. But what he recommended and wrought was no more than the administrative completion of the moral programme of British nineteenth-century nonconformism. Other welfare states went much further.

The combination of welfare state and employment policy in Sweden represents the apogee of the concept of the nation as the improver of man's lot. The Myrdals argued in 1934 that the state should alter the philosophy of its welfare provision towards preventing social problems rather than merely treating their symptoms.[31] In this context unemployment clearly became a social problem and full employment policy an integral part of the

---

[31] A. Myrdal and G. Myrdal, *Kris i befolkningsfrågan* (Stockholm, 1934).

welfare state. As early as 1932 the leading theoretician of the Swedish Social Democratic Party, Ernst Wigforss, had introduced into the party programme Keynes's idea of deficit spending by the state to promote a return to equilibrium levels of employment at a higher level and it became a vote-winning commitment.[32] This resumed the vision of the Swedish eighteenth-century enlightenment, the model of a comprehensive interventionist state which would make the national economy more efficient and more prosperous. When Sweden was under threat during the war of invasion by two different hostile economic systems, the vision of a distinctively Swedish economic model gathered great popular appeal behind the Social Democratic slogan of a 'Peoples' Home'. One of its ultimate expressions was thirty years of compulsion of the central bank by the state to force other banks to provide long-term credit to the housing sector for standardized subsidized housing ahead of other sectors.[33]

How, in a world of such nationally dominated conceptions, apparently justified by the remarkable economic prosperity which attended them, could integration and the surrender of national sovereignty be born? Not as the intellectual counter-current to European nationalism, which it is so often said to represent, but only as a further stage in the reassertion of the role of the nation-state. The common policies of the European Community came into being in the attempt to uphold and stabilize the post-war consensus on which the European nation-state was rebuilt. They were a part of the rescue of the nation-state.

It is not the intention of this book to argue that they were the most important part. Most of the history of that rescue would, perforce, be a national history. Nevertheless, one of the inherent instabilities of the political economy of the post-war nation was that it had to be internationalized at certain points if it was to survive. All history is movement, and in its rescue the European nation-state was from the outset laying the basis of a new international order for the continent. Yet the feasibility of that order was, and continues to be, determined by the evolution of national economic life.

The basis of the rescue of the nation-state was an economic one, and it follows that the Europeanization of its rescue had also to be economic. The interdependence of European states was, however, by no means purely economic. The single greatest problem within that interdependence was political, the future of Germany, as it had been in 1848, in 1864, in 1870, in 1914, and since 1933. No European rescue of the nation-state was of any validity, unless it also offered a solution to this problem. Although therefore the European rescue of the nation-state was necessarily an economic one, it is at the point where that economic rescue intersected with the

---

[32] N. Unga, *Socialdemokratin och arbetslöshetsfrågan 1912–1934. Framväxten av den 'nya' arbetslöshetspolitiken* (Stockholm, 1976).

[33] U. Olsson, 'Planning in the Swedish Welfare State', in *Studies in Political Economy*, vol. 34, 1991.

problem of Germany's future in Europe that the common policies of the European Community developed. What, after all, was personal security for Europeans in 1945 without personal security against Germany? It needs no more than that question to make the point that the European nation-state could not be rescued within its own frontiers. The chapters that follow trace the way in which some national policies aiming at national reassertion had to be internationalized in order to make them viable, and trace also the point at which, where they intersected with the fearful question of the future of Germany, the reinvigorated nation-state had to choose the surrender of a degree of national sovereignty to sustain its reassertion.

3 Coal and the Belgian nation

On those heavy, sodden summer days, so common there, when the broad-boughed trees droop with the weight of wet chestnut spikes and the fresh shoots of willow herb cover the spoil tips, the Borinage is a green lethargy. It closes about the traveller, instilling a deep unwillingness to leave. Along the canals the fishermen doze at regular intervals. Their rods, unmoving, dip into the black stagnant water. Rows of soot-stained, dull brick houses reflect from blank windows only the fatigue of the past. They are scattered in a pattern whose rationale is wholly industrial, to be understood only by the location of mines and factories now closed. Once, this pattern asserted the unfettered vitality of a new industrial civilization to which church, castle and market square had become unimportant. Streets led to mine entrances and the perspective was closed not by steeples but by winding-gear.

The landscape now has become a museum, scattered clues to a past society. Vitality has moved to the lorries speeding with cargoes of furniture and cakes on fast motorways through the region and to the tarmac spaces surrounding the exits and junctions with their complexes of offices, garden centres and do-it-yourself shops. Where once the location of everything depended on coal, the new civilization makes no locational demands other than ease of access and dispatch. In the old culture the roads were narrow and winding, not meant for travelling far. Life was lived with little interest in the rest of the country and little need to visit it. Roads and windows turned away from distant views. The mental effort needed to replace this life can be seen in the jagged new buildings, frantic colours, and dislocated abbreviations of the advertisements which cling around them, the triumphant symbolism of the replacement of a local culture by a worldwide pattern of production.

The Borinage is typical of a long swathe of southern Belgium, before 1958 one of the three major coal-producing regions of western Europe, after it the classic and much-studied case of the coal industry in decline. In reality its decline had begun much earlier. Competing only with difficulty with other regions in the 1920s it was dealt a blow by the Great Depression of 1929–32 which would have been mortal had not government for a mixture of reasons preserved it in almost the same size until the outbreak of war. During and immediately after the war it was a valuable resource, at first for the Germans and after 1944, in the worldwide coal shortage, for Europe's reconstruction. When that coal shortage was over, coal mining in southern Belgium continued to be preserved in almost the same size until the falling price of coal on world markets overwhelmed it at the end of the 1950s.

There is no more striking example anywhere in Europe of the post-war concern for employment and of the increased influence of labour over government than this preservation of the coal mines of southern Belgium at their level of output and employment of the 1920s. Even when the collapse eventually came, employment remained a central concern. Yet from the moment when the Treaty of Paris was signed the Belgian national government was only one of the two authorities with ultimate responsibility for the Belgian coal industry. The other was the High Authority of the European Coal, Iron and Steel Community. The Treaty told the High Authority to preserve 'the continuity of employment' and forbade it to 'harmonize' living and working conditions of workers by reducing wages. But it cannot be said that it contained any strong expression of social or employment policy. Yet even during the 1950s the process of integration internationalized employment and welfare policies which, left to its own devices, the Belgian government would have found extremely difficult to maintain on such a level.

The coalfields on which the new industrial civilization of the late eighteenth century was built stretch in an arc through the whole of southern-central Belgium from the French frontier near Maubeuge in the west to the town of Charleroi in the Sambre valley, along that valley to Namur where it joins the Meuse, and thence along the Meuse to Liège close to the Dutch frontier of Limburg. The difficulties which faced the Belgian coal industry after 1929 were common to all this southern area. But it was in its most westerly part, the Borinage, that they were the hardest to come to terms with.

The only town of any size in the Borinage is Mons, the provincial capital. From the late eighteenth century to 1960 its administrative services provided the only important source of stable employment in that area not based on coal. Whereas Charleroi and Liège and their regions early in the nineteenth century developed into important engineering centres in the forefront of technological development, extracting coal remained the main business of the Borinage. The ironworks which used so much of the increased output settled less in the Borinage than near to the larger towns which had a greater range of customers for iron products. In 1957 out of 64,800 people recorded as being in employment in the Borinage 23,000 worked in the coal industry. Only 7,000 people worked in services, although in Belgium as a whole 49 per cent of employment was in the tertiary sector. Metallurgical industries, still almost entirely dependent on

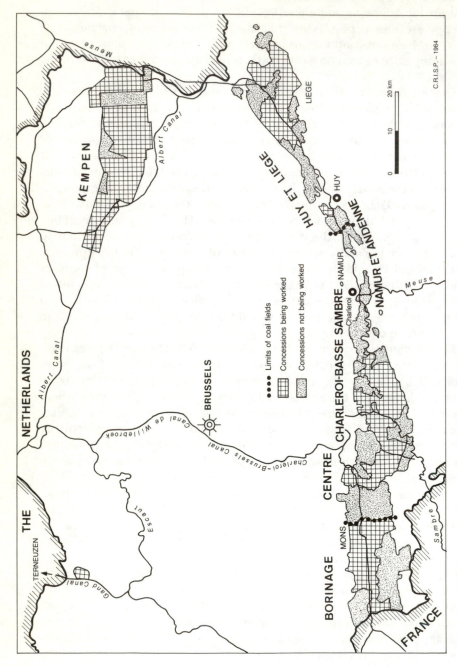

Figure 3.1 Mining concessions in the Belgium coalfields (1 June 1964)

coal, employed 4,800 people, the mining and quarrying of minerals about the same number, often in pits which had once yielded coal.[1] So half the labour force of the Borinage still depended directly or almost directly on coal. The chemical plant at Tertre, built in the 1930s as a development project to use the coke made from Borinage coal, cheap and unsold because of the slump in steel demand, as the basis for making fertilizers and related products, employed another 5 per cent of the labour force. Its pipes still twist around the new road system but the inputs no longer come from the area.

The mines of southern Belgium, particularly those of the Borinage, were old. Some had been digging coal before the eighteenth century. They were deep, increasingly difficult to work, with broken, narrow and steeply pitched seams and high temperatures. In the 1920s increases in output, such as that which corresponded with the 1926 miners' strike in Britain, were achieved only by adding labour. After the economic crash of 1929 the response of the coal industry was to hold down wages and to clamour for protection. In the 1930s Belgian miners' real wages were well below those in other western European coal-mining areas. One consequence was an increasing proportion of immigrant labour, for few Belgians sought unpleasant and dangerous jobs underground for low pay in an industry which seemed to have little future.[2]

In the 1920s the development of a new coalfield in the north of Belgium, the Kempen, which promised to be more profitable, went ahead rapidly. Although there were many disappointments on the way, by the early 1930s its mines were more profitable than those in the south and operated at higher levels of productivity. When the demand for coal fell steeply in 1929 the competition on domestic markets between the two coalfields threatened to reawake the linguistic division in the Belgian state, for the Kempen was entirely Flemish and the southern coalfield entirely francophone. Regulating competition in coal on the internal market and not leaving the coal mines of southern Belgium to the brutal self-adjustment which the free play of internal market forces would have meant, followed almost automatically. Coal determined the income of an important proportion of voters, especially socialist voters in southern Belgium and regulation of the domestic market in coal was a contribution to preserving Belgium as a national entity. It was, though, francophone Belgium which was subsidized by the state through these arrangements.

In the world of the 1930s there were, certainly, good arguments for retaining capacity in an industry vital to defence. An additional motivation

[1] ECSC, *Etude du développement économique des Régions de Charleroi, du Centre et du Borinage*, Collection d'économie et politique régionale no. 2. Programmes de développement et de conversion (Luxembourg, 1962), pp. 22–3.
[2] 'People decided to work in the mines hoping to find another job as quickly as possible.' J. Chapelle-Julière, 'La mobilité des mineurs du charbonnage du Bois-du-Cazier (1900–1945)', *Revue du Nord*, vol. lxxii, January–March 1990.

came from the great Belgian investment banks which had financed the development of the Kempen. They had equally important investments in the southern coalfield, as well as in the industries which used the output of both. Their interest lay in cartelizing the Belgian coal industry to preserve these investments in the face of the worldwide slump. Regulating the internal market in this way required protection on the national frontier and in the 1930s the Belgian coal industry became a highly protected and regulated sector of what remained overall a relatively open economy.

The consequence was that on the eve of the Second World War coal still employed more than 10 per cent of the national industrial labour force and still accounted for about 12 per cent of the value of all industrial production. Protection during the 1930s had preserved its size. After 1945 the demands of reconstruction and the temporary worldwide coal shortage meant that the search for national consensus and economic reconstruction came to rest on government support for an industry which could not possibly have maintained itself at the same size in an open economy in the face of international competition.

PROTECTION, WELFARE AND EMPLOYMENT

In the world coal shortage of 1945, when the only coal available on world markets was allocations from the United States to the European Coal Organization, it appeared logical that there could be no question of reducing the size of the Belgian industry. Coal and the need to mine it were exalted into major national symbols by the post-war socialist majority government. The prime minister Achille van Acker proclaimed a 'battle for coal' reminiscent of the production drives of more authoritarian political systems of the 1930s.[3] As a consequence both of this and of the early emergence of the post-war consensus in the Belgian state there was nowhere in western Europe where the changed position of labour in the immediate post-war world was more evident than in Belgian coal mining.

During the war wages had been frozen at a level less than 10 per cent above their pre-war level, although even on the evidence of the falsified official cost of living index this had meant a fall in the standard of living of coal miners of about a third. Mining, however, was a protected occupation during the war, and to escape labour drafts to Germany the labour force accepted the situation. It was in any case almost impossible to leave for

---

[3] Achille van Acker, 1898–1975. One of six children of a basket maker. Left school at the age of ten to work in the same trade, becoming boatman, docker and bookbinder before his election as a socialist to parliament in 1927. He stayed there for forty-seven years. During the German occupation he drafted the proposals of the banned socialist party for the Belgian welfare state, which he then implemented as minister of labour and social security, 1944–5; prime minister, 1945–6; minister of communications, 1947–9; prime minister, 1954–8. Notorious for his rudeness, he became a much respected president of the parliament. His life exemplified the transition of the economy of Flanders from pre-industrial poverty to post-industrial wealth.

other paid employment, because of the controls imposed by the occupiers. The German military administration itself repeatedly protested about the low pay for miners, because it had to face one obvious consequence, lower labour productivity.[4] At the liberation when well-paid work was liberally available for the Allied armed forces there was a mass departure from the mines. About 30,000 workers left in 1944 and early 1945 and monthly output fell by about a half. The response of the van Acker government was a series of increases in miners' wages and welfare allowances which took them from being one of the worst-paid groups in the Belgian labour force to being the best-paid.

The increase in real wages for a hewer in the Borinage in 1947 as compared to 1938 was of the order of 30 per cent.[5] The lowest-skilled group of surface workers received wages much higher than unskilled labour in other industries.[6] In western Europe only British miners received equivalent pay, and they did not get the same range of supplemental benefits. The Belgian social security laws of 1944 included special dispensations for miners, better accident and retirement insurance provision, large starting-work bonuses, free train tickets, cheap housing loans (where there was no free housing), exemption from military service, free coal, and sometimes free electricity and free water.

Yet in spite of such rewards and in spite of persistent post-war unemployment Belgian citizens still showed no great desire to work underground. This was not only because of memories of the earlier period. Between the end of the war and the end of 1955 1,000 men died in mining accidents in Belgium. For three weeks in August 1956 television screens throughout Europe showed the crowds waiting at the pit-head of the Bois du Cazier mine in Marcinelle while rescue workers brought up the 262 bodies, 136 of them Italians, who had died in an underground fire caused by careless working practices.[7] The shortfall of labour was made up by recruiting immigrants and retaining prisoners-of-war.

Until March 1947 Belgium retained 64,000 German prisoners in its mines.[8] Starting with an agreement to exchange coal for immigrant labour in 1945 an organized effort was made by the government to recruit Italians. After 1947 immigrants made up about three-quarters of the total under-

---

[4] J.R. Gillingham, *Belgian Business in the Nazi New Order* (Ghent, 1977), *passim*.

[5] Real wages for hewers in the Borinage before tax (1938 = 100)

    1938 = 100
    1947 = 130.3
    1948 = 117.6
    1951 = 177.7

Wages from *Annales des Mines de Belgique* deflated by the official cost-of-living index of the Ministry of Economic Affairs.

[6] W. Degryse *et al.*, *Le Borinage* (Brussels, 1958), p. 58.

[7] F. Dassetto and M. Dumoulin, *Mémoires d'une catastrophe. Marcinelle, 8 août 1956* (Brussels, 1986).

[8] P. Sunou, *Les Prisonniers de guerre allemands en Belgique et la bataille du charbon, 1945–1947* (Brussels, 1980).

ground labour force, and of them about three-quarters were Italians. Only in the more profitable and newer Kempen coalfield were these proportions lower. While post-war national reassertion thus concentrated on the status and future of the national coal industry, the composition of the labour force was already indicating that the management and future of the industry could not be reasonably regarded as decisions for Belgium alone. In fact in the 1950s the Italian government twice placed a stop on migration to the Belgian coal mines in an attempt to enforce improvements in safety.

After 1929 the industry had tried to save itself by international cartel arrangements which would preserve capacity, and when that failed, to use state action to get protection from all competition. International cartels broke apart in the face of falling prices and the collapse of inter-governmental cooperation. In the face of German dumping in 1931 the Belgian government followed the trend of the times and imposed quotas on coal imports. These were followed in 1933 by import duties whose proceeds went, apart from a brief period in 1934, directly to the owners to prevent mine closures and to retain their labour force. From then onwards the industry was concerned mainly with keeping the whole of the domestic market as far as possible for itself and retaining capacity in that way. The percentage of domestically mined coal used by Belgian industry grew. Protests from coal users who would have preferred cheaper foreign coal got nowhere in the face of what was, domestically, a highly cartelized structure and which in the 1930s was able to operate as such with open encouragement from the government. A Coal Commission was set up in 1931 to associate government with the supervision of the industry. It included two delegates from the Ministry of Industry both from the Mines Administration, which in the 1930s and after the Second World War was staffed with ardent defenders of comprehensive protection for the whole sector.[9]

Agreement on this domestic regulation of the market was easier because of the 29 million tonnes of coal a year which the industry mined at full capacity about 13.5 million tonnes in the 1930s were produced by collieries under the ultimate financial control of the two greatest financial holding companies in the country, the Société Générale and the Brufina group in which the Banque de Bruxelles had the dominating influence. The other nominally independent collieries were often in fact ultimately dependent on the same two holding companies. Joye, whose estimates are probably somewhat exaggerated, suggests that through the indirect control of independent mines half the total output was in fact controlled by the two major trusts and as much as 90 per cent by trusts of some kind or other.[10]

The origins of this control were various. The Société Générale was an

[9] R.L. Hogg, *Structural Rigidities and Policy Inertia in Inter-War Belgium*, Verhandelingen van de Koninklijke Academie voor Wetenschappen, Letteren en Schone Kunsten van België, Klasse der Letteren, Jaargang 48, Nr. 118 (Brussels, 1986).

[10] P. Joye, *Les Trusts en Belgique. La concentration capitaliste* (Brussels, 1964).

extremely diverse group which had been responsible in the nineteenth century for much of the development of the southern coalfield and also had important steel interests. The Banque de Bruxelles had extended its interests into coal in the 1920s because of the stability which the coal market then seemed to offer. A third large financial group, Coppée, which had been a pioneer of coke-oven engineering, also had extensive cartelized interests in steel and coal. One outcome of this ownership structure was a high degree of vertical integration by steelworks to secure regular coal and coke supplies of the right quality. Most coke used in Belgian steelworks, up to about 80 per cent of the total, was made in coking plants attached to the steelworks themselves. The mines themselves, unlike their counterparts in Germany, were thus often confined to extraction only, without having the opportunity to expand into the higher-value-added processing activities which constituted an increasing share of whatever profits the industry as a whole made. The holding companies supported the import duties on coal in the 1930s against the opposition of independent coal users as a way of sheltering their investments in steel and coke-making from the blasts of the depression. By the mid-1950s the quantity of coal output which they directly controlled in the country as a whole had risen to 17 million tonnes.[11]

In general the cartelized structure of the industry was used to provide a rent from its activities at the expense of higher fuel prices for other Belgian industries and in the 1930s it was probably maximizing employment in coal mining, albeit at low wages, at the expense of employment elsewhere. The political weight of steel and coal together could overcome objections from elsewhere in Belgian industry, especially when the policy could be seen as a patriotic one; the most obvious European competitor was the Third Reich and there were good arguments against depending on imports from that quarter should demand improve. In 1935 the trusts managed to bring all producers together into one national coal syndicate, the Comptoir Belge des Charbons (Cobéchar). It was in the same year that receipts from the import duties began to be used to subsidize exports, giving Belgium a coal export surplus for the two years 1935 and 1936. Rearmament brought a resurgence of demand late in 1938 and this was held up at the time, as it was to be in 1950–1, as a justification for having retained capacity. In 1939 coal imports would indeed have been difficult to obtain.

Under the German occupation coal producers were forced to sell their product at the prices prevailing in Germany and to meet a nominal freight charge calculated on the basis of its carriage to the German town of Oberhausen. To enable them to do this they were heavily subsidized directly by the Belgian administration. Eventually in 1943 the coal price to Belgian users was increased, but a direct rebate was provided by the Belgian administration to coke plants and steelworks using Belgian coals.[12]

[11] ECSC, *CECA 1952–1962. Résultats. Limites. Perspectives* (Luxembourg, 1963), p. 224.
[12] J.R. Gillingham, *Belgian Business . . .*, op. cit., p. 135.

Production of coal fell from January 1941 onwards. Lack of investment for more than a decade and an ageing and unwilling work force left the industry demoralized and poorly equipped to face the continuation of high demand into peacetime. The post-war 'battle for coal' did not improve the industry's long-run situation in this respect. The employment underground of prisoners-of-war and untrained immigrants exerted a downward pull on productivity trends negating the upward pull of returning to full capacity working.

The van Acker government identified the need for an increase in employment and output in the coal mines with the survival of the Belgian nation. Van Acker actually styled himself additionally 'minister for coal', 'Achille Coal' the population called him. Because it saw coal as the first essential of post-war recovery his socialist government also saw a cheap coal price as a necessity. Post-war sales prices remained strictly controlled at too low a level to encourage the quantity of new private investment needed if the industry was to come to terms with the much higher post-war labour costs. The sales cartel (Cobéchar) and the management association (Fédéchar)[13] were tightly bound by government decrees behind which lurked the constant threat of nationalization, several times debated in parliament. The first post-war minister for reconstruction, Albert de Smalle, tried to restructure coal-mine ownership into five limited companies, one for each coalfield. The ultimate objective was to rationalize and amalgamate mines by linking their underground workings and so improve productivity. The existing companies, through the Social Christian Party, vehemently attacked the scheme in parliament as an interference in the rights of private industry and the idea was dropped, the fate that would befall similar proposals in the 1950s.

Nevertheless, it was acknowledged that the industry would not return to functioning in a merely private capacity because the demand for coal was once more high. Coal had become a part of the post-war mixed economy, in which its objectives would be strongly and directly influenced by government. In August 1947, as a compromise on the nationalization question, the National Coal Council (Conseil National des Charbonnages) was set up. The Council, with twenty-four members equally divided between representatives of government, industry and the unions, was given an overall supervisory role in determining long-term policy and objectives. It was also supposed to report within eighteen months with proposals for restructuring the industry and merging mines in order to improve productivity, but this area of its activities came to nothing. By the unions, it was seen as acknowledging the post-war gains made by organized labour, a public commitment that the days of low wages and unemployment in coal mining would not return. This, in itself, did not bode well for the chances of a really radical set of proposals.

---

[13] Fédération Charbonnière Belge.

In exile, socialist and christian trade unions, employers and government had put together the basis of the post-war consensus in their negotiations for a social security pact. This was at once implemented after liberation by legislation in 1944 for an integrated social security system for wage earners and in subsequent years by the creation of various Enterprise Councils, including workers' representatives, of which the National Coal Council can be seen as a special case.[14] It is hardly surprising that the Council, which was charged with the general supervision of the whole industry, should have approached its task with caution. The coal companies themselves showed little enthusiasm for closing marginal mines, whose retention, they continued throughout the 1950s to believe, helped to increase the flexibility of output in the face of changing demand. They were strongly opposed to company mergers. Workers, of course, were not interested in closing down their own industry. The Council saw its primary task rather as stimulating the investment which had been foregone.[15] Its problem was how to do this when the government controlled the coal price at a level which did not meet the high production costs.

A tax was levied on all coal sales to finance investments. In continuation of the policy of equilibrating regional disparities in profits and investment the sales tax was higher on Kempen coals than on those from the southern coalfield, so that the more productive coalfield was being taxed to finance part of the investment programme in the areas of lower productivity. At 45 Belgian francs a tonne, the initial burden of the levy, Kempen coals were paying a tax of 6.3 per cent on their average sales price. Southern coals taxed at 35 Belgian francs a tonne were paying a levy of only 5.1 per cent.[16] To the sums raised by this levy was added part of the Marshall Aid counterpart funds. It was, admittedly, one way of forcing the financial trusts to finance some of the investment. But at the same time they were in effect receiving government aid, because the coals purchased by their steelworks had to be sold at controlled prices.

Measuring productivity in mining is a hazardous statistical business. But, if we take output per shift as one of the less meaningless measures usually used, its level in the Kempen in 1951 was more than a third higher than that of the average of the southern coalfields. This was a consequence of larger coal seams, a higher net coal yield from the material extracted, newer workings, and a larger size of firm. The average height of coal seams worked in Belgium in 1954 was between 100 and 120 centimetres. In the Borinage 135 of those worked out of 202 were less than 120 centimetres, in

[14] G. Kurgan-Van Hentenryk and J. Puissant, 'Industrial Relations in the Belgian Coal Industry since the End of the Nineteenth Century', in G.D. Feldman and K. Tenfelde (eds), *Workers, Owners and Politics in Coal Mining. An International Comparison of Industrial Relations* (New York, 1990), pp. 260 ff.

[15] And for which the industry itself had recognized the necessity at the end of the war. See Belgium, Fédération des Associations Charbonnières, *La Belgique devant le problème charbonnier* (Brussels, 1945).

[16] Average coal sale prices from *Annales des Mines de Belgique*, January 1953.

the Kempen only 99 out of 219.[17] There was a geological advantage in the
north, increased by the greater evenness of the seams, but it was not so
telling as other differences. The 19.2 million tonnes mined in the southern
coalfields in 1950 came from 157 pits; the 8.1 million tonnes mined in the
Kempen from only 11 pits.[18] The average annual output per underground
worker in the Kempen was 321 tonnes; in the south 250 tonnes.

Kempen output gradually came to account for a larger share of national
output, rising from 28 per cent of the total in 1949 to 36 per cent in 1957, so
that the overall international competitiveness of the Belgian coal industry
tended to improve through this shift in the regional balance. It did nothing,
of course, to solve the political problem. Given the extent of protection,
subsidization and cartelization the true profit and loss account of Belgian
colliery companies is probably undiscoverable. But the estimate made by a
member of the Mines Administration, that in 1948 only one-fifth of the
colliery companies would have been operating at a nominal profit had they
not been subsidized, demonstrates clearly enough the grim outlook for the
southern mines, for only one pit in the Kempen was operating at a nominal
loss.[19] Of course the cartelized structure of coal and steel meant that few
colliery companies or individual mines had their viability judged by their
own individual balance sheets. Nevertheless, limiting price competition
and competition for capital between the regions did not stop the relative
decline of the south in the face of its northern rival.

No less than 80 per cent of the nominal post-subsidy profits of coal mines
as they were reckoned in 1949 were siphoned off for distribution to the
non-profitable mines.[20] Coal prices remained fixed within a complex zonal
pricing system, not only to equilibrate returns between north and south but
also between collieries producing the coals more in demand and those
whose output mix veered more towards the less wanted coals. Government
aid to the mines to compensate for these price ceilings amounted between
1 September 1944 and the end of September 1949, when the system was
changed, to 9,535 million Belgian francs ($237 million).

The argument for preserving this subsidization was that demand was
high. Steel exports dominated Belgium's foreign trade in the recovery
period. With the whole of western Europe suffering from acute steel
shortages, Belgian steel sold at such premium prices that in 1948 its exports
were more than 40 per cent of all Belgium's export earnings. It was steel

---

[17] A. Meyers, 'Aspects techniques de l'exploitation charbonnière belge en 1954', *Annales des Mines de Belgique*, 1956, no. 1, January.

[18] P. Wiel, *Untersuchungen zu den Kosten-und Marktproblemen der westeuropäischen Kohlenwirtschaft* (Essen, 1953), p. 70.

[19] J. Martens, 'Evolution du droit minier et certains aspects de l'industrie charbonnière belge', in *Annales des Mines de Belgique*, December 1950, September 1951.

[20] C. Demeure de Lespaul, 'L'industrie charbonnière belge devant la menace des importations', in *Bulletin de l'Institut de Recherches Economiques et Sociales de Louvain*, vol. xv, no. 1, 1949. The author contrived to hold a regular place in the journal through the late 1930s and well into the 1950s with lengthy arguments for protection.

above all which gave Belgium a favourable trade position when neighbouring economies depended on American aid to balance their payments.
Because there was an even greater shortage of coke and coking-coal than
of coal in general, these export earnings were dependent on the utilization
of Belgium's own national coking-coal resources. Steel exports provided an
argument for subsidizing even the most unprofitable pits if they produced
the coking-coal from which was made the coke charge going into Belgian
blast furnaces. Of all the southern Belgian coal basins none mined a higher
proportion of top quality coking-coal in its total output than the Borinage.
This was what sustained the region after 1945 and it was for this above all
that men continued to crouch and crawl 3,000 feet below the earth's
surface. For other kinds of coal, although demand was very high, the
possibilities of substitution were, as we shall see, greater and the argument
for subsidization weaker.

Coking-coal is an imprecise term, since a wide range of coals can be
turned into coke. Much effort and money was, for example, spent in
France in this period in experimenting with the coking of mixtures of
different grades and mixtures of coal in the hope of reducing the French
steel industry's dependence on imported coke and coking-coal. Coking-
coal in Belgium was more often broadly defined as the two grades *gras A*
and *gras B*, corresponding most closely to the *Fettkohle* of the Ruhr, which
was the product used to produce most of the coke charge in blast furnaces
in Germany and eastern France. Coke itself was made in various grades
some of which were for heating purposes and would not serve as metallurgical coke for making pig-iron. The coke input into pig-iron manufacture in
Belgium was mainly, but not solely, from *gras A* and *gras B* coals. These
grades accounted for 56.8 per cent of total output in the Borinage in 1954,
rising to 63.3 per cent in 1956, falling to 50.7 per cent in the 1958 recession
and rising again to 54.5 per cent in 1959.[21] In 1954 the Borinage supplied
18.8 per cent of total Belgian coking-coal output defined in this way, 2.43
million tonnes out of a national total of 12.88 million tonnes.[22] The other
southern coalfields together produced only 1.21 million tonnes of coking-
coal. In the same year the Kempen mined 9.24 million tonnes of coking-
coal, but it was not usually reckoned to be of the same high quality as that
of the Borinage.

The Kempen's output was theoretically sufficient, extrapolating from the
national average conversion ratio of coal into coke, to make 7.11 million
tonnes of coke, 1 million tonnes more than national output and 1.9 million
tonnes more than apparent consumption. If all Kempen coking-coal been
coked, and if its coke yield had been as high as that of the best Borinage
coking-coal, and if it had been possible to switch types of coking-coal
inputs into coke plants and of coke inputs into blast furnaces, the Kempen

---

[21] *Annales des Mines de Belgique*, various issues.
[22] ibid., January 1956, p. 105.

coalfield would by itself have met national demand for coking-coal in the recovery period. But none of these conditions held good and this fact alone, leaving aside the acute regional and linguistic issues, led the coal and steel industries as well as the unions to support the general subsidies and the price controls which were their basis. It was essential, they argued, to keep open southern mines which produced coals in demand, even if they did so at a loss, in order to ensure that there was no shortage of coal and particularly of coking-coal in cyclical peaks in steel production.

The National Coal Council's deliberations led to the changes in the subsidization regime which eventually were introduced in 1949 after the loss of the socialist majority in June and the switch to a Social Christian–Liberal coalition government in August. This political change coincided with the collapse of the steel export boom as the production of other countries rose. Pig-iron output fell steeply in Belgium from its 1948 peak, not to recover the same level until late in 1950 (table 3.1), and the output of metallurgical coke fell more steeply, below its 1938 level in fact (table 3.2). But given the continuing restrictions imposed on German steel output by the occupiers and the quick return to buoyant demand for steel in 1950, it could be argued, as the steel industry claimed, that the fall in output of pig-iron in 1949 was merely a temporary adjustment to lower export prices, which would make the need for subsidized and guaranteed coal inputs into its coking plants more imperative.

Table 3.1 Output of pig-iron in Belgium, 1938–60 (thousand tonnes)

1938	2,426
1939	3,059
1945	735
1946	2,161
1947	2,817
1948	3,929
1949	3,749
1950	3,695
1951	4,868
1952	4,790
1953	4,232
1954	4,625
1955	5,385
1956	5,770
1957	5,581
1958	5,519
1959	5,697
1960	6,553

Source: Belgium, Ministère des Affaires Economiques, Institut National de la Statistique, *Annuaire Statistique de la Belgique et du Congo Belge*

Table 3.2   Output and consumption of coal and coke in Belgium, 1938–60 (thousand tonnes)

	(A) Output of coal	(B) Apparent consumption of coal*	(C) Output of coke	(D) Apparent consumption of coke*	(E) Output of metallurgical coke
1938	29,585		5,106		4,398
1946	22,852		3,900		2,840
1947	24,436		4,793		3,535
1948	26,691	29,102	5,629	4,537	4,481
1949	27,854	26,257	5,034	4,189	3,788
1950	27,321	26,069	4,598	4,034	3,564
1951	29,651	30,905	6,096	5,553	4,783
1952	30,384	28,014	6,407	5,549	5,055
1953	30,060	26,670	5,945	4,953	4,629
1954	29,249	27,554	6,146	5,245	4,884
1955	29,920	28,946	6,597	5,964	5,346
1956	29,461	29,979	7,270	6,404	5,912
1957	29,001	28,908	7,156	6,230	5,839
1958	27,062	24,025	6,906	5,906	5,595
1959	22,757	24,891			
1960	22,469	25,024			

* Output + imports − exports − △ stocks

Sources: A, C, E; *Annales des Mines de Belgique.* B; trade from UN, *Quarterly Bulletin of Coal Statistics*, stocks from Ministère de l'Èconomie, *L'Èconomie belge.* C; trade from UN, *Quarterly Bulletin of Coal Statistics*, stocks from *Annales des Mines de Belgique*

Pig-iron output responded in 1950 to the renewed buoyancy of world demand. Afterwards, as table 3.1 shows, the fluctuations in demand were, as always in the iron and steel industry, marked, even in a period of such continuing prosperity as that of 1950–60. Output as well as consumption of coke followed both the rising trend and the sharp fluctuations of pig-iron output, as table 3.2 shows; and fluctuations in the consumption of coal reflected this pattern of fluctuations in coke consumption. The long-run trend of coal consumption in general was downward. Output was stable between 1951 and 1958. The strong increase in industrial production after 1953 was accompanied by only a mild upward movement in coal production which did not last. Partly this was because sudden expansion of coal output is difficult, partly because the increase in demand was met by sales from stocks accumulated when demand was lower, but mainly it was because the increase in the demand for primary energy inputs was also met by oil which was beginning to replace coal for a wide range of purposes. A vigorous if highly fluctuating demand for coking-coal with a general persistent upward trend was co-existing therefore up to 1958 with a slow downward trend in the demand for coal in general. As oil replaced coal for firing ovens and for powering railway locomotives, falls in demand for coal for these purposes were cancelling the effects of increased demand from power stations and coking plants.[23]

These patterns of demand, if foreseeable, were not apparent in autumn 1949 and the basic motivation of the new government when it altered the subsidy regime from 1 October that year was not to provoke a reduction in output but to save money, to reduce the disincentive to investment which the previous subsidy regime appeared to place on the more efficient mines, and to look after the interests of the steel industry. From that date the coal subsidies were made more selective. They would be paid directly by government for a fixed term of twenty months and in degressive quantities. The producers of good quality coking-coal in the Borinage, were exempted from this regime. They signed special agreements with the government to last to the end of 1954 under which government aid would continue to be provided at more or less the same level as before in return for specific commitments to rationalization and investment.

How rigorously the government would in fact have been able to run down subsidies to the non-profitable, non-coking-coal sector in the south was never put to the test. Schuman made his proposals for a common market in coal, iron and steel in May 1950. Negotiations interfered with policy making, and control over prices once the Treaty of Paris came into force passed to the European Coal, Iron and Steel Community. The outcome of the negotiations again altered the subsidy regime. The net effect of the treaty was to provide new subsidies while retaining the old prices. What the price policy of the Belgian government might have been under the new subsidy regime of 1949 is hard to guess. The principle of the differentiation between mines on the basis of the kind of coals they produced, not only on their levels of profitability, was subsequently upheld by independent inquiries as the basis of a sound price and investment policy. It carried with it, though, the implication that in periods of high demand for good quality coking-coal prices would have to move upwards. Would the Belgian government have been able to allow that? And, even more serious, would it have accepted the converse position that for coals in low demand prices should fall? It is probable that it would have not wished to face the political consequences.

As part of the process of permitting the allocation of Marshall Plan counterpart funds to the investment programme in the mines the United States Economic Cooperation Administration (ECA) commissioned an inquiry into the Belgian coal industry from a firm of American mining consultants, Robinson and Robinson. Their report argued that large parts of the industry now unprofitable could in fact be made profitable and at the same time the sale price of Belgian coal be reduced by a drastic programme of rationalization. A proliferation of separately managed collieries each

---

[23] ECSC, *Sixth General Report on the Activities of the Community*, vol. 2 (Luxembourg, 1955), p. 117.

with a small output and few if any centralized surface processing activities had led to a proliferation of separate machine shops, repair shops and other small-scale activities. These were as much responsible, the report argued, for lower productivity as the lack of rationalization of the mine workings below ground.[24] The fragmentation of the firms also prevented the investment in coal treatment and processing plant which could increase the value added of the output.

Here the Robinson report was laying its finger on two highly sensitive political issues. One was the power of the government over the holding companies. The attempts of government since 1945 to rationalize company structure had failed. The special subsidy regime introduced in 1949 for the Borinage was one more attempt along these lines and the Robinson report encouraged it. The report emphasized the likelihood of sustained demand for coking-coal and pointed out that there was therefore an even stronger case for rationalization of company structure in the Borinage than else-where. The second issue was that of employment. Rationalizing the surface activities of mines meant that the main reductions in the size of the labour force would fall on Belgians, not immigrants.

The report was available from spring 1950 and there were many rumours about its content, but the government would not release it, and after May and the onset of negotiations on the Schuman proposals it was not likely to do so, because its contents would have embarrassed the stand which the government took. The proposal for a common market in coal was likely to raise serious problems in setting coal prices. The government hardly wanted in those circumstances widespread publicity for an argument that Belgian mines would need less protection and that prices might be liberated if government acted more boldly.

In the light of subsequent history the Robinson report, like the proposed changes in government aid in October 1949, seems optimistic. Belgium's southern mines had the highest unit labour costs and probably the lowest productivity of all western Europe's coal-mining areas. Labour costs per man/shift, which were 65 per cent of total output costs, compared to 56 per cent in the Federal Republic, amounted to $5.84 compared to $5.13 in France, $4.39 in the Federal Republic, and only $3.51 in the Netherlands.[25] Labour costs per tonne of output were $13.07 compared to $8.74 in France and $7.33 in the Federal Republic, the difference between this comparison and the previous one reflecting the lower output per shift (table 3.3). The disparity in other costs between Belgian mines on the one hand and German or Dutch mines on the other was often even wider than the disparity in labour costs, for the weak competitive position of the industry was only in part to be blamed on the great social advances which

---

[24] MAECE, 5216, Report by Robinson and Robinson to the ECA Mission in Belgium and Luxembourg.

[25] 'The Coal and Steel Industries of Western Europe', in UN, ECE, *Economic Bulletin for Europe*, 2nd quarter, 1950.

its labour force had obtained since 1945. The investment which had taken place had stayed well short of the radical restructuring which the Robinson report deemed necessary. To undertake such a restructuring in 1950 was likely to be harder than in the immediate aftermath of the war when it might have been done in return for the concessions then made to labour.

Table 3.3   Average output per man/shift in European coal-mining areas 1951 (kg.) (monthly average)

Netherlands	1,420
Lorraine	1,264
Ruhr	1,124
Saarland	1,043
Kempen*	917
Aachen	585
Nord and Pas de Calais	761
Southern Belgium*	626–724

* June only.

Sources: Deutsche Kohlenbergbau-Leitung, *Die Kohlenwirtschaft der Welt in Zahlen. Statistische Übersichten über die Kohlenwirtschaft Deutschlands und des Auslandes* (Essen, 1952); Belgium from *Annales des Mines de Belgique*

The accusation, commonly made, that the capital stock of the industry was being run down while Italian workers were ruthlessly exploited had no substance. Not only were the immigrants very well paid,[26] the absolute level of investment after the war compared reasonably well with coal industries elsewhere in Europe. Real gross fixed assets in 1957 were 44 per cent higher than in 1948, a rate of increase comparable to that in the steel industry or the food and drink industry and higher than that in the textile industry.[27] Indeed, the problem is rather to explain why so much investment continued in so unpromising an area.

Total investment per tonne of coal produced between 1952 and 1961, $1.89, was higher than in Germany ($1.57) or than in the Netherlands ($1.67).[28] The best explanation seems to be that of Lamfalussy, that this was defensive investment. Because the life-span of the fixed capital was long, because the planning horizon of the firms was short, because the break-up value of their assets was lower than their profit value while they were still being worked, a stream of investment continued, most of it capital deepening, to enable the firms to stay in production, which they could only do if their competitive situation did not deteriorate further.

[26] Making it more or less impossible for the National Coal Board in Britain to compete for them, even where chauvinistic British miners reluctantly agreed to work with these former enemies.

[27] A. Lamfalussy, *Investment and Growth in Mature Economies. The Case of Belgium* (London, 1961).

[28] ECSC, *CECA 1952–1962*, op. cit., pp. 10, 259.

Subsidization and the continuation of the sheltered regime which had begun in 1931 meant that defensive investment of this kind could continue to provide a rent for the shareholders, employment and a relatively high income for the workers, and a guaranteed national source of supply of coal and coke to the steelworks. It precluded, however, anything so bold as company mergers and the rationalization of workings.

For the unions, maintaining the southern mines in production was seen not merely as employment policy but also as generally symbolic of the great national gains which labour had won since liberation. There was a tendency for the smaller of the two unions involved, the Centrale des Francs Mineurs, which was associated to the Christian Union Confederation and which recruited mainly in the Kempen coalfield, to break ranks in defence of jobs and wages in the more profitable northern pits, but this was of real political significance only in the late 1950s. For the coal owners the politics of this situation could be turned to their advantage. Faced with pressure for job preservation it was easy for them to ask for further subsidization. The one likely source of opposition was coal consumers. Where these were independent they did in fact come together in their own pressure group, the Union des Utilisateurs et Négociants Belges de Charbon. Its ineffectiveness is in part explained by the sympathy of public opinion for miners and the coal industry in the aftermath of the war. It was also weakened by the continuing underlying threat that the coal industry would have to be nationalized if the regime of subsidies had to be renounced. The examples of France and Britain were only too near at hand and in defence of the freedom of enterprise, no matter how little meaning that had in the circumstances, support from other businesses rallied to the coal industry. High coal prices and high public expenditure on the industry were always in the last resort seen by industrialists as better than what was feared would be only the start of further nationalizations in Belgium.[29]

There was therefore a powerful combination of political interests behind the preservation of an autarkic regime for the coal industry. Subsidized output and wages, no imports until domestic output had been sold, subsidized exports, and subsidized domestic sales to consumers such as electricity producers who might otherwise have moved more quickly away from coal, this was a policy mixture which appeared absolutely incompatible with a common market. On balance the country would be more or less self-sufficient in coal provided the regime was maintained. Foreign trade could be limited to a small exchange of different kinds of coal. Any alteration appeared to touch too many vital political interests.

In 1950 coal in its natural and processed forms, briquettes and coke, accounted for about 75.8 per cent of all energy consumption in the economy.[30] Imported sources of energy – coal, oil and natural gas – still came to

[29] J. Meynaud *et al.*, *La Décision politique en Belgique* (Paris, 1965) pp. 277–8.
[30] G. Marchal, 'Bilan énergétique de la Belgique. Année 1950', in *Annales des Mines de Belgique*, 1952, 6, table 7.

only 13.5 per cent of total consumption.[31] Certainly the sudden weakening of demand in 1949 and the long-run tendency for coal to be replaced by other forms of fuel both suggested that the regime of the post-war years could not survive indefinitely, if only because the opportunity costs of such policies were very high. With coal carrying so much weight in the economy, accounting for 13 per cent of total value added, such a misallocation of resources was bound to slow down the rate of growth of national income, as indeed it seems to have done. Nevertheless it was not domestic politics which first effectively challenged this autarkic framework in spite of the subsidy changes in 1949, but foreign policy and the unsettled question of Germany's future. With Schuman's proposal on 9 May 1950 every proposition on which the national management of the Belgian coal industry rested was brought into question.

BELGIUM ENTERS THE COAL AND STEEL COMMUNITY

For Monnet and Schuman, when they drew up their proposals for the ECSC, the Belgian coal industry was only instrumental to the grander scheme of things, a future framework for Franco–German relations within which their own aspirations for the future of France and Europe could be realized. Had Belgium understood in advance the nature and contents of the working document which was to be drawn up by Monnet and his associates as the sole initial base for the negotiations, it would 'in all probability' have taken the same attitude as the United Kingdom and refused to negotiate from that basis.[32] Such was the view of François Vinck, the head of the Fuel and Energy Administration in the Ministry of Economic Affairs.[33] The prior commitment to achieving a common market spelled out in that working document, although it had been implicitly accepted in the Ministry of Foreign Affairs, combined with the other propositions in the document to place Belgian negotiators in a weak position when it came to defending the interests of their coal industry. 'Madness', Vinck called it.[34] Monnet's ideological predisposition to denounce all forms of business association and to extol at length at crucial moments in the negotiations the virtues of free competition made the original basis of the negotiations seem even more unwise. Eventually,

---

[31] Recalculating the data in Marchal (op. cit.) to allow for the small volume of natural gas imported from the Netherlands.

[32] PRO, CAB 134/295, 'Note of a Conversation with the Belgian delegates to the Paris negotiations', 20 September 1950.

[33] François Vinck, 1906– . Socialist son of a ship's carpenter. Director of the Coal Allocation Office, 1945–7; director-general for fuel and energy in the Ministry of Economic Affairs, 1948–52; director of the marketing division of the High Authority, 1952–60 (which he found complacent); director-general for labour, health and reconversion problems in the UN Economic Commission for Europe, 1960–73; director-general for social affairs in the EEC, 1973. A lover of the cinema.

[34] PRO, CAB 134/295, Conversation between UK labour attaché in Brussels and Vinck, 6 July 1950.

however, Monnet was forced in autumn 1950 to abandon this constricting framework which he had sought to impose, although the commitment to reach agreement on a common market for coal was preserved.

Monnet had originally envisaged a common market with a simple price structure in which the High Authority set a maximum and a minimum coal price and the mines were left free to compete between those bounds. The assumption was that existing discrimination in freight rates would also be removed. Underlying this conception of a future price structure was an important political decision which had not been initially apparent to the Belgians. Monnet's intention was that Belgian coal output should be reduced by about 5 million tonnes a year to make room for an equivalent volume of German coal to be exported to Belgian markets. While this was by no means an unreasonable prediction of the outcome of a common market in coal, it was also a convenient bait for the Federal Republic to sign the treaty. To be fair, in Paris the Planning Commissariat was initially willing also to see an equivalent reduction in French output, although such ideas tended to disappear rather quickly once the Korean War came and in the face of domestic political pressures.

The assumption that Belgian output would fall to make room for the Germans was a poor initial ground for winning Belgian acceptance of the political goals of the proposed treaty and the Belgian attitude hardened as soon as Monnet's underlying assumptions about Belgian output became clear. 'The political aspect', the foreign minister Paul van Zeeland told his negotiators, 'must be the consequence of what is achieved economically and not the opposite.'[35] The degree of surrender of national sovereignty demanded by Monnet was not necessary, he argued, to regulate the coal question.[36] 'You', the head of the Belgian delegation to the negotiations, Max Suétens, told Monnet, 'see the solution to our problems through the High Authority. We see the High Authority through our problems and their solution.'[37]

As soon as it was ascertained that the Dutch felt much the same about the powers which Monnet was demanding for the High Authority, Dirk Spierenburg their chief negotiator describing them as 'dictatorial', it became clear to the Belgian delegation that a division of labour was possible. They could concentrate their efforts mainly on the economic issues and on repelling the threat to their coal industry. Their close agreement with their Benelux partner on the constitutional issues meant that these could safely be left to the Dutch negotiators.[38]

---

[35] MAECE, 5212, 'Compte rendu de la réunion de la délégation belge chez M. van Zeeland, le 29 juin', 30 June 1950.

[36] ibid., 'Note concernant les conversations du 20 au 24 juin sur le Plan Schuman', 27 June 1950.

[37] ibid., 'Echange de vues entre M. Monnet et ses adjoints et les chefs des diverses missions', 23 June 1950.

[38] MBZ, 996.1, Plan Schuman, Alg. III, 'Kort Verslag van de bespreking inzake het Plan Schuman met de belgische luxemburgse delegaties op 3 Juli 1950'. Dirk Pieter

Suétens was a foreign ministry official. His delegation was made up of civil servants and two prominent industrialists, Pierre van der Rest[39] from the steel industry and Pierre Delville[40] from the coal industry. Delville, the president of the Association Charbonnière du Centre, was the head of the coal section of the Coppée holding company, a man with an immediate economic interest in the fate of the southern mines. It became clear by the close of the negotiations that the industrialists regarded themselves as watchdogs over the foreign ministry officials, while on the foreign ministry side they were thought of as being there to provide a measure of public support for what was likely to be a diplomatic agreement at first reached in secret but afterwards requiring widespread public debate before acceptance. This was not a relationship that would have a happy ending.

The negotiations took place against the reflation, rising inflation and soaring coal demand of the start of the Korean war, whereas the French proposals about the future status of Belgian coal in the common market drawn up in early 1950 had been influenced by the fact that the demand for coal was slackening. When coal had been a scarce commodity at the end of the war western Europe had depended on imports of American coal, as in the immediate aftermath of the First World War. It had been assumed in France that 1949 had marked the end of these imports and that planning for the different shares of output would take place in a self-sufficient common market. American coal exports to the six countries had fallen steeply from their peak in 1947, as table 3.4 shows, and had almost disappeared from western European markets by the time the Schuman proposals were made. During the negotiations countries again however began to import American coal and in 1951 imports exceeded the level of any previous year except 1947. In 1950, when dollars began to flow into western European reserves, imports from America were seen by some of the negotiating states as preferable to European coal. By the start of 1951 however, the dollar shortage was temporarily reappearing and demand for coal switching to European suppliers. In general, therefore, Monnet's wish to reduce the size of Belgian output became increasingly unrealizable and impractical as an immediate step as the negotiations proceeded.

Spierenburg, 1909– . Director-general of foreign economic affairs in the Foreign Ministry, 1945–52; member of the High Authority of the ECSC, 1952–67. His commentaries on the negotiations are the most percipient of those of any of the major civil servants involved.

[39] Baron Pierre van der Rest, 1916– . Eldest of seven children of the chairman of the Central Committee of Belgian Industry. Studied law and economics at Leuven. Head of the Price Administration, 1944–6; of the central representative committee of Belgian iron and steel manufacturers, 1946–77. His father and grandfather had been in the same industry. The patriarch of an extensive family network of Belgian and American business.

[40] Pierre Lucien Marie Delville, 1905– . Third of nine children of a prominent civil servant. Studied mining and religious thought at Leuven. Made his whole career in the Evence Coppée holding company, of which he was a director, 1950–71. Served as president of Fédéchar and of the Belgian Christian Employers Federation. In spite of his initial opposition to the Treaty of Paris he not only served in 1965–6 as president of the Coal Producers' Advisory Committee of the Community but also, in 1974, as President of the

Table 3.4 Imports of United States coal into ECSC countries, 1946–62 (thousand tonnes)

1946	11,200
1947	25,800
1948	15,300
1949	8,800
1950	100
1951	18,200
1952	16,302
1953	6,684
1954	6,164
1955	15,935
1956	30,389
1957	37,828
1958	25,820
1959	14,102
1960	12,484
1961	11,734
1962	14,980

Sources: 1946–52, W. Degryse *et al. Le Borinage* (Brussels, 1958); ECSC, *Sixth General Report on the Activities of the Community*, 1957–8; ECSC, *CECA 1952–1962. Résultats. Limites. Perspectives* (Luxembourg, 1963)

The same increased demand for coal from summer 1950 also called into question the capacity of German coal mining to replace the Belgian production which was to be forgone. By April 1951 the minister for the economy in the Federal Republic, Ludwig Erhard, was complaining that the economy was short of 15 million tonnes. Despite its ulterior purpose – ensuring that the Ruhr Authority's power to enforce exports of German coal was taken away in return for Germany's acceptance of the common market – this complaint was not unfounded. What had been unforeseen by any of the negotiating powers, was the general tendency for Germany to change between 1951 and 1957 from being a coal exporter on a major scale to becoming a net importer.[41] German coal exports were sustained throughout those years at their 1951 level only because of imports of coal from the United States and elsewhere for use on the German market. Furthermore Monnet's unquestioned assumption of 1950, that German coal would always be produced at a cost so much lower than Belgian coal that it could be delivered in Belgium below Belgian producers' prices, also proved uncertain. Such were the consequences of the sustained high

Steel Producers' Advisory Committee, an industrial transposition which was probably only open to a Belgian.

[41] Net exports of German coal fell from 10.7 million tonnes in 1950 to 3.5 million in 1951 and to 300,000 in 1952. In 1953 and 1954 there were large exports but throughout the cyclical upswing of 1955–7 the Federal Republic was on balance a large coal importer, with a net import surplus of 9 million tonnes in 1957.

growth rates of industrial output in Germany, which French planners like almost everyone else had failed to predict.

At the start of the negotiations the Belgian coal industry took up a defensive position which nevertheless accepted some of the assumptions behind the French calculations. It would, its representatives argued, be impossible to operate the common market with simple maximum and minimum prices, because the German pit-head coal prices would be so much lower than the Belgian that even with the addition of the transport cost from the Ruhr to Belgium they would still eliminate much of Belgium's production. The wholesale coal price in the Federal Republic in 1950 was $7.10 a tonne.[42] The average domestic sale price of Belgian coal in the same year was $14.07 a tonne.[43] A rail journey of 500 km. added about 50 per cent to the price of a tonne of Ruhr coal.[44] Its delivery price in Charleroi, a much shorter journey, would thus have been roughly $8.52 had it been sold originally at the domestic market price, a reasonable assumption since the practice of higher pricing for exports was supposed to end with entry into the common market. This price disparity applied also to coking-coal. The price of Ruhr coking-coal after January 1950 was between DM32.50 and DM37.00 ($7.62–$8.80) a tonne. The price of Belgian *gras A* varied between 640 and 670 Belgian francs a tonne ($12.75–$13.35).[45] Ending higher pricing for German coal exports while removing the Belgian coal tariff did seem to mean therefore on the basis of 1950 prices an adjustment in Belgian coal output at least as violent as that which Monnet envisaged, providing there actually were German exports. In fact Monnet's figure of 5 million tonnes of coal to be imported into Belgium from Germany seemed, given the prevailing assumptions on both sides, more of an attempt at a political compromise than the full acceptance of the economic rationale of a common market.

It was however a compromise flatly turned down from the outset by the Belgian coal industry. High prices, its representatives insisted, were due to geological problems which prevented substantial productivity improvements and had therefore 'an irremediable cause'.[46] This was an argument which relied for its force on the abnormal conditions of the Korean war. Behind it was the conviction that if coal were to continue to sustain welfare in Belgium, either it must get a permanent form of protection within the common market or the wage and social security costs falling on German employers must be increased to the level of those in Belgium. If the second path was adopted there would still need to be a lengthy transition period before the common market could be opened. It was thus a cardinal point in

---

[42] OECD, *General Statistics*.
[43] *Annales des Mines de Belgique*, January 1953, p. 95.
[44] P. Wiel, *Untersuchungen . . .*, op. cit., p. 137.
[45] ECSC, *Recueil statistique*, 1953, p. 199.
[46] MAECE, 5212, Cobéchar, 'Observations de l'industrie charbonnière belge à l'issue de la première semaine de négociation', 27 June 1950.

the negotiations for Belgium that the proposed common market in coal should not include the Belgian industry at the start.

To expect the Germans to forgo the advantage which lower wages seemed to give them, when exports appeared to be the only way forward for their economy, was a forlorn hope, particularly after Monnet and Schuman had offered them the bait of steady sales in Belgium. They and the Dutch refused to contemplate any increase in miners' wages and welfare to the average level prevailing in the Community. By September 1950 the idea of an equalization of living standards for Community coal miners, which the Belgians tried to present as being in accord with the social aspirations expressed in Monnet's original working document, had been rejected.[47] The treaty text was nevertheless eventually to accord one power over wages to the High Authority; they could not be reduced to improve competitiveness in the industries covered by the treaty unless as part of a general national reduction of wages.

If wages elsewhere could not be forced up, the best available outcome was likely to be a transition period in which Belgian mines would improve productivity so that prices, in spite of higher wages, came closer to those elsewhere. The government had already committed itself in autumn 1949 when it changed the subsidy system to eventually ending general subsidization of the industry and affirmed its determination to reduce mining costs through improving productivity. It still wished to reach those objectives and hoped now to use the proposed Community as an aid. Supranational authority might well dissipate political opposition to mine closures or restructuring which would otherwise have been focused entirely on national government. But the improvement in demand for coal since 1949 had weakened its position in relation to the companies and unions. An immediate reduction in Belgian capacity would mean higher dollar expenditure for the Six if German exports could not plug the gap. And politically it would have been unwise to allow German coal to replace Belgian output too soon in large quantities, because the Belgian coal industry in the winter of 1950–1 was once more in a strong position to make its favourite argument – that even if the existing capacity was retained in full, at cyclical peaks of activity Belgium would be left dependent on imports which would not necessarily arrive.

It was politically crucial for Monnet, as it was for the German negotiators, to be able to symbolize the achievement of the Franco–German agreement by opening the common market at the earliest possible date after the ratification of the treaty. In the circumstances of 1950–1 a return to subsidization above the level to which the Belgian government had been intending to reduce it in autumn 1949 appeared to be the only way to achieve this, and this in turn meant that the others would have to pay. This

---

[47] R.T. Griffiths, 'The Schuman Plan Negotiations: The Economic Clauses', in K. Schwabe (ed.), *Die Anfänge des Schuman Plans 1950/51* (Baden-Baden, 1988), pp. 40 ff.

was recognized overtly by Walter Hallstein, the head of the German delegation to the negotiations. Providing that this return to higher subsidization met two conditions, firstly that it was confined to the length of the necessary transition period, and secondly that it was degressive, the Germans were prepared from an early stage to accept that they themselves would pay. The Belgian government could then circumvent the accusation that it had altered the course of policy set in 1949 by claiming that an increase in subsidies was now necessary in order to provide the extra investment needed to improve productivity even faster and shorten the transition period before entering the common market.

In a subsidiary negotiation between Vinck and Etienne Hirsch, Monnet's deputy in the Planning Commissariat, it was agreed that the treaty could permit the governing body of the Community, the High Authority, to impose a levy on the coal production of countries whose average coal production costs were lower than the weighted average of costs in the Community. This meant Germany and the Netherlands. The far greater volume of German output compared to Dutch would mean that it was on Germany that the levy would mostly fall. The device was known as *péréquation*. Of its total yield over the period when it was imposed, 56.6 million ECSC units of account, 52.09 million were in fact paid by German mines.[48] The levy was to last for the length of the transition period before Belgium entered the common market in coal on equal terms, five years. Its upper limit was set at 1.5 per cent of receipts on each tonne of coal sold in the first year of the common market. It was then to degress by one-fifth for each year of the five-year period. In the event the High Authority fixed the levy in the first year at only 1.1 per cent of receipts. The purposes for which the levy could be used were defined as: bringing the Belgian coal price as close as possible to prices prevailing in the common market; reducing the price of Belgian coal to the Belgian iron and steel industry; offsetting losses on the sale of Belgian coal within the common market. This covered most things.

Hirsch, accepting the obvious strength of the opposition to closing coal mines in the circumstances of late 1950, saw the agreement as a way of ultimately realizing the objective of replacing Belgian coal with German coal on the Belgian market. He found in Vinck, as later events were to show, a man with whom it was not hard to agree. Both had a common interest in raising productivity levels in Belgian mining and Vinck saw the agreement as a way of realizing Belgian government policy of 1949. *Péréquation* payments would, he intended, be tied to an improvement in productivity in Belgian mining whose main aspect would be the restructuring of companies and the consequent rationalization of workings that the Robinson report had suggested. If this could not be achieved by the Belgian national government, and events between 1945 and 1950 suggested

---

[48] ECSC, *Sixth General Report . . .*, op. cit., vol. 2, p. 28.

it could not, perhaps it could be achieved by the new concept of supranational government which Monnet and Schuman had invented.

The calculation of the size of the levy was made by Hirsch and Vinck from the starting-point that the Community should subsidize through *péréquation* the equivalent of the quantity of Belgian coal consumed in Belgium by coking-plants, iron and steelworks, exports and the mines themselves. This amounted to 41 per cent of the total consumption of domestic output. The sum of money required to meet the difference between the existing official Belgian prices for this coal and the price schedules which would be published by the High Authority would thus be the sum which it would be necessary to levy from the value of German and Dutch sales. The sum eventually raised in the first year of operation of this levy worked out at an average of 29 Belgian francs ($0.58) for each tonne of Belgian coal. It was additionally agreed that the Belgian coals not covered by this subsidy, all other coals for general industrial purposes as well as domestic and heating coals, would be subsidized by an equal sum of money to be provided from the Belgian government irrespective of the volume of output. This was to be made available over the same transition period of five years from the opening of the common market and was also to be used for investment within a rationalization programme.

In the Borinage however these new arrangements did not replace the special subsidy regime for that coalfield which had been instituted in 1949. The companies which had then signed special contractual agreements with the Belgian government for five years had only received exemption from the otherwise general reduction in subsidy for the industry in return for specific promises of rationalization and productivity improvement. It was pointless to weaken the force of those agreements, which were much stronger and more detailed than anything foreseen in the Schuman Plan negotiations. The mines which had been earlier singled out in this way would continue therefore to receive the same degree of assistance from the national government which had been promised, independently of *péréquation*.

The *péréquation* agreement left it free to producers and the Belgian government to decide between themselves on the nature of any rationalization programme. Belgian collieries were effectively guaranteed the same level of receipts as before the entry into force of the common market. The regime of *péréquation* would subsidize a wider range of coal sales while it lasted than had been intended by the national changes to the subsidy regime introduced in 1949 and now superseded. The chances of a really trenchant rationalization programme had in the circumstances diminished. This outcome was firstly a reflection of the favourable change in the coal market during the negotiations. Secondly, it was a consequence of the way in which Monnet and his associates had initially approached the problem. It was their initial ideas which eventually determined the time-scale over which *péréquation* would be paid, for five years was the period of time over which they had initially envisaged the reduction of Belgian annual output by 5 million tonnes when they were preparing the Schuman proposals. Thirdly, the fact that the problems of the Belgian coal industry threatened to prevent the successful conclusion of a major diplomatic settlement gave the industry an opportunity to demand better terms than it might otherwise have obtained. Had the Treaty of Paris not been the first treaty in which the Federal Republic was offered equality of status as a negotiating partner, an equality which was to be continued into the constitution of the ECSC, it is hard to believe that the German negotiators would have agreed to penalize their own coal-mining industry with the *péréquation* levy.

Once the Hirsch–Vinck agreements encountered a full discussion in the Belgian government they ran, though, into strong opposition on the grounds that the five-year period was too short, in spite of the safeguards to prevent too sharp a reduction in coal output in any one year. The agreements stipulated that if total Community coal output did not fall in any year, Belgian output would not be allowed to fall additionally by more than 3 per cent. If Community output fell, Belgian output would not be allowed to fall by more than the coefficient of 3 per cent of the decline in Community output. When this was presented to ministers who had been outside the negotiation they demanded to know what the situation would really look like in five years from the opening of the common market. On Vinck's own estimates the average sale price of Belgian coals would still only by then have been reduced to $12.35 per tonne, assuming that the common market and *péréquation* began almost immediately after the ratification of the treaty. Even assuming that the high demand for coal induced by the Federal Republic's booming economy and western Europe's rearmament persisted, it was hard to imagine that the delivered price of Ruhr coal in Charleroi in 1958 would have increased by the 40 per cent above its 1950 level which would be necessary to equalize its price in that year with that of this forecast average sale price of Belgian coals. The German delegation, well aware of this, had tried to construe the Hirsch–Vinck agreements as a guarantee that on the expiry of the five-year period of *péréquation* the Federal Republic would automatically have a coal market of 5 million tonnes a year in Belgium. It seems clear from Vinck's own subsequent actions that he felt the Belgian coal industry should indeed shrink by this much and that any longer transition period would prevent the needed rationalization. But some ministers argued that in the final treaty the agreement should be defined as only setting the bounds of a maximum adjustment to be made.

Their opposition was made stronger by the vehement opposition of the coal industry itself. It saw well enough where the danger lay. The government might be able to use the new supranational authority to enforce a restructuring policy on the industry and do so in the name of Europe. Exalted as the pillar of the nation's security only five years earlier, coal would now be represented as interposing its selfish interests between the nation and a European peace agreement. From the outset the industry declared an absolute opposition to the Hirsch–Vinck agreements, and this was carried forward into a political campaign against the treaty. It was not possible, the coal companies argued, to bring down the cost of Belgian coal to a level which would make it competitive. The five-year period was too short to make any effective difference at all to productivity and prices and the gap would be as wide at the end as at the start.

At first van Zeeland incorporated the Hirsch–Vinck agreements into Belgium's official negotiating stance on condition that at the end of the five-year period the ultimate authority of the Community, the Council of Ministers, should be empowered to pronounce on whether some extension of the transition period was needed. This would still leave the matter in national hands, because unanimity would be required at that level. But his colleagues were unhappy suspecting that van Zeeland himself was of much the same opinion as Vinck. Faced with such strong opposition, he determined on a safeguard clause, allowing if necessary a temporary severance of the Belgian market from the common market.[49] The demand to include this in the treaty he left until the last moment of the negotiations, knowing that it would have to be conceded if refusing it meant that the other powers would lose the treaty. Much of the last stage of the treaty negotiations was taken up with discussion of the terms and conditions under which Belgium might be allowed to invoke this safeguard and with the terms and conditions of any prolongation of the five-year transition period.

In December 1950 it was accepted that there should be a further clause in the draft text that on the expiry of the five-year period of *péréquation* the Belgian coal industry could be given a further three-year transition period over which the Belgian government could continue to pay national subsidies under Community supervision but without further *péréquation* payments from the other producers.[50] At the last moment when this was brought to the full conference for drafting into the treaty Monnet insisted that it contain a statement that its sole justification would have to be to subsidize the gradual substitution of Belgian production by cheaper coal. The negotiations temporarily broke down because this was unacceptable to the Belgian delegation. Soothing words by Hallstein on the subject of Germany's desire to help Belgium with its 'geological difficulties' had to be spoken, some of them in private to Monnet, before he finally accepted the change.[51] There still remained van Zeeland's safeguard clause, the terms for which had not yet been settled. It was agreed, after more prolonged argument, that if member-states should eventually agree at any time that there was a 'manifest crisis', a temporary separation of the

[49] The clause was eventually invoked by the High Authority itself at the end of the decade to protect the Belgian industry, which by then was contracting sharply, not from German but from American competition.
[50] MAECE, 5216, 'Note pour les chefs de délégation', 13 December 1950.
[51] ibid., Suétens to van Zeeland, 18 December 1950.

Belgian market from the common market could take place.

The attitude of the Belgian government as a body at the time and its actions afterwards must call into question the firmness of its commitment to the terms of the treaty and the adjustment required. Most ministers knew well enough that something had to be done to make Belgian coal mining less uncompetitive. Van Zeeland, who admittedly saw the foreign policy aspects of the treaty as more important than its domestic implications, was in favour of what had been obtained, albeit expressing himself cautiously, and might indeed at first have been satisfied with an absolute limit of five years on all further subsidies. He had, though, close connections to the world of Belgian high finance and under pressure supported most of the subsequent treaty modifications to the Hirsch–Vinck agreements. But he did this in order to retain their core. In contrast to this was the chauvinistic attitude of Joseph Meurice the minister for foreign trade.[52] His arguments were typical of the coal industry as a whole. The output of the Borinage should be fully maintained throughout the period of the agreement, he insisted, and that of the Kempen increased by 2 million tonnes, because these were the fields producing a large proportion of coking-coal in their final output. This would leave room for a reduction of output by 2 million tonnes in the other southern coalfields of Charleroi, Liège and Namur while maintaining the total volume of national output unchanged and leaving the Belgian steel industry still free of any dependence on German supply. This redistribution of output would also have the advantage of shifting supply more towards those coals for which demand was not showing a falling trend. He was also probably relying on the greater capacity of the Charleroi and Liège regions to absorb a redundant work force. The Secretary General of the Mines Administration pressed similar views. A reduction in annual output to 25 million tonnes would necessarily, he argued, mean a loss of some of the best quality Borinage coking-coals whose quality was such that they were not properly substitutable even by Kempen coking fines, which required mixing before use. The Hirsch–Vinck accords should not be allowed, the Mines Administration insisted, to result in a treaty which could allow the Community even indirectly to exert pressure for running down Borinage mining.

Van Zeeland's attitude was the shrewder. If demand stayed high, he had clearly calculated, the agreements might have little real meaning and the government could both sign them and avoid mine closures. Should it fall, as it began to in 1952, and Belgium be forced by the Community to take 1 million tonnes of imports, it would nevertheless in practice remain a Belgian decision as to what kinds of coals were imported. This was uncertain. But if, van Zeeland argued to his fellow ministers, the High Authority tried to shift the composition of Belgium's imports towards

---

[52] Joseph Meurice, 1896–1972. One of the post-war founders of the Social Christian Party. Minister for foreign trade, 1950–4.

coking-coal and thus threaten employment in the Borinage, 'this decision would be difficult to put into practice'.[53] There was some discussion about the possibility of taking the money and then leaving the Community after the five years, if a genuine common market still looked at that time as though it would be really damaging. Because this was judged unrealistic the rest of the government, urged on by the young minister for economic affairs Albert Coppé, backed van Zeeland's policy, which was linked to the commitment that he would insist on the 'manifest crisis' clause.[54]

Coppé was to become a member of the High Authority, so his views are of particular importance. He had begun his career as an academic economist publishing in 1939 a study of the impact of price and demand elasticities on the Belgian coal industry in the 1930s and deriving policy conclusions from his study. The industry's problems, he had then argued taking the side of the industry, were cyclical as much as structural, a consequence of the low elasticity of output in response to changes in demand. Because foreign coal industries had similarly low elasticities, protection in periods of falling demand would not increase the domestic coal price. However, it would prove superfluous and inflationary once demand increased. What was therefore needed was a cyclical policy, a minor Keynesian remedy for this one industry. This could, he had then argued, best be achieved through an international agreement which would regulate competition outside domestic markets by European coal industries. This would allow Belgium to retain a national capacity close to that needed at the peak of the cycle on the basis of a protected domestic market. This was an ideal perspective, not a real one in 1939. 'In order to understand the interest that there is in a sound and supple coal industry it suffices to imagine what would happen if one day by bad luck in business we were deprived of it', he had written on the eve of the war.[55] Once an international agreement was achieved, cyclical policies in all countries based on the same premiss could evolve into a common European management of the coal market, although not necessarily retaining all national capacities at their existing level. A necessary component of these policies would be seasonal and cyclical aid to collieries to finance coal stocks in periods of low demand. This European perspective, an abstract consideration in 1939, now opened up.

It was the perspective which Coppé took to the High Authority and he was to argue strongly for it in the mid-1950s.[56] Financing stockpiles had been a main plank in the attempts of the holding companies to cartelize and stabilize the market for industrial coals after 1931. The variations in

---

[53] MAECE, 5216, 'Compte-rendu de la Conférence tenue au Ministère', 10 January 1951.
[54] ibid.
[55] A. Coppé, *Problèmes d'économie charbonnière. Essai d'orientation économique* (Bruges, 1939).
[56] Thirty years afterwards M. Coppé still had cogent arguments that this should have been national and Community policy. Interview with M. Coppé on 22 November 1985.

stocks however had been too wide for their policy to succeed. Coppé's arguments can be seen as a request for supranational aid to support efforts to preserve cartel policy. Vinck also went to the High Authority, as Director General of the Labour Division. He took with him the contrary view, which he had upheld in the negotiations: that the problems of the Belgian coal industry were not cyclical but structural and that it was the task of the ECSC to reduce its size and improve its productivity quickly. To achieve that it was essential to ignore the argument that major structural changes could not be made in periods of high demand when it was necessary to give first priority to its satisfaction. There was also, in his eyes, nothing to be gained by attempts at cyclical stabilization until the industry was on a new and smaller basis.

This was a clearer division of opinion than that in the Belgian government. As in all governments ministers were doubtless concerned to give themselves the greatest possible room for manoeuvre. They were on no account going to say publicly that Belgian coal output would be reduced by entry into the ECSC, not least because the industry's own organizations were loudly insisting that a reduction in output was inevitable and intended and were enlisting trade union support for rejecting the treaty. The extent to which ministers would use the period of *péréquation* to put into practice a restructuring plan which would include a reduction in output would be left as far as possible, as such things are in governments, to last-minute opportunistic decisions. The uncertainty of the future pattern of demand for coal, it could reasonably be held, fully justified such an attitude. It was evident that the Belgian government as a whole felt no particular allegiance of principle to the underlying intentions of *péréquation* and was quite prepared to allow the more generous subsidy regime which was its outcome to prop up the industry relatively unchanged, should that prove the easier political choice.

The attitude towards the future Community of Belgian political parties was as ambivalent as that of the government. The president of the Liberal Party Roger Motz was one of van Zeeland's collaborators in the League for European Economic Co-operation, a pressure group for lower tariffs and currency convertibility. He took van Zeeland's view that internationalization of the problem might give the national government extra strength in dealing with it. 'For our country', he declared, 'it is a political and at the same time a social problem of unprecedented seriousness, which risks setting one race against another in the bosom of the fatherland.' 'Yet', he added, 'we think that the Schuman Plan can serve to remedy certain disorders which we would perhaps be incapable of curing by our own means.'[57] It is hard to believe that van Zeeland's own position was uninfluenced by his business friendships in the Brufina holding company and

---

[57] M. Dumoulin, 'La Belgique et les débuts du Plan Schuman (mai 1950–février 1952)', in K. Schwabe, *Die Anfänge . . .* , op. cit., p. 274.

thus his involvement with the coal and steel interests of the Banque de Bruxelles. As for the socialists they covered a wide spectrum of opinion, from militant federalists like Spaak, who was in favour of the treaty on the simple grounds that it brought nearer the federal Europe which he now preached, to the former prime minister van Acker who strongly opposed the Schuman Plan. The same divisions can be seen in the trade union movement, for while the treaty promised official international recognition of its post-war public status in the corporate management of the industry and stipulated firmly that wages should not be reduced as a device to stimulate competition, its terms also threatened their members with a reduction in employment. Ambivalence reached its heights inside the christian trade unions, well represented in the Kempen coalfield where employment was not threatened, who contrived in the interests of maintaining union solidarity not to mention for several months those parts of the treaty dealing with coal.

Only the management of the coal industry itself, as represented by Fédéchar, seemed entirely unambivalent in its public utterances. But Fédéchar had been the creation of the holding companies and it was obvious that at the higher levels within those large financial groups opinion could only be divided, for the steel industry could have no long-term advantage in supporting the cause of dear coal. This further ambiguity was successfully exploited by the government and does much to explain van Zeeland's remarkable coolness in the face of seemingly implacable, intemperate and increasing public opposition from the coal industry. Indeed the violence of its opposition was turned to good effect in his negotiating tactics, for conceding his last-minute demand for a safeguard clause in the treaty looked all the more necessary to those in France and Germany who had read the Belgian coal industry's ferociously nationalistic diatribes against its terms.

Fédéchar's denunciations of the Treaty of Paris suggest that it had in fact been relatively confident of mitigating the effects of the 1949 changes in subsidies and feared that the new supranational authority might be beyond its reach and influence. It was the High Authority which was especially denounced. The most common attack was that it was a form of nationalization through the back door. It is tempting to dismiss this as mere humbug given the already existing extent of government intervention and control. But the purpose of the financial trusts in financing Fédéchar to carry out a national propaganda campaign against the terms of the Treaty of Paris was more to modify the powers which the treaty gave to the High Authority over the iron and steel industries than it was to rescue of the coal industry. The coal industry was being used to campaign against clauses in the treaty which seemed to give the High Authority powers of detailed intervention in the management of the steel industry. The precise juridical relationships between on the one hand the High Authority, which was clearly intended to be led by Monnet, a man who in Belgian eyes was an arch-interventionist, and on the other hand the Belgian steel firms was a strongly contested issue at the diplomatic and governmental level. This high-level diplomatic struggle was accompanied by a noisy and public campaign over coal. Demagogy was more appropriate for coal, because the public propaganda that the industry was vital to the survival of the nation was still fresh in all minds and the question of the industry's nationalization had long invoked political sentiments which went far beyond questions of the coal industry itself. Coal could once more be represented as the artery of the Belgian nation now in danger of being severed by foreigners, even if the ulterior purpose of the campaign was to keep the steel industry from falling into their interventionist clutches.

By early 1951 the steel manufacturers' association was accusing the High Authority of 'arrogating to itself the dictatorial right to insert itself into private affairs', something which 'does not fit the Belgian political system'.[58] The Belgian steel industry, 40 per cent of whose output was exported, was never in any position to resist the basic concept of the proposed treaty if the other signatories wanted it. Its concern in the negotiations was with the details of input prices, sale prices and market regulation and with the extent to which it could continue to keep its affairs private. But it was never able to explain convincingly to the public at large why it should not be subjected to the same framework of public supervision that the Dutch, French, German and Italian steel industries all accepted after 1945. It was easier to try to force alterations in the treaty by stirring up against the powers of the High Authority a public campaign of sympathy for the coal industry. Reducing output, creating unemployment, making Belgium dependent on supply from a country which had cruelly occupied and exploited it only five years earlier, the text of the treaty looked like a vulnerable target.

The campaign could also be represented as a campaign to save the welfare advances since 1945. If the price of coal on Belgian markets had to be reduced by one-third in five years this, the coal industry could claim, would not even pay the current level of miners' wages, let alone the social security charges. The transition period once over, they argued, even some mines in the Kempen would be obliged to close. 'Such perspectives, which can be termed revolutionary, are far too dangerous for our Government and the Representatives of the Nation not to greet the Schuman Plan as it exists without extreme caution.'[59] Without permanent aid a substantial part of the national market, in reality more than 5 million tonnes, would have to be sacrificed to German producers. Permanent aid was justifiable to enable Belgium to retain one of its basic industries and it should be provided by the ECSC. This would support the cause of the preservation

---

[58] MAECE, 5216, Groupement des Haut-Fourneaux et Aciéries Belges. 'Position de l'industrie sidérurgique belge à l'issue des négociations', 13 February 1951.

[59] ibid., Fédération des Associations Charbonnières de Belgique, 'Quelques réflexions sur le Plan Schuman'.

and methodical exploitation of European resources.[60] 'Yes or no', the president of Fédéchar, speaking in Liège in November 1950 asked his audience, 'shall our national industry agree to accept its daily bread from foreign hands', or 'does it prefer to stretch out its own hand to its national bread every morning without fear?'[61] It was never necessary to spell out the exact meaning of the word 'foreign'.

The decision to descend into the battlefield of popular politics was taken as early as October 1950 when the industry's objections to the treaty as it was emerging had not been sent to the government only but also to mayors of coal-mining communes. The temptation to strengthen this popular campaign with a dose of xenophobia was too strong to resist. The theme of the nation reverberated the louder when memories of two occupations were evoked. Belgium should not be forced, 'on the simple grounds that there was a surplus in Germany' to reduce production.[62] In the final campaign against ratification one year later the argument was to run that 'the whole of the transition regime supposedly established in favour of Belgium in fact only had as its objective the disposal of the surpluses from German production; the *péréquation* payments all in all were the price which the Germans were paying to buy our market.'[63]

Behind this crude chauvinism can be discerned the concentration of the holding companies on the defence of the existing private management structure of the steel industry. The High Authority represented the post-war view which had come to prevail outside Belgium that government should have a constitutional role in the overall direction of an industry of such apparent basic importance in the economy. Monnet was most tena-cious on the point that the constitution of the Belgian steel manufacturers' association was unacceptable to the High Authority because it excluded representatives of trade unions and consumers. This was not, he argued, politically appropriate for the post-war world and he insisted on a uniform pattern of constitutional management structures for all the steel industries of the Community. Included in this was an obligation that private invest-ment plans in steel must be reported to the High Authority for information and for judgement. It was certainly not easy in the context of international comparisons to explain why such proposals, accepted with little discussion by other governments and which already applied in the Belgian coal industry, were a threat to Belgian national interests, but they were issues for which Belgian steel was prepared to risk a campaign against the whole treaty.

---

[60] ibid., Fédération des Associations Charbonnières de Belgique, 'Situation des entreprises charbonnières belges dans le cadre du Plan Schuman', 22 October 1950.

[61] E. Devos, *Le Patronat belge face au Plan Schuman (9 mai 1950–5 février 1952)*, (Brussels, 1989), p. 65.

[62] MAECE, 5216, 'Positions communes de l'industrie charbonnière et de l'industrie sidérur-gique belges vis-à-vis le Plan Schuman', 7 December 1950.

[63] ibid., Fédération des Associations Charbonnières de Belgique, 'Les conséquences du Plan Schuman pour la Belgique', 5 November 1951.

In a joint document that itself looked not unlike a treaty between two nations, the coal and steel industries agreed on a set of common positions at the start of December 1950. The steel industry committed itself to full support for the coal industry's objectives in the negotiations including permanent subsidization in the Community. In return the coal industry promised full support for limiting the powers to be given to the High Authority which 'completely curb the initiative and responsibility of firms and establish a complete *dirigisme* of the High Authority equivalent in fact to a disguised nationalization'.[64] It was, though, a treaty of alliance of only short duration. It would last only until Monnet had been forced to accept changes in the two treaty articles 60 and 61 which governed the recognition of business associations by the Community. Once those articles were modified, as they eventually were in March 1951, the coal industry was left to its own devices. It was noticeable throughout the three months of this tactical alliance that whereas the steel industry's propaganda was aimed against interference with private enterprise it was never aimed at the 'foreigners' who were the coal industry's target.

A campaign of this kind could not have been successful had it not been able to draw on the strong political insistence that there should be no threat to welfare and employment, and it was in the defence of those causes that public opposition to the Treaty of Paris was stepped up. The rallying cry was that Belgian jobs were threatened by Germans in France's interests, because that was the point of sensitivity at which electors could be aroused. It was something of a forlorn hope that in the post-war world even the Belgian government would continue to regard the management of steel as not a matter for public supervision. The modification of the treaty articles 60 and 61 did not go as far as Belgian steel wished and the negotiations for and the establishment of the ECSC can be seen as marking the moment of commitment of the non-socialist parties in Belgium to the mixed economy. Even before Christmas 1950 the Belgian government was agreeing with the leader of its delegation to the negotiations that it was 'ridiculous' to sustain the more extreme constitutional objections of the steel industry to the High Authority's powers 'when in every other country concerned there was government control in one form or another over investment in the steel industry'.[65] Conceding to the High Authority the right to full knowledge of and free comment on private investment plans in steel would ensure that Belgian national government would for the first time have the same rights.

The steel industry's chief adviser to the negotiating team, van der Rest, continued nevertheless repeatedly to speak in public before the ratification of the treaty against the extent of the powers which the High Authority had been granted over private firms. The attitudes which Monnet displayed in

---

[64] ibid., 'Positions communes de l'industrie charbonnière et de l'industrie sidérurgique belge', 7 December 1950. A.S. Milward, 'The Belgian Coal and Steel Industries and the Schuman Plan' in K. Schwabe (ed.), *Die Anfänge . . .*, op. cit.
[65] MAECE, 5216, Biernaux to Meurice, 22 December 1950.

the negotiations had greatly increased anxieties about the way in which the treaty might be used to extend the High Authority's power.[66] Certainly Monnet had a deep distrust of private associations between businessmen and a great belief in the power of public authority to make them compete, influenced perhaps by his experiences of the United States. But there were other, less personal, reasons for his dislike of the Belgian management structure.

These sprang from the determination of the French government to use the Schuman Plan to implement the Allied policy of breaking up the links between German steel producers and Ruhr coal by limiting the extent to which German steelworks would be allowed to control their own coal supply. In this French diplomats found themselves supported by the American High Commission in Germany.[67] Belgian steelworks and the holding companies which controlled and financed so many of them could see no reason why they should be caught by French attempts to pry out of the hands of German steelmakers the control of coal which French steel-makers wanted for their own post-war expansion, by American determi-nation to force through the Schuman proposals in their own foreign policy interests, or by radical American trust-busters lingering on in Germany. To have to accept that kind of intervention when, as van der Rest argued, a free-for-all inside a common tariff would probably give Belgian steel-makers inputs at a cheaper price, seemed the ultimate folly.[68]

But a common market free of price controls and free of power relation-ships between steelworks and coal mines was only a flight of fancy. It was on the long history of politically influenced relationships between French and German industry that Schuman's proposals had been built.[69] Van Zeeland understood that whereas support for the French insistence on the deconcentration of the German steel industry by the Americans was essential to the treaty, Belgian industry, whatever powers Monnet himself might be seeking over it, was not a concern of the United States so long as Belgium accepted the treaty. When the American high commissioner in Germany finally forced Adenauer to accept the clauses in question in March 1951, van Zeeland also accepted them on behalf of Belgium. But before he did so William Tomlinson, an American official who had worked

---

[66] Discussion with M. Pierre van der Rest on 27 February 1987. When in the first week of December 1950 Monnet threatened to abandon the negotiations unless the two draft articles 60 and 61 on business associations were accepted in substantially the form in which he had submitted them, van der Rest was convinced that the situation was dangerous for the future.

[67] There is a full account in I. Warner, 'Allied–German Negotiations on the Deconcentration of the West German Steel Industry', in I.D. Turner (ed.), *Reconstruction in Post-War Germany. British Occupation Policy and the Western Zones 1945–1955* (London, 1989).

[68] MAECE, 5216, 'Remarques de l'industrie sidérurgique belge concernant la note du 13.12.1950'; van der Rest to van Zeeland, 23 January 1951.

[69] For a survey of these relationships and the way the proposals emerged from this long history, J.R. Gillingham, *Coal, Steel and the Rebirth of Europe, 1945–1955* (Cambridge, 1991).

closely with Monnet from the embassy in Paris throughout the negotiations, was empowered by his government to make a statement that as far as the application to Belgium of the articles relating to deconcentration was concerned, 'The United States would be content with a satisfaction in principle and that in practice it would tolerate certain agreements and concentrations.'[70] This was good enough for the Belgian government, but the steel industry continued to regard articles 60 and 61 as an unwarranted intrusion on private management.

Although maintaining these objections, Belgian steel was ready to accept the treaty and work to modify it afterwards. Its strategy all along had been close to that of the government. 'We have limited ourselves to trying to reduce the inconveniences which this initiative might have for us', wrote the economist Fernand Baudhuin, who was close to van Zeeland, in April 1951.[71] But a campaign as vehement as that of the coal industry could not simply be called off. In the Conseil National de l'Economie, where the provisional treaty text was debated between February and April 1951, and where the various economic interest groups were supposed to be represented according to their weight in the economy, the coal industry won the almost unanimous support of businessmen and farmers' representatives for its case by presenting the ECSC as creeping nationalization. But its seeming success – the Conseil gave its advice approving the draft treaty only by the casting vote of the chairman – was the last moment before the industry moved into political isolation. It was to prove not too difficult for the government to turn the tables on it after this troublesome debate by representing it as a welfare industry depending on the public purse while hoarding its own cash.

By the time of the ratification debate its only hope lay in the support of those who opposed the treaty on constitutional grounds. The Belgian constitution declared roundly that 'all powers emanate from the nation' and a variety of opponents of the treaty sought to construe this as meaning that the treaty was unconstitutional unless the constitution were changed, a lengthy and complicated business. Otherwise the coal industry's campaign by 1952 attracted little support outside the endangered areas of the south. The press was in large part against it, particularly after (in circumstances which remain obscure, but which certainly favoured van Zeeland) the details of the Robinson report were leaked to the newspaper *La Dernière Heure*. Less emphasis was placed by the paper on the report's optimistic conclusions that many southern mines could be made profitable than on its numerous demonstrations of over-employment and lack of rationalization.[72]

In all this debate no trace of idealism about the wider advantages to

---

[70] MAECE, 5216, 'Note concernant les articles 60 et 61 du Projet de Traité', 30 March 1951.
[71] F. Baudhuin, 'Le plan Schuman prend forme', in *Revue Générale Belge*, no. 66, April 1951, p. 971.
[72] E. Devos, *Le Patronat . . .*, op. cit., p. 82.

mankind of European integration can be discovered. It was taken for granted that peace between France and Germany was essential for Belgium's security, and that this was the strongest reason for accession to the treaty. After that acceptance it was vital to ensure that Belgium's other national interests were not trampled into the ground in the rush of the French, Germans and Americans to find a common framework for the future. What emerged as a definition of Belgium's national interest was then strikingly clear. Firstly, national survival, which the Schuman proposals guaranteed better than any earlier peace proposals. Secondly, support from the proposed new arrangements for the new basis of the state in welfare, higher employment and a measure of government influence and management in key industrial sectors, all of which appeared safeguarded in principle by the treaty. Thirdly, supranationality brought a new advantage. A genuine restructuring of the coal industry might well be easier if the immense political problems which were bound to arise – large-scale shifts in employment, regional regeneration, quarrels between Walloons and Flemings – could be shared with supranational management, or blamed on it. The Treaty of Paris can be understood not just as the diplomatic substitute for a peace treaty, but also as the moment when Belgium formally entered the mixed economy and so ratified the changes which had taken place in its government and society since 1944. It ratified the shift to public responsibility in management, to the incorporation of the labour force into that responsibility, and to the commitment of the state to welfare and employment, a ratification of change all the more striking in contrast to the earlier history of the coal industry. The Belgian state did not emerge weaker in the face of a liege authority but stronger in the face of an unruly subject.

THE BELGIAN COAL INDUSTRY IN THE COMMUNITY

The Treaty of Paris, while ratifying post-war political trends, also announced a future struggle between Belgian coal, national government and supranational government that would not be quickly resolved. The coal industry's calculation had been that in a strictly national system it would exercise more leverage over political decisions. It was not prepared to change its attitudes because the treaty had been ratified, but hoped still to mobilize opinion against the Community. Pierre Delville, who had resigned from the negotiating team earlier, denounced the treaty in print in November 1951. Deploying technical arguments from an article published by a member of the Mines Administration in 1950, he argued that the national output of coal should actually be increased.[73] Schuman's promise that the Community would mean an upward levelling of wages and living standards had already been broken, Delville claimed. *Péréquation* would

[73] J. Martens, 'Evolution du droit . . .', op. cit.

be of no help in the investment programmes because it would still result in coal being sold at prices which would reduce the incomes of the colliery companies below the level which would have completely compensated for the losses they would have to bear. 'In sum, in accepting submission to this apparatus Belgium will renounce once and for all everything which up to now has built its greatness and prosperity: courage and the spirit of initiative of its industries, the extraordinary flexibility of its economy.' European coal output would shift to the Ruhr and in cyclical booms Belgian industry would be left 'at the mercy of Germany'.[74]

It is not only in Belgium since 1950 that the coal industry has fallen into a rancorous political isolation, as all British readers will be only too aware. No union leader appeared in Belgium to give the industry the national political platform which Mr Arthur Scargill was to occupy for the British coal industry thirty years later. The Belgian industry was not nationalized and the government's interests could be perceived as separate from those of the industry's management, which led the opposition to government, although its subsequent relations with the unions were too manipulative to be called an alliance. But the support of the mining trade unions for the campaign of opposition to the treaty was solid. Given the apocalyptic vision of the future put out by management this was not surprising. The industry's spokesman told the Conseil National de l'Economie when it debated the treaty that the common market would mean that 'the Belgian coal industry including our best collieries would be condemned over a more or less short period of time and in normal cyclical conditions to disappear.'[75] 'Belgium would be deliberately accepting for 50 years, which is as good as saying for ever, consequences which it knows in advance will for the most part be catastrophic for itself', proclaimed Fédéchar.[76] The outcome would be 'total ruin'.[77]

There was a campaign of equal vigour by the French iron and steel industry against the ratification of the treaty. This is rightly interpreted as a moment of transition in France from an older protectionist elite to more modern and less parochial leaders who were to take over once the treaty was ratified.[78] It was almost as much about divisions in the industry as

---

[74] P. Delville, 'L'industrie charbonnière devant le plan Schuman', in *Etudes Economiques*, no. 81/82, November 1951. Compare the remark of G. Delarge, 'The big loser of two world wars will triumph economically', G. Delarge, 'Le plan Schuman et l'industrie houillère du Borinage' in ibid.

[75] MAECE, 5216, Communication au Conseil Central de l'Economie par M.L. Canivet, 20 January 1951

[76] ibid., Fédération des Associations Charbonnières de la Belgique, 'Les Conséquences du Plan', op. cit. Fifty years was the period of validity of the Treaty of Paris.

[77] ibid., Fédération des Associations Charbonnières de la Belgique, 'Déclaration des Producteurs Charbonniers au Gouvernement Belge au sujet de l'état des negociations relatives au Plan Schuman et à la position qui en découle de la part de l'industrie Charbonnière Belge', 24 January 1951.

[78] P. Mioche, 'Le patronat de la sidérurgie française et le Plan Schuman en 1950–1952: les apparences d'un combat et la réalité d'une mutation', in K. Schwabe (ed.), *Die Anfänge* . . ., op. cit. H.W. Ehrmann, 'The French Trade Associations and the Ratification of the Schuman Plan', in *World Politics*, vol. 6, no. 4, 1954.

about the Schuman Plan. The same divisions of opinion were present in Belgian industrial and financial circles, but no such story can be told about Belgian coal. Isolated and united, it stood in a resentful, sullen and pessimistic determination to resist the treaty's implications, isolated as van Zeeland implied in his closing plea to the senate for ratification against 'a turning-point in history'.

Monnet was determined to set the date for the opening of the common market in coal as early as possible. It opened on 10 February 1953. Under the terms of the treaty Belgium could choose between the safe-guarding clause which had been incorporated as article 26.3 and the subsidized regime of *péréquation* whose terms were set out in article 25. As everyone had intended, it was *péréquation* which was chosen. This was paid from the opening of the common market until 10 December 1957, although the small payments under this head from the Netherlands were suspended earlier from 1 May 1957. The total sum made available from the *péréquation* levy amounted to $38.13 million, almost the whole of it from Germany, with an equal sum paid into the account by the Belgian government. In addition the aid provided by the Belgian government's earlier agreements with Borinage collieries amounted by the end of 1958 to more than the government's equivalent payments to *péréquation*. In 1954 a further supporting fund was authorized, of which the High Authority was liable to pay only about a third and eventually paid less. Finally, export subsidies to make Belgian coal exports possible, which had also been allowed under the terms of *péréquation*, were paid from June 1953 and the joint contribution of national government and Community to these eventually came to $10.3 million. The total aid received by the Belgian coal industry from the opening of the common market in coal to the end of 1958, was therefore $141.42 million (table 3.5).

This was much less than the $237 million received between September 1944 and September 1949 and the contribution by the Belgian government itself was reduced by more than 60 per cent compared to the earlier period. More than a third of the total subsidies after the start of the common market was paid to those Borinage collieries with which the Belgian government had signed agreements in 1949, almost one-half of the aid from the national government. The treaty gave the High Authority vague supervisory rights over the disposition of these earlier national arrangements and these subsidies were at least directed to that sector of the industry whose output was still subject to rising demand. *Péréquation*, however, was conceived as a subsidy to the whole industry, and so appeared to rule out discrimination between collieries producing different types of coal. As we have seen, coke and coking-coal output although always marginally higher than consumption followed it extremely closely. Nor was the steep fall in demand for coal after 1956 accompanied by a parallel fall in demand for coking-coal. The appropriateness

Table 3.5   Subsidies paid to Belgian collieries, 10 February 1953 to 31 December 1958 (million current $US) (average exchange rate, 50.05 Belgian francs = $1.00)

	Paid by Belgium	Paid by ECSC	Total
General *péréquation* subsidy	38.13	38.13	76.26
Conventional subsidies to specific collieries	43.64	5.90	49.54
Supplementary conventional subsidies	0.86	0.86	1.72
Supporting fund	3.56	0.04	3.60
Export subsidies	5.15	5.15	10.30
	91.34	50.08	141.42

Source: ECSC, *7th General Report on the Activities of the European Coal and Steel Community*, pp. 92–3

therefore of a general subsidy to all Belgian coals was not evident. Nevertheless if the subsidy regime was more selective than before 1949 and also a degressive one, more than half the total subsidies were in principle inappropriately general in their incidence.

The opening of the common market in February 1953 coincided with a return to slack demand. Coal consumption in Belgium in 1953 fell from its 1951 level back almost to its 1949 level. So much for Monnet's plans; in this year of slack demand Belgian coal output exceeded its level in the 1938–9 rearmament boom. The increase in output in 1952 had already been almost completely achieved by June and stocks were beginning to accumulate after March.[79] On 1 January 1954 more than 3 million tonnes of coal were in stockpiles. With the return of boom conditions in 1954 however, the stockpiles began to be used up and in 1956 apparent consumption of coal exceeded national output. Output was more or less exactly what it had been when the text of the treaty had been agreed.

When demand reached its peak in 1956 it was still met almost entirely from Belgium's own resources. Over the period of *péréquation* the highest annual figure for coal imports from the Federal Republic was the 2 million tonnes imported in 1954. In face of increasing demand in 1955 and 1956 German exports to Belgium in fact fell, because of the even greater pressure of demand in Germany itself. Those exports that did reach Belgium were only possible because of German coal imports from the United States. Total coal imports into Belgium did reach 5 million tonnes

[79] OEEC, *The Coal Position in Europe in 1953 and 1954. Report of the Coal Committee*, 20 November 1953.

in 1957. However it was not the Ruhr which was the main supplier but the United States. Nothing had turned out as the Schuman proposals had supposed.

Belgian coal imports and exports are set out in tables 3.6 and 3.7. As domestic demand for coal fell in 1952, exports rose. With the opening of the common market in 1953 exports continued to rise, but not sufficiently to avoid stockpiling of coal in greater quantities as the decline in domestic demand persisted. The decline was not, though, evenly spread. Demand was becoming more selective as changes in the pattern of coal consumption developed. The increasing stockpiles were made up mainly of low-quality coals for general industrial use. Subsidized exports of other grades mainly to France, Italy and the Netherlands partly made up in those countries for the fall in exports from the Federal Republic. It was in fact foreign demand which first began to reduce the Belgian stockpiles in 1954. Exports to the Netherlands doubled and for the first time the United Kingdom became a big purchaser of Belgian coal. These were indications of a general European boom and they heralded an upsurge in demand for coal in Belgium itself through the years 1955 and 1956. In 1956 domestic demand was so high that export quantities fell steeply.

The year 1956 was in fact one of those peaks of cyclical activity in which, as the Belgian coal industry had argued, any reduction in capacity would have left the nation without adequate supply. The industry claimed that its attitude in the Schuman Plan negotiations had therefore been justified: that it would have been foolish to close mines in a slack year such as 1953 when their output could still be exported and the capacity thus retained justified by sales in the eventual upswing on the domestic market. It was an implausible argument. Many of the exports had only been possible because of the Community regime of subsidization. Furthermore, even at the peak of the boom there was no shortage of coal on offer, not the Community coal from the Ruhr which Monnet had envisaged, but American coal. The Belgian industry's claims would only have been truly justified if Belgian coal had been cheaper than imported American coal. It was in fact cheaper between August 1954 and April 1957. But, as we shall see, that was for only temporary reasons and also because the ECSC was subsidizing the Belgian coal price.

Those subsidies which the treaty had granted to Belgium during the transition period specifically to assist exports began to be paid from June 1953 and lasted until March 1955. They covered exports only to the Netherlands, Italy and the Federal Republic, because France, whose northern coalfields might themselves have laid a reasonable claim to *péréquation*, objected to the treaty being used to subsidize the hauling of coal across its northern frontier to French steelworks. Exports to Britain were unaffected by the subsidy, but until late 1954 Belgian coal would not have been bought on grounds of price alone by the Netherlands, and possibly not by Italy either, had it not been subsidized to make its price

Table 3.6   Imports of coal into Belgium, 1938–60 (thousand tonnes)

From:	Federal Republic	Netherlands	France/ Saarland	USA	USSR	UK	Total
1938	2,167[1]	795[2]	342[3]		11	667	4,233
1945	–	–	–	474	–	–	474
1946	–	–	–	1,423	–	–	1,423
1947	–	–	–	4,182	–	–	4,182
1948	1,201	–	–	959	–	94	2,602
1949	734	–	1	4	–	133	929
1950	345	2	7	9	–	232	648
1951	360	1	1	1,454	–	352	2,194
1952	324	7	111	794	23	337	1,615
1953	726	171	150	664	46	420	2,179
1954	2,019	517	337	253	63	525	3,724
1955	1,260	346	574	783	124	485	3,633
1956	1,187	341	435	1,981	69	598	4,787
1957	1,538	394	350	2,138	50	563	5,102
1958	2,035	659	205	1,879	71	389	5,250
1959	2,352	845	241	1,050	35	348	4,874
1960	2,020	716	233	801	2	131	3,903

[1] Third Reich (includes briquettes)
[2] includes briquettes
[3] France only
Source: 1938–48, W. Degryse *et al.*, *Le Borinage* (Brussels, 1958); 1949–60, UN, *Quarterly Bulletin of Coal Statistics*

lower than American coal. These two markets alone absorbed roughly 1 million tonnes of output which could not be sold in Belgium. Since both countries always strongly resisted any suggestion by the Community that Belgian coal should be seen as a European resource whose sales must be guaranteed at the expense of cheaper imports from the United States, it is likely that their choice of Belgium as a source of imports was decided by prices or by a reluctance to spend dollars, and thus by temporary phenomena as well as by the subsidization of Belgian coal.

In early 1955 the delivered price of American coal in western Europe climbed steeply above that of Belgian coking-coal and there was no longer any need for the export subsidies agreed under the treaty to be paid. What made Belgian coal cheaper than American coal in Europe in the upward swing of the cycle in 1954–5 was not however any increase in American coal production costs or domestic coal prices but an increase in Atlantic freight charges. Had these remained constant, the price of American coal at European ports would have been only marginally more expensive than subsidized Belgian coal and for only one year from midsummer 1955 onwards. But transatlantic freight charges soared upwards uninterruptedly from February 1954 to late 1956. Figure 3.2 which shows these price movements, probably slightly overstates the price advantage of Belgian

Table 3.7   Exports of coal from Belgium, 1938–60 (thousand tonnes)

	To France	To Italy	To Netherlands	To Federal Republic	To Switzerland	To UK	Total
1938	3,545	112	519	–	81	–	4,516
1945	–	–	–	–	–	–	–
1946	44	–	–	–	104	–	168
1947	85	565	–	–	184	–	841
1948	261	3	82	–	229	–	598
1949	730	500	159	–	110	–	1,547
1950	759	1,065	486	–	120	–	2,699
1951	442	570	324	–	96	–	1,728
1952	1,091	668	478	19	50	–	2,537
1953	1,577	836	1,049	107	51	192	3,812
1954	1,303	577	2,148	226	230	911	5,295
1955	1,223	182	2,818	731	350	1,537	7,051
1956	1,141	99	1,721	294	300	746	4,461
1957	1,411	23	1,435	202	161	615	3,847
1958	1,111	–	868	44	77	645	2,771
1959	797	53	846	115	238	93	2,172
1960	636	279	782	192	267	–	2,275

Sources: 1938, W. Degryse, *Le Borinage*; 1946, UN, Economic Commission for Europe, Coal Division, *Bulletin of Statistics*; 1947, ibid., *Monthly Bulletin of Coal Statistics*; 1948–60, UN, *Quarterly Bulletin of Coal Statistics*

coal in that period, because freight rates were usually lower for long-term purchase contracts. Nevertheless, the influence of the rise in freight rates on delivered coal prices was far too great over the years 1955–6 to be seriously weakened by the time-scale of the contracts.

The comparison of the price of American coal in figure 3.2 is made with the price of Belgian coking-coal, because a large part of American coal exports to Europe was coking-coal to replace the shortfall of supply from the Ruhr. As the figure shows, the price of Belgian coking-coal was allowed to climb from summer 1956 by the High Authority in response to the increase in the sale price of American coal. It also shows with what dramatic suddenness the relative prices then changed when Atlantic freight rates plunged steeply late in 1956 as a result of the increase in shipping space. The fall in Atlantic freight rates was then supplemented by a fall in the price of American coal on board ship in Hampton Roads from early 1957. From summer 1957 the American wholesale price for coal began a long downward movement.

The causes of the fall in the price of American coal were not merely cyclical, they were long-run. The movement away from coal to other fuels had begun earlier there and was more marked. The impact of the 1958 recession on the American coal market was more emphatic even than in Europe, so that the price of American coal on offer fell more steeply, suggesting that the price difference between American and European coal

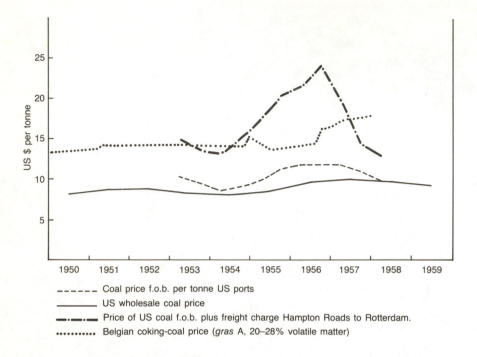

Figure 3.2   Movement of coal prices, 1950–9

would become a permanent one. The impact of the falling price of American coal can be seen from the trend of coal prices in Italy, the one ECSC member-state which was almost entirely dependent on imports (figure 3.3). Although wholesale coal prices continued to increase there in 1956 because of the increased cost of American coal, they did so by much less than the increase in the wholesale price of coal in Belgium. From late 1957 the gap between the price of coal in Italy and its price in Belgium widened remorselessly, even though the price of Belgian coal fell steeply. In retrospect 1958 can be seen as the turning-point in the history of the European coal market.

The productivity improvements in American coal mining in the 1950s had been greater than those which the Community's cautious policies had brought about in Europe and this, too, accounted for the widening gap in price trends. The employment of continuous mining machines where higher, less broken seams made this practicable, and the switch to open-cast mining both gave opportunities for improving productivity in the American coal industry which were not present to the same degree in Europe. In the Virginia, West Virginia and Pennsylvania coalfields, from where the coals exported to Europe came, output per man day doubled

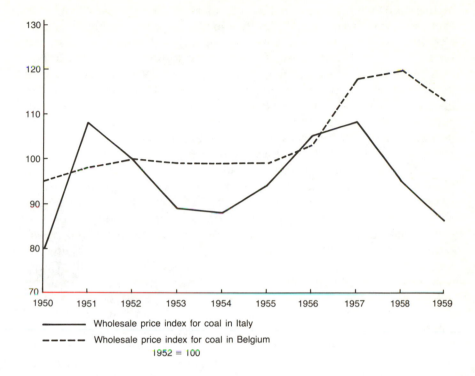

Figure 3.3 Wholesale price indexes for coal in Italy and Belgium, 1950–9

between 1950 and 1961, excluding the effect of the greater contribution of open-cast mining to total output. Labour costs per tonne of output had already begun to fall in 1952, although this trend was interrupted by demand-led wage increases in the course of 1956.[80] After 1957 the fall in labour costs was especially marked, so that in 1960 they were 25 cents per man/tonne lower than in 1957, although hourly wage rates did not fall. It seemed that American mining had a greater organizational capacity to respond to shrinking demand by improving productivity. It was also hard to avoid the conclusion that America's coal reserves were so vast that wherever transport costs did not exclude that possibility American firms would try to maintain operations by exporting. If the price trends shown in figure 2 were continued into the strong cyclical upswing of 1960–1 they would show no increase in the price of American coal landed in Europe over the level it had fallen to by 1958.[81]

Productivity improvements in European industries also played their part

---

[80] M. Liebrücks, *Die technische und wirtschaftliche Entwicklung der amerikanischen Steinkohlenförderung* (Berlin, 1961), p. 72.

[81] The pit-head price of US coking-coal (Pocahontas) was $6.50 tonne in 1960. Transport to Hampton Roads was $4.50 per tonne and the Atlantic freight rate $3.50. ECSC, *Etude sur*

in this fundamental break in the coal market. Energy consumption in Western Europe rose more slowly than industrial production in the 1950s. Even for coking-coal, which as we have seen stayed in high demand, this factor operated. The quantity of coke needed to produce a tonne of pig-iron began to fall. By 1964 the Community forecast was that even if steel output increased by 50 per cent in the decade 1960–70 coke consumption in blast furnaces would increase only by 12 per cent.[82] The same pattern held good in electricity generating. Whereas in the aftermath of the war it had needed roughly a kilogram of coal to produce one kilowatt/hour of electricity, by the close of the 1950s the figure was only 350 grammes.[83]

These productivity improvements were linked in many cases to a move away from coal consumption. While, for example, consumption of coal in Belgium for domestic and handicraft purposes fell from 6.69 million tonnes to 5.41 million over the period 1959–60, the consumption of coal for general industrial purposes (omitting coking-plant, gasworks and power stations) fell from 5.19 million tonnes to 2.96 million tonnes.[84] Railways, too, were converting rapidly to other forms of traction. Within the ECSC solid fuel, responsible for 82 per cent of primary energy consumption by industry in 1950, was responsible for only 48 per cent in 1960.

Belgium, because of its ample coal resources, began that period with a still higher proportion of primary energy consumption by industry depending on coal, 88 per cent. By 1960 this had fallen to a much lower figure than the ECSC average, 34 per cent.[85] High production costs meant that the move from coal to oil in the 1950s progressed further and faster in Belgium, despite its ample coal resources, than in any other European coal-producing country. By 1960 oil accounted for 53 per cent of industry's primary consumption, roughly the same proportion as in the Netherlands, higher than in Italy whose coal resources were small but which had larger reserves of natural gas, and much higher than in France and Germany. In the economy as a whole primary energy consumption derived from oil, expressed as a proportion of the primary energy consumption derived from coal, increased from 10.5 per cent in 1950 to 39.2 per cent in 1960. Imports of crude oil rose from 446,000 tonnes in 1950 to 6,508,400 tonnes in 1958. The shifts to oil were particularly striking in the slack years 1952–3 and 1958, whereas the boom year 1956, when restrictions on oil imports were first introduced, saw a slowing down in the switch to oil. In spite of restrictions on oil consumption, which included an increase in the tariff on

---

les perspectives énergétiques à long terme de la Communauté Européene (Luxembourg, 1964), p. 77.
[82] ibid., p. 39.
[83] F. Vinck, 'Le problème charbonnier', in Université Libre de Bruxelles, Institut de Sociologie, *Les Régions du Borinage et du Centre à l'heure de la réconversion* (Brussels, 1962).
[84] J.D. von Bandemer and A.P. Ilgen, *Probleme des Steinkohlenbergbaus. Die Arbeiter-und Förderverlagerung in den Revieren der Borinage und Ruhr* (Basel, 1963), p. 38.
[85] ECSC, *Etude sur les perspectives*, . . . op. cit., p. 125.

crude oil to almost 25 per cent, the tendency to substitute oil for coal was especially strong in years of slack demand as firms sought to cut costs.

As the Belgian coal industry felt the first effects of the 1954 boom national government policy veered towards Coppé's view that the retention of capacity in 1953 had been justified and that what was needed was not so much a fundamental restructuring of the industry as a cyclical policy. By 1955 restructuring had clearly been pushed aside as the prime objective. It is evident that this short-term policy was wrong and only served to increase the difficulties of 1958. This is not a judgement which could only be made with historical hindsight. There was sufficient contemporary evidence for it to be made. Even in the peak year 1955, for example, Belgian coke output had not expanded until the end of the year, in spite of the large rise in pig-iron output, because accumulated stocks had been large enough to cater for the increased demand. When the increase in Community pit-head coal stocks began again in December 1956 it was Belgian stocks which over the next twelve months made up three-quarters of the increase.[86] They increased to 3 million tonnes by the end of March 1958. When Belgium had entered the ECSC the government had looked favourably on the idea of supranational support to help with the immensely difficult problem of restructuring the coal industry and it was inherent in the Treaty of Paris that that would take place. Why, in spite of five years of subsidization, had it not happened?

This question was asked thirty years ago in interesting works by two economists sympathetic to the idea of western European integration, in William Diebold's pathbreaking work on the Schuman Plan and in the study of Benelux by J.E. Meade and his co-authors.[87] There is an air of pained disappointment about their answers. Both express a humane understanding of the industry's problems and of national policies of job protection. But the move to supranational management, both imply, should have been a move to more rational management, where decision-making, while equally humane, could have been distanced from short-term national political pressures. Even if keeping open the mines was a politically justifiable response to the sustained demand for coal, Meade and his collaborators argued, the investment which accompanied this policy was an error. It should have gone elsewhere. Even from the strictly national perspective the Belgian government's support of its coal industry was thus misguided. An ideal European Community should have been able to moderate policy errors of this kind and achieve a more rational allocation of resources. Do these verdicts still hold good?

Firstly it should be said that the high demand for coal in 1951 was still

[86] ECSC, *4th General Report on the Activities of the Community (April 11 1955 to April 8 1956)* (Luxembourg, 1956), p. 118.

[87] W.J. Diebold, Jnr, *The Schuman Plan. A Study in International Cooperation* (New York, 1959), J.E. Meade, *et al.*, *Case Studies in European Economic Union. The Mechanics of Integration* (London, 1962).

influencing opinion in 1952. That year the fall in coal consumption in Belgium made no impact on the general feeling in OEEC that the coal shortage was still a serious impediment to European economic expansion. Imports of American coal into Western Europe in 1952 were as high as 20.4 million tonnes. A third of this quantity was for the Federal Republic, whose coal imports from the USA increased by 1.6 million tonnes over the level of the previous year. In midsummer 1952 the OEEC was calling for a 4.5 per cent increase in Belgian coal output over 1951 levels. Even in 1953, when Western Europe's coal imports from the USA fell to 7.5 million tonnes, attitudes in OEEC and in ECSC still did not change until late in the year, because the problem was seen as one of coking-coal supply. Coke consumption in Western Europe in 1953 was still, taking the year as a whole, at its 1952 level. Virtually the whole of the American coal imported into Europe in 1953 was coking-coal. At the opening of the common market the High Authority's public attitude was that it was one of Belgium's tasks to reduce this dependence of the European steel industry on America.[88] It froze coking-coal exports to non-Community countries at their level of the first quarter of the year.

Although this meant there was no initial pressure on Belgium to begin restructuring its mines, the early Belgian attitude to the High Authority suggests that any such pressure would have been rebuffed, for it was one of watchful, defensive hostility. Coppé adopted a 'minimum' attitude to his new colleagues.[89] The rumour actually ran in the High Authority that he was in the pay of the British. Every job allocated to a Belgian citizen was carefully recorded to make sure there was no unjust attempt to deprive Belgium of its share. Even the appointment of a driver entered into the diplomatic correspondence. The Belgian minister in Luxembourg disapprovingly relayed every instance of Monnet's early attempts to increase the High Authority's powers. 'The foundation of his character', he wrote, 'is autocracy. Some consider him to be a supra-national-socialist, only recognizing the "Führerprinzip".'[90] The cause of most complaints was Monnet's attempts to merge the secretaryship of the Council of Ministers with that of the High Authority, his support in the High Authority for suggestions that it be given control over imports into the Community and over coal allocation within the Community, and his insistence on an early opening of the common market for coal.

It was crucial to the terms on which Belgium had entered the ECSC that the Council of Ministers should still retain complete independence of decision-making at the end of the five-year transition period. Belgium also

---

[88] ECSC, *The Activities of the ECSC. General Report of the High Authority (10 August 1952–12 April 1953)* (Luxembourg, 1953), p. 35.

[89] MAECE, 5216, Vicomte Berryer to van Zeeland, 18 November 1952. 'Of all my colleagues, only Albert Coppé seemed to present a problem.' J. Monnet, *Memoirs* (London, 1978), p. 374.

[90] MAECE, 5216, Berryer to van Zeeland, 6 December 1952.

strongly opposed control over non-Community imports, and coal allocations inside the ECSC, seeing both as steps towards the power which would allow the High Authority to force reductions in Belgian output against the wishes of the Belgian government. Monnet's attempts to control coal allocation within the Community were supported by the French and Dutch, because for both countries one intention of the ECSC had been to guarantee an adequate supply to them of German coking-coal.[91] The Belgians, the Dutch complained, were exploiting the coal shortage to force them to take a proportion of unwanted inferior coals with the coals they needed.[92] Fortunately for Belgium, it could rely at this early stage on support from Germany. The Germans had not got rid of the International Ruhr Authority in order to see it brought back in another guise.[93] The Belgian coal industry still believed itself in the first half of 1953 to be operating in a sellers' market and preferred to postpone as long as possible the proclamation of the common market in coal and to live without subsidies from *péréquation* until conditions worsened. It was only when the rapidly accumulating coal stocks changed these ideas in the course of 1953 that the initial bleak hostility to the High Authority was replaced by an attempt to use the Community machinery to get help. This coincided with the beginning of Community pressures to reduce output.

There were various ways in which opinion inside the Belgian government looked for support from the High Authority, but they were not complementary. One was that the High Authority could be used to increase the pressure for a restructuring of the industry. A second reflected a different view of the problem. They were that the ECSC could be used to subsidize coal stockpiles. This was the cyclical view of the problem, that Belgium, as in the 1930s, needed aid to sustain the industry in temporary periods of low demand. Between this view and the view that a long-term restructuring, with the reduction in the labour force that it would imply, the Belgian government was as divided as it had been during the treaty negotiations. In October 1953 the minister for economic affairs, Jean Duvieusart, formally requested the Community to provide financial aid for stockpiling coal in Belgium.[94] When he did so, he specifically indicated in parliament that he was in effect asking the Council of Ministers of the ECSC and the High Authority to decide whether the problems of the Belgian coal industry were structural or cyclical.

[91] ECSC, CEAB 2, no. 219, 'Mémorandum présenté par la Délégation Italienne . . .', 3 March 1953.

[92] ECSC, CEAB 2, no. 236, Head of Dutch delegation to the ECSC to Monnet, 4 February 1953.

[93] BA, B102/12608, 'Zur Frage einer Ausgleichskasse der Montan-Union für Kohleinführen', 21 July 1953.

[94] Jean Duvieusart, 1900–1977. A lawyer who built his political career in the Social Christian Party. Mayor of his home town Charleroi, 1944–9; minister for economic affairs, 1949; prime minister, June to August 1950, at the height of the abdication quarrel; minister of economic affairs, 1952–64; president of the European Parliament, 1964–5. He became a

In reality this was more a threat than a request. To emphasize its commitment to welfare and employment the treaty had made provision for a Readaptation Fund to provide help with relocation and retraining for workers whose jobs were lost. If the High Authority and the Council of Ministers decided that the problems of the Belgian economy were structural and refused the stockpiling subsidies, Duvieusart implied, this would commit it to financing out of the Readaptation Fund the redeployment of 17,000 workers whose jobs would be in immediate danger.[95]

The applicability of the appropriate treaty clauses to specific cases of closures and unemployment had not been tested and would be a matter of legal and administrative trial and error. It would obviously be preferable for the Community not to have to begin that trial with so large a number of people. Nothing on such a scale had ever been envisaged, for it had been assumed that the Redeployment Fund would be used only in cases of necessity to back up a much more gradual restructuring of the Belgian coal industry spread over five years. Even by the end of 1957 the number of workers in all member-states who had benefited in some way or other from the Readaptation Fund was 18,600. Most of these were Italian workers. In effect, the Readaptation Fund supplemented Italian social security payments under the guise of help with employment relocation. The Community, as Diebold argues, was unenthusiastic about taking up the challenge thrown down by Duvieusart because this would not be to supplement national policy but to substitute for its lack.[96] The game the Belgian government was playing was in fact a double bluff; it was not itself going to put 17,000 workers out of work almost immediately and it knew the Community was not prepared to do so either. The intention was to force the High Authority into an empirical acceptance of the argument that the economic problem of the coal industry was cyclical, not long-term.

If European coal were thought of as a European resource, and there had been plenty of indications in early 1953 that the High Authority would think that way, then cyclical aid in this form for Belgium would appear more logical and the national policy of the 1930s be transformed into the supranational policy of the 1950s. The Treaty of Paris, however, offered no obvious way of imposing a common import policy on the member-states without an extension of the High Authority's powers, that very extension to which Belgium had been so opposed over the first months of the High Authority's existence. The Germans, losing their apprehension that the High Authority would turn out to be a second International Ruhr Authority, and protectionist in the extreme about their national energy resources, were considering asking for such a policy by autumn 1953 in

militant supporter of linguistic nationalism in the next decade, a founding member of the Rassemblement Wallon and a supporter of a federal constitution for Belgium.

[95] MAECE, 5216, Direction Générale du Commerce Extérieur, Note for the minister for the special meeting of the Council of Ministers, 22 October 1953.

[96] W.J. Diebold, Jnr, *The Schuman Plan . . .*, op. cit., p. 419.

order to guarantee their place on western European markets, not envisaging that their earlier coal shortage would soon return. Belgium followed the discussion in Germany with interest, for it was now in Belgium's interest to have the ECSC promote its coal exports within the Community by imposing a ban on coal imports from the United States. The opposition from the coal importers Italy and the Netherlands to any such attempt to extend the High Authority's powers was, however, extremely vigorous. Germany eventually took the easier way. The treaty allowed individual states to maintain their own national quotas against non-Community imports. The Federal Republic, to the anger of American coal producers, imposed its own quotas against American coal.[97] This unilateral action at once made it more difficult to persuade the High Authority to finance Belgian stockpiles, for the Germans, set on maintaining output in the new conditions of slack demand, were fixing their eyes once more on the Belgian market.

If the main thrust of Belgian national policy was to win acceptance of the idea that coal resources must be preserved, it did not only rely on subsidization to do this. There was an awareness that the structure of demand for coal was changing. The other side of policy was to provide a better market for the low-grade industrial coals of which the accumulating stockpiles were mainly composed. Linked to the demand for help with stockpiling was a request for Community aid for investment in building coal-fired power stations to increase the demand for lower-grade coals. France had actively supported a policy of heavy investment by the High Authority from the outset, perhaps under the influence of Monnet's vision of the ECSC as a French plan transposed to Europe. It was known that the United States was prepared to encourage a loan from Wall Street to the ECSC so as to demonstrate its support for Monnet and integration. Requesting part of the proceeds of the loan to build power stations in Belgium would surely get Monnet's support, because it would enhance the High Authority's role. Such a request could easily be presented as a step towards integration, because some of the electric current produced would be sold to France and Holland.

The American loan did eventually contribute $14 million to investment in four new coal-fired power stations in southern Belgium. But the discussions on Duvieusart's request for stockpiling aid brought home rather sharply the distinction between supranational and national government. The actual progress, or lack of it, made with restructuring the mining industry in southern Belgium, and particularly in the Borinage, now became for the first time the subject of expert international attention,

---

[97] Described as 'discrimination of the rankest sort' by the Coal Exporters Association of the United States in their evidence to the President's Committee on Foreign Economic Policy (Randall Committee). They persuaded the State Department to protest, unsuccessfully, on their behalf. EL, Records of the President's Commission on Foreign Economic Policy 1953–1954, Box no. 56, 29 October 1953.

especially from the countries which preferred cheap imports to the idea of using European resources. What had been in 1948–9 an argument, of little importance on a European scale, between Belgium and America over aid to Belgian mines and then a subject of argument between diplomats who were less than expert in the question, became now a matter of detailed economic investigation and decision in five other countries. The power station loan was only approved by the High Authority in return for additional powers over the use of the subsidies paid under the 1949 national agreements for restructuring the Borinage mines. Had the Belgian government been united, this point would not have been conceded. But, of course, it was not, and those who wished to see a speedier restructuring were in favour of bringing in the ECSC to their help.

Sales of Belgian coal on the domestic market were increasingly confined to two major outlets, power stations and steelworks. But of these two, as we have noted, only one had an underlying upward trend in demand, because technological improvements and the shift to oil were also reducing inexorably the long-term demand for coal by the power industry. Should the High Authority have acquired its additional influence in Belgium by investing in a declining market for non-coking-coal? The coking-coals of the Borinage were not mined without a substantial proportion of lower-value coals. These could have retained a market if mines elsewhere in the south which produced no coking-coal had been closed. The High Authority had not, it was to emerge, been given sufficient political leverage by the Treaty of Paris or by its modification to achieve that outcome. Its increased powers arising out of the loan agreement were to prove relatively effective, but only in the collieries in the Borinage which had signed the original 1949 agreements.

The agreements between the Belgian government and four of the six companies which held the mining concessions in the Borinage had set targets for productivity improvement. These targets had not been achieved by 1953 and in most cases the restructuring plans on the basis of which they were drawn up had barely begun to be implemented. A typical case was that of the most southerly of the Borinage concessions, Les Charbonnages Belges et d'Hornu Wasmes. On this company alone 693 million Belgian francs ($13.8 million) had been lavished in aid between the 1949 agreements and October 1953. Its mines produced the highest grade coking fines in Belgium. They supplied the Cockerill steelworks in Seraing with coking fines to mix with lower-grade coking-coals from Cockerill's own mines in the Kempen and they also supplied the coking plant at the Tertre complex. One of its mines, Crachet-Pigny, was by itself a profitable operation; the others in spite of this massive subsidization had remained deeply unprofitable. The Robinson report had suggested that with a proper rationalization of the underground workings the whole of the coking-coal seam worked by the company's other mines could eventually be worked profitably, while seams of non-coking-coal were abandoned. Rationalization in this case meant not only reducing the number of separate mines operated by the company in its concession but also a merger with the company operating the most easterly of the Borinage concessions, Levant et Produits de Flénu in order to reduce the number of mines owned by that company working the same coking-coal seams.

Levant et Produits de Flénu had fulfilled by 1954 most of the targets for rationalization set out in the 1949 agreement which it had signed. But these agreements had never insisted on the company mergers which the Robinson report had deemed necessary for an effective return to profitability in the Borinage. Les Charbonnages Belges was far from completing even the rationalization of its own workings underground and its surface activities which had been stipulated in the 1949 agreement. The excuse was that high demand prevented rationalization and that the price of coal was in any case too low to justify such investment.

While discussion in Luxembourg about the possibility of financing stockpiles and the uses to which the American loan might be put was under way, the Belgian government officially requested Community permission to increase its own aid to the Borinage companies.[98] Before the request could officially be placed before the High Authority and the Council of Ministers, Les Charbonnages Belges issued an ultimatum which typified government–industry relations in coal since the Schuman proposals. Perhaps encouraged by Duvieusart's challenge to the ECSC in October 1953, it announced it would cease mining on 1 March 1954 unless there were an immediate decision that the subsidies which kept it going would continue after the close of the transition period to the common market, as well as extra subsidies to cover the increase in social security costs since the 1949 agreement.[99] No more obvious signal to the work force could have been devised. On cue the miners in six of the company's seven pits for which closure was threatened came out on strike in the week before Christmas. In the mining township of Wasmes street barricades appeared. Speaking to the lower house Duvieusart publicly opined that there should be no mine closures, that increased subsidies would have to be paid, and that the High Authority should now take an initiative in helping to carry out restructuring in the Borinage. He was thus able to straddle the political arguments within the government, and the High Authority was able to extend its powers.

Financial trusts, colliery companies and the trade unions, while each apparently acting out their traditional roles in conflict were in reality presenting a united front to the High Authority. If increased subsidies were not paid, the Community would have to appear responsible for unemployment and pay for its relief from the Readaptation Fund. The High

[98] ECSC, AMH, 23/5/1, Division du Marché, 'Rapport provisoire sur la visite à l'Administration des Mines Belges relative à la fermeture de la division des Charbonnages Belges et d'Hornu-Wasmes', 17 December 1953.
[99] ECSC, AMH 23/5/2, 'Note au sujet des Charbonnages Belges et d'Hornu-Wasmes', n.d.

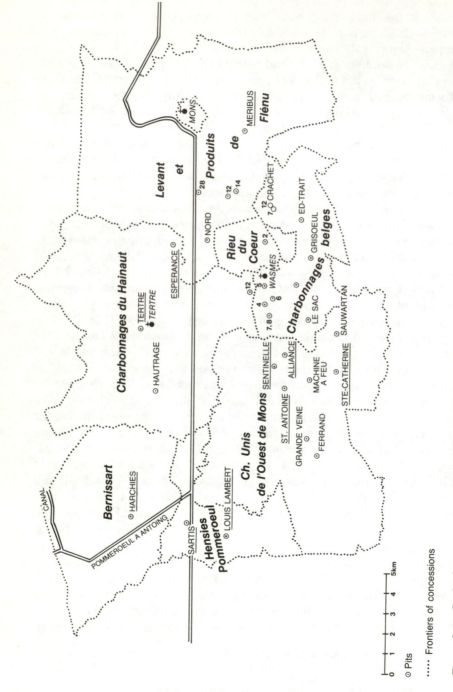

Figure 3.4 Coal mine concessions and pits in the Borinage

⊙ Pits

..... Frontiers of concessions

0 1 2 3 4 5km

Authority could refuse to allow extra subsidies, defy the company to close its mines, take the opprobrium of this decision, see its refusal in all probability disputed by the Belgian government, and appear as the enemy of the post-war consensus on employment, or it could use the opportunity to extend its influence and at the same time perhaps accelerate productivity improvements. Under article 26 of the treaty Belgium had an undisputed right to continue paying national subsidies after the five-year transition period, and even the powers of the High Authority to prevent it increasing its existing level of subsidies were most uncertain. There was really little choice in the matter for the High Authority. It could be the opportunity, as Monnet's advisers pointed out, to insist that aid was provided only to companies which would be able to manage after the end of the transition period without further payment.[100] In return for a small increase in its financial contribution the High Authority could exercise a more immediately effective influence than it obtained from the large sums it transferred in *péréquation*.

Even in so short a time the ECSC had acquired all the habits and processes of a bureaucracy. Its first move was a joint committee of inquiry with the Belgian government, not only into the two companies in question, but also into two other companies in the Borinage which had signed agreements in 1949. The Belgian government agreed in late January 1954 to create an additional temporary support fund for Les Charbonnages Belges until the joint inquiry should be complete. One-third of this additional fund, it suggested, should come from a national levy on all coal sales, one-third from existing government revenue, and one-third from the ECSC.[101] The High Authority however refused to allow any further subsidization from Community funds until the joint inquiry had been completed. Under the terms of the 1949 agreements the level of subsidy provided by the Belgian government to the four Borinage companies should have fallen by almost half in 1954 compared to 1953. In view of the High Authority's refusal to increase its contribution the Belgian government imposed an extra levy of 120 million Belgian francs ($2.4 million) on coal sales to be used as additional aid to coking-coal producers in the Borinage. The money would go to Les Charbonnages Belges, Levant et Produits de Flénu, and to a third company, because the mines of all three 'could ultimately be judged necessary for supplying the common market'.[102]

The composition of the joint committee of inquiry was not agreed until 17 February 1954. Its report was not available until September. The same change in background conditions occurred as during the Schuman Plan

[100] ECSC, AMH 23/5/11, Division des Finances, Investissements et Marché, 'Note pour M. Monnet', 21 January 1954.
[101] ECSC, CEAB 4/414, Division du Marché. 'Note à Messrs. les membres de la Haute Autorité', 9 February 1954.
[102] ECSC, AMH 23/5/14, Duvieusart to Zijlstra, 12 February 1954.

negotiations; demand for coal again began to rise as the report was being written. The argument that this proved that the problems had, after all, been merely cyclical was vigorously advanced by the Belgian representatives on the joint committee. The committee was sufficiently influenced by the increase in demand to recommend, as the Robinson report had, continued support for Borinage mining to increase the quantity of coking-coal mined. But this, it insisted, would have to be in the context of a more far-reaching restructuring plan than that imposed by the 1949 agreements. Of the twenty mines worked by the four companies receiving aid under those agreements only nine, the joint committee recommended, should be kept in operation, and only two of those belonging to Les Charbonnages Belges. Company mergers which would allow a realignment of underground working to exploit the better seams immediately at the expense of the more marginal would, it suggested, eventually make three of the four companies profitable, their output would even increase. Les Charbonnages Belges, the company which had precipitated the crisis, though, could not by itself again be run at a profit, the report indicated. The case for keeping some of its workings was only the case for maximizing coking-coal output, and for that the merger with the separate concession Levant et Produits de Flénu was indispensable.[103]

The report envisaged an increase in labour productivity of between 25 and 30 per cent, whereas the investment and rationalization which had taken place since 1949 had resulted in very little improvement in labour productivity. But that depended not only on company mergers but on facing up to an equally difficult problem, so far avoided, the closure of eleven Borinage mines. The eventual collapse of the market in 1958 showed that the report was in fact too optimistic. It required high investment for its implementation, 3,349 million Belgian francs ($66.32 million), more than the Belgian government wished to make. While it was ready to meet the full cost of restructuring the two Borinage companies where the least investment and the fewest political difficulties were involved, for Les Charbonnages Belges and Produits de Flénu it demanded a fifty–fifty participation by the Community.[104] This was to make sure that the political difficulties were shared by the supranational authority.

One remarkable aspect of the discussions on the joint committee's report was that there was no disagreement over the recommendation that coking-coal should be mined in increased quantities. The hold of steel on the imaginations and policies of European governments in the 1950s was a powerful one and it was the perspective of a constantly increasing steel production which influenced the High Authority towards so optimistic a view of the future of Borinage mining. As far as the prognosis for demand

[103] ECSC, CEAB 9225, *Expertise relative à la rentabilité présente et future des Charbonnages Borains . . . par une Commission Internationale d'Experts réunie à l'initiative de la Haute Autorité de la Communauté Européenne du Charbon et de l'Acier*, September 1954.
[104] ECSC, AMH 23/5/18, Rey to Monnet, 10 November 1954.

for coking-coal by the European steel industries went, their view was well-founded. It was also, though, very Eurocentric. The fall in the European price of American coking-coal took place only two years after the publication of the report of the joint committee.

In the event the Community paid only a small part of the aid provided under the new agreements with the Borinage companies, $6.76 million, and was proved correct in its assumption that sharing the political burden in the Borinage would be the thin end of the wedge in making the general subsidies from *péréquation* more appropriate and better targeted on the industry's problems. Low-grade industrial coals and coals for power stations, the grades which had accumulated in 1953, should, the joint committee suggested, no longer be subsidized at all. It also recommended the removal of all *péréquation* subsidy from lower-grade coking-coal, *gras B*, mined in the Kempen, because the Kempen companies were profitable. To both these alterations to the *péréquation* regime the Belgian government was ready to agree. For the coal industry this was the test of the treaty for which it had been waiting. It took the High Authority and the Belgian government to the new Court of Justice of the Community, arguing that they were in breach of the treaty, which in their view did not permit discrimination between producers. The Court decided in favour of the High Authority and thenceforward subsidies under *péréquation* were adjusted in favour of coking-coal producers, which meant that of the total paid over the whole transition period the southern mines eventually received a larger sum per tonne of coal mined.

Since October 1953, following a request from the Council of Ministers, a joint committee of experts of the High Authority and the Council of Ministers had begun to survey the whole energy market. Although this was mainly a low-level bureaucratic exercise, the High Authority could already draw on its work in 1954 to support the view that output of lower-grade coals should be allowed to decline relative to that of coking-coal. The committee's work could also be used to refute the continued claim that capacity should be kept large enough to satisfy the peak of cyclical demand.[105] Whatever policy was applied to coking-coal, it would, the High Authority now belatedly began to argue, be entirely wrong to retain a general coal production capacity which coincided with the peak of cyclical demand. This was a view supported by all member-states except Belgium and Luxembourg. The acceptance of the report of this joint committee as well as the report of the joint committee with the Belgian government into the Borinage, and the final agreement to finance a programme of restructuring there, can be seen as a definite rejection by the High Authority of the argument that the problems of the Belgian coal industry were cyclical.

On 23 April 1954 van Acker returned again as prime minister as the head

---

[105] ECSC, CMI/1955/245, Mémorandum de la Haute Autorité sur la Politique Charbonnière, 1 February 1955.

of a Socialist–Liberal coalition. The conflict of views between the Community and the national government at once became more marked. It was under van Acker's prime ministership that the package of agreements with the Community was concluded. But agreements which had been intended to force on to supranational management a visible shared public responsibility for the necessary painful restructuring of the industry were now seen by the Belgian government more as committing supranational management to going at Belgium's own speed, dictated by domestic politics. As boom conditions pushed the price of American coal above Belgian coal in 1955 the intended restructuring of the Borinage began to be scaled down from the joint committee of inquiry's proposals. The Conseil National des Charbonnages produced an alternative plan under which the number of closures in the Borinage would be reduced to eight, and the High Authority was asked to support this version.

The High Authority's third annual report published in April 1955 was sharply critical of these tendencies. 'The High Authority', it declared,

> is of the opinion that the production capacity contemplated cannot be centred on the maximum of foreseeable requirements, such as would result from maximum general expansion and the most favourable peak periods in market conditions. Such a solution would lead to an increase in production costs, and a weakening of the competitive position of coal.[106]

Keeping open marginal mines would not preserve employment, the report insisted, but would lead on the contrary to a loss of jobs by making it more difficult for coal to compete with other forms of energy.

The counter-argument of Belgian producers by that time was once more that the control of coal prices was robbing them of justified returns and that output was more important than restructuring programmes. It was coal-importing countries in the Community, they argued, who were being subsidized by an artificially low coal price. Fédéchar demanded an increase in the price of coking-coal to acknowledge the boom conditions. Even if this should again make American coal competitive, the Mines Administration argued, 'the present glut of American coal cannot be considered permanent and there is a risk that in the future the American steel industry will absorb all the country's coal production in spite of its great elasticity.'[107] This was the most far-fetched of all its arguments for protection.

Fédéchar, preparing its court case against the High Authority, refused to participate in the committees whose task was to determine whether

---

[106] ECSC, *Third General Report on the Activities of the Community*, 12 April 1954 to 10 April 1955 (Luxembourg, 1955), p. 122.
[107] ECSC, CMI/1955/245, Comité Ad Hoc Pour l'Examen du Mémorandum de la Haute Autorité sur la Politique Charbonnière. Compte-rendu analytique des débats, 16 May 1955.

Community coal prices should be increased by the new price scale due to be published in May 1955. The decision on whether to increase the price of coal had to be taken on the same day as the High Authority was due to conclude the final details of the package agreement on aid to Belgium, 26 April 1955. Every member, as well as close observers in national governments, was aware that this was the first great test of the capacity of supranational governance to display genuine political independence and take a set of optimum economic and managerial decisions rather than reach a fudged political compromise.

Monnet, as all who worked with him in the ECSC agree, had little interest in or knowledge of the details of the coal, iron and steel industries. For him, they were merely instrumental to his higher political goals. As president of the High Authority he had tried to give a political leadership to the other members, each of whom had been allocated a specialized supervisory administrative function. This had not resulted in their emancipation from their national governments. Functionalists must seek evidence of their thesis elsewhere. At this crucial moment at the end of April each member of the High Authority faithfully represented the position of his national government.

The members who represented coal-importing countries, Enzo Giacchero and Dirk Spierenburg, voted for an increased subsidization of coal prices in the Community to mitigate the rising cost of American coal.[108] The French, German and Luxembourg members voted to support the alternative, that is subsidies to support the package agreement with Belgium. They also voted for a proposal that the Community and the Belgian government could jointly establish a higher Belgian coal price if necessary, even though the original purpose of *péréquation* had been to reduce the price of Belgian coal. Coppé abstained. Monnet voted with the French, German and Luxembourg members, for the Belgian package, greater intervention, and the possibility of a subsequent increase in the price of Belgian coal.[109]

Vinck was severely critical of him afterwards, holding that he had failed to give any true economic or European leadership. The decisions, Vinck believed, were contradictory. Even if the price of Belgian coal were raised in defiance of the intentions of the Treaty of Paris, the producers would not be satisfied. The incentive for the restructuring of the Borinage would be reduced. It was, he complained, a short-sighted response to short-term influences and a mistaken concession to vested interests in Belgium and their 'deliberate manoeuvres and obstructions'. It made a genuine common

---

[108] Enzo Giacchero, 1912– . Taught engineering in Turin Polytechnic, 1936–40; a military leader of resistance units, 1944–5; prefect of Asti, 1945–6; member of the Constituent Assembly 1946; elected deputy, 1948; member of the High Authority, 1952–9; director-general of SATAP, a motorway concern, 1963–74. A pianist.

[109] ECSC, AMH 7/1/297, Procès-verbal de la 258ème séance de la Haute Autorité, 26 April 1955.

market in coal look much further away, possibly indeed having 'fatal consequences for integration'.[110]

The Belgian law of 12 July 1955 promulgated the new Borinage investment programme and backed its funding by a state guarantee. As much as 2,300 million francs ($45.5 million) was earmarked for the Borinage companies on the basis of the new agreements reached with the High Authority. The counterpart to this was a High Authority decision in May that subsidy payments would be withheld from companies not complying with the restructuring plan and that *péréquation* would now be made discriminatory by withdrawing it from certain grades of coal, according to the earlier proposals. It had taken a year and a half from Duvieusart's first threatening request to the High Authority for aid. Restructuring had lost something on the way and the price of Belgian coal had not come closer to that of other coals in the common market. But in spite of the return of the van Acker government the broad agreement on lines of action had been preserved. What was the outcome?

There were only three mine closures announced, but not completed, in 1956 and a further one in January 1957. They were insignificant in their impact. Foreigners were being recruited in increasing numbers for underground work in 1956. Overall employment in mining increased in 1957. The committee of inquiry had written that financial viability depended on Borinage mining increasing its daily output from 6,525 tonnes to 7,950 tonnes.[111] In the event by the end of 1957 it had scarcely increased at all. In summer 1956 the Belgian coking-coal price was finally increased. The productivity figures reveal the heart of the failure. It is probably true, as Belgian mining engineers claimed when the crash came in 1958, that given the conditions in which they had had to operate they had achieved remarkable productivity levels. It is very hard to find any evidence that methods of working were less modern than in mines in other countries with comparable geological conditions. Indeed they seem usually to have been more mechanized. But in the boom productivity gains were small. Annual output per underground worker in the Borinage in 1957 was only three tonnes more than in 1954.[112] Costs stayed higher and output per man/shift stayed lower than elsewhere. This was not due to lack of investment. Capital expenditure per tonne of coal in the southern coalfields rose in 1956 to its 1951 level, not counting the investment in the new power stations.

When Belgian coal stocks again began to increase at the end of 1956 the High Authority's unease was public. The subsidies from *péréquation*, its main leverage, had little time to run. Under renewed High Authority pressure the Belgian government was forced to accept a reclassification of

[110] ECSC, AMH 20/9/1, Division du Marché, Vinck to Monnet, 27 April 1955.
[111] ECSC, AMH 23/5/19, Division du Marché, 'Rapport à la Haute Autorité sur l'ensemble des problèmes charbonniers belges', 13 December 1954.
[112] Annales des Mines de Belgique, 1954, 1957.

Table 3.8   Average monthly employment in Belgian coal mining, 1952–60

Year	Total employed	Of which foreigners
1952	159,777	70,014
1953	156,518	67,614
1954	149,946	60,782
1955	146,292	60,736
1956	144,908	64,119
1957	146,292	67,622
1958	146,127	68,323
August 1959	125,899	56,555
August 1960	105,402	46,684

Source: UN, ST/ECE/COAL/5. *The Coal Situation in Europe*

all Belgian collieries into three groups. For one group, representing about half the total coal output, it was decided that no further assistance at all from the Community would be provided. This group included all the Kempen mines. A second group consisted of mines which it was believed could become viable if subsidies were continued to the end of the transition period. The third group was mines now declared to have no chance of financial viability at the end of the transition period. For them all subsidies from *péréquation* would end in February 1957. There was of course nothing to stop the Belgian government itself continuing to subsidize them even after the transition period, although in the case of the Borinage mines it would now only have been able to do so with High Authority authorization.

Belgian government subsidies under the terms of the agreements with the Borinage companies did in fact increase from 396 million Belgian francs ($8.06 million) in 1956 to 640 million ($12.75 million) in 1957. The van Acker government appeared quite prepared to continue these subsidies while only half-heartedly carrying out the restructuring programme. The failure of labour productivity to improve is hardly surprising when extra output was being achieved with extra labour. In the late months of 1957 government attitudes were revealed when the Kempen producers were refused permission to cut the prices of their coking-coals because it would endanger the survival of the Borinage mines. 'The problem of the integration of Belgian coal', the High Authority announced in its 1958 report, 'therefore remains unsolved.'[113] Then came the collapse. In 1958 output fell by 2 million tonnes. In the next year it fell by 4.3 million tonnes. Only then did restructuring really begin.

The Community could only have been used to restructure and rationalize the Belgian coal industry if the Belgian government itself had consist-

---

[113] ECSC, *Sixth General Report on the Activities of the Community 1957/8* (Luxembourg, 1958), vol. 2, p. 45.

ently wished to do so. Only between late 1954 and spring 1955 was it really committed to such a programme and even then it was divided and wanted to go slowly. The Community began to apply consistent pressure only in spring 1955. But its devices were weak. The reclassification of the collieries for subsidy in 1956 could not bring sufficient financial pressure to bear. The time to do that would have been when the financial contribution from *péréquation* was a larger share of the total subsidy. The Treaty of Paris did not give that opportunity to the Community. It had to be created by political action afterwards. The delay imposed on the changes in *péréquation* by the legal action of Fédéchar further weakened the High Authority's financial leverage. The conclusion must be that the Treaty of Paris itself was an inadequate instrument.

The adjustment of Belgian coal mining to the realities of an interdependent world was not brought about through the supranational machinery but more brutally through the old familiar mechanism of bankruptcy. Ironically, after delaying the use of the supranational structure to help in a rational restructuring of the industry, the Belgian government found itself facing the coal industry's collapse at the very moment when de Gaulle's seizure of power in France confined all Community action to the strict letter of the Treaties of Paris and Rome and so prevented further recourse to the Community's financial resources.

Even in 1959 the government clung to the illusion that the problems of the industry could be solved by cyclical policy. It asked the High Authority to formulate a common policy to restrict imports from America and to devise a price-stabilization plan which would subsidize stockpiles in periods of slack demand while allowing more rapid price increases in periods of high demand. Although the Federal Republic repeated its earlier action by unilaterally introducing restrictions on imports of American coal to limit them in 1959 to their 1958 level, neither the German regional coal sales organizations nor the government were prepared to support these Belgian requests.[114] They no doubt felt they had paid their due. It needed little more than a show of coolness by the French and Italians, insisting on the prior need for structural change in Belgium, to incite the liberal Dutch minister of the economy Jelle Zijlstra into a wholehearted denunciation of any attempts at cyclical regulation. 'If the High Authority is a supranational institution, it cannot however be or become a "superbusiness".'[115]

In response Belgium, like the Federal Republic, took unilateral measures, imposing extra import duties on oil and cajoling collieries and oil importers into agreements to slow down the growth in oil consumption. In the face of unilateral measures by two countries limiting extra-Community imports the weakness of the High Authority was cruelly exposed. Its only

---

[114] ECSC, CMI/1958 266, Extrait du Compte-rendu de la 75ème Réunion de la Commission de Coordination, 22–23 April 1958.
[115] ECSC, CMI/1958 267, Extrait du Projet de Procès-Verbal de la 50ème Session du Conseil, 29 April 1958.

policy was to try to preserve the illusion of a common policy. The zonal system of fixed coal price parameters, which had begun with the start of the common market in coal, was terminated in February 1958 and producers were allowed to set their prices with reference to those of any other Community producer. Very few took advantage of this. The market was still shifting towards purchases by large-scale consumers and this trend corresponded with the beginnings of market regulation by the producers and consumers themselves through the use of extensive rebates for long-term contracts at stable prices and other similar devices. Its significance was more that it marked a stage in the collapse of the ECSC.

Yet it was Belgium which most needed a common policy and the political support it could bring, more indeed in 1958 than earlier. As the full measure of the changed perspective for coal was taken, the Belgian government began to press most urgently for a different kind of common action to deal with the economic and social crisis of the southern mining areas, not cyclical aid but a long-term economic programme. By the Dutch and Italians, benefiting from falling coal prices, these requests were at first seen only as further efforts to keep up the price of coal, by de Gaulle and his ministers as a dangerous incitement to a further and unwanted stage of European integration.

On 14 May 1958 the Council of Ministers rejected the original Belgian request for cyclical aid and the introduction of unilateral measures of protection. The Mines Administration drew up the details of a more drastic restructuring plan. Production in each of the four Borinage companies which had been the object of the joint committee inquiry was now to be concentrated in only one mine in each concession. This projected increase in closures also reflected Van Acker's defeat at the elections in the middle of the summer when Gaston Eyskens was returned as prime minister of a Social Christian government, at first in office by itself and then in a coalition with the Liberals. The Eyskens government was ready to go ahead with the drastic restructuring that now seemed inevitable, but it preferred to do so in the framework of Community rather than national policy. The problem was that the restructuring, delayed when times were good, now had to take place in the 1958 recession and because of that the government wanted a measure of protection against coal imports in order to slow the pace of change.

The High Authority too was in search of a common policy. But to find it in imposing a common protection on the frontier of the Community against coal imports looked impossible. It would never receive Italian or Dutch support, because these countries wanted the cheapest possible imports. The High Authority did approach the Council of Ministers in autumn 1958 for permission to impose a temporary quota on coal imports into the Community, confining them to the same quantity as in the previous twelve months. It asked that all governments should consult with it before they took further unilateral action to restrict imports. And it asked that it be allowed to finance out of its own resources, rather than out of a levy on coal sales as the Belgians had proposed in the spring, all new additions to stockpiles after the end of October. It was made clear to the Council of Ministers that these proposals were considered only as a stopgap defence until the search for a common policy on production had been successful.

The Belgians regarded these requests as far too weak, but it was only they who in the end supported them all. The Germans having already done the same thing unilaterally through their quotas, were in favour of maintaining extra-Community imports at their 1958 level. As far as the Dutch were concerned, however, prices must fall and any import controls would impede that. So, too, they argued, would financial aid for stockpiles. The German coal sales syndicates were also opposed to this. The French were not unwilling to consider some form of long-term market regulation which would shift all variations in demand on to extra-Community imports, but only at a lower level of Community output. Even this was unacceptable in Italy and the Netherlands. Furthermore, the French were not prepared to tolerate any declaration of principle that member-states should be obliged to consult with the High Authority over details of commercial policy where the Treaty of Paris had not stipulated that obligation, as this 'could bring about a limitation of governmental sovereignty in the area of commercial policy'.[116]

What was the point, the new Belgian minister for economic affairs van der Scheuren asked, of a Community whose decisions were plunging more than half the Belgian coal industry into immediate bankruptcy?[117] Unless all additional stockpiles over 5 million tonnes were financed Belgium would demand a proclamation of 'manifest crisis', invoke the safeguard clause which van Zeeland had negotiated and ask for a temporary separation from the common market. Of the 6 million tonnes of coal already in stockpiles in Belgium, the government claimed, 2 million tonnes were from America and 2 million from the rest of the Community. The government was not prepared in these circumstances to put thousands of miners out of work.[118]

The Federal Republic had already eliminated about 10,000 jobs in coal mining in 1958 by October when van der Scheuren made his protest and it could hardly be argued that this had produced a social crisis. In a rapidly growing economy all workers, except those close to retiring age, had been quickly re-employed elsewhere. All other member-states agreed that the Community could not go on looking after Belgian coal miners for ever. If the problems were more acute in Belgium than Germany, because of the greater number of miners relative to total employment and the slower

[116] ECSC CMI/1958 264, Compte-rendu de la 81ème réunion de la Commission de Coordination du Conseil de Ministres, 9 October 1958.
[117] ibid.
[118] ibid., Extrait du Procès-Verbal de la 53ème session du Conseil Special des Ministres, 13–14 October 1958.

growth of the Belgian economy, those, as the Dutch and Italians commented, were Belgian national problems, not ones for which they themselves should be made to pay in higher manufacturing costs.

Had the Treaties of Rome not been signed, the ECSC, which had virtually collapsed, would probably have been unable to find a common course of action, because there was no least common denominator of national policies. Once there was a commitment by the Six to a common market for all industrial products, however, it was impossible to argue that for coal each member-state should permanently have its own import policy. There had to be some compromise. The Council of Ministers in autumn 1958 allowed the High Authority to continue to subsidize out of its own funds certain Belgian collieries whose difficulties could be proved to be genuinely cyclical. These could not include any of those recommended for closure by the joint committee of inquiry.[119] The Belgian government itself however was still free to subsidize such mines under the terms of the 1955 agreements, which meant in certain cases until the end of 1962.

This appeared to leave the decision to the Belgian government whether it would implement the much more drastic 1958 plan of the Mines Administration for closures. A wave of strikes throughout the Borinage in winter 1958–9 attempted to deter any such decision. This time, because of other political troubles, they received massive support from outside the coal industry. The rhetoric of the strikes, though, had changed from that of winter 1953–4 towards accepting realities. The demands were more for regional help, a regional development policy which would rescue francophone Belgium from the hard times to come. The new president of the High Authority was Paul Finet, a Belgian trade unionist.[120] Negotiations in February 1959 between Finet and prime minister Eyskens finally offered the High Authority some chance of achieving a common policy. Finet persuaded the mining unions to accept a restructuring plan on the understanding that there would now be some special regional support from the national government and the Community, and offered Eyskens support for the more drastic proposals which the Mines Administration had drawn up.

Finet was on shaky ground in making any sort of promise of regional help on behalf of the ECSC. The Council of Ministers was not prepared in March 1959 to support such a proposal. Their refusal was accompanied by an outraged French commentary that no one had ever intended to set up a

---

[119] D.A. Sexter, 'The Belgian coal mines in the European Coal and Steel Community' (Ph.D. Dissertation, University of California, Davis, 1969), p. 115.

[120] Paul Finet, 1897–1965. A metal worker and trade unionist who was an ardent supporter in the 1930s of de Man's attack on state financial orthodoxy. Became national secretary of the Federation of Belgian Trade Unions in 1945 on its foundation and thereafter pursued the typical post-war career of a trade union bureaucrat, even to becoming president of the International Federation of Free Trade Unions and president of the High Authority of the ECSC. Some accounts of his life express surprise that a workman could be both educated and polite.

European Community to finance and manage regional policies. This was on the eve of the steepest fall in output and employment in Belgian coal. The government, still with a promise of financial support as far as it could be legitimated without changing the terms of the Treaty of Paris, began the restructuring plan in November 1959 for a reduction of almost a third in coal-mining capacity. Before the plan was promulgated 16,000 workers had left the industry in one year. Over the next year almost 25,000 were to leave.

Table 3.9 Output per man/shift and employment in Belgian coal mines, 1953–61 (monthly average) (kg.)

	Underground	Surface and underground	Number of underground workers
1953	1,060	758	95,500
1954	1,098	787	90,700
1955	1,145	824	87,200
1956	1,156	838	88,700
1957	1,146	836	90,500
1958	1,153	842	90,200
1959	1,262	907	77,800
1960	1,430	1,018	62,300
1961	1,541	1,092	53,100

Source: Banque de Belgique, *Revue de l'économie belge en 1961*, p. 42

The improvement in productivity which followed this reduction of capacity left no doubt that the failure to carry out the restructuring plans earlier had been partly responsible for the high cost of Belgian coal. When labour was being slowly reduced in the period of slack demand in 1953–4 productivity slowly improved. When demand was rising in 1955 and labour was being added, productivity stagnated. The first true indications that Belgian coal mines might indeed be able to operate at levels of productivity comparable to those of the Ruhr came only with the loss of 28,000 underground workers over the period 1958–60 and a further 8,200 in 1961. It was in 1960, seven years after the opening of the common market and in entirely changed circumstances that output per man/shift in Belgian mines reached approximately the 1951 level in the Ruhr (table 3.9). That meant a fall in output over the period 1957–60 of roughly 6.5 million tonnes, or 22.4 per cent. It meant an overall decline in employment, underground and surface, over the same period of roughly 41,000, with a further decline in 1961 still to come.

In the Borinage over the period 1957–60 output of coal fell from 4 million tonnes to 2.2 million. Ten collieries were closed down. By the end of 1961 only five mines were still working there, although some of these incorporated the underground workings of earlier smaller mines, as the restructuring programme was put into operation. The Tertre plant had to be supplied from elsewhere and the biggest of the new coal-fired power stations built with the American loan to the Community, the Inter-borinage, when it opened depended on coal from outside the region.[121] The closures elsewhere in southern Belgium were on a still greater scale. Over the same period a further twenty-eight mines with an output of 5 million tonnes were closed in the Centre, Charleroi and Liège.[122]

PRESERVING THE WELFARE CONSENSUS

There may in the history of the post-war high employment state before 1968 be other examples of so many being kept in industrial work at the expense of higher productivity by such a wide and expensive range of public subsidies. But they do not readily spring to mind, and the special interest of this case is that so large a part of the subsidies was provided by the nascent European Community. And there is no other example of the same state and the same international framework then having to cope with so many workers permanently losing their employment in one industry over so short a time. The contradictions which lay at the heart of the post-war political consensus stand uncovered by this Belgian experience: full employment versus economic growth; the preservation of the nation versus the need to internationalize the policies by which it was preserved. The story is the more appropriate because it was in Belgium, that European microcrosm, that the European Economic Community chose to settle in 1957. The collapse of the coal market in 1958 was a crisis of the post-war Belgian state, of the post-war consensus on employment in general, and of the internationalization of that consensus through the Community institutions.

The consensus remained in place. The Six rejected the choice of treating Europe's coal as a European resource; that would have been too high a price to pay in terms of productivity and growth. But when it came to welfare and employment what had seemed in 1958 like the complete disintegration of all common authority, or even common decision-making was replaced by that readiness to act in common which springs from shared assumptions.

The Belgian government's own prevarications in 1958 and its unilateral measures to deter energy imports and oil consumption had a fortunate outcome. The steepest drop in coal output and employment came after autumn 1958 when the economy was entering a vigorous upswing. The first wave of unplanned closures before the acceptance and initiation of the

---

[121] R.C. Riley, 'Recent Developments in the Belgian Borinage. An Area of Declining Coal Production in the European Coal and Steel Community', in *Geography*, vol. 50, part 3, 1965.

[122] J.D. von Bandemer and A.P. Ilgen, *Probleme . . .*, op. cit., p. 47.

autumn 1959 restructuring plan coincided therefore with a vigorous upturn elsewhere in the economy. Perhaps even more to the point it coincided with an equally vigorous upswing in the Italian economy. Italy's industrialization in the 1950s made it a ready market for trained industrial labour returning home. Of the loss in labour between 1958 and August 1960, 53 per cent was accounted for by foreigners, whereas they had been only 47 per cent of the total labour force in 1958. Mostly they returned home. The total number of Belgians leaving the industry over the same period was 19,086. By the end of April 1960 only 4,412 workers had been officially laid off since the start of 1958; the rest had left voluntarily, some measure of the ease with which alternative employment, albeit at lower wages, could be found. In July 1960 the officially recorded unemployment rate for the Borinage region was only 1.6 per cent, compared to a national rate of 4.8 per cent.

For all those compulsorily laid off generous Community provision was made on top of the already extensive social security provision of the Belgian state. The High Authority paid a readaptation allowance for one year to every worker obliged to change job by the restructuring schemes in the Borinage. For industrial retraining all Belgian miners received a guaranteed identical wage to that in their former job and allowances for transport to a new location and for settling in there. The Community paid a proportion of the cost of the industrial retraining centres which were opened in 1959. In April 1959 it began to provide financial aid for miners affected by collective short-time working agreements. This was continued until the end of September 1960. The financial burden on the Readaptation Fund of these decisions was in fact much less than foreseen because of the vigorous labour market. Almost all except those close to retiring age found new employment within two years. The readiness to supplement national social security was there however, and the fact that the Treaty of Paris had accepted all the implications of the welfare state was a theme on which Finet played loudly in his settlement of the Borinage strikes. A substantial part of Finet's negotiations with the miners and the Belgian government over the winter of 1958–9 was about how much welfare beyond that guaranteed by the treaty he could persuade the other member states to make available.

These extra welfare payments had been foreshadowed by similar relocation and retraining payments offered when the High Authority, after the report of the joint committee of inquiry in 1955, had shared the responsibility for restructuring the Borinage mines. At the time in June 1955, it was thought that these special provisions would be needed for 1,100 workers, the number it was estimated would lose their employment in mining, less than 1 per cent of the labour force.[123] Over the period 1952–6 the number of Belgians employed in the coal industry had fallen by about 9,000 without

---

[123] W.J. Diebold, Jnr, *The Schuman Plan . . .*, op. cit., p. 207.

adding significantly to the unemployment rate. Assuming the labour market to be equally absorptive between 1958 and 1961, would lead to the conclusion that at the time of Finet's negotiations the serious risk of adding to long-term unemployment was confined to about 2,000 workers. In the event, less than 1,000 workers joined the long-term unemployed. Where now is the government in western Europe which would show such concern over so small a number?

Furthermore, although Finet's efforts to push the Community towards financing a rudimentary regional programme for the Borinage were an extension of Community powers well beyond anything the French government was then prepared to countenance, the intense concentration of policy on the Borinage, beginning with the decision in 1949 to single out coking-coal production for special treatment, eventually did give birth to the idea of Community regional policy. The lavish expenditure on the region by the Belgian government, even though some of it was only replacing the lavish subsidies to coal mines, constituted an experiment in regional policy which attracted sympathetic attention elsewhere in western Europe, if only because regional policy was seen as another form of employment policy. When the United Kingdom finally entered the European Community one of the concessions made to it was support for already existing British regional policies. This was not something sprung anew on the Community, indeed the supplementary welfare it provided to Belgian workers, like its earlier subsidies, clearly had a regional bias in their distribution.

Was the Borinage really a region? It is only 30 kilometres from east to west and 20 kilometres from north to south, a tiny stretch of plain in one of the world's most developed and modernized industrial areas, criss-crossed by roads and railways. Labour mobility could not, physically, have been easier. It is only 55 kilometres from Mons, its central town, to the industrial city of Charleroi and only 67 to Brussels itself. The efforts of geographers, sociologists, historians and economists in the early 1960s, once regional development plans had been launched, to describe and define the unique regional nature of the Borinage are an exercise in academic pedantry of a high order. They perfectly reflect though the persistent concern with employment and welfare throughout the 1960s.

The definition of the Borinage as a region exposes the conservatism which lay at the heart of the post-war consensus. It was understandable that the strength of this conservatism should have been particularly great in southern Belgium. It gained force from the increasing insecurity of the francophone communities there as one of the firmest pillars of their former economic strength was eroded. In the 1960s employment policy, including regional policy, can be seen as a conscious attempt, firmly supported by the Community, to hold together the Belgian nation. Workers, companies, whole towns, seemed so trapped in their own history as to be unable to envisage any other way of existence than the miserable, dangerous occupations which had sustained them for so long, until foreign investment, attracted on more favourable terms by regional policy, changed their perspectives away from economic security as the first goal of the post-war economic and political system. Most of the time in the 1950s the national government seemed to construe this demand as meaning security for all Belgians in the place where they actually worked and lived.

On almost every count Belgium's entry into the European Coal and Steel Community reinforced national policy. Without supranational support that policy would have been harder to carry out. Where there were differences of opinion national policy was never in danger of having to change, except slowly and marginally. The real reason for this was the strength of mutual assumptions about stability, welfare and the need for a managed interventionist response to economic change. In circumstances like that it was easy to internationalize policy. The wonder is that Belgian governments did so at first with such trepidation; it shows how strong national sentiments actually were in 1950.

What difference did supranational management of the Belgian coal industry actually make? The High Authority exercised a constant pressure towards the necessary restructuring of the industry, provided subsidies to that end, and eventually was able to make the arrangements for paying those subsidies have some effect on the will of the companies to comply. Its impact, though, was much less than that of the real economic forces for change, the long-run structural changes in the energy market and their culmination in the collapse of the coal market in 1958. That collapse almost broke the Community. It survived because it was still a valuable support to national welfare objectives. In more effectively bringing financial and political pressures to bear on the Belgian coal industry before 1958 the Community was only doing most of the time what the Belgian government wanted it to do. From the start of the negotiations over the Schuman proposals in 1950 to the beginnings of a regional plan for the Borinage the Belgian government always saw the purpose of the supranational authority as a buttress for national policies. It was a source of authority outside the nation which could be appealed to for help, blamed for unpopular policies which were also those of the government itself, and, when it suited the mood, caricatured as a technocratic dictatorship trampling the rights of Belgians underfoot. It was only under the second van Acker government that there were serious conflicts of political will.

Belgium received $44.83 million in subsidies from the Community in less than six years from the opening of the common market to help defray the costs of managing the decline of the coal industry. Approximately $37 million of this was a direct transfer from the Federal Republic. This sum was the equivalent of more than a fifth of total investment in the Belgian coal industry in that period.[124] If the concept of defensive investment

---

[124] Calculated from ECSC, *Seventh General Report on the Activities of the European Coal and Steel Community*, statistical appendix, table 40.

provides a rationale for the relatively high level of investment in the Belgian coal industry in the 1950s, it seems unlikely to have been so high without this contribution from the new supranational regime. Investment in southern Belgian collieries per tonne of coal mined was, for example, at least the equivalent of that in the Ruhr. *Péréquation* could hardly have been without its effect here. And then there was the $14 million invested by the ECSC in four new power stations in southern Belgium. Furthermore, in the period 1953–5 Belgium got the foreign exchange returns on coal exports which would probably have been impossible without the $5.15 million export subsidies paid by the ECSC. It is true that all these subsidies committed the Belgian national government to equivalent sums, but there can be little doubt from the evidence that these, and more, would have been spent anyway.

There was never any question that the ECSC would be able to make Belgium do anything it did not want to do. It presented no threat to the independence of national policy formulation. When there was a difference of opinion over the extent to which an agreed policy should be executed, as in the case of the restructuring of the Borinage mines between April 1955 and 1957, events went at the pace set by the Belgian government in spite of the elements of financial leverage which the Community had acquired. Community policy itself could only arise from harmony of national policies. The High Authority, as the decisions at the end of April 1955 made clear, was not the triumph of functionalism, but a powerful international committee within which separate national representatives argued for separate national policies. Common decisions and policies were only possible where there were wide areas of agreement between the nations. Where there was wide disagreement, as over the extent to which the members should be free to import American coal at world market prices, there was a complete failure to formulate a coherent policy. There was, though, enough agreement for the ECSC to become a buttress to any national policy which was in conformity with the political and economic trends in the other member-states.

Gradually the spoil tips of the Borinage have been turned into parks and all-weather ski slopes. Regional policy drove a motorway through an ever-greener landscape. Canals which carried coal now carry pleasure boats. The stagnant waters left by mining subsidence have become marinas or centres of ornithological interest where Sunday visitors from Brussels try out their new telescopes. It takes some effort to think of the Borinage as a tourist region, but by the end of the 1960s the leisure industry had seized on what it could and gave employment to more people than coal. As the mines closed sociologists began to write nostalgic articles about the closeness and alleged supportiveness of working-class life in coal-mining towns, contrasting it unfavourably with the anomie they believed was replacing it. They were less observant about the parochial and uncreative conservatism of the culture of coal. The local nature of the concerns of these close communities, although they could be translated into an extremely influential political force at national level, had found little defence against the tide of international economic change. The way that tide was setting was more clearly recognized in the ECSC than in the national government at Brussels. But the Community could do little more than nudge Belgium to swim with it rather than against it. In that sense the Belgian government had judged correctly in 1950 that integration would provide needed, and unembarrassing, support for combining the management of industrial decline with high welfare and high employment. It had had very little to lose and much to gain.

4 Foreign trade, economic and social advance, and the origins of the European Economic Community

Those who see the creation of the European Community as a special act of political will tell an essentially political story about its formation. After the successful creation of the Coal, Iron and Steel Community the political will to integration focused, they tell us, on the European Defence Community. The defeat of this project by national resentments in August 1954 could have been, they imply, a mortal blow to the idea of a united Europe. Gloriously, however, the idea was 'relaunched' (the favourite word in all languages of writers on this theme), albeit on a less ambitious scale, by the two great federalists Monnet and Spaak in the twin projects for Euratom and the common market. The Treaties of Rome were the culminating triumph of this relaunch. This is the story as usually presented in summary accounts for general readers and students.

Most of this is myth, nurtured by federalists and other advocates of political unification as an end in itself. The reality is that two lines of negotiation, one for the economic security of a customs union and the other for the military security of the Defence Community, flowed in parallel between 1950 and 1954. The second was foredoomed to failure. The military security of the post-war state did not require integration, indeed a sovereign German army in a politically unified western Europe was seen almost as much as a threat to security as its future guarantee. This was a security problem resolved by the traditional method of military alliance.[1] Once this had been done, the first line of negotiation, which was the crucial one, briefly and only by fortuity mixed up with the military problem, was able to resurface where it had been submerged. What was unavoidable in the future, in a way that German military primacy was not, was the primacy of Germany's economic role in Europe's economic development. It could perhaps only have been avoided by the ruthless destruction of the German economy and state after 1945, but that course was wisely rejected. European security, in the full sense of the word, did not crucially depend on a German army. It did crucially depend on German prosperity. This was the issue which had to be resolved and which had

[1] The best account remains, E. Fursdon, *The European Defence Community, a History* (London, 1980).

become more pressing every year since the great revival of the Federal German economy in 1949–50. There was a continuity of proposals for resolving it. The widespread notion of the failure and the relaunch of the project for European integration over the years 1954–6 is mainly fanciful political propaganda in favour of one particular view of the European Community, and the idea that the Treaties of Rome were a substitute for the Defence and Political Community is altogether wrong.

The project for a customs union was of much earlier gestation than the notion of a relaunch implies. At first attracting little enthusiasm, it began to accumulate in its support a coalition of interests which came to have an increasing influence. There were two important reasons why this was so. One was that western Europe's foreign trade with the new West German State became of central importance to the growth and stability of the whole region, so important that commercial policy guarantees became an indispensable part of any policy to bind West Germany to western Europe. The second was that national tariffs were decreasingly seen as useful to post-war national economic development. Politically cumbersome, economically ineffective, they came to be seen as superfluous between countries which could devise more effective ways of regulating and protecting particular markets without having to pay the cost of the restrictions on the growth of trade and national income which tariffs would have demanded. Since 1931 tariffs had become so much less important in western Europe than non-tariff barriers, particularly quotas, that the customs union was in fact a policy response to the removal of quotas. It marked a new epoch in national commercial policies in western Europe. Whereas 1873–1931 was the classic period of tariff bargaining between European nations, 1931–50 saw an attempt to regulate foreign trade by physical controls, and the period since 1950 has been dominated by the attempt to combine protection with the rapid growth of foreign trade through agreement between western European countries on the non-tariff regulation of markets. Tariffs have been reserved for dealing with countries like the United States where they still have a constitutional role.

It is of course generally true that high rates of growth of national income and foreign trade diminish fears to which the removal of tariffs might otherwise give rise. It is no less generally true that national existence at higher levels of output and consumption requires some international commercial order to facilitate the exchange of goods across frontiers. All explanations of the Treaties of Rome recognize that the common market was a response to the expansion of foreign trade. But this observation is too vague and truistic to be of much use as historical explanation. Once the great importance to national economic resurgence in western Europe of three things – trade with Western Germany, trade expansion in general and protection in specific areas – is understood, the common market can be seen as the best possible arrangement to combine these three elements in a new form of international commercial regime.

THEORY, IDEOLOGY AND PRACTICE IN FOREIGN TRADE

The idea that liberalizing foreign trade can have benign results is an old one. Its classical form was the philosophy of free trade, that without trade restrictions comparative advantages would reallocate production to the point where marginal domestic costs do not exceed international costs. Its more modern form is more typically the argument that wider markets encourage larger-scale production, fiercer competition, and gains in productivity. It was this more dynamic conception which was the intellectual basis for American pressure on Western European countries under the Marshall Plan to form a customs union.

The historical reality however has been that short-lived periods of trade liberalization in the nineteenth century, in the sense that tariffs and excises were reduced, were followed by increases in protection, because they had not helped in the building of a stronger political consensus except in the dominant trader, Britain. On the contrary, they were more usually followed by a vigorous clamour from a variety of interest groups demanding protection against British exports and branding free trade as a philosophy designed to strengthen Britain's economic hegemony. Until the early 1950s historical experience seemed to offer no solid guarantees that freer foreign trade would make national economies prosper. That was one reason for the unwillingness of European countries at first to pay any more than lip service to the ECA's wishes for a customs union and for the slowness with which they approached the reduction of tariffs by other means as well as the removal of non-tariff barriers.

In the mid-1950s, and especially as a result of the great boom in foreign trade of 1954–7, opinion shifted. In some quarters the idea of 'export-led' growth became almost a slogan. Exaggerated though these ideas were in the thought of the time, there were precise mechanisms which in the 1950s connected the rapid growth of intra-West-European trade to the historically unique rates of growth of national incomes. As we shall see when we examine these in detail West Germany was the pivot of these mechanisms. It was the exemplar of the fast growing economy, whose exports grew faster than its imports, and much faster than its own GDP. The profits from exports provided the wherewithal for its higher levels of savings and investment. In those countries where the growth of exports only kept pace with imports, the growth of exports to Germany made the greatest quantitative contribution to the growth of exports overall and was responsible for much of the qualitative shift in the structure of exports towards those modernized sectors of higher-value-added manufacturing which governments wanted to encourage. If West Germany were not firmly secured in its place as the pivot of this trade expansion income growth would be less. How it should be secured however was the matter of at least a dozen contradictory plans.

The earliest proposals for a European customs union emanated from

Paris before the Marshall Plan and had an almost entirely political content: they were designed to organize western Europe into a political bloc around France to provide security against a restored and resurgent Germany in the future. The American proposals too had an essentially political rationale, the creation of a strategic political bloc in western Europe of which West Germany would be a member as part of America's security system. But underlying this there was also an economic argument. A larger market, it was argued, by increasing the levels of productivity in European manufacturing would reduce the prices of European manufactured goods so that Europe would become less dependent on American aid. It was only in the early 1950s that proposals for a western European customs union which had genuinely strong backing from domestic economic interests began to be put forward. They coincided with other schemes for liberalizing foreign trade; the global schemes for reducing tariffs in GATT, and from 1949 the OEEC trade liberalization programme for removing quota restrictions on intra-Western-European trade. It was only when it was clear that the Federal Republic had become the pivot of Western Europe's prosperity that the advantage of the customs union for regulating trade with Germany, its irreversibility, came to the fore. As it did so, so did its other advantage, its capacity both to expand trade and to provide the requisite measure of specific protection.

A noteworthy aspect of the period was that customs unions at first received little encouragement from academic economists working within the traditional body of trade theory. The fundamental assumption of most of the theory of foreign trade was that existing trade in the 1950s was the consequence of comparative and competitive advantages of some nations over others, which themselves were the outcome of different factor endowments. The assumption of advocates of the reduction of trade barriers in the 1950s was that every nation still had some unexploited advantage, so that if freer trade prevailed there would be an increase in mutually advantageous specialization. The implication of trade theory's initial assumption about the causes of foreign trade was that tariffs were a measure of the cost of resource misallocation and that their removal would increase trade and income. Once the question was asked however, by how much this political effort would actually increase income, the answer was that the net gain in income could only be a fraction of that newly created trade, not greater than the percentage rate of the *ad valorem* tariff which had excluded it. When this estimated net gain was represented as a proportion of GNP it did not seem worth the political effort required to create a customs union, much less one which involved surrenders of national sovereignty and a promise to proceed towards political unification.

Scitovsky forecast in 1958 that the Six would gain an average increase of only 0.05 per cent of GDP from the increment in trade caused by tariff removal in a customs union.[2] Johnson predicted that the net gain to

Britain's GDP from entering the customs union of the Six would be 1 per cent at the maximum.[3] Wemelsfelder set the additional increase to GDP in the Federal Republic from the first round of tariff reductions in the common market at the same level as Scitovsky.[4] Later, after the British entry, Miller and Spencer estimated that the gain to British GDP had in fact been only about 0.15 per cent.[5] These meagre increases also correspond with Denison's calculations of the increase in growth rates of national income to be attributed over the period 1955–62 to the whole process of reduction of barriers to trade. He concluded that, had levels of foreign trade in economies been as high at the starting-point of this period as at the end, the rate of growth of British national income would in fact have been only 0.02 percentage points lower. The corresponding figure for France would have been only 0.07 percentage points and for Belgium, Italy and the Netherlands 0.16.[6] In an age when the expansion of national income was such a high priority such figures can have done little to encourage government to place hope in the benefits of trade liberalization, much less in the idea of a customs union.

From the same assumptions about international trade Viner in 1950 developed a theory of customs unions which posed the question, to what extent such increases of trade as might arise between states forming a customs union would be offset by trade which it excluded.[7] Not only might the net benefits of replacing high cost domestic production with newly created intra-trade turn out to be relatively small; additional net costs would arise from the diversion of trade which a customs union would cause when low-cost suppliers from outside the union were replaced by higher-cost suppliers inside it who no longer had to pay tariffs on their exports.

How should we reconcile this type of theorizing with the accumulation of real economic interests in Europe behind proposals for a customs union? The question must be asked whether decision-makers actually believed these calculations to have any meaning in the real world. They are static calculations based on once and for all additions to the value of trade caused by the removal of tariffs. The ideas which motivated statesmen and industrialists at the time were not based on a static world but referred rather to a dynamic process of change which would be set loose by the removal of

[2] T. Scitovsky, *Economic Theory and Western European Integration* (London, 1958), pp. 48 ff.

[3] H.G. Johnson, 'The Gains from Freer Trade with Europe: An Estimate', in *The Manchester School of Economic and Social Studies*, vol. xxvi, no. 3, 1958.

[4] J. Wemelsfelder, 'The Short-Term Effect of the Lowering of Import Duties in Germany', *Economic Journal*, vol. lxx, 1960.

[5] M. Miller and J. Spencer, 'The Static Economic Effect of the UK Joining the EEC: A General Equilibrium Approach', in *Review of Economic Studies*, vol. xliv(1), no. 136, 1977.

[6] E.F. Denison, *Why Growth Rates Differ* (Washington DC, 1967), pp. 260–2.

[7] J. Viner, *The Customs Union Issue* (New York, 1950).

trade barriers and would result in a long-run improvement in the rate of growth of national income.

The reason why productivity in manufacturing industry in the United States was more than twice as high as in some western European countries (and wages correspondingly higher) was frequently said to be a direct consequence of the continental size of the American market. That was a message which the ECA endlessly relayed to European countries during the Marshall Plan and one in which Monnet and many other advocates of European integration believed. If western European industry could operate within an untrammelled market the size of the American it would, they argued, close the gap in productivity levels with the United States and generate striking gains in income per head. These dynamic processes though could not be quantified and their potentiality was largely a matter of faith. They were discussed by Scitovsky, who suggested that their consequences in terms of gains to income could well be much greater than the single net addition from tariff removal.[8] What he has to say about them however, is not noticeably different from the commonplaces of journalistic discussion at the time.

If this persistent iteration of the alleged dynamic benefits of trade liberalization implies a certain scepticism about the existing theory of foreign trade, it seemed justified by the signal failure of theory to predict the remarkable surge in foreign trade between Western European countries which took place after 1945. While foreign trade continued to be explained by patterns of comparative and competitive advantage, the reality was that foreign trade between Western European countries increasingly consisted of the interchange of similar manufactures between the richer, more industrialized economies. That this was so was first comprehensively demonstrated in 1963 by Maizels.[9] There was nothing in existing theory which could explain why trade increasingly took the form of train loads of manufactures destined for one national market passing train loads of exports of almost identical products going in the reverse direction.

The awareness among businessmen that this was in fact the nature of much of the increase in Western Europe's foreign trade after 1945 perhaps explains why, whatever the strict conclusions to be drawn from theory, the belief, even perhaps among trade theorists, that there was a dynamic relationship between market expansion and higher levels of productivity seems to have been so prevalent in the 1950s. The key concept used to explain this relationship was that of economies of scale. In a larger market a longer run of output of standardized products will lower unit costs in manufacturing and also sale prices. The observation that manufacturing plant was larger in the United States than in Europe and production runs often longer suggested that the formation of a larger market in Western

---

[8] T. Scitovsky, *Economic Theory . . .*, op. cit.
[9] A. Maizels, *Industrial Growth and World Trade* (Cambridge, 1963).

Europe might well provide European manufacturers with similar opportunities for these scale economies. They proved however as hard to specify and describe as they were to quantify.

Scale economies only began to be incorporated as a concept into models which could be quantified in the 1960s and there have been few attempts to measure them. Such measurements as have been made suggest that their size and importance is a function of the particular manufacturing sector in question, but that they are rarely large.[10] Some studies on intra-Community trade starting from such models however show that additions to trade and GDP resulting from the formation of a common market were in fact much larger than the earlier static calculations implied and the additional trade created much greater.[11] It has proved harder to justify the hope that scale economies of the common market would finally close the gap in productivity with American manufacturing. That did happen to a small extent with German industry, but eighteen years after entry into the common market its productivity levels were still roughly only half those of American manufacturing.[12] Nevertheless a detailed microeconomic study of the trade in cars and consumer goods such as that by Owen, not only suggests that there were indeed in appropriate industries substantial economies of scale to be derived from entry into a customs union or common market, but also that these could be translated into high profits by firms that were able to implement them. Increases in a firm's output through exports significantly reduced in these industries, he argues, the costs of all its output. When investment was sufficient to maintain this increase and the consequent economies of scale in advance of its rivals, it could eliminate marginal higher-cost producers at home and abroad at the same time by the same process. A customs union could thus extend the opportunities for larger low-cost producers by bringing a greater number of markets occupied by vulnerable high-cost producers within their range. This was the success story of a car manufacturer such as Volkswagen, a washing-machine manufacturer such as Zanussi, or a refrigerator manufacturer such as Ignis. Even though within this competition there are more losers than winners, a process of this kind might still constitute a motive to form a customs union. This would more usually, but not invariably, be a motive of larger firms.[13]

---

[10] Z. Griliches and V. Ringstad, *Economies of Scale and the Form of the Production Function: An Econometric Study of Norwegian Manufacturing Establishment Data* (Amsterdam, 1971) found them most noticeably in such products as footwear, bakery products, canning, but also in non-electrical machinery and transport equipment.

[11] N. Owen, *Economies of Scale, Competitiveness, and Trade Patterns within the European Community* (Oxford, 1983). J. Williamson and A. Bottrill, 'The Impact of Customs Unions on Trade in Manufactures', in *Oxford Economic Papers*, vol. xxiii, no. 3, 1971.

[12] S.J. Prais *et al.*, *Productivity and Industrial Structure*; *A Statistical Study of Manufacturing Industry in Britain, Germany and the United States* (Cambridge, 1981).

[13] Maizels calculated that only half the increase in manufactured imports into developed economies in the 1950s was to be attributed to the rise in domestic purchasing power. The other half was to be attributed to the dismantling of trade restrictions, so their removal

What might look like the triumphant result of scale economies might also be the outcome of a variety of possible business arrangements and these too could also no doubt constitute a motive for supporting a common market. There have been virtually no studies of the precise relationships between industries and governments on the details of the market extensions that were made. Long-protected sectors such as French steel were divided over entry into the ECSC and similar divisions of opinion appear to have characterized industry in general in most countries in the debate over the formation of the common market. But general studies of opinion before the event are less useful than studies of business behaviour within the newly integrated markets, and they are lacking.

The mismatch between existing theory on the one hand and the reality of economic change on the other in the 1950s was not merely a matter of academic interest. When governments sought advice about the advantages and disadvantages of customs unions, as did Britain in 1945 or the Netherlands in 1950, it was on the basis of existing theory that the advice, not enthusiastically in favour of such arrangements, was given.[14] The fact that in the 1950s the exports of some countries increased faster than production, and that rates of productivity increased the most rapidly in those countries and industries where the rate of increase of exports was the most rapid, had to last for some time before this comparative statistical information could be considered as hard evidence. Businessmen, though, may have sensed these trends before they were described and identified as one of the main characteristics of the decade.

There is a strong analogy between the ideological and political consequences of the great trade boom after 1954 and that after 1852. As in that earlier boom there was an outburst of literary and economic predictions that national government would fade away and that foreign trade would unite the warring nations in the Tennysonian parliament of man. There was, too, a similar spate of predictions that technology would unite mankind by annihilating distance. The theories of interdependence and integration discussed in chapter one were partly an offshoot of this intellectual fashion of the 1950s. This was most noticeably the case in the Federal Republic of Germany where attributing the country's economic and political success to exports became a political cult.[15]

The converse of this cult could later be observed in studies of the British

---

must have presented investment opportunities in manufacturing industry which were certainly not there between 1929 and 1939. A. Maizels, *Industrial Growth . . .*, op. cit., pp. 415 ff.

[14] PRO, FO 371/62554, BOT memorandum, 'A European customs union or unions', 10 October 1947. P.J. Verdoorn, 'Welke zijn de achtergronden en vooruitzichten van de economische integratie in Europa, en welke gevolgen zal deze integratie hebben, met name voor de welvaart in Nederland?', in Netherlands, Vereniging voor de Staathuishoudkunde, *Prae-Adviezen*, 1952.

[15] W. Michalski, *Export-und Wirtschaftswachstum. Schlussfolgerungen aus der Nachkriegsentwicklung in der Bundesrepublik Deutschland* (Hamburg, 1972).

economy which concentrated on the failure of British exports to grow as quickly as those of other Western European countries as the best explanation for the comparatively slow rates of income growth there and all the country's woes. To an economy suffering from balance of payments constraints, which were sometimes said to be the unavoidable consequence of the higher investment, higher employment and higher welfare of the post-war years, 'export-led growth' seemed to offer a way forward. All other methods of increasing demand in an economy regulated by demand-management, so Kaldor argued, incurred either an increase in inflation or an increase in imports. 'Export-led growth', by contrast, liberated the post-war consensus from this trap by stimulating investment while avoiding the difficult balance-of-payments consequences which would follow.[16] The rapid development of exports in the 1950s, Lamfalussy argued, had raised the ratio of both savings and investment in some continental European countries, so that capacity and productivity had grown fast without setting an even faster-growing rate of inflation in motion. In contrast, countries with more slowly-growing exports, of which the United Kingdom was the obvious example, experienced a slower rate of income growth, a higher rate of inflation, and a recurring balance-of-payments constraint.[17] Although such views never became orthodoxy, they had growing political currency, some measure of the way that the observed realities of the 1950s changed the nature of economic thinking.

The proposals for trade liberalization and customs unions that were made fell therefore on to a receptive soil. Theory was at odds with facts. Governments whose main desire was to sustain the growth of productivity and incomes were eager for any device which made this seem possible. No matter what rigorous theory suggested, they turned eagerly to the belief that in the circumstances of the 1950s a faster growth of foreign trade would entail a faster growth of national income.

The facts, as table 4.1 shows, were that while there were striking cases in western Europe of exports growing faster than output, the experience of different countries was varied. At constant prices the manufactured exports of the Federal Republic and the Netherlands grew more than twice as fast as GDP. In Italy manufactured exports also grew much faster than either total output or manufacturing output. Those of the United Kingdom may have grown somewhat more slowly than GDP, and did grow more slowly than total manufacturing output. For France much depends on the method used to deflate the prices and also on the choice of years. In general, France had a high rate of growth of GDP and a relatively low rate of growth of exports until the period 1958–60. The evidence on which this eager turning by governments towards foreign trade as an engine of growth was based was, at least on this macroeconomic level, most uncertain. As

[16] N. Kaldor, 'Conflicts in National Economic Objectives', in *Economic Journal*, vol. lxxxi, no. 321, 1971.
[17] A. Lamfalussy, *The United Kingdom and the Six* (London, 1963).

Table 4.1 Growth of volume of output and exports compared in western Europe, 1950–8

	Annual percentage growth rate of GDP		Annual percentage growth rate of manufacturing output		Annual percentage growth rate of manufactured exports	
	1950–8	1951–8	1950–8	1951–8	1950–8	1951–8
France	4.4	4.2	5.3	4.8	3.8	1.4
German Federal Republic	7.8	7.3	10.6	10.0	19.7	15.0
Italy	5.0	5.8	6.8	6.8	9.2	8.9
Netherlands	4.3	4.5	n.a.	n.a.	11.7	9.8
United Kingdom	2.0	1.9	2.5	2.3	1.8	1.8

The value of output is at constant 1963 prices. Manufactured exports are SITC 5, 6, 7 and 8 deflated by an index of their average value.

Sources: OEEC, National Accounts Statistics; ibid., Statistical Bulletins of Foreign Trade, Series IV

Table 4.2   Exports of goods and services as a proportion of GNP, 1950 and 1960

	1950	*1960*
France	16.4	15.6
German Federal Republic	11.6	20.7
Italy	12.0*	15.4
Netherlands	43.1	52.9
United Kingdom	26.9	23.0
	* 1951	

Source: OEEC, *National Accounts*

we shall see however, at the microeconomic level and where it concerned trade with Germany it was stronger.

There were however other aspects of the 1950s which brought foreign trade to the forefront of political considerations. Were we to seek one defining characteristic of the period 1945–60 we might well find it in the astonishing increase in the manufacture, exchange and ownership of objects. There is no period of similar length in European history in which purchasing power grew so rapidly. Western European homes were filled by a yearly increase in the manufactured symbols of social ease and advancement. That the winning and losing of parliamentary elections came to depend on the ability of national governments to satisfy their citizens' demands for these material symbols seems well attested, as does the fact that governments varied their policies in this respect according to the nearness of general elections. Maintaining the political consensus increasingly came to depend on satisfying the aspirations to this increasing ease of life, usually defined in the 1950s in a rather narrowly materialistic way. The intellectual fashions of the time reflected a similar materialism, at times even an obsession with the world of objects. As electors became more able to make international comparisons of material success the task for governments was made harder. Foreign trade was integral to satisfying electors' needs, for one consequence of the new sensibilities and needs which arose from the combination of higher incomes and the expectation that they would continue to increase was the demand for a greater choice of objects. The import acquired a symbolic prestige of its own. Fulfilling the expectations of the reformed capitalist economy came to mean facilitating international exchanges. The greater range of choice which ensued was held up as the superiority of Western Europe over the undemocratic governments of eastern Europe, with missiles and sputniks but without washing machines and cars.

Yet the rejection of the extreme protectionism of the 1930s and the cautious moves towards trade liberalization in the pursuit of the economic goals of the post-war consensus inevitably also endangered the position of some elements of that consensus, and it was this which gave the commer-

cial policies of the period their peculiar mixture of liberalism and protectionism. The transition was not, as so many commentators suggest, a
transition from pre-war protectionism towards classical free trade, but
towards a new form of neo-mercantilism appropriate to the changed
political conditions. By 1960 foreign trade was still less liberalized than
between 1925 and 1929. One aspect of this was the exemption of the
agricultural sector from the process of trade liberalization. Whereas for
example in the great trade boom after 1852 some governments had believed that cheap food imports would encourage income growth, with
farmers so important to the political basis of the post-Second World War
state the opposite view prevailed. Similarly the insistence on policies of
national economic development through industrialization produced a mixture of liberalization and protection of manufactured trade which was
highly selective. While it was believed that liberalization of foreign trade
would encourage the growth of productivity and incomes and satisfy
consumer demands, it was also believed that protection would stimulate
technological modernization and a more sophisticated manufacturing
sector.

It was in the pursuit of this difficult compromise that governments
developed another typical characteristic of the period, close links between
industrial policies and commercial policy. Tenuous or non-existent in the
1930s, such links became an inherent part of the political and economic
system after 1945. Their existence alone meant that the internationalization of commercial policy could not be, as it had been before, merely a
matter of mutual tariff reductions or trade agreements. Some attempt had
to be made to safeguard national development policies and the new and
more sophisticated mix of liberalism and protectionism had to be made
operative at the international level.

The need to support policies of industrialization and modernization was,
though, by no means the only influence which demanded that post-war
commercial policy be shaped along lines to which history was very little
guide. The mass unemployment of the 1930s had to be avoided, and
protectionism was associated with its avoidance. As we saw in the Belgian
case in the last chapter, even the possibility of avoiding long-term unemployment for about 1,000 workers in a declining industry could justify very
large sums in public money as well as continued protection. The historical
inheritance from the nineteenth century of 'general' and 'special' tariffs for
bargaining with other nations was only appropriate to states which did not
directly try to influence the course of trade, did not reorganize industries,
did not try to target the level of growth, were not responsible for a large
share of aggregate consumption and for huge transfer payments, did not
significantly own and run their own industries, and rarely intervened in
capital markets except as a borrower. All these aspects of state action were
typical of post-war government. It was the problem of combining them
with the removal of trade controls and the lowering of tariffs which led in

the 1950s to a form of internationalized neo-mercantilism which is still the stamp of the commercial policy of the developed countries.

The chief link between industrial policy and commercial policy and the principal basis for these neo-mercantilistic policies immediately after 1945 was not tariffs but non-tariff barriers. This was not because tariffs had fallen from their high levels of the 1930s, but because other barriers had reduced their significance or even rendered them inoperative. Industrialization and modernization policies in particular depended on the support of non-tariff barriers. The traditional confrontation of national governments in tariff bargaining, the activity which American post-war plans for an International Trade Organization hoped to promote, was, even if successful, not likely to reduce greatly the protectionism of the 1930s, for the maintenance of some non-tariff barriers was still seen as indispensable for national economic development. The core of the problem was to remove non-tariff barriers, especially quotas, but for Western European countries this meant doing so within a framework which would permit the maintenance of those non-tariff barriers still considered essential within a generally more liberalized framework. GATT was an ineffectual organization in the 1950s precisely because its activities were confined to tariff bargaining. The OEEC by contrast became a forum of more genuine inter-governmental commercial bargaining, because it was there that the conflicts between liberalization and the sophisticated use of non-tariff barriers in national development policies could be compromised.

The adjustment of national tariffs to reconcile the conflicting interests of economic and social groups within the nation had lain at the heart of the constitutional process when, as was the case in many nations before 1914, the powers of parliamentary assemblies remained very limited. The regular adjustment of the national tariff in a country like the German Empire served the constitutional purpose of putting together a parliamentary majority, which was a distant image of a national political consensus. In that sense the national tariff served in some countries as an alternative constitution, rewarding or penalizing particular social groups.[18] This became increasingly impossible as links between domestic economic policies and national commercial policy began to be developed through the medium of non-tariff barriers and as both the complexities of consensus building and the powers of parliaments grew. Consensuses fell apart in 1929–32 and governments sought to preserve or rebuild them through piecemeal, incoherent, protectionist concessions. The proliferation of non-tariff barriers was a haphazard business in the 1930s as governments conceded privileges unsystematically to particular pressure groups. It was this hodge-podge of quotas, subsidies, exemptions, incentives, other non-tariff protectionist devices – and the old tariffs themselves, which no matter

---

[18] A.S. Milward, 'Tariffs as Constitutions' in S. Strange and R. Tooze (eds), *The Management of Surplus Capacity* (London, 1981).

how irrelevant or inoperable remained on the statute books – that was inherited by governments struggling to turn it into a coherent instrument for national reassertion.[19]

Even in the early years of the Marshall Plan conflicts of interest between development policy requiring more coherent elements of protection on the one hand and trade liberalization on the other can be observed. The programme of trade liberalization supervised and mediated by OEEC proved to be a contentious and uneven process. There were acrimonious differences relating to specific industrial policies in the larger countries. Thus, for example, Italy protected its car industry with quotas so as to provide a market for its projected developments in steel and also to make a large increase in engineering exports a foundation for post-war national economic development.[20] In France general measures of liberalization were accompanied by the use of specific measures of non-tariff protection to make sure that the OEEC programme did not bring into jeopardy any of the modernizing and industrializing objectives of the French state as expressed in the successive five-year plans. The plans were based on maintaining a sufficient measure of trade control over appropriate industrial sectors until they had been brought to the point where they could effectively compete in a more open economy.[21] Important industrial sectors – cars, steel, oil refining for example – were considered by planners as infant industries to be protected by a variety of non-tariff barriers against unwanted competition.

The French case is especially revealing, for it was in the foreign trade sector that the five-year plans were least able to forecast and maintain stable growth. Liberalization of trade was seen by French planners as a dynamic agent of modernization and growth, ready to be deployed once the plans had modernized industrial sectors to the point where they could successfully compete. Fitting these twin goals of protection and liberalization into a coherent commercial policy would have been difficult enough at any time. In the great surge of intra-Western-European trade of the 1950s it was impossible. Import and export growth always far exceeded the targets of the plans. The forecast of the volume of imports was the least accurate forecast made by the Second Plan, drawn up in 1952, as well as by the Third and Interim Plans which served as guidelines from 1956.[22] Import growth was estimated by projecting the import ratio of the base

---

[19] Its lack of relevance to post-war conditions and the superfluousness of some of it is illustrated in W.J. Diebold, Jnr, *Trade and Payments in Western Europe: A Study in Economic Cooperation 1947–1951* (New York, 1952).

[20] R. Tremelloni, 'The Italian Long-Term Program Submitted to the OEEC', in *Banca Nazionale del Lavoro Quarterly Review*, vol. ii, no. 8, 1949; V. Zamagni, 'Betting on the Future. The Reconstruction of Italian Industry, 1946–1952', in J. Becker and F. Knipping (eds), *Power in Europe? Great Britain, France, Italy and Germany in a Post-war World, 1945–1950* (Berlin, 1986).

[21] J.H. McArthur and B.R. Scott, *Industrial Planning in France* (Boston, 1969).

[22] V. Lutz, *Central Planning for the Market Economy. An Analysis of the French Theory and Experience* (London, 1969), pp. 87–9. Dutch planners had a similar experience. The

year of the plans and adjusting it downwards to take account of the import substitution which the plans aimed to generate. The growth of domestic demand, however, was always higher than estimated and swamped the capacity of planners to regulate imports. Export growth was estimated by extrapolating the share of French products in markets in the base year, assuming no relative price changes and deriving estimated growth rates of demand in those markets.[23] This only exaggerated the underestimation of the demand for imports elsewhere.

It is true that the planners had few ways to limit the growth of domestic demand. But to have drawn up a plan in 1952 which forecast no increase in the volume of imports for five years and a 25 per cent rate of increase of national product shows how protectionist they were still unsuccessfully attempting to be. The forecast in the Second Plan that there would be no increase in the volume of imports was based on the assumption that foodstuff imports would be reduced by 40 per cent. And what can be said about the Second Plan's attempt to hold capital goods imports to the average volume of the years 1949–52, when investment in the French economy was forecast to rise by one-quarter above its average level under the First Plan? The French economy could not in fact produce those investment goods itself. It is not surprising that by the mid-1950s the view was gaining ground that a more effective way of modernizing the French economy would in fact be to open it much more freely to the influence of international trade and particularly of intra-Western-European trade. This was the view strongly advocated by the former secretary-general of the OEEC, Robert Marjolin, when in February 1956 he became adviser to foreign minister Christian Pineau, with the specific brief to prepare industrial and agricultural opinion for the common market.[24]

Such conflicts between protectionist import substitution and trade liberalization were not confined to the larger economies. Even highly trade-dependent smaller economies like Norway and the Netherlands made extensive neo-mercantilist efforts to create their own national steel industries and to develop other new industrial sectors. The Netherlands maintained a wide range of quotas on infant industries which it wished to develop after 1945. Norway maintained both quotas and selectively high tariffs for the same purpose. Like any small country, neither had any effective bargaining power in international tariff negotiations; they had learned from their experience of the 1930s that it was non-tariff barriers that mattered. The organizations which had been envisaged by American post-war planning were worldwide, while the precise mechanisms which linked the expansion of foreign trade to the rapid growth of national

Netherlands, Centraal Planbureau, Monografie Nr. 10, *Voorspelling en realisatie. De Voorspellingen van het Centraal Planbureau in de jaren 1953–1963* (The Hague, 1965).

[23] M.C. MacLennan, 'The Common Market and French Planning', in *Journal of Common Market Studies*, vol. iii, 1964–5.

[24] R. Marjolin, *Le Travail d'une vie; Mémoires 1911–1986* (Paris, 1986), pp. 255 ff.

income in Western European countries were European, especially for the smaller economies.

Given the tendency of the post-war west European state to justify itself ideologically as the guarantor of the social and economic advance of its citizens; given the ensuing tendency to take a somewhat exalted view of the power of foreign trade and particularly of exports; given the velocity with which foreign trade in western Europe did grow; given the way in which this growth did contribute to the growth in efficiency, incomes and choice; a European solution was necessary. Domestic policy was not in the end sustainable unless this neo-mercantilism could be guaranteed by its Europeanization.

Europeanization had to incorporate the Federal Republic as the core of the system. The hoped-for advantages of trade liberalization across Western Europe as a whole were imprecise and subject to repeated political challenges and economic difficulties. The advantages of expanding trade with the Federal Republic were precise and indispensable to the process of industrialization, modernization and growth. The Federal Republic had to be embraced in a commercial and political clasp from which it could not readily escape.

WESTERN EUROPE'S TRADE WITH GERMANY AS THE PIVOT OF ECONOMIC ADVANCE

If the Treaties of Rome and the common market were the resolution of the problem of combining these two essential elements of a post-war West European economic order, the question remains to be answered, in what precise way was West Germany so essential to the growth of incomes elsewhere in Western Europe? No matter how favourably the expansion of foreign trade was regarded in the 1950s, the real origins of the common market were not in the increase in the number of Tennyson's costly bales landed on foreign shores, either by pilots dropping from the purple twilight or as is usually, but regrettably not always, the case, from somewhere more readily identifiable from official foreign trade statistics. They were much more related to the precise content of those bales and the way it was determined by trade with one country, the Federal Republic of Germany.

It is easy to see that the Federal Republic was the dominating influence on the remarkable expansion of intra-Western-European trade in the 1950s. It was the country the growth rate of whose exports was most in excess of the rate of growth of manufacturing output and of GDP, and the country whose output grew the most rapidly. It quickly became the most important supplier and also the most important market for most other western European countries. Furthermore, exports to Germany were one cause of Western Europe's economic stability, because they immunized it against American economic recessions.

After 1950 the Federal Republic registered massive surpluses on commodity trade which showed no sign of diminishing. Over the whole period 1951–8 its commodity exports exceeded the value of its imports by roughly DM 44,541 million ($10,605 million), which was about the value of all the imports into Europe financed between 1948 and 1952 by the Marshall Plan. This contributed to a current account surplus over the same period of roughly DM 30,472 million ($7,255 million).[25]

The reasons for the persistence of such a massive disequilibrium were intensively studied.[26] It did raise interesting theoretical problems for those starting from the text-book assumptions of trade theory and the consequence was that little attention was paid to German imports, except to see them as one possible explanation of the trade surpluses because their level was held by some commentators to be too low. This concentration on trying to explain the persistence of German export surpluses has diverted attention away from the fact that it is both aspects of Germany's foreign trade, imports and exports, which are essential to explaining European integration, but imports even more so than exports. Dominant though German goods became in Western European markets, the Federal Republic was even more dominant as a market for Western European goods. As far as the rate of growth of foreign trade is concerned Western Europe in the 1950s needed Germany even more than Germany needed Western Europe.

Table 4.3 gives an overall impression of the importance to Western European countries of their export growth to the Federal Republic. It shows the relative rate of increase of exports to the Federal Republic compared to that of exports to other areas. The increases are measured in current values on the assumption that in a non-inflationary era these will fairly reflect the true relative values of the goods. Finding an appropriate period over which to measure is a difficult problem to which there is no entirely satisfactory answer. In 1950 the Federal Republic had a deficit on commodity trade caused by a massive influx of imports which must be described as untypical because they fulfilled a demand which was not translated into an import surplus in later years. In 1951 on the other hand the full inflationary effect of the Korean war was present and trade values were well above trend. Furthermore 1958 is a trough in foreign trade, whereas 1951 represents a peak. If measurement is made from 1952, a different problem is encountered; the countercyclical importance of European exports to the Federal Republic is not captured. Exports to the rest of Western Europe fell steeply in 1952 compared to exports to the Federal Republic, which means that any measurement starting from 1952 will exaggerate any subsequent rate of growth of exports to the rest of

[25] The figures are those derived by P.M. Boarman, *Germany's Economic Dilemma* (New Haven, 1964), pp. 38–9.

[26] For a review of the discussion see C.P. Kindleberger, 'Germany's Persistent Balance of Payments Disequilibrium', in R.E. Baldwin *et al.*, *Trade Growth and the Balance of Payments* (Chicago, 1966).

Table 4.3 Relative growth of exports of Western European countries to the world, to Western Europe, to the Six, and to the Federal Republic, 1951–8 (percentage increase in current $ values)

Country	All exports	Exports to Western Europe excluding Germany	Exports to the Six	Exports to USA and Canada	Exports to the Federal Republic
Austria	102	55	151	85	257
Belgium–Lux.	16	8	49	30	121
Denmark	49	22	96	317	137
France	25	10	74	−11	168
German Federal Republic	154	–	135	186	–
Italy	54	24	75	145	185
Netherlands	67	67	99	71	126
Norway	20	14	28	47	119
Portugal	10	1	60	−23	82
Sweden	17	20	29	33	68
Switzerland	44	39	65	21	174
United Kingdom	25	22	59	70	147

Source: OEEC, *Statistical Bulletins of Foreign Trade*, Series IV

Western Europe as against exports to the Federal Republic. Continuing the measurement beyond 1958, however, would begin to invalidate the exercise, whose object is to stop before the first effects of the Treaties of Rome are captured. These problems remain a difficulty throughout the chapter, in which various solutions have been applied without any being perfect.

It is nevertheless evident from table 4.3 in spite of these problems of measurement that exports to Germany grew much faster in all cases than exports to the rest of Western Europe or than exports to the six ECSC countries. Whereas the Federal Republic's own exports grew faster to the whole world than to Western Europe, the exports of the majority of the other countries behave in the opposite way, mainly because of the importance of the German market. The history of Western European exports to North America in the 1950s was an extremely variable one. In general the growth of exports to the North American market was more rapid from 1956 onwards and the last three years of the period inflate the percentage figures in that column. For the Federal Republic after 1956 it was by far the most rapidly growing large market. Only France, Switzerland and Portugal have a slower growth of trade to North America than to Western Europe without Germany. Denmark is alone in having had throughout the period a faster rate of growth of exports to North America than to the Federal Republic.

Another way of measuring the importance of the German market is to compare the annual average percentage growth of exports to the Federal Republic and to the rest of Western Europe. Measured in this way the dependence of a country like Belgium whose overall exports grew relatively weakly emerges particularly clearly (table 4.4). Had it not been for its exports to the Federal Republic, Belgium's export performance to Western Europe would in fact have been worse than that of the United Kingdom, which has been so heavily criticized. The predominant influence of Germany, as distinct from Western Europe, can also be seen more clearly for Denmark and France, two other countries whose overall rate of export growth was not among the most dynamic in Europe. Through its contribution to both the volume and growth of their exports the Federal Republic became indispensable to the Benelux countries, to Austria and Switzerland and to Denmark. To Norway and Sweden it was also of major importance, although to Sweden its importance lay in the absolute size of the market more than in its growth. For France and Italy it was by far the most rapidly growing market and this was especially important for France, whose exports elsewhere in Europe grew only sluggishly.

Table 4.4 Average annual percentage increase of the value of exports to (A) the Federal Republic and (B) the rest of Western Europe, 1951–8

	(A)	*(B)*
Austria	21.3	6.7
Belgium–Lux.	13.8	1.8
Denmark	13.9	3.2
France	16.2	2.6
Italy	16.4	4.4
Netherlands	12.6	7.7
Norway	12.7	2.7
Sweden	8.1	3.1
Switzerland	15.7	5.1
United Kingdom	13.9	3.5

Source: OEEC, *Statistical Bulletins of Foreign Trade*, Series IV

Table 4.5 measures the share of the German market in the exports of Western European countries. From 1951 the increasing proportion of total exports going to the Federal Republic was everywhere a persistent trend; it led to a situation in which Germany received more than 10 per cent of the exports of every Western European country by value except those of the United Kingdom and Portugal. For Austria, Denmark and the Netherlands the importance of the German market was much greater.

Table 4.5 Western European exports to the Federal Republic as a percentage of all exports (by value), 1950–8

	1950	1951	1952	1953	1954	1955	1956	1957	1958
Austria	14.3	14.2	20.1	19.6	23.5	25.1	23.4	23.8	25.1
Belgium–Lux.	6.8	6.1	9.6	9.3	9.6	11.7	10.2	10.2	11.6
Denmark	17.4	12.6	12.5	11.5	12.8	17.0	18.5	19.5	20.1
France	7.8	4.9	5.9	7.4	8.4	10.5	10.5	10.9	10.5
Italy	5.9	7.7	10.0	11.0	11.2	12.6	13.3	14.0	14.3
Netherlands	20.9	14.0	14.0	14.1	15.9	17.1	18.0	18.5	19.0
Norway	11.3	7.7	8.8	9.1	10.2	11.2	11.9	13.3	14.1
Portugal	3.6	4.7	6.3	7.2	6.9	7.8	7.1	6.8	7.7
Sweden	12.4	9.9	11.8	11.5	12.3	13.2	13.6	14.2	14.2
Switzerland	9.3	8.5	10.8	11.8	12.2	13.4	13.9	14.3	16.3
United Kingdom	2.0	1.9	2.0	2.3	2.6	2.6	2.9	3.2	3.8

Source: OEEC, *Statistical Bulletins of Foreign Trade*, Series IV

Table 4.6   Value of exports to the Federal Republic in 1957 as a share of GNP

Netherlands	5.5%
Austria	4.6%
Denmark	4.4%
Switzerland	3.3%
Belgium–Lux.	3.1%
Sweden	2.8%
Norway	2.5%
Italy	1.0%
France	1.0%
United Kingdom	0.5%

Sources: OECD, *National Accounts Statistics 1950–1968*; OEEC, *Statistical Bulletins of Foreign Trade*, Series IV

What this growth of exports to the Federal Republic meant in terms of export-dependence is shown in table 4.6 where their value is expressed as a part of national income.

The Netherlands by this measure was almost twice as dependent on the German market as Hungary had been in 1938, when accusations of German economic exploitation of central Europe were rife. Belgium and Denmark also had shares of their national product dependent on sales to Germany as high as some of the central and south-eastern European countries before the war. Of course the circumstances were entirely different. Dutch earnings on the post-war German market were in a currency transferable into any other Western European currency and the nature of the German government was much altered. Nevertheless, the tendency of the pre-war Reich to form a trading web with the smaller trade-dependent economies of central and south-eastern Europe was replaced after 1948 by the tendency of the Federal Republic to form a trading web with the smaller trade-dependent economies of Western Europe.

The comparative importance of the other major market, North America, was very variable. For the United Kingdom it accounted for 14.4 per cent of exports by value in 1958, for France a mere 4.8 per cent. Except in the case of Denmark there is a marked difference between the behaviour of exports to North America and exports to Western Europe. Exports to North America were more volatile, owing to the less stable nature of American demand and the arbitrariness of United States commercial policies.[27] The volatility is especially marked in the fall of the share of total exports going to North America in 1954 as compared to 1953, a consequence of the American recession. Only Denmark and the Federal

---

[27] Swiss exports to the United States, for example, did not increase in 1955 in response to improving demand as America recovered from recession, because the American tariff on watches was increased to protect its own ailing watch and clock industry. There had been a similar episode earlier when changes in the American legislation sharply reduced Dutch cheese exports.

Republic of all the Western European countries showed an increase in exports to North America in 1954 as compared to the previous year (table 4.7). For others, exports to the United States fell by more than 10 per cent in value and some, such as France and Switzerland, never recaptured the lost ground until the end of the decade. Although North America was the fastest-growing market for German exports from 1955, this was largely due to exports of one product, cars; for most other German manufactured goods the American market was not growing any faster than the European one.

Table 4.7 Average percentage rate of growth of value of exports in 1953 and 1954 to: (A) the Federal Republic; (B) the rest of Western Europe; (C) the United States and Canada

	(A)	*(B)*	*(C)*
Austria	19.70	6.69	− 9.6
Belgium–Lux.	−2.24	−0.81	−18.4
Denmark	10.99	2.93	+19.8
France	24.89	12.49	−14.5
German Federal Republic	–	7.08	+2.56
Italy	15.60	12.22	−11.2
Netherlands	14.75	6.30	−7.6
Norway	10.85	0.77	−13.2
Sweden	3.38	5.56	−25.4
Switzerland	12.42	6.38	−24.8
United Kingdom	9.13	6.92	−5.3

Source: OEEC, *Statistical Bulletins of Foreign Trade*, Series IV

The volatility of the American market over the period 1953–4 reflected the similar experience of 1949–50 and was to be experienced once more in 1958. It contrasted starkly with the stability of the Western European market, itself very much a function of the stability and growth of the German market. In American recessions German demand continued to grow and exercised a powerful countercyclical effect on Western European exports. This was especially marked in 1954, a year of relatively poor export opportunities to the United States but the first year of an extremely powerful boom in exports to Western Europe. The impact on the formulation of commercial policy in Western Europe of this contrast was a greater one than in longer-term perspective it perhaps merited. Nevertheless it was understandable that commercial policy should have responded so noticeably when the Federal Republic was not only the most rapidly growing export market for most Western European countries, as well as being for many the largest in absolute size, but was also the stabilizer of their exports and thus to some extent of their economies.

Both in 1948–9 and in 1953–4 the index of manufacturing production in the United States fell steeply. In 1953–4 the fall was almost 7.5 per cent and if the special circumstances attaching to coffee and cocoa imports are discounted the fall in import values was of the order of 9.5 per cent.[28] Both of these movements in the American economy were moments when the post-war boom in Europe might have come to its expected end. In the 1948–9 recession Western Europe's exports to the United States fell back to their level of 1947 and in the last quarter of 1949 the value of Western Europe's extra-European exports was no higher than at the end of 1948. Intra-Western-European exports, by contrast, increased by 27.6 per cent in value in 1949.[29] The main cause of this increase was the reopening of the German market and for some countries, notably France where the domestic economy was experiencing a sharp deflation, exports to Germany were an important source of growth in an otherwise faltering economy. In the cycle of 1953–4 the upward pull exerted on Western European economies by the German market was no less important. United States imports from Western Europe fell between the last quarter of 1953 and the last quarter of 1954 by 12 per cent in value, by much more than the fall in imports from other sources. A major component of this fall was a 50 per cent reduction in the value of steel imports. This movement fortunately was more than compensated in most Western European countries by the expansion of their exports to Germany. As in 1948–9 France was one of the main beneficiaries of the German expansion, but the effects on Austria, Denmark, the Netherlands and Norway are also very striking.

The stabilizing importance of the German market seems to have been the greater in as much as countries whose overall export performance was relatively weak in the 1950s tended to do worse on non-German markets, while the demand for their goods still remained high in Germany. To countries whose all-round export performance was very good, such as Italy, Germany made less difference in spite of its weighting in their total trade. The countercyclical force of the German market uncoupled the rhythm of growth of intra-Western-European trade from the rhythm of growth of world trade. In so doing it became one of the forces which sustained the great post-war European boom uninterrupted through movements in the American economy which otherwise might have brought it to its generally expected end and would certainly have slowed it down.

In the course of 1954, when the American recession was neutralized by Germany's growth, there was a noticeable change of opinion in Europe, a confidence that the harmful effect of cyclical fluctuations on employment

[28] H.K. Zassenhaus, 'Direct Effects of a United States Recession on Imports', in *Review of Economics and Statistics*, vol. xxxvii, no. 3, 1955.

[29] A.S. Milward, *The Reconstruction of Western Europe, 1945–1952* (London, 1984), pp. 349 ff.

and growth had at last been mastered, that Keynesian demand-management could work, and that a structural break in the historical experience of capitalism had occurred. So overwhelming a presumption could not help but increase the weight which governments placed on the foreign trade sector as an instrument of policy. When they did so their first concern was to fix the commercial bonds with Germany more securely in place. Their experience with Germany in the inter-war period had left no room for risk. The crucial importance of the German market suggested that political arrangements of equally crucial importance might have to be made and that these too could mark a structural break in the historical experience.

The earlier discussion of foreign trade and politics suggested that the conscious development of links between commercial and industrial policy was an important new post-war political element, one of the indispensable components of post-war neo-mercantilism. It was at this microeconomic level, in the details of what was actually traded, that the role of trade with Germany was also crucial. The stabilizing influence of exports to the Federal Republic was linked to their composition. Whereas before the war the highly protectionist Third Reich could be characterized as exporting manufactured goods in return for foodstuffs and raw materials, the post-war Federal Republic was increasingly engaged in an exchange of manufactures. Whereas trade theory at the time would have predicted that an increasing specialization in engineering exports by the Federal Republic would have occurred in parallel with an increasing specialization by other Western European countries in exports of labour- or land-intensive goods to Germany, this did not happen. Exports of engineering products to Germany grew faster than those of raw materials or foodstuffs. This shift in the commodity composition of German imports, which was one reason for the stability of German demand, gave to the German market a particular importance because of its modernizing effects on the commodity composition of the exports of other Western European countries. Since the establishment of more technologically sophisticated forms of manufacturing was seen as fundamental to national economic development, the trade with Germany appeared to exercise a constant pressure to improve on the structure of manufacturing.

To demonstrate this it is first necessary to confront the substantial body of economic and historical argument which blames the persistent German export surpluses on Germany's inability or refusal to provide an adequate market for its trading partners in Europe. The Federal Republic's export surpluses were occasionally held to be the consequence of fiscal and other commercial policies which unfairly supported exports with public funds.[30]

---

[30] See the analyses by K. Häuser, 'West Germany', in National Bureau of Economic Research and Brookings Institution, *Foreign Tax Policies and Economic Growth* (New York, 1966), and H.J. Jung, *Die Exportförderung im wirtschaftlichen Wiederaufbau der deutschen Bundesrepublik* (Cologne, 1957).

More typically, though, it was German imports which were blamed. Four different, although not necessarily unrelated, arguments have been made. One is that the earlier Nazi autarkic economic policies aiming at strategic independence had reduced the structural importance of imports in the German economy through the successful development of import substitutes. A second is that the Federal Republic was too protectionist. A third is that the Federal Republic's terms of trade were too favourable, encouraging exports and reducing the value of imports, although the reasons given for this are by no means a matter of agreement. Fourthly, the Federal Republic is accused of pursuing monetary and fiscal policies which encouraged saving at the expense of expenditure on imports. How much force is there in these arguments?

It is true that the Federal Republic had a lower proportion of raw materials in its total imports than there was in total German imports before the heavy investment of the Third Reich in import-substituting industries. It had a lower proportion also than had the United Kingdom, a country of roughly the same size and with a roughly similar industrial structure.[31] In 1936 on the eve of the Four Year Plan, which inaugurated the large investments in synthetic substitutes for imported raw materials, raw materials were 40 per cent of the value of total imports of the Third Reich. In the early 1950s they were only about one-third of those of the Federal Republic. The Nazi industrial investments in synthetic oil and rubber had indeed made a difference, for compared to Britain imports of natural oil and rubber per capita were much lower. However, the apparent reduction in the absolute value of all raw material imports, allowing for the difference in size of the Federal Republic compared to the Third Reich, is much less than the great increase in imports of manufactured goods, both in absolute volume and value and as a proportion of total imports into the Federal Republic as compared to the Third Reich.[32] For most of the countries in table 4.3 it was manufactures which made up the bulk of the increase in their exports to the Federal Republic. This in itself might seem a better explanation of the lower proportion of raw material imports than the changes in industrial structure in the late 1930s and during the war.

Alternatively, it is alleged that the Federal Republic was too protectionist. This might seem at first sight nonsense in a country whose tariffs on manufactures were consistently lower than those of the other large European economies and which was a leader in quota removal and other forms of trade liberalization throughout the 1950s. It is not, though, an accusation entirely without substance; there were areas of high protection in the German economy. Two in particular attracted much criticism, agriculture and energy. For agriculture protection was as comprehensive,

[31] A comparison used to suggest that German imports were inadequate by, for example, H.C. Wallich, *Mainsprings of the German Revival* (New Haven, 1955), p. 221.
[32] The territorial area of the Federal Republic is estimated to have accounted for 71 per cent of the imports of the Third Reich.

perhaps more so, as under the Nazi regime. Nevertheless food imports, because of the loss of agricultural areas after the war, were still a larger share of total imports than in the 1930s. Part of the difference between German and British food import levels was attributable to lower consumption in the Federal Republic. A decidedly lower level of per capita meat consumption, for example, was reflected in the fact that Britain's annual meat imports were usually more than 1 million tonnes and the Federal Republic's about 150,000 tonnes. Had Germany's per capita calorific consumption in 1959 been only 3 per cent less than that of the United Kingdom – per capita national income was roughly 3 per cent lower than in the United Kingdom – and had the Federal Republic had the same ratio of food imports to food consumption as Britain, then the value of German food imports would have been 45 per cent higher than it actually was.[33] As a rough measure of the import saving in foodstuffs resulting from agricultural protection this does amount to almost 80 per cent of the value of the export surplus. But agricultural protection, as the following chapter suggests, had costs which may well have resulted in a lower level of exports than would otherwise have been achieved, for the effect of higher food prices was not confined to holding down consumption.

Compared to the United Kingdom the Federal Republic also maintained high duties on imported oil products. Imports of crude oil were only about one-third those of the United Kingdom. If its per capita fuel imports had also been at a level only 3 per cent less than those of Britain the whole difference in value between the German and British balances on commodity trade would have been cancelled out by German protection against food and oil imports. The Federal Republic, unlike Britain, did have a domestic source of oil, mainly the synthetic production developed in the 1930s which provided for about one-third of the relatively low level of oil consumption in the mid-1950s. The high duties on imported crude oil which protected this sector were later supplemented by the levy on coal imports from outside the ECSC. Again, though, the costs of this must also have been partly borne by German exports, which with cheaper fuel prices would have reached a higher value.

Even in manufactures there were areas where Germany was no less protectionist than other countries, cars and car engines, tyres, paper, and porcelain for example. But in general, across the whole range of manufactured products Germany was the least protectionist of the larger west European economies. The unweighted mean of German tariffs was decidedly lower than that of the United Kingdom, France or Italy and on engineering and chemical products much lower. In addition, to be sold in Britain imports had also to bear the purchase tax, usually 15 per cent, levied on the price after customs had been paid.

[33] J. Markus, 'Some Observations on the West German Trade Surplus', in *Oxford Economic Papers*, vol. xvii, no. 1, 1965.

Table 4.8 Selected *ad valorem* tariff levels on manufactures, United Kingdom and German Federal Republic, 1957 (per cent)

	Federal Republic	United Kingdom
chemicals	10–15	12–33.3
general engineering products	0–15	12–33.3
electrical engineering products	0–15	15–33.3
cars	17–21	33.3
aircraft	free	17.5
railway locomotives	8–12	17.5–25
railway wagons and carriages	8–10	10
metal manufactures	6–19	15–33.3
cotton yarn	5–11	7.5
cotton fabric	10–13	17.5
woollen fabric	13	17.5
clothing	15	12–33.5
hosiery	13–17	20–33.3
footwear	12–19	10–20
leather	3–12	10–20
bricks	5–12.5	10
cement	5	5
porcelain and earthenware	15	3–6
sanitary ware	9	25
furniture	8–19	10–20

Source: Economist Intelligence Unit, *Britain and Europe. A Study of the Effects on British Manufacturing Industry of a Free Trade Area and the Common Market* (London, 1957)

As far as non-tariff barriers were concerned, as soon as large trade surpluses began to appear the Federal Republic removed them more quickly than Britain and France. By March 1953 84 per cent of its quotas on private trade with other OEEC countries on the 1948 basis which OEEC used as the yardstick for measuring its trade liberalization programme had been removed. By the same date and on the same basis the United Kingdom, which had temporarily suspended all trade liberalization in 1951, had removed only 44 per cent of its quotas.[34] When the United Kingdom reached the stage of 75 per cent liberalization in February 1954, the Federal Republic was at the 90 per cent mark, only Italy, which still maintained high tariffs, having a better record. This steady progress from 1951 onwards was unlike the trend in Britain and France, both of which reneged on trade liberalization as a consequence of adverse balance of payments movements in 1951–2.

The volume of total German imports in the early 1950s in fact rose faster than the volume of exports; it was only the improvement in the terms of trade which meant that their value rose less. And since the improvement in

[34] GATT, *International Trade*, 1953, p. 100.

the terms of trade was largely a consequence of the fall in raw material prices, the value of imports coming from Western Europe rose as fast as exports, because the structure of imports from the continent was skewed towards manufactured products. Imports of machinery and metals from the continent grew faster than German exports to Europe and, as will be seen later, this was also the case in other dynamic sectors of world trade in the 1950s. The big German trade surplus, growing as an absolute magnitude, was made up of manufactures, where levels of protection were low. But imports of these manufactures grew even more quickly. The higher tariff rates on manufactures in Britain, in any case, presumably reduced their import into Britain in comparison to the Federal Republic. Whereas British exports lost ground throughout Western Europe to German competition over the period 1953–9 and the United Kingdom lost 1 per cent of its share of the Federal Republic's own market, there was a more or less even balance on the mutual trade in manufactures between the two countries. Would that have been so had British and German tariffs been of the same height? With equal levels of protection the German trade surpluses would probably have been yet greater than they were.

Although the rate of growth of the volume of manufactured imports, adjusted for differences in the growth rate of GNP, was similar in the Federal Republic and Britain, the rate of growth of their value was not, and this provided another explanation for the persistence of the German surpluses. The Federal Republic's terms of trade were, it is frequently argued, exceptionally favourable.

There were in fact two years in which Germany's terms of trade did improve sharply. One was during the price fall after the Korean war commodity boom, and the other was in 1958. Each of these sudden movements in the terms of trade was very large in monetary terms. In 1958, for example, the difference in the terms of trade compared to the previous year accounted for nearly half the export surplus of DM 5,900 million ($1,412 million) recorded in that year.[35] Yet the biggest growth in German trade surpluses was during the trade boom of 1954–7, when the terms of trade remained relatively unaltered. These are the years least disturbed by any macroeconomic shocks. The increasingly favourable trend in the terms of trade over the whole period from 1950 to 1960 is about the same for both Germany and the United Kingdom. It was not until 1958 that average German import prices again fell by more than average British import prices, while the trend after 1954 was for average German export prices to rise more slowly than the average price of British exports. Changes in the terms of trade therefore, while certainly adding to the monetary value of German surpluses in particular years, can hardly be held responsible for the persistent large annual surpluses. This may well, on the other hand, have been the main reason for the surplus registered by

---

[35] P.M. Boarman, *Germany's Economic Dilemma*, op. cit., p. 123.

the United Kingdom in 1956, perhaps for the first time since the late eighteenth century.[36]

Another explanation for German trade surpluses is sometimes alleged to be the Federal Republic's high savings ratio, which in turn is attributed variously to tight monetary and fiscal policies and to the unequal distribution of income. Such policies are said to have created a smaller home market for domestic and foreign suppliers.

As a share of disposable income, private consumption in the early 1950s seems to have been lower in the Federal Republic than in countries with a comparable level of GNP per capita. At the same time savings ratios were higher than in most other countries, reflecting the desire to reconstitute savings after the post-war inflation and the drastic monetary reform. On the other hand, investment ratios were correspondingly high, and this was reflected in a high level of manufactured imports. The increase in German imports over the period 1950–5, when personal disposable income was at its lowest in relation to comparable countries, was mainly in manufactures, whose value increased by $1,209.27 million over that period. Of that increase $184.49 million was made up by machinery and transport equipment, $115.06 million by chemicals, and $863.71 million (almost three-quarters of the total) by the large miscellaneous category of SITC 6 which embraces metals and metal goods, intermediate manufactures, and textile yarns and fabrics. Of this total, yarns and fabrics accounted for only $100.8 million, so for only 8.3 per cent of the total increase in manufactured imports. The German private consumer might have been offering a more sluggish market for imports than some of his European counterparts before 1955, but if this was indeed so it was only likely to increase the interest of German manufacturers in export markets, and, as these figures show, the growth of German manufactured exports was based on a remarkable increase in imports of semi-finished manufactures, the intermediate goods on which the huge variety of German manufactured exports ultimately depended.

Monetarists and other anti-Keynesians cannot be wholly wrong in seeing tight control over the money supply and balanced budgets as one cause of the flood of German exports, but to propose these as the fundamental cause is to overlook the structure of Western European trade within which those exports grew and which had so dynamic an impact on them. Ultimately it was not monetary and fiscal policies within the Federal Republic which were responsible for the export surpluses but the unsatiable demand from Western Europe for German engineering goods and the interlocking demand in the Federal Republic for imports of metals and

---

[36] Cairncross suggests that it was the better terms of trade rather than any favourable structural change in the relationship of exports to imports which did account for the United Kingdom's equilibrium on current account in the 1950s compared to its earlier deficits. A. Cairncross, 'The Postwar Years, 1945–77', in R. Floud and D. McCloskey (eds), *The Economic History of Britain since 1700*, vol. 2 (Cambridge, 1981), p. 390.

machinery, largely satisfied by other European countries, which sustained this trade. This can best be seen by looking at the arguments advanced by those who see the causes of German surpluses not so much on the import side of the German trade balance as on its export side.

The Federal Republic was frequently accused by Britain in the early 1950s of giving unfair incentives to exporters. This trivial issue used up so much ink and political time that it needs to be put in perspective. German exporters did receive help both through the fiscal system and from special institutions created for the purpose. The major tax concession was the rebate of the turnover tax on exported commodities, a device to which the British government took such exception that it had to be abandoned in 1955 in response to their frequent and energetic protests. Apart from this, exporters were allowed to deduct from their taxable income an amount which averaged 3 per cent of the value of their export sales. These tax provisions had at first only an emergency status, supposedly until the serious balance of payments deficits of 1949–50 had been corrected and a sufficient reserve accumulated to pay off foreign debts. German exporters, though, pressed hard in 1952 to have them made more systematic and they received a good measure of support from the Ministry for the Economy. The Finance Ministry, however, refused to extend or regularize the system.[37] Before they were ended in 1955 these tax concessions could have favoured large companies seeking extra funds for investment and encouraged them to link export successes to investment privileges.

Häuser estimates that over their four years of operation these fiscal privileges resulted in a loss of government revenue of between DM 850 million and DM 1,000 million ($202.4 million and $238.1 million).[38] In addition exporters received financial assistance through guarantees given to them for medium-term repayment contracts on the export of capital goods, at first from the Reconstruction Credit Corporation (Kreditanstalt für Wiederaufbau) and with the expiry of Marshall Aid from an export-finance corporation linked to the central bank. The state also created an export-insurance company, Hermes AG., which provided trade insurance at rates which were occasionally below the private rates for export contracts with deferred repayment. Both export credit organizations operated on strict banking principles. The Kreditanstalt, for example, in 1951 provided credits of only DM 76.5 million ($18.2 million). Its better funded successor agency, the Ausfuhrkredit AG., provided credits of DM 2,000 million ($476.2 million) covering export credits of about DM 4,000 million ($952.4 million) over the years 1952–4, roughly equivalent to about three-quarters of the value of exports in any one year to the ECSC countries.[39] Over the period 1952–7 its credits financed about one-quarter of the value

---

[37] BA, B102/12683, Kurzbericht über die Sitzung der Steuersachverständigen der Länder im BFM am 2 und 3 September 1952; 6 September 1952.
[38] K. Häuser, 'West Germany', op. cit.
[39] H.J. Jung, *Die Exportförderung*, op. cit., pp. 86–97.

of all German exports. Almost the whole of them supported exports of capital goods.[40]

The role of these export credit institutions however was not peculiarly German. It reflected a general trend in commercial finance in the 1930s, most notably in the United States. In a period when capital was short the Ausfuhrkredit was offering the type of government-supported financial service which would become increasingly common and to see this as unfair trade competition was to get the issue wholly out of historical perspective. There was a gradual, long-run tendency of government everywhere to take over the provision of export credits.[41] It is hardly surprising that in a country where capital was so scarce and so high a proportion of exports consisted of capital goods, which were usually only sold on medium-term deferred repayment schemes, government should have intervened. The service the German government provided was less comprehensive than that of the Export–Import Bank of the United States, and German industrialists not infrequently expressed their discontent by demanding something more like the American model. The range of direct export subsidies provided by the French government was at least as extensive as that in Germany, on many commodities more generous, and continued after 1955.[42] The Bank of England when it surveyed German policy, did not regard it as unfair competition. Although the Ausfuhrkredit could provide eight year credits, four-fifths of those provided were for no longer than the two years which was also the usual limit in Britain.[43] The rebate of turnover tax, however, was more open to criticism that it infringed the principles of non-discriminatory trade enshrined in the trade rules of the European Payments Union and it was on these grounds that it had eventually to be modified.

Of more comprehensive importance is the claim that the Deutschmark was undervalued and that German export successes were a function of the unfairly favourable exchange rate. Under a fixed exchange rate regime an improvement in economic efficiency, such as occurred in the Federal Republic, may well cause the currency to appear undervalued in terms of other currencies. To avoid confusion between cause and effect the specific question needs to be asked, whether the Deutschmark was initially undervalued and whether this gave an initial favourable impetus to German exports?

After the general European devaluations against the dollar in September 1949 there was a sharp argument between Americans, French and

[40] 'Le commerce extérieur de l'Allemagne occidentale depuis 1954', in *Etudes et Conjoncture*, no. 5, May 1959 (14e année), p. 515.

[41] C. Segré, 'Medium-Term Export Finance. European Problems and Experiences', in *Banca Nazionale del Lavoro Quarterly Review*, no. 11, 1958.

[42] G. Marcy, 'Libération progressive des échanges et aide à l'exportation en France depuis 1949', in *Cahiers de l'Institut de Science Economique Appliquée*, série P, no. 2, no. 81, May 1959.

[43] BOE, OV 34/39, Report on Visit to Frankfurt by Mr J. Rootham, 7–8 May 1953.

Germans as to what the par-rate of the Deutschmark should be, the Germans wanting a higher rate than they ended up with, the French wanting them to be saddled with an even higher one, and the Americans wanting a rate lower than the German government in order to stimulate German exports. In the end the rate that was set made some concessions to French demands for a higher rate. The argument for subsequently revaluing the Deutschmark upwards only gained ground in the late 1950s as a way of reducing the German surpluses and the idea that the Deutschmark was initially undervalued often appears as a tautological assertion that it must have been so because where there is a persistent surplus there is by definition a misvaluation. There do not seem to be any better grounds for determining the correct relative values of fixed currencies. It should be noted therefore that the most severe problem in making settlements in intra-Western-European trade for the first six months after the par rate for the Deutschmark had been set was Germany's export deficit.

Under a fixed exchange rate regime any initial undervaluation of the currency would tend to be eliminated by inflation. Money wages and export prices, although not domestic prices, in fact rose more rapidly in the Federal Republic than in many of its competitors, including the United Kingdom. By 1956 German wage rates, which had been well below those in Britain at the start of the decade, had reached roughly the same level. Over the decade 1950–60 the index of German export prices also rose more than that of British export goods. This was mainly attributable to the increasing share of capital goods exports in total German exports. In volume and value over the decade, they increased by almost 30 per cent more than that of consumer goods.[44] The index of consumer good prices tended to have a falling trend over the decade, while that of capital goods rose more steeply than prices in general. In fact if we compare solely the relative prices of capital goods exports, they had a more steeply increasing upward trend in the Federal Republic than in most other Western European countries. Even supposing that the Federal Republic had had the initial advantage of a misaligned exchange rate or indeed any other factor which gave its machinery exports a price advantage in 1950–1, this advantage would have been quickly eroded.

Had the Federal Republic enjoyed an overall advantage because of an undervalued currency it is likely that all its exports would have made gains against British exports of all kinds. But any study of manufactured exports in the period shows that in spite of the retreat of British exports in the face of German competition there were clear and important exceptions to the overall pattern. Some British exports, such as chemicals and heavy electrical engineering equipment, retained a greater share of post-war markets than they had held in the pre-war period and did so at the expense of German exports in that sector, which did not regain their pre-war market

44 P.M. Boarman, *Germany's Economic Dilemma*, op. cit., p. 114.

share.[45] Faced with the complex and variable pattern of the productivity improvements which compensated for a higher level of costs in the Federal Republic, with the even greater complexity of the causes of these productivity improvements, and with the fact that the most important and most rapidly growing category of German exports was increasing in price relatively more rapidly than that of its main rivals, the argument that the Deutschmark exchange rate was initially too favourable seems too simple and very difficult to substantiate.

The fact that the German trade surplus continued to grow as export prices increased more rapidly than elsewhere is much more likely to have been the outcome of the relatively more rapid gains in productivity in the Federal Republic. The steeper rise in money wages and the lower increase in labour costs per unit of output indicate a much faster rate of physical productivity improvement than in Britain, for example. Between 1953 and 1959 wage costs per unit of output rose by about 7 per cent compared to 20 per cent in the United Kingdom.[46] Other input costs appear to have been higher than in Britain. It was the improvement in labour productivity which kept the prices of German consumer goods exports in line with competitors and prevented those of capital goods exports from going too far beyond them.

No method of making international productivity comparisons has yet proved sensitive enough for historians to trust unless the differences in productivity which are demonstrated are very wide indeed. In this case however much of the evidence does point to a very wide gap in productivity levels between Germany and Britain, in 1950 in Britain's favour, which had either disappeared or become much narrower by 1955. All estimates of West German productivity in manufacturing industry in 1950 put it not only well below the British level but below that of the pre-war Reich too. Most estimates suggest also that by 1955 the Federal Republic and the United Kingdom were on roughly similar levels of industrial productivity, although Prais's estimates, the most carefully worked out, suggest the gap was not finally closed until the end of the 1950s.[47]

The change between 1950 and 1955 is not surprising. The obstacles to a rapid recovery of output in the Federal Republic were bottlenecks in supply and transport which caused low levels of utilization of the new industrial plant created by the high levels of investment in fixed capital

[45] A. Maizels, *Industrial Growth . . .*, op. cit., appendix F2.
[46] E. Benoit, *Europe at Sixes and Sevens. The Common Market, the Free Trade Association and the United States* (New York, 1961), p. 162.
[47] M. Gilbert and I. Kravis, *An International Comparison of National Products and the Purchasing Power of Currencies* (OEEC, Paris, 1954); M. Gilbert *et al.*, *Comparative National Products and Price Levels* (OEEC, Paris, 1958); United Nations, Economic Commission for Europe, *Economic Survey of Europe in 1958*, Appendix A-8; United Nations, ECE, *Some Factors in Economic Growth in Europe During the 1950s* (Geneva, 1964); S.J. Prais, *Productivity and Industrial Structure*, op. cit.

between 1933 and 1944.[48] Many were administrative bottlenecks imposed by the cumbersome administrative procedures of the occupation authorities, by the rigid administrative divisions between occupation zones, by the lack of a general law and common government, by uncertainty about frontiers, and by the lack of a satisfactory medium of exchange. The mere fact that the western allies reintegrated their occupation zones and created a German state was bound to improve productivity levels irrespective of levels of capital investment, which were also high. This sharp upward movement in productivity in the first years of the Federal Republic's existence seems, furthermore, to have been a return to a long-term trend dating from at least 1870 for productivity in Germany to improve more rapidly than in Britain.

All these explanations, whether they attribute the Federal Republic's export surpluses to its protectionism or to special circumstances favouring its exports, tend to portray the success of German trade as in some way accidental, temporary, or even unfair. However, direct comparisons between the relative success of German and British exports in the 1950s, particularly an inquiry conducted by the Board of Trade in 1956, suggested more fundamental explanations for the Federal Republic's success.[49] It began from three assumptions. Firstly, the Federal Republic might have had a competitive advantage over the United Kingdom in prices, either because of initially lower prices or a more rapid improvement in physical productivity, or from non-price factors like salesmanship, marketing and servicing. Secondly, the commodity composition of the Federal Republic's exports appeared more favourable to their growth than that of British exports, which were more heavily concentrated on textiles, the demand for which grew more slowly than for other goods. Analogously the geographical distribution of Germany's exports was more favourable to their expansion, because they went mainly to rapidly expanding European markets, whereas the Commonwealth and North American markets to which British exports were still mostly sent grew more slowly.

The Board of Trade inquiry attempted to attribute between these causes the success of German exports in displacing British goods from foreign markets. The method used was taken from an earlier longer-run study by Tyszynski and was also later to be used by Kindleberger and by Krause to try to measure the relative causes of changes in the shares of all countries in

[48] W. Abelshauser, *Wirtschaft in Westdeutschland 1945–1948. Rekonstruktion und Wachstumsbedingungen in der amerikanischen und britischen Zone* (Stuttgart, 1975); Abelshauser, 'Wiederaufbau vor dem Marshall-Plan. Westeuropas Wachstumchancen und die Wirtschaftsordnungspolitik in der zweiten Hälfte der vierziger Jahre', in *Vierteljahrshefte für Zeitgeschichte*, Bd. 29, Heft iv, 1981. Abelshauser's index of industrial production is criticized by A. Ritschl, 'Die Währungsreform und der Wiederaufstieg der deutschen Industrie', in *Vierteljahrshefte für Zeitgeschichte*, Bd. 33, Heft i, 1975, but the revision of the index does not disprove these particular conclusions.
[49] *Board of Trade Journal*, 30 March 1957.

world trade.[50] Through a counterfactual representation of what each country's share of world exports would have been had it held the same share as a selected base year in, firstly, each geographical market, and, secondly, each commodity group, the relative impact of changes in geographical distribution and changes in commodity composition were assessed against each other as causes of the loss (or gain) of market share. The percentage of loss (gain) of share not accounted for by those two causes was attributed to all other causes, 'the residual'. If an exporting country did not become any less competitive, in the terms of this definition, its percentage shares of each submarket would remain fixed. Even in that case its share of the total market might nevertheless fall simply because income and demand in its traditional markets grew more slowly than average.

The conclusion reached by the Board of Trade inquiry was that, compared to the base year 1951, as much as one-quarter to one-third of the United Kingdom's loss of world market share for exports (mainly lost to German competition) was due to their geographical distribution and commodity composition, the former being more important than the latter. It was in Western European markets that the major loss of share had occurred. The rest of the loss of share, more than two-thirds of the total, was due to 'the residual', competitive disadvantage, a result confirmed by the observation that the loss of market share in all markets was attributed in roughly the same proportions to the same three causes, thus, it was claimed, eliminating the explanation that their geographical distribution was a prime cause of their relative decline. By analogy, the Federal Republic's gain in market share could be attributed in roughly the same proportion, between one-quarter and one-third, to the geographical distribution and commodity composition of its exports. All the rest was due to changes in their competitive advantage. The Board of Trade report conceded that, although German gains in share were roughly of the same order all over the world, the fact that the bulk of German exports went to Western European markets, which were the fastest growing, while half of British exports in the same period by contrast went to sterling area markets, which were stagnant, did give the Federal Republic a geographical advantage, which the United Kingdom over so short a period could have done very little to reduce. Nevertheless, almost three-quarters of the British loss of market share (and three-quarters of the German gain) were attributable, the report concluded, to other causes, most probably to the Federal Republic's overall competitive advantage.

It is necessary to be cautious about what this method really demon-

---

[50] H. Tyszynski, 'World Trade in Manufactured Commodities, 1899–1950', in *The Manchester School of Economic and Social Studies*, vol. 19, 1951; C.P. Kindleberger, *Europe's Postwar Growth. The Role of Labor Supply* (Cambridge, Mass., 1967); L.B. Krause, 'Britain's Trade Performance', in R.E. Caves *et al.*, *Britain's Economic Prospects* (Washington DC, 1968).

strates, even if we are as complacent as the Board of Trade about a fraction of lost shares in world imports which would represent a considerable magnitude in relation to the balance of payments. In the Tyszynski method differences between the effects of geographic distribution and those of 'competitiveness' are logically distinct by formal definition. The ability to capture shares in submarkets from other exporters is presumed to be independent of the initial configuration of the export pattern. Such a method takes no account of the possibility that the rapid expansion of exports in markets where competition is fierce may have dynamic effects on the economy as a whole. Where success in export competition requires a high level of technological innovation, which appears to have been the case with manufactured exports to high per capita income Western European markets, this might well stimulate a higher rate of technological innovation and a faster rate of productivity improvement throughout the economy. Curiously, the corollary, that a high proportion of manufactured exports directed to slow-growing and still-protected sterling area markets, which were also much less competitive, might in comparison have retarding effects on technological innovation and productivity change did not enter into the official discussion in the 1950s. Looked at another way, the method tries to separate increasing competitiveness relative to rival exporters from the accident of selling the right goods in the right place. But suppose that in the 1950s competitiveness largely was a question of selling the right goods in the right place. The Board of Trade inquiry was based on data up to 1955, the last year in which complacency about sterling area markets was possible. What they were surveying was to some degree the result not of an accident but the conscious post-war strategy of regarding Europe as the third-best market and its consequence, ceding to Germany the task of re-equipping Europe's investment programme.

It is here that we can best begin to understand the real reasons for the remarkable growth of German exports and the persistence of the trade surpluses which resulted, for the connection between the geographical distribution of the Federal Republic's manufactured exports and their commodity structure was a dynamic one. The growth of Germany's exports was a function of the exceptionally high levels of investment in western Europe. It was German industry which re-equipped western European industry from 1949 onwards. But German manufactured exports grew in a modernizing symbiosis with the exports of other western European economies to Germany; the German market was as important to modernization as German supply.

From at least 1890 Germany had been the main European supplier of investment goods (machinery, transport equipment and steel), to other European economies. Their demand for these goods fluctuated in relation to their levels of investment. As these reached much higher levels after 1945 than in the 1930s the demand for that particular category of German exports also reached unprecedented heights, especially as the only alternative source of provision was often the United States whose currency was in short supply and where international payments were more difficult because it was not a member of the European Payments Union within which settlement could be made in credits. Inability to find the dollars to purchase an increased quantity of American investment goods in 1947 had been the immediate cause of the European balance of payments crises which precipitated the Marshall Plan.[51] The Marshall Plan had funded the continued import of these capital goods, sustaining high levels of investment and employment in Western Europe while it did so. But as Marshall Plan funds declined and as German manufactured exports returned, European importers switched eagerly to German goods to replace imports from the United States. The Federal Republic quickly re-occupied the pivotal role in continental Europe's trade which the German Empire had filled before 1914, but with greater dynamic effects because it was less protectionist.

The existence of a much larger engineering and capital goods sector than in any economy other than the United States, and also of an intensive network of trading contacts in all neighbouring western European countries, could, however, do no more than provide a favourable opportunity.[52] Whether it could be taken depended not only on post-war conditions in other European economies but also on Allied post-war policies towards Germany. From the start of the Marshall Plan it became a cardinal point of American foreign policy that the Federal Republic should be reintegrated into the international economy with all possible speed and that the severe controls on German trade imposed by the occupation forces be removed.[53] The first German government removed controls even faster than the Americans wished and the Federal Republic was from its origin in a position to respond to the demand for goods arising from the high investment levels in Europe. For those countries for which data exists table 4.9 shows how much higher investment was than in the inter-war period. The increase in investment as a ratio of national product started in fact not in 1950 but in 1945, so that the figures in the second column of the table represent a trend already in existence for five years, and the figures in the first column would be lower if the period 1945–9 were excluded.

The more directly relevant comparison is between non-residential investment and capital goods imports but it is not unfortunately possible to extract the residential component of investment in a consistent way from the figures. In some countries, particularly in the United Kingdom and the Federal Republic itself, this share was high. Nevertheless the evidence

[51] A.S. Milward, *The Reconstruction . . .*, op. cit., pp. 19 ff.
[52] Before the end of the war certain circles in the Nazi party, as well as many industrialists, already envisaged this as Germany's best hope of post-war recovery from the imminent ruin. L. Herbst, *Der Totale Krieg und die Ordnung der Wirtschaft. Die Kriegswirtschaft im Spannungsfeld von Politik, Ideologie und Propaganda 1939–1945* (Stuttgart, 1982).
[53] C. Buchheim, *Die Wiedereingliederung Westdeutschlands in die Weltwirtschaft 1945–1958* (Munich, 1990).

Table 4.9   Investment and imports of capital goods in western Europe, 1914–55

	Total gross investment as a percentage of GNP at current prices		Capital goods imports as a percentage of total imports at current prices	
	1914–49	1950–60	1929[c]	1951–5[d]
Belgium	n.a.	16.5	6.2	9.97
Denmark	12.6[a]	18.1	2.7	8.15
Italy	13.5	20.8	4.7	9.1
Netherlands	n.a.	24.2	6.9	10.93
Norway	15.4[b]	26.4	4.9	11.73
Sweden	15.5	21.3	5.5	10.06

[a]   1921–49
[b]   1914–38
[c]   all machinery
[d]   SITC 71 + SITC 72

Sources: A. Maddison, *Economic Growth in the West. Comparative Experience in Europe and North America* (New York, 1964); OEEC, *Statistical Bulletins of Foreign Trade*, Series IV; Belgium, Ministère de l'Intérieur et de l'Hygiène, Statistique Générale, *Annuaire Statistique de la Belgique et du Congo Belge*; Denmark, Danmarks Statistik, *Vareomsætningen med Udlandet*; Italy, Istituto Centrale de Statistica, *Annuario Statistico Italiano*; Netherlands, Centraal Bureau voor de Statistiek, *Maandstatistiek van den In- Uit-En Doorvoer*; Sweden, Sveriges Officiella Statistik, *Handel*

Table 4.10   The share of different manufactures (by value) in the total exports of the Weimar Republic and the Federal Republic

	Percentage of Total Exports		
	Machinery	*Metals*	*Textiles*
Weimar Republic 1928	9.5	18.1	16.8
Federal Republic 1956	18.9	19.1	5.9

Sources: Weimar Republic: Statistisches Bundesamt, *Der Aussenhandel Deutschlands*; Federal Republic: Statistisches Bundesamt, *Der Aussenhandel der Bundesrepublik Deutschland*

does point to the fact that in the 1950s the share of investment directly related to the demand for capital goods was higher than in other historical periods.[54] The impact of this on the commodity structure of West German exports can be easily seen from table 4.10. In 1928 machinery had accounted for 9.5 per cent of the total exports of the Weimar Republic at

[54] UN, ECE, *Some Factors* . . ., op. cit., chapter III, Table A2.

Table 4.11   Proportionate contribution made to the total increase in West German exports by some European markets, 1949–51 (at current $ prices)

	July–Dec. 1949	Jan.–June 1950	July–Dec. 1950 %	Jan.–June 1951	July–Dec. 1951
Belgium–Luxembourg and Netherlands	17.9	44.0	19.7	12.1	17.9
Austria and Switzerland	9.8	4.6	7.8	12.1	9.0
Denmark, Norway and Sweden	12.1	10.0	13.6	11.0	11.6

Source: Statistisches Amt des Vereinigten Wirtschaftsgebietes/Statistisches Bundesamt, *Der Aussenhandel der Bundesrepublik Deutschland*, Teil 3. The definition of manufactures is groups IIb and IIc of the German classification, not the SITC classifications used elsewhere and thus not strictly comparable with other tables.

current prices. The equivalent figure for the Federal Republic in 1956 was 18.9 per cent.

On the German side, with levels of disposable income still so low in 1949 and 1950 that much of their increase went on extra food consumption, with the population increasing rapidly, and with no financial reserves, the only way forward for manufacturers and for government alike was through exporting. As table 4.11 shows, this took place at first to those neighbouring smaller economies whose need for capital goods imports was greater because of the more restricted scope of their own manufacturing industries. It was these economies which brought the strongest pressure to bear during the occupation of Germany for the Americans and British to relax their rigid controls on trade, because their need for the German market was also greatest. Over every six-month period from the rebirth of West German manufactured exports to the end of the Marshall Plan, between 33 and 40 per cent of each total half-yearly increase in the value of exports was accounted for by eight small European economies, Belgium–Luxembourg and the Netherlands, Austria and Switzerland, and Denmark, Norway and Sweden. In the first six months of the Federal Republic's so-called economic miracle the Benelux countries alone were responsible for 44 per cent of the increase in the value of its exports.

Over the period 1946–8, before the restoration of a unitary West German economy, the ratio of gross domestic capital formation in all these markets taken together had averaged 31 per cent of net national income. Without supply from German manufacturing industry such ratios were already in 1949 treading the limits of feasibility, in spite of Marshall Aid. By 1959 the Federal Republic's exports accounted for 22.6 per cent of Sweden's total imports, for 20.7 per cent of Holland's, for 20.5 per cent of those of Denmark and for 20.1 per cent of Norway's. If we narrow the calculation down to imports in the SITC 7 category which includes machinery and transport equipment, Sweden's imports from Germany amounted to 45 per cent of the total for the whole category, those of the Netherlands and Denmark each for 38 per cent, and those of Norway for 31 per cent. The geographical pattern established in the first surge of German exports persisted, not surprisingly because all these economies except Denmark continued to record gross investment ratios near to 20 per cent of national income until the end of the decade.

Because of their smaller manufacturing capacity these eight economies continued to sustain higher levels of capital goods imports per head than the larger economies. Between 1950 and 1959 almost one-third of the increase in world exports of capital goods was attributable to their demand. The first markets into which West German goods were able to insert themselves at the birth of the Federal Republic became therefore the most dynamically growing markets of the decade and especially so for the capital goods in which German manufacturing industry was so heavily specialized.

Although by 1959 around 60 per cent of German exports by value still went to Western European markets and the smaller Western European countries remained the driving force behind their expansion, the path forward was not direct. In 1950 the Federal Republic's share of world manufactured exports was still only 7 per cent compared to the 21.8 per cent of the pre-war Reich. Its share of world exports of machinery and transport equipment one year later was still only 9.9 per cent compared to the United States' share of 39.8 per cent. That the European investment boom would continue throughout the 1950s did not then seem probable and, indeed, with the end of the Korean war inflation there was a clear faltering of the rate of growth of output in several countries. It was not until the last quarter of 1953 that there was again a general upward movement and only in early 1954 was every Western European country again in a vigorous cyclical upswing. For most Western European economies the vigorous upward trend which resumed in 1953 persisted until the end of the first quarter of 1957 and in France until the end of the first quarter of 1958. The only countries whose output turned down earlier were those whose general growth record in the 1950s was poorer. In Denmark there was a slowdown in the third quarter of 1954, in the United Kingdom in the last quarter of 1955, and in Belgium in the first quarter of 1956. It was only in this 1954 upswing, which initiated for three years the greatest of all western European foreign trade booms, that the pattern which determined the growth of German exports finally became fixed.[55]

Before this great resurgence of growth in output and trade swept away the last gloomy prophecies about the inescapability of a post-

[55] Of the export credits granted by the German export credit association (Ausfuhrkredit AG.) in 1954, 62 per cent were in Europe, compared to only 41 per cent in 1953. UN, ECE, *Economic Bulletin for Europe*, vol. 7, no. 3, November 1955, p. 9.

reconstruction crash, there was a period of anxious and relatively unsuccessful experimentation by German exporters in markets outside Europe.[56] If the export of particular types of machinery from the Federal Republic is studied in detail it can be seen that in 1952 the United States, because of rearmament there, was the second biggest market for German exports of metal-working machinery. The impact of rearmament can also be seen in the fact that the United Kingdom was the biggest German market for goods in this category in 1951 and 1952. Brazil, as a consequence of the German trade drive there, was also an important market for German machinery in 1951 and 1952. But the role of industrialized and industrializing Western Europe dominates the picture even in those years (tables 4.12 to 4.14). After 1954 in the great trade boom it became more dominant.

The continuing contribution of the smaller trade-dependent economies to the increase in Germany's exports to Western Europe in the trade boom of 1954–7 is compared in table 4.15 to that of the more protectionist larger economies, the United Kingdom, France and Italy. The three major western European economies made a contribution to the increase in German manufactured exports over these years much less than half that of the smaller, more trade-dependent economies on which German exports had first sold in large quantities. It was evident to German exporters that progressing beyond the rather narrow base on which German export growth still mainly occurred was ultimately necessary. One appeal of a customs union was that it would extend that base by forcing down levels of protection in France and Italy, and perhaps eventually the United Kingdom.

For the Federal Republic's trading partners the advantage of a customs union would be that the interchange in manufactured goods which had been built up would be made easier and its continuation guaranteed. As the pattern of trade in manufactures shows, they had nothing to fear. In all the German manufacturing sectors where output, productivity and exports grew the most rapidly, with the exception of shipbuilding, there was also a very rapid growth of imports, frequently more rapid than that of exports. The shipbuilding sector itself must also have depended on the great increase in steel imports. One general measure of this tendency is the increase in finished manufactures as a percentage of the value of all imports. They rose from an average of 11.7 per cent of total imports in the two years 1950–51 to 23.85 per cent in 1957–8. Semi-manufactured products rose from 18.8 per cent of total imports in 1951 to 33.4 per cent in 1955.[57]

[56] A.S. Milward, 'The Marshall Plan and German Foreign Trade', in C. Maier (ed.), *The Marshall Plan and Germany. West German Development within the Framework of the European Recovery Program* (Oxford, 1991).

[57] H.H. Liesner, *The Import Dependence of Britain and Western Germany: A Comparative Study*, Princeton Studies in International Finance No. 7 (Princeton, 1957).

Table 4.12 Percentage share of market in rank order of exports of general machinery from the Federal Republic, 1950–5

1950		1951		1952		1953		1954		1955	
Netherlands	11.03	Netherlands	10.56	Netherlands	7.69	Netherlands	8.00	Netherlands	8.85	Netherlands	9.45
Belgium–Lux.	9.41	France	8.03	France	7.51	Italy	7.91	Italy	7.21	France	7.64
France	9.31	Brazil	6.53	Italy	7.37	Belgium–Lux.	6.41	France	6.65	Italy	7.54
Italy	5.57	Belgium–Lux.	6.31	Brazil	7.28			Belgium–Lux.	6.18	Belgium–Lux.	6.40
		Sweden	6.05	Belgium–Lux.	6.60			Switzerland	5.52	Switzerland	5.96
		Italy	5.75	Sweden	5.25					Austria	5.60
		Switzerland	5.72	Switzerland	5.15						

The calculations are by value. All countries with more than 5 per cent of the market are included.

Sources: UN, Statistical Papers, Commodity Trade Statistics, Series D; Statistik des Aussenhandels der Bundesrepublik Deutschland, 1951

Table 4.13 Percentage share of market in rank order of exports of metal-working machinery from the Federal Republic, 1950–5

1950		1951		1952		1953		1954		1955	
Sweden	10.18	UK	13.36	UK	20.31	UK	13.82	France	11.07	France	12.13
Netherlands	9.28	Sweden	10.64	USA	9.99	Italy	10.85	Italy	9.66	Italy	8.93
Belgium–Lux.	8.47	France	8.88	France	8.44	France	10.51	Belgium–Lux.	8.11	UK	8.79
France	7.89	Netherlands	8.62	Italy	8.41	USA	7.17	UK	7.99	Sweden	6.64
Czechoslovakia	7.67	Brazil	7.41	Switzerland	6.68	Switzerland	6.61	Switzerland	6.71	Belgium–Lux.	6.34
Italy	7.49	Switzerland	6.95	Belgium–Lux.	6.01	Belgium–Lux.	6.41	Yugoslavia	5.68	Switzerland	6.12
Hungary	7.15	Italy	6.90	Sweden	5.79			Netherlands	5.17	Netherlands	5.51
Switzerland	6.05			Brazil	5.63			Brazil	5.15		
Brazil	5.13			Netherlands	5.01						

The calculations are by value. All countries with more than 5 per cent of the market are included.

Sources: UN, Statistical Papers, Commodity Trade Statistics, Series D; Statistik des Aussenhandels der Bundesrepublik Deutschland, 1951

Table 4.14   Percentage share of market in rank order of exports of electrical machinery from the Federal Republic, 1950–5

1950		1951		1952		1953		1954		1955	
Netherlands	15.2	Netherlands	11.63	Sweden	9.32	Netherlands	8.82	Netherlands	10.38	Netherlands	11.61
Sweden	8.65	Sweden	10.85	Netherlands	7.81	Sweden	7.48	Sweden	7.40	Sweden	7.8
Belgium–Lux.	6.69	Turkey	5.81	Belgium–Lux.	6.57	Italy	6.94	Belgium–Lux.	6.49	Belgium–Lux.	5.91
Austria	5.15	France	5.63	Turkey	5.33	Belgium–Lux.	6.77	Italy	5.42	Italy	5.27
		Belgium–Lux.	5.03			Switzerland	5.19				
						Norway	5.17				

The calculations are by value. All countries contributing 5 per cent of the market in any one year are included.

Sources: UN, Statistical Papers, Commodity Trade Statistics, Series D; Statistik des Aussenhandels der Bundesrepublik Deutschland, 1951

Table 4.15   Percentage contribution to the increase in total exports (by value) of the Federal Republic made by different European markets, 1954–7

Belgium–Lux. and Netherlands	16.01
Denmark, Norway and Sweden	12.13
Austria and Switzerland	10.96
	——
Total contribution of above to percentage increase	39.10
	——
France and Italy combined	13.15
United Kingdom	3.99

Source: OEEC, *Statistical Bulletins of Foreign Trade*, Series IV

The mechanical engineering industry, whose 4,060 firms in 1958 employed 12 per cent of the total employed labour force, was the central pillar of the Federal Republic's exports. Yet Germany's own machinery imports rose from 1.5 per cent of the total value of its imports in 1950 to 4.1 per cent in 1958. The single biggest category of machine imports was textile machinery, the imports of which increased fourfold over the period 1950–8, but as a rate of increase this was slow in comparison to other machinery imports. Imports of machine tools increased more than sixfold in value over the same period. Imports of engines, insignificant in 1950, increased more than twenty times, of pumps and compressed air machinery twenty-eight times. Over the period 1954–8 slightly more than a quarter of these machinery imports came from the United States, about one-half from Europe. In most years the value of machinery imported from Switzerland equalled that from the United States. It was much the most important European supplier. The United Kingdom, Europe's largest machinery producer after Germany, came well down the list.

If we compare the structure of Swiss and British machinery exports to the Federal Republic one possible reason for this can be suggested. A high and growing proportion of total exports directed to Germany encouraged specialization in more modern goods related to newer technologies. Britain, excluded from the benefits of having so high a proportion of its trade concentrated in this exchange of manufactures with Germany, did not show the changes in industrial output which occurred elsewhere. In 1950 both Britain and Switzerland were still leading exporters of textile machinery, as they had been since the nineteenth century. Textile machinery remained in the 1950s the most valuable component in British machine exports to Germany, followed by agricultural machinery. For Switzerland, while textile machinery was initially much the biggest item and still remained the most valuable category in 1958, there was an increasing proportion of machine tools and office machinery in the total and they were among the categories that grew most rapidly.[58] There was a much less marked change in the commodity structure of British machine exports to Germany; they retained their structure of the early part of the decade.

The value of German imports of electrical machinery grew ninefold over the period 1950–8. For some products, such as domestic electrical appliances, imports grew slightly faster than exports, but generally exports and imports in this sector grew at about the same pace. About 80 per cent of all these imports were of European provenance. Here, by far the biggest European supplier was the Netherlands, which over the last three years accounted on average for 21.5 per cent of the value of all imports in this sector. This exceeded the share of the United States, 21 per cent over the same period. Two other suppliers, the United Kingdom and Switzerland, each had roughly half the Dutch share of the German market. Electrical engineering was one of the few sectors where British exports performed well in the 1950s. But the country whose exports of electrical machinery to Germany grew the most rapidly, France, puts the British performance in perspective. Relatively small in 1950–1, French exports to Germany in this sector by 1956–8 had reached the same value as those of Britain and Switzerland.

Germany's imports of chemical products grew as fast as its exports, remaining throughout the decade at just over a quarter of their level. They rose from 2.3 per cent of total imports in 1950 to 3.7 per cent in 1958. By value, between 55 and 60 per cent of them came from Western Europe, the rest almost entirely from the United States. Of the European suppliers Switzerland was the most important, in most years accounting for about 12 per cent of the total. Four other suppliers of roughly equal importance accounted for between 8 and 9 per cent of total chemical imports; Belgium, France, the Netherlands and the United Kingdom.

The importance of the large, expanding market which the Federal Republic offered was underlined by the protectionism and slow growth of the British market in the same period. If we measure the extent of import penetration into the two economies over the period 1950–8, excluding agricultural imports, it can be seen that in the United Kingdom this reached a peak in 1951 from which it was subsequently brought down by trade controls to a low point in 1955. From there the upward trend was too slow to have brought it back to its 1950 level by 1958. In the Federal Republic levels of import penetration were much lower over the period 1950–3 and then moved upwards on a gradually rising trend so that over the period 1955–8 they were higher than in the United Kingdom.[59]

---

[58] 'Le commerce extérieur de l'Allemagne depuis 1954', in *Etudes et Conjoncture*, 1959, op. cit.

Between 1952 and 1958 when the value of imports of metalworking machinery into the Federal Republic rose by $25.4 million, imports into the United Kingdom of goods in the same category fell by $109.6 million. Into all other ECSC countries they rose by $11.2 million, and into all other OEEC countries (excluding both the United Kingdom and the Federal Republic) by $9.6 million. The increase in value of German imports of mining, construction and other industrial machinery (SITC 716) over the same period was $145.8 million, compared to an increase in imports of the same category into the United Kingdom of only $91.6 million. In a somewhat different market, sales of office machinery to the Federal Republic in that period rose by $25.1 million, 67 per cent of the increase coming from Western Europe, which was one-quarter of the total increase in imports of goods of this category into all OEEC countries. For non-electrical machinery as a whole (SITC 71) the increase in imports into the Federal Republic accounted for 22.3 per cent of the increase in imports into Western Europe, with 18.9 per cent of this increase originating in OEEC Europe itself.

The effect of Germany's replacement of the British market is probably best observed in the Netherlands, the corresponding changes in whose commercial policy are analysed in the following section. The relationship between these changes in the pattern of trade and the rapid process of Dutch industrialization after 1945 may however be briefly noted here. The fact that the Netherlands became the greatest European supplier of electrical machinery to the Federal Republic should be seen in the wider context where exports of non-electrical machinery and transport equipment (SITC 71 + 73) to the Federal Republic rose from 0.5 per cent of all exports by value in 1951 to 1.9 per cent in 1958. The Netherlands had no car industry to swell this figure and of all the Western European countries it is probably the most striking example of modernization and industrialization depending on an ever-closer attachment to Germany. It explains much of the reorientation of Dutch foreign policy away from attachment to the United Kingdom.

The German market provided an equally powerful stimulus to exports of metals and this was of prime importance to the process of industrial development in France. Imports of base metals from Western Europe, the largest component being steel, more than doubled in value between 1953 and 1956. The slowness in the recovery of German steel output up to 1950 and the bottleneck in supply which resulted, together with the steep increase in domestic demand, caused a suspension of steel tariffs in mid-

[59] Import penetration is estimated as $\frac{M}{N+M-X}$ where M = imports in current values excluding all agricultural imports, N = value of domestic output excluding all agricultural output, and X = value of exports in current values excluding agricultural exports. By this measure the average ratio of penetration of imports of manufactures and raw materials into the United Kingdom over the period 1950–3 was 0.399, over the period 1955–8 0.306. The corresponding figures for West Germany are 0.266 and 0.337.

1952, before the common market of the ECSC was formally initiated. Over the next three years there was an increase in annual net steel imports from the ECSC of 1.2 million tonnes. The main suppliers were Belgium–Luxembourg, the traditional exporter, and France. This was the largest increase in value of imports into Germany of any single category of goods and an important part of the increase in French exports to Germany. The access to southern German markets for their steel exports, for which the French had manoeuvred in the negotiations for the Coal and Steel Community, was hardly something Germany would have wished to resist by 1952. In the great boom of 1954–7 German steel remained in short supply. The big post-war investments in France in continuous strip-rolling mills, on which the first Plan had laid such heavy emphasis, were justified by their large and valuable exports to Germany. They were to provide the thin steel sheet from which the ever-increasing spate of Volkswagen exports was made.

The pattern of the Federal Republic's trade in the most rapidly growing sectors could thus be characterized as a dynamic growth of both imports and exports of which two-thirds was focused on Western Europe and which was closely linked to the rapid industrialization of much of the Western European area in that period. The trade deficit with the dollar zone increased threefold over the period 1951–7, while the surplus with Western Europe increased by about three and a half times. At the same time Germany provided the main market for the new manufactured products of Western Europe's industrialization. In doing this it was taking over the role of mid- and late nineteenth-century Britain.

One measure of comparison of the importance of this openness is to estimate the rate of growth of European exports in two of the most rapidly growing manufacturing sectors to the Federal Republic, to Britain, and to a large protectionist economy with a smaller manufacturing capacity such as France. This is done in table 4.16. Single very large export orders in one year can make so great a difference to the annual index number for small economies, whose trade in these commodities was still at a relatively low level, that some have been omitted from the table. The figure for Italian exports of SITC 7 products to Germany in 1957 is not however a freak number, but fairly represents the trend of Italian exports in this category, which surged so remarkably at the end of the decade. The picture which emerges is clear. In these two sectors, where output and productivity were improving especially rapidly, the German market was not only a much greater stimulus to export growth from the other Western European countries than the British or French markets, but after 1954 it was increasingly so. The superior rate of productivity improvement in German manufacturing industry compared to the United Kingdom may to some extent have been a function of the greater openness of German manufacturing to competition on the domestic market. That, though, would open up another subject.

A combination of long-run development trends and new post-war policies in western Europe and Germany made the Federal Republic indispensable to the rescue of the European nation-state. This rescue had
come to depend on a country that was not really yet a country, without
full national sovereignty until 1955, an artificial creation whose future was
highly uncertain, still the subject of a possible deal between America and
Russia, and still deeply distrusted. It mattered little that the European
Defence Community failed, for it would never have been capable of
guaranteeing that the Federal Republic would stay in place. It met neither
the needs of the Germans nor the other Europeans. It was commercially,
as the pivot of West European trade that West Germany had to be bound
in place, and it was this necessity, particularly as the trade boom accelerated after 1953, that gave increasing force to the idea of the customs
union.

THE SIX AS A TRADE NETWORK

Underlying and accompanying the reshaping of Europe's trade by the
Federal Republic can be seen a separate tendency for foreign trade between the six member countries of the ECSC to grow faster than foreign
trade elsewhere in Europe. Tables 4.17 to 4.20 show the growth in the
period before the Treaties of Rome of exports from ECSC members except
the Federal Republic to other members of the Community in comparison
to the growth of their exports to the United Kingdom and to the smaller
non-ECSC trade-dependent countries. This gives a closer picture of the
commercial background to the Treaties of Rome. Whereas for every ECSC
country except the Federal Republic the share of exports going to the
British market shrank, the share going to the ECSC market increased, and
as the tables show this was not merely a function of the increase in exports
to the Federal Republic. During the great trade boom after 1954 the rate of
growth of Belgian exports to France and to the Netherlands was as fast as
to the Federal Republic. The same is true for Italian exports to France and
to the Netherlands and for Dutch exports to Italy. Although exports from
the ECSC countries to the smaller non-ECSC countries grew rapidly, they
grew even more rapidly within the ECSC itself. The share of these non-
ECSC countries in French exports hardly varied and their share in Belgian
exports fell.

The geographical pattern of Western Europe's foreign trade thus began
to resemble before 1957 the pattern which has sometimes been regarded as
the result of the creation of the common market itself and the trade which
it generated. It is not in doubt that the common market after its creation
did generate either an increase in trade or a diversion of existing trade.
However, some studies which have shown that there was a significant
increase in trade between the member states of the EEC as a result of
the tariff changes incorporated in the Treaties of Rome, tend to

Table 4.16 Indices of export growth of chemicals (SITC 5) and machinery and transport equipment (SITC 7) of Western European countries to the Federal Republic, the United Kingdom and France, 1951–7 (1953 = 100) (by value)

Exporter	To: Federal Republic			United Kingdom			France		
	1951	1954	1957	1951	1954	1957	1951	1954	1957
Austria									
SITC 5	105	139	223	228	283	486	299	224	307
SITC 7	107	146	342	119	107	199	147	139	257
Belgium–Lux.									
SITC 5	152	163	174	175	87	112	137	121	204
SITC 7	89	129	223	98	72	164	114	104	166
Denmark									
SITC 5	72	75	150	132	110	266	84	111	141
SITC 7	42	112	399	49	141	124	115	85	87
Italy									
SITC 5	106	291	343	178	178	101	106	137	200
SITC 7	84	106	412	73	56	153	80	149	230
Netherlands									
SITC 5	73	135	267	122	81	112	103	110	257
SITC 7	56	126	399	76	161	447	147	80	75
Sweden									
SITC 5	66	131	153	174	144	354	196	136	155
SITC 7	80	114	178	56	105	137	69	108	158
Switzerland									
SITC 5	62	95	133	121	135	189	110	107	126
SITC 7	67	111	214	71	100	121	100	106	134

Source: OEEC, Statistical Bulletins of Foreign Trade, Series IV

Table 4.17 Index of comparative growth of exports of Belgium–Luxembourg to ECSC and other countries, 1951–6 (1953 = 100) (by value)

Importing country	1951	1953	1956
France	137.1	100	192.8
German Federal Republic	76.0	100	153.2
Italy	73.6	100	86.0
Netherlands	117.3	100	172.4
As % of total exports	35.2	38.0	44.5
United Kingdom	150.4	100	115.2
As % of total exports	10.0	7.7	6.4
Austria	177.2	100	111.3
Switzerland	169.6	100	161.9
Denmark	93.7	100	107.8
Norway	118.2	100	111.6
Sweden	133.4	100	123.0
As % of total exports	12.4	10.7	9.7

Source: OEEC, *Statistical Bulletins of Foreign Trade*, Series II and IV

Table 4.18 Index of comparative growth of exports from France to ECSC and other countries, 1951–6 (1953 = 100) (by value)

Importing country	1951	1953	1956
Belgium–Luxembourg	100.5	100	146.5
German Federal Republic	70.9	100	168.7
Italy	77.1	100	144.0
Netherlands	188.6	100	144.4
As % of total exports	15.4	18.5	24.8
United Kingdom	161.6	100	130.4
As % of total exports	8.1	5.3	6.0
Austria	144.8	100	177.9
Switzerland	134.6	100	184.2
Denmark	157.4	100	134.8
Norway	118.2	100	130.2
Sweden	117.2	100	98.0
As % of total exports	8.6	6.9	8.9

Source: OEEC, *Statistical Bulletins of Foreign Trade*, Series II and IV

Table 4.19   Index of comparative growth of exports from Italy to ECSC and other countries, 1951–6 (1953 = 100) (by value)

Importing country	1951	1953	1956
Belgium–Luxembourg	102.4	100	130.0
France	188.4	100	195.1
German Federal Republic	76.6	100	173.2
Netherlands	118.6	100	189.9
As % of total exports	21.1	20.6	25.3
United Kingdom	203.2	100	127.8
As % of total exports	13.5	7.2	6.5
Austria	81.8	100	188.1
Switzerland	89.7	100	156.5
Denmark	84.0	100	102.9
Norway	139.4	100	135.0
Sweden	95.4	100	118.0
As % of total exports	12.0	14.4	15.0

Source: OEEC, *Statistical Bulletins of Foreign Trade*, Series II and IV

Table 4.20   Index of comparative growth of exports from the Netherlands to ECSC and other countries, 1951–6 (1953 = 100) (by value)

Importing country	1951	1953	1956
Belgium–Luxembourg	85.9	100	122.4
France	91.1	100	166.2
German Federal Republic	90.0	100	172.1
Italy	68.2	100	179.5
As % of total exports	34.4	35.7	40.7
United Kingdom	90.1	100	146.8
As % of total exports	15.9	10.7	11.7
Austria	127.1	100	223.5
Switzerland	88.5	100	140.9
Denmark	57.6	100	110.4
Norway	96.7	100	123.9
Sweden	87.1	100	148.7
As % of total exports	9.5	11.3	11.9

Source: OEEC, *Statistical Bulletins of Foreign Trade*, Series II and IV

underestimate, because of the methods they use, the remarkable increase in trade between those same countries over the three years before they signed the treaty.

The difficulty is to find normal years between which to measure. The solution adopted by Walter in his discussion of this problem was to compare the growth of intra-trade between these countries over the periods 1953–8 and 1958–63.[60] But a more detailed short-term analysis indicates that the geographical pattern of trade which became identified with the common market began in 1954. Inclusion of the year 1953 in any comparative measurement will inevitably make any increase in intra-trade in the period after the Treaties of Rome appear greater compared to the pre-common market period. This is even more the case, as Walter readily admits, if the year 1958 is included in the first of the two periods for comparison. This was a year of recession with a rate of growth of foreign trade which was clearly abnormally low for the period, so that the statistical outcome of such a comparison has much less force as a demonstration of the effects of the initial stages of the common market than is claimed. That is not to deny that the common market did have a powerful effect on increasing the value of trade between its signatories. But this increase in their trade was a continuity in which the Treaties of Rome and their subsequent implementation were stages.

The growth of trade between the Six did not follow a uniform pattern; it would be more enlightening to view it in terms of separate, especially expanding trades. Two may be singled out as of special importance economically and politically. One, by magnitude the most important, was the trade triangle between the Benelux and the Federal Republic. If Belgium–Luxembourg's exports to the Federal Republic grew more slowly than those of the Netherlands this has to be seen in a context where the Netherlands remained, as it had become during the reconstruction, the main market for Belgium–Luxembourg's manufactures (as it was for those of Germany), while the Federal Republic and Belgium became the main market for new Dutch manufactures and for increasing quantities of Dutch food. In 1956 Belgium–Luxembourg and the Federal Republic together accounted for 32.4 per cent of the value of Dutch exports. The high Dutch demand for imports from Belgium depended on German demand for Dutch exports, so that Belgium–Luxembourg was an indirect beneficiary of Germany's role, but the triangular pattern created also strengthened intra-Benelux trade.

Secondly, the growth of Italian exports was one of the more remarkable aspects of Western Europe's foreign trade in the period and to this growth the Six were particularly important. After 1955 the rate of growth of Italian exports was much faster even than those of Germany. The basis for that

[60] I. Walter, *The European Common Market. Growth and Patterns of Trade and Production* (New York, 1967).

growth was the fall in their price, absolutely and even more so relatively to the prices of other exporters. This was not because of the improving world terms of trade for raw material and foodstuff exporters. The share of those categories in Italian exports did not increase. The share of the Italian mechanical engineering industry in total exports, by contrast, increased from 20.4 per cent in 1953 to 25.8 per cent in 1957 and to 32.0 per cent in 1960. Over the same period the OEEC price indices for total exports show a fall in Italian export prices from 100 to 95 and then to 87. The export price index produced by the Italian Central Statistical Office for manufactures containing a large element of labour, many of which were finished manufactures, fell even more steeply, from 100 to 89.6 and then to 84.4 over the same period. The level of the overall export price index was in fact higher because of the influence of raw material and food prices, which in Italy actually increased in price against the tendency of the world movement in the terms of trade.

Some of the growth in exports of finished manufactures was in textiles, clothing products and shoes, labour-intensive industries where Italy had the advantage of lower wages. But engineering, where Italy had the most rapid increase in physical productivity per man hour, was far more important in absolute value and also in its relative rate of growth. By the later 1950s this had been transformed into an Italian competitive advantage in consumer durables. Only Spain of the countries in western Europe had a similar fall in export prices, but the structure of its exports was far too unsophisticated to compete with Italy.[61] The advantage which Italian machinery and consumer durables had in Western European markets was reflected in the high export ratios by the mid-1950s for cars, motorcycles, typewriters and calculating machines.[62] For cars and motorcycles about a third of the output was being exported by 1957. In 1951 21.1 per cent of Italian exports by value went to ECSC countries, this proportion had risen to 25.0 per cent in 1956, and to 28.5 per cent by 1958. Demand from the Six was probably effecting a shift in the commodity composition of Italian and other exports, independently of the same response to the German market alone.

Confirming this are trends in the export of machinery and transport equipment (SITC 7). Exports of goods in that category to the Six were 2.5 per cent of the value of the total exports of Belgium–Luxembourg, France, Italy and the Netherlands in 1951. In 1956 this percentage had increased to 4.3 per cent. Of this share the percentage accounted for by exports to the Federal Republic rose from 0.33 per cent to 0.75 per cent. The average growth rates of GNP in the ECSC countries tended, except for Belgium, to

[61] A.S. Milward, 'El sector exterior en la expansión de los años cincuenta: comparación de las exportaciones españolas, italianas y portuguesas', in L. Prados de la Escosura and V. Zamagni (eds), *El desarrollo económico en la Europa del Sur: España e Italia en perspectiva histórica* (Madrid, 1992).

[62] V. Cao-Pinna (ed.), *Le esportazioni italiane* (Turin, 1965), p. 27.

be higher than elsewhere in Europe and the three large economies which were members showed especially high growth rates. But the detailed exploration of trade in capital goods in the preceding section shows that it would be far too simple to see the rapidity of growth of exports within the ECSC market, compared for example to the growth of exports of the same countries to the United Kingdom (which are also shown in tables 4.17 to 4.20), as merely a function of differences in the rate of growth of manufacturing output or of differences in the propensity to import which were themselves merely a function of differences in the rate of growth of GNP. Across the decade, imports into slow-growing Belgium tended to grow faster from the Six, with or without Germany, than from the EFTA countries, with or without the United Kingdom. It reflected the same tendencies towards greater specialization and an increased technological competitiveness, perhaps also to scale economies, as did the growth of trade with the Federal Republic. The growth of Italian exports and the change in their commodity structure is evidence enough of that. Later in the book in chapter 7 we shall consider the impact on the foreign trade of the United Kingdom of its much smaller degree of involvement in these trade circuits.

THE NETHERLANDS AND THE ORIGINS OF THE COMMON MARKET

How were these commercial trends reflected in commercial policy? Their impact can best be shown by an account of the way that commercial policy in the Netherlands, the most trade-dependent of the Western European economies and the one whose dependence on the Federal Republic increased the most, gradually changed to take account of the new circumstances, so that this change came eventually also to alter the whole stance of Dutch policy.

Although the Netherlands was always included in the early French proposals for a customs union, as a serious objective of Dutch policy itself the idea of a West European customs union can be traced back no earlier than late 1952. The Dutch in fact remained firm opponents of the earlier French schemes, regarding them as attempts to create a west European power bloc dominated by France. The view still prevailed within the Dutch government that security required an Atlantic cooperation with Britain and the United States and that membership of any purely continental bloc had very little to offer. One measure of the power of the economic forces which were reshaping western Europe is the shortness of the period over which the Netherlands abandoned this position.

The essence of this change was the redefinition of the concept of security to emphasize economic rather than military security. Before 1955 military security looked in any case almost impossible to achieve. With only a very small army and with no other forces between its frontier and the Red Army other than a few Allied occupation troops in Germany, a land defence against a possible Soviet attack looked out of the question. The feeling that it was so was strengthened by knowledge of early American and NATO strategic plans. Initially, these were to not defend the Netherlands at all and later only to defend about one-third of its territory. American pressure on the Netherlands in 1950–1 to rearm by creating a substantial land army provoked searching questions about the real meaning of security. After 1945 Dutch rearmament had been mainly concentrated on rebuilding the navy. American demands to divert scarce resources into rearmament for a land war were strongly called into question across almost the whole spectrum of Dutch politics, especially when backed up by threats to withdraw Marshall Aid if the Dutch government did not comply. Did not, many members of the governing coalition and the majority Labour Party asked themselves, extra expenditure on rearmament actually endanger security by endangering economic security? Where did the real danger lie? In a land attack by the Soviet Union? Or in losing the battle for reconstruction and thus the economic and social competition with the Soviet system? Many, including prime minister Willem Drees, gave the second answer.[63]

The shift of opinion in favour of a much wider definition of security to embrace long-run economic security coincided with American and French pressures to participate in the European Defence Community, something to which the Netherlands was unwilling fully to commit itself until a year after the French first proposed it in October 1950. It led to Dutch demands for an economic as well as a military foundation for the supranational structure of the European Political Community (EPC) which was to be brought into being at the same time as the Defence Community. The Dutch terms for accession to the European Political Community became that its basis should be a customs union. To understand how this proposal could arise after so much earlier opposition to similar French proposals it is necessary to consider more closely the precise grounds for that earlier opposition.

When in 1945 the Dutch government together with its Benelux partners signed with France the Agreement on Mutual Economic Consultation (*Accord Economique de Consultation Mutuel*) its motive was to gain greater influence over the policy of the occupying powers in Germany. In January 1946 when the French proposed that this group should produce plans for a customs union or, alternatively, a preferential trade area, it was the Dutch who led the opposition, arguing that no such area could benefit the Netherlands unless it were much larger and would also include

---

[63] Willem Drees, 1886–1990: bank clerk, 1903–06; shorthand writer in the States-General, 1906–19; socialist leader of the city council of the Hague 1913–41; interned in Buchenwald concentration camp 1940–1; minister of social security and deputy minister-president, 1945–8; minister-president, 1948–58. An architect of the Dutch welfare state. He alarmed his ministers by making rapid shorthand notes of their comments in cabinet. A man of pacifist tendencies, he was married to the same person for 64 years.

Germany itself.[64] The French again proposed talks on creating a future customs union between France and Benelux during the meetings of the Committee of European Economic Cooperation (CEEC) in 1947, partly to comply with American insistence on integration as the price for Marshall Aid. The Italian government, moved by similar motives, had also proposed a customs union between Italy and France. The French, while accepting participation in negotiations with Italy and using this to good propaganda purpose in Washington, were uninterested in a customs union with Italy alone. Their objective, as in the 1946 proposals, was to create an economic area wide enough to provide protection against a future Germany.

With everything still undecided about the future of Germany and with the Dutch, as well as the Belgians, not so much interested in controlling Germany and keeping it weak as in restoring it economically as quickly as possible, the proposals could, once more, go no further. They petered out in the Study Group for a European Customs Union which never got further than a bland examination of the technical aspects of tariffs.[65] The separate Franco–Italian negotiations got as far as a draft treaty for a customs union, proclaimed as the future with much accompanying propaganda in Cavour's former house in Turin. They were never to reach the French national assembly. The draft treaty was in fact far too protectionist to be used as propaganda for the support of either country for American objectives.

The French initiatives did however concentrate the minds of the Dutch as to what the conditions for a western European customs union should be if it was to serve Dutch national interests. Two conditions had been judged to be necessary. Firstly, both Britain and Germany would have to be members. Secondly, the external tariffs would not have to be higher than any external tariff eventually arrived at by the Benelux customs union.

Dutch policy was further clarified when the French, in response to the American demand in OEEC in October 1949 for further progress towards integration, came forward with a modified version of their earlier proposals. Now they suggested a multilateral payments association with Benelux and Italy which would be tied to a special programme between those countries for the removal of non-tariff barriers. The OEEC had accepted a British programme of mutual phased removal of quotas. An important point in the new French proposals was that participants in the proposed payments association would remove non-tariff barriers on their intra-trade faster than the general trade liberalization programme within OEEC. As far as the Dutch were concerned, this would only bring forward

[64] R.T. Griffiths and F.M.B. Lynch, 'L'échec de la "Petite Europe": Le Conseil Tripartite, 1944–1948', in *Guerres mondiales et conflits contemporains*, no. 252, 1988.

[65] The French approach to Benelux in CEEC is discussed in A.S. Milward, *The Reconstruction* . . ., op. cit., pp. 232 ff. The best account of the Franco–Italian customs union negotiations is P. Guillen, 'Les vicissitudes des rapports franco-italiens de la rencontre de Cannes (décembre 1948) à celle de Santa Margherita (février, 1951)', and E. Serra, 'L'unione doganale italo-francese e la Conferenza di Santa Margherita (1947–1951)', in J.B. Duroselle and E. Serra (eds), *Italia e Francia 1946–1954* (Milan, 1988).

the moment at which the existing high French and Italian tariffs would again become effective. This would accentuate what they saw as the inherent unfairness toward low-tariff countries of the OEEC trade liberalization programme; it would allow large protectionist countries like Britain and France to bring their tariffs into operation while forcing the removal or widening of small countries' quota restrictions. Although the French were prepared to give guarantees that quotas once removed would not be replaced by new tariffs, they rebuffed any suggestion that they should lower existing tariffs, maintaining that these were strictly the province of GATT. Initially the Dutch pressed for the inclusion of both Britain and Germany in the proposed payments association.[66] It was very quickly made clear by the British however that they would not participate.

The OEEC trade liberalization programme took little account of the commercial interests of a country like the Netherlands. It excluded all imports on government account from the liberalization process and so penalized exporters of agricultural products. Most of the food imports into the two biggest food markets in Europe, Britain and Germany, were on government account. In Britain food importing was mostly done by the government. In occupied Germany it was done by the agencies of the Military Governments. After the foundation of the Federal Republic it was eventually done by committees of farmers and civil servants who were classified by OEEC as importing on government account. Food exports constituted about 40 per cent of the value of all Dutch exports. Furthermore, because the base year for calculating the percentage of potential trade excluded by quotas was 1948 and for Germany 1949, Germany, whose imports had been low in that year could easily satisfy the initial requirements of the programme without much increase in its imports, even where these were in private hands. Escape clauses for countries encountering balance of payments difficulties while implementing the programme were also generous. They would be invoked by Britain in late 1951 and by France in early 1952. In spite of the trade liberalization programme, the three largest potential markets in Western Europe remained closed to many of Holland's new manufactured and old agricultural exports.

The programme threatened to deal severely with Holland's own attempts to industrialize. It foresaw the removal of 50 per cent of quota restrictions on the total value of 1948 imports by December 1949, 60 per cent by June 1950, and 75 per cent by December 1950.[67] Initially countries were only required to meet these targets on total trade, so that the percentage figure could be reached while keeping quotas on foodstuffs, providing there was a wide range of other quotas which could be removed.

[66] R.T. Griffiths and F.M.B. Lynch, 'L'échec de la "Petite Europe": les négociations Fritalux/Finebel, 1949–1950', in *Revue historique*, vol. cclxxiv, no. 1, 1985.

[67] The best account is W. Diebold, Jnr, *Trade and Payments . . .*, op. cit. The Dutch participation is discussed in J.M.M.J. Clerx, *Nederland en de liberalisatie van het handels-en betalingsverkeer (1945–1958)* (Groningen, 1986).

In conditions of industrial boom it was normal for countries to remove quantitative restrictions on raw material imports. Most economies also had numerous quotas on manufactures which served no useful purpose because they were appropriate only to the world of the 1930s. As a competitive agricultural exporter the Netherlands had had little need of quotas on foodstuffs and its quotas on manufactures were often the result of post-war industrialization policies. In order to reach the percentage targets for quota removal the Netherlands would have to start removing them over a wide range of manufacturing which it wanted to encourage; iron and steel products, agricultural machinery, aluminium, synthetic fabrics, fertilizers, plastics, detergents, telephones, cars, lorries, and typewriters.[68] At the same time the 40 per cent of its own exports which were agricultural produce scarcely benefited. It is no wonder that the Netherlands was the last OEEC country to subscribe to the trade liberalization programme.

The situation was made more difficult as it became clear by 1950 that the hopes of a worldwide reduction in tariffs held out at Bretton Woods would only be realized to a limited extent by GATT. The tariffs registered at the GATT conference in Annecy in 1949 were generally high and, although for the most part intended as bargaining positions, they were beginning to become operative in 1950 as quotas began to be removed and there was no particularly good prospect of reducing them at the next GATT conference to be held in Torquay in that year. The Torquay conference made it clear that in a worldwide organization like GATT protectionist interests would always have a strong voice, because these were the preponderant interests in the less-developed world, and also because, for all its fine rhetoric, the United States administration saw all pressures to reduce tariffs through concerted action in GATT as presenting a domestic political problem which it preferred itself not to face, whatever it called on others to do.

Table 4.21 can give no exact indication of the effective level of protection in any of the economies, and says nothing about the protection of particular goods, but it does show that the historical pattern of a low-tariff group of small countries in western Europe faced with relatively protectionist larger economies, which had persisted since the late 1870s, was once more emerging after the Second World War. The only change in the pattern had been that Britain had joined the protectionists. The low-tariff group's struggles in the inter-war period through the Ouchy and Oslo agreements, in which the Netherlands had been an active participant, to create its own trading links and influence the higher-tariff countries, had been squashed by the demands of the larger countries that most-favoured-nation treatment continue to be extended to them on the basis of earlier agreements. Memories of this strongly suggested that collective action on tariffs after 1945 would not improve the bargaining prospect.

In table 4.21 the Benelux tariff rates have been used, because by 1951

[68] W. Asbeek Brusse, 'The Stikker Plan', in R.T. Griffiths (ed.), *The Netherlands and the Integration of Europe 1945–1957* (Amsterdam, 1990).

Table 4.21 Average *ad valorem* percentage incidence of import duties, 1952

	Benelux	Denmark	Sweden	Norway	Federal German Republic	United Kingdom	France	Italy
cotton, yarn and thread	4	1	2	7	16	13	17	25
synthetic yarn and thread	11	11	6	14	19	41	18	28
newsprint	10	0	0	n.a.	12	10	25	17
rubber tyres and tubes	24	12	17	6	30	27	19	24
woollen and worsted fabrics	16	4	6	21	22	21	18	22
plate glass	16	14	12	34	25	12	20	31
internal combustion engines	9	1	4	19	15	16	18	26
tractors	9	5	10	1	20	23	22	36
machine tools	6	5	7	17	9	18	16	17
cars	24	7	15	30	32	33	30	40
bicycles	18	6	23	37	15	20	30	50
clothing	24	6	11	26	24	24	23	28
watches and parts	9	10	3	6	14	33	15	7
toys and games	18	8	15	19	20	23	32	33

Sources: UN, ECE, *Economic Survey of Europe in 1956*, ch. IV, p. 15

the remaining differences between Dutch and Belgian external tariffs were small. The German tariff is the one that emerged from the Torquay conference and it should be borne in mind that it was reduced for many products after 1951 as the Federal Republic's dependence on manufactured imports became clearer. It can be seen that over the range of sample manufactures Benelux, Denmark and Sweden had a much lower level of tariffs than other countries. Norway displayed a different, but still relatively typical, post-war pattern for a small country by heavily protecting certain development sectors of its economy while maintaining only revenue tariffs on others. The larger economies were all in comparison very protectionist, except where, as in the case for example of the Italian watch industry, they had nothing to protect.

The difficulty was made worse by the fact that in the first post-war years the Netherlands had the most intractable balance of payments deficit in Western Europe. This was accentuated by its small number and value of dollar-earning exports, although American aid made a large contribution to closing the gap. The outcome of numerous disputes in a divided government during those years was usually that existing import levels should be maintained, even when in 1947 Marshall Aid was still uncertain and its quantity unguessable, because the general aim of developing a more sophisticated industrial structure for the Dutch economy in the post-war world was an overriding one.[69] The level of gross fixed industrial investment did not drop in 1948. It was 9.8 per cent of national income at factor cost in current prices in spite of the acute balance of payments difficulties.[70] The long-term goal of reducing the overall weight of the agricultural sector as an employer and an export earner was a pervasive influence on economic policy.[71] The pursuit of these objectives, to which after much resistance a greater commitment to rearmament had to be added in 1951, inevitably meant an increase in imports. These rose as a share of national income from less than 33 per cent over the years 1947–9 to more than 40 per cent in 1950–1.[72]

The main hope of reversing the balance of payments deficits lay in the lower manufacturing costs of the Netherlands. Like Italy, Holland was a relatively low-wage economy. As non-tariff barriers elsewhere began to be removed and high tariffs again came into effective operation it seemed essential that if this hope was to be realized European tariffs would have to come down. The need for this was accentuated by Belgian insistence, strong in 1949 and 1950, that the Benelux customs union itself should become a reality rather than a promise.

[69] P. van der Eng, *De Marshall-Hulp: een perspectief voor Nederland 1947–1953* (Houten, 1987).

[70] K.G. Groot, *De Financiering van de industrialisatie in Nederland* (Leiden, 1957), p. 79.

[71] P.E. de Hen, *Actieve en re-actieve industriepolitiek in Nederland* (Amsterdam, 1980); H. de Liagre Böhl, *et al.* (eds), *Nederland industrialiseert!* (Nijmegen, 1981).

[72] J.L. van Zanden and R.T. Griffiths, *Economische geschiedenis van Nederland in de 20e eeuw* (The Hague, 1989), p. 191.

The Benelux union stands as the first and best example of the super-fluousness of tariffs to the smaller post-war western economies. The three governments in exile having agreed during the war on a post-war economic union as a way of exercising a greater influence on Allied policy, particularly over Germany, found that the easiest aspect of this was to remove the tariffs between their countries and agree on a common external tariff. It made little difference to their mutual trade or to their economies. Indeed, it would be hard to find between 1945 and 1951 two countries where domestic economic policies were more different than those of Belgium and Holland. Trade between them remained severely restricted by Duch quotas, by radically different fiscal measures including big differences in excises, and by the resolute non-tariff protection of Belgian agriculture against Dutch food exports.[73] Here, too, under the OEEC programme Holland would have to sacrifice its quotas on manufactured imports while Belgium would keep most of its food quotas. Yet the Dutch trade deficit with Belgium–Luxembourg was the most persistent and in per capita terms the most serious in intra-Western-European trade in the post-war years, requiring large transferable export earnings in Germany or Britain for its settlement.

Table 4.22   The balance of trade and balance of payments of the Netherlands, 1946–60 ($ million)

	Balance of trade	*Balance of payments*
1946	−501.3	−494.5
1947	−693.1	−628.3
1948	−607.6	−428.1
1949	−359.9	−75.5
1950	−456.0	−280.5
1951	−275.2	−23.6
1952	+162.1	+492.1
1953	+39.2	+358.1
1954	−226.6	+65.9
1955	−173.4	+212.0
1956	−494.2	−184.1
1957	−459.4	−145.1
1958	+31.9	+416.0
1959	+19.6	+486.7
1960	−107.3	+318.9

Source: IMF, *Balance of Payments Yearbook*

One way forward seemed to be to tie the question of tariff reduction to the trade liberalization programme. This was the way chosen by the Plan of Action proposed by foreign minister Dirk Stikker to the OEEC in June 1950. This found its origin in an intensive consideration of the difficult

[73] J.E. Meade, *et al.*, *Case Studies in European Economic Union* (London, 1962), pp. 61 ff.

Dutch situation in Europe by the Ministry of Economic Affairs from April onwards. Stikker's Plan of Action proposed a method for freeing trade from quotas and tariffs together through a lengthy process of 'sectoral integration', a concept which it was hoped would be seen as building on the sectoral nature of the Schuman proposals. It proposed that OEEC undertake detailed comparative studies, industry by industry, of Western European manufacturing with a view to equalizing costs within sectors and so eventually allowing tariff and quota removal sector by sector until a genuine and complete liberalization of trade in manufactures had been achieved. What would then have been the level of the external protection around this free trade area in manufactures was left unclear. Although OEEC did undertake pilot studies of this kind few governments showed enthusiasm. The British government was particularly unwelcoming and Stikker seems to have blamed the eventual failure of his proposals on the British attitude.[74]

Their weaknesses, however, were inherent. Holding lengthy inquiries into single industries was an open invitation to businessmen to lobby against the removal of protection, which in fact Dutch industrialists themselves were not slow to do. To launch such a programme effectively it would have been essential to find an industry which could be liberalized across the whole of the OEEC area without there being a serious loser; for Stikker was prepared to accept only very limited financial support for such losers. Such an industry might well not have existed. Certainly OEEC did not find one.[75] Such a programme would in any case have taken an extremely long time to complete as it approached industries where production costs and import prices were wider apart and where the real benefits of free trade were to be reaped. Stikker's own liberal leanings, on which the Plan of Action was optimistically based, were by no means so prevalent in some other small economies, such as Norway or Austria, more inclined to persevere with economic controls. If the sectoral proposals had any chance at all it was not over the whole OEEC area but between the countries in the contemporaneous ECSC negotiations. That idea did emerge, for in those negotiations between the Six the Dutch were realizing that they had considerable political leverage. But Stikker himself would not countenance it.

Stikker's proposals coincided with a brief phase of liberalism in France associated with the increase in dollar earnings in 1950. In November the French proposed Western European tariff reductions on 80 per cent of trade, to be achieved by a cut in tariff levels of 10 per cent annually for five years. The Dutch had a valid objection to this: it was a procedure evidently favouring countries which started from a higher level of minimum tariffs. It

---

[74] D.U. Stikker, *Memoires, Herinneringen uit de lange jaren waarin ik betrokken was bij de voortdurende wereldcrisis* (The Hague, 1966), p. 166.

[75] The OEEC studies began with paper and pulp and with textiles, proceeding to cement, nitrogenous fertilizers and plate glass.

did, though, much more than the Plan of Action, take into account the realities of post-war policy. The exemption of 20 per cent of all trade was intended to provide for infant industries such as those the French and Dutch had been protecting by quotas. For this to be acceptable to the Dutch, the 20 per cent of goods excepted would have had to be equally spread over the three different categories, of manufactures, raw materials, and agricultural products, in order to prevent a blanket tariff protection against Dutch agricultural exports reinforcing the existing inequities of the trade liberalization programme.

More of France's own foreign trade was classified as state trade (34 per cent of its West European trade in 1952) and thus as outside the scope of the OEEC trade liberalization programme, than that of any other participating country. Quota removal up to the 75 per cent level within that programme would still have affected only about one-quarter of total French imports at their 1950 level. Automatic tariff reductions, from which 20 per cent of commodities could be excluded, would have hardly breached French protection, when quotas were still so extensive.

The quiet burial given to Stikker's Plan of Action left the Netherlands with only two small consolations. The OEEC accepted that the 75 per cent mark in the trade liberalization programme could be postponed beyond February 1951 in the Dutch case because of the effect on Dutch exports of German import restrictions, themselves recommended by the OEEC; and the OEEC acknowledged also that high tariffs did tend to nullify the effects of quota removal. This did not offer any prospect of real political action in OEEC to bring tariffs down, but it did provide the opportunity for a set of joint Benelux proposals for tariff reduction to GATT in early 1951. The essential point in these proposals was that the low-tariff countries should offer to bind their tariffs at their existing levels for some years in return for tariff reductions by the high-tariff countries.[76]

As with Stikker's proposals in 1950 it was an obvious weakness that the Benelux was not speaking for all low-tariff countries in Western Europe. Even to present an agreed set of Benelux proposals had proved difficult enough. After the devaluation of the guilder in 1949 by more than the Belgian franc, Dutch wage-rates were on average 40 per cent lower than those in Belgium. In spite of the gradual relaxation after 1952 of the strict control of wages in the Netherlands this disparity reduced only slowly. A uniform lowering of tariffs which still left most countries' tariffs higher than those of Belgium, where manufacturing costs were greater, was not a particularly appealing policy in Brussels, and it was especially unappealing as long as Dutch tax policy and direct controls continued to limit the flow of Belgian exports to their main market, even though that was the one market where Belgian exporters did not face a tariff. Seen from Brussels the Plan

---

[76] R.T. Griffiths, 'The Abortive Dutch Assault on European Tariffs 1950–1952', in M. Wintle (ed.), *Modern Dutch Studies. Essays in Honour of Professor P. King* (London, 1988).

of Action looked like a device to make everyone reduce tariffs while allowing the Netherlands itself to maintain its quotas and fiscal barriers against Belgian exports.

Even with a stronger common front between the Netherlands and Belgium, even with more support from other small European economies, it was unlikely that these proposals to GATT could have achieved anything. The Americans did show some sympathy, but only up to the point where it was suggested that tariff negotiations become part of the activities of OEEC. This they opposed, and the United Kingdom did so even more resolutely. The United States made it clear that in the future it could consider nothing other than the existing multilateral tariff-bargaining framework, within which Congress allowed the executive only to make reciprocal concessions and on which it also imposed strict limitations.[77] If there was to be American support for a purely European organization for reducing tariffs, it was only going to be for a customs union, and that, it was now accepted in Washington, could not include all OEEC members and in all probability might be just the Six.

The French proposals for mutual tariff reductions which had been made in November 1950 were submitted to the Council of Europe. The Benelux countries' reaction to them revealed once again their lack of harmony on commercial policy. Tariffs, under the French proposals, were to be reduced by 10 per cent a year, but the reductions were to be on the weighted average level of tariffs for each sector. Everything turned on what was meant by a sector. France proposed there should be only five. The Dutch wanted four sectors in agriculture alone, so that their agricultural exports would not be blocked. The Belgians, determined not to relax their own agricultural protection, insisted that agriculture, as the French had proposed, be treated as one single sector.[78] In February 1952 France followed the British action of November 1951 by invoking all the escape clauses in the trade liberalization programme and reimposing quotas.

This experience of the inequity of non-tariff barrier removal in OEEC and the hopelessness of tariff reduction agreements either in GATT or the Council of Europe contrasted strongly with the experience of integration in the ECSC. In the former organizations a long and energetic diplomatic effort had ended in complete failure. In the latter the Netherlands had exercised from the start of the negotiations weight and influence beyond its size. The Treaty of Paris had incorporated most of the safeguards for national political power on which the Dutch negotiators had insisted. It could not be said that any one of Holland's vital national interests had been ignored or overridden. It was understandable that interest in tariff reduction would in those circumstances begin to focus on the Six as a more

[77] K. Kock, *International Trade Policy and the GATT, 1947–1967* (Stockholm, 1969), p. 71.
[78] I. Frank, *The European Common Market. An Analysis of Commercial Policy* (New York, 1961). The United States referred the French proposal to the Randall Presidential Commission in 1953, whose report never mentioned it.

manageable political framework and one where some support might be obtained from Washington for such a cause.

The rules of GATT, largely at American insistence, had proscribed customs unions, on the grounds that they were preferential arrangements for trade discrimination, unless they resulted in an external tariff lower than the previous average level of the national tariffs of their members. The tariffs on coal, iron and steel products of the ECSC did not meet this requirement; yet the signatory powers of the Treaty of Paris were able to secure such strong American diplomatic support in GATT, against British opposition there, that they were granted a waiver. The grounds were that once the process of harmonization of their external customs duties on the products concerned had been completed the common market in coal, iron and steel would eventually have lower external tariffs than the general incidence of the separate national tariffs in 1951.[79] When it was considered that Holland's two biggest markets by 1952 were ECSC members (table 4.23) and that these were also the fastest growing markets, and when it was considered that the two large high-tariff economies France and Italy were members, the attractions of widening the common market of the ECSC to other products were evident. It was this long chain of disappointing events which eventually led to the Dutch proposal in 1952 that the European Defence Community and the European Political Community should also be a customs union.

Table 4.23   The geographical distribution of Dutch exports, 1938–57

Percentage of total exports by value going to:			
	United Kingdom	*West Germany*	*Belgium–Lux.*
1938	22.1	14.6	10.6
1946	10.9	6.4	20.8
1947	12.8	3.1	15.6
1948	14.5	5.9	15.6
1949	16.3	10.7	13.3
1950	14.7	20.6	13.5
1951	15.9	13.9	14.8
1952	12.4	13.9	15.4
1953	10.6	13.9	15.5
1954	11.5	15.7	14.0
1955	12.4	17.1	13.9
1956	11.8	18.2	14.3
1957	10.9	18.6	15.6

Sources: 1938–51: Netherlands, Centraal Bureau voor de Statistiek, *Tachtig Jaren Statistiek in Tijdreeksen, 1899–1979* (The Hague, 1979); 1952–7: OEEC, *Statistical Bulletins of Foreign Trade*, Series IV

[79] G. Patterson, *Discrimination in International Trade. The Policy Issues 1945–1965* (Princeton, 1966), pp. 107 ff.

While the Netherlands was reactively thinking its way towards a customs union of the Six, France, which had initiated the idea, was however moving in the opposite direction. French interest in a Western European customs union as a foundation for the political reconstruction of the continent faded as the French balance of payments, rapidly improving in 1950, began to deteriorate badly in 1951. A concept originally intended to revitalize the French economy and control Germany looked by the start of 1952 more like an arrangement to remove France's protection against a country with which it could not compete. This increasing economic anxiety added force to the mounting domestic opposition to Pleven's proposals for a European Defence Community.[80] By the time the Netherlands belatedly and reluctantly committed itself to the EDC the whole concept of a federal European Political Community to control the EDC was already in serious political trouble in France. When the price for this Dutch commitment became the reduction and eventual elimination of tariffs between the six member states, those political difficulties were made much worse.

The credit for reorientating Dutch commercial policy and diplomacy in this direction must go very largely to one man, Johan Willem Beyen. Beyen succeeded Stikker as one of two foreign ministers named when Drees formed his third administration in September 1952. 'In the extension of the common market for coal and steel into the general common market, into the European Economic Community, Dutch diplomacy played, for example, a decisive role', wrote the subsequent German foreign minister Walter Hallstein, who was a central figure throughout the negotiations for that extension.[81] Yet in the hagiography of European integration Beyen is usually presented as a relatively minor background figure. He is portrayed as a banker and businessman whose vision of European integration did not extend beyond the narrow, and in the eyes of European federalists somewhat ignoble, commercial interests of his own country. Yet Beyen has as much claim as anyone to be the first architect of the European Economic Community and his achievement shows how unfair such a portrayal is.[82]

---

[80] René Pleven, born 1901, son of an army officer. Trained as a lawyer. European managing director of the Automatic Telephone Company 1929–39; joined de Gaulle 1940; member of the provisional government in exile; elected to parliament 1945; minister of finance 1945; of the national economy 1945; of defence 1949; president of the Council of Ministers 1950–2; minister of defence 1952–4; French delegate to the European Parliamentary Assembly, 1958–69, where he sat as a liberal; president of the Committee for the Regional Economic Development of Brittany, 1964–73 and much responsible for the rapid economic transformation of his own province in that time. An angler.

[81] W. Hallstein, *Die europäische Gemeinschaft* (Düsseldorf, 1975), p. 17.

[82] Johan Willem Beyen, 1897–1976. Civil servant, businessman and banker. Studied law at Utrecht. Ministry of Finance 1918–24, where he observed the post-World War I financial reconstruction; executive with the Philips Co., 1924–5; international banker 1925–35; president of Nederlandse Bank, 1935–7; president of the Bank for International Settlements 1937–9; financial adviser to the Dutch government in exile and director of Unilever, 1940–5; one of the directors of the International Bank for Reconstruction, 1946–7; Dutch representative to the Economic and Social Council of the UN, 1947–8; a director of the IMF, 1948–52; foreign minister, 1952–5. A cellist.

Beyen who had spent much of his life in the world of international finance, had been present at the Bretton Woods negotiations. He had been an enthusiastic supporter of the agreement as a viable international basis for the political economy of the post-war state, but had soon come to realize that more was needed, because Bretton Woods had failed to anticipate the full nature of political developments in the post-war state. The problems of his own country's trade and payments problems from 1945 onwards strengthened that sentiment. He was clearly sympathetic to the idea that integration might provide a better support for domestic policies than the international cooperation envisaged at Bretton Woods, even if he did not think the reality could be brought any nearer by enthusing in public about the ideal. He was in any case a quiet man, not a professional politician, who before 1952 had stayed well away from the world of propaganda and publicity. Not a member of any political party, with no unqualified support from his ministry or within the government, and against some firm pockets of opposition in both, he almost single-handedly swung Dutch commercial policy in this new direction.

As it stood, the draft EDC treaty declared that the European Defence Commissioners who would be in charge of the European army would themselves be controlled by a parliamentary assembly in the way the High Authority was. The draft treaty made provision however only for a temporary assembly, because from early 1952 onwards the French and the Italians had insisted on a greater measure of democratic control over the EDC than that exercised over the High Authority by the parliamentary assembly of the ECSC. Schuman, de Gasperi and Adenauer, the three European architects of the draft treaty, had all spoken of the EDC as needing to be governed by a supranational democratic parliament. It was decided therefore that a temporary assembly would draft proposals for a permanent federal parliament as part of a federal constitution. Discontented with this delay and, as they saw it, deliberate postponement of the question of political unification, the Council of Europe demanded that a democratic constitution to control the EDC should be ready by the time the treaty had been ratified. When Beyen came into office the situation was that a resolution to this effect was to be submitted to the foreign ministers of the Six when they next met in Luxembourg in September 1952 to consider once more the draft treaty.

He at once seized one element of the discussions and policy reviews which had occupied much time in the Dutch foreign ministry since the Pleven proposals. This was the argument that any attempt to move towards a political structure for Europe without provision for giving economic powers to such a structure was only likely to make it even more difficult in future to reach agreement on a commercial framework in the Dutch interest. Virtually his first public act as foreign minister was to persuade his fellow foreign ministers at the Luxembourg conference to agree on an apparently anodyne resolution that the temporary EDC assembly, when it considered the draft federal constitution, should also examine the question of economic integration. Within the Dutch government there was no clear idea of what this should imply.

The task of reviewing policy relating to European integration had been handed over for study before Beyen's appointment to an inter-ministerial committee. When it made its first report after the Luxembourg meeting it recommended, satisfactorily enough for Beyen, that the Netherlands should not join the federal constitution unless it did receive commercial recompense, and it suggested that the foreign ministers of the Six set up a separate economic study group. As to what propositions the Dutch would then make to this group, there was much division. Civil service advice was pessimistic and cautious. It was Beyen himself who proposed that the recompense should be that the EPC become a customs union. Furthermore, he proposed that automatic steps by which the tariffs between its member-states would be progressively eliminated should be written in detail into the draft EPC treaty by the assembly.[83] Previous experience demonstrated, he argued, that tariffs would not be lowered except by a supranational authority which had been set up to enforce a preordained, irrevocable course of action.

This was a new kind of thinking about the tariff problem and it was undoubtedly influenced by the experience of the ECSC. Beyen himself had been trained as a lawyer and the concept of a treaty as an instrument of detailed, binding law which would determine a long series of future actions enforceable by an international court appealed to him because it came from that experience of the ECSC. Once the treaty was signed it would, at least between the Six, end the long history of national tariff bargaining bringing tariff removal into harmony with quota removal. The OEEC trade liberalization programme had in any case come almost to a standstill in 1952 because of British and French actions. As these proposals were shaped into the Beyen Plan, taking its name from the analogy with Stikker's earlier Plan of Action, they came to contain the additional stipulations that a date for final completion of the customs union should be set and that any safeguard clauses to be incorporated into the schedule of tariff cuts should also be administered and supervised by a supranational body, which would itself be bound by the detailed legal clauses of the treaty.

It is hard to know how seriously Beyen considered the chances of any immediate political success coming from this initiative. By the time the plan took final form in March 1953 the EDC treaty as it stood was surely already condemned to defeat in France, even without any additional clauses about a customs union. In January a new government had been formed and Schuman's long spell as foreign minister had come to an end.

[83] R.T. Griffiths and A.S. Milward, 'The Beyen Plan and the European Political Community', in W. Maihofer (ed.), *Noi si mura. Selected Working Papers of the European University Institute* (Florence, 1986).

His successor, Georges Bidault, who had to face opposition to the treaty from Gaullist members of his coalition, was more concerned to reduce its scope than to extend it by giving it an economic basis. It may well be that Beyen's real intention was to establish a firm line for Dutch commercial policy, to commit the country to pursuit of a European customs union as a way of reducing tariffs if a more realistic opportunity should present itself in the future.

The Beyen Plan was debated only once in the Dutch cabinet, in April 1953. Prime minister Drees was convinced that the EDC treaty would not be ratified in France as it stood and was firmly opposed to any attempt to reduce its scope to make its acceptance in Paris easier. For him, Beyen's proposal was acceptable, but only if it did guarantee the achievement of a customs union by an automatic procedure. If it failed to do this and the Netherlands had to sign a commitment to the European army and a federal European government with only a vague commitment by its partners to change their commercial policy, he would have no choice, so he informed his colleagues, but to resign. The one federalist in the cabinet, the minister of agriculture Sicco Mansholt, took the opposite view, arguing that a wide range of concessions should be made by weakening the treaty to help the French government to pass it through the national assembly. The economic issues could, he thought, be settled afterwards by the European organs that would be created.

In between came a variety of opinions from indifference to the vigorous insistence of the minister of economic affairs, Jelle Zijlstra, that a mere customs union, as Beyen proposed, would not serve the purpose. Tariff removal, especially if it was to be an automatic procedure, required, he argued, common policies on taxes, wages, prices and employment policy. It would mean not a customs union but a common market with a wide range of rules about many other matters than tariffs. This in turn would perhaps mean the surrender of much greater powers to an equivalent of the High Authority than Beyen appeared to be contemplating.[84] Nobody in fact in the cabinet appears exactly to have agreed with Beyen. The British ambassador described him as a 'simple' man, who thought like the American officials in the ECA and who only carried his colleagues with him in his proposal because they were so disappointed about the present state of European commercial policy and so anxious about the future.[85]

The opinions of Zijlstra were close to those of the Belgian government, where the Beyen Plan made little appeal as it stood. The Belgian reaction was as it had been to the ECSC. The higher level of wages and welfare

---

[84] W. Asbeek Brusse and R.T. Griffiths, 'The Dutch Cabinet and The Rome Treaties', in E. Serra (ed.), *Il Rilancio dell'Europa e i Trattati di Roma* (Brussels, 1989).

[85] PRO, FO 371/105999, British Embassy at the Hague to FO, 25 March 1953. Certainly Beyen's own account is so simple as to be disturbing; J.-W. Beyen, *Het Spel en de Knikkers. Een kroniek van vijftig jaren* (Rotterdam, 1968), pp. 219 ff. But politicians' memoirs are often so.

payments in Belgium would have to be defended. The mere removal of tariffs would only lead to the same disappointments, because of the differences in prices and earnings, as those to which Benelux had given rise. Without policy harmonization costs would not be equalized, because the disparities would be so great as to provoke new forms of protectionism.[86] The view of many in the Belgian government and certainly of van Zeeland and of Meurice was that currency convertibility and the free movement of capital throughout Western Europe was more likely to reduce these disparities than a customs union confined to six countries. When van Zeeland and Meurice met the German minister for the economy Ludwig Erhard before the foreign ministers' meeting in Paris on 12–13 May 1953 which was to hear French pleas to amend the draft treaty, they found themselves in agreement that tariff reductions plus the legal convertibility of all Western European currencies into the dollar should be objectives to be reached together across the whole of Western Europe. Commercial arrangements between the Six, they agreed, were more likely to impede this outcome than to advance it.

Their agreement hid a disagreement. A customs union embracing a greater number of Western European countries would still, van Zeeland believed, require many common policies to harmonize welfare and wages, otherwise Belgium with its high labour costs would not be able to enter. That was too interventionist a stance to be acceptable to Erhard.[87] Yet the first and most obvious effect of Beyen's proposed customs union would be that the 30 per cent of Belgium's exports which were sold in the Netherlands would be subjected to a competition on equal terms which they had previously been spared and which high prices made them ill-suited to bear. Belgian civil servants had good grounds for arguing that the Beyen Plan would not necessarily increase Belgium's trade.[88]

It mattered less to Beyen's plans that one German minister was opposed to them than that they would not be supported by Belgium and thus not be presented as Benelux plans. The mandate from his own government, which accorded with his own strong personal conviction, was that no customs union could serve the Dutch interest unless it contained from the outset automatic and irrevocable procedures for its completion. Introducing the idea of policy harmonization into this would, he believed, make the treaty unacceptably complex and lengthen intolerably the period of time over which the customs union would be achieved. It was evident also from the discussion of his proposals in the Dutch cabinet that no modification of

86 MAECE, 17.771/1, 'Considération d'ordre économique sur le mémorandum néerlandais relatif à la création d'une communauté politique européenne', 12 December 1953; ibid., 'Etude du 3e mémorandum néerlandais concernant la Communauté Européenne'.
87 ibid., 'Entretien du 4 mai entre Mm. Erhard, van Zeeland et Meurice', 7 May 1953.
88 ibid., Comptes-rendus des séances de la Commission Interministérielle, 1 June, 5 June, 9 June, 17 July, 28 August, 1953.
89 An inflexibility with which their leader in the negotiations J. Linthorst Homan increasingly disagreed. Interview with J. Linthorst Homan, 4 March 1985.

them would be allowed. This explains the extreme inflexibility of the Dutch negotiators after the proposals had been made.[89]

Yet whatever the current tide of opinion and the genuine difficulties which appeared, Beyen had laid the basis of a plan for the Six which, if not yet sufficient, already met necessary conditions for European advance towards a better regulation of commercial policy as no other scheme did. It offered the best prospects of fulfilling Dutch commercial interests. It offered France the least painful way out of the protectionist womb, in which almost everyone agreed it could not remain for ever. It was a useful second best to German industry, and, since it underlined the equality of political rights for the Federal Republic, satisfied German foreign policy objectives. Belgian objections to the scheme were, essentially, that it did not go far enough.

Of course the Netherlands was far too small a power to effect any change on its own; Western European commercial policies were hardly going to change because the Dutch wanted them to. Nor was the context of the EDC and the EPC the one in which such plans could succeed. Nor did the particular Dutch proposals go far enough to satisfy the general demand for economic security, for they seemed to endanger the position of important groups in countries with higher wage and cost levels. The general drift of discussion over the EDC treaty in 1953 and 1954 was in fact more in favour of Zijlstra's or van Zeeland's views, that common policies were needed to make a customs union work effectively.[90] The Italian delegation particularly pleaded for economic policy coordination as the only way to cope with a programme of automatic tariff reductions. The new European body should have powers by itself to make laws on policy coordination, they argued.[91] Beyen's objections to this remained firm, although it is hard to see that a common market of this kind between the Six would have created greater economic difficulties for the Netherlands than did Benelux. But the debate had become abstract; the European Defence Community and the European Political Community were to all intents and purposes in early 1954 already dead and the discussions lacked 'life and sense'.[92]

'The more or less academic events', nevertheless, 'took place in a friendly atmosphere'.[93] The interesting aspect of them is how far-ranging was the discussion of the Beyen Plan. For anyone contemplating the discussions in 1990–1 on European Monetary and Political Union the arresting fact is that virtually every question which they have raised was discussed with equal fullness and frankness more than thirty years earlier. Should Western Europe have one currency and one monetary policy?

[90] MAE, 17.771/3, 'La position de la délégation belge en matière économique à la lumière des premiers travaux de la conférence de Paris', 26 January 1954.
[91] BA, B102/11412, 'Zusammenfassendes Exposé über die in der Zeit vom 7 Januar bis zum 5 März 1954 auf wirtschaftlichen Gebiete durchgeführten Arbeiten', 6 March 1954.
[92] MAE, 17.771/1. 'Problème de la Communauté Européenne. Où en est-on?', 10 June 1954.
[93] BA, B102/11413, von Boeckh to Erhard, 13 July 1954.

Should the monetary policy of the German central bank be imposed on the other states? Should there be freedom of movement for labour? Should there be a mutual recognition of professional qualifications? Should there be a common company law? Should there be a free capital market? Should there be common criteria for safety at work? For standards of manufactured goods? For foodstuffs? The range and scope of the discussion was much wider than anything which had previously taken place and the solutions proposed often much bolder. There was, of course, no intention of implementing them. Nevertheless, as the prospect of the Defence Treaty became less real, committees convoked to discuss an apparently utopian solution to what was now an artificial problem boldly spoke their minds over Europe's future.

After the rejection of the Defence Community Monnet and Spaak made energetic efforts to keep alive the idea of political union between the Six. But it was not from their efforts that the Treaties of Rome sprang. They sprang from a renewal of the Beyen proposals. Monnet announced that he would not seek renewal as a member of the High Authority, in order to dedicate himself to the Action Committee for the United States of Europe, which he was creating. His contacts with Spaak became frequent and close. Neither had been involved in the discussions about the possibility of EDC becoming also a customs union or shown any interest in the idea. Monnet indeed gives the impression in his memoirs of discovering the existence of the customs union proposals and thinking of them as a possible way forward to European unity only in autumn 1955.[94] Even then he preferred other ways. Yet the realistic discussion about European integration had already focused in 1953 on the issues which the Beyen proposals raised. They did not die with the rejection of EDC but remained an active subject of discussion.

Opinion about the chances of a common market was obviously made more pessimistic in Belgium by the vote on EDC in the French national assembly. Its obvious implication was that common policies requiring supranational institutions to enforce them would meet much opposition in France. There was also support in the Belgian government for an alternative to the Beyen Plan, a free trade zone covering as much of Western Europe as possible. Its objectives would merely be to remove tariffs where possible and avoid all the complications of policy harmonization. With this alternative in mind, Belgium proposed after the failure of the EDC treaty that Benelux should make one more effort to persuade OEEC to tackle the tariff question. The suggested initiative was to propose that the OEEC countries should all move gradually to becoming a low-tariff, if possible even a free-trade, area for manufactured goods. This free-trade area, although it was not intended to modify the tariff autonomy of its members to the outside world, could nevertheless, it was suggested, in the course of time become a customs union which would conform to the GATT requirements for recognition. This would not be done by the infinitely painstaking

[94] J. Monnet, *Memoirs*, op. cit., pp. 400 ff.

procedures of the Stikker Plan of Action in 1950, but by establishing targets to be reached at set dates, like the trade liberalization programme. The proposal emanated from Baron Snoy et d'Oppuers, a civil servant in the foreign trade section of the Ministry of Foreign Affairs and Foreign Trade.[95]

The timing of these Belgian proposals appears to have been a response to the anxiety caused by the French prime minister Mendès-France's bilateral dealings after the collapse of EDC with the Federal Republic.[96] These culminated in the Franco–German bilateral agreement of 26 October 1954, which covered not only foreign trade but also joint investments in French and German industries and an agreement to proceed with the joint canalization of the Moselle, something which had been originally promised as part of the ECSC. Anxiety in Belgium and the Netherlands that this would usher in a world of direct bilateral dealings between the larger European economies at the expense of the smaller and repeat the pattern of the inter-war period was high. Mendès-France had shown little enthusiasm for any association of the Six and a distinct preference for regulating the future of Franco–German relations between the two countries. Coppé gave his support in Belgium to the free trade zone proposals because he thought it essential that Benelux make it clear that a purely Franco–German agreement about the framework of Western European interdependence was every bit as unacceptable as a further stage of integration replicating Monnet's 'authoritarian methods'.[97] Beyen was not enthusiastic about repeating earlier unavailing efforts in OEEC, but had to accept that as long as Mendès-France was in power the customs union proposal had no chance.

Spaak, restored as foreign minister by the van Acker government at the end of April 1954, lent little support to this Belgian commercial initiative, even though it emanated from the foreign trade section of his own ministry. His interest was in creating a further layer of political machinery for the Six and his hopes now centred on the idea of a common transport policy governed by another High Authority, or by the existing one with

---

[95] Later Snoy took the view in various interviews including one with the author on 3 March 1985 that the primary purpose of the proposals was the 'relaunching' of Europe, for which he was prepared to envisage a wide variety of commercial foundations. For example, Commission of the European Communities, Information Universitaire, *La Naissance de l'Europe Contemporaine, Interview du Comte Snoy et d'Oppuers* (Brussels, July 1984); J.C. Snoy et d'Oppuers, 'Le rôle du Bénélux dans la relance européenne en 1955', in *Belgische buitenlands beleid en internationale betrekkingen. Liber amicorum Prof. Omer de Roeymaker* (Leuven, 1978).

[96] Pierre Isaac Isidore Mendès-France, 1907–82, son of a Jewish shopkeeper. Elected to parliament 1932 for the Eure; under-secretary of state for the Treasury 1938; member of the provisional government in exile 1943; minister of the national economy 1944–5; governor of the International Bank for Reconstruction and of the IMF, 1946–58; president of the Council of Ministers and minister of foreign affairs 1954–5; afterwards a journalist and political commentator. Author of fifteen books. A man of integrity, whose career shows that that was not the quality required of a politician, nor even one which would make him trusted.

[97] MAE, 17.771/4, 'Note pour M. le ministre', 29 October 1954.

additional powers. In functionalist terms transport was the ideal next step for sectoral integration on the model of the ECSC. Alternatively, or in parallel, he was prepared to support Monnet's idea that there should be a common programme of civil nuclear energy development between the Six which could be achieved by extending the powers of the High Authority to cover all forms of energy.

To these ideas which tried to preserve and build on the idea of the High Authority Beyen was opposed. International transport was in any case a sector where the Dutch had a long tradition and a competitive advantage, as well as one which made a big contribution to Dutch income. Its supranational regulation, Beyen thought, was likely to reduce this Dutch advantage. Dutch ministers as a body were antagonistic to the idea of a nuclear energy Community. In nuclear energy the Netherlands would be marginal to the Franco–German developments. As for electricity, coop- eration between OEEC members on traditional lines was all, they argued, that was needed. And if oil were brought under the aegis of the Community, as Spaak had suggested, they feared this would mean the permanent institutionalization of subsidies for coal output and levies on oil imports, to which, as we saw in chapter 3, they were already strongly opposed in ECSC.[98]

Reviewing the situation for his colleagues in November 1954 Beyen reached the conclusion that while Mendès-France was prime minister of France all such initiatives were a waste of effort and a diversion from what was now the main task, preserving the ECSC.[99] It was for the collapse of the Mendès-France government that he was waiting. As soon as Mendès- France fell from power in February 1955 he decided to revive his proposal for a customs union and went back to cabinet in March to ask for per- mission to do so. This time the proposal was more flexible. Beyen pro- posed a special transition period to allow France to enter the customs union. But the insistence on a treaty, enforceable by law, which would determine in advance the reduction of tariffs by automatic stages, was as firm as before. The aim, Beyen wrote in his memorandum to fellow ministers, was the development and stabilization of the market for Dutch exports.[100]

Opinion inside the Dutch cabinet echoed that of 1953. Drees thought there was even less chance than before of the proposals succeeding. Mansholt still argued that a political community should be created first and then left to do its own economic work.[101] But although there was still little positive enthusiasm in cabinet for the Beyen Plan, none of the doubters or

[98] MBZ, II, 913.100, no. 139, Beyen to Spaak, 14 April 1955.
[99] ibid., 'Het beleid van de Nederlandse regering ten opzichte van de Europese samenwerk- ing', 19 November 1954.
[100] ibid., 'Nota inzake de Europese integratie', 24 March 1955.
[101] A.G. Harryvan and A.E. Kersten, 'The Netherlands, Benelux and the Relance Européenne 1954–1955', in E. Serra (ed.), *Il Rilancio . . .*, op. cit.

critics could argue convincingly that outside the framework of the Six there actually was any real chance of altering the commercial policies of Europe in a way that met Dutch needs. The Belgian free trade area proposals, in keeping with all later similar European attempts at free trade areas, including EFTA, excluded agricultural trade. The compromise could only be what it had been before; the Beyen Plan could again go forward.

Within a week of this decision, on 2 April 1955, Spaak without consultation with Beyen sent to the ECSC foreign ministers a set of proposals on which he and Monnet had earlier agreed, to call a general conference of the Six to discuss the creation of a new High Authority for energy or transport. It is hard to believe that the timing of Spaak's proposals was decided without regard to the Dutch cabinet decision. Spaak's suggested conference would replicate the method used in negotiating the Treaty of Paris, to which Monnet, wrongly, attributed the success of those earlier negotiations. The participants would be required to make an initial declaration of their commitment to the principle of further sectoral integration either in energy policy, including nuclear energy, or in transport. They would then call a working conference under Monnet's chairmanship to establish the details of the next step in that direction. Two days after the Spaak proposals were made, the Beyen Plan was reissued to the foreign ministers of the Benelux, 'to achieve the economic integration of Europe in the general sense by travelling on the road through a Customs Union to the realization of an Economic Union'.[102] The Benelux foreign ministers were thus confronted with three different and opposed suggestions for the future of their nations in Western Europe, a European free trade area, an extension of the High Authority to further sectors of the economy, and a customs union of the Six.

Inevitably, much turned on estimates of the balance of political power inside the French government. The new prime minister, Edgar Faure, governed only with the participation of the Gaullists whose opposition to Monnet and all further European integration was vehement. Monnet, acting as the interpreter of the shifting opinions in the French cabinet, naturally did not emphasize that much of it was becoming hostile to himself. To Spaak he insisted that his own was the only viable political way forward, because given opinion inside the French government, there was no point in Beyen's challenging French protectionism.[103] The outcome of the Benelux foreign ministers' meeting was a compromise in which none of the possible initiatives was completely ruled out.

The three foreign ministers decided on two parallel lines of action. One was a very much reduced version of the Spaak–Monnet proposals. They would support a common development programme for road construction, railway electrification and other transport improvements supported by a common investment fund, but not a common transport policy. They would

[102] MBZ, II, 913.100, no. 19, 'Nota'.
[103] Interview with Baron Snoy et d'Oppuers, 3 March 1985.

support a programme of joint research, but not necessarily of joint production, in atomic energy. In the rest of the energy sector they would not support anything more than a strengthening of cooperation. The second line of action was, that without eliminating the idea of a free trade area they would also support at the same time a proposal for a customs union of the Six provided it had some of the attributes of a common market. The ultimate aim of the common market would have to be the harmonization of a range of economic policies which affected foreign trade, but no time-span was set for the adoption of the common policies that would achieve this, whereas Beyen maintained his insistence that there must be a timetable for the tariff reductions which would be its foundation. A European Fund, to be used to mitigate the disruptive effects of tariff changes became a part of this initiative. An agreed statement to this effect was sent to the other foreign ministers of the Six on 20 May. The Beyen Plan had begun its transformation from customs union to common market and had returned to the international agenda.

Until the end of 1955 the Belgian officials, including Snoy, seem to have convinced themselves that their own free trade area proposals and the Beyen Plan were compatible and that the numerous technical problems which would arise from the merger of a customs union (in the process of becoming a common market) and a free trade zone, with as many external tariffs as nations, would be a suitable area for regulation by a supranational authority. This belief that the Beyen Plan, if adopted by the Six, could serve as the start of a wider process of tariff-reduction across Europe and thus as the bridge between a more integrated Six and the rest of the continent was important to its advance. It was influential in establishing the customs union proposal as a suitable basis for negotiation in the Federal Republic. The British counter-proposals at the end of 1956 for a European free trade area were made with a view to capitalizing on these same sentiments. But commercial negotiations have to deal with what is practical and achievable. When the Italian foreign minister Gaetano Martino, who wished to support the Benelux initiative, asked his officials which was the better proposal, a customs union or a free trade area with or without Britain, all they could answer was that they could not see how a free trade area could be realized.[104]

At the Messina meeting of the foreign ministers of the Six called to discuss the Benelux proposals in May 1955, together with those for an atomic energy Community, all the proposals were referred for further study to an *ad hoc* committee chaired by Spaak. In much of the historiography of the European Community this is a hallowed event. Those who were at Messina have retold their story to so many conferences of historians that it has become the chronicle of a miracle. They went there with no hope that the Benelux proposals would be allowed to go any higher than the desks of

[104]   E. Serra, 'L'Italia e la Conferenza di Messina', in *Il Rilancio . . .*, op. cit.

working groups of civil servants before being dropped again into the waste-paper basket. They came away with an agreement to set up a high-level, independent committee chaired by the most prominent and one of the most enthusiastic advocates of a federal Europe, whose task was to choose among these proposals for their next meeting. The kindly Italian sun warmed all hearts, for various reasons to do with local politics the meetings took on an unexpectedly informal air, and on the ancient site of Taormina to where they had been taken on an excursion a mystical grace descended on them.[105] Europe was 'relaunched'.

To start the history of the European Economic Community with a moment of divine inspiration is a pleasing conceit, for it has often needed a certain amount of religious fervour to sustain its appeal to the populace. But there is no reason to single out the Messina conference from the long continuity of commercial negotiations inside and outside OEEC. If any clear starting date for the history of the European Economic Community has to be chosen, it should be when the Beyen proposals for a customs union were first made. They were the bridge which led from the ECSC to the EEC.

THE TREATIES OF ROME

The historical narrative has so far been confined largely to the role of the Netherlands, as a way of showing how changes in the post-war state shifted the perspectives for commercial policy. Although the choice of the Netherlands to illustrate this process had heuristic merit and also a certain logic because international commerce had for so long been so important there, it could not explain why the common market emerged as a matter of general agreement among the Six. The criterion for acceptance which the various proposals before the *ad hoc* Spaak Committee had to meet was that they should satisfy the economic interests of the negotiating parties and especially the supreme interest of retaining the Federal Republic as the commercial and economic pivot of Western Europe's growth. In 1955 the common market proposal still received unequivocal support only from the Netherlands, and then only in a form where it would have the minimum necessary common policies and would come as close as possible to Beyen's first idea of a tariff union only. Belgium supported it, but gave equal support to the free trade area, while Spaak himself energetically promoted Monnet's quite different plans. The Netherlands was certainly not a strong enough country to make its own interests prevail.

As the study of intra-Western-European trade earlier in the chapter showed, even though more than 60 per cent of German exports by value went to Europe they were by no means concentrated on the market of the Six. On the contrary, Austria, Denmark, Norway, Sweden, Switzerland

---

[105] D.H. Lawrence had a similar experience there earlier.

and the United Kingdom were all markets of major importance to German industry. A customs union which through an external tariff higher than that of the Federal Republic made trade with these countries more difficult was going to be regarded with stern suspicion by much of German industry. If it conceded the Belgian, and what was soon to become even more strongly the French, argument, that the prior harmonization of levels of wages and social security payments was necessary, this would only deepen those suspicions. Satisfying economic interests might involve offering a market for Dutch, or French, food surpluses and so weakening the protection of German agriculture.

These serious objections to the common market or customs union were counterbalanced by one major economic appeal which they held out to German industry: access on much easier terms to the French and Italian markets. As we have seen (table 4.15, p. 163) over the period of the Federal Republic's greatest trade boom, 1954–7, France and Italy together accounted for only 13.15 per cent of the total increase in value of German exports, only 1 per cent more than Denmark, Norway and Sweden. All German industry was conscious that here, potentially, were two of its greatest markets, and also that the smaller European economies could not continue to support so rapid a rate of growth of exports. It was clearly worth paying some economic price in terms of greater trading difficulties elsewhere to build the links with France and Italy to the level of those with Scandinavia and Benelux.

From a political point of view the issues were much clearer, or at least were made to seem so by Adenauer and his immediate aides. When the Beyen Plan had first appeared in 1952 it was referred to the head of the western European section of the Foreign Office, Carl Friedrich Ophüls. Ophüls was a convinced federalist who saw the proposal as an obstacle to completing the EDC treaty.[106] His view however, like that of Adenauer, was that it was not possible to reject the proposal if the equality of rights which the Federal Republic sought depended on it. When objections arose from other ministries to the excessive simplicity of the proposal, the German Foreign Office argued that if common policies would indeed be necessary to make it operative, this would be a stronger incentive to create another supranational authority where the Federal Republic would gain a further measure of equality. It went even further in pointing out that a larger number of countries than the Six would make that impossible and that in any case it was desirable that a project of this kind should at first be confined to the Six, because the reassurance which that context gave to France would make it easier to gain the chief objective of re-establishing full German sovereignty.[107]

---

[106] H.-J. Küsters, *Die Gründung der europäischen Wirtschaftsgemeinschaft* (Baden-Baden, 1982), pp. 79 ff.

[107] BA, B102/11418, Bericht über eine Besprechung im Auswärtigen Amt über Wirtschaftsverhandlungen zwischen den sechs Montan-Union-Ländern, 15 January 1953.

The issues, though, went deeper than those of restoring equality of rights. Even after equality had been conceded by the Western European Union in 1955, the Foreign Office and the chancellor were as firmly in favour of the Beyen Plan as before. Adenauer was unswerving in his idea that Western European integration must be the basis of the Federal Republic's security and that it was ultimately the only chance of German reunification. There is some evidence that Adenauer at first preferred the alternative proposals for a common atomic energy authority for the Six, Euratom. When the reception of the Euratom idea by German industry proved to be almost entirely hostile, and when the proposals were weakened to the point where they seemed no longer to guarantee the integration which he sought, he naturally turned to the common market proposal.

The story of the acceptance of the common market in Germany makes a complete contrast to that in France. For all the early post-war enthusiasms of some Quai d'Orsay officials for European integration, as the way in which a modernized France could cope with Germany, the Quai d'Orsay's advice in 1955 was not really in favour of the common market, at least in the shape in which it finally emerged from the Spaak Committee. But it was overridden by favourable advice from economic ministries concerned with France's modernization. In Germany the opposite happened: adverse opinions in the economic ministries were overridden by what were seen as the political imperatives of foreign policy.

In the Federal Ministry of the Economy the minister's own opposition to the proposals was energetic. Although at the highest level Erhard officially accepted that political interests must come first, he did so with an ill grace, still criticizing the terms of the Treaties of Rome on the eve of their signature and inciting the Americans to opposition. From the moment the Beyen Plan was first announced Erhard argued that it would redirect German exports into a still smaller area and leave the Federal Republic's economic policies wide open to the unwholesome influence of an inflationary France.[108]

Below the level of the minister himself, however, opinion within the ministry was divided. His two closest associates, Alfred Müller-Armack and Rolf Gocht in the Basic Policy Division (*Grundsatzabteilung*) took different and conflicting views. Gocht was opposed to it. He, like his minister, was a militant exponent of the virtues of free trade and currency convertibility. But Müller-Armack took a more complicated position, tending towards support for the proposal providing it did not result in insurmountable barriers to an ever-widening association of European states.[109] And in the special section of the ministry created to deal with

[108] BA, B102/11408, Erhard to Auswärtiges Amt, 19 February 1953; BA, B102/11418, Erhard to Auswärtiges Amt, 4 March 1953.
[109] A. Müller-Armack, 'Fragen der europäischen Integration', in E. von Beckerath, *et al.*, *Wirtschaftsfragen der freien Welt. Festgabe zum 60 Geburtstag von Bundeswirtschafts-minister Ludwig Erhard* (Frankfurt-am-Main, 1957); Müller-Armack, 'Institutionelle Fragen der europäischen Konjunkturpolitik', in *Wirtschaftsordnung und Wirtschafts-politik* (Freiburg im Breisgau, 1966).

ECSC affairs the two leading figures, Hans von der Groeben and Hans von Boeckh, had become convinced that the supranational structure of the ECSC, which both saw as vital to the Federal Republic's status in Europe, would collapse unless there was a further stage of integration. Both therefore showed strong sympathy for Beyen's proposals and tried to influence the minister more favourably towards them.

Like Erhard, finance minister Fritz Schaeffer was reluctant to see any customs union of the Six delay the establishment of free convertibility for the Deutschmark on international exchanges, as it seemed it must do if it were to be tied into any permanent links with the French franc from which it could not escape. But unlike Erhard he was prepared to envisage a closer coordination of monetary policies with the other members of the Six as a genuine possibility.[110] The Ministry of Finance agreed with the standpoint of the Belgian government, that for a customs union to be feasible the countries would have to agree on a codex of international rules covering far more issues than tariff reductions and the removal of non-tariff barriers. Some of these would have to be designed to forbid inflationary policies.[111]

The ministers represented their views to a cabinet meeting on 20 February 1953, where Beyen's memorandum of December 1952 was discussed. There was support from the Ministry of Transport and the Ministry for the Marshall Plan for Beyen's argument that the full details of any economic powers to be given to the EPC would have to be written into the draft EDC treaty. In the Chancellor's eyes, this was a cogent reason for postponing the whole question of a customs union. The immediate objective for him was the Defence Community and rearmament. Anything which made the treaty text more complicated was to be rejected unless it was absolutely unavoidable.

Studies of the German economy's response to the OEEC trade liberalization programme indicated that for some industries, especially the capital goods industries, quota removal was a major advantage, and the assumption therefore was that this would also hold good for tariff removal. For others, such as woollens, cement and cars, the verdict was uncertain. For some sectors, cotton for example, further trade liberalization was thought by the manufacturers to be dangerous. This was even the case for some exceptional areas of capital goods, agricultural machinery for example, where British producers had a large market in Germany, and textile machinery, where the smaller firms who had resettled in the Federal Republic would suffer severely from outside competition. In aluminium

[110] BA, B102/11418, Erhard to Hallstein, 26 February 1954.
[111] BA, B102/11408, Bundesminister der Finanzen to Auswärtiges Amt, 14 February 1953, 'Gutachtliche Ausserung zu der Kabinettsvorlage des Herrn Bundesministers der Finanzen vom 16.2.1953 über finanz-und wirtschaftspolitische Zielsetzung der EPG', 19 February 1953.

the firms objected that they were too new to benefit from a larger market, which would be exploited by their rivals.[112] The balance of opinion was difficult to strike.

A serious question for most producers was the geographical extent of the customs union. Quota removal was advantageous to some because it covered all OEEC Europe. A customs union of the Six was only seen as advantageous to German trade if it created no serious difficulties for trade with the other members of the Federal Republic's western European trade web. Although the leading employers' association, the Bundesverband der Deutschen Industrie (BDI) gave its opinion in favour of political action such as a customs union to support market extension, it warned against 'partial unions'.[113]

This was still of course the same when the Beyen proposals went forward with the other proposals to the Spaak Committee and may have been one reason why Adenauer was at first inclined to favour the project for a European atomic agency. The Federal Republic, obliged by Western European Union unilaterally to renounce the development of nuclear weapons, was beginning to build the administrative structure for a civil nuclear programme. Behind the French proposals was the idea that cooperation with this German programme would provide financial and technological help for the French nuclear energy programme while also allowing for French, and perhaps American, surveillance and control of German developments.[114]

The Euratom project however ran into strong opposition from the economic ministries in Bonn and from the industrialists in the Atomic Energy Commission, which was established in January 1956. The engineering firms involved were vehemently against the degree of government and supranational control which another High Authority would involve. They were upheld in their resistance by the new minister for atomic energy, Franz-Joseph Strauss, not in general a supporter of integration. He was convinced that the control of fissile materials by the equivalent of a High Authority would limit German developments. The Federal Republic would stand, he believed, a much better chance of acquiring the supplies it needed as an independent negotiator, not least because it was a part of Monnet's conception that the High Authority would negotiate for supplies and technological help directly with the United States. When it then emerged that supplies of fissile material for France's military nuclear programme would be excluded entirely from the purview of Euratom, as well as all information about it, the idea no longer served the Federal

---

[112] BA, B102/11409, Bundesminister für den Marshallplan, 'Integrationsstudien in Rahmen der OEEC, Stand 15 January 1953'.

[113] ibid., 'Die Integrationsaufgabe der OEEC. Entschliessung des BDI', 28 March 1952.

[114] P. Weilemann, *Die Anfänge der Europäischen Atomgemeinschaft. Zur Gründungsgeschichte von Euratom 1955–1957* (Baden-Baden, 1983) gives a full account; Weilemann, 'Die deutsche Haltung während der Euratom-Verhandlungen', in E. Serra (ed.), *Il Rilancio . . .*, op. cit.

Republic's interests. Monnet stuck firmly to his task of promoting Euratom throughout 1956, but there was virtually nothing that it now offered the Federal Republic which would not also come from the common market. The various proposals for the ECSC foreign ministers' proposed meeting at Messina did not offer any clear optimum choice for the Federal Republic and remained a subject of intense bureaucratic struggle until late May 1955.

The crucial decision on the German attitude to be taken at the Messina meeting was made at an all-day session in Müller-Armack's country house on 22 May 1955.[115] It was attended by the main disputing partners in the Ministry for the Economy, by Josef Rust the head of the Ministry's raw materials division, because he was a personal confidant of Adenauer, and by von Brentano the foreign minister who was not known for his independence from the chancellor's views. The chancellor, through Rust and the Foreign Office, made it clear that the foreign policy interest should come first and that this was in supporting an initiative which would mean a further degree of integration for the Six. The Dutch proposals had the majority of supporters in the meeting and looked better to fit the foreign policy requirement than Euratom.

For the Ministry of the Economy, the issue then became one of how to prevent the customs union proposals from developing into proposals which would harm German trade. Erhard had no doubt that under French influence the external tariff of a customs union would be high. He saw the best way forward now as an insistence on a parallel move to dollar convertibility for Western European currencies. This would force French prices into line with other customs union members and make the union less protectionist. Others in the ministry argued in the contrary sense, that a strong supranational institution could concentrate on measures of policy harmonization within the Six. Positions on the form and likely economic consequences of a customs union did not get closer, but everybody in the ministry agreed that a customs union must be an automatic and durable arrangement for the reduction of trade barriers and not a repeat of the experience of the inter-war years or of trade liberalization within OEEC.[116] There lay the core of the problem. Was such an arrangement politically feasible? Would France agree?[117]

In 1950 it was France which had been the campaigner for programmes of automatic tariff reduction in Western Europe. By 1952, when this became Dutch policy, France had become a strong opponent of the idea. The reversal in French policy is mainly explained by the swings in its external

---

[115] H.-J. Küsters, *Die Gründung . . .*, op. cit., p. 116.

[116] A. Müller-Armack, *Auf dem Wege nach Europa. Erinnerungen und Ausblicke* (Tübingen, 1971), pp. 99–100.

[117] BA, B102/56578, 'Zum Vorschlag einer Zollunion zwischen den Staaten der Montangemeinschaft', 24 May 1955; ibid., 'Westeuropäische Integrationsprobleme unter Zugrundelegung des Gedankens einer Zollunion', 1 April 1955.

position. By summer 1950 the current account of metropolitan France was no longer showing the large deficits it had shown since 1945. The net deficit on the balance of payments of the French overseas territories with foreign countries in 1950 was $123.1 million, so that on current account the area of metropolitan France itself was probably recording a small surplus over the whole year. In the last two months of 1950 however the Korean war was to change this. Most of the year 1950 appears as a small island of relative comfort in what was the most uncomfortable area of the French economy, its balance of payments. In the years before 1950 huge commodity trade deficits had been covered; firstly by running down the remaining gold reserves; secondly by Marshall Aid; and thirdly, as Marshall Aid diminished, by the increased inflow on capital account. In 1951 the balance both of trade and of invisible earnings again deteriorated rapidly. It was not until 1952 that the balance of payments first began to show a surplus on invisible earnings and not until 1953 that, together with American aid, this covered the trade deficit – by then more than four times larger than it had been in 1950. Although not as desperate as in 1947, the payments position in 1951 was dangerous, and now there were no reserves to spend. Experiments with tariffs now found little political support; what had looked politically feasible in 1950 looked impossible by the end of 1951.

Table 4.24   Balance of payments of the franc area with the rest of the world, 1946–57 (million current $)

	Balance of trade	Balance of invisibles
1946	−1,527.2	−224.9
1947	−1,451.7	− 61.4
1948	−1,428.3	−101.8
1949	−467.6	−71.6
1950	−78.3	−36.6
1951	−770.3	−199.7
1952	−618.5	+27.6
1953	−338.5	+221.9
1954	−179.4	+441.4
1955	+86.2	+516.4
1956	−809.5	+125.6
1957	−850.5	−254.5

Source: France, Ministère des Finances et des Affaires Economiques, Institut National de la Statistique et des Etudes Economiques, *Annuaire Statistique de la France*

While attempts to bring down tariffs were gradually abandoned in 1951, quotas were retained to a greater extent than elsewhere. It was against France that more than half of all the complaints in the OEEC trade committee were filed.[118] France was reduced from a bold initiator to

[118] AN, F60*ter* 469, ECA, 'Comments on French Trade Policy in Europe', n.d.

powerlessness in the debate about commercial policy in Western Europe. The earlier visions of France as the leader of Western Europe's reconstruction around a customs union were not abandoned. Because France could now play only a defensive role however, the initiative passed to Britain, firstly through the OEEC trade liberalization programme, and secondly from spring 1951 through its insistence on the restoration of currency convertibility as the next stage in reconstruction.

This powerlessness began to change with the current account surplus of 1954. In 1955 there was a trade surplus and in particular a dramatic improvement in France's net payments position with Western Europe. By December 1953 France had reached a cumulative deficit position of $800 million in the European Payments Union. In 1954 it began to register surpluses in the EPU with other European countries and the European settlement debts, together with the outflow of gold which they entailed, began to be reduced. This trend continued well into 1955. France resumed participation in the trade liberalization programme and advocates of tariff reduction once more began to make themselves heard.

In order to achieve the resumption of the trade liberalization programme, however, an import surcharge, in some cases as high as 15 per cent, was applied to all commodities on which quotas were removed. The intention was to use the surcharges at first to measure the extent to which domestic prices were out of alignment with those of other OEEC members and then gradually to reduce them and bring price levels into line. French governments spent much time collecting evidence to show how much higher French prices were than those of their competitors. This evidence was used in the national assembly to influence it to reject the EDC treaty.[119] The surcharge was intended to be temporary, but given French trade practices since the end of the war it was not a device which inspired much confidence in France's trading partners. What, they were inclined to ask, would bring French prices into line other than a devaluation or an exposure to competition?

One of the most worrying aspects of the balance of payments after 1951 had been the virtual stagnation of exports. If the balance of trade was painfully brought to the point over the two years 1952–3 where the balance of payments deficit had become financially manageable, this was by a sharp contraction in imports brought about by the reimposition of quotas at the start of 1952. Although a Second Plan to follow the Plan for Modernization and Equipment was ready in 1952, it was more or less abandoned for two years in favour of this short-term reaction and only officially launched in

[119] J. Vernant, 'L'économie française devant la C.E.D.', in R. Aron and D. Lerner (eds), *La querelle de la C.E.D.* (Paris, 1956), For the evidence as collected, France, Ministère des Finances, *Rapport général présenté par la Commission créée le 6 janvier 1954 pour l'étude des disparités entre les prix français et étrangers* (Paris, 1954). For a review of the evidence, A. Armengaud, 'L'Europe, problème économique et social', in *Politique étrangère*, numéro spécial, *L'Union Française*, 1954.

1954. Yet this Second Plan laid out a line of economic policy no different from the first. The determination not to surrender import-substitution policies was made clear by the decision to use commercial policy to support them.[120] The selective surcharges were added to the existing instruments of persuasion over industry and capital at the disposal of the Ministry of Finance, as a way of enforcing compliance with the plan's guidelines.[121] When France's participation in the trade liberalization programme was resumed in April 1954 the extent of quota protection was greater than in 1951; and to that was added the new import surcharges. The state's bargaining power over industry, in as much as it depended on the degree of protection that could be kept or removed, was thus much larger than at the close of the Monnet Plan.

As elsewhere, the debate was not only about the way in which commercial policy could be made to support domestic objectives, but also about France's relationship with Germany. It was that relationship which planning was supposed eventually to make more economically equal. Yet protection against German exports accorded ill with the extent to which the increase in the value of French exports depended on the German market. As far as France's European trade was concerned, the Federal Republic was much the biggest outlet for the increase in its exports. France had a much smaller share of its total trade with Western Europe than most other European economies, but empire trade, the biggest share of total trade, grew only sluggishly. Furthermore, exports to the French empire were more heavily made up of lower-value-added goods such as textiles. The great intra-Western-European trade boom which began in 1954 brought the need to choose between protection and liberalization much more sharply into focus.

The relatively sluggish growth of French exports was attributed by some to the fact that protection caused output costs to rise faster than those of France's competitors. Others argued that exports were being impeded by an overvalued currency. The debate became sidetracked by the claim of protectionists that French exports were not in any case price-elastic.[122] So far-reaching and implausible a claim contradicted the whole of Western Europe's experience since 1950. The reappearance of the Beyen Plan in April 1955 represented a sudden and serious increase in the external pressures on France to resolve this domestic argument. For France to decline any tariff arrangements for Western Europe which were now supported by those very states which it had itself first tried to organize into a customs union looked like a confession of economic weakness of the first magnitude.

---

[120] J. Weiller, 'Relations commerciales et financières de la France au cours de la reprise des années 1952 à 1956', in *Cahiers de l'I.S.E.A.*, P9, no. 145, January 1964.
[121] A. Bienaymé, 'La réorientation de la croissance planifiée française et les risques de freinage par le commerce extérieur', *Cahiers de l'I.S.E.A.*, Série P. no. 4, August 1960.
[122] W.C. Baum, *The French Economy and the State* (Princeton, 1958), pp. 102–3.

The parallel proposals for Euratom also had French origins. They developed with the beginning of the increased demand for energy in 1954, but their deeper origins were in the exaggerated hopes placed on nuclear power as a future source of energy. The argument over imports of American coal had led to long debates in ECSC and OEEC about Europe's dependence on the outside world. OEEC had commissioned an expert report on the subject by the French engineer Louis Armand.[123] Armand, famous as the driving force behind the reconstruction and electrification of the French railway system after 1945, also held a post in the French Atomic Energy Commissariat. He was an enthusiastic advocate of the development of nuclear power to reduce or even eliminate dependence on middle eastern oil imports as well as those of American coal. It was his report which introduced the idea of European collaboration in nuclear energy production and it was he who put the idea in Monnet's head that such collaboration could be another step towards political integration.[124]

But Monnet's conviction that he had discovered a new functional foundation for integration was also closely connected to the evolution of American atomic policy and the Atoms for Peace programme announced by President Eisenhower's speech to the General Assembly of the United Nations in December 1953. Monnet easily saw himself as the bridge between a nuclear America and a nuclear Europe, the Americans' most trusted man in Europe and thus the most appropriate head of a new functional, supranational agency, to which the United States, under the terms of Eisenhower's speech, would release fissile materials and information on nuclear technology. After the irritating, wearisome struggle with the details of an old declining industry like coal, the regulation of nuclear energy had a strong and more positive appeal; a science-based industry, a new and more potent symbol of modernization, one that all governments were hesitant to see in private control, and a business unencrusted with the barnacles and weeds of long years of national regulation. A programme of European cooperation would have the advantage for France that it could draw on German technological and financial help with the construction of the necessary isotope separation plant.

But as a proposal for re-establishing French leadership in the integration of Western Europe Euratom was a poor one precisely because it did put so much emphasis on public regulation. A High Authority with supranational powers had been accepted as the necessary political keystone to the Treaty of Paris, the guarantee that Germany would indeed have equal rights. But the political arrangement had been disliked and continued to be thought of as something not to be tried a second time, except of course by the more committed federalists. Monnet's attempts to turn the High Authority into a

---

[123] OEEC, *Intra-European Economic Cooperation in the Production and Distribution of Power* (Paris, May 1955).

[124] P. Guillen, 'La France et la négociation du traité d'Euratom', in *Relations internationales*, no. 44, 1985.

strong centre of decision-making had made him as well as the High Authority disliked. 'M. Monnet', the Belgian commercial attaché in London told the Foreign Office in January 1953, 'was a hard little man and his attitude was one of *l'Etat c'est moi*. It would be much better for all concerned if he returned to France and ran the French government.'[125] The announcement in November 1954 of his impending resignation appears to have been received with some relief in Paris, where many had similar sentiments.[126] When in spring 1955 he let it be known that he was after all willing to serve again, in his own mind probably as the prelude to the presidency of Euratom, Edgar Faure was quick to appoint his successor.[127]

Euratom, however, was the one further step in European integration which the Gaullists in the government were prepared to tolerate.[128] The National Defence Committee concluded its discussion on 30 March 1955 by empowering the minister of foreign affairs 'to establish the necessary contacts with a view to creating a European organization for atomic energy'.[129] When foreign minister Antoine Pinay visited Bonn at the end of the month, after the Benelux initiative for the customs union had been reopened, he came back with German agreement that the peaceful development of atomic energy was necessary to any attempt to renew the process of integration. This was the preferred step forward for the French at the Messina conference. To have vetoed the customs union proposal there would have been to lose essential support for Euratom, as well as to take a negative decision which some members of the government would have opposed, so the Spaak Committee was allowed to begin its discussions of the Benelux proposals also. The subsequent French contribution to that discussion was somewhere between discouraging and non-committal, the essential tactic being to play for time.

[125] PRO, FO 371/105951. Record of a conversation with M. Jean de Bassompierre by R.C. Hope-Jones, 20 January 1953.

[126] Edgar Faure had long been of the opinion that Monnet must go. FO 371/115999. Conversation between W.N. Hugh-Jones of the British Embassy in Paris and M. Pierre Ricard, president of the French Steel Manufacturers Association, 1 July 1955, who said of Monnet that, 'He had always given the idea of being bored with technical matters and he had no idea of administration.'

[127] Jean Edgar Faure, 1908– , son of an army doctor, he became a lawyer; member of the provisional government, 1944; assistant prosecutor at the Nürnberg trials; elected to parliament as a radical socialist for the Jura, 1946–58; secretary of state to the ministry for the budget, 1949–51; minister of justice 1951; president of the Council of Ministers and minister of finance 1952; minister of finance and economic affairs, 1953–4; of foreign affairs, 1955; president of the Council of Ministers 1955–6; minister of finance, 1958; of agriculture 1966–8; of education 1968–9; minister of state for social affairs, 1972–3; president of the national assembly, 1973–8. Author of popular histories, popular philosophies, very many detective stories (Edgar Sunday), songs, and piano music. Member of the French Academy. Like so many post-war French politicians a 'man of letters' in the nineteenth-century style. 'He is', the British Embassy reported in 1945, 'constitutionally incapable of arriving at any destination by the direct route and can be relied on to judge every issue in the light of his own interests.'

[128] R. Massigli, *Une comédie des erreurs 1943–1956* (Paris, 1978), p. 507.

[129] P. Guillen, 'La France . . .', op. cit., p. 282.

When Faure was replaced as prime minister on the last day of January 1956 by the leader of the socialist party (SFIO) Guy Mollet, the political balance shifted somewhat in the direction of the common market as a political possibility. Mollet had 'a favourable bias' towards the common market proposal as it was emerging from the Spaak Committee, as did his foreign minister Pineau.[130] Pineau brought the first OEEC Secretary-General Robert Marjolin into his planning staff specifically to try to influence policy making in favour of the common market.[131]

Marjolin had served the provisional government in exile in London and Algiers, and had been one of the strongest supporters of the Monnet Plan, for him the foundation of a French renaissance. The international implications of the Plan and its successor were, he thought, clear. 'It was the European question which inspired me to the exclusion of almost all others – the European question, that is to say the French question, of its economy, of its necessary renaissance within the framework of a unified Europe.'[132] Any arrangement like that of the ECSC, he and Mollet both believed, would never be any more than a highly imperfect market. The French renaissance had to be completed by pushing the whole of protectionist French manufacturing into a competitive common market. The implications of this for the ultimate political unity of Europe were not, Marjolin argued, of much immediate significance. One great advantage for him of the common market was that it avoided, as he hoped, attempts to impose a federal structure on the Six, which Monnet's plans for Euratom or the alternative proposals for a High Authority for transport raised.

The awareness that protectionism at the current level had to end if there was to be genuine economic security and advance underlay the French decision not to block any of the proposals about European integration

[130] R. Marjolin, *Le Travail . . .*, op. cit., p. 282. Guy Mollet, 1905–75, schoolteacher (of English). Secretary-general of the Schoolteachers' Association, 1932–40; prisoner-of-war in Germany 1940–2; escaped 1942; in resistance movement 1942–5; elected to parliament as a socialist, 1945; minister for European Council affairs, 1950–1; president of the Council of Europe, 1954–6; president of the Council of Ministers, 1956–7. His English was not particularly good.

[131] Paul Christian Pineau, 1904– , son of an army officer. Trained as an economist. Banker 1931–8; secretary of the Economic Council of the CGT, 1936–40; member of the constituent assemblies 1945–6; elected socialist deputy for the Sarthe 1946–58; minister of food 1945; of public works 1948–9; of foreign affairs 1956–8; managing director of a holiday village and motel company 1963–70. Instigator of the Franco–British invasion of Egypt in 1956. In a second marriage his mother married the playwright Jean Giraudoux. The author of a large number of successful childrens' books, some of which were perhaps read by his own seven children by three marriages.

Robert Marjolin 1911–87, economist, educated at Yale during the New Deal, a young socialist converted to capitalism while working with Monnet in the French Purchasing Mission 1944–5, director of foreign economic relations in the Ministry of the National Economy, 1945–6; Planning Commissariat, 1946–8; secretary-general of OEEC, 1948–55; professor of political economy, University of Nancy, 1955–7; deputy leader of the French negotiating team for the Treaties of Rome 1956–7; European Commissioner, 1958–67; professor of economics, University of Paris, 1967–9; businessman and administrator in steel, oil and car industries, 1969–87. Married to an American, he succeeded in being trusted by both Americans and British, and sometimes by his own side.

[132] R. Marjolin, *Le Travail . . .*, op. cit., p. 255.

presented to the Messina meeting. Most industrial and agricultural opinion in France at the time however seems still to have been against a customs union. Certainly the foreign ministry thought this to be so and wanted to avoid any general consultation of economic interest groups in case, as with the EDC treaty, its scope for manoeuvre was severely restricted.[133] It was clear that the Beyen proposals had acquired a sufficient measure of support outside France for the discussions in the Spaak Committee to be of genuine political significance for the future. By early spring 1956 it became clear, too, that France's negotiating partners would try to tie an agreement on Euratom to agreement on the common market. To turn down the Beyen proposals as a subject for negotiation was to turn down all other steps to European integration.

Following so hard on the rejection of the EDC treaty, this would have killed the issue beyond resurrection and brought the story to an end. And where then would France be? Through timidity all its bold plans for post-war European reconstruction would have been finally abandoned, above all the hope of living safely and equally with Germany. As the discussions in the Spaak Committee gradually revealed, alternative structures – Euratom, a common transport policy – did not satisfy the interests of the other parties as well as the emerging conception of a common market. France either had to join or reverse the whole course of its post-war policies.

The argument of this book should not be misunderstood. In bringing together so much evidence relating to the economic and social foundations of the Treaties of Rome there is no intention to deny the political motivations which are conventionally and correctly ascribed to the Treaties. These are, that it was a further guarantee of the peace settlement in western Europe; that it made central to this peace settlement a still closer Franco–German association; that in doing so it reasserted French political leadership in western Europe; and that it represented a yearning that Europe should have a greater voice in world affairs. At the close of the peroration in which he asked the French parliament to ratify the treaty it was to this last sentiment that Maurice Faure, minister of state at the Ministry of Foreign Affairs, made his appeal; 'Well, there are not four Great Powers, there are two; America and Russia. There will be a third by the end of the century: China. It depends on you whether there will be a fourth: Europe.'[134] The argument accepts all these political motivations, but asserts that, except in Germany, the economic foundation of the treaties was more fundamental, because without it they could not have achieved their additional political objectives. These were, in any case, not truly separable from the economic ones.

---

[133] *DDF*, 1956, I, no. 122, Note du Département, 23 February 1956.
[134] France, Assemblée Nationale, *Débats*, 5 July 1957. Cited by M. Camps, *Britain and the European Community 1955–1963* (Princeton and London, 1964), p. 88.

A complete account of the negotiation and signing of the Treaties of Rome will have to await the opening of all the French and German Foreign Office records. There seem, though, as a result of the general opening of other records no important mysteries to be revealed. The economic reasons for France to sign became more persuasive during the negotiations, leading in November 1956 to a rapid acceleration towards concluding the Treaties. Either France renounced liberalization, modernization, and its hopes for the future, or it took the economic risk. The speed with which the text was drafted from mid-November is clear testimony to the collective sense that the risk had to be taken. The Benelux proposals, though, were greatly altered between summer 1955 and November 1956 in France's favour by safeguards and additions which left much disgruntled opinion afterwards in the Dutch government.

Opinion of French Foreign Office officials on the discussions in the Spaak Committee and on its subsequent report was divided, but generally still not in favour of the common market. The Spaak Committee's eventual report to the foreign ministers insisted, as Beyen always had, on irreversibility: progress towards a common market could not be stopped at an intermediate stage. There was therefore no possibility of trial and error, for France signing the treaty meant removing tariffs within a fixed timetable until the process was complete. This was one of the two great hesitations which officialdom voiced. The other was the effect of the common market on the French empire, especially in North Africa. Could France run the risk that the new statute for the French Union would be weakened in its effects by new economic relationships to Europe? Olivier Wormser, the official who directed the French negotiating team on the Spaak Committee, was opposed to taking these risks and felt that France should be prepared to go no further than the first stage of any customs union, with the right to withdraw if it was not working. It was certainly necessary, he agreed, to regulate European markets rather than progress towards a liberal free-for-all. Would not the wiser way to do this however, he suggested, be by agreements between the major firms in each area of production? Such arrangements could be closely supervised and even controlled financially by the states, who would thus effectively be creating national investment companies in all the major areas of industrial development that they wished to pursue and regulate.[135] It is quite impossible to imagine Germany accepting any such solution. In Bonn the idea was that in a common market disparities between wages, social benefits, manufacturing costs, and prices would be gradually eliminated without government effort. The role of the state in regulating markets would be confined to the one it already occupied at the national level.

[135] *DDF*, 1956, I, no. 293, Note de la Direction des Affaires Economiques et Financières, 3 March 1956.

Once the Dutch demand that the customs union treaty must incorporate automatic procedures by which tariffs would be removed became the standpoint of Belgium, Germany and Italy, as it quickly did inside the Spaak Committee, the scope for negotiating merely one round of tariff cuts with no guarantee that they would continue had gone. Had something weaker been possible, or had it been possible for France to commit itself only to the first four-year stage and then, if it wished, withdraw, the fears that the tax, social security and wage burden on French manufacturing costs would remain much higher than in Germany would not have had to be translated into demands for prior harmonization and these into the beginnings of a European Community social policy. In reaction against the concept of the High Authority, most countries approached the negotiations from the standpoint that supranationality should be no more than what proved minimally necessary. This only increased the need to write into the treaty text the maximum possible detail of the actions that must be taken in the future, and this in turn made French hesitations and resistance greater.

The French 'had played a rather sorry part' at Messina, making it clear 'that they must consider not what they *should* do, but what they *could* do without the French government having to face a debate in the Chamber'.[136] It was essential for the French negotiators to produce a text which would not meet the fate of the EDC treaty. The British, until the last moment thought this could not be done. The Germans, especially Adenauer, often had doubts. The Italian foreign minister, Gaetano Martino, was more optimistic from the start, believing that the political balance in France pointed the way to the customs union.[137] When the French elections in January 1956 saw a collapse of the Gaullist movement and massive electoral gains to the Poujade protest movement, the communists, and the socialists, Adenauer judged this to be 'a severe set-back for the idea of European integration' and Spaak thought it so 'disastrous' that he wondered 'what could happen to small countries like Belgium and Holland, which could not really exist on their own. There were moments when he thought that the sensible thing to do would be to join the British Commonwealth.'[138]

In fact the election results meant that European integration was one plank of a possible agreement within a governing coalition of socialists and MRP. It may well have been this possibility that made the new socialist prime minister Guy Mollet more favourable to the Six than he had shown himself at the time of the negotiations for the ECSC. But the greater dependence of the governing coalition on socialist votes increased the strength of the

---

[136] PRO, FO371/116039, 'The Messina Conference and the OEEC', Report by J.E. Coulson, 13 June 1955.

[137] ACS-VCM, 12 July 1955.

[138] PRO, FO371/124421, Sir F. Hoyer-Miller, Bonn Embassy, to FO, 5 January 1956; Sir George Labouchère, Brussels Embassy, to FO, 6 January 1956.

demands for harmonization, for a treaty which would solidify French welfare gains, rather than endanger them in a direct manufacturing competition with Germany. 'The French view', said the new foreign minister Christian Pineau about the Spaak Committee's work,

> was that while the common market was quite possibly desirable in the long run, it was essential that it should not give rise to any ideological conflict, such as was provoked by the EDC. For this reason the French would urge on their Messina colleagues the importance of going slow on this front, and contenting themselves with long and patient studies concerning wages, social benefits, protection of industries, etc.[139]

Euratom looked easier to get through parliament. But at the Venice meeting of the foreign ministers of the Six on 29–30 May 1956 to which the Spaak report was presented, the other countries were not prepared to negotiate Euratom without also negotiating the Spaak Committee's report on a common market. The French government therefore adopted a position in which it accepted inter-governmental discussions on the Spaak Committee's common market proposal, while reserving the right to reject any agreement which would not offer an escape from further automatic stages of tariff reduction at the end of the initial four-year period which the report proposed. This was clearly unacceptable to the others as a final position and was tolerated as temporizing in order to appease domestic opposition or give more time to convert it.

The need for harmonization was raised by the French at the Venice meeting which accepted that this harmonization would have had to be achieved before the end of the first stage of the customs union, which the Spaak report suggested should last for four years. It was only on the basis of this understanding that France entered into the inter-governmental negotiations on the Spaak report. In those inter-governmental talks the French delegation took their own awkward view of what the initial period should be. They asked for it to be defined in terms of objectives to be reached, rather than as a specific period of time, with the implication that if these objectives had not been attained, the four-year period might be extended. This was still the French position as late as mid-October 1956.

Furthermore, France still insisted on the right to keep its temporary import surcharges and export subsidies until it judged that levels of prices, wages and manufacturing costs had been harmonized sufficiently to allow their removal. This was acceptable to the others only if a schedule and a method of reducing both surcharges and subsidies was prescribed by the agreement. This, however, was in turn unacceptable to France, because it appeared to be the equivalent of allowing other countries to prescribe the timing of a devaluation of the franc. On what had become for the French

---

[139] PRO, FO371/122023, Conversation between M. Pineau and Sir Gladwyn Jebb, 10 February 1956.

the essential points on which they must obtain concessions to be sure of winning enough support at home the discussions and negotiations, including those in the Spaak Committee, had now lasted intermittently for sixteen months without any agreement being reached. The common market was, Spaak said, being held up by France's 'impossible demands'.[140] The German foreign minister von Brentano thought in late October that 'if this state of affairs was allowed to continue it might be a long time before any agreement on the common market or on Euratom emerged'.[141]

Between July and October the French government however made up its mind to sign the treaty and was only looking for a reasonable show of public concession by the others on the issue of harmonization.[142] It viewed with alarm the vehemence of some German reactions to its negotiating stance. This came to a head over the two days 21–2 October which had been set aside to try to reach agreement on the issue of harmonization. It was well enough understood in French government circles that what could be gained under the heading of harmonization of wage and social security costs would not in fact make a significant alteration to the relative prices of French and German goods. Indeed before the two days of negotiations Marjolin described the specific points on which France required concessions as 'nonsense' and 'a sacred cow'.[143] Yet for parliamentary reasons they were necessary, and it was precisely on those points that the German opposition to the treaty seized and disrupted what the French hoped would be a satisfactory compromise.

The persistent demand for harmonization can be traced back to the inter-ministerial committee to inquire into relative manufacturing costs in France and Western Europe at the time of the resumption of France's role in the OEEC trade liberalization programme. Among the complaints that French car manufacturers, for example, had made to the committee was that the working week in France was only forty hours, whereas it was forty-eight in Germany and Belgium. Because actual hours worked were very similar, overtime pay at higher rates was a larger part of weekly take-home pay in France.[144] These findings were translated into the demand that the working week in manufacturing in the common market should be standardized, at least as far as the basis of calculating pay was concerned, and that overtime payment rates should also be standardized. France had, in principle, equal pay for men and women. In the other countries women's pay was on average only 60–65 per cent of men's pay. Equal pay for the sexes

---

[140] PRO, FO371/122036, Report from the Paris Embassy on the meeting on 21–2 October of the foreign ministers of the Six, 23 October 1956.

[141] ibid., Sir F. Hoyer-Millar, Bonn Embassy, to FO, 23 October 1956.

[142] PRO, FO371/122037. Note of a meeting between R.F. Bretherton and Robert Marjolin, 17 October 1956.

[143] ibid.

[144] AN, F60^{ter} 470, Secrétariat Général du Comité Interministériel pour les Questions de Coopération Economique, 'L'industrie française de l'automobile et la libération des échanges', December 1954.

became also therefore one of the demands for harmonization. So too did the demand that other countries provide the same amount of paid holiday as France.

It was in fact by no means clear that French employers paid a heavier burden in social security contributions than Italians or Belgians. German employers certainly had to meet smaller social security charges, but with the increase in social security benefits in Germany in 1955 occasioned by the pensions law in that year the gap was beginning to close. In general the higher levies on French employers and the differences in provision for holidays and overtime were relatively trivial when set against the whole range of manufacturing costs. Meeting the French demands would not have imposed any great burden on German manufacturers, nor any they would not soon meet in any case as a result of domestic pressures. The more serious objection to concessions to France in this respect was that it was necessary to secure the support of German trade unions for the treaty. Even a clause which implied a levelling up of German wages could not be written into the treaty if it appeared to threaten the principle of free collective bargaining.

Erhard seized on French persistence and elevated their demand for harmonization into a genuine threat to the future competitiveness of German manufacturing. Before the meetings on 21–2 October France proposed that the other countries should agree to legislate for equal pay for the sexes within two years of the signature of the treaty and that they should devise a method of harmonizing working hours and overtime payments, as well as holidays with pay, by the end of the first stage of tariff removal. If they had not met these conditions, France could be exempted from the automatic progress to the second stage. The first stage satisfactorily completed, the member-states should equalize wages during the following stages and before the final achievement of the customs union. This left ample time for the equalizing effects of a common market to work themselves out, without any excessive interference, and avoided the problem of circumscribing the rights of German unions to free collective bargaining. There were some objections from other quarters to the idea that the treaty would try to regulate the path of future wage changes.[145] But it was Erhard who seized on the French compromise proposal as an example of the damage the treaty would do.

He was simply not in favour of any treaty which would internationalize the increases in welfare to which both French and German governments were committed. This emerged unambiguously from his conversations with Maurice Faure on 16 September. He judged French welfare legislation to be 'baneful' (*néfaste*). Inevitably in a common market its influence would spread to Germany. France too would find cause to regret the economi-

---

[145] PRO, FO371/122035, Summary of a memo on the French position in the negotiations by Spaak. Copy provided to the embassy in Brussels, 18 October 1956.

cally detestable pensions legislation just passed in Germany.[146] He demanded to be allowed to attend the negotiating sessions on 21–2 October. When this request was turned down by the other countries, he nevertheless still attended, to the great embarrassment of foreign minister von Brentano.

Studies presented to the negotiators beforehand showed that arrangements for paid holidays over the course of a whole working year in the different countries were in fact very similar. No country dared object to the inclusion in the treaty of a promise to legislate for equal pay for the sexes.[147] This left only the French demand that overtime payments must be standardized on the basis of a forty-hour working week. Erhard fiercely opposed it. Because for the French negotiators harmonization was a necessary condition for accepting the automatic timetable for tariff reductions, they could not then agree that the customs union could move automatically to its second stage. The transition, they insisted, would require the unanimous agreement of the Council of Ministers. That of course would have destroyed the main point of the treaty, its irreversibility. Erhard then deliberately leaked the discussions to journalists. Negotiations, he told them, were now in a deadlock which would never be resolved and had become futile. It was the opinion of the Dutch that, had he wanted to accept a solution, a form of words which avoided the quarrel over the forty-hour week could easily have been found during the negotiating session.

Even had the full range of concessions on overtime and pay been made to France, it would have increased wage costs in the Federal Republic over the four-year initial period of the common market by an average of about 4 per cent. Such a percentage would have been no higher than the normal rate of wage increases. Erhard's fear was perhaps that German unions might use the treaty text to demand higher basic wages, or that French wage rates would continue to increase and in so doing lead to further wage demands in the Federal Republic. Underlying his actions however was his belief that his own government's foreign policy was placing crippling future burdens on the economy by maintaining the close links with France.

It is sometimes suggested that the Treaties of Rome would not have been signed and the long negotiations have been in the end as futile as Erhard implied had international circumstances not taken the turn they did at the end of October. The Hungarian rising; its brutal suppression; the Anglo–French–Israeli invasion of Egypt; the direct threats to the invaders by the Soviet Union; the refusal of the United States to support the pound sterling until Britain ended the invasion; all these things happened between the apparent deadlock of 22 October and a meeting between Adenauer and Mollet which had been fixed for 6 November. But the truth is that France

---

[146] *DDF*, II, 1956, no. 184, Conversation entre M. Maurice Faure et M. Erhard, 16 September 1956.

[147] That turned out not to be the same thing as providing it.

was looking for a way to conclude the treaty before these dramatic events took place and that Adenauer was looking for a way to repair the damage done by his minister of the economy. Mollet's personal message to Adenauer on 31 October makes it clear enough that he saw the purpose of their meeting as removing the obstacles to agreement and signature.[148] Obviously it was not without effect that the Adenauer–Mollet meeting did take place at the height of the Suez crisis. But there is no evidence that American failure to support the Franco–British invasion of Egypt changed Mollet's and the French government's opinion about the treaty. What seems to be closer to the truth is that both men felt 'that in view of the magnitude of other recent world events it was absurd to argue about points such as the harmonization of social charges'.[149]

Germany, Adenauer agreed, would allow France to delay tariff reductions at the end of the first stage unless by that time there was effective standardization of overtime regulations or it could be shown that pay increases elsewhere had been faster than in France. Germany dropped its demand for a fixed time limit on the duration of French import taxes and export subsidies. In return France accepted that there would be periodic consultations about these items and acknowledged an obligation to remove them. What this implied for the powers to be given to the new European political machinery, however, was not so clear. The principle of irreversibility had been accepted, but the control of political decisions was still, if France had its way, to be left to a Council of Ministers where unanimity would be required to allow the progress from first to second and successive stages. There, Mollet and Adenauer could do no more than agree that they would find a solution later. As the French foreign minister wrote of Adenauer, it was evident that he 'did not intend to come back from a trip which had raised criticism in parliamentary circles in Bonn without a substantial result in the area of the "relaunching" of Europe'.[150] Mollet and Adenauer indeed came to so quick an agreement on 6 November on how to settle the remaining points at issue in the negotiations that they scarcely read through the text of what they had agreed. From that moment the negotiations proceeded at speed to a completed treaty text.

How open the competition to which the agreement on harmonization committed France really was, is a question which would deserve separate investigation, if it could yet be properly answered. The car manufacturers, for example, who had been so responsible for starting the hare of harmonization, had other ways of adjusting to competition. The treaty included a protocol, agreed in the Mollet–Adenauer meeting, that the member-states considered it desirable that overtime hours and rates by the end of the first

---

[148] *DDF*, 1956, III, doc. 75.
[149] PRO, FO371/122038, Report of a conversation with Karl Carstens by Sir F. Hoyer-Millar, Bonn Embassy, 10 November 1956.
[150] *DDF*, 1956, III, doc. no. 146, circular letter from Pineau to ambassadors.

stage should be similar to those in France in 1956; if they were not, France would be allowed to impose certain safeguards. There was no pressure from the French car industry subsequently to invoke the safeguards. When marketing surveys by Simca revealed that one in three of the potential car buyers in France wanted a German car, the firm's response was to try to reach an understanding between French and German producers to bias the flow of imports into both countries towards the models least competitive with domestic production.[151] As soon as the Treaties of Rome were signed French and German industrialists began to meet in large numbers for frequent, regular detailed discussion under the auspices of their official organizations. Meanwhile the French employers' federation continued with only one junior employee on a low salary to look after relations with Britain.

Yet if the issue of harmonization was subordinate, it would be a mistake to see the time and energy it consumed as merely an accident of negotiating tactics. The problem genuinely was how to construct a commercial framework which would not endanger the levels of social welfare which had been reached. The shift to a much higher level of public welfare provision in the mid-1950s in the Federal Republic, for which German employers had to meet some of the bill, was important. It was rapidly rising wages and welfare in the Federal Republic which took much of the force out of the demonstrations of cost differences which the French inquiries had revealed in 1954. If French civil servants and politicians could take a sceptical view, as they did, of the arguments of their own manufacturers about harmonization, they could not take the same attitude to welfare in general. The public commitment of the Treaties of Rome to improve the level of welfare provision to that of the most generous provider repeated that of the Treaty of Paris for the same reasons. Erhard was defending a position that was anachronistic and electorally unpopular. The Treaties of Rome had to be also an external buttress to the welfare state.

Three issues were left undecided which were to be extremely troublesome. One was that of the relative power of the supranational bodies, the European Commission, the Court and the Parliament compared to those of the Council of Ministers. A second was the relationship of the French empire to the common market. A third was the question of agricultural trade.

At the opening session of the Spaak Committee Hallstein had made it unambiguous that Germany wanted the eventual outcome to be another set of supranational institutions. The Spaak report however recommended that the main decision-making body should be the Council of Ministers, a body solely representative of the national governments. The European Commission was to be essentially an executive for enforcing the treaty, although with the power of initiating proposals under certain limited

---

[151] NA, SD, RG59 440.002/12-158, 'French Automobile Industry Attitudes Towards the Common Market', 4 December 1958.

circumstances. The Council of Ministers should be allowed, it recommended, in some circumstances, especially when it was considering policy initiatives from the Commission for approval, to reach decisions by a qualified majority, thus eliminating the right of national veto over some policies. The suggestion was, that after the second stage of tariff reduction had been successfully achieved the number of circumstances in which the Council of Ministers would not be required to reach unanimous decisions might be extended. The French negotiating position until mid-October 1956 was that progress itself beyond the first stage of implementation of the customs union would require a unanimous decision by the Council of Ministers. This would not merely give France the right to veto further tariff changes after the initial small reductions; it meant that the treaty would have no supranational content if France decided to exercise that right. Although French negotiators took a compromise proposal to modify this stance to the meeting on 22 October, they withdrew it in the face of Erhard's attitude.

The compromise that eventually emerged was not far from what France had demanded. There would have to be unanimous agreement in the Council of Ministers that the first stage had been completed in either four or five years. If a unanimous decision had still not been reached at the end of six years the Council of Ministers would be able to decide by a qualified majority vote to proceed to the next stage. If this happened, however, any member finding itself outvoted could require the decision to be referred to an Arbitration Board. From the ruling of that body there would be no escape. There was a further complicated struggle to define the qualified majority voting system, so that the smaller countries would not be inevitably outvoted, during which there were even attempts to define one that would be suitable for a later British entry.

The distribution of powers between nations, as represented in the Council of Ministers, and supranation, as represented by the Commission, inclined much more to the nation-states than Hallstein had indicated as desirable from the German standpoint when he had first addressed the Spaak Committee. It did not satisfy civil servants such as Ophüls or von der Groeben who had fought inside the German government for the common market.[152] But it was not the outcome only of France's objections to any greater degree of supranationality; it also appeased opposition inside the Federal Republic. The Dutch too would have wished a greater extent of supranational powers, but once Mollet and Adenauer had laid out the path for the rest of the negotiations the smaller countries simply had to take what was handed down to them by the French and Germans. The Dutch constitutional proposals, for example, had been to allow the Council of Ministers to act only on initiatives from the Commission, almost the

[152] A. Müller-Armack, *Auf dem Wege . . .*, op. cit., p. 117.

reverse of what was finally decided, and to give to the Commission decisive powers over agricultural exports, trade policy with non-Community countries, and cartel and competition policy. If the treaty gave fewer powers to the Commission and fewer powers of supranational decision-making to the Community as a whole than the Spaak report had recommended, it yielded more than France had appeared ready throughout most of the negotiations to concede. Some of these powers were to be retaken by de Gaulle's governments in the 1960s, but more in word than deed, which tended to show that the powers that had been conceded were indeed necessary.

The biggest concession was to France's last-minute demand that its overseas territories be included in the common market. When Anthony Nutting, under-secretary at the Foreign Office, was escorting his counterpart Maurice Faure back to London airport after his visit in June 1956, Faure 'dwelt at length upon the importance of Europe and Africa getting together as the counterbalance to the growing expansion of the Soviet Union. He had no illusions about the future of competitive co-existence and he said that Europe must unite its efforts with Africa or go under in this competition.'[153] France did have great trade advantages with its empire because it had not yet applied the OEEC trade liberalization rules to trade with its overseas territories. It could not develop a system of preferences because some of the overseas territories did not have tariffs, even inoperable ones, against the metropole. Decisions about a future colonial tariff regime had been in abeyance since Vichy because trade and currency controls had made existing tariffs largely superfluous. The 1955 decision to conform to OEEC rules meant that for this technical reason alone, although there were many others, the Treaties of Rome required some change in French imperial commercial policy. The French demand that goods from its overseas territories be admitted to the common market on the same terms as French goods was, though, a part of a much wider adjustment of French attitudes to the imperial role. It was linked to the demand for an investment fund which would attract the capital of the EEC member states for investment in the French empire.

While the achievement of a common market had seemed a decision which might still be postponed, the question of its economic impact on the empire's future, although examined in several reports, had also been postponed. The agreement at Venice to enter into official inter-governmental negotiations was accompanied by official notice that France's imperial interests would also have to be catered for. As things stood in 1956 there seemed large advantages to France and imperial producers in retaining existing arrangements. France had a virtual monopoly of its imperial markets. But producers in the overseas territories

---

[153] PRO, FO371/122029, Report by Anthony Nutting on the visit of Maurice Faure to London, 15 June 1956.

received prices on French markets for their products at least 25 per cent above world prices. The head of the French branch of Lever Brothers paid, for example, 40 per cent above the world price for the palm oil and related products which the French commercial system obliged the company to buy from the empire.[154] These arrangements were in conflict with the objectives of French industrial policy: modernization and successful competition in Europe. There was, furthermore, a widespread understanding that the political imperialism still practised in the 1950s could not survive and a growing conviction that, because the French empire was crucial to France's survival as a major power, it had to be linked to France's security policy in Europe. Acceptance in principle of the common market as the basis of that security policy provided the moment to change the relationship with the overseas territories.

The existence of the Commonwealth wherein large countries had tariff autonomy and would not have welcomed removing protection against European manufactured exports would have prevented any similar move by Britain. The French empire was transformed from a system of direct rule, increasingly costly, enfeebled, and resisted, into the complex system of economic and cultural dependencies which was created in the 1960s. In spite of the attachment shown to Commonwealth and empire as a support for Britain's status as a world power, the subsequent history of the empire was marked by indifference to the future of its poorer colonial territories; a lingering and commercially disadvantageous attachment to the 'Old Commonwealth' which was said to be an insurmountable barrier to entry into a European common market; a realization that this had been a mistake; an inability to decide on a European policy which would rectify that mistake and be acceptable enough to gain it entry to the European Community; and the subsequent disintegration of the empire into many separate units whose cultural and economic attachment to Britain in most cases rapidly withered away. Of course, the steps in France between deciding that the empire must be part of a European common market and the imperial arrangements of the 1960s were many, but the first bold step was taken in 1956 with the decision that producers in France's overseas territories must have access to the common market on equal terms, and that that in turn meant removing non-tariff barriers as well as tariffs on common market exports to its overseas territories.

When the decision was made it was assumed that it would be supported by the two other colonial powers, Belgium and the Netherlands, since it was Germany that would bear most of the cost. Adenauer accepted the French decision in his November talks with Mollet and the French introduced into the negotiations for the first time on 16 November 1956 a joint Franco–Belgian proposal along these lines. It was never vitally important in Belgium whether the Congo was in the common market or not, how-

[154] PRO, FO371/122046, R.S. Isaacson, Commercial Dept. of Paris Embassy to FO, 23 October 1956.

ever, and the Dutch were strong opponents of the whole idea. When at the crucial negotiating session of 26–8 January 1957 the Dutch sought to reject the French demands, and the Germans were damply discouraging, Italy, Belgium and Luxembourg were in favour.[155] The way was opened to the later Yaoundé and Lomé agreements which formalized the trade links between most of Africa and the Community.

The problem of agricultural protection and the marketing of agricultural surpluses was not resolved at all before the treaty was signed. The issue was fudged in the treaty text which recorded that all parties had agreed that the agricultural sector should be the subject of a common agricultural policy to be supranationally administered. The whole question of agricultural protection and its relation to European integration is considered at length in the next chapter. Here, it need only be said that agreement on this way forward was only reached in late January 1957 and that the French government had to pledge itself formally before the national assembly that it would actually succeed in negotiating a common agricultural policy that would advance the interests of French agriculture. In the first four- to five-year stage of the common market France was guaranteed long-term purchasing contracts for its food surplus exports to the other members which were to be larger than the average value of contracts over the previous three years and at higher prices. This amounted to a temporary preference system combined with guaranteed minimum export prices. This had been the goal of French agricultural policy for some time. But it was explicit that it was a temporary solution only, to allow France to sign, and that in the initial stage of the union it would begin to be replaced by the common agricultural policy where France would have to start bargaining again.

Almost everything France wanted out of the treaty it got. The supranational authority was weak. The initial stage of the customs union could be prolonged if France had still not brought its manufacturing costs and balance of payments into what was judged a satisfactory state. The treaty made an explicit commitment to maintain the high levels of welfare payments and the short working week to which most French governments had been committed since 1936 and the Popular Front. The French empire would be given preferential markets in the Six and benefit from an investment fund to which the whole community would contribute. French farmers, albeit temporarily, were given the guaranteed good prices and markets outside France which they had been demanding. The treaty was easily ratified by the national assembly in July 1957 by 341 votes for to 235 against.

The treaty text was drawn up around the principle on which Beyen had insisted from the outset, that each stage of progress towards the customs union would be achieved automatically by the application of a method

---

[155] *DDF*, 1957, I, no. 86, French ambassador in Brussels to Pineau, 28 January 1957.

already laid down in the treaty. It stipulated an initial tariff cut of 10 per cent on all tariff posts. Thereafter the reductions in tariffs would not apply to each commodity but to average tariffs for groups of commodities weighted by the value of imports from the other member states. The problems of nomenclature which this might have posed were resolved by allocating commodities to these groups solely according to the height of the tariff on them. This had the advantage of forcing down especially high tariffs at the start and there was also, to strengthen this tendency, a special provision to reduce all tariff posts over 25 per cent.

The first stage of establishing a common external tariff was to last either four or five years. The period was left imprecise because of a political compromise to cater for France. Once the first stage had been achieved there would begin a second stage which would involve reductions in the national tariffs of a further 30 per cent within a four-year period, followed thereafter by annual reductions of 10 per cent. The base level for calculating these reductions was the average of tariffs levied over the period 1953–5. The treaty text also made recommendations on how the common external tariff was to be established. The relevant duty for each country to be used in the calculation was to be the lower of two figures, either the most recent duty before the treaty's ratification or the mean of the previous three years. The arithmetic mean of the duty on each item for all countries having been established, it was to be used as the common tariff for all commodities whose actual duty did not differ from the mean by more than 15 per cent. Where an actual duty exceeded the mean by more than this margin, actual duties were to be reduced to a stipulated level for raw materials (10–15 per cent), for semi-manufactured products (20–25 per cent), and for finished products (35–40 per cent), and the average was to be recalculated. There were in addition lists of commodities, almost entirely raw materials and semi-manufactured products, on which duties could not go beyond a fixed ceiling.

On the treatment of quotas the treaty did not aim at the same precision. The OEEC trade liberalization programme was to apply up to the date of the first 10 per cent tariff cut. After that, no new quotas were to be allowed on trade which had been once liberalized. After the first tariff cut the size of all remaining quotas was to be uniformly increased. State-trading would no longer be an exception to this procedure, a provision only possible because agriculture had been set aside as the subject of a special common policy. Existing quotas would not be allowed to discriminate between member-states, so that any bilateral quotas had to be extended to the whole Community from 1 January 1959. Where existing quotas were so low a percentage of national production that their progressive enlargement would still leave intra-Community trade distorted, at the end of the tenth year their number would have to be reduced to the point where they were

---

[156] US T, EUR 3/12 v. 2, 'Italy and the Common Market', reporting a conversation between Mr Hunter of the US Treasury and ambassador Cosmelli, 28 February 1957.

at least 20 per cent of national output in that commodity.

On the face of things Beyen, who had left office in summer 1956, could not have wished for anything more precise, the sacrifice of tariff autonomy within a common set of rules and with the possibility of relapses excluded, a more gradual relaxation of quotas, and all the safeguard clauses subject to a common and not a national determination. However, an important number of the most difficult commodities, particularly those for which the method for calculating the external tariff meant an increase over the height of the existing Benelux tariff, was set aside for later consideration as List G. List G covered 20 per cent of the Community's imports by value. Nor had Beyen or his colleagues accepted, when they made their original proposals, that there would be an overall increase in Benelux tariffs as they were replaced by the common external tariff, but that was now the certain outcome.

The Dutch, whose persistence from 1952 had been the foundation of the whole enterprise, were left to contemplate ruefully. The temporary agricultural arrangements did not please them and it was not sure how much bargaining power they would now have in getting something better. They were opposed to the inclusion of the French empire, but getting no support from the other five, even from their Benelux partners, had to abandon outright opposition and ended up claiming a derisory sum from the proposed investment fund for their own remaining empire. The arrangements for removing quotas were not what they would have preferred. The Euratom treaty which was linked to the European Economic Community Treaty in the ratification process committed them to budgetary contributions higher than they would have wished in a cause in which they had little interest. Their tariffs to non-Community countries would be increased by the terms of the treaty. The price they had paid for the guarantees of commercial policy and the removal of tariffs was a much higher one than they had intended. Nevertheless the treaty did enshrine Beyen's main idea, on which the Dutch refused to make any compromise, that the common market was an irreversible, unbreakable agreement.

Nevertheless, if the common market was more protectionist from the outset than Beyen had anticipated, if the Netherlands in particular, which had pressed so hard for the customs union, felt that at the end of the negotiations it had suffered more than the others, it was still a commitment to guarantees of future commercial policy without precedent in European history. And the solemnity of that guarantee was emphasized by the promise to reach an 'ever-closer union'.

It was that central point, accepted by France at the end of the long chain of concessions for which it bargained, that gave the Treaties of Rome their immense significance in Europe's history. The solemnity of what was to be agreed was never called into question by the most pernickety of the French officials who worked over the text. Indeed, it was what incited them to pursue the grand bargain in its finest details. Their bargaining position was a strong one. While the Italian ambassador to the USA agreed 'with

chancellor Adenauer's reported disgust with some of the undignified trading tactics indulged in by the parties to the conference' and thought that
France had taken advantage of the situation while thinking only of immediate gains, he put his finger at the same time on the strength of France's
position. 'Europe', he said, 'cannot organize without France and, to get
her in, prices must be paid which may seem exorbitant. As the soldiers say,
France has the geography.'

If we ask why Europe had to be 'organized' in this particular way the
answer seems clear. The will of the European nation-state to survive as an
organizational entity depended on the prosperity which sustained the
domestic post-war political compromises everywhere. The importance of
foreign trade to that prosperity was great and was magnified in the political
and economic thought of the time. West Germany was the pivot on which
the increases in foreign trade, investment and prosperity turned. It was
essential for political and economic reasons that West Germany be bound
to the west, but it needed an arrangement that satisfied the economic
interests of Western European countries if a durable way of doing this was
to be found. The common market was the one durable way that had been
found.

It was the fact that it rested so firmly on the economic and social
foundations of post-war political change and in so doing reinforced the
post-war nation-state that gave the European Economic Community its
strength and marked out the Treaties of Rome as a turning-point in
Europe's history. The EEC rested firmly on its recognition of two dominant and interconnected developments in Western Europe after 1945. It
recognized and formalized the reality that changes in the political economy
of the post-war state invalidated all earlier models of international commercial relations between those Western European states where the
changes had taken place, and it created an entirely different model which
would buttress that new political economy. It recognized and formalized
the central role of Germany in those relations. Only twelve years after the
overthrow of the cruellest of anti-parliamentary regimes there this was a
remarkable fact. It was the proof that Western Europe could create a more
durable and more harmonious foundation for post-war society than its rival
beyond the Elbe.

5 The Europeanization of agricultural protection

In the 1960s anyone attempting to explain the origins and purpose of the European Economic Community might have been tempted to seek that explanation in the history of European agriculture. The Community's survival seemed repeatedly menaced by noisy public quarrels whose immediate cause was trade in some foodstuff or other. To judge from contemporary newspapers the most serious question in the middle of that decade for the future of a united Europe was the price of wheat. The Community's Common Agricultural Policy (CAP) by the end of the decade took up four-fifths of its administrative effort and 70 per cent of its budget. Yet the member-states were among the most industrialized countries in the world and the Treaties of Rome had been overwhelmingly concerned with trade in manufactures. Agricultural trade was a matter of only secondary importance and the previous chapter found little need to consider it when explaining the background to the treaties. The agricultural sector, furthermore, was of rapidly diminishing weight in the economies of each of the member-states. Nevertheless the economic, social and political problems of agriculture became a central aspect of the Community from the moment the Treaties were signed.

Agricultural protection and the maintenance of a satisfactory level of income in agriculture had become a basic policy in each European nation. Support for agricultural incomes led to support for agricultural output, which in turn led to food surpluses which had not previously existed, high-priced in relation to non-European food. As early as 1950 there were already attempts to create a common European framework for trade in agricultural products. These attempts showed how extraordinarily difficult the problem was. It manifestly required an international solution if domestic policies were not to change, but any international solution appeared to require more sacrifices than the beneficiaries of national agricultural policies were prepared to make. In agriculture Western Europe had some easily perceived interests in common against the rest of the world. Reconciling them in common action already appeared so difficult in the 1950s that the strife and effort of the 1960s was easily predictable.

The objective of achieving a common market in manufactures would have been more easily secured by leaving agriculture out of the arrangement, as was done in the case of EFTA. There was, however, no possibility of this solution, partly because agricultural exports were so important to Dutch export earnings (and by no means a negligible part of Italy's), and partly because France had made expensive efforts since the war in the name of economic progress to generate agricultural exports for which by 1957 it wanted a guaranteed outlet. In these circumstances the architects of the common market treaty made the bold declaration that its signatories would shape a Common Agricultural Policy, without having reached any agreement on what its principles would be and having already manifestly failed in an earlier attempt to do so.

In accepting this commitment the signatories set themselves a political task of an altogether different political order from that of regulating coal, iron and steel markets or harmonizing general rules of foreign trade. To agree to shape the details of production and prices which affected the incomes of millions of farmers and workers, for the most part operating extremely small enterprises, was to accept a vast political and economic task, as well as to descend much more deeply into the realm of national electoral politics. To understand why this commitment had to be accepted it is necessary to see the great extent to which the problems of Western European agriculture were already common before 1957, as well as the increasingly clear evidence that they were not easily able to be resolved within a national framework.

THE ECONOMICS AND POLITICS OF POST-WAR WESTERN EUROPEAN AGRICULTURE

While western Europe was being transformed after 1815 from a society in which income came mainly from agriculture to one in which it came mainly from industry and services, there were very few periods anywhere where agricultural income grew as fast as industrial income. Only where countries were able to respond to the increasing demand for food from the rapidly growing industrialized and urbanized populations beyond their own frontiers was it occasionally possible to increase farm incomes at the same rate as those in other sectors of the economy. Such cases were infrequent and the investment costs were high. The successful concentration of Danish agriculture after 1880 on providing bacon and butter to the British market and the similar concentration of Dutch farmers on a range of specialized products such as cheese, eggs and flower bulbs for the German and British markets were both examples of what might be done to make the returns to agricultural activity as high as those in industrial production. But even in Denmark, which is the most striking case, it was only for a brief period of twenty-five years before the First World War that incomes in the agricultural sector rose as fast as those in industry. Of course the incomes of the largest landowners or farmers might improve as rapidly as those elsewhere in the economy and frequently did not lag so far behind. This, together with the very wide national differences in the social structure of agriculture, in tenurial arrangements and in the average size of farms, meant that the political response to this long-term tendency of agricultural incomes to fall behind was very varied. Nevertheless it would be hard to deny that in general the machinery of constitutional government in Europe found it increasingly hard between 1873 and 1929 to cope with these widening economic and social disparities.

Their first cause was the tendency for productivity to grow more rapidly in industry than in agriculture. In part this was because technological innovation seemed to produce more dramatic improvements in industry. In part it was because the income elasticity of demand for food was less than that for manufactured goods. There were not the sudden increases in consumption which speeded up the pace of industrial production as countries grew richer. In part it was because agriculture was not an activity in which rapid adjustments of capital and labour were easily made. The landholding arrangements were not only extraordinarily varied and complex but they were in most countries the social foundation of the political system and of the army. Changes in managerial systems in agriculture were thus complex political decisions. Although incomes increased more rapidly elsewhere in the economy, large numbers of people were retained in the agricultural sector, where their marginal productivity was nil, in the sense that if they had migrated the only consequence would have been an improvement in per capita productivity; output would not have fallen.

Where new markets could be opened up these problems were less acute. Specialization of output in those foodstuffs for which there was a higher elasticity of demand, usually livestock products, could be combined with a more rapid reduction in the size of the labour force and a narrower gap in incomes between those employed in agriculture and those employed elsewhere. In part this is what occurred in Denmark and in the Netherlands. In both cases, however, the population was only small, so that the foreign markets to which more specialized commodities could be exported also needed to be only small. In the United Kingdom early industrialization and a large service sector reduced the share of agriculture in the national income to a level much lower than elsewhere by the late nineteenth century, and its weight and influence in the political system was consequently diminished. Elsewhere in western Europe maintaining incomes in the agricultural sector became a prime objective of state policy because agricultural interests were so powerful at the political centre. It is hard to conceive any other possible political outcome in France, Germany and Italy, for example, once cheaper foodstuffs began to arrive in quantity in the 1870s from North America and from Russia, than the protection of the agricultural sector from which in the three countries together more than 30 million people still drew their livelihood. This does not mean that the kind of protection given was well-designed to permit economic adjustment or that it solved the problem of the widening gap in rates of sectoral income growth. On the contrary, it was for the most part no more than an attempt to prevent political stability from being threatened by an even wider disparity in rates of growth of income. As such it was not particularly successful, and the rise of violently authoritarian politics from the last quarter of the nineteenth century owed much to the widespread economic and political discontent in the agricultural sector.

Although experiences were somewhat different from country to country, an increase in agricultural incomes relative to others was brought about by the First World War. It proved, however, only temporary and after 1919 the gap between industrial and agricultural incomes again began to widen. Food was not short in international markets and farmers were unable to exercise the leverage on the political system which they had been able to apply during the war. Among their responses to the resumption of pre-war trends may be cited the high degree of political mobilization and violence in the Po Valley and Giulia which was so influential in bringing the fascist regime to power. In Austria, in Hungary, and in eastern and south-eastern Europe similar authoritarian political movements drew their support from the agricultural sector, developing a political rhetoric in which agriculture was exalted as the foundation of a distinct national culture and the bedrock of the nation-state. This reached its apotheosis in the exaltation of the mystical links between blood, race and soil with which the ideology of the National Socialist Party in Germany made such play. In the depression of 1929–32 agricultural prices in many European countries fell by two-thirds and everywhere much more steeply than industrial prices. The Nazi party made its first big electoral gains as the result of a massive protest vote in the heavily agricultural province of Schleswig-Holstein and the difficulty of maintaining constitutional democracy without major concessions to agriculture was demonstrated to the whole of Europe. In a world where the prices of agricultural products in international trade remained depressed and where persistent large-scale industrial unemployment made it politically very difficult to raise food prices at home it was hard for democratic governments to find a satisfactory response to these dangers.

The response in the 1930s was an increasing regulation of certain commodity markets. For some crops, typically wheat, this often went as far as the fixing of prices. In Germany the response was much more comprehensive. The Nazi regime imposed a total control over agriculture and food through a national corporation, the Reichsnährstand. Elsewhere policy was only piecemeal. Typically, it began to take the form of government- or producer-sponsored marketing boards and similar organizations to regulate the output and sales of some products. Although these policies brought agricultural prices up from their catastrophically low levels of 1933, incomes in agriculture in most countries still continued to improve more slowly than in other sectors. The Second World War, like the First, interrupted the trend.

During the Second World War the demand for food rose steeply. The war brought full employment to all combatant countries and even where wage rates did not rise, actual earnings did. Rationing sometimes controlled the extent to which these higher earnings were spent on food, but in many countries, particularly occupied countries, black markets thwarted rationing. Outside occupied economies there was no tendency for rationing to reduce food consumption below its overall pre-war level until the last year of the war. On the contrary, the average level of food consumption was often higher because rationing and price controls improved the level of consumption of the poorer social groups. Soldiers' rations were everywhere higher, usually much higher, than pre-war levels of civilian consumption. While demand was higher, supply fell, because of the shortages of labour and other inputs, the disruption to supply caused by the war, the loss of land to military purposes, and the damage caused by military campaigns. In spite of the rigid government control of the food sector farmers enjoyed much greater prosperity and outside occupied countries a position of relative political power.[1] Even in occupied territories their position was much better than that of other groups.

After 1945 the change in politics combined with a difference in the prevailing economic conditions to preserve the privileged position which the agricultural sector had had during the war. Agricultural output in Europe did not attain its pre-war level until 1951 and for much of that time the only available food surpluses were in the United States and Canada and so purchasable only in the scarce currency, dollars. All increases in domestic food output, expensively obtained though they were, could be justified as dollar saving. At the same time the strategic lessons of the war seemed to be that agriculture should not be allowed to shrink to the point where a country was over-dependent on foreign food supply. Countries which depended heavily on food imports, such as Britain, Germany and Switzerland, had found themselves particularly endangered by the strategies by which the war had been fought, and this led to reversals of earlier policies independent of the post-war supply problems.

These circumstances provided a favourable background against which the representative interest groups of the agricultural sector could press for a far more systematic approach by government than anything that had been tried outside Germany or the United States in the 1930s. The effect of changes in agricultural income on local and regional economies was so important in elections, that, given the changes in the state's overall objectives, such pressure was quickly and strongly effective. Agriculture was brought into the new post-war political consensus as one of the pillars of political stability. To buttress the political system farmers were now treated as if they were providers of a public good.

---

[1] B. Martin and A.S. Milward (eds), *Agriculture and Food Supply in the Second World War* (Ostfildern, 1985).

In every western European country agriculture became the equivalent of a large nationalized industry, managed by interventionist policies which sought to impose macroeconomic objectives in return for exemption from the forces of open economic competition. In some countries the obligations which government accepted were far greater than any it could exact from the agricultural sector in return, obligations which it would never have accepted in the management of a nationalized manufacturing industry. In Norway and Sweden, for example, there was a political guarantee, impossible to uphold though it proved, that incomes in agriculture would be maintained at a level equivalent to those in industry. Elsewhere the avowed purpose of supporting incomes in the agricultural sector was expressed more cautiously. In Austria, France, Germany and the United Kingdom, for example, there were specific legislative undertakings that the level of agricultural incomes would stay in a fixed relationship to that in other sectors of the economy and would not be allowed to fall behind them in periods of income growth. In other countries the political bargain was a tacit one, as in Italy, but none the less significant in its effects.

Ironically, the only thing that gave such a commitment by the state any real chance of success was the tremendous pace of industrialization in western Europe between 1945 and 1960. Although the differential in elasticity of demand for industrial and agricultural goods was even more marked than before, it proved far from an immutable law that labour productivity would grow faster in industry than in agriculture. Much higher rates of growth of industrial output in the great industrialization boom of those years led to a much more rapid absorption of the agricultural labour force into the rest of the economy and this in itself produced remarkable per capita productivity improvements in agriculture. It is impossible to disentangle the effects on the agricultural sector of full employment and a high demand for labour from those of government policies. However the main thrust of government policies in the 1950s in agriculture was certainly not to improve productivity but to maintain incomes and improve output. Had the industrial sector not performed as vigorously as it did it is most improbable that agricultural incomes could have been maintained in such a stable relationship to incomes elsewhere, because average productivity in the agricultural sector would not have risen so rapidly as the simple consequence of the loss of so much redundant labour to other sectors.

Not infrequently one reads that net productivity actually grew faster in the 1950s in agriculture than in manufacturing industry. Calculations of this kind are subject to such large margins of error that their results are extremely variable. It seems wiser to go no further than agreeing that, in comparison to earlier historical periods, the movement of labour productivity in agriculture in western Europe in the 1950s was much closer to the level of that in manufacturing industry and did in some cases actually exceed it. The figures in table 5.1 for the growth rates of productivity in manufacturing industry are not adjusted for man hours worked but are

Table 5.1   Annual average rate of growth of labour productivity in Western
European agriculture and industry, 1949–59

	Agriculture	*Industry*
Austria	1.8	3.7
Belgium	4.6	3.7
Denmark	4.9	2.3
Federal Republic	5.5	5.1
France	4.9	4.7
Ireland	2.5	2.6
Italy	4.7	7.2
Netherlands	3.8	4.6
Norway	3.1	3.2
Sweden	1.7	2.7
United Kingdom	3.8	2.4

Source: UN, ECE, *Some Factors in Economic Growth in Europe during the 1950s* (Geneva,
1964), chapter III, p. 15

related to the size of the labour force, because it seems futile to attempt to
adjust figures for productivity growth rates in a peasant agricultural system
to the number of hours worked. With such rapid changes in the size and
composition of the agricultural labour force changes in hours worked were
probably much more sweeping in agriculture than in industry. That is only
one reason why the figures should be taken as no more than a rough
approximation. They do seem to indicate, though, that in Belgium,
Denmark, and the United Kingdom the growth rate of labour productivity
in agriculture was decidedly higher than in manufacturing. It is perhaps a
more striking fact that in France and Germany, where the growth rates of
industrial productivity were higher, average labour productivity in agriculture at least kept pace and probably slightly exceeded that in industry. It
was a phenomenon of a quite different order that the large protected
agricultural sectors in France and Germany should keep pace in this way
and it is the best indicator of the fundamental changes which took place in
the conditions of agricultural production after 1945.

The nature of these changes as they affected agricultural productivity
was twofold. Rapid technological improvement in agriculture increased
rates of marginal productivity. At the same time the even more striking
improvement in marginal productivity rates in manufacturing, reflected in
higher wages, drew large numbers of workers out of agriculture so that
average productivity in agriculture also improved. In a country such as
Denmark or the United Kingdom, where the average productivity of
agriculture was already relatively high, technological innovation in agriculture after 1945 combined with a relatively lower rate of growth of labour
productivity in manufacturing to make the rate of growth of labour productivity higher in the agricultural sector. Similar forces were probably at work

in Belgium too. For the three countries in table 5.1 which show the highest rates of growth of labour productivity in industry, France, Germany and Italy, the more important force operating to improve agricultural productivity was probably the sustained huge shift of labour away from the farm and into the city. In these cases the rise in average productivity of farm workers mainly reflects the great superiority in marginal productivity of workers in manufacturing. Big gains in marginal physical productivity in industry could make for big gains in average productivity in agriculture, even if marginal rates of productivity in agriculture did not improve. The fact that between 1945 and 1960 average labour productivity in agriculture improved much more rapidly than it seems to have done in any earlier period did not automatically lead to an improvement in farm incomes relative to those elsewhere in the economy.

It is not possible to know how much of the improvement in average productivity in agriculture was merely a function of the improvement in marginal productivity elsewhere, but one of the best indicators that the major component in this change was the inter-sectoral transfer of labour is that the increase in labour productivity in Europe as a whole was generally higher in the industrialized north-west where labour markets were tightest. That proportion of total agricultural investment whose main objective was labour saving was estimated at about two-thirds in north-western Europe and at about only one-third in southern Europe.[2] Output per unit of land rose in most countries by roughly 2.5 per cent yearly. Output per worker was often rising at twice this rate. The share of agriculture in total employment fell steeply even in countries such as Belgium and Britain where it was already small. More than half a million people were leaving agricultural employment annually in Western Europe, mostly for employment in construction, transport and the service sector.

In some countries, as in Belgium, France and West Germany, wage earnings of adult workers in agriculture seem to have increased more rapidly in the 1950s than in manufacturing industry. Partly this was because the exodus from the land sometimes caused regional labour shortages.[3] But the major part of labour and of earnings in the agricultural sector in all those countries was made up of family labour. It is not wages which are the proper measure of agricultural income but profits on the family enterprise. If the rural exodus maintained a steady pressure forcing up wages of farm employees in western Europe, this was as likely to reduce overall income in agriculture as to increase it. The general conclusion of attempts to measure the movement of total farm income compared to the movement of income in industry was that the gap between the two did not close between 1945 and 1960.[4]

[2] UN, ECE, *Economic Survey of Europe in 1960*, chapter III.
[3] ibid., p. 17.
[4] OEEC, *Trends in Agricultural Policies since 1955, Fifth Report on Agricultural Policies* (Paris, 1961), chapter 1; UN, ECE, *Survey of the European Economy in 1960*, chapter 3.

Table 5.2   Employment in agriculture as a percentage share of total employment in Western Europe, 1949 and 1959

	1949	*1959*
Austria	34	29
Belgium	11	8
Denmark	27	21
Federal Republic	25	16
France	29	24
Ireland	43	38
Italy	41*	33
Netherlands	14	10
Norway	31	24
Sweden	21*	15†
United Kingdom	6	4

* = 1950;   † = 1960

Source: UN, ECE, *Some Factors in Economic Growth in Europe during the 1950s* (Geneva, 1964), chapter III, p. 28. Data for Sweden refer to active population, for the Netherlands and for Norway to man–years, elsewhere to the employed labour force

Table 5.3   Average annual reduction of the total active work force in agriculture in Western Europe, 1951–9

Austria	6,444	Italy	114,444
Belgium	10,333	Netherlands	11,222
Federal Republic	110,555	Norway	6,333
France	120,000*	United Kingdom	17,333
Ireland	8,444		

* = 1945–54

Sources: OEEC, *Trends in Agricultural Policies since 1955* (Paris, 1961); for France, M. Latil, *L'évolution du revenu agricole* (Paris, 1956), p. 82

Low incomes remained a characteristic of smaller farm units run by increasingly older families especially in more remote areas. In the 1950s the number of non-family workers fell on average in those countries for which there is data by more than 20 per cent, whereas the number of families operating farms did not decline so far.[5] There may have been a diversification of earnings on low-income farm units by an admixture of non-agricultural activities as employment in other sectors grew in more remote areas and as tourists reached those areas in greater numbers. This admixture of non-agricultural activity to the farm income was in general nothing new however. It seems to have been discovered by statisticians

[5] OECD, *Low Incomes in Agriculture. Problems and Policies* (Paris, 1965), p. 27.

only in the 1950s, although they could certainly have known it earlier from the numerous books by economic historians explaining that this had been a common pattern since at least the sixteenth century.

There is general agreement that these new sources of income were insufficient to alter the trend. Although the estimation of farm income is a hazardous business, it seems a reasonable conclusion that it was only on the larger farm units that the income gap with other sectors did in fact narrow. Elsewhere the nature of the new policies towards agriculture was essentially that of extended public welfare, because it increased the financial contribution from government which was essential to prevent agricultural incomes falling further behind.

The main thrust of government intervention was to support prices, by subsidies, by import levies, by official purchasing at set prices, by tariffs, or by quotas, usually by a mixture of all these devices. These methods of intervention alone could frequently raise the price of a European crop 40 per cent or more above its sale price on markets outside Europe. But protection and subsidy went much further than this in sustaining agricultural incomes. Let us take the Federal Republic as an example. Government support there also went to agricultural research, to education and advisory services, to programmes for the prevention of pests and diseases, to low interest rate loans for infrastructural improvements, to agricultural credit and mortgage institutions, to storage costs and centralized storage facilities, to the provision of cheaper diesel fuel, to the provision of cheaper fertilizer, to reducing the cost of commercial loans from joint-stock banks, and to the remission of taxation especially of turnover tax.[6] This was a fairly typical range of government activity for most other western European economies as well. In Italy after summer 1952 the Agricultural Credit Institutes were provided with a regular supply of funds for subsidizing purchases of machinery and infrastructural improvements. Under the land reform programmes the Cassa per il Mezzogiorno could make similar low interest loans to new smallholdings which also qualified for tax relief.

The extensive nature of state support for agriculture must be seen as a major stimulus of technological change in the 1950s. In Italy, for example, between the start of October 1952 and the end of 1959, of the 243,535 million lire ($389.73 million) made available as low interest loans by the Ministry of Agriculture, just over a half was used for purchasing machin-

---

[6] The list is compiled from German Federal Republic, Bundesministerium für Ernährung und Landwirtschaft, *Grüner Bericht* (Bonn, 1956). The total of budgetary allocations whose purpose could be said to be that of improving farmers' incomes in the short term amounted in 1956 to DM 2,148.8 million ($511.06 million). This was roughly half the cost of meeting the difference between cheaper non-German grain prices and the price at which imported grains were sold in Germany in order to sustain the price of German-grown grain. Consumers, very roughly, were meeting the rest of the bill, because German farmers could shift the cost of more expensive feed grains on to consumers of livestock products.

ery.[7] Improvements in agricultural technology, reflected in remarkable increases in yields, were not extraneous or fortuitous; they were the consequence of government policies which financed their introduction into an area of production where the majority of enterprises were unable to afford such innovations out of their earnings. Cheap loans for purchase and the subsidies for fuel, for example, are part of the reasons for the increase from 69,000 to 620,000 over the period, 1947–57, in the use of tractors in the Federal Republic.[8]

Even with this range of public subsidies the average costs of operating a farm in western Europe in the 1950s rose more steeply, except in Belgium, than the average increase in the value of output. In some cases, as in Germany, Italy and the Netherlands, they rose almost twice as much.[9] This was mainly due to the increase in capital costs of machinery and construction, although in the Netherlands increases in the cost of fuel and power were also greater than the increase in the volume of output. The few detailed calculations about particular enterprises which have been attempted show that government aid could be more than one-third of annual income in an enterprise which would have been classified at the time in Germany as 'a viable unit'. What the German Ministry of Agriculture classified as 'direct aids' to agriculture (payments made directly for milk and eggs, subsidies on fertilizers and diesel oil, tax remissions) amounted, for example, to one-quarter of the annual income of farms in North Rhine-Westphalia in all farm categories larger than five hectares.[10] 'Direct aids' of this kind were only about 44 per cent of all aid to the agricultural sector.

In spite of universally adopted policies of price support and subsidization, real prices received by producers may in fact have been falling throughout the 1950s leaving farm income even more dependent on all other forms of subsidy.[11] The only hope of reducing the number of farms and farmers effectively dependent on this system of public welfare was that continuing high government outlays would ultimately lead to improvements in productivity sufficient to make European farming competitive at an acceptably high standard of living for those employed in it. This, though, required not only the movement of labour out of agriculture but also the elimination of smaller, uneconomic units of production.

This elimination did occur in the 1950s. The lowest recorded percentage fall in the number of holdings was in Denmark, where between 1946 and 1961 it fell by 6 per cent. In the Federal Republic, for example, it fell by 19 per cent between 1949 and 1962. In Belgium and the Netherlands between

[7] C. Bonato, 'Il piano dodecennale per lo sviluppo dell'agricoltura: 1952–1960', in *I Piani di Sviluppo in Italia dal 1945 al 1960. Studi in Memoria del Jacopo Mazzei* (Milan, 1960).
[8] B. Oury, *L'Agriculture au seuil du marché commun* (Paris, 1959), p. 231.
[9] UN, ECE, *Economic Survey of Europe in 1960*, table III–5.
[10] OECD, *Low Incomes . . .*, op. cit., pp. 211–12.
[11] F. Duchêne, *et al.*, *New Limits on European Agriculture* (Totowa, 1985), p. 14.

1950 and 1959 the average size of holdings increased by 21 and 22 per cent respectively, in the Federal Republic between 1949 and 1962 by 19 per cent.[12] The background political rhetoric that agriculture was the immutable bedrock of national society, echoing from pamphlets and speeches after 1945 to the accompaniment of general official approval, was surely provoked by the wish to hide reality. The Swiss delegation to OEEC, as befitted the country which probably took post-war agricultural protection to greater heights than any other, was especially fluent in resonant declarations about the need to maintain a 'blooming peasantry' as the backbone of the nation.[13] The old rhetoric of nineteenth-century French agrarians, that agriculture was the fabric of '*la France éternelle*', enjoyed a splendid revival across the whole of western Europe. It was the counter-harmony to the harsher modern notes of industrial modernization.[14] The one thing post-war agricultural policy most conspicuously did fail to do was to protect agriculture as a way of life. The number of farms, farmers and workers decreased more rapidly over fifteen years from 1945 than in any previous period and it may well be that for those remaining, non-agricultural activities supplemented their incomes on a greater scale than before. Given the commitment of politicians in the post-war world to getting support from the farming sector, there is nothing surprising in the fact that political rhetoric should have risen to a frenzy of concealment.

In spite of its very high rates of productivity improvement post-war agriculture had many of the characteristics of a declining sector of the economy: inability to compete, over-employment, unprofitability, and an increasing dependence for its survival on large transfers of public funds. The argument in favour of these transfers was ultimately its importance to the nation. In the interests of the national community food consumers were being asked to make a substantial long-term transfer of income. It is not only that tax-payers paid the state subsidies to agriculture, they also had to meet the difference between low non-European food prices and high European prices. If, for example, fodder grains had been priced inside the Federal Republic at the price at which they could have been purchased on world markets, a policy which would have reduced the prices to consumers of all the livestock products for which the fodder grains were inputs, the hypothetical increase in available consumer purchasing power in one year alone, 1956, would have been DM 4,472.4 million ($1,064.1 million).[15] Of course if the Federal Republic had abandoned most grain-growing, which is what abandoning price support would have implied, and had Britain, France and other European countries done the same, the impact of the increased demand on world supply patterns would have so altered world

---

[12] OECD, *Low Incomes . . .*, op. cit., p. 29.
[13] A fine example may be found in PRO, CAB 134/1012, 'Report on the Preparatory Conference held in Paris on 25 March 1952', 5 April 1952.
[14] P. Barral, *Les Agrariens français de Méline à Pisani* (Paris, 1968).
[15] W. Boerckel, *Einfuhr-und Vorratsstellen als Mittel der Agrarpolitik* (Mainz, 1959), p. 74.

prices that a calculation of this kind loses all meaning, except as an indication of the size of the commitment which every national community was expected to make. Even so, in an age when the growth of national income appeared often to dominate all other economic considerations, the readiness to sacrifice a potential increase in real income of up to 2.7 per cent argues for the political force which this declining sector drew from its new role as a necessary element in the political consensus.

It was on the institutionalization of this role that the political leverage exercised by agriculture soon came to depend, because the rapid decline of the overall weight of agriculture in the economy (table 5.4) together with that of the number of voters whose incomes depended on agriculture, weakened its capacity to exercise the simpler threat of the ballot. The new circumstance that everywhere it was government which had made itself responsible for annual variations in agricultural incomes simplified the channels through which agricultural interest groups brought pressure to bear on the political system. They became an integral part of the political system themselves. But the reason for their continued apparent success in making it respond to their wishes was not their sharpened political skills, nor the greater ease with which these could be brought to bear, but the way in which the overall objectives of the post-war state across the whole range of economy and society continued to be construed as depending on the maintenance of incomes and output in agriculture.

Table 5.4 Agriculture as a percentage of GDP in Western Europe, 1949 and 1960

	1949	*1960*
Austria	16.6	11
Belgium	8.6	6
Denmark	19.1	14
Federal Republic	11.4	6
France	12.1	9
Ireland	29.2	22
Italy	27.5	13
Netherlands	13.5	9
Norway	16.1	9
Sweden	12.3	7
United Kingdom	5.1	4

Sources: For 1949, UN, ECE, *Some Factors in Economic Growth in Europe during the 1950s* (Geneva, 1964), pp. A-2ff.; for 1960, B.R. Mitchell, *European Historical Statistics 1950–1970* (London, 1975)

When the financial costs of agricultural policy were more strongly called into question in the late 1950s the political costs of altering it seemed hardly worth risking, precisely because the economic weight of the agricultural sector was so rapidly diminishing. Responsible for more than a quarter of Italian GNP in 1949, it accounted by 1960 for but 13 per cent. By then, only in Ireland, Spain and Portugal was agriculture still making the large proportional contribution to GNP which it had done quite widely in 1949 (table 5.4). It was possible to respond to political criticism by arguing that a humane management of the problem by the state had succeeded in transferring labour while improving productivity and avoiding unemployment, genuine hardship and social unrest. It appeared as though the financial costs of these policies would diminish as the whole sector was eventually made profitable with a much smaller labour force. It was this happy ending, however, about which critics, with good reason, became increasingly sceptical, not only because it was by no means evident that a reduced agricultural sector was actually profitable, but because the links between the state apparatus and agriculture's own representative organizations became so close that it was not easy to see how the state could take a dispassionate and more distanced view of the problem.

AGRICULTURAL PRESSURE GROUPS AND THE STATE IN POST-WAR EUROPE

The systematic attempts at market regulation after 1931 mark the beginnings of the transformation of agricultural interest groups into instruments of state management. Government needed representative bodies with which to deal once intervention became systematic in so huge and regionally differentiated a sector of the economy with so many separate enterprises. The Second World War sharpened the awareness of this need. Although national production programmes and national price policies were quickly established, the conditions of agricultural production are so local that their implementation in detail depended on turning the farmers' organizations into the local and regional executive of the state apparatus.[16] In occupied countries this was just as necessary. They were faced with massive demands on their food production capacity by the German occupiers. Rational planning, as far as was possible, became essential in order to ensure a proper food supply to sustain the native population, albeit at a wretched level. In these countries the indigenous farmers' organizations tended to become at one and the same time an indispensable part of the German administration and a defence against it. In Germany itself, within the Reichsnährstand the producers were supposed to function as both representatives of the agricultural interest and executives of government policy.[17] At the end of the war agricultural interest groups were thus in a

---

[16] The process has been partly analysed in I. Boussard, *Vichy et la corporation paysanne* (Paris, 1980); M. Cépède, *Agriculture et alimentation en France durant la deuxième guerre mondiale* (Paris, 1961); P. Maurer, *Anbauschlacht. Landwirtschaftspolitik, Plan Wahlen, Anbauwerk 1937–1945* (Zürich, 1985); K.A.H. Murray, *Agriculture* (London, 1955); E. Whetham, *British Farming 1939–1949* (London 1952).

[17] J. Farquharson, *The Plough and the Sword; The NSDAP and Agriculture in Germany 1928–1945* (London, 1976).

much stronger position than in the 1930s, well placed to take advantage of the economic and political circumstances in their favour.

They did so in strikingly similar fashion across western Europe. In Germany the Allied Military Governments kept in place the comprehensive food control of the Nazi regime and also the Reichsnährstand officials until the start of 1948.[18] The producers themselves, however, were quick to organize politically within a different political context. The key figure in the process was Andreas Hermes, who had been the first minister of agriculture of the Weimar Republic and later the organizing spirit behind the Green Front which had campaigned for agricultural protection and programmes of self-sufficiency in Germany after 1928.[19] In 1945 he had been one of the founders of the CDU in Berlin.[20] After crossing to the western zones he succeeded in bringing together in one organization the various regional agricultural organizations, cooperatives, and specialized commodity interest groups which had sprung up after the war. The head of the Bizonal agricultural administration (Verwaltungsamt für Ernährung, Landwirtschaft und Forstwirtschaft) Hans Schlange-Schöningen wanted a post-war organization as nationally comprehensive as the Reichsnährstand, because he envisaged the continuation for some time of food controls.[21] It may have been Schlange-Schöningen's influence which got through the Bizonal Economic Council a law financing for three years from a levy on agricultural land a new producers' representative body, the Deutscher Bauernverband, to fill the gap left by the dissolution of the Reichsnährstand. This was an organization which Hermes had created in October 1948 as a federation of the existing regional associations and of which he was to become the first president. He joined to his presidency that of the Deutscher Raiffeisenverband, the corporate organization of the Raiffeisen local cooperatives. The Bauernverband's first electoral address, sent out to all members in the first federal election, asked them to vote only for those who would represent the interests of agriculture and who were christians, in short the CDU/CSU.

---

[18] J. Farquharson, *The Western Allies and the Politics of Food. Agrarian Management in Post War Germany* (Leamington Spa, 1985).

[19] H. Barmeyer, *Andreas Hermes und die Organisation der deutsche Landwirtschaft. Christliche Bauernvereine, Reichslandbund, Grüne Front, Reichsnährstand 1928–1933* (Stuttgart, 1971).

[20] Andreas Hermes, 1878–1964. Son of a parcel-carrier. Doctorate in agronomy at Bonn, 1905; director of the International Agricultural Institute in Rome, 1911–14; minister of agriculture, then finance, 1920–3; member of Zentrum; organizer of the Green Front, 1928–33; imprisoned by the Nazi regime for four months; agricultural adviser to the government of Colombia, 1936–9; sentenced to death for alleged implication in the attempted assassination of Hitler, 1944; released from gaol by the invaders before the sentence could be carried out; founder member of CDU in the Russian zone, 1945; began his career as the leader of the western zone agricultural organizations, 1946; president of the Society for the Reunification of Germany, 1950.

[21] A. John, *Andreas Hermes und der Deutschen Bauernverband* (Hennef, 1978), p. 17. F. Reichardt, *Andreas Hermes* (Neuwied-am-Rhein, 1953) adds a few details to this still relatively obscure story.

Henceforward the power of Hermes and the Bauernverband was exercised over the government from outside parliament by controlling the agricultural vote and by serving as an instrument of state policy. Hermes may have excluded himself from membership of the government by his presidency of the Society for the Reunification of Germany and his opposition to the Basic Law of the Federal Republic on the grounds that it would prevent reunification.[22] When the Federal Ministry of Food, Agriculture and Forests was established several of its most important officials, including the state-secretary Theodor Sonnemann, were recruited from the Bauernverband.[23] The head of the Food and Agriculture Division of the United States Military Government described the new ministry in February 1950 as 'little more than a sideshow for the Bauernverband'.[24]

In spite of strenuous opposition from the United States, at first from the Military Government and then from the High Commissioner, the Bauernverband found an immediate acceptance of its protectionist policies in the German government. The basis of protectionism was to replicate the earlier control of imports by the Reichsnährstand through import monopolies operated by the new farmers' organizations, in order to sustain high fixed domestic prices. The first attempt to lay down the legal foundation for these monopolies was the Law on Import Equalization, under which the government sought to levy duties on imports to support domestic prices to producers, while at the same time protecting domestic consumers by subsidizing imports whose prices were higher than domestic prices. The law was opposed by the American High Commissioner who, having first allowed it only to the end of 1949, then allowed its extension, against strong protests from his own Food and Agriculture Division, until 30 June 1950. Although the United States gained the point that no general law of this kind could be passed, subsequent German legislation achieved similar results by dealing in detail with separate commodities.

Its new starting-point was the Grain Law, of which in May 1950 the head of the Food and Agriculture Division gave such a 'strong and broadly sweeping criticism' that the US High Commissioner demanded its modification.[25] The law was to replace the expiring Allied legislation on grain prices. The US disagreed over the level of the official price of wheat to

---

[22] Adenauer preferred him outside the CDU's leadership, fearing his rivalry. H. Heitzer, *Die CDU in der britischen Zone 1945–1949. Gründung, Organisation, Program und Politik* (Düsseldorf, 1988), pp. 198 ff.

[23] Theodor Sonnemann, 1900–   . An official of the Reichsnährstand, 1934–6; of the Reichs Ministry for Armaments and War Production, 1936–45; chief officer of the Verband des Niedersächsischen Landvolkes, one of the constituent federal parts of the Bauernverband, 1947–9; state-secretary, Ministry of Agriculture, 1950–61; president of the Deutscher Raiffeisenverband, 1961–73. His way into the post-war CDU led through the nationalistic Deutsche Partei.

[24] H.G. Schmidt, *Food and Agricultural Programs in West Germany 1949–1951*, Historical Division, Office of the Executive Secretary, US High Commissioner for Germany (Bonn, 1952), p. 46.

[25] ibid., p. 39.

domestic millers to be set by the law. The Americans would have liked to see a higher price to reduce the subsidy on the price of bread to consumers. For the German government, faced with the steep rise in other consumer prices after the September 1949 devaluation and threatened with a national miners' strike over the steep rise in the cost of living, the issue was seen as crucial. Neither the British nor the French gave much support to the Americans, the British indeed voicing the opinion that the legislation was much like their own agricultural marketing acts of the 1930s. There was more support for the United States inside the German government, where in spite of Adenauer's pressing appeals to establish a new grain price control system, Erhard succeeded in getting the proposed law sent back for redrafting. Eventually in September, however, the redrafted law established a compromise favourable to the original legislation. The proposed official grain price to millers was increased, but by less than the Americans had demanded and only for grain released from stocks. The so-called 'consumers' bread', standard loaves at subsidized prices, continued to be subsidized. It was, Erhard lamented, 'a turning-point in economic policy and in practice a retreat from the basic principles of the free market economy'.[26]

The Grain Law set the pattern of all subsequent commodity laws. It fixed an annual supply plan for the crop year and established an Import and Stock Board (Einfuhr- und Vorratsstelle) to purchase and stock both imports and the domestic crop. The Import and Stock Boards were staffed by a mixture of civil servants, members of the producers' own interest-group organizations, representatives of domestic trade in the product concerned, and consumers. Their status was that of an executive agency of the Ministry of Agriculture.[27] All imports covered by subsequent commodity laws had to be offered for sale to these agencies which sold them at the fixed domestic price. The Sugar Law, the second commodity law to be introduced, was opposed in cabinet for three weeks but then accepted for submission to the Bundestag. The Meat and Livestock Law was accepted in spite of Erhard's 'basic misgivings'.[28] The Milk, Dairy Products and Fats Law was first rejected by the cabinet, because it relied on an equalization tax on margarine to subsidize butter producers, a tax which fell mainly on poorer consumers who preferred margarine to butter. At this the minister of agriculture Wilhelm Niklas threatened resignation if a solution acceptable to agricultural interests were not found. The outcome was a changed law which allowed the government only to propose, not to establish, butter and margarine prices, which then had to be accepted at Land level before becoming law. But the proposed prices were in the event rejected only by the almost wholly urban Länder of Bremen and Hamburg.

If the post-war system of agricultural production in the Federal Republic

---

[26] *Die Kabinettprotokolle der Bundesregierung*, vol. 2, 1950, pp. 313–4.
[27] W. Boerckel, *Einfuhr- und Vorratsstellen . . .*, op. cit.
[28] *Die Kabinettprotokolle . . .*, op. cit., vol. 2, 1950, p. 352.

remained almost as closely controlled as in the 1930s – only the internal distribution of food being completely free from government intervention – it was not as protectionist as the Bauernverband would have wished. The Bauernverband's claim was for parity of income with employees in the industrial sector, the claim which Swedish farmers' organizations had already won. This was the claim pressed on Adenauer in return for Bauernverband support in the 1953 federal election. What was achieved, under very strong pressure when the government began to drag its feet after the election, was the Agriculture Law of 5 September 1955, the so-called Green Law. By this law the 'social situation' of people working in agriculture was to be brought up to the same level as that of 'comparable professional groups'. This vague language left much room for subsequent dispute, in which, however, the agricultural sector did not lack a powerful voice at the political centre. In the late 1950s about one-fifth of the CDU deputies in the Bundestag are estimated to have represented agricultural interests in some form or other.[29]

A comparable case, although one that has been even less studied, seems to be that of the Stichting voor de Landbouw in the Netherlands. It was legally established in 1945 as a federation of six representative agricultural organizations, two of which had formerly represented only agricultural workers. The decision to merge these organizations into one corporate body was taken in 1941 during the occupation because of the government's desire for a common response in the face of German exploitation. The Germans banned the resulting organization, so that it came into existence only with the liberation government. The intention in 1945 was that the whole of the agricultural sector should be represented by one common interest group not only at the national but also the international levels. To 'prepare for the establishment of a public organization for agriculture', the government published a draft bill in 1946 confirming the Stichting as the first stage. The 'public organization' which eventually replaced it, the Landbouwschap, was not created until 1954, by which time the Stichting had firmly established its control of agricultural politics.[30] Membership of the Stichting was compulsory. It had quasi-autonomous powers over the regulation of production, storage, distribution, and working conditions in agriculture, subject only to its regulations being approved by the Economic and Social Council. The Ministry of Agriculture held formal monthly conferences both with the Stichting and its successor organization. There were more frequent informal meetings between officials concerned with particular products. As in the Federal Republic the differences between Ministry of Agriculture and first the Stichting and later the Landbouwschap were often fine. Indeed the Dutch organization was a

---

[29] M. Tracy, *Agriculture in Western Europe. Challenge and Response 1880–1980* (2nd edn, London, 1982), p. 251.
[30] A.D. Robertson, *Dutch Organized Agriculture in International Politics 1945–1960* (The Hague, 1981), pp. 55 ff.

more pliable organ of ministerial control, because its origins lay more in central government initiative than did those of the Bauernverband.

Like the Bauernverband, the Stichting was prepared to take on government over the issue of prices.[31] In the 1950s only about twenty of the 150 members of the Dutch second chamber were farmers or in related occupations, but as elsewhere it was not the numerical strength of the sector's representatives in national parliamentary assemblies that mattered as much as its local influence on elections. The Stichting kept up a steady stream of political propaganda about the importance of maintaining the large number of small farms in the Dutch economy, the dangers which post-war industrialization programmes meant for the peasant farm because of their tendency to increase labour costs, and the crucial role of exports in sustaining the farming sector with its existing social structure. As in Germany it was not only the central national organization of agricultural interest groups which became an agency of government management. The marketing boards which had started as voluntary bodies in the 1930s to limit production of certain commodities and to raise levies to help in price and income maintenance, became statutory organizations, the Productschappen, under the Industrial Organization Act of 1950. They were then built up from the Stichting membership, so that the Stichting became to all intents and purposes the local administration of the Ministry of Agriculture.

In France the story is more complicated. The failure of any political party to capture most of the agricultural vote in its own interests gave a much greater disunity to the rural world. Vichy had succeeded in imposing a unified corporate structure, the Corporation Paysanne, but its insistence on paternalism as the basis of French society was hardly designed to make it popular with the liberation government.[32] The first post-war minister of agriculture, Pierre Tanguy-Prigent, swept it away and created instead the Confédération Générale d'Agriculture (CGA) to be, as he hoped, an instrument of his own very different policies. He was looking for an instrument to help in agricultural modernization, which would push agriculture towards changes in the pattern of output and towards the utilization of labour-saving production methods.[33] The CGA was supposed to serve as the highest, federal, policy-making structure of a series of democratically elected associations for producers, cooperatives and technicians. The producers were constituted in one association of this federal body, supposedly equal in power to the other associations, in order to give greater weight to the technocratic, reforming influences from the other groups. The CGA was thus seen from the outset by a majority of farmers not so much as a democratic replacement of Vichy's Corporation Paysanne but as

[31] *Jaarverslag van de Stichting voor de Landbouw*, 1947, pp. 14–19; ibid., 1948, p. 39.
[32] I. Boussard, *Vichy et la corporation . . .*, op. cit., pp. 235 ff.
[33] G. Wright, *Rural Revolution in France* (Stanford, 1964).

a body gerrymandered to ensure compliance with new central government policies.

When the voting for the associations took place in 1946 the representatives whom the voters returned to the producers' association, the Fédération Nationale des Syndicats d'Exploitants Agricoles (FNSEA), were men whose spiritual allegiance was nearer to the earlier regime. They set about running the constitution of the CGA in such a way as to make sure that power actually lay with the producers themselves.[34] The driving force in the FNSEA, René Blondelle, had in fact been a strong wartime advocate not only of a national corporation of agricultural producers but also of a corporate state. It was not long before his effective political power within the CGA was greater than that of the CGA's secretary-general, originally envisaged as the key post.

Opposition to Tanguy-Prigent may have been reinforced by the fact that the first versions of the Monnet Plan ignored the importance of the agricultural sector to the French economy. Where they dealt with it at all, the planners at first saw agriculture as merely instrumental to industrial modernization. Only about 4.5 per cent of public investment was in agriculture between 1945 and 1947, when public investment was roughly a half of total investment in the economy. Monnet's only obvious interest in agriculture at that time seems to have been that it should promote one of the modern industries he was determined to establish in France, tractor manufacture. There were in fact plans which had been developed inside the socialist party in exile to expand post-war agricultural output in France on an ambitious scale and Tanguy-Prigent had thought of his political reforms as a step on the road to their fulfilment. But the Planning Commissariat showed no interest in them before Marshall Aid.[35] Its emphasis was on diverting investment to industry as the most rapid route to modernization and recovery.

This situation only changed when the catastrophic harvest of 1947 coincided with the violent political disturbances in November of that year. In part the bad harvest, the worst of the century, was attributable to climatic circumstances which produced similarly bad harvests over all northwestern Europe. A bitterly cold winter was followed by a summer drought. But the outcome was worse in France, in part because of the relative neglect of agricultural recovery after the depletion of the capital stock and the reduction of fertility during the occupation, in part because of errors of pricing policy which had resulted in an insufficient crop of wheat being sown. The high food prices which by autumn 1947 were the outcome, together with the need to mix maize with wheat in bread manufacture, coincided with the attempt by the Communist Party to foment popular discontent against the Marshall Plan. Strikes and riots brought food supply

---

[34] J.T.S. Keeler, *The Politics of Neocorporatism in France. Farmers, the State, and Agricultural Policy-Making in the Fifth Republic* (New York, 1987).
[35] M. Cépède, *Agriculture et alimentation . . .*, op. cit., pp. 473 ff.

to the centre of the political stage and the Ministry of Agriculture, not hitherto a route to advancement in French political life, to an important role in government. A young and vigorous minister, Pierre Pflimlin, was installed with an immediate commission from Robert Schuman the prime minister to solve the food supply problem and with a great increase in central government resources to help him to do so.[36] The promised increase in investment was linked to a sweeping revision of the Monnet Plan, in which agriculture was promoted from being merely a background permissive factor in modernization to one of the 'key' sectors for investment.

Exactly what difference this made to the volume of public investment in French agriculture is difficult to estimate even within fairly wide parameters. Between the time the Modernization Plan was revised in 1947 to 1951 the share of public funds in agricultural investment rose from about 4.5 per cent to 7.5 per cent, excluding the flow of public funds through the agricultural credit organizations which, if counted, would probably make the increase much greater. The largest single investment categories were those related to improving the infrastructure (housing conditions, electricity, water supply and so on), which depended on an admixture of mortgage finance through the credit organizations, and those related to mechanization, essentially the provision of tractors, part of the original programme of the earlier 1945 Monnet Plan.[37]

Pflimlin relates that he was only able to interest Monnet in the idea that agriculture was important to the French economy by devising a way of showing him that it was important to its modernization. He did this, apparently, by showing him a map of France on which the wide regional variations in the standard of living were indicated. The number of rural homes with their own piped fresh water supply was only about one-third of the total in Monnet's native Cognac, far below the European average, compared to a figure of more nearly 80 per cent in Pflimlin's native Alsace. It was this, according to Pflimlin, that awoke Monnet to the idea that the development and modernization of his country also depended on raising the living standards and changing the outlook of the 7.5 million farmers and agricultural workers who made up 30 per cent of the active French labour force.[38] The increased government expenditure on agricultural

[36] Pierre Pflimlin, 1907–   . Under-secretary for public health 1946; minister of agriculture 1947–51; of commerce and foreign economic relations 1951–2; of France overseas 1952–3; of finance 1955–6, 1956–7; president of the Council of Ministers 1958; member of the Consultative Assembly of the Council of Europe and mayor of Strasbourg 1959–67; president of the Consultative Assembly of the Council of Europe, 1967–86. His own version of his political role may be read in J.-L. English and D. Riot, *Entretiens avec Pierre Pflimlin* (Strasbourg, 1989). An energetic and able man. The author has a happy memory of him complaining at an academic conference in 1986 that some of the proceedings were in English.

[37] L. Boyries, 'La répartition d'après les modes de financement des investissements réalisées dans l'agriculture française au cours des plans de modernisation et d'équipement', in *Economie rurale*, January, 1957; J. Klatzmann, 'La modernisation de l'agriculture', in *Revue économique*, no. 5, 1953.

[38] Interview with M. Pierre Pflimlin on 14 November 1985.

investment was then channelled through the Planning Commissariat, because the Ministry of Agriculture had no adequate machinery for such a task. This involvement of the Planning Commissariat in the agricultural sector and the revision of the planning priorities, established in June 1948, was a part of the preparation of the medium-term plan which each Western European country was supposed to submit to OEEC.

When these changes in planning targets are looked at in detail the degree to which they represented rational economic choices for modernization looks less obvious than the degree to which they represented concessions to the political power of organized agriculture. The main increases were in traditional areas of production, particularly wheat and sugar beet, the two crops of the large arable farms of central and north-eastern France. These were the farmers who dominated the FNSEA. Thus, for example, whereas the 1946 version of the Monnet Plan had forecast a total wheat output of 8.2 million tonnes in 1950 (compared to an average annual output over the period 1934–8 of 8.1 million tonnes), the output target for the new terminal date of the Plan, 1952, was now set at 9.5 million tonnes. The projected increase in sugar output was not so clearly expressed. In the 1946 version of the Plan there had been no target for sugar output, because of a political dispute. Sugar surplus to requirements in the 1930s had been bought by the state at a guaranteed price and turned into industrial alcohol. During the war contracts of ten to fifteen years' duration had been signed with some of the alcohol distilleries and they came to be regarded after the war as guaranteed quotas for sugar beet output over and above the quantity made into sugar.[39] Monnet wanted to end this policy, so no target was set for sugar in the first versions of the Plan. But in the revised plan a target for sugar output for 1952 was set which was two-thirds higher than the average pre-war level. The state-supported quotas for beet production for alcohol were not reduced until the law of 9 August 1953. But the revised plan appeared to assume an increase in sugar output for all purposes. This was another concession to the political power of the larger farmers.

The changes in the plan must be seen in the context of the state's decision that the political allegiance of the farming community was indispensable and must take precedence over attempts to alter the structure of French agricultural output. It was in November 1947, in the worst period of political disturbance, that Blondelle began the long campaign to make himself president of the FNSEA (eventually successful in 1950), and carried with him the National Association of Wheat Producers which established itself as a separately represented group in the association.[40] The economic and political implications of the revision of the Monnet Plan

[39] In 1947–8, 68,000 hectares out of the total surface area of 301,000 hectares planted to sugar beet were for fulfilling those contracts to distilleries alone. Part of the rest of the crop was also turned into alcohol. H. Cayre, *Vingt ans d'économie betterave sucre en Europe* (Strasbourg, 1966), p. 64.

[40] G. Wright, 'Agrarian Syndicalism in Postwar France', in *American Political Science Review*, vol. xlvii, no. 2, 1953.

were heavy for the future. Bread, it is true, and dollars were immediate political problems in 1947–8. For the future, though, increasing the output of wheat could bring only limited import savings, because France was at least 90 per cent self-sufficient in wheat in a normal harvest year, and the cost of those import savings on the rest of the economy would be high. It was partly to be paid, as we shall see, in government subsidies for exporting wheat surpluses in the 1950s.

These concessions did not bind the agricultural interest to the French version of christian democracy. No alliance of interest between the Mouvement Républicain Populaire (MRP) and organized agriculture akin to those between other christian democratic parties and the agricultural sector was ever forged. Why this was so would be a fascinating study in the differences between politics in France and its neighbours. It may well have been partly related to the failure of agricultural policy and planning to overcome the striking differences in income, class and economic interest between French farmers.

The large farm sector actually suffered more from government policy between 1945 and 1947 than the small farm sector. Conditions in 1947 for the smaller peasant farms, whose income typically came from sales of animal products, essentially milk, butter and meat, were relatively favourable. In part this was due to the long-run shift of consumers' preferences towards animal products as their incomes and diet improved. Mainly, however, it was because of the effects of the war. The depredations of occupying armies had fallen heavily on livestock. In France these depredations had reduced the quantity of livestock in some categories by almost a half. Output in the animal sector took longer after the war to recover than arable output because the destruction had been greater and because the time needed to restore animal stocks is naturally longer. Reducing bread prices by subsidizing consumption or by direct price controls increased the demand for animal products even more rapidly, thus focusing the main increase in demand on the sector where supply was recovering most slowly. Peasant producers of livestock and milk sold their output in markets where prices rose rapidly until 1951, the year in which the pre-war level of animal stocks was regained. While the small farm sector continued in its earlier patterns of political behaviour the arable farmers of the large farm sector, in revolt against government policy, captured the new organizations which Tanguy-Prigent created. Government concessions to the arable interest in 1947 strengthened this political control. It was noticeable that when in 1951, and then even more in 1953, the prices of livestock products fell steeply, as supply and demand came into equilibrium, the protest which rose from the peasant farming sector was frequently not channelled through the FNSEA and the CGA but took the form of riots and public disturbances at local level.

Pressures to favour arable farming in the allocation of government subsidies were not confined to France. When the member-states of the

OEEC submitted their provisional medium-term plans to the ECA as requested in December 1948 the most striking aspect of their forecast that agricultural imports would be reduced over four years by 30 per cent was the proposed reduction in wheat imports.[41] The publicly expressed motivation was dollar-saving, against which it was difficult for the ECA to argue. But the underlying motivation was political concessions to the arable interest across the whole of Western Europe. The output of wheat was forecast to increase in the 1950s in the Federal Republic, Italy, Switzerland and the United Kingdom, relative to the 1930s level, by much more than in France. In Switzerland indeed it eventually rose to twice its 1930s level. By the end of the decade four countries, Belgium, the Federal Republic, Switzerland and the United Kingdom, had actually increased the area of farmland devoted to wheat farming at the expense of other forms of production, while in three of them the average yield of wheat per hectare had increased in that time by between one-quarter and one-third.[42]

In this European light French concessions to grain farmers look relatively restrained. They none the less had the effect before 1953 that the democratic political organization through which post-war governments hoped to manage the agricultural sector was not seen by the mass of peasant farmers as being genuinely representative of their interests but more of those of large arable farmers. While the CGA continued officially to represent agriculture to the government, the real battle for political power was fought within the FNSEA between the larger arable farmers, who had the time and money to spare on political organization and the small farm interest with the latter staying relatively free of state regulation and support until the collapse of prices in 1951. When prices did collapse, it reacted vigorously. The general election of June 1951 returned about sixty deputies with official backing from the FNSEA. Of these, twenty-seven were actually its officials. The MRP, Pflimlin's party, could count only eight of these deputies in its ranks.[43] Pflimlin ceased to be the minister of agriculture, and after July 1951 the minister always came from the parliamentary alliance of the FNSEA deputies and the Amicale Parlementaire Agricole, a loose parliamentary group coming together to vote in common only on agricultural issues. After the brief tenure of Pflimlin's successor, Paul Antier, had ended over his failure to support government increases in public expenditure occasioned by the rearmament programme, the new minister, Camille Laurens, a farmer and a wartime associate of the Corporation Paysanne, was the choice of the agricultural bloc, as were to be his successors.[44]

[41] OEEC, *Interim Report on the European Recovery Programme* (Paris, 1948).
[42] UN, ECE, Committee on Agricultural Problems, *Review of the Agricultural Situation in Europe at the End of 1958* (Geneva, 1958).
[43] J. Fauvet and H. Mendras, *Les Paysans et la politique dans la France contemporaine* (Paris, 1958).
[44] Camille Laurens, 1906– . A farmer from Auvergne. Founder of the Fédération des Syndicats Agricoles du Cantal; delegate to the Corporation Paysanne, 1940; minister of agriculture, 1952–6. Described by the Dutch agricultural attaché in Paris as 'a cattle-merchant, but not stupid'.

In September 1953 the law recognized the need to defend the interests of farmers in the animal sector by giving them the same guarantees of prices and incomes that arable farmers already had. It allowed specialized professional groups (Comités Nationaux Interprofessionels) to be established which in the guise of 'Sociétés Professionelles d'Intervention' could organize and regulate markets by signing guaranteed purchase contracts with the Ministry of Finance and the Ministry of Agriculture. They were to be aided in this by a government-backed fund (Fonds de Garantie Mutuelle et d'Orientation de la Production Agricole), which would support the financial intervention necessary to equilibrate prices for those products for which there was no official intervention system. The 1953 laws can best be understood as an increment to existing policies designed to respond to the political pressures from the small farm sector which reached a crescendo in 1953. The Société Interprofessionelle du Bétail et des Viandes (SIBEV) was the first outcome of the change in the law, created to sign government purchasing contracts for meat. Interlait was formed in April 1955 to do the same thing for milk.

After the German Green Law of 1955 the demand for similar legislation became part of the programme of the FNSEA. The decrees of September and the law of December 1957 integrated the existing miscellany of producers' and marketing groups into the planning structure for the Third Plan. They were to be part of a committee structure which would set 'indicative' commodity prices for agriculture in 1958, 'target' prices to be reached by the last year of the Plan (1961), and support and intervention prices for commodities in each intervening planning year. All these prices were to be based on an official composite indexation of farmers' input prices, agricultural labourers' wages, and the retail price index. Much of the ground gained was almost immediately temporarily lost when there was briefly a different balance of political power at the origin of de Gaulle's regime. Indexation was terminated in January 1959 on the grounds that it was too inflationary. But de Gaulle's attack on the position which agriculture had gained could not be sustained. In 1960 the government accepted the same obligation as that laid on the Federal German government to present a detailed annual report on the state of national agriculture and accepted too that its policies must be geared to 'increasing the contribution of agriculture to the development of the French economy and national social existence'. This was an attempt to define as loosely as possible the parity with other sectors which, following the German example, the farmers had claimed and which finally appeared in the law of 5 August 1961 whose first clause read, 'the purpose of the law on the orientation of French agriculture is to establish parity between agriculture and other economic activities in the framework of economic and social policy'.[45]

[45] J. Chombart de Lauwe, 'Avons-nous une politique agricole aujourd'hui?', in *Vingt ans d'agriculture française 1948–1968*, numéro spécial de la *Revue française d'économie et de sociologie rurales*, nos. 79 and 80, 1969.

The political role of the Bauernverband was more nearly duplicated in Italy by the Confederazione Nazionale dei Coltivatori Diretti (Coldiretti). The fascist regime had juridically integrated the federation of agrarian cooperatives (Federazione Italiana dei Consorzi Agrari) into the state apparatus. Nominally, at least, the wide range of economic functions carried out by cooperatives was brought into a framework of state capitalism. These activities were juridically privatized by the Italian republic after the war, but the federal organization of the Consorzi Agrari remained in place. Power within it was increasingly exercised by one of its components, Coldiretti, an organization representing peasant farmers which was closely linked to the Christian Democratic Party. Its leader Paolo Bonomi was elected as president of the cooperative federation in September 1949.[46] The advantages which accrued to Coldiretti through a measure of control over the services which the cooperatives provided gave Bonomi a power base much like that which Hermes and the Deutscher Bauernverband had through their links with the Raiffeisen cooperatives, or the Stichting with the Productschappen.

Access to cheaper fertilizers, seed, and insurance, help with a wide range of financial and administrative problems, useful political patronage and leverage in local disputes, all came with membership and were responsible for the very high membership figures, which in turn enabled Coldiretti to exercise much weight in Christian Democratic Party councils. Above all Bonomi's control of the local welfare insurance funds for farmers, the Casse Mutue, made it distinctly unprofitable not to be a member, so that membership of the older alternative left-wing associations, once large, became very small.[47] Under the law of 25 July 1952, by 1960 $185.8 million dollars had been made available for cheap building loans which were allocated through the Casse.[48] Whereas only 35 per cent of French farmers were members of the FNSEA, the membership figure for Coldiretti was over 80 per cent, as it was for the Bauernverband. In the Italian case this meant 7.76 million people in 1958, enough to influence directly the election to the lower house of between 50 and 66 deputies who were expected to look after the peasant farmers' interests there.[49]

The link between membership of agricultural organizations and the economic advantage of cooperatives run by the same organizations was equally evident in Belgium. The Boerenbond had close links to the Flemish wing of the Social Christian Party. Estimates suggest that twenty-five Flemish catholic deputies directly represented the agricultural interest in

[46] I. Barbadoro, *La Federconsorzi nella politica agraria italiana* (Rome, 1963) pp. 210 ff. F. Bertini, 'La DC e la politica agricola dal 1947 al 1955' in *Il Ponte*, vol. xxxvi, no. 2–3.

[47] E. Rossi, *Viaggio del feudo di Bonomi* (Rome, 1965).

[48] C. Bonato, 'Il piano dodecennale . . .', op. cit.

[49] J. La Palombara, *Interest Groups in Italian Politics* (Princeton, 1964).

parliament in the mid-1950s, together with five francophone catholics, about one-tenth of total parliamentary representation.[50] The Boerenbond was a confessional organization, adherence to catholicism was a condition of membership. Its parliamentary influence was exercised in conjunction with the francophone members of the Alliance Agricole Belge, which also had links with catholic politicians. The power of the Boerenbond was demonstrated in 1950 when it secured the rejection of the first genuine attempts to reduce the level of protection of Belgian agriculture against its Benelux neighbours. In that same struggle Luxembourg's farmers also showed the extent of their influence. There, the Centrale Paysanne had been created after the war to replace the Reichsnährstand, maintaining the German concept of an organization which would represent the interests of everyone who depended on the agricultural sector. Those members of parliament who represented the agricultural interest were expected to conform strictly to the policy of the Centrale Paysanne and political parties were openly threatened before election with a withdrawal of support if they did not conform to the organization's wishes.[51]

Although historians of the United Kingdom are not given to making the analogy, the pattern there was the same, although as in France the links were not to Christian Democracy. The National Farmers' Union (NFU) found its power enhanced by the post-war persistence of the Labour government with controls. In 1946 when it seemed that policy might be different the NFU was protesting that there was a need for agricultural planning and was claiming its place as a quasi-official organ of government. The die was cast by the government's decision in the 1947 balance of payments crisis to opt for increases in domestic agricultural output. The Agriculture Act of 1947 guaranteed markets and prices for the most important food products and led to an understanding that increases in farmers' costs would be met by annual government agricultural price reviews which would take them into account. The only subsequent danger to the NFU's position came with the move to decontrol food imports in 1953. In spite of the Conservative Party's preference for free markets, the method of setting agricultural prices survived the decontrol of the economy substantially unchanged. The wartime direct subsidization of consumer food prices was continued by keeping these roughly in line with world prices, while the producers received 'deficiency payments' to make up the difference between these prices and the higher prices they themselves were due under the government annual price reviews. Each review lasted for six or seven weeks and its complicated and detailed nature meant that the NFU became an integral part of the bureaucratic structure of administration.

---

[50] F. Debuyst, *La fonction parlementaire en Belgique: méchanismes d'accès et images* (Brussels, 1966), pp. 211 ff.

[51] G. Tholl, *Die Luxemburger Agrarpolitik in der Nachkriegszeit (1945–1959) und ihre ordnungspolitische Problematik* (Dissertation, Diplom-Volkswirt, Bonn, 1963).

In terms of the improvement of farm incomes relative to others, Britain in fact went further in the reconstruction period than most of the continental countries. Average farm incomes in 1949–50 before tax were seven and a half times their pre-war level, those of industrial workers about two and a half times higher.[52] To some extent, however, this is explained by the fact that a greater proportion of total output in the British agricultural sector than of that of any continental country was produced by large farms whose income gains over most of Europe were greater than those made by smaller enterprises. The NFU was dominated by the larger, wealthier and more influential arable farmers. In theory the annual price reviews could be used to produce alterations in the pattern of output. In practice the influence of the NFU leadership was preponderant.[53] It was usually exercised in the direction of securing advantages for the arable sector. In the long period of Conservative Party rule after 1951 the NFU, although it was not officially committed to any political party, found political influence easier to exercise, for it was with this party that it shared mutual sympathies and for this party that its members mostly voted.

The way that the farmers' representative organizations became a quasi-official part of the administration of so many countries has been dealt with in detail here, as far as it is yet known, because it is the key to understanding the great difficulties of regulating agricultural production and trade within the new post-war commercial framework. For all the high priority given to employment, the role of trade unions remained essentially a consultative one. The same can be said of the official representative organizations of manufacturers, who were in any case more divided because they represented a larger and more diverse interest. Farmers, more than either of these other groups, were able to gain a position where they regulated themselves.

Farmers' organizations, for all the post-war circumstances that so favoured their rise to power, could not have wielded such powerful influence as they did had there not been a deeper political commitment to the policies that were pursued than that dictated by the ballot box. It is to be found in the pervasive belief that the land was a national resource which had been long neglected. In a universal mood of national reassertion patriotism turned to the idea that the land should now be more fully utilized.

Ultimately it was increases in output at which national management of agriculture aimed. In France, denunciations of the neglect of the countryside since the mid-nineteenth century joined with an archaic agrarian rhetoric to generate a new political vision of France as Europe's greatest and most efficient agricultural producer, another Denmark on a vast scale.

[52] D. Seers, *Changes in the Cost of Living and the Distribution of Income since 1938* (Oxford 1949).

[53] P. Self and H.J. Storing, *The State and the Farmer* (London, 1962).

Increases in output from that long-neglected resource could bring, so it was fervently argued, improvements in productivity which would create consensus between agriculture and industry where division threatened. Agriculture, too, could be modernized, bringing old agrarians and new technocrats together in a common vision of a greater national future. Plans to expand agricultural output in Britain were often couched in a similar rhetoric of national development; the great national resource left untilled from the mid-nineteenth century because of free trade would now once more be brought into use. The same rhetoric launched the Cassa per il Mezzogiorno in Italy. The revitalization of the land in the eroded, infertile areas in the south and Sicily would be both symbol and reality of national revival. Land reform schemes were creating new small farming units in those areas even as large numbers of similarly sized units were being abandoned or amalgamated elsewhere in the country.

The revision of the Monnet Plan in 1948 was aimed not only at reducing imports. The new targets were set so that there would be a sufficient volume of agricultural exports by 1952 to cover the balance of payments deficit on total commodity trade. What this might mean statistically was as vague as most of the calculations of the Monnet Plan, but at the end of December 1948 it seems to have been taken to mean that agricultural exports in 1952 should attain a value of $560 million.[54] This was not to think merely in terms of import saving to help the balance of payments, but in terms of a permanent change to agriculture as a major export resource. When the Second Plan was being prepared in 1949, Libert Bou, who was mainly responsible in the Planning Commissariat for the work, saw agricultural exports as a step towards economic modernization, 'because it is a fact attested by history that there can only be true progress in agriculture in countries orientated towards the export market'. 'No other western European country', he wrote,

> has the same possibilities as France to put into effect the technical revolution which would allow it to satisfy Europe's food needs. She has in effect so far realized only in the elite farming sector the fundamental transformation which in the last fifty or a hundred years has allowed certain countries to take the lead in agricultural development.[55]

Compare this vision of a transformed, modernized peasant farming sector serving Europe's food import needs to the offhand remark in the first published version of the Monnet Plan in 1946, that if improved productivity did generate occasional surpluses in agriculture 'they would serve to

---

[54] France, Institut National des Statistiques et des Etudes Economiques, *Notes et études documentaires*, no. 1040. Situation et perspectives de l'agriculture française en 1948, 20 December 1948.

[55] AN, 80 AJ 14, Commissariat Général au Plan, 'Agriculture. Note sommaire concernant le Plan 1952', 9 March 1949.

combat malnutrition in North Africa'.[56] It was only two years after that benevolent thought that policy began to concentrate instead on selling food exports to the much less undernourished population of Germany. The underlying sentiments elsewhere were not different. The utilization of resources weighed in the political balance more than the cost of their utilization.

The more the search for a way of internationalizing and guaranteeing the post-war commercial order developed in the 1950s, the more keenly did farmers feel the threat to the positions they had won in the aftermath of the war. When the search for a guarantee turned towards the customs union and integration the political task for farmers became to try to secure at the supranational level the political position they had acquired within the nation. That the motivation was a defensive one, because agriculture's position within the economy was being so rapidly eroded, only intensified the struggle. For agriculture, economic security in a new international order implied a wholly different set of rules and principles from those which governments were seeking to apply to trade in manufactures. For most European farmers the advantages of international trade in providing opportunities for economies of scale and productivity improvement were illusory. Most enterprises could not compete. Removing barriers to foreign trade was not an opportunity but a threat to their incomes.

PROTECTION, PRICES AND CONSUMPTION IN EUROPEAN AGRICULTURE IN THE 1950s

The political power of farmers' representative organizations everywhere was directly linked to protection and the twin pillars of protection were trade controls and price controls. Although there was wide variety in the methods of price manipulation, they depended in every case on the prior control of imports in order to support incomes.

The most obvious difference in practice was between the United Kingdom and the continental countries. British food consumers were allowed to consume at prices nearer to the level of world prices, usually much lower than Western European prices. A large volume of food imports was purchased and sold to consumers at world market prices, while farmers' income was raised to the level deemed appropriate through the so-called deficiency payments, which made up the difference between these prices and the higher national prices set in negotiation between them and government. There were other countries where the prices received by national farmers were set for most products by the government; the Netherlands, Norway, Sweden and Switzerland. Imports however were not sold at the lower prices to consumers. They had to pay the prices received

---

[56] France, Commissariat Général au Plan, *Rapport général sur le premier plan de modernisation* (Paris, 1946), p. 163.

by farmers. Next on this scale might be placed the Federal Republic, France and Italy, where only the prices of more important products were fixed in this way, although in Germany and as we have seen after 1953 in France the number of products for which the price was not fixed was small. Belgium might be placed lower down this scale, because the prices fixed in negotiations with government were only target prices and not a fixed commitment. At the bottom of the scale would come Denmark, where there was substantial protection in various forms against imports as well as much other aid, but where prices to farmers were left to move freely within the system.

Measured by the degree of protection at the frontier, the extent of agricultural protection in the different countries would appear differently. By that measure the Federal Republic would appear as a country with a higher level of agricultural protection than Belgium or the United Kingdom. Its quotas seemed designed to exclude all foodstuffs in which it could become self-sufficient, while its domestic prices in these products were set so high as to bring that self-suffiency ever nearer. The system of deficiency payments by contrast allowed Britain to maintain a relatively low level of protection at the frontier, which allowed it also to claim that world prices continued to exercise some influence on the prices received by farmers. Even where a certain latitude was allowed for the influence of imports, as in the British case, too sharp a variation in prices invariably provoked demands from farmers for government action, to which the usual response was the imposition of temporary quotas or bogus health restrictions, an even more effective and absolute method of protection. Although the trade in fresh fruit and vegetables was the only one in Western Europe that could lay any claims to being generally free from national price support measures, it was the constant complaint in the OEEC Food and Agriculture Committee that quotas on these products were everywhere imposed without prior warning as soon as domestic prices fell, leaving goods to rot at frontier stations and raising prices received by domestic farmers.

The British claim that a lower level of protection on the frontier genuinely distinguished British agricultural protection from that elsewhere by leaving it more open to the influence of world prices must be regarded sceptically. The element of subsidy to the producer was built into the system, no matter what his real need for it, because those with the resources and ability to produce at costs close to world prices still received their share of the total deficiency payments, probably in unjustly favourable proportion. The political possibility of choosing this method of protecting farmers' incomes existed only in the United Kingdom, because it was only there that the agricultural sector had so relatively small a number of producers. Elsewhere direct subsidies would have constituted too large and visible an item in the budget paid to so many people, so the consumer had to pay more instead. Neither did the theory that world prices could still be used as guidelines in the annual price reviews mean that the British system was less costly to the central exchequer than others. Far from it; per head of the total population, price support levels in the United Kingdom were higher in 1955–6 than in any other Western European country except Switzerland, Sweden and France. Per head of the active agricultural population they were higher than anywhere, even than in Switzerland.[57] The taxpayer, not the food purchaser, was subsidizing the British farmer and in addition was subsidizing a certain proportion of the food bought by poorer food purchasers. It was a system which managed to combine a greater measure of social justice by providing cheaper food than on the continent, with a bigger measure of income support for farmers. Whether the non-farm population in Britain subsidized the farmer more for every unit of food consumed than did non-farmers on the continent is a more difficult question to resolve.

The obvious consequence of trade and price controls was that Western European prices were for many products much higher than world prices. The world price for wheat, to give an example, could be considered as the average of the price on the one hand of Canadian wheat purchased officially in Canada for export by the Canadian Purchasing Board plus the transport costs to Europe, and on the other hand that of Australian wheat delivered at European ports. They were the two cheapest bulk producers. Until the end of the 1950s the price of delivered Australian wheat was higher than the official Canadian export price at Canadian ports, but the transport costs for Canadian wheat to Europe were between 25 and 30 per cent of the domestic Canadian price (table 5.5). Both were below the official price paid to American farmers for wheat for storage. However the situation was more complicated because most Canadian wheat exports consisted of hard wheat for mixing with European soft grain to make bread. In the circumstances an increase in low-priced Canadian imports might indicate an increase in demand for higher-priced European soft wheat. Table 5.5 does show that Western European wheat prices varied from 60 per cent above this nominal world price (in Italy) to 15 per cent above it (in France by the end of the 1950s). The United Kingdom and the Netherlands, with relatively low prices, were producers on too small a scale to matter.

It was trade in wheat and other grains that formed the bulk of the trade in agricultural produce between Europe and North America. For grains other than wheat the tendency for New World prices to fall throughout the decade is a marked one (tables 5.6, 5.7). In general, barley prices were 30 to 60 per cent higher at the end of the decade in Western Europe than in North America. Only Sweden, in some years, and France, towards the end of the decade, could match the North American prices for oats. Maize

[57] G. McCrone, *The Economics of Subsidizing Agriculture. A Study of British Policy* (London, 1962), p. 51; E.F. Nash, 'The Competitive Position of British Agriculture', in *Journal of Agricultural Economics*, vol. xi, no. 3, 1955.

Table 5.5 Wheat prices 1950–60 (US cents per kg) (crop years)

	Canada	USA	Australia	Belgium	France	Germany	Italy	Netherlands	UK
1950–1	7.4	8.4	–	8.7	7.4	7.9	10.5	6.0	7.6
1951–2	8.5	8.9	–	9.4	10.3	10.5	10.6	6.3	7.8
1952–3	8.2	8.5	–	9.5	10.3	10.0	12.0	6.7	8.1
1953–4	7.0	8.3	–	9.5	10.3	10.0	11.3	6.7	8.6
1954–5	6.5	8.7	7.3	9.3	9.7	9.7	11.7	6.7	8.7
1955–6	6.3	8.0	7.4	8.9	9.7	9.9	10.9	6.6	8.3
1956–7	6.4	8.1	7.9	9.4	10.7	9.6	11.0	6.9	8.3
1957–8	6.2	7.9	7.3	9.4	8.0	10.0	11.1	7.3	7.8
1958–9	6.3	7.1	6.8	9.3	7.8	10.0	10.0	7.6	7.7
1959–60	6.4	7.3	6.7	9.4	7.7	10.1	10.4	8.0	7.5
1960–1	6.2	7.1	6.8	9.3	8.1	9.8	10.9	8.2	7.4

Canada   Export price (class 2) outside IWA quota
USA   No. 2 hard winter, spot price, Kansas City
Australia   In European port, c.i.f., nearest forward shipment
Belgium   Average producer price, excluding taxes and premiums, leading markets
France   Average quality, official price to producers including taxes and bonuses
Germany   Standard producer price
Italy   Soft wheat producer price at Padua
Netherlands   Average producer price
United Kingdom Through 1953–4, average producer price of millable wheat, England and Wales only. Afterwards, all grades including deficiency payments

Source: FAO, *Production Yearbook*, 1961

Table 5.6 Barley prices, 1950–60 (US cents per kg) (crop years)

	Canada	USA	Denmark	France	Germany
1950–1	5.9	6.7	8.6	4.9	7.5
1951–2	5.8	6.2	9.2	7.8	8.9
1952–3	5.9	7.0	7.7	8.1	8.9
1953–4	4.5	6.4	6.3	6.9	8.6
1954–5	5.3	6.1	7.3	7.0	8.0
1955–6	4.9	5.3	5.7	8.0	8.8
1956–7	4.6	5.5	6.3	7.1	8.8
1957–8	4.3	5.4	6.0	6.3	8.7
1958–9	4.6	8.3	6.8	6.3	8.9
1959–60	4.6	5.0	6.5	6.6	9.1
1960–1	4.5	4.9	5.7	6.7	9.0

Prices are for barley for animal feed.

Canada	No. 2 quality, export price from Great Lakes stores
USA	No. 3 wholesale price, Minneapolis
Denmark	Spot price on Copenhagen exchange
France	Government fixed price to producers 1951 onwards, average of quotations on Paris Commercial Exchange
Germany	Average producer price

Source: FAO, *Production Yearbooks*, 1960, 1961

Table 5.7 Maize prices, 1950–60 (US cents per kg) (crop years)

	United States	European Ports	Italy
1950–1	6.8		10.2
1951–2	7.2		8.7
1952–3	6.3		10.0
1953–4	6.0		7.2
1954–5	5.8	7.3	7.8
1955–6	4.9	8.2	7.8
1956–7	5.2	8.2	7.8
1957–8	4.8	6.7	6.7
1958–9	4.8	5.8	6.9
1959–60	4.6	5.8	7.2
1960–1	4.3	6.0	6.5

United States	No. 3 yellow, wholesale price, Chicago
European Ports	Argentinian maize, c.i.f. nearest forward shipment
Italy	Producer price, Venice

Source: FAO, *Production Yearbooks*, 1960, 1961

prices in France and Italy were between one-third and one-half higher than in North America. In all grains the generally prevailing situation between 1945 and 1960 was that imports from North America, Argentina or Australia would have been substantially cheaper than domestic production at almost all times and in almost all Western European countries.

In other products the situation was much less clear cut. The competition between beet sugar and cane sugar producers had long been regulated through a network of commercial agreements between the imperial countries, including America, and their non-European possessions. In these, relative prices played little part. It was more a matter of guarantee-ing markets for tropical producers of cane sugar, for domestic beet growers, and for sugar refiners. In the fruit trade, although prices for American apples and pears undercut by a large margin those of many northern European producers, they could not undercut prices in the Netherlands, where production was on a more capital-intensive scale than elsewhere in northern Europe. Both America and Holland were then themselves increasingly undercut during the 1950s by Italian apple and citrus fruit prices. American pork and mutton prices, transport costs aside, were lower than the European averages, while beef prices tended to be higher. Comparing the more efficient European pigmeat producers with their main outside competitors gives the results shown in table 5.8. Once transport costs were added the more efficient European meat producers could usually compete successfully with New Zealand and American prices, although not in all meats. Their exports were often highly special-ized trades geared to particular consumer tastes, so that prices were not the only determining factor. In the pork trade, for example, Danish exports were mainly of bacon produced specifically to meet the taste of the British market. This specialization allowed Denmark to maintain higher pig prices than some competitors but still sustain high exports of pork products.

Fresh milk of course was protected by nature, but butter and cheese from Australia and New Zealand could be sold more cheaply in Europe than the European product. In the cheese trade the great number of specialized varieties meant that prices were of less relevance. In many varieties the European product was preferred. A better test of competitive-ness in the dairy farming sector is butter. The only European producer able to compete with Australia and New Zealand was Denmark (tables 5.9, 5.10). As table 5.10 shows, once prices of butter imports were set free on British markets in April 1954 New Zealand butter sold for less than Danish.

European producers came closer to being able to compete internation-ally the more they concentrated on capital-intensive production methods for specialized markets in non-arable products. A good example would be the trade in eggs and poultry. For poultry the market was transformed in the 1950s by the advent of the broiler chicken industry. This began in the United States and its earlier start there meant that Western Europe's

Table 5.8 Pig prices 1950–60 (US cents per kg)

	USA	New Zealand*	Denmark	Netherlands	France
1950–1	40.5	30.9	56.6	42.6	41.2
1951–2	45.7	34.7	61.4	48.7	60.9
1952–3	40.3	42.4	64.7	52.9	58.3
1953–4	48.6	42.4	59.6	46.3	49.7
1954–5	48.8	43.7	58.1	47.9	60.3
1955–6	33.4	45.0	59.4	44.7	54.6
1956–7	32.4	45.0	65.3	46.8	53.1
1957–8	40.3	48.9	56.0	45.0	60.4
1958–9	44.7	41.2	57.0	46.3	55.1
1959–60	32.7	50.2	58.5	47.1	45.2
1960–1	35.4	55.3	57.8	42.1	50.2

* production years October to October

United States	Barrows and gilts, wholesale price, Chicago. Live weight
New Zealand	First quality bacon pigs, opening schedule prices of meat exporters. Slaughter weight
Denmark	First quality bacon pigs, price paid by cooperative slaughter-houses. Slaughter weight
Netherlands	Average producer prices, leading markets. Live weight
France	Second quality, wholesale price at Paris excluding tax and live weight

Source: FAO, *Production Yearbooks*, 1960, 1961

poultry imports from the USA moved up sharply before the mid-1950s. As soon as a similar investment had taken place in Europe, however, poultry imports fell without the impact of any import controls. The nearest thing to a completely uncontrolled trade was that in eggs. A specialized producer such as Denmark using capital-intensive methods could produce eggs at little more than half their sale price in France where agriculture was less capitalized.[58]

As the survey of the politics of agricultural interest groups showed however, the protection of European agriculture as it developed after 1945 was usually biased towards the interests of arable farmers. To take the example of France, French wheat farmers could produce at prices which would undercut other European prices and other European producers were increasingly protected against them. They, in their turn, could only do so because they were protected against North American and Australian producers. Yet this was the sector of food production where income elasticities of demand grew the slowest. It was not only the livestock sector of European farming which was more efficient measured by world prices, it was also for livestock sector produce that income elasticities of demand were highest.

[58] OEEC, *Trends in Agricultural Policies since 1955* (Paris, 1961), Statistical Appendix, p. 89.

Table 5.9 Butter prices 1950–60 (US dollars per kg)

	Australia*	Belgium	Denmark	France	Germany	Ireland	Netherlands	Sweden	Switzerland
1950–1	0.71	1.56	0.83	1.55	1.17	0.96	1.10	0.96	1.99
1951–2	0.95	1.66	0.81	1.61	1.30	1.06	1.03	1.10	2.03
1952–3	1.06	1.72	0.90	1.84	1.36	1.10	1.12	1.13	2.08
1953–4	1.08	1.70	0.96	1.83	1.31	1.18	1.03	1.17	2.15
1954–5	1.05	1.66	0.95	1.54	1.35	1.19	1.02	1.17	2.14
1955–6	1.03	1.67	0.98	1.63	1.44	1.19	1.11	1.19	2.17
1956–7	1.01	1.66	0.95	1.74	1.47	1.19	1.10	1.28	2.25
1957–8	1.00	1.71	0.80	1.53	1.50	1.19	1.10	1.23	2.28
1958–9	1.05	1.61	0.65	1.51	1.46	1.15	0.87	0.99	2.23
1959–60	1.06	1.64	0.94	1.60	1.49	1.16	1.07	1.06	2.25
1960–1	1.03	1.65	0.83	1.53	1.37	1.24	0.94	1.01	2.25

* crop year, July–June

Australia	Average return to producers for domestic and export sales including subsidies and storage charges
Belgium	Average producer price, excluding tax, leading markets
Denmark	Average producer price paid by Export Commission
France	Wholesale price, including tax, Paris
Germany	Standard sale price of best dairy butter, packaged, from free producers' station. Before 1954 Lower Saxony only
Ireland	Net return to dairies, wholesale lots
Netherlands	Average producer price
Sweden	Official bulk selling price, f.o.b. dairy. From May 1953 one brand only
Switzerland	First quality guaranteed producer price

Source: FAO, Production Yearbooks, 1961, 1962

Table 5.10   Prices of Danish and New Zealand butter in the United Kingdom, 1950–60 (US dollars per kg.)

	Denmark	New Zealand
1950–1	0.45	0.45
1951–2	0.61	0.61
1952–3	0.69	0.69
1953–4	0.84	0.84
1954–5	1.03	1.03
1955–6	1.10	0.98
1956–7	1.07	0.89
1957–8	0.88	0.78
1958–9	0.76	0.65
1959–60	1.06	0.95
1960–1	0.90	0.85

All prices until May 1954 are official butter prices of Ministry of Food. After May 1954 first quality butter ex-store in London.

Source: FAO, *Production Yearbooks*, 1960, 1961

Income per head in Western Europe grew between 1950 and 1958 at the unprecedentedly high compound rate of 4.6 per cent annually. The consumption of cereals per capita, however, fell by 1.1 per cent annually. Sugar consumption rose on average by only 3.3 per cent annually, mainly due to the increase in consumption of confectionery, but this was still comfortably below the rate of income growth. The consumption of some non-arable foodstuffs, on the other hand, rose faster than the rate of growth of per capita income. This was true of poultry, beef, veal, fruit and cheese, and to a lesser extent of pork. Less protection for arable farming would have meant lower prices of grain inputs for livestock farmers. Had that encouraged increasing specialization in the livestock sector it might have lowered prices still further. This, it is true, would have depended on access to markets, which in the prevailing political circumstances farmers' organizations saw no reason to concede.

Specialization in the products of more capital-intensive farming had often to be confined to national markets. On those markets the chances of success were restricted by the absolute size of the market, often small, and by the fact that in the highest per capita income countries elasticities of demand even for livestock products were lower. At the top end of the per capita income scale, in Sweden, agricultural policy did make serious efforts in spite of protection to avoid generating food surpluses. There was nevertheless an increasing tendency to produce them because of the sluggish increase in food consumption of the national population. It would have required a 10 per cent increase in disposable purchasing power to generate a 2 per cent increase in food consumption in Sweden in the

1950s.[59] At the other end of the income scale, in poor countries such as Ireland and Italy domestic consumption still did not offer a way out of the trap, because there the income elasticity of demand for arable products was still relatively high. In Ireland the government felt obliged to subsidize the consumption of butter and bacon on the domestic market, thus probably increasing costs to a majority of the agricultural population more than it was increasing producers' prices.[60] Subsidizing the butter consumption of the Irish population, whose per capita income on a Western European scale was low, so that they had a level of calorific consumption amongst the highest in the world was no substitute for exports, as the very low rate of growth of the Irish national income in the 1950s testified. In Italy the income elasticity of demand for grain products was still relatively high in the south. It was only in the richer north in the 1950s that consumers' preferences were shifting.

The growth of agricultural output between 1950 and 1962 was greater than the per capita expenditure of consumers on food for many western European countries for which we have satisfactory data. It was so in Belgium–Luxembourg, Denmark, France, Ireland, the Netherlands, and the United Kingdom.[61] There seem to have been only five countries where it was slower. One of these, Austria, is a special case because of the abnormally low level of food consumption still prevailing even in 1950. Another, Sweden, is perhaps a special case too, the one country where policy deliberately made an effort to restrict increases in output and to avoid surpluses. A third, Norway, has peculiar agricultural difficulties because of its terrain, with comparatively little good arable land. That leaves only two others, Italy and Portugal. Both were low per capita income countries, where the percentage of GDP spent on food was still more than 30 per cent in 1960 and where in certain products an increase in output would still be eaten domestically. Generally the figures indicate an inexorable tendency of policy, if left unchanged, to produce surpluses. Here was a policy problem of the first magnitude, for without a way of disposing of these growing surpluses political consensus would become more difficult to maintain. Surpluses were far from being a chance outcome of the pursuit of self-sufficiency, as governments sometimes argued. They were the logical outcome of the political choice which had been made. How to dispose of them when every Western European country was doing the same thing and when most of the produce was at prices well above those prevailing outside Europe?

When faced with this particular critique of their policies governments fell back on the argument that import substitution and sales of surpluses

---

[59] The elasticity calculation is that of H. Niehaus and H. Priebe, *Agrarpolitik in der sozialen Marktwirtschaft* (Ludwigsburg, 1956).

[60] R.D. Crotty, *Irish Agricultural Production; Its Volume and Structure* (Cork, 1960).

[61] OECD, *Agriculture and Economic Growth* (Paris, 1965), p. 38. The calculations are based on an index calculated in 1954 prices.

improved the national balance of payments. It is by no means clear that in the 1950s they were doing so. Protection of arable farming may not have increased self-sufficiency in grain overall, for example, but may have led to a switch to the highest-priced arable crop, wheat, at the expense of other grains, and this in turn may have reduced the level of self-sufficiency in fodder grains below what it might have been. The higher income elasticities of demand for livestock products required an increase in total inputs of fodder grains, of which the import proportion often rose, while import-saving was achieved by increasing the output of the commodity for which the income elasticity of demand was lowest, bread-grain. There were few exceptions to this in Western Europe; Norway, where domestic wheat output could in any case only be a very small part of supply because of the climate and terrain, Ireland, France (after 1958), and Denmark. The two major grain importers, the Federal Republic and the United Kingdom, both became markedly less self-sufficient in other grains while becoming more self-sufficient in wheat.

To decide whether one outcome of this policy was also to make Western European countries less self-sufficient in livestock products is extremely difficult. The commodity for which the income elasticity of demand was highest, meat, provides some evidence, though, that this was so. Table 5.11 shows the meat imports from outside Western Europe of the Federal Republic, the biggest Western European meat importer other than the United Kingdom and a country in which the switch to wheat farming was especially noticeable. The increase in the Federal Republic's meat imports coming from outside the region was much greater than could be accounted for by the relatively low level of consumption in 1951 and the figures are the more telling because the 1959 imports are after the Federal Republic had made its commitment to take more agricultural imports from France in putting its name to the Treaties of Rome.

Table 5.11 Meat imports of the Federal Republic from outside Europe, 1951 and 1959 (thousand tonnes)

	1951	*1959*
SITC 001, livestock for food	13,112	66,099
SITC 011, fresh meat etc.	19,258	116,407
SITC 012, dried meat etc.	3,913	1,515
SITC 013, canned meat etc.	4,859	21,876

Source: UN, *Commodity Trade Statistics*, Series D

Imports of fresh, chilled and frozen meat into the OEEC from non-OEEC countries doubled over the period 1952–9, mainly because of the increase in German imports. Over the same period imports of wheat and wheat flour into OEEC countries from non-member countries fell by more than 40 per cent, while imports of barley showed a very slight rising tendency and imports of maize for cattle feed doubled. Not only may Western European governments not have been reducing their balance of payments problems by preferring wheat to other arable crops, they may have been neglecting an opportunity of reducing them by subsidizing arable output at the expense of more profitable exports which would also have been less of a problem to dispose of. As we shall see, a vast amount of time and trouble was spent by French governments on trying to get rid of wheat surpluses in Germany. Furthermore, French wheat exports in the 1950s required a large subsidy. As the following section of this chapter illustrates, French export subsidies on wheat and sugar by the mid-1950s were probably costing about a third of the balance of payments income from agricultural exports.

The trend of output itself, as well as these financial contradictions, casts doubt on the argument that the ultimate purpose of agricultural policy was import-saving, no matter how much this may have initially weighed in the period 1945–51. When the dollar shortage was at its most acute in summer 1947 on the eve of the Marshall Plan the United Kingdom drew up plans to reduce the level of agricultural imports by 35 per cent compared to pre-war. Half of the expansion of agricultural output was to be in the animal sector.[62] Because half the fodder imports into this sector came from the dollar zone, dollar import-saving could only be achieved by drastic changes imposed on the use of grain. British millers used a fixed proportion of hard wheat, imported from the dollar zone, while British farmers produced the soft wheat component of the mixture of grains used for baking. The consequence was that the plans included an increase in the domestic output of wheat, which could only take place on land which could have been used to produce substitutes for fodder imports from the dollar area. The plans were not implemented in full, but they showed the hold of wheat farmers over the system, for the United Kingdom was less uncompetitive with the USA in feed grains than in wheat. This may be compared with the revision of the Monnet Plan in 1948. This set agriculture the target of feeding France and the Saarland by 1952 at a level of food consumption 15 per cent higher than before the war while eliminating most dollar imports. As in Britain an increase in bread-grain production was to be achieved, while not reducing, perhaps indeed increasing, fodder imports.

It would be wrong though to claim that the argument on behalf of agricultural protection from the balance of payments problems of the period was wholly false; it was a question of relative priorities. When so much, for example, of France's balance of payments deficit was due to food imports there was a plausible case for increasing output. In a bad year like 1956 the deficit on commodity trade in food, drink and tobacco (SITC

---

[62] A. Robinson, 'The Economic Problems of the Transition from War to Peace: 1945–49', *Cambridge Journal of Economics*, vol. 10, 1986.

0+1) accounted for 62 per cent of the deficit on France's visible trade and the increase in the deficit in these categories of imports due to the poor harvests accounted for 42 per cent of the total deficit. This was a priority too, but a shorter term one because as a policy it was not import-saving in the long run.

Because the thrust of policy was to produce more output, because increases in output were not an accident of policies designed for other purposes but the inevitable consequence of the political regime within which agriculture operated, the real international problem for agriculture in the 1950s was not how to reduce imports, for there was no political difficulty there, but how to get rid of the surpluses which the national management of agriculture would produce. Who would consume the increased output? If the mould of political consensus was to keep its form, exports would be the only solution, for there would surely come political objections to subsidization of output which could not be sold. How to combine an undiminished protectionism with increased exports of produce which was usually produced at a price well above average world (or even European) levels, and when every European country wanted to reduce its agricultural imports? That was to square the circle indeed, a puzzle far more complex than any posed by trade in manufactures.

FINDING A VENT FOR SURPLUS

New surpluses, those which could be attributed to post-war protection, were still small in the 1950s, in a few products only, and at first not consistently produced. Yet small though they were, because of the government policies of which they were the outcome they presented a political and economic problem out of all proportion to the quantities involved. Disposing of them in an environment so protectionist that to try to do so appeared seriously to threaten the political and economic interest of farmers in another country required the utmost ingenuity. The fact that there were few products where European prices were lower than world prices meant that Europe appeared the only possible terrain on which this ingenuity could be exercised. There was no way out within a strictly national framework, no possible alternative to it other than a European framework, and seemingly little chance of a European framework. History offered little guidance, protectionism not having been devised in order to generate a mutual increase in exports.

It was in France that this problem was first posed when the Monnet Plan was revised in 1948. The impact of this revision can be seen from table 5.12. The target for wheat output was increased to 1.5 million tonnes above pre-war production and the target for sugar output to more than one-third above its pre-war level. The milk output target was also revised upwards. The text of the Second Plan drawn up in 1951–2 foresaw an increase of 20 per cent in agricultural production by 1957 and only a 10 per cent increase in domestic consumption.[63] Specific export targets were laid down for 1957; 2 million tonnes of wheat, 200,000 tonnes of meat, the equivalent of 20 million hectolitres of milk in dairy products, and 250,000 tonnes of sugar. The Third Plan covering the period 1958–61 foresaw a further 20 per cent increase in the overall value of agricultural exports.[64] It made a break however with the priorities of earlier plans and attempted a switch of resources to the livestock sector. There was to be only a small increase in wheat output, to 11 million tonnes by 1961, and within grain output a switch of emphasis towards fodder grains. The output of barley was to increase by more than 80 per cent to reach 4.5 million tonnes in 1961. The output of maize was to double, so that it reached 2 million tonnes by the same year. The programmed increase in feed grains and the switch from wheat and sugar beet was to help in increasing the output of milk, from 189 million hectolitres to 240 million hectolitres, as the basis for a further increase in dairy exports. There was also to be an increase in output and exports of all kinds of meat, of poultry and of eggs.

The successive medium-term plans thus set specific increases in agricultural exports, at first in wheat, sugar and livestock products and after 1958 mainly in livestock and dairy products as a goal of French agriculture and allocated resources to that purpose. There is, though, only a most rough and ready statistical similarity between these supposedly coherent targets and the actual trend of exports.

To take first the example of wheat. The cereals sub-committee, responsible for drawing up the revision of the Monnet Plan appear to have had no doubts about the feasibility of finding a market for the increased output. It would, they suggested, not be difficult once account was taken

> of the needs of the countries of central Europe, needs actually unsatisfied because of the growth of the population of these countries, the increase in their standard of living and, equally, of the difficulties which these populations have of acquiring in the dollar zone the foodstuffs which they need.[65]

That, presumably, meant Germany. Yet important though the German market was, the United Kingdom was by far the largest European wheat importer and it was more in that direction that Monnet's own interests first turned. In his conversations with Sir Edwin Plowden in February 1949, when he proposed some form of coordinated planning response by France and the United Kingdom to American requests for medium-term planning by OEEC, one of the main French proposals was that the United Kingdom

---

[63] *Deuxième Plan de Modernisation et d'équipement (1954–57)*, Loi no. 56–342, 27 March 1956.

[64] *Troisième Plan de Modernisation et d'équipement (1958–61)*, Decret no. 59–443, 19 March 1959.

[65] AN, 80 AJ 14, Commissariat au Plan, 'Procès-Verbal de la Réunion de la Commission "Objectifs de Production-Céréales" tenue le 20 juillet 1948'.

Table 5.12 Public planning targets for agricultural output in France, 1946–57

	Average output (1934–8)	1950 target (in 1946)	1950 target (1948 revision)	1951 target (1948 revision)	1952 target (1948 revision)	1957 target (in 1954)	1961 target (in 1957)
wheat (million tonnes)	8.15	8.2	8.1	8.8	9.5	9.5	11.0
feed grains (million tonnes)	4.71	6.68				6.68	11.1*
sugar (million tonnes)	7.7	n.a.	10.0	12.0	13.0	15.0	15.0
milk and milk products (million hl. milk equivalent)	138	150	150	160	170	200	240
of which:							
butter (hundred tonnes)	200	200		280			
cheese (hundred tonnes)	250	300		300			
wine (million hl.)	6.3	5.0				4.9	5.5

* = target for barley and maize plus actual 1957 output of oats

Sources: France, Commissariat Général au Plan, Rapport général sur le premier plan de modernisation, 1946, pp. 163–4; ibid., Quatre ans d'exécution du plan de modernisation, 1951, p. 194; ibid., Cinq ans d'exécution du plan de modernisation, 1952, p. 133; ibid., Rapport sur la réalisation du plan de modernisation et d'équipement de l'Union Française, Année 1952, 1953, p. 29; ibid., Deuxième plan de modernisation et d'équipement. Projet de loi portant approbation, 1954, p. 33. Ministère de l'agriculture, Notes et études documentaires, no. 1314, Le plan quadriennal (1948–1952); ibid., Commissions de la Production Agricole et de l'Equipement Rural, Résumé du Rapport Général, 1953. OEEC, Interim Report on the European Recovery Programme (Paris, 1948). OEEC, Price and Income Policies. Second Report on Agricultural Policies in Europe and North America (Paris 1957)

commit itself to taking 1 million tonnes a year of French wheat exports. The United Kingdom was predictably uninterested in substituting expensive for cheap wheat, opposed to European integration in the form in which Monnet wanted it, and furthermore was rightly sceptical that France would have a wheat surplus of that size by 1952.[66]

Germany too was not a market of the size these plans required. The pattern of German wheat imports was that the Federal Republic bought wheat as part of trade agreements of limited duration in exchange for manufactured exports shipped to Argentina, Australia, Turkey and occasionally other suppliers. It topped up its remaining large import needs by switching between Canada and France. But fluctuations in German wheat imports from France in the 1950s did not correlate with fluctuations in French harvests. Thus, for example, the steep increase in German imports from France in 1955, the only year when they climbed above 500,000 tonnes, came in a year when the French harvest was slightly smaller than in the previous year. The fluctuations in imports from France do, however, correlate highly (and, of course, negatively) with fluctuations in imports from Canada. One implication of this is that French wheat exports to the Federal Republic had to follow prices set in Canada. This was even more the case with wheat exports to the British market (table 5.15).

It was only in 1953–4 that there was in fact a decisive upward movement in French wheat output. In the four years of high French wheat exports, 1954, 1955, 1958 and 1960, Britain and Germany fell far short of taking the surplus. In 1954 they bought 72 per cent of it, but in 1956 this proportion fell to 56 per cent. French sales to other Western European countries were small. Over the decade 1950–60 sales to Holland amounted, for example, only to 4.3 per cent of total Dutch wheat imports, by volume, when supply from North America amounted to 68 per cent.[67] Italy was to disappear as a potential market during the 1950s as the sustained high domestic price of wheat there eliminated an average import deficit of 1.5 million tonnes of imports a year in the immediate post-war period, and Belgium–Luxembourg made only insignificant purchases from France. In 1955 French wheat exports were sustained by exceptional large sales to Hungary and Poland. In 1960 sales to Algeria saved the situation, when they were almost a third of all exports.

Wheat was the only commodity for which the 1943 Hot Springs conference, called to stabilize post-war food markets, eventually succeeded in producing agreement on a stabilization scheme. The International Wheat Agreement, the basis of this, signed on 26 January 1949 and to which thirty-eight countries finally adhered, set up a structure of quasi-

---

[66] PRO, FO371/71982, cabinet working paper on OEEC long-term programme, 4 December 1948.
[67] Netherlands, Centraal Bureau voor de Statistiek, *Maandstatistiek van den In-Uit-En Doorvoer van Nederland*, various years.

Table 5.13 Agricultural production in France, 1946–60

Crop year	Wheat m.tns	Barley m.tns	Oats m.tns	Maize m.tns	Wine m.hl	Beet sugar m.tns (raw value)	Butter 000 tns	Cheese* 000 tns	Condensed milk** 000 tns	Dried milk** 000 tns
1946–7	6.76	1.06	3.77	0.21	36.2	0.41	152	160	–	–
1947–8	3.27	1.12	2.81	0.20	44.2	0.69	143	155	21	–
1948–9	7.63	1.27	3.39	0.46	47.4	0.60	160	180	24	3
1949–50	8.08	1.43	3.22	0.19	42.9	0.86	183	240	28	6
1950–1	7.70	1.57	3.31	0.39	65.1	0.79	250	250	43	6
1951–2	7.03	1.67	3.69	0.69	52.9	1.30	275	260	68	6
1952–3	7.11	1.73	3.35	0.46	53.9	1.47	240	278	54	16
1953–4	8.98	2.24	3.66	0.80	59.1	1.64	280	296	52	16
1954–5	10.56	2.52	3.60	0.95	40.9	1.69	305	324	58	16
1955–6	10.36	2.67	3.60	1.09	61.1	1.63	323	350	60	20
1956–7	5.68	6.41	4.60	1.74	51.7	1.37	284	320	50	10
1957–8	11.08	3.63	2.58	1.39	33.3	2.38	319	390	92	48
1958–9	9.60	3.89	2.64	1.67	47.7	1.56	340	400	91	48
1959–60	11.54	4.93	2.81	1.82	60.3	1.05	330	385	97	54
1960–1	11.01	5.71	2.73	2.81	63.1	2.73	380	420	–	–

* Includes skim-milk cheese
**Includes both whole and skim-milk

Source: FAO, Production Yearbooks

Table 5.14   French imports and exports of wheat, 1948–60 (000 tonnes)

	Imports	Exports	Balance
1948	793.2	88.2	−705.0
1949	592.9	275.6	−317.3
1950	222.2	679.7	+457.5
1951	278.4	510.1	+231.7
1952	764.9	115.4	−649.5
1953	238.6	233.5	−5.1
1954	253.8	1,227.7	+973.9
1955	231.7	2,276.6	+2,044.9
1956	1,526.3	582.7	−943.6
1957	699.6	922.7	+223.1
1958	291.9	1,311.3	+1,019.4
1959	539.1	897.7	+358.6
1960	333.2	1,325.7	+992.5

Source: FAO, *Commerce Yearbooks*

Table 5.15   United Kingdom wheat imports from France and Canada 1946–60

	Imports from France volume (tonnes)	Imports from France as % of total	Imports from Canada as % of total
1946	–	–	85.5
1947	–	–	82.0
1948	18,239	0.02	78.6
1949	17,395	0.02	76.5
1950	49,872	1.5	75.3
1951	32,619	0.8	55.5
1952	21,629	0.5	70.9
1953	18,070	0.4	69.4
1954	337,758	9.6	56.6
1955	628,695	13.8	50.2
1956	187,147	3.8	55.1
1957	332,727	7.2	47.0
1958	529,742	11.5	53.1
1959	51,749	1.2	53.6
1960	94,312	2.3	51.2

Source: United Kingdom, Board of Trade, *Accounts Relating to the Trade and Navigation of the United Kingdom*

guaranteed imports to help in the disposal of surpluses. Importers allocated part of their imports to the exporters in the agreement, providing exporters could meet the fixed upper and lower price limits. Its coverage was imperfect. Neither Argentina nor the Soviet Union, both major prewar wheat traders, joined. About a third of the potential imports allocated

Table 5.16   Wheat imports into the Federal Republic by country of origin,
1950–60 (000 tonnes)

	Total	From France	From USA	From Canada	From Argentina	Imports from France as % of total
1950	1,724.4	110.0	1,096.8	0	192.4	6.4
1951	2,754.7	228.6	1,903.9	197.8	149.4	8.3
1952	2,120.0	54.0	1,240.0	619.0	0	2.5
1953	1,853.0	176.0	884.0	535.0	0	9.5
1954	3,358.5	280.9	776.9	623.7	594.7	11.3
1955	2,434.9	597.9	616.6	537.7	327.6	24.6
1956	2,969.8	288.8	779.7	964.4	369.7	9.7
1957	2,901.9	357.0	789.0	995.3	350.9	12.3
1958	2,268.5	415.5	517.7	886.1	255.6	18.3
1959	2,472.0	367.0	381.6	920.9	273.4	14.9
1960	1,988.0	449.3	199.4	741.7	250.8	22.6

Source: German Federal Republic, Statistisches Amt, *Statistische Jarhbücher der Bundes-republik Deutschland*

were into the United Kingdom and about three-quarters of the potential exports covered by these quotas were from the United States, reflecting the temporary dislocation of agriculture elsewhere and the absence from the agreement of Argentina.[68]

The one major surprise of the agreement was the demand of France that it be registered as an exporter rather than as an importer, so claiming the chance to compete for the import quotas of the thirty-five registered importers. However, the prices set meant that France was obliged to subsidize its wheat exports if it wished to take advantage of the agreement. Before April 1953 the upper limit of the agreement price was only two-thirds the level of the unsubsidized French export price. When it was then increased, the United Kingdom refused to buy at the higher price.[69] The cost of Canadian imports into the United Kingdom when the International Wheat Agreement began to operate was 13 per cent below the price at which the French national grain-purchasing board (ONIC) purchased French wheat.[70]

[68] Dollar shortages encouraged purchasers to buy in soft-currency areas, and unsubsidized American exports, those outside the quotas, were not in such plentiful supply as to force non-American exporters to reduce their prices to compete. In these circumstances the agreement made little difference to the market. If the 'world' price was stabilized, that was because the American and Canadian governments stabilized the domestic price. This, of course, was done at a level far lower than anything France could meet. A. Binder, *Internationale Regulierungen auf dem Weltweizenmarkt*, Kieler Studien, no. 23 (Kiel, 1952).

[69] P. Fromont, 'Les équivoques du pool vert et les projets d'expansion agricole européenne', *Revue économique*, no. 5, 1953.

[70] AN, F60^ter, Secrétaire-Général du Comité Interministériel pour les questions de coopération économique. 'Listes particulières et communes – Blé'.

The official price paid by ONIC was set every year by the French government in consultation with agricultural interests, a process which had begun in 1932. At the same time the government determined a standard quantity which was to be bought at the fixed price. This exceeded the quantity estimated as being necessary for domestic human consumption by no less than 1.5 million tonnes. Before 1959, when it was lowered as the emphasis shifted towards livestock farming under the Third Plan, the standard quantity to be bought at guaranteed prices was fixed at 7.2 million tonnes. The price paid for the remaining crop was then allowed to depend on prices received on the export market. Until 1959 farmers paid a contribution, the *taxe de résorption*, toward the cost of marketing abroad officially purchased quotas. They were themselves contributing to the subsidy needed to remove the discrepancy between the official price paid for wheat by ONIC and the price paid for it by foreign importers. Although this discrepancy shrank, as table 5.17 shows, the cost of subsidizing wheat exports remained very high. Over the two years 1954 and 1955 it was 37,000 million francs ($105.72 million). Of this, 14,000 million francs ($40.0 million) was borne by the producers in the *taxe de résorption*, government aid contributing the remaining 23,000 million francs ($65.7 million).[71] The relative prices of French wheat exports to Britain and Germany show that the export subsidy on French wheat to Europe's two biggest markets had to be between 60 and 70 per cent of the international c.i.f. selling price (table 5.17).

Table 5.17   Domestic and export prices for French wheat, 1954–8 ($ per tonne)

	Official ONIC quota price to French farmers	Average export price to United Kingdom	Average export price to Federal Republic	Average price of all exports
1954	103.0	59.5	66.7	63.6
1956	97.0	59.9	65.0	66.8
1958	80.0	55.9	57.3	66.8

Source: Official prices as in table 5.5; average export values derived from UN, *Commodity Trade Statistics*, Series D

The problem and the high cost of selling wheat surpluses has been examined in some detail because it was to be one of the most salient political issues in the first decade of the European Economic Community. It exemplifies the financial effort which France had to make to vent agricultural surpluses. The true costs, if the cost of subsidized imports into

[71] AN, 80 AJ 71, Commissariat Général au Plan, Comité d'intégration économique de la métropole et des Pays d'Outre-mer, 'La politique céréalière de l'Union Française', 12 July 1955.

agriculture were taken into account, were much higher. With the other arable crop whose output was increased after 1947, sugar beet, the costs were at least as high, although the marketing system was more complicated.

Sugar had already been a regulated international market since the late nineteenth century in order to accommodate the competition between the cane sugar producers of the tropical and semi-tropical zones, many of which were colonial territories, and the beet sugar producers of the temperate zones. Arrangements between imperial powers and their overseas territories were embodied in a series of International Sugar Agreements. The International Sugar Conference in 1937 allocated import quotas for the major markets to surplus producers. In abeyance during the war, these arrangements were reintroduced in 1946 and revised in 1954. They covered the so-called free market in sugar. Two very important areas of world sugar trade were entirely excluded from this 'free market'.

The import trade of the United States, which accounted for about half of its huge domestic consumption, was governed by the Sugar Acts. These allocated import quotas to a long list of suppliers, of which Cuba was the most important. Trade within the French Union was also excluded and governed by its own rules. France's arrangements were, though, similar to those prevailing elsewhere. It imported raw sugar from its dependencies, kept out refined sugar by high tariffs, and exported refined sugar to its dependencies and associated territories, especially in North Africa. These arrangements with North Africa were incorporated into the general law on agricultural policy of 9 August 1953 which allocated the markets of Morocco, Tunisia, French tropical Africa, and Indo-China to French and franc-zone producers. A state export subsidy was to be paid on sugar exports to these areas up to a maximum quantity of 300,000 tonnes annually. The subsidy applied also to producers in Guadeloupe, Martinique, Madagascar, and the French Congo. They also were given a market in France, where cane sugar imports were supposedly balanced against domestic raw sugar production from beet by the 1953 law.

In the pre-war period France had not succeeded in venting the whole of the surplus production of refined sugar of metropolitan France. Since the 1930s, beet for sugar refining had been sold up to a fixed quota at guaranteed prices to sugar producers. A proportion of the output in excess of the market for refined sugar was additionally sold at low fixed prices for conversion into alcohol. During the war this was a useful additional source of an important industrial raw material and longer-term contracts were passed between distillers and beet growers to continue the system. In this way, following the typical pattern of other countries, the emergency aid of the 1930s became an integral part of the post-war agricultural support programme. By the early 1950s however, the alcohol distilled from beet was increasingly being added to unsaleable stocks. Yet its output continued to increase as a result of the general subsidization for increasing sugar output. This policy came under heavy pressure from the Ministry of Finance and from those interests seeking to develop a larger oil-refining sector in France. In response, the 1953 laws reduced the quantity of beet subsidized for distilling. In compensation an export subsidy, largely contributed to by the sugar producers themselves, was allocated to sugar, in order to prevent a contraction of beet output caused by this contraction of the domestic market. It was set at 30 per cent of the gap between the domestic and the 'world' price for sugar. Although the area of land devoted to beet growing was stabilized, output still increased because there was an upward trend in yields, although these were extremely variable according to weather conditions.

There were better economic grounds in the post-war world for encouraging an increase in the output of sugar than of wheat. Sugar consumption in Western Europe by 1960 was between 30 and 60 per cent higher, according to country, than in the 1930s. But by 1958 the expansion of consumption in France was already slowing down, partly because of a slowing down in the growth rate of confectionery output and partly because of public awareness that the increase in sugar consumption, no matter how beneficial to some French farmers, was far from beneficial to the health of the population.[72]

These trends in consumption in France were common to most of Western Europe, where sugar beet production was protected and subsidized in most countries in similar fashion. Belgian sugar beet production was controlled, for example, by a system of regional quotas in which each region was allocated a fixed percentage of national output. These quotas were further subdivided into quotas for individual producers for deliveries to specific refineries.[73] Trends in beet production followed a similar path in almost all Western European countries, only distantly affected by international competition. By the mid-1950s they had risen further above the level of pre-war output than those of any other major crop except wheat, one more indication that the targets of French planning were not, in agriculture at least, doing much more than adding a spurious element of statistical cohesion to generally pervasive economic and political forces throughout Western Europe.

The sophisticated gloss added to these general European trends by the planners' argument that agricultural exports would improve productivity in the primary sector was a measure of how their world was still confined by the national frontier of France. The target figures for sugar output in the French plans correspond well in the 1950s with the actual increases in output achieved, but it is hard to believe that the Planning Commissariat could have been sufficiently prescient to forecast in 1948 the much greater increase in sugar consumption compared to the 1930s. In spite of this stroke of good fortune, surpluses were still accumulating and increasingly

[72] J. van Leynseele, *La Politique de la betterave* (Paris, 1967), pp. 27 ff.
[73] K. Rogge, Jnr, and W. Schubert, *Die Zuckerwirtschaft der Benelux*, (Marktforschungsstelle Zucker, Bd. 31–2, September 1959), p. 62.

so in the later part of the decade. The expansion of beet and sugar output in the 1950s was much more rapid in Italy and Germany than in France and it was not at all clear to where, even with the export subsidy, sugar would be exported beyond the confines of the franc zone. And even in the franc zone, the major market, North Africa, hardly looked secure in the long run except to the most determined of French imperialists.

Table 5.18　Refined sugar exports from France by major markets, 1951–60 (tonnes)

	Total exports	To Africa	To USA	To Switzerland	To German Federal Republic
1951	472,826	267,597	65,157	25,384	15,705
1952	355,170	247,449	43,232	15,700	7,812
1953	313,102	260,673	9,547	10,934	–
1954	652,084	323,654	68,485	30,731	–
1955	879,047	384,750	81,543	55,081	3,123
1956	805,631	404,934	62,812	94,337	18,557
1957	622,621	415,675	73,768	72,423	12,618
1958	524,386	389,104	46,085	73,068	345
1959	497,066	322,950	49,609	58,015	17,964
1960	654,939	442,102	54,429	76,029	31,564

Source: UN, *Commodity Trade Statistics*, Series D

Refined sugar exports grew in 1954 and 1955 partly through the increased sales to Algeria and French African colonies for which the 1953 legislation provided. A bigger influence was large sales through bilateral trade agreements with India and Pakistan. After 1955 exports fell steadily until 1959, because of a general restriction of markets and the particular loss of a substantial share of the Tunisian market. Sales to Tunisia and Morocco could only be sustained by government pressure on producers to subsidize them (out of guaranteed home sales) to an even greater degree than provided for in the 1953 law. In good harvest years considerable quantities had to be added to stocks when they could not be sold abroad at subsidized prices.

As with wheat the hope immediately after the war had been that surpluses could be vented in Germany. Whereas the pre-war Reich had been an important exporter of sugar, partition left the Federal Republic at first as a substantial net importer with a net average import surplus of 575,750 tonnes annually over the period 1948–52, about half of which was imported as refined sugar. The United Kingdom was an importer on four times that scale, the Netherlands on about half of it, but both were tied to supply from their dependencies as well as to import contracts with non-colonial cane sugar producers. The British import surplus was largely filled by quotas to the Commonwealth and to Caribbean possessions and the Dutch offered large quotas to Indonesia. German net imports, although subject to violent fluctuations, showed a declining trend under the influence of protectionist policy, until in the crop year 1958–9 the Federal Republic's own domestic output was greater than its consumption. Before that a substantial part of German imports was committed by bilateral trade agreements to exports from Cuba, the Dominican Republic and Peru. Under the first Dutch–German post-war trade agreements Indonesian sugar refined in Rotterdam was also passed on to the Federal Republic. Following its surplus in the crop year 1958–9 the Federal Republic imposed quotas for the next year on the quantity of beet which would be bought by refiners at the official fixed price and followed the French practice in providing subsidies for refined sugar exports. This coincided with the introduction of similar quotas in Italy. Even in the Netherlands, where a large and growing confectionery industry led to a greater increase in consumption than elsewhere in Europe, from 1959–60 the government found itself obliged to limit the quantities of beet for which it offered price guarantees. At the end of the decade the signs of a glutted market were omnipresent in Western Europe.

The French law of 10 October 1957 struggled to overcome this problem by once again attempting a comprehensive organization of the sugar trade within the franc zone. After estimating the total needs of the zone to the end of the crop year 1961–2 it provided that three-quarters of the total would be met from metropolitan France. The outcome was a new surge in French output culminating in the record harvest of 1960–1, a further surge in stocks, largely unsaleable, and renewed restrictions on the quantities for which support prices would be paid.

As in the case of wheat, the costs of sugar exports were very high, making nonsense of the argument that increases in output would lead to balance of payments savings. If the money set aside for the subsidy on exports to the franc zone after 1953, for example, was not claimed, it could be used to refund export losses on the free sugar market, controlled by the International Sugar Agreement. Generally the prices obtained for exports to Western European markets were only a half those for exports within the franc zone, and for exports to the United States less than a quarter.[74] Since even the highest-priced sugar exports needed a public subsidy to beet growers, the loss on the lower-priced markets indicates a desperate effort to clear stockpiles.

To what degree was the policy of subsidizing increases in arable output actually piling up surpluses of grain and sugar which could not be vented at all? In the case of wheat this is a difficult question to answer, because there

[74] Prices for sugar were so variable, and often so secret, that coherent price series would only be works of imagination. These are spot prices from International Sugar Council, *The World Sugar Economy: Structure and Policies* (London, 1963).

is no data for stockpile levels and consumption can only be estimated indirectly. We could assume that output plus imports minus exports equals the sum of consumption plus additions to stocks ($Y+i-e=c+\triangle$ stocks). If on this basis we make various estimates of probable consumption, it does seem that in spite of the very high level of exports in 1955 and the relative failure of the wheat crop in 1956, additions to stocks were increasing during the 1950s and that stocks eventually amounted to more than one year's consumption. If, for example, we assume that consumption was 8 million tonnes yearly, which is slightly under the pre-war output level to allow for the decline in per capita consumption after 1945, this indirect method would give a quantity of available output net of imports which was always higher after 1956 than this estimate for consumption. Since consumption was not constant but falling, the probability of an increasing trend of additions to stockpiles seems high.

Sugar stocks averaged about 70 per cent of annual consumption.[75] In this case, however, the increase in stocks which did occur over the 1950s has to be seen against the 30 per cent increase in consumption. The rise in consumption, though, was not a smooth trend. There was a steep upward movement from about 1.2 million tonnes in 1956 to about 1.45 million tonnes in 1958, otherwise the increase was much slower. Over the decade as a whole stocks rose faster than output. Correlating year-to-year changes suggests that exports and changes of stocks varied with movements in the previous year's output, while output and consumption moved independently. A successful campaign to increase consumption after 1956 was reflected in declining exports and increased imports, but this consumption trend could not continue indefinitely, and it could not have been brought about at all for wheat.

The evidence therefore is persuasive that French surpluses of wheat and sugar were increasingly difficult to vent, could only be vented at high cost to the public purse, and that the perspective was one in which they might not be vented at all. The Ministry of Agriculture estimated the sum of money set aside from public funds in 1955 to help agricultural exports at 75,000 million francs ($214.3 million) and to lowering agricultural costs at 50,000 million francs ($142.9 million). If we attribute a quarter of the second sum to lowering export costs, the subsidization of agricultural exports could be estimated in 1955 at $250 million, that is to say at 64 per cent of the value of agricultural exports in the previous year. The commercial department of the British embassy estimated the subsidies from the public purse on wheat and sugar exports to amount to 36,000 million francs ($102.9 million) and 12,000 million francs ($34.3 million) respectively in 1955, a calculation which seems as plausible as anything else which can be done with the highly confusing official figures.[76] Without the subsidies to

---

[75] ibid., vol. I, p. 27.
[76] PRO, FO 371/118137, Dispatch from P.A.R. Brown to Board of Trade, 17 January 1955.

infrastructure, mechanization and fuel, the subsidization of wheat and sugar exports was alone costing about one-third of the income from all agricultural exports.

The Planning Commissariat had been well enough aware in 1948 of the weakness of any policy of developing exports on the basis of the arable sector. Pierre Maestracci, who served as Pflimlin's *chef de cabinet* and as link between the Ministry of Agriculture and the Planning Commissariat, attempted to push the revision of the Monnet Plan towards development of exports from the livestock sector, something which, he argued, would modernize a much greater number of French farms and which would direct exports to areas where per capita consumption was growing more rapidly.[77] Studies in 1948 suggested that exports of 200,000 tonnes of meat in one form or another would be possible by 1952.[78] The early drafts for the Second Plan however described wheat, sugar and dairy products as the three future staple exports of French agriculture, omitting meat. In part this seems to have been because the proposals for meat exports of 200,000 tonnes annually required too much investment before producing the required return and in part because dairy products were thought to represent a higher stage of modernization. Although these required a great investment in packaging, warehousing and refrigerating plant, they represented a higher level of value added. The gulf between the French cross-channel butter trade, in which small quantities of fresh butter were sold from the barrel in local grocery stores in southern English ports, and the highly organized selling of packaged Danish or New Zealand brand-name butter in modern chain-store retail outlets throughout the United Kingdom summed up more than half a century of difference in investment trends. Those countries sold their packaged product in 1949 in Europe for about half the domestic price of French butter.[79] In all these livestock-based trades France would be entering into direct competition with the only three countries in Western Europe, Denmark, Ireland and the Netherlands, which were net agricultural exporters and which, by adaptation to international markets over a long period, had well-established positions.

The weakest of the three was Ireland, but as events were to show it was still capable of competition with France in one of the few markets that seemed possible in the future, Germany. Before 1956 Irish exports went to the British market, which on average took three-quarters of their value up

[77] Pierre Maestracci, 1918– , son of a judge. Chargé de mission in the Planning Commissariat, 1946–55; head of the French delegation to the OEEC Food and Agriculture Committee, 1947–51; *chef de cabinet* of René Pleven in the ministry of trade, 1951–2; ministry of the interior, 1953–4; bank administrator, 1955–62; vice-president of the National Syndicate of Sugar Manufacturers, 1963–7. He left this sheltered existence to become a university teacher, 1968–72.

[78] AN, 80 AJ 14, Commissariat au Plan, 'Note sur les possibilités de réalisation d'exportation de certains produits alimentaries en 1952', 29 May 1948; FJM, AMF 15/43, Maestracci to Pflimlin, 2 November 1948.

[79] AN, F60*ter* 469, Secrétaire-Général du Comité Interministériel pour les questions de coopération economique. 'Listes particulières et listes communes, – Lait, Beurre, Fromage.'

to that date. Of this proportion 38 per cent of the value on average consisted of live animals and only 29 per cent of processed animal products, including both meat and dairy products. The live animal trade consisted almost wholly of cattle to be slaughtered and, together with the smaller numbers exported to Germany, made up virtually the whole of Europe's import trade in unprocessed meat. The weight of live cattle in the total exports meant that Irish agricultural exports had a much lower value-added than those of Denmark or the Netherlands. The only significant processed item was butter. Cattle and butter together sustained growth in Irish exports to the end of 1953, after which they stagnated because British purchases did not grow. This stimulated a search for other markets in Europe. The Irish government in a series of annual trade agreements with the Federal Republic sought to weaken the monopsonistic position of British official and private purchasers. The Irish–German trade agreement of July 1950 conceded, but only after some delay, a maximum quota of £1 million ($2.8 million) for butter imports from Ireland, about a third of the total value of the permitted Irish exports under the agreement. But the subsequent trade agreements closed down this outlet again. Ireland was not able to break out of this situation until the trade agreement of October 1955 allowed fresh beef exports to the Federal Republic instead of the small quantities of frozen beef previously imported. This was an important breakthrough; the Federal Republic replaced the United Kingdom as the main market for fresh Irish beef after that date.

If Ireland could only be a small competitor, with Denmark and the Netherlands the situation was very different. Both countries exported butter, cheese, and also milk itself in various processed forms, powdered, evaporated or concentrated. Denmark in addition had a powerful grip on part of the British market for meat, because of its well-established bacon trade. Yet reliance on its agricultural sector, which was the object of French planners' admiration, did Denmark little good in the post-war world. Shaped by free trade and designed to compete in open markets, Danish agriculture was much less viable in a world of agricultural protectionism and closed markets in which Denmark was too small a country to exercise effective bargaining power. The large quantities of many products taken by the British market meant that bargaining between markets to enhance prices proved impossible.[80] After the mid-1950s protectionist policies elsewhere were forcing Danish governments increasingly to subsidize farmers' incomes in spite of their superior levels of productivity, which continued to grow more rapidly than elsewhere in Western Europe. How could France break into markets of this kind when their restricted size was

---

[80] Between January and September 1951 sales of Danish butter outside the United Kingdom were at export prices 30–40 per cent higher than the price paid under the United Kingdom purchase contract. The difference in the relative prices for eggs sometimes went as high as 80 per cent. E.F. Nash and E.A. Attwood, *The Agricultural Policies of Britain and Denmark; A Study in Reciprocal Trade* (London, 1961).

slowing down the rate of national income growth of even the most efficient producer?

The Danish–British trade agreement of June 1949 committed the United Kingdom to purchase 75 per cent of the Danish butter export surplus up to a ceiling of 115,000 tonnes annually until September 1955. This amounted to between 75,000 and 88,000 tonnes of butter a year. The rest of the market was taken up by allocations of import licences to the Netherlands, Ireland and Commonwealth producers. The first revisions of the Monnet Plan in 1948 envisaged butter exports of about 20,000 tonnes by 1952. For these there appeared to be only three possible markets, the residue of the British market after fulfilment of the Anglo–Danish agreement, the Federal Republic, and Belgium. In Britain the best that could be hoped for was import licences for small quantities. Total butter imports into the Federal Republic were not easy to forecast in 1948, but in the event they amounted to slightly more than 30,000 tonnes a year before 1955 and about 26,000 tonnes over the period 1956–60. Of these however the Netherlands and Denmark quickly established themselves as supplying more than half, while competing fiercely with each other through trade agreements for a hold on the market. Sweden provided a further 17 to 18 per cent. All these were lower-cost producers than France. It was to be not until 1959 that France for the first time sold large quantities of butter to the German market. Belgium was a smaller market, with imports of about 12,500 tonnes a year. Until 1949 these came mainly from Denmark but after the conclusion of the Anglo–Danish trade agreement in June and the Benelux Pre-Union agreement, by which Belgium was obliged to extend a first import preference to the Netherlands, they came mainly from Holland.

Alternative dairy product exports were processed milk and cheese. Before the war 90 per cent of the world's output of condensed and evaporated milk and 75 per cent of that of powdered milk had been produced in three countries, the Netherlands, the United Kingdom and the United States. The war altered this pattern. Powdered milk, economical of shipping space in the Allied shipping pool, was shipped around the world as a substitute for fresh milk from new processing plants erected in the United States. To try to sustain its output and exports after the war the United States bought domestic milk surpluses to turn into powdered milk to be exported under food-aid schemes. Denmark had also entered into this trade under the stimulus of German military demand. Post-war demand was mainly from low-income tropical countries and the growth prospects unexciting. Condensed milk, too, had only a very limited market in Europe, mainly in the United Kingdom, whose imports were confined to the product of Swiss and Dutch food-processing companies.

The unpromising prospects for butter and milk exports were already leading the Danes and the Dutch to diversify into cheese exports. The consumption of cheese was growing more rapidly than that of butter and the market was less tied up by trade agreements. As table 5.19 shows, milk output in both Denmark and the Netherlands was increasingly diverted to cheese-making. Here, the two big export markets were Belgium and the Federal Republic. Again, however, the implementation of the Benelux accords from 1949 onwards meant that the Belgian market was taken up by the preferences which had to be offered to the Dutch. On the German market Denmark and the Netherlands together supplied between 85 and 95 per cent of the imports between 1950 and 1960. They also shared the British market with Commonwealth suppliers. The only remaining market of any size was Italy, entirely taken by imports from Denmark. There was more scope perhaps for inserting French exports into this pattern, but only by very hard trade bargaining.

After early failure however, France did succeed in disposing of an increasing total of dairy exports in the 1950s, essentially because this was

Table 5.19   Annual average output of butter and cheese in Denmark and the Netherlands, 1947–61 (000 tonnes)

	1947–9	*1950–2*	*1953–5*	*1956–8*	*1959–61*
Butter					
Denmark	134	167	173	166	169
Netherlands	69	86	80	82	92
Cheese					
Denmark	56	75	85	97	117
Netherlands	97	139	165	176	207

Source: FAO, *Production Yearbooks*, various issues

Table 5.20   French exports of dairy products, 1951–60 (tonnes)

	Butter	*Cheese*	*Concentrated and dried milk (skim and whole)*
1951	1,695	17,550	17,984
1952	1,229	17,903	17,789
1953	1,489	16,697	15,188
1954	2,816	18,626	16,588
1955	11,935	19,333	16,381
1956	4,742	20,260	14,585
1957	10,136	26,095	26,416
1958	12,462	27,637	32,237
1959	12,192	28,210	42,492
1960	23,145	31,261	62,000

Source: FAO, *Commerce Yearbooks*, various issues

one area where consumption was growing more rapidly. But the success was more in butter and processed milk, not in cheese. The strong growth of butter output up to 1952 was accompanied by only weak exports but, as with wheat, a breakthrough came in 1955. Before 1954 Algeria was the only worthwhile market for French butter exports. Sales of butter to the Federal Republic and to Italy began in 1954 and from 1955 onwards the United Kingdom and occasionally Switzerland were also purchasers, although in very small quantities compared to Danish sales. By 1960 through this process of persistent bargaining French butter exports were more than half those of the Netherlands and surpassed those of Ireland. Milk exports did not increase until 1957, but in that year production and exports of processed milk also took an upward turn. Even so, the increase in French milk exports across the 1950s was but one-fifth that of Dutch milk exports. Exports of concentrated and dried milk remained confined to underdeveloped economies under French domination, mainly Algeria and Indochina, and mainly for military consumption, until sales of evaporated milk to the Federal Republic began in 1957. The big expansion between 1957 and 1959, however, was not in Europe but in sales to Algeria and Indochina.

Cheese exports at first depended on the Algerian market, although almost all Western European countries as well as the United States bought small quantities of French cheese. The notable exception was the Federal Republic. Germans did not eat French cheese until 1957. Exports to Western European markets did show a persistent slow growth. But if we compare the rate of growth of French cheese exports to that of the dominant exporters the picture does not look as rosy as table 5.20 might suggest. Compared to the period 1948–52 French butter exports by 1958–60 increased by 45,700 tonnes, while Danish and Dutch exports had not increased. Danish cheese exports, though, had increased by 39,700 tonnes over the same period and Dutch exports by 43,000 tonnes. France's increase was a mere 13,500 tonnes. France, in fact, had forced its way into the less rapidly expanding dairy product market, butter, where it had difficulty meeting the prices which importers would pay, largely because its main rivals Denmark and the Netherlands were leaving that market for better prospects in the higher value-added cheese market.

When French policy changed in 1953 towards extending more support to the small-farm livestock sector as a response to the riots and protests in that year, butter exports were accorded an emergency subsidy of about 80 per cent of the Danish price. Like other dairy products their encouragement and subsidization then became a matter for the Fonds de Garantie Mutuelle et d'Orientation de la Production Agricole. The proportion of subsidy relative to production price became roughly the same as for wheat. The subsidy was only less expensive because the exports were less. The gap between butter prices in France and those in Denmark and the

Netherlands did not shrink in the 1950s. As French butter exports increased it must therefore be assumed that the costs of subsidizing them rose correspondingly. The financial advantage of the alternative policy of concentrating on livestock sector exports, at least as far as dairy exports were concerned, was only that it distributed the largesse of the state more widely and to those who needed it more.

As for meat exports they, too, initially proved costly. They first began to develop in 1954, partly as a response to a shortfall in the beef exports of Argentina and Uruguay to their traditional European markets, but also because of the creation of SIBEV and the support provided to it for exports from the Fonds de Garantie. About a quarter of the 100,000 tonnes of meat exported in 1954 were subsidized exports to the USSR made at a loss to appease the political crisis caused by the protests from the small-farm sector. However meat was a less regulated market and as French prices became competitive over the course of the 1950s, exports began to grow and the need for subsidy to decline.

It is clear that for French agriculture single discontinuous sales to underdeveloped economies or to eastern Europe were not a satisfactory policy because they provided no consistent guarantee to producers that there would be a vent for surplus. Empire markets were economically safe, but politically increasingly uncertain. Nor were they growing fast enough to provide a solution. Although Western Europe appears statistically in the 1950s to have been only a supplementary outlet as surpluses grew, it was nevertheless the only possible long-run solution. Both empire and Western Europe offered the possibility of continued protection, but if full development of national resources was at stake, the transformation of agriculture into a high value-added exporter, it was in Western Europe that the future had to lie.

One of the most common explanations found for the Common Agricultural Policy of the EEC is that it represented a Franco–German deal in which Germany, in return for a common market for its industrial exports, conceded to France a market for its agricultural exports. This cliché, so often repeated, ought to be laid to rest. Agricultural exports were only a secondary, subordinate issue for both countries and in no way a proportionate counterbalance to industrial trade. Having decided in favour of an industrial common market France made it a precondition for concluding the treaty that it would vent more of its agricultural surpluses on the market of the Six, because no other solution had yet been found. The concept of a Common Agricultural Policy, however, embracing the regulation in common of output, prices and sales was not a French idea, but came much more from the Netherlands. France would have been satisfied with preferences for its wheat, sugar, dairy and meat exports on Western European markets in the form of long-term purchase contracts, the kind of arrangements which the Dutch and Danes had with Britain and Germany. French agriculture remained until almost the last moment suspiciously antagonistic of anything more complicated, especially anything that would provide a market for other peoples' surpluses in France. It was the primacy of the industrial common market that finally forced France to cede to the wishes of its partners for a genuine supranational regulation of agricultural output and sales rather than merely a preference scheme.

Yet ultimately it was the whole path of French agricultural development since 1948, stimulated and directed by the state towards ever greater output and surpluses, which left France no choice but to accept the more comprehensive arrangements demanded by its partners in the common market. They were either rivals in agricultural trade like the Netherlands and Italy, or markets like Germany and Belgium. It was in these markets that France desperately needed a corner. There was nowhere else to go unless domestic policy was thrown into reverse.

THE SEARCH FOR A POLITICAL SOLUTION

That this was the true situation seemed already clear to Pflimlin by 1950 and had been glimpsed by Monnet as soon as the Monnet Plan began to be revised in 1948. Both were advocates of a federal Europe in some form and this made the leap to the idea of a European solution to the problem of venting French surpluses easier to make. In 1950 Pflimlin embarked on a political crusade to match the ECSC with a European Agricultural Community complete with another High Authority. Its purpose was to place projected French agricultural surpluses, which as yet still did not exist, on European markets.

The beginnings of the idea are to be found two years earlier in one of Monnet's fertile schemes to plan for Europe. As soon as he became interested in agriculture as a part of France's modernization he thought of a Europe whose agricultural markets would be regulated and planned in common by the official farmers' representative organizations in each country. They would sign planning and trade agreements between themselves for the exchange of products, guaranteeing the quantities to be traded, quality standards, and distribution. In France this would have been a way of using the CGA and the FNSEA as the Planning Commissariat's executive.[81] Why not, Monnet seems to have thought, encourage the same development everywhere so that each country would have a similarly planned agricultural sector and each official farmers' representative group have a similar role in it?

The FNSEA naturally did not see things this way. It was hoping to have the same role in policy making at the same time maintaining its political independence. Farmers do not seem to have been impressed by the

---

[81] FJM, AMF 14/4/10(a), 'Moyens d'exécution du Plan 1952', 10 January 1949; AN, 80 AJ 14, Commissariat au Plan, 'Plan 1952 Révisé Agriculture', handwritten note by Libert Bou, 'Agriculture. Mesures générales à prendre pour réaliser les objectifs 1952', n.d.

juggling with planning figures for future exports. They wanted guarantees that export markets were indeed there before they increased output, because they had no wish to repeat the experience of low prices of the 1930s. And they were only too aware that exports might require bargains which would open a breach in French protectionism. This was, for example, their reaction to Maestracci's enthusiasm for meat and dairy exports.[82] Reviewing the difficulties of finding a future vent for surplus in July 1948 the Planning Commissariat had concluded with platitudinous optimism that, 'it suffices to say that markets do exist and that the rest will be a function of the aptitude of the French in presenting good quality products at normal prices on the market and what will not be realizable in 1952 certainly will become so later'.[83] When the final report of the Monnet Plan and the drafts for a second Plan were under discussion in 1951 this view was flatly rejected by the representatives of the agricultural organizations themselves who served on the consultative committees. More government effort, they claimed, was needed to find guaranteed markets.

> We would not know how to hide from you that in the course of recent weeks a growing unease has dominated their work, an unease which has its profound cause in the fear, felt particularly by the representatives of the profession, of overproduction bringing on a crisis like that which struck agriculture between 1930 and 1936[84]

So wrote the two chairmen of the Committee for Agricultural Production and the Committee for Rural Infrastructure when asked to comment on their past and future activities in the Plan.

They were especially troubled by the fall in animal product prices in 1951 and by the failure to achieve any guarantee of export markets beyond the framework of the existing international agreements on wheat and sugar. The bias of the Plan towards supporting the large arable farms of northern and eastern France allegedly in the interest of balance of payments policy was sharply criticized, especially in contrast to its apparent bias against wine producers. The Monnet Plan indicated a decrease in wine production of 1.3 million hl. by 1952 compared to the pre-war period (table 5.12, p. 267) and there were, the chairmen of both committees complained, wine-growing areas where neglect was deliberate, especially in marginal hill-farming areas from which the loss of labour was more rapid than from other areas. The current rate of labour migration out of the agricultural sector was, they argued, far too high for a country with such limited

---

[82] Maestracci imagined a large trade in pork offal products to Britain. French farmers, rightly, were more sceptical. In 1949 only the lowest-income groups in Britain ate pork-butchery products in any quantity while their beef-chewing superiors shuddered at their insanitary habits. Now it is the smart classes who eat pork offal, having learned (one measure of the final success of the French planners) to call it *charcuterie*.

[83] AN, 80 AJ 14, Commissariat au Plan, *Procès-verbal de la réunion du 20 juillet 1948*.

[84] ibid., Commissariat au Plan, Commissions de la Production Agricole et de l'Equipement Rural. *Résumé du rapport général*, op. cit.

industrial and energy resources as France and must be slowed down by more generalized price support for agriculture. They were ready to agree that an expansion of agricultural output was the only way forward, but this meant finding markets for what peasant farmers actually produced rather than encouraging an expansion of output of things which it might not be possible to export. Prices would, they agreed, fall if markets could be extended, but until this happened the only answer was a more active government role in finding those markets, before indicating planning targets.

Export drives had never been any activity of the Ministry of Agriculture. Its only previous interest in foreigners was in keeping out their products. Monnet's successor as head of the Planning Commissariat, Etienne Hirsch, relates that he did not sense there was any change in the Ministry's attitude until the grand portrait of Méline, the political father of the French tariff of 1892, was removed from the minister's office after 1952.[85] It was for this reason that Pflimlin had so quickly turned to the Planning Commissariat for help. But the Planning Commissariat itself was a small body. Its consultative committees were staffed with expert advisers from the producers' own associations who, through their much greater influence on the political system, determined what was actually produced. Wine production did not fall. Indeed, when the first attempt at implementing something like Monnet's vision by attempting a regulation of European markets with other representative groups of organized agriculture was made, the French producers showed much more interest in regulating the wine than the meat market.

In fact, at the international level national representative organizations of farmers were very early organized after the war. The role they played there tells strongly against functionalist explanations of European integration. Although they had a considerable capacity to resolve some of the technical problems of international trade in agricultural products to the mutual advantage of all parties, they consistently expressed a narrow, protectionist view of the national interest and less of a spirit of compromise than national bureaucracies and governments. Their role was particularly strong in the Food and Agriculture Committee of OEEC. Governments pursuing the goal of trade liberalization through other OEEC committees regarded the Food and Agriculture Committee with despair as an immoveable concentration of vested interest. That interest groups of this kind could be used to find a political solution to the problem of venting surpluses was unreal optimism.

In 1948 the elements of an international organization of producers' groups were already in place. Hermes, who had been interested since 1918 in developing such an organization under the auspices of the League of Nations, was one of the architects of a post-war organization, the

[85] E. Hirsch, *Ainsi va la vie* (Lausanne, 1988), p. 122.

Confédération Européene de l'Agriculture (CEA), founded in October 1948. The timing of its foundation reveals much. It was intended to resist the unwelcome American pressures, accumulating under the Marshall Plan, to reduce the extent of national protection in European agriculture. While offering itself as part of the political framework of European integration, it was really a defensive organization against such pressures. However it was condemned to obscurity from the start by the refusal of the British and Scandinavian farmers' organizations to join. They appear to have regarded it simply as an organization to represent the interests of central European peasants. With such limited participation it could never be officially recognized by OEEC.

Another reason for the British attitude was that the National Farmers' Union had been faster off the mark and had played a leading role as early as May 1946 in the creation of the International Federation of Agricultural Producers (IFAP), intended as a representative organization for European farmers to the United Nations Food and Agriculture Organization (FAO). By the time of the Marshall Plan seven western European countries were already members of IFAP, including Britain, France, Belgium and the Netherlands, making it possible for this earlier organization also to stake a claim to represent the European agricultural interest-groups within OEEC.[86] The Economic Recovery Committee of IFAP was formed to deal with the European Recovery Programme in 1948 and to try to have IFAP recognized as a semi-official part of the OEEC committee structure. The Economic Recovery Committee's first chairman J. Linthorst Homan was soon to become a member of the Dutch delegation to OEEC and the dominant figure in the OEEC Food and Agriculture Committee, one example of how the national ministries of agriculture which nominated the members of the OEEC Food and Agriculture Committee were so permeated by the sector's own interest groups as to blur the difference between OEEC and private sectional interest.[87] In April 1949 the CEA

---

[86] There are brief accounts in M. L'Eplattenier, *Die Träger der internationalen Zusammenarbeit auf dem Gebiete der Landwirtschaft* (Winterthur, 1961) and G. Noël, 'Les tentatives de communauté agricole européenne entre 1945 et 1955' (Thèse de doctorat, Faculté de droit et des sciences économiques, Université de Nancy-II, 1982). Noël's thorough and informative thesis is an excellent guide to the international politics of European agriculture. Noël, *Du Pool Vert à la Politique Agricole Commune. Les tentatives de Communauté agricole européene entre 1945 et 1955* (Paris, 1988), which contains most of the material in the thesis, had regrettably to be published without footnotes.

[87] Johannes Linthorst Homan, 1903–87, son and grandson of a provincial governor; a lawyer trained in Leiden and Dijon. Governor of Groningen, 1937; founder of a political party for national regeneration, Nederlandse Unie, based on a corporatist and colonialist rhetoric, 1940; chairman of OEEC Food and Agriculture Committee, 1948–52; director for integration in the Foreign Economic Relations Section of the Ministry of Economic Affairs, 1952–8; member of Dutch delegation to the Spaak Committee, 1955–6; head of Dutch delegation in the negotiations for the Treaties of Rome, 1956; permanent Dutch representative to the EEC and Euratom 1958–62. Author of numerous books and articles on the need to combine national individuality within a common European spiritual and cultural inheritance.

agreed to form a joint committee at OEEC with the IFAP Economic Recovery Committee.

At the Hague conference in August 1948, inspired by the federalist movement, which created the European Unity Movement, French delegates initiated a debate about the need to harmonize national agricultural policies. Mainly this was the effort of the socialist agricultural reformer Michel Cépède and it was obvious that his enthusiasm for structural reform of post-war agriculture was not shared, even within the French delegation, by producers' organizations. The economic questions raised by European unity were referred to the second conference of the European Unity Movement at Westminster in the following year. That conference, where free-trade integrationists predominated, was clearly unhappy with agricultural questions and called for a further conference in Munich to deal with agricultural issues only. The conference received only lukewarm support.[88] Far from being interested in the removal of trade restrictions in Europe, farmers' organizations were digging in to oppose the threat of quota removals which the trade liberalization programme raised.

At first the threat was limited. Imports on government account were exempted, so that British and German farmers could rest easy. The high proportion of West European food imports going to Britain and Germany meant that food imports on private account in Western Europe in 1951 were only about 30 per cent of the total. The complaints came more from the food exporters, Denmark and the Netherlands, who found themselves removing quotas on manufactured imports in return for negligible concessions to their agricultural exports.

Even in the Benelux, where on the Dutch side one of the principal objectives of the wartime agreements on the customs union had been to acquire a preferential treatment for agricultural exports, Belgian agricultural protection was little disturbed, while within the Belgian–Luxembourg economic union itself the agriculture of Luxembourg was protected by a special convention from competition by Belgian farmers. It had its own purchasing boards and its own distinct prices to producers, maintained by tax barriers on the frontier. Over virtually the whole range of agricultural output Dutch prices were lower than Belgian, partly the result of higher productivity and lower wages, but the agricultural protocol to the Benelux agreements signed in May 1947 did not permit Dutch farmers to capitalize on these advantages. Each country was allowed to fix its own minimum prices for any agricultural product and could use any measure it wished to maintain them. The only timid step taken towards a customs union in agricultural products was that the countries would extend the first preference in imports to each other.[89] Although this gave certain Dutch exports,

[88] G. Noël, 'Le Congrès d'Agriculture de Munich 1949: échec d'une initiative "européenne" ', *Revue historique*, no. 266, 1981.

[89] T. Mommens, 'Agricultural Integration in the Benelux', in R.T. Griffiths (ed.), *The Netherlands and the Integration of Europe 1945–1957* (Amsterdam, 1990).

such as butter, a stronger position on the Belgian market than those of their rivals and had immediate consequences in a steep decline of Danish butter exports to Belgium, it still protected the Belgian farmers' right to supply their own market first. The grandiosely styled Pre-Union Agreement of 1949 did virtually nothing to change this. It permitted joint agreements between the countries on mutual price fixing, but no such agreements were reached.

It was only the Luxembourg protocols, signed in October 1950 as a consequence of Dutch protests about the inadequacy of the Pre-Union Agreement, which first allowed Dutch exporters more than the right to a first preference on the Belgian market. The Luxembourg protocols deemed that where the joint machinery failed to agree on prices there might be a resort to independent arbitration for specified products. The right to impose quotas on certain items of agricultural trade was removed. The breach in Belgium's walls did not last long. The Boerenbond mobilized opposition so effectively that by December the Belgian government was already obliged to renounce the agreement.[90] It met the same fate in Luxembourg. The idea of independent arbitration was abandoned and the right to impose quotas on the frontier restored. Luxembourg was allowed to establish a list of products which would be entirely exempt even from such feeble powers as remained to the joint price-fixing committees.

Better success for the Dutch came through their trade agreement with the Federal Republic in September 1949. In the last quarter of 1949 Dutch exports to the Federal Republic doubled.[91] By December however the Bauernverband was already campaigning vigorously against any further relaxation of quotas on imports of milk, cheese and eggs and against any renewal of the trade treaty on the same terms. In May 1950 the Ministry of the Economy had to protest against an attempt by the Bauernverband to influence the Ministry of Agriculture to impose an embargo on Dutch butter imports. The Bauernverband then negotiated directly with its Dutch counterpart, the Stichting, to spread imports more evenly over the year in order to reduce the fluctuations in prices.

The Dutch–German trade agreement seemed to establish a pattern for Europe's post-war agricultural trade, hard bilateral bargaining with which the professional groupings themselves were closely associated. Pflimlin early encouraged a direct approach by the CGA to the Bauernverband. There was, the CGA was reported to have told him in November 1949, 'only one solution: the opening up to France of another regulated market which imported foodstuffs, namely Germany'.[92] The Dutch and French governments however thought about the German market in different organizational ways. Both, because of their interest in Germany as a

[90] A. Coninx, 'L'agriculture belge et le protocol de Luxembourg', in *Etudes économiques*, no. 79, 1950.
[91] A.S. Milward, *The Reconstruction of Western Europe, 1945–1952* (London, 1984), p. 353.
[92] PRO, T232/148, Paris Embassy to London, 14 November 1949.

market, responded to the request of the Westminster economic conference to submit studies to the Munich agricultural conference on how a European agricultural market might be organized, the only two countries to do so. The French argued for bilateral agreements on particular products, the Dutch, inspired by their representative on the OEEC Food and Agriculture Committee, for some common European policy.[93] If the OEEC trade liberalization programme did come to the point where quotas on agricultural imports were genuinely threatened, Holland's position would be seriously undermined by Denmark, whose prices across the range of similar products which they exported were mostly lower. Freer trade in agriculture was not in the Dutch interest, a comprehensive regulation of European markets which froze the situation as it existed in 1950 was greatly preferable, preferable also to allowing France and Germany to indulge in bilateral trade bargaining at Holland's expense.

It was into this situation that Schuman's proposals for the Coal, Iron and Steel Community erupted with dramatic effect. Pflimlin, who had been one of the founders of the federalist parliamentary group in the national assembly, set out to use the new diplomatic circumstances to produce a solution to the problem of agricultural surpluses which suited his political views. He wrote to Monnet in May 1950 congratulating him on the initial success of the Schuman proposals and adding 'Perhaps you remember certain conversations where we discovered the coincidence of our views, on this problem as on so many others.'[94] On 6 June Gabriel Valay, his close collaborator who had briefly replaced him as minister, specifically asked Monnet to link proposals for a European Agricultural Community to the Schuman proposals.[95] French agricultural exports to Germany, he wrote, 'can only find an effective solution in the progressive realization of an economic union which releases the reciprocal commerce of the two countries from the vicissitudes of industrial or agricultural protectionism – from bilateralism and from financial disequilibrium'.[96] This was accompanied by three days of lobbying and debate in the national assembly between 12 and 15 June 1950 when Pflimlin and Valay succeeded in passing a resolution asking the government to call an international conference on European agriculture. It demanded the 'organization' of markets as a stronger incentive to producers and claimed that within a larger, regulated market 'an equilibrium could be more comfortably achieved'.[97]

---

[93] J. Linthorst Homan, *Europese landbouwpolitiek, 2ᵉ Rapport ingiedend bij de Europese Beweging* (Assen, 1951).

[94] FJM, AMG 26/2/21, Pflimlin to Monnet, 30 May 1950.

[95] Pflimlin was minister of agriculture from 24 November 1947 to 1 December 1949 and from 2 July 1950 to 11 August 1951. From 1 December 1949 to 2 July 1950 the post was filled by Gabriel Valay.

[96] FJM, AMF 15/6/14 bis, Valay to Schuman, 6 June 1950.

[97] France, Assemblée Nationale, Session de 1950, no. 10254, 'Proposition de résolution tendant à inviter le Gouvernement à prendre l'initiative d'une organisation européene des principaux marchés agricoles'.

In his speech to the assembly Pflimlin spoke of a European body with a common executive authority and called on the government to enter into negotiations for a possible common market in wheat, sugar, feed grains, dairy products, meat products, and fats. Meanwhile the Wheat Producers' Association sketched out a plan for a Franco–German wheat board, which would simply have been an extension to the Federal Republic of the French central grain-purchasing organization.[98] The Bauernverband representatives were invited to visit Paris in July to form a 'Permanent Committee' with the CGA. That Pflimlin was well aware that French farmers did not share his and Monnet's European enthusiasms is shown in his subsequent written statement to the government where he indicated that France should 'as a general rule' allow imports only when there was a deficit of that particular commodity in the French Union.[99]

German farmers were of course no more enthusiastic. They were willing to recommend that their government should buy wheat from France, provided this did not threaten German producer prices, but not to commit themselves to agreements about any other commodity. Philippe Lamour, the secretary-general of the CGA, described them as 'cool' toward the French ideas and seemingly more interested in signing agreements with Italy whose agricultural exports were not so competitive with their own produce.[100] It turned out that the strongest common interest of the CGA and the Bauernverband was in keeping out Italian wine exports. Both France and Germany had controls on wine labelling, because both countries had established foreign markets for high-value, vintage wine. They believed these markets to be threatened by the absence of effective quality and labelling controls, combined with cheap prices, in the largest producer, Italy. The idea was to stop the Italians competing against quality wine by forcing them to adopt an equally strict system of controls on labelling. They decided to hold a conference on wine marketing to be held in February.[101]

This was hardly the central issue for Pflimlin. The Planning Commissariat was by no means averse to French wine output shifting away from the cheaper lines towards the vintage wine trade, but it was evident that French farmers hoped to use the conference to keep cheap Italian wines out of France. For the French Foreign Ministry it was a big embarrassment that French and German farmers should conspire in this way. The issue of a Franco–Italian customs union was still on its agenda. The CGA, however, refused to pass on any invitation to its Italian counterpart.[102] The producers of cheaper wine in France, not in favour in government and

---

[98] Noël, 'Les tentatives . . .', op. cit., p. 272.
[99] AN, 81 AJ 172, 'Communication du Ministre de l'Agriculture', 15 June 1950.
[100] BA, 116/7292, Memo. von Mangoldt, 'Austausch landwirtschaftlicher Produkte zwischen Frankreich und Deutschland', 16 January 1951.
[101] MAE, Ambasciata de Parigi, Pool Agricolo, 'Résolution adoptée par la Commission Permanente franco–allemande', 4 July 1950.
[102] MAE, Ambasciata de Parigi, Pool Agricolo franco–tedesco, 7 July 1950, 2 August 1950.

planning circles, had their own different protectionist recipe for the future. For them, a better policy would be a Franco–Italian export cartel which would monopolize the import surpluses of the other Western European countries.[103] The French CGA drew up proposals under the terms of which Italy would not only have to agree to restrict its rapidly increasing output, but also to accept French laws on quality controls and labelling, agree to ban exports of table wine for current consumption to any other member of the cartel with a 'sufficient' supply (France), and accept common minimum prices in third markets.[104] Even before the wine conference met, Pflimlin had added wine to the list of staple exports for which he wished to organize a European market. He called on his officials to design a plan under which a European Agricultural Community, following the pattern of the ECSC, would provide a regulated market for French staple exports of wheat, sugar, dairy products and wine. Meat was not mentioned. The objections which were always to dog this idea were at once raised. Would the United Kingdom participate, and if not was it useful or even possible? Would French farmers accept it? The CGA and FNSEA declared their opposition to any model based on a High Authority with supranational powers.[105]

Pflimlin pursued his ideas in the Consultative Assembly of the Council of Europe, where any talk of European unity could be assured of an enthusiastic reception. One of his close associates in the MRP René Charpentier proposed there on 10 August 1950 that the Consultative Assembly set up a special committee to study the possibility of a common market for agricultural products in western Europe. A similar proposal was submitted for discussion to the French Council of Ministers on 22 August. The difficult issue of the United Kingdom's attitude could be avoided, so Pflimlin argued in his submission to his fellow ministers, by setting up separate study groups of experts for each of the four product groups in question and allowing the geographical extent of the regulated market for each product to be determined separately according to the recommendations of the separate reports. This was also of course a convenient way of allaying the opposition of the farmers.

Monnet received an advance copy of Pflimlin's submission to the Council of Ministers while he was on holiday on the Ile de Ré during the brief summer break in the Schuman Plan negotiations. It was highly unwelcome. The last thing he wished was that the problems of European agriculture should obstruct the negotiation of the Coal, Iron and Steel Community. He had made up his mind that the ECSC must first be created and without the United Kingdom. An urgent telegram to Pflimlin described the timing of the proposals as a 'great mistake' and begged him to postpone the

[103] AN, F 10/5359, Sous-commission d'études 'Vins', 'Organisation des marchés européens', 3 April 1950.

[104] ibid., Procès-Verbal de la réunion de la Commission d'Etude de l'Organisation du Marché Européen du Vin, 27 September 1950.

[105] Noël, 'Les tentatives . . .', op. cit., pp. 272–85.

submissions to the Council of Ministers.[106] Pflimlin agreed, arranging to dine at the end of August with Monnet and Schuman, before submitting them. The proposals he did submit in September were much less ambitious than the grand scheme contemplated in August. They requested support for preliminary studies of markets in the four commodity groups in question with a view to making definite proposals only after the conclusion of the ECSC treaty. To this ministers agreed.

Monnet could envisage an Agricultural Community as a second stage in the uniting of Europe. It would, though, have to be achieved, he insisted, through the same negotiating methods as the ECSC treaty and would have to replicate the institutions to be created by that treaty. The partners to the negotiations would have to accept a prior commitment to create a supranational authority and would then be presented with a working paper which would constitute the sole basis of negotiation. It followed that the negotiations would have at first to be limited to the six members of ECSC.[107] While wheat producers were unenthusiastic about anything larger than an agreement with Germany,[108] the sugar producers argued that a western European common market in sugar made no sense.[109] Dairy farmers were opposed to supranational institutions.[110]

Submitting these conclusions to ministers on 25 October Pflimlin retreated still further from his first ambitions. It was, he told them, 'necessary to foresee the creation of one or several European institutions which it would no doubt be advantageous to link in some way to the Organization for European Economic Cooperation'.[111] His proposals were for a series of European Commodity Boards 'to ensure a guarantee of the disposal at normal prices of the output of the participating countries', for a transition period before one common High Authority would govern the Community.

For 'deficit' products, in which category sugar as well as wheat were listed, both the transitional and the final regimes should be such as to encourage an increase in output. For wheat, a European wheat price would be fixed by a European Wheat Board which would control the quantity, price, and distribution of all imports of wheat into the Community. For sugar, a similar body would place upwards of 300,000 tonnes a year of French sugar on the German market. This calculation allowed for some production increase in Germany too, but one less rapid than the projected increase in consumption. France would remain the sole supplier of its own

---

[106] AN, 81 AJ 172, Monnet to Pflimlin, 19 August 1950.

[107] FJM, AMG 58/1/2, Monnet to Pflimlin, 28 December 1950.

[108] AN, 81 AJ 172, 'Création d'un marché européen des céréales', 23 September 1950.

[109] ibid., Groupement National Interprofessionel de la Production Betteravière et des Industries de Transformation de la Betterave, 'Etude d'un marché commun du sucre ouest-européen', n.d.

[110] ibid., Commission pour l'Etude de l'Organisation du Marche Européen des Produits Laitiers, 'Note du Rapporteur-Générale . . .', 10 October 1950.

[111] ibid., 'Communication du Ministre de l'Agriculture . . .', 21 October 1950.

overseas territories, and where these were sugar exporters they would be included in the common regime, so guaranteeing their sales in Europe. No adjustment would therefore be necessary to the existing sugar regime of the French Union. For products where supply and demand were in equilibrium, such as dairy products, a different regime would be necessary. A continuous increase in Western Europe's standard of living and a continuous increase in consumption of these products could be expected. This meant a common programme of stockpiling, price supports and price equalization methods, the suppression of 'unfair competition' and a common programme to increase consumption. For wine an immediate 'common discipline' was needed, a regime which would stop production increases of cheaper wines, impose common quality controls, stop imports into those member countries which already had a surplus, and share out between the surplus countries exports to those which had a deficit.[112]

Pflimlin added to these proposals a draft 'Declaration' which was obviously intended to reawaken the spirit and form of Schuman's declaration of 9 May. 'Europe', it declared, 'is a great agricultural land. In its social as well as in its economic aspects the state of their agriculture commands the destiny of European countries.' What was needed was 'a healthy and lasting equilibrium' and this could only be achieved in 'a unified European market'. This meant an 'institutional organization analogous in its structure and its working rules to the High Authority'. 'It would in effect provide a further foundation for the creation of a European Federation on which the political future of Europe depends.'[113] Only the negotiating parties to the Treaty of Paris, Pflimlin suggested, should at first be invited to discuss the 'Declaration', whereas the Commodity Boards would be open to all other OEEC members who accepted the principles set out in it, but not necessarily as a matter for immediate action.

This provoked a cacophony of disharmonies. Guy Mollet, who had received his first ministerial appointment as minister with special responsibility for the Council of Europe, wanted to avoid what he thought of as the initial mistake of the Schuman Plan and not exclude the United Kingdom. Maurice Petsche, the minister of finance, who at one stage asked the British government to intervene against his own government's support for the Treaty of Paris, insisted that any negotiations on agricultural markets must include all OEEC members. The FNSEA made public its objections to any scheme restricted to the Six.[114]

It would be difficult to think of a stronger contrast to the speed, relative secrecy and lack of prior discussion within the government which had characterized the issuing of the Schuman proposals. Pflimlin's proposals were referred to an inter-ministerial committee, which included Mollet, Petsche and Schuman. Pflimlin wanted to include Monnet, but some

[112] AN F60^ter 474, Communication du Ministre de l'Agriculture . . ., 25 October 1950.
[113] ibid., 'Projet de "résolution" du gouvernement français', 25 October 1950.
[114] H. Delorme and Y. Tavernier, *Les Paysans français et l'Europe* (Paris, 1969), p. 20.

ministers took a strong constitutional objection. It was not until March 1951, once the text of the Treaty of Paris was assured, that the invitation to discussions and the accompanying 'Declaration' were issued. That the invitations were issued at all seems to have been the outcome of a compromise in mid-February to pursue the same negotiating procedures as for the Schuman Plan but to do so at first with all seventeen OEEC members. To make confusion worse the invitations were issued through the Council of Europe, to emphasize their general west European nature.

The proposals which Charpentier had submitted to the Council of Europe in August 1950 had been accepted for study there and had led to the formation of a sub-committee to report on the possibilities of a common market in European agriculture. When its report was being prepared its British member, Sir David Eccles, had drawn up a minority report rejecting all need for any supranational authority. The Danish representative, Per Federspiel, who was generally regarded as the spokesman there of Venstre, the farmers' party, took his side. The majority report, inspired by Charpentier, requested a common agricultural policy managed by a High Authority. Eccles then gave a press conference saying that there 'should be no more division of Europe along the lines of the Schuman Plan'.[115]

Apart from the light it casts on the readiness of some important figures in French political life to take up the cause of a united Europe as a solution to immediate economic problems, it may not at first seem worthwhile to have related this episode. Neither the French government nor French farmers saw a European Agricultural Community in 1950–1 as a practical proposal, and indeed it was not. The significance of the episode, however, lies elsewhere. Firstly it lies in the reaction to it in the Netherlands. When the dismantling of tariffs on intra-Western-European trade became a high policy priority there, as it first did in 1950 with Stikker's Plan of Action, it inevitably raised the question of what would protect agriculture. A permanent retention of quotas on agricultural trade was not a happy answer in a country 40 per cent of whose commodity export earnings came from agriculture. The general removal of quotas was, as we have seen, not favoured by Dutch governments either. Even if the general removal of all Western European quotas on agricultural imports could have been realistically envisaged, there would always have been the more competitive Denmark to contend with. It is understandable that Pflimlin's and Monnet's ideas should have seemed more promising in the Hague than in Paris.

Secondly, the negotiations between the national farmers' associations, and their activities in OEEC, had made it clear that they had no solution to the problem of surpluses other than hoping that governments would continue buying them for storage. The European Agricultural Community,

[115] *FRUS*, vol. IV, 1951, p. 13.

muddled and impractical though it was as a political idea, did at least grasp the one essential point that if a political solution could be found it had to be in Europeanizing the problem.

When the Stikker Plan of Action was proposed to Dutch ministers in June 1950 it faced very strong objections from the minister of agriculture, Sicco Mansholt.[116] While Stikker's ideas were not inconceivable as a programme for the removal of tariffs on manufactures, they had no relevance, Mansholt protested, to agriculture. Freeing intra-Western-European trade in agriculture, he argued, would not be achieved by removing tariffs but by equalizing the impact of government policies on prices and costs. This was certainly true; agricultural tariffs were an insignificant barrier to trade compared to the complexity of government intervention. The Plan of Action was submitted to OEEC with a paragraph, insisted on by Mansholt, stipulating that agriculture would require 'a special treatment'.[117]

Mansholt was an ardent European federalist. The 'special treatment' he devised reflected these views. It took until September to get agreement in the Dutch cabinet on what it should be, by which date Mansholt's earliest proposals had been considerably reduced in scope. He proposed a European Board for Agriculture and Food to standardize the prices of agricultural commodities in intra-Western-European trade and develop a common trade policy towards the rest of the world. Each country could keep its own domestic prices if it wished, providing they were lower than the standardized prices. Such a state of affairs, he argued, need be only temporary, because a guaranteed vent for surpluses would speed up the rate of productivity improvement and reduce prices, the same argument as that of the French planners. Prime minister Drees, his minister of economic affairs Johannes van den Brink, and the head of the delegation to the Schuman Plan talks, Dirk Spierenburg, all disagreed. Dutch food prices would, on the contrary, they maintained, be forced upwards, an accurate vision of the 1970s.[118] Nevertheless, the proposals were accepted as a basis for negotiation.

How far there was collusion between Mansholt and Pflimlin is hard to judge. The Dutch Ministry of Agriculture was kept well informed of the struggles inside the French government. In November 1950 officials of the

[116] Sicco Leendert Mansholt, 1908–   . Agronomist and farmer. Began farming in the mid-1930s in the Netherlands as agricultural prices fell, and so fulfilled the predictions of his grandfather who had unsuccessfully campaigned for agricultural protection in the 1880s. His wartime role in the resistance brought him appointment as minister of agriculture, 1944–58. European commissioner for agriculture, 1958–72. A socialist, he believed in April 1989 that food prices in Europe were too low and that a widespread agricultural population based on family farms was an indispensable foundation of the modern social order.

[117] MBZ, DGEM 6117/1262, 'Statement by Dr. Stikker on the Netherlands Plan of Action made at the Council Meeting of OEEC on July 7 1950.'

[118] AR, MR (588), 'Nota betreft: Integratie Europese Landbouw', 12 August 1950. R.T. Griffiths, 'The Mansholt Plan' in Griffiths, (ed.), *The Netherlands . . .*, op. cit.

French and Dutch ministries met in Paris to try to take the idea of a European Agricultural Community further. Among the ideas they discussed was that the European Board would also control agricultural imports into Western Europe, and that it might establish a central investment fund, financed from the income which it would receive from a common external tariff.[119] It is difficult to see this meeting other than as a conspiracy against their own governments by the two ministers and their close officials. The French council of ministers had certainly not agreed either to the idea of a single European Board for agriculture or a central investment fund. Two young and remarkably vigorous ministers, each with strongly favourable views about European unity, each eager to pursue a forward policy in ministries whose affairs do not normally rank so high in the scale of government priorities – it is not hard to see how they could have persuaded themselves that they would be able to break through the political constraints surrounding them.

It was not uncommon in Britain until recently to hear the view expressed that the Treaties of Paris and Rome were a conspiracy between a small group of federalist politicians, acting with political skill but little popular support. Federalist politicians were obviously not above attempting such conspiracies. Monnet himself was soon to join it, as ready as Pflimlin to present the French government with a *fait accompli*. That such tactics were doomed to failure however is shown by their outcome.

The responses to the French invitation to all the OEEC countries to discuss the possibility of an Agricultural Community were, as could only have been expected, most discouraging. Even the Dutch government made a point of not returning its reply directly to the Council of Europe and wondering whether the USA and Canada should not also be invited. The Germans gave Maestracci the chance to address the Bauernverband and other professional representative bodies at a conference to discuss, and bury, the whole affair. 'The French plan', he told them, 'foresees the creation of an economically and politically united Europe. In spite of the different circumstances and methods it follows the way pointed out by the Schuman Plan.'[120] The addresses by members of the Bauernverband did not respond. At the most the Bauernverband could envisage two separate boards, one for wheat or grains only, the other, a more remote possibility, for cattle and meat. Both would have to be controlled by the interest

---

[119] ML, GS Arch 2, Int. Eur. Land, corresp. en bespr. met buitenland, 'Verslag van de bespreking met ambtenaren van het Franse Ministerie van Landbouw betreffende de Franse plannen tot integratie van de landbouw', 10 November 1950. G. Noël, 'Les tentatives . . .', op. cit., pp. 292 ff.

[120] A photograph of this singularly unagricultural personality, looking as though he had never before left the 17th *arrondissement* of Paris, may be seen saying something of the kind to the broad-shouldered, horny-handed ranks of the Deutscher Bauernverband in German Federal Republic, Bundesministerium für Ernährung, Landwirtschaft und Forsten, *Sicherheit und Landwirtschaft, Vertragsfolge der internationalen öffentlichen landwirtschaftlichen Tagung am 9 und 10 Mai 1951* (Hiltrop, 1951).

groups themselves.[121] The Ministry of Agriculture, of course, agreed with this position.[122]

These views were positively welcoming compared to the reaction of the Ministry for the Economy. In a long and repeatedly reworked draft Erhard and his officials rehearsed every possible theoretical argument against a European Agricultural Community and against most of the Federal Republic's post-war domestic agricultural policy as well. Ever since the First World War, they argued, Europe had been developing high-price farm surpluses, so that none of the talk of higher productivity generating lower prices could be credited. The first thing that was needed was to correct the external values of overvalued currencies like the French franc and to move as rapidly as possible to international currency convertibility. The proposed agricultural arrangements were actually intended, Erhard argued, to be a barrier to this, by institutionalizing artificially supported differences in national prices.[123]

Even before the French invitations had been issued the Italian Ministry of Agriculture had already firmly decided to oppose Pflimlin's ideas. The surplus products France wanted to vent were all protected in Italy and Italian agricultural exports hardly seemed to require any new European regulatory machinery. The highly specialized apple, pear, and peach farms of the Po Valley and the table grape farms of Puglia were successfully competitive in northern European markets even with American produce. From 1.55 million tonnes in 1951, exports of fruit and vegetables rose to 3.57 million tonnes in 1961, an average annual rate of increase of 8.7 per cent.[124] The main support of this remarkable growth was the increase in demand from the Federal Republic. There were also large and growing values of exports to Austria, France, Switzerland and the United Kingdom. The only area where Italian farmers saw a need for regulation was to curb arbitrary and seasonal quotas on this trade. If Italy for political and diplomatic reasons had to accept the French invitation, it should, the Ministry of Agriculture decided, insist that talks cover a range of products which the French did not wish to talk about. Officials enjoyed themselves listing these; fruit, rice, perfume essences, tobacco, fresh vegetables – the list grew ever longer. The head of the economic section of the Foreign Office summed up the position by saying that Italy, because it might be harmed by staying out of them, should participate in any discussions with 'a

---

[121] BA, B102/11305, 'Stellungnahme zu der Note der französischen Regierung hinsichtlich eines Grunen Schuman Planes', 20 April 1951; B116/7292, Plan eines europäischen Agrarunion, 22 May 1951.

[122] AN, F10/5694, François-Poncet to Schuman, 15 June 1951. The statistical materials of the report were published as German Federal Republic, *Auswärtiges Amt, Gutachten zur Fragen eines Europäischen Agrargemeinschaft* (Bonn, 1953).

[123] BA, B102/11305, Drafts of a letter from Erhard to Hallstein, 11 April 1951 onwards.

[124] G.E. Marciani, *Andamenti e linee evolutive delle produzione agricole 1951–1981* (Milan, 1972), p. 83.

prudent scepticism'.[125] The Italian CGA saw the French proposals as 'detailed international dirigisme'.[126]

In Belgium the agricultural sector was too insignificant on a European scale to gain from Pflimlin's ideas, but it would be damaging in other respects if Belgium were left out of any Agricultural Community.[127] Opposing any commercial diplomatic initiative supported by its Benelux partner was obviously difficult. Belgium did have surpluses of which it might hope to dispose within the proposed arrangements; its sugar surplus in fact in 1950 had been greater than that of any other Western European country. It was an exporter of market garden produce such as chicory and grapes to France and the Federal Republic. In the inter-war period it had been an exporter of eggs and, although very small by Dutch and Danish standards, exports were beginning again. The danger was that an Agricultural Community might force Belgium to take unwanted surpluses from elsewhere.

Baron Héger, the Minister of Agriculture, who was himself a member of the Alliance Agricole Belge, believed that agricultural protection and high producer prices would inevitably lead to occasional surpluses; that a vent for them was necessary to equilibrate the system; that this might well mean some form of European organization to regulate agricultural trade; but that such an organization should not have powers over domestic policy like those of the ECSC.[128] Even this stance was too favourable for the Boerenbond. It could not accept any European organization unless wages and costs in agriculture elsewhere, especially in the Netherlands, were brought up to the Belgian level, the same welfare argument as that made by coal miners.

In Luxembourg the government discussed the invitation with the Centrale Paysanne, which insisted that Luxembourg refuse to attend any conference without a prior guarantee that the protected status of Luxembourg's agriculture within Benelux would be completely preserved in any wider European structure.[129] As the prime minister Joseph Bech explained; 'everybody believes that the government is itself governed by the steel magnates and notably by Mr. Meyer, the president of Arbed. Even so it signed the Schuman Plan, but the government

[125] MAE, Ambasciata Parigi, Resoconto della riunione tenuta sabato 10 febbraio 1951.

[126] ibid., 'Appunto per il Ministro Pella: osservazioni preliminari sul "pool verde" ', 5 March 1951; ibid., Resoconto della riunione interministeriale tenutasi il 24 marzo 1951.

[127] J. Forget, 'De Belgische landbouw tegenover de internationale vraagstukken', *Landbouwtijdschrift*, iv, April 1951. Forget had been an employee of the Boerenbond in the 1930s. See also the discussion by L. van Molle, 'Le milieu agricole belge face à la "concurrence européene" 1944–1958', in M. Dumoulin (ed.), *La Belgique et les débuts de la construction européene* (Louvain-la-Neuve, 1987).

[128] Baron Charles Héger, 1902–   . Lawyer and farmer. Member of parliament and senator for the Social Christian party, 1946–73; minister of agriculture, 1950–4, 1960–71; of the interior, 1958; member of the European Parliament, 1971–4. He farmed 150 hectares.

[129] AN, F 10/5694, Letter from French ambassador in Luxembourg to Ministère des Affaires Etrangères, 17 May 1951.

is in fact much more frightened of the farmers.'[130]

The British reply was merely to restate British policy; nothing beyond OEEC was needed. On 24 April 1951 Guy Mollet wrote a personal letter to the Foreign Secretary Herbert Morrison urging him to send a British representative to the proposed conference and explaining that it was at his personal instigation that the invitation had been issued through the Council of Europe as a way of allowing Britain to attend. This made no impression at all on Morrison. When the United Kingdom finally decided to attend, it was only because it could not rely on all its usual supporters in OEEC to refuse to participate.

In summer 1950, when first tentatively apprised by the French of the idea of 'a Schuman Plan for agriculture' the Danes had indicated to the British that they 'could not help feeling that the proposals had certain attractions'.[131] The attitude of the two dominant agricultural interest groups there, the Agricultural Council and the Federation of Smallholders, was by no means as hostile to the idea of European-wide market regulation as the British had hoped it would be. They were restless about the depressing effect on their export prices of dependence on the British market and well aware that nothing remotely like free trade in agriculture would return. As the Federal Republic in early summer 1951 began to lift the import controls imposed at the end of 1950, it was of central importance for Denmark to be present in every forum where trade with Germany would be discussed.

Britain could firmly rely only on neutrals. The Swedish government announced that it had no intention of joining any international scheme which would cut across its policy of 'self-sufficiency in times of war'.[132] The Swiss attitude was set out by an official spokesman in a published speech; 'The matters which are in question here, however, are exclusively matters for individual nations. It is unthinkable that the individual nation should want to surrender them out of its hands and entrust them to an international body.'[133] This was not sufficient to organize a bloc to oppose the talks and left the French government, no doubt to the displeasure of some of its members, in a position where Pflimlin's initiative must go ahead.

After the June 1951 election Pflimlin was moved to the post of minister for France overseas, with a supervisory brief over the proposed agricultural conference. His successor at the Ministry of Agriculture, Paul Antier, showed no enthusiasm for the project. It was only with his resignation in November and the appointment of Camille Laurens as minister that renewed pressure was brought from the Ministry on the government to pursue the issue.

[130]   PRO, FO 371/94346, Luxembourg Legation to FO, 22 May 1951.
[131]   PRO, FO 1009/31, Note by Sir E. Hall-Patch on a conversation with Mr Bartels, 17 July 1950.
[132]   PRO, FO 371/94348, Stockholm Embassy to FO, 22 May 1951.
[133]   O. Howald, 'Agrarwirtschaftliche Zusammenarbeit in Europa', in W. Abel, *et al.*, *Probleme einer europäischen Agrarintegration* (Vienna, 1953).

Mansholt kept up the pressure by publicizing his own proposals to the annual IFAP meeting in September 1951 and in October tried to persuade the French government to call a conference of the ministers of agriculture of the Six alone. Pleven's proposals for the EDC helped to keep the possibility of a European Agricultural Community of the Six clinging to life. Nine months after the original invitations to the conference had been sent, the decision was taken to call it. 'A European Agricultural Community', the FNSEA observed on its eve, 'has been discussed. It is obvious that the variety of output and the diversity of positions does not allow so general an objective to be envisaged from the start.'[134] When officials from the French Ministry of Agriculture attended the annual agricultural show in Brussels shortly before the conference, Héger, in his official speech of welcome, told them that he wished the French government shared the opinions of its farmers.[135]

The conference opened with an address from Schuman. Pflimlin introduced the French proposals for 'a European co-ordinating organization' which would begin the task of harmonizing production, marketing and consumption policies, something rather vaguer than Mansholt's plans. Laurens was even more reticent. Mansholt by contrast pleaded fervently for a further stage of European integration under a supranational authority, one unified market with common prices for as many products as possible. The Dutch government considered it impossible 'to restrict, even at the start, agricultural integration to a limited number of products'.[136] There was no support for this from anywhere else, but general agreement that OEEC was proving unsatisfactory as a forum for regulating agricultural trade. All governments were discontented with the obstructionist attitude of the Food and Agriculture Committee to trade liberalization. Their ministers of agriculture on the contrary were more discontented with the pressures brought on them there to liberalize trade and with the thought that they might not always be in a position to resist them. The conference voted to set up a series of study groups and present their reports to a further conference. At once it acquired the unofficial appellation of 'Green Pool'.

The study groups were bound to duplicate OEEC activities, but the Green Pool was independent of any control of the OEEC Executive Committee. Spain, excluded from OEEC, was a member, its first participation in any of the post-war European international organizations. The ministers of agriculture saw the Green Pool as a useful forum for advancing the vested interest of agriculture even further. The German delegation had not even been led by the minister of agriculture, but by Hermes, and

---

[134] AN, F10/ 5694, Note de la FNSEA, 'La Création de Marchés Communs Européens de Produits Agricoles', 13 February 1952.

[135] ibid., Brussels Embassy to Paris, 20 February 1952.

[136] PRO, CAB 134/1012, 'Report on the Preparatory Conference held in Paris on 25 March 1952'.

immediately on the close of the conference the Bauernverband demanded that its wishes be given the fullest consideration by the government in settling all the questions which would subsequently arise there.[137] It demanded: that a future Agricultural Community should not be allowed to deliver German farms 'into foreign hands'; that foreign aid should be provided for German agriculture; that the capacity of the Federal Republic to supply itself in 'abnormal times' must not be weakened; and that the existence of the Green Pool must not prejudice the possibility of German reunification.[138]

The Green Pool was not in fact in German eyes intended to reach an understanding for the vent of French surpluses in Germany, but to defend German farmers' interests better than OEEC might be capable of doing in the future. The Bauernverband was opposed to the idea of a High Authority or a European Board for agriculture.[139] It was still ready to support the idea of French wheat exports to Germany, but only providing it and the CGA were themselves allowed to determine the annual volume of trade and the prices.[140] The Ministry of Agriculture was opposed to any attempt to restrict a new European organization for agriculture to the Six.[141]

Yet none of this in any way deterred Mansholt. He told the Danes they were not wanted in the new organization unless they were prepared to accept a common market and a High Authority.[142] They had, he said, 'never formulated a single constructive idea'.[143] On his return from the conference of ministers of agriculture he told his officials that he had privately agreed with Monnet to produce an experts' report in a year's time recommending a European Agricultural Community.[144] A small working group in the Dutch Ministry of Agriculture henceforward collaborated closely with a working party set up by Monnet under the direction of an official from the French Ministry of Agriculture, Louis Rabot.[145]

When the Beyen Plan was launched in September 1952 it gave extra strength to Mansholt's position in the Dutch government. He did not

---

[137] BA, B116/7292, Vermerk über einer Rücksprache zwischen Herrn Dr. Hermes und Herrn Staatssekretär Dr. Sonnemann, 3 April 1952.

[138] BA, B102/11304, Material für die Verhandlungen über eine Agrar-Union, 12 May 1952.

[139] BA, B116/7293, Treffen der landwirtschaftlichen Organisationen Belgiens, Luxemburgs und der Bundesrepublik, 3 January 1953.

[140] BA, B102/11305, Deutsch–französische Zusammenarbeit. Besprechungen über Agrarfragen in Bonn, 14 June 1952.

[141] ibid., Niederschrift über die Besprechung des dänischen Landwirtschaftministers Sonderup mit Staatssekretär Sonnemann, 17 December 1952.

[142] ML, GS Arch 1, Int. Eur. Land 3, de Waal to Min. Land., Bezoek Minister Mansholt Januari 1953 aan Denemarken, 22 January 1953.

[143] ML, GS Arch 2, Int. Eur. Land, Corresp. en Bespr. met buitenland 1, Besprekingen te Kopenhagen, 14–15 January 1953.

[144] ML, GS Arch. 1, Int. Eur. Land., Notitie betreft: bespreking met minister Mansholt, 10 April 1952.

[145] ML, GS Arch. 3, Int. Eur. Land., Interim Werkgr. Parijs (Alg.), Verslag der besprekingen op het Bureau Monnet betreffende het in gemeen overleg op te stellen basisdocument, aangaande agrarische integratie, 28 May 1952.

believe that the European Defence Community would be a sound foundation for European integration.[146] But if the EPC was only to come into existence if it had the foundation of a customs union, 'special arrangements' for agriculture were evidently again on the table. In November, after discussing with Spaak the possibility of submitting a separate report on the possibility of agricultural integration within the customs union of the EPC, Mansholt invited Laurens to the Hague to discuss the relationship of the Green Pool to the EDC treaty. There the two ministers signed a protocol which went well beyond what the French government would have accepted. The purpose of the second Green Pool conference, they agreed, should not only be to accept the studies but to draw up proposals for a supranational authority for agriculture within the customs union of the Six. The protocol recorded that this European Authority for Agriculture should be 'noticeably different' from the High Authority of the ECSC.

There followed a determined effort by Mansholt to persuade the other members of the Six to subscribe to the terms of this agreement. Fanfani, the Italian minister of agriculture, only agreed with reluctance, and by January 1953 he was already telling the Dutch ambassador in Rome that it had now become unacceptable and impossible because of the forthcoming Italian elections.[147] It was all very well, Fanfani was reported as saying, for de Gasperi to talk about the political and economic integration of Europe, it was not he who had to deal with Italian farmers.[148] In Germany, knowing what to expect from the Ministry of Agriculture, Mansholt went directly to Adenauer. Adenauer, by then desperate to save the Defence Community, supported him fully. Any sacrifices which Germany would have to make in the cause of agricultural integration, he told Mansholt, would amply be compensated by gains made from economic integration in other areas. To this Sonnemann, the state-secretary in the Ministry of Agriculture, remained however 'absolutely opposed'.[149] Erhard, too, argued that the acceptance by the foreign ministers of the Six of the Dutch demand for EPC to be based on a customs union was far too vague to commit the Federal Republic to any attempt at constructing an Agricultural Community. While he warmly supported the view that agricultural tariffs in the Federal Republic might be reduced in order to obtain reductions in tariffs elsewhere, tariffs were nevertheless, he insisted, a

[146] Interview with Dr Mansholt, 19 April 1989.
[147] Amintore Fanfani, 1908– . Professor of economic history in three universities. Joined the Christian Democrats, 1945; member of parliament, 1946; minister of agriculture, 1951–3; once minister of labour and social security, once minister of foreign affairs, twice president of the Council of Ministers, once stopgap president of the Republic. For more than forty years high in the councils of his party. Author of a book on the sixteenth-century price revolution.
[148] Bonomi took the same view, arguing that as far as Italy was concerned the Green Pool remained a protectionist device against Italian agriculture unless it also permitted the free movement of labour. F. Bertini, 'La DC . . .', op. cit.
[149] ML, GS Arch. 2, Int. Eur. Land., 'Besprekingen te Bonn op 15 Januari 1953', 18 January 1953.

more acceptable form of protection than the supranational regulation of markets, which could only lead to a further stage of agricultural protectionism.[150]

Laurens may have felt like a man being forced against his better judgement into a polygamous marriage when his limited desires were as likely to be satisfied without a marriage at all, particularly as only one of the future brides appeared to want him. It may have come as a relief when the Pinay government fell just before Christmas 1952 and Bidault returned in January 1953 to take charge of French foreign policy. He was as opposed to any Agricultural Community of the Six as he was determined to modify the EDC agreements. When Laurens revealed the existence of the Hague protocol, the council of ministers rejected it as an agenda for the second Green Pool conference. The conference's purpose, the council of ministers laid down, could be no more than an effort to reach separate single-product marketing agreements on surplus commodities.

At the end of February 1953 when Mansholt's chief official visited Paris he was told that the European Agricultural Community was now, in French eyes, dead. As the Green Pool conference was now due in little more than two weeks' time the French suggested that it should receive separate proposals from the French and Dutch governments, one based on the Mansholt–Laurens protocol, another to create a set of working parties to examine the prospects for single-product agreements.[151] This the Dutch refused, demanding a separate meeting of the ministers of agriculture of the Six to which Mansholt could present the plan for a Community. At the last moment the French government gave way and a conference of the agriculture ministers of the Six was called, as a 'preparatory' conference, on the two days preceding the full meeting of the Green Pool.

The six ministers met on 14 March 1953. The proceedings could only in the circumstances resemble one of Labiche's better farces. The play opened with Laurens warning Mansholt that the joint protocol needed some 'small adjustments'. As adjusted by the French it declared the purpose of the preparatory conference to be solely to discuss the agenda and proceedings of the full conference. The Dutch insisted on their original proposal as the main item on the Green Pool agenda. Nobody else would even agree that it should be on the agenda at all, unless at the end and if there was time. The Six ministers then set to work drawing up a list of possible single-product agreements to be discussed in the Green Pool conference, to the background of a sulky silence from the Dutch. This culminated in an explosion by Mansholt, calling the meeting a conspiracy and threatening to leave. Hastily, it was agreed that the Laurens–Mansholt protocol would after all be discussed.

[150] BA B102/11408 Erhard to Adenauer, 19 February 1953.
[151] AN, F10/5694, Note relative à la Conférence Européene de l'Agriculture, 10 March 1953; ibid., F10/5696, 'Directives données par M. le Ministre sur les diverses questions que soulève la préparation de la conférence européene de l'agriculture'.

When it was, Fanfani explained that the decisions of the foreign ministers of the Six had nothing to do with Italian agriculture at all and that he would certainly not commit himself to any kind of common market or Community. It was, he insisted, not up to ministers of agriculture to settle questions relating to the major issue of European integration. This was a view supported by Héger who found himself unable to understand why a Dutch minister of agriculture should aspire to settle major political questions at all.[152] Mansholt, for his part, could not understand how a Belgian minister of agriculture could desert his own government. It was left to Hermes, still the leader of the German delegation, to clear the stage for the final curtain with a resolution that the ministers should submit to the full conference a recommendation that only separate single-product marketing agreements were likely to be achieved, but that it would be desirable to preserve an organization separate from OEEC in which to achieve them.[153]

There was therefore, six years before the Treaties of Rome, a reasonably purposive attempt to create a common market for Western European agriculture. It probably would not have taken the form it did, a central supranational authority, had it not been for the Schuman Plan. To that extent it followed the political fashion in which advocates of a federal Europe took their cue from Monnet's success in making the Coal, Iron and Steel Community a political reality. Nor was the European Agricultural Community a subordinate consequence of an industrial common market; it preceded the Beyen proposals by two years, although they gave a powerful additional motivation to it in the Netherlands when they came. It was the political creation of two federalists, something close to the federalist conspiracy which defenders of national sovereignty were always trying to detect, although in each case their motives were also economic. The length of time over which the idea of a European Agricultural Community held the stage, from May 1950 to March 1953, compared to the expiry immediately after birth of similar projects which copied the Schuman Plan, is testimony to the seriousness of the problem and the lack of an alternative solution. Yet the idea was a risible failure.

The one alternative that was pursued, long-term contracts for the purchase of surpluses had met with no greater success by 1953, whether in the form of bilateral trade agreements or organized in a comprehensive Western European framework by OEEC or some European Board. Bilateral trade was looked on with deep disfavour in OEEC and no one outside France and Holland including French farmers had wanted a European Board.

For the farmers' own organizations immobilism was an easy and viable course of action. In 1952–3 the trade liberalization programme remained in

---

[152] MAE, DAE, 'Appunto per il ministro', 26 March 1953.
[153] AR, MR (487), 'Verslag van de bespreking tussen de Ministers van Landbouw', 14 March 1953.

virtual suspension. The producer groups could rest safely in their protectionist cocoon by doing nothing and there were still no French surpluses to trouble the existing disposition of exports. The great trade boom of 1954–7 would wreck this immobilism. Government would not be willing to allow the agricultural interest to block the process of quota removal indefinitely once it became in the interest of the industrial sector to pursue it. Surpluses would grow and the existing disposition of exports would not endure. And the combination of economic and political forces behind the common market would overwhelm the entrenched position of organized agriculture.

AGRICULTURE IN A HIERARCHY OF POWER

The United Kingdom was always opposed to the Green Pool. The government had accepted it only because it had been unable to mobilize enough support to stop it and waited for the moment when it could end it. Dutch opposition after the failure of the Green Pool conference was much fiercer. The Netherlands had wanted a European organization to make exporting agricultural products easier, a common agricultural policy which would have enabled Beyen's industrial customs union to function. It had got the opposite, a club in which ministers of agriculture could maintain barriers against imports. The proposals that began to emerge from the Green Pool working groups after March 1953 were highly protectionist. They pointed 'unmistakably in the direction of forming a high-cost club'.[154] 'It is quite likely', the British representative on the working group on livestock and meat commented, 'that the next version of the group's report will say that "the experts do not regard liberalization of trade as a practical method of achieving their aim of liberalizing trade".'[155]

The cautious moves back towards trade liberalization in OEEC in 1953 did not affect agricultural trade. France, freed from the constraints of the idea of the Agricultural Community, decided in April that more than a quarter of the import savings it wished to make over the next six months could be made at the expense of meat imports from Denmark and the Netherlands. It also reimposed quotas on imports of Dutch cheese.[156] Although Britain in that year began to replace government purchase of food imports by the free market, it did not remove quotas on them. France saw the continuation of the Green Pool solely as a way of reaching long-term single-commodity trade agreements, beginning with an agreement on wheat exports. The French argument was that grain prices were too low and too fluctuating to provide security and stability to European farmers at the levels appropriate in the post-war world, so that both protection and a

---

[154] PRO, CAB 134/1019, Report by the United Kingdom representative on the Interim Committee of the European Conference on Agricultural Markets, 5 November 1953.

[155] PRO, FO371/106037, Third Session of the Group of Exports on Livestock and Meat, 5 December 1953.

[156] *International Trade*, 1953, pp. 101 ff.

general agreement that Western Europe should buy European grain surpluses was necessary. Danish and Swiss representatives on the Green Pool
working party on grains advanced the contrary argument, that for
countries dependent on large imports of grain the lowest possible import
price was the best, because domestic producers could always be protected
against its effects if necessary. The Dutch put forward proposals for a
common market in grains.

The French position was that it was Europe's duty first to buy Europe's
food. In the discussions on the meat trade the French representatives were
perfectly willing to envisage a common authority. Its task would be to
establish national import and export quotas by compiling an annual
European balance sheet of needs and supplies. Import licences would then
be issued by the authority for multilateral use up to the agreed total of
imports. This however was only another way of venting French surpluses in
that particular commodity group. While Mansholt continued his campaign
for a common agricultural policy run by some form of High Authority,
Pflimlin had almost completely abandoned the idea.[157] 'I think', Pflimlin
said in a speech in March 1954,

> for my part that it is not necessary to envisage the installation for
> agriculture of a High Authority equipped with power and majesty.
> Henceforward it is a question of simply applying correctly a certain
> number of relatively simple technical mechanisms according to rules and
> criteria which will be clearly defined. It would suffice to create a
> technical organization with the necessary competence to operate the
> system without having to attribute to it too great a power, nor the
> possibility of intervention at the level of production, which seems to me
> perfectly useless.[158]

The Green Pool turned out not to be this 'technical mechanism'. It failed
to produce the marketing arrangements which France wanted. It was kept
alive everywhere by ministries of agriculture against the wishes of their
foreign ministry colleagues who all soon came to see it as a waste of time
and a diplomatic embarrassment. This was so in Italy for example where
the Ministry of Agriculture wanted to use it to win long-term guarantees
for fruit and vegetable exports.[159] In Belgium the minister of agriculture
was under such strong pressure from the farmers' organizations that he too
insisted, against the wishes of other ministers, that the Green Pool continue.[160] By November 1953 the Quai d'Orsay was ready to admit that it
was tired of the whole affair and would abandon it were it not for the

---

[157] Speech by Mansholt to the Wirtschaftspolitische Gesellschaft 1947, Frankfurt-am-Main,
20 March 1954.
[158] Speech by Pflimlin to the Section Etudiantine du Mouvement Européen, 30 March 1954.
The author would like to thank M. Pflimlin for lending him the text of the speech.
[159] MAE, DGAP, 'Appunto di CORRIAS', 30 June 1954.
[160] PRO, MAF 83/3391, 'Note for Record' by Sir H. Ellis-Rees, 24 February 1954.

pressure of the agricultural interest groups and the Ministry of Agriculture.[161] There was, though, one advantage in continuing,

> for in its European partnership the French government is constantly pressed to become more liberal and by its industrialists and farmers to become more protectionist. For them the only policy is to gain time and put off the evil day when fundamental decisions will have to be taken. The Green Pool serves this purpose admirably. Here they can talk of stimulating exports and protecting imports without much disturbance.[162]

Eventually it was wound up by a Franco–British agreement to turn it into a special ministerial committee of OEEC. The ministers of agriculture did not accept this solution at once. It was not until January 1955, when an acceptable form of words was found and the problem of Spain's membership resolved, that the Green Pool was dissolved. In so far as France had made any progress in disposing of its surpluses it was not through the Green Pool but by bilateral trade bargaining with Germany.

Even there, although the Federal Republic was prepared in the 1955 trade agreement to take 500,000 tonnes of wheat for the first year falling to 400,000 tonnes in the two succeeding years, no offer of any kind was made on sugar and no increase in dairy imports was proposed. Attempts to bargain for more only opened the door to German demands that they be allowed more manufactured exports to France in the non-liberalized sector. All that could be gained was a commitment on the German side to take other cereals up to an annual level of 200,000 tonnes.[163] This bilateral bargaining did, it is true, raise the value of French agricultural exports to Germany to roughly the same level as that of exports of semi-manufactures. But a ceiling appeared to have been reached just as the projected French surpluses were arriving in quantity. By the time France had cautiously entered the inter-governmental negotiations on the Spaak report it was difficult to believe that bilateralism would offer a vent for surpluses. The common market proposed in the Spaak report did offer the attraction that it might provide a way forward which otherwise was difficult to see.

In 1955 about one-third of the agricultural imports of the OEEC countries by value was still subject to quantitative restrictions, either because they were imports on government account or because quotas had still not been removed. It was still possible to remove quotas in statistical

[161] PRO, CAB 134/1017, Ellis-Rees to Salisbury, 1 August 1953.
[162] PRO, FO 371/106037, Lloyd to Crawford, 4 November 1953; FO 371/106034, Horpham to Crawford, 20 November 1953.
[163] In fact with the failure of the 1956 wheat harvest France had to ask for a waiver on the obligation to supply 500,000 tonnes and Germany accepted 200,000 tonnes of barley instead. 125,000 tonnes of wheat exports were postponed to the 1957 harvest.

conformity with the rules of the OEEC programme without making much difference to agricultural imports. Belgium, for example, in December 1955 could take an apparently giant step towards removing quotas over a wide range of imports, but because prices of most of the foodstuff items did not meet Belgian target prices they could not be admitted, even though no import licence was necessary, and when they could be admitted the Benelux agreements meant that most of them came from the Netherlands under the preference scheme. It was just as difficult to sell in Holland. The response of the German Ministry of Agriculture to Dutch complaints in 1954 about German protectionism was that the regulation of food marketing in the Netherlands itself was 'actually more restrictive than that of the former Reichsnährstand'.[164] France, though, could hardly complain about the difficulty of exporting. When in April 1955 it liberalized 60 per cent of agricultural imports this affected 'none of the main sectors of metropolitan production'.[165] Of its agricultural imports from Western Europe 42.9 per cent were subject to quota restrictions.[166]

When Beyen revived his proposals for a customs union in 1955 he was prepared to incorporate a series of exemption clauses for French agriculture, but the Dutch cabinet rejected this as a premature concession on a fundamental issue.[167] In the Spaak Committee and afterwards in the intergovernmental negotiations the French representations reiterated the point they had always made in the Green Pool working groups, that it should be established as a first principle that European agriculture would be protected against the rest of the world, and European surpluses consumed in the common market before extra-European imports. This could be achieved, they argued, by a straightforward preference scheme without any need for the complications of standardizing prices and external tariffs. All that France in fact wanted was still a guaranteed disposal of its surpluses. A common agricultural policy, not wanted by French farmers, appeared altogether too high a price to pay.

It was with the representatives of agriculture that Marjolin had his 'longest and for a time most difficult discussion', when he set about the task of persuading French interest groups to support the policy of entry into the common market.[168] There was remarkably little discussion between the Messina and Venice meetings of how French agriculture would be fitted into the common market. The Spaak Committee got as far as agreeing that

---

[164] BA, B102/11419, 'Vermerk über die Besprechung am 18.6.1954 zur Prüfung der zollpolitischen Erörterungen, die im Rahmen der Verhandlungen über die EPG stattgefunden haben', 25 June 1954.

[165] OEEC, *First Report on Agricultural Policies in Europe and North America*, 1956, p. 62.

[166] G. Curzon, *Multilateral Commercial Diplomacy. The General Agreement on Tariffs and Trade and its Impact on National Commercial Policies and Techniques* (London, 1965), p. 158.

[167] A.G. Harryvan and A.E. Kersten, 'The Netherlands, Benelux and the Relance Européene 1954–1955', in E. Serra (ed.), *Il Rilancio dell'Europa e i Trattati di Roma* (Brussels, 1989).

[168] R. Marjolin, *Le Travail d'une vie: Mémoires 1911–1986* (Paris, 1986), p. 292.

agriculture could not be brought into a common market without a transitional period and that

> an attempt should also be made to seek a means to establish in the near future a common market for certain agricultural products, in cases where the markets and the prices seem to be already balanced. Nothing would be more important than to destroy the prejudice that agriculture in all cases and without exception presents the most difficult problem.[169]

In its final report to the foreign ministers however, the Spaak Committee came close to acknowledging that it had found no solution for agricultural trade.

Agriculture would have, nevertheless, to be included, it reported, in the common market and there would have to be a transitional period. In that period countries would still be able to maintain quotas. For agriculture, the common external tariff might have to be reinforced by other means of protection, because the objective would still have to be to maintain a level of European prices high enough to maintain the living standards of European farmers.[170] It would, the report suggested, be the task of the European authority which would govern the common market to begin, within two years of the start of the market, the task of aligning national agricultural policies so that a common agricultural policy would eventually become possible. The acceptance by the French of the Spaak report at the Venice meeting, against the wishes of the Ministry of Agriculture, underlined that agriculture was not the first priority, although in the subsequent negotiations France continued to demand some form of preference scheme.

In Germany too the subordinate position of agriculture was left in no doubt by the Venice decision. Sonnemann argued within the Ministry of Agriculture that the Spaak report was unacceptable as a basis for negotiations.[171] But Niklas's successor as minister of agriculture, Heinrich Lübke, was a firm supporter of Adenauer's foreign policy.[172] To the American observers in OEEC in 1955, 'Mr. Luebke justified the German policy of bilateralism and European agricultural protection on a political basis. His economic argument was secondary. Luebke's position was that European

---

[169] Comité Intergouvernemental Créé par la Conférence de Messine, Document de Travail, no. 5, 11 January 1956.

[170] Comité Intergouvernemental, *Rapport des Chefs de Délégation aux Ministres des Affaires Etrangères*, 21 April 1956.

[171] H.-J. Küsters, *Die Gründung der europäischen Wirtschaftsgemeinschaft* (Baden-Baden, 1982), p. 258.

[172] Heinrich Lübke, 1894–1972. Like Hermes he had created a representative political organization for agriculture, the Deutsche Bauernschaft, of which he was director from 1926 to 1933. Elected to parliament for the Zentrum, 1931; in prison, 1933–4; an engineer, 1934–40; head of a firm which made spare parts for V2 rockets, 1940–4; joined CDU, 1945; deputy to the Landtag of North Rhine Westphalia, 1946–9; Bundestag deputy, 1949–50 and 1953–9; minister of agriculture, 1953–9; federal president, 1959–69. In this last capacity he was frequently derided for his verbal infelicity.

unification was essential to Europe's survival, and the key to this was French and German unification.'[173] In that perspective, unification could equally well demand an end to bilateralism and the agricultural interest be depicted in a rather distant background.

In both countries the Venice meeting marked the start of really serious negotiations about the way agriculture could be fitted into the common market, but not of any worthwhile progress. German agriculture was all the more determined to keep up prices and keep out imports. French negotiators had to try to fit their objective of guaranteed long-term export contracts into the much more comprehensive schemes for managing agriculture which the Dutch brought forward. The problem was made worse with the decision to incorporate the empire into the common market.

Edward Lloyd, the official in the United Kingdom Ministry of Food and Agriculture most concerned with the Green Pool, thought that it was not until March 1952 that Pflimlin had realized that the biggest problem of a European Agricultural Community might well be the integration into it of France's overseas territories.[174] As we have seen, the overseas territories and the North African protectorates absorbed more French food surpluses in the 1950s than Western Europe. They were even more important as a source of food imports which could be paid for in francs. Seen from the standpoint of the overseas territories themselves the French market was often their one slender hope of economic development, or in some cases of survival. The minister for overseas territories at the time, François Mitterand, criticized Pflimlin's ideas as incompatible with imperial policy as it existed. Probably, he argued, no European country other than Denmark would be prepared to admit agricultural imports from the French Union, if France alone became a member of a European Agricultural Community.[175]

Most of the committees which then studied the problem agreed that this was so and were critical of Pflimlin's ideas. A sub-committee of the Conseil Economique concluded that an Agricultural Community would be inimical to the interests both of France and the French Union unless the French Union as a whole was a member.[176] Including it raised many difficulties. It would force citrus fruit producers into a losing competition with more efficient European producers. It would mean the end of the local imperial monopolies of French sugar refiners. If imperial producers switched exports to Germany the outcome for France might be a loss in dollar and sterling earnings. In some cases Germany might well refuse to make a market for them at the expense of its Latin American trade treaties. From

[173] FRC, ECA, Box 60, 'FAS Administrator Garnett's Report on OEEC Agricultural Ministers' Meeting, 4/5 July 1955', 15 July 1955.
[174] PRO, MAF 83/3388, Lloyd to Foreign Office, 20 March 1952.
[175] AN, F10/5694, Mitterand to Pflimlin, 5 March 1951.
[176] France, Conseil Economique, *Incidences du Pool Vert sur la production agricole dans les territoires extra-métropolitains de l'Union Française*, Rapport présenté au nom de la Commission de l'Economie de l'Union Française, 4 February 1954.

where the Germans would buy their bananas was in fact destined to become a big issue in the CAP. As things stood there seemed a large advantage to France and imperial producers in retaining existing arrangements.

It is hardly surprising that in the three weeks of dramatic diplomatic activity after the Mollet–Adenauer meeting on 6 November, when almost every obstacle fell, it was on the common agricultural policy alone that no progress was made.[177] No one now intended to delay the treaty to meet the demands of French or German farmers, yet all recognized that including the French overseas territories made the agricultural issue more complex even as the others were all simplified.

The attitude of metropolitan French agriculture did change in the course of 1956; Marjolin described French farmers as being 'quite enthusiastic' by mid-October at the idea that a common market would guarantee them wheat and meat exports.[178] But their enthusiasm, it would seem, still depended on long-term fixed contracts rather than on a common agricultural policy. Adenauer may well have made the crucial concession in his talks with Mollet on 6 November. The day after that meeting Maurice Faure told the FNSEA leaders that it had been decided that during the transitional period of the common market, before a common agricultural policy was established, the treaty text would make provision for agricultural trade between the Six to be carried on by long-term single-product export contracts.

During the same transition period each country would be allowed to set its own minimum import prices for food and anything offered at less than these prices might well be kept out, if necessary by the additional protection of quotas.[179] French farmers would thus get more of the German market and would lose none of their protection, at least until the details of the common agricultural policy had been worked out. On 16 January 1957, presenting the text of the treaty to the national assembly, Edgar Faure pledged the government to obtain a common agricultural policy that would not reduce the incomes and level of protection of French farmers.

The treaty text laid down in article 39 a number of objectives which a future common agricultural policy should meet. They repeated the general objectives of national agricultural policy, heavily emphasizing welfare and incomes, the protection of rural life and the need to improve productivity. Three years were set aside to devise a common policy which would achieve these incompatible goals. This timetable was imposed by the timetable for the removal of industrial tariffs. The task was to be undertaken by the

---

[177] PRO, FO371/122056, R.F. Bretherton to FO, 'Note of a Meeting in Brussels', 8 December 1956.

[178] PRO, FO 371/122037, Note by R.F. Bretherton of a discussion with Marjolin, 17 October 1956.

[179] PRO, FO371/122046, Commercial Dept. of the UK Paris Embassy to FO, 10 December 1956.

ministers of agriculture. If they were unable to agree it would be up to the European Commission to bring forward its own proposals.

Mansholt became the European commissioner for agriculture, taking with him Louis Rabot as his chief official. When the ministers failed at their Stresa meeting in July 1958 to shape a common agricultural policy the task thus fell to two of the original architects of that federal dream, the European Agricultural Community of 1950–3.

This is not the place to begin a history of the CAP as it subsequently emerged. But what occurred after the Treaties of Rome should be placed in the perspective of the events which led up to it. The similarity between the European Commission's proposals for a common policy in late 1959 and Mansholt's proposals at the time of the Stikker and Beyen plans was no coincidence. Most of the Commission's ideas were already there in Mansholt's first rejected proposals to the Dutch cabinet in 1950 for 'special arrangements' in agriculture to allow the Stikker Plan of Action to go ahead. Whereas at Stresa the French minister of agriculture had continued to insist that all that was necessary was an obligation on members of the Community to allocate first preferences in food imports to other members, Mansholt's proposals as commissioner repeated his insistence when he had been Dutch minister of agriculture that a common policy meant common prices, at least by the expiration of the ten-year period for removing industrial tariffs. They repeated also the suggestion he had first made in 1950 during the arguments in the Dutch government, that prices could be gradually brought into harmony by the temporary establishment of variable levies on the national frontiers, supplemented in the case of exports from high-price countries by export subsidies. This had the advantage of leaving the existing arrangements undisturbed for some time, while securing agreement on the principle that the basis of the CAP would in fact be common prices and common policies.

During the negotiations for the treaty France had demanded a formal statement, to fulfil Edgar Faure's pledge, that protection for agriculture would not be at a lower level than existing national protection. While refusing this, the other parties had agreed on a vaguer form of words; there would be a right of veto against any common policy which did not give guarantees of an equivalent standard of living and an equivalent amount of employment in the agricultural sectors of national economies to those which national policy provided. Adopting a system of variable levies on national frontiers left governments free to determine themselves the standard of living of their own farmers. But for how long? Italy's reaction to Mansholt's proposals, for example, was to demand that the right unilaterally to impose minimum prices on national markets be confined only to the first transitional period for the removal of tariffs. The FNSEA and the Bauernverband succeeded in getting a motion accepted in the European Parliament that in any future system common prices should not be fixed below the German level, which was generally the highest.

The approval of the Commission's proposals in June 1960 led to the acceptance by the Council of Ministers at the end of 1961 of the list of products for which there should be common policies; cereals, pigmeat, poultrymeat, eggs, fruit, vegetables and wine. It was in the negotiating marathon between 18 December 1961 and 14 January 1962 that this was achieved. This covered most French surpluses except sugar, where the European-wide surplus was too daunting a problem for the ministers to tackle. Sonnemann resigned his post in the Ministry of Agriculture in a last protest.

In 1962 and 1963 the divergences between national prices scarcely closed and the system of levies and subsidies only differed from what had gone before by virtue of its requiring the approval of the Brussels machinery and being labelled temporary. It was only with Mansholt's initiative in early 1964 to begin the task of setting common prices by establishing a price for wheat that the resistance of German farmers was overcome. Even then the struggle was hard. The price of wheat had to be fixed closer to the German than the French level. When in July 1964 the Federal Republic eventually agreed to the proposed price it was with effect only from July 1967.[180] German farmers had to be offered a lump sum in compensation. At the same time Italian livestock farmers were also given direct monetary compensation, because of the higher feed grain prices which must inevitably follow when the price of other grains was also fixed not far below the German level. Italy also only agreed on the supplementary condition that the Commission establish a policy for fruit and vegetable exports, thus finally fulfilling the one consistent Italian demand in the earlier negotiations for the European Agricultural Community.

The 1964 agreement meant an increase of 6.4 per cent in the official price at which French wheat was purchased. This was the herald of fixing a generally higher price level for all products than the average of national prices, as other common prices were set. The overall level of agricultural protection was higher, except for sugar, after its Europeanization than under the separate national systems, for many products more than twice as high in percentage terms.[181] For a feedstuff importer like the Netherlands this was a sacrifice to the French interest.

On the other hand, in effectively excluding Danish exports of pork products, eggs and cheese from Germany until Dutch surpluses had been sold there at favourable prices, and holding out the likelihood that other products too would come under a common policy, the CAP gave great advantages to Holland, from a commercial point of view justifying the support which Dutch governments had given since 1950 to the concept of a common agricultural policy. Over the period 1951–4, 52.3 per cent by

---

[180] For a full account, E. Freisberg, *Die Grüne Hurde Europas. Deutsche Agrarpolitik und EWG* (Cologne, 1965).

[181] H.B. Malgren and D.L. Scheckty, 'Technology and Neo-mercantilism in International Agricultural Trade', *American Journal of Agricultural Economics*, no. 1326, 1969.

value of Denmark's exports of foodstuffs and fodder (SITC 0) had been sold in the United Kingdom, only 14.9 per cent on the German market. As a result of strenuous efforts over the period 1955–8 the proportion sold in Germany rose to 23.4 per cent, while that sold in the United Kingdom fell to 42.5 per cent. The CAP ended this trend. The loss of German markets by Danish agricultural exporters in the 1960s was dramatic. Danish exports to the Federal Republic had shrunk by 1972 to three-quarters of their 1962 value, while those of the Netherlands had increased almost fourfold and those of France almost fivefold.[182]

Of the increase in value of total agricultural imports (SITC 0) into all Community countries over the period 1962–72, 39 per cent was accounted for by the increase in imports from France and the Netherlands. By 1972 15.8 per cent of the value of all Community food imports came from France. In the specific case of the Federal Republic, imports from France and the Netherlands accounted for 20 per cent of the food import bill in 1962 and 38 per cent in 1972. The Federal Republic was surely importing from Holland and France things which could have been more efficiently produced in Denmark or outside Europe. Krause estimates that the United States lost between $150 million and $200 million of agricultural exports as a consequence of Community policy even in the initial period 1958–66.[183]

In retrospect therefore the CAP was the Franco–Dutch agricultural trade bargain for which both countries had been searching from the first revisions of the Monnet Plan in 1948 and the French decision to become a greater food exporter. As is the nature of such bargains, however, the country with the higher productivity was overall the greater beneficiary. The increase in French arable output and exports between 1964 and 1974 was much more striking than that in output from the animal farming sector. French agriculture became orientated towards an increased development of cereal farming, the very tendency which French planners had been struggling against since the mid-1950s. The growth of Dutch butter, cheese and processed milk exports continued to exceed those of France. Only in exports of dried milk, the product with the lowest value-added in the range of dairy products, was France as successful as the Netherlands. Between 1964 and 1970 at constant prices and exchange rates the Netherlands had a greater increase in share in the total final value of the Community's agricultural product than France.[184]

The outcome of the CAP, easily predictable from the political tendencies we have traced in this chapter, was much more favourable to the agricultural vested interest than to the planners and economic reformers

---

[182] Belgium–Luxembourg's agricultural exports to Germany, only one-fifth the value of those of the Netherlands in 1962, increased more than sixfold over the decade.

[183] L.B. Krause, *European Economic Integration and the United States* (Washington DC, 1968), p. 101.

[184] J. Le Guennec, *L'Agriculture dans la C.E.E.*, vol. 1, *24 ans de production*, Collections de l'INSEE, no. 528 (Série E, no. 104), 1987.

who had originally pushed for the Europeanization of agricultural market-ing. Between 1968, the first full year of Germany's effective operation of the common wheat price, and 1979 the real increase in net farm income per person in France was higher than anywhere else in the Community.[185] Average farm income grew at about the same speed as average income elsewhere in the economy. For the large grain and sugar beet farmers of the Ile de France this was a good result. For the two-thirds of French farmers whose income was less than 80 per cent of the non-agricultural income for their region it meant, though, that they were falling further behind producers in other sectors in absolute terms. They were the ones who, for the most part, were producing the commodities which planners had wanted to encourage.

For farmers elsewhere in the Six incomes per head rose steadily in real terms, although not by more than elsewhere in the economy until 1976–9, after which, except at first in the Netherlands, they began to fall. The same disparities as in France between large producers, whose incomes grew more rapidly, and small producers was evident. In the Federal Republic, where large farm units were few, income per person employed remained less than half that elsewhere in the economy. In the Netherlands, essen-tially because of higher productivity, relative income per person employed was about 90 per cent of that elsewhere in the economy, so that although the farms were small the outcome was, in the circumstances, satisfac-tory.[186]

These results have to be looked at realistically in the light of our initial survey of the economics of Western European agriculture. The chances of closing the income gap with other sectors of the economy were extremely small. It took the Europeanization of the regime of protection and subsidi-zation, which meant an increase in both, even to prevent the income gap from widening before 1979. Without Europeanization the political power of the agricultural interest would have been too weak even to achieve this result. Integration fixed its power for some time within the limits it had achieved by the end of the 1950s, an extremely favourable outcome when it is considered how rapidly shrinking a part of the electorate the agricultural interest constituted and how clearly this was indicated in the decision to create the EEC.

As the CAP increasingly relied on the machinery of intervention prices, levies and rebates, so did the farmers' own purchasing and marketing organizations acquire an even more official role as the executive of the Community than they had acquired as executives of national policy. It is true that the relationships between the major corporate representative bodies and these purchasing and marketing organizations were ambivalent

---

[185] B.E. Hill, *The Common Agricultural Policy: Past, Present and Future* (London, 1984), p. 107.
[186] UN, ECE, *Economic Survey of Europe in 1971, Part 1, The European Economy from the 1950s to the 1970s* (New York, 1972), p. 66.

and differed from country to country. At one extreme in the Federal Republic the Einfuhr- und Vorratsstellen remained official state organizations, functioning to all intents and purposes as part of the civil service. At the other extreme in Italy the Federconsorzi remained constitutionally strictly a farmers' organization, although still linked intimately to the governing Christian Democratic party. The *interprofessionel* organizations in France, such as Interlait or SIBEV, had an intermediate status. It was, however, through the common executive role of these organizations that the political power of farmers was expressed, for their representation on these lower-level organizations and their influence over them was in all cases preponderant and the rapid weakening of their national electoral strength could not easily touch that position.

Would national taxpayers and voters have continued so long to pay the costs of income support for agriculture as the size of the agricultural sector and its weight in the national economy rapidly declined, had the decision been set in a purely national context? Surely not. But once the CAP became not only the most prominent symbol of European integration, but also that aspect of it which required a large European civil service and which could show a wide range of genuinely common policies, any political attack on it involved issues far more serious than those of agriculture. It was usually judged better not to raise them and to allow the agricultural sector to continue its institutionalized, managed, extremely expensive reduction in employment. Because it was shrinking so rapidly, Western European agriculture was the most vulnerable of all the elements in the post-war political consensus. It has proved to be, however, because of the Europeanization of agricultural policy, one of its most durable components. The Common Agricultural Policy has lumbered on like some clumsy prehistoric mastodon, incapable of evolution into the present world where the political influence of agriculture on parliamentary systems is small indeed, an awesome reminder of the strength which integration could add to the rescue of the nation-state.

6 The lives and teachings of the European saints

The historiography of European integration is dominated by legends of great men. Most histories emphasize the role of a small band of leading statesmen with a shared vision. For the Community's supporters they have become saints, men who held fast to their faith in European unity and through the righteousness of their beliefs and the single-mindedness of their actions overcame the doubting faithlessness of the world around them. Monnet, Schuman and Spaak are honoured above others in the calendar, although Adenauer and de Gasperi stand in almost equal rank. Their photographic ikons decorate the walls of the Berlaimont building, while cheap coloured reproductions of the arch-saint Monnet adorn the desks of their faithful servants on earth.

The miraculous doings of these European saints, as recited by disciples and set down in hagiographies, may seem to have little place in that reassertion of the earthly nation-state with which this book has been concerned. The founding fathers of the European Community appear in most histories as the harbingers of a new order in which the nation no longer had a place. Their associates have testified to so many conferences, spoken so frequently in the media, and given so many oral history interviews, all to the effect that the start of the Community was an act of conversion, that they appear to have convinced most opinion that this was so. On one side had stood the believers, on the other the heathen opposition. The history of the Community was a struggle between the forces of light and darkness.[1] For the European saints it was the moment of rejection of the old order which was exalted as the most important moment of their lives, the conversion on the road to Damascus expected of all the Community's labourers on earth, including those who wrote its history. Only by a myriad replications of these conversions would a united Europe be built.

Widely held though it is, this is a view which entirely misrepresents the

[1] Written within the constraints of this conformity are H. Brugmans, *L'Idée européenne, 1918–1965* (Bruges, 1965); ibid., *Prophètes et fondateurs de l'Europe* (Bruges, 1974); W. Lipgens, *A History of European Integration, 1945–1947*, vol. 1, *The Formation of the European Unity Movement* (Oxford, 1982).

historical significance of the early fathers. Far from renouncing the nation-state as the foundation of a better European order, they achieved prominence and success because they were among those who developed an accurate perception of the positive role it would play in the post-war order and who also recognized or stumbled upon the need for those limited surrenders of national sovereignty through which the nation-state and western Europe were jointly strengthened, not as separate and opposed entities, but within a process of mutual reinforcement. Their perceptions of the links between the changed nature of the post-war state and the process of integration were fragmentary. We are dealing with busy politicians, not theorists, men whose antennae governed their actions much more frequently than any logical consistency of intellectual belief. From their speeches and writings our perceptions of them can also be only fragmentary. But from the traces they did leave it is none the less possible to arrive at an understanding of their role in integration unobscured by any received theology or the accounts of fabulists. The beliefs of these revered figures were of far more moment than those of the national bureaucrats whose memoranda provide much of the historical evidence in this book, not least because as politicians they had to go out and get votes, in general a powerful constraint on abstract thought. How did these practical politicians envisage both the role of the nation-state and European integration?

The question is best approached, initially, through the example of Spaak. He was a citizen of a state whose claims to historic nationhood are not usually regarded as having so long an authenticity as those, say, of France or the Netherlands, a state which had twice in the twentieth century proved virtually indefensible when involuntarily caught in wars between greater powers. Both facts give the question extra point, for they were central to the evolution of Spaak's ideas.

What has been written about Spaak, including his own memoirs, does little to explain the deeper springs of these ideas. To judge from his actions and speeches he saw himself as a pragmatist whose role was in promoting political action by others and, like many who prefer that self-image, he may not have been adept at discerning his own motivation. Nevertheless from what he said and wrote a pattern emerges. His sudden and surprising elevation to the role of foreign minister in 1936 when still only 37, and at the very time when the external menace to Belgium's national independence from a regime which he detested was becoming evident, led to a drastic reordering of his political priorities. He came to office as a militant socialist mainly concerned with altering the nature of Belgian society. He left it for exile in 1940 convinced that the first problem was the security of the nation and the international arrangements which would guarantee it. He became foreign minister in the wake of a bitter dispute over the merits of the military alliance with France as a system of national defence. The dispute's origins lay in the exaggerated hopes so often placed in the 1930s on the alternative policy of neutrality. Would alliance with France not be more likely to unleash a German attack on Belgium? His term of office was dominated by a no less acrimonious quarrel over the feasibility of a third system of security, an independent defence of the national territory. This was the policy which he advocated. When independent defence failed abjectly, there followed flight, danger and exile. It is easy to understand how the question of national security kept its precedence for him.

According to Spaak himself he was already convinced early in 1941 that Europe must be politically united because no military defence of the nation-states by themselves was now possible.[2] The evidence for this does not amount to much, one private letter to an unimportant recipient. His public statements during the war certainly reveal that the problem of the military defence of the nation predominated in his thinking, and that he had rejected both the concepts of conventional military alliance and of an independent national defence as solutions to the problem of the security of Belgium and other small European countries. His speeches and writings suggest that his goal was to restore Belgium's national independence within a new framework of security which he could not yet clearly formulate, but which required some form of closer institutional links between states than in the pre-war period. 'The formula: solidarity in war but isolation in peace did not survive yesterday and has no chance of living tomorrow', he declared in 1941.[3] But the numerous remarks to this effect were invariably accompanied by a sturdy defence of the value of small states to Europe. Small states had not, Spaak repeatedly insisted, proved to be an inadequate foundation of the continental order, as so many statesmen, Churchill most prominently with his schemes for European regional councils, were alleging. They had not been the cause of Europe's tragedy. Their sense of nationality could and must be turned towards preserving Europe's security, of which it could in fact become a pillar. 'What we shall have to combine is a certain reawakening of nationalism and an indispensable internationalism.'[4]

Three possible ways of preserving and strengthening the small states in a security framework recur as themes. One was to persuade the United Kingdom to abandon its former policy of maintaining a balance of power on the continent and take the lead in creating a new collective security in western Europe. A second was to persuade the Dutch government in exile into a far-reaching agreement for mutual diplomatic support and economic reconstruction, which might serve as a model for a network of similar agreements between western European states. A third was to achieve international agreement on a more effective version of the League of Nations. All three of these were, in Spaak's mind, ways of preserving Belgium's nationhood against the cosmic juggling of the greater powers,

[2] P.-H. Spaak, *Combats inachevés*, vol. 1 (Paris, 1969), pp. 147–8.
[3] P.-F. Smets (ed.), *La Pensée européenne et atlantique de Paul-Henri Spaak* (Brussels, 1981), vol. 1, p. 17. Speech by Paul-Henri Spaak at the Belgian Institute in London.
[4] ibid., p. 22.

although not necessarily preserving the full extent of pre-war sovereignty. They were also, he hoped, ways of getting some say in the question of what was to happen in Germany, whose speedy post-war reconstruction seemed to be essential to the future welfare of Belgium.

These motives are evident in the wartime negotiations in London for the Benelux accords. It was not Spaak, as his memoirs suggest, who thought of the idea of a customs union as the basis of the association with the Netherlands. This course was suggested to him by the finance minister of the government in exile, Camille Gutt, later governor of the World Bank, apparently with the support of the man who was to become finance minister at the end of 1942 in the Dutch government in exile, Johannes Vandenbroek.[5] It was not such a break in historical continuity, a customs union being the basis of the association between Belgium and Luxembourg, but according to Gutt Spaak rejected the idea, and there was certainly no suggestion of anything as far-reaching as a customs union when he addressed the Consultative Council of the government in exile in May 1942 on the subject of the Benelux discussions. He spoke there only of a regional association, whose purposes he conceived as helping the countries to represent their post-war aims to the Allies more strongly after liberation and as strengthening their mutual economic security.

It seems to be in early 1942, perhaps as a result of the arguments over the scope of the Benelux accords, that he began to speak on the theme of economic as opposed to merely military security. Military guarantees by themselves, he well knew, were insufficient to preserve the Belgian state, and his interest in Benelux increased with his increasing belief that economic security was a fundamental aspect of overall national security. Even after the small group of Belgian and Dutch ministers in exile had signed the monetary agreements in the Savoy Hotel on 22 March 1943 and had instructed their experts to prepare agreements for a customs union and for an ultimate economic union Spaak, however, was still insisting that the purpose of the agreements was not to merge the three nations but to permit their separate survival in the post-war world.

The actions of the Benelux governments, like much of the airy discussion during the war about future European federations, have to be seen in the context of the ignorance about post-war Allied reconstruction plans in which exiled politicians were kept by the British and American governments. The British and Americans, as we now know, did not in any case spend much time talking together on this question and, when they did, did not often agree with each other. Spaak was near enough to British government circles to be alarmed by some of Churchill's more ambitious and improbable ideas about European reconstruction, and the proposals which he began to press on the British government towards the end of the war were conceived as alternatives, which would better

[5] C. Gutt, *La Belgique au carrefour, 1940–1944* (Paris, 1971), pp. 154–5.

permit the survival of an independent Belgian national state.

Spaak thought of a Benelux customs union, a concept which he always had difficulty in defining even in the later 1950s, as a step towards a larger and more effective association of states, in which Belgium and the Netherlands would play a more effective role, because they would speak with one voice. Among these possible associations, his speeches dwelt most on the idea of a post-war League of Nations administering an international army to which all states would contribute, and which would be the guarantor of an international economic as well as political order, permitting small states to pursue those domestic policies which would give them greater political and economic security and stability.

It was at this point that he reconciled his original interest in socialism, now meaning income redistribution and welfare, with the issue of the preservation of the state's security which had increasingly dominated his outlook since he became foreign minister. The security of small states, he became convinced, was first and foremost a question of their capacity to provide a secure economic and social framework for their citizens. Some better military guarantee of their security was also indispensable, but without a new social and economic order this would not suffice. The new international organization, he suggested, should manage exchange rates and have the authority to enforce on nation-states a minimum level of welfare legislation.[6] This insistence on a basic minimum of welfare under-lay all his subsequent proposals for a new European order, although here as in other areas his ideas were never clearly formulated. His position anticipated the persistent Belgian demands in all intra-European negotiations after 1945 that other nations should raise their level of wages and welfare to that attained in post-war Belgium.

The Benelux customs union agreement, eventually signed on 5 September 1944, was no more than an accord to implement a tariff community at some later date and to discuss the many changes in fiscal and commercial policy which would be needed to turn it into a true customs union and single market. Spaak in fact seems to have been far from certain that a customs union would allow for the increases in welfare which he saw as necessary to a secure post-war order and showed no great enthusiasm for the concept later as a more general basis for western European reconstruction. A customs union with France, he told the British foreign minister Anthony Eden, would be impossible for Belgium because of the difference in size of the economies.[7] His model for association with larger economies seems to have been what he proposed to Britain, a binding commitment on the British side to defend the national territory of Belgium, combined with agreements to coordinate industrial and agricultural production, to initiate a common full employment policy and a

[6] P.-F. Smets, *La Pensée* . . ., op. cit., vol. 1, p. 34. Address to the Belgian Council of Ministers, 18 May 1943.
[7] ibid., p. 47. Conversation with Eden.

common transport policy, especially in civil aviation. In common with several other Belgian and Dutch ministers he saw the Benelux agreements as only a minor contribution to post-war economic security. They would resolve long-standing national disputes of a traditional kind, such as the right of access of Belgium to the Scheldt waterway and the related freight and canal disputes of the 1930s. Should the agreements succeed at this lower level, the goals of a customs union and an economic union might become feasible, provided they still served the purposes of all parties to the agreement. It was the failure of the United Kingdom to show much interest in anything other than a bilateral commercial treaty with Belgium which made Spaak elevate the Benelux agreements to a greater level of importance.

Even then, it was some time before Benelux could genuinely advance his quest for economic security. The Netherlands was a low-wage economy before 1950 with a comparatively low level of social security provision and with large international debts. The more difficult aspect of 'constructing Europe', he told the press after the first session of the Consultative Assembly of the Council of Europe in Strasbourg in September 1949, would always be the economic one. On cultural policies, on questions of human rights, even on the details of a draft European constitution (providing it was not actually a question of implementing such a constitution), agreement between parliamentarians would be easy, he ironically remarked. But even at the level of principle, a discussion of economic policy would show sharp disagreements even before the details of the policies themselves were reached. Many such disagreements emanated, he said, from statements of pure economic liberalism, to which he had listened with growing irritation in the debate. He thought such statements misguided, because some measure of control and organization was inevitable both domestically and internationally if it was necessary one day to harmonize the different economies. Ultimately there had to be a compromise between on the one hand the kind of controls with which socialists and other interventionists wanted to guarantee welfare and stability and, on the other, the liberty of individual enterprise.[8]

In this apparently impromptu statement, which received wide publicity, the beginnings of his later indiscriminate advocacy of Western European political unification in the period up to the signing of the Treaties of Rome, and of the disillusionment which followed can be detected. By 1949 he believed that to guarantee economic and military security some measure of national sovereignty could be surrendered. But he never clearly thought out the economic mechanism by which this could be achieved. As projects to achieve the same objective began to proliferate from other quarters, which he often suspected did not fulfil what he thought were the necessary minimum conditions for security, and as the difficulties and disagreements

---

[8] ibid., vol. 1, p. 209. Press conference at close of first session of the Consultative Assembly.

he encountered at the international level became great, he increasingly took refuge in rhetoric, for he lacked the economic understanding properly to formulate his own proposals or criticize those of others.

Having heard the Consultative Assembly at its ineffective work and having glimpsed the real difficulties of coordinating expansionary domestic economic policies and welfare at the international level in a Western Europe where financial conservatism was returning to fashion, he began to reach indiscriminately for anything which seemed to represent definite progress towards European unity, no matter that it avoided the central issues. His earlier pragmatism became mixed with utopianism. The first signs of this appear in his press statement after the Consultative Assembly meetings. 'For me', he told the journalists, 'everything which tends towards European organizations is good.' And indeed he commended a proposal for common European postage stamps as having equal value with any other proposal and concluded that, 'It is when we will have worked in directions which will sometimes appear perhaps as a little opposed, even contradictory, that it will even so be possible after all to make a synthesis.'[9] He had already enough evidence to know that this would not be so and subsequent events were cruelly to expose such vagueness.

The motives for his indiscriminate support for integration are to be found in the interaction between his conviction that a new post-war order was needed and the missionary zeal of the Americans, once the Marshall Plan was launched, for integration as the basis of that order. What the British had declined to undertake in Western Europe might now be undertaken by the Americans. A long American intrigue to make him 'director-general' of the OEEC with the mission of wrenching that organization out of the paths of cooperation and into those of integration meant that he only incurred greater political distrust from some other national governments. As the tension between his desire that the American wish for political integration in Western Europe be fulfilled, because it would be the best available guarantee of Belgium's future economic and military security, and the opposition of other statesmen to those American plans, grew, his pragmatism was increasingly tainted with utopianism and then with cynicism. Any form of integration, any form of common authority in Western Europe, had become the indispensable guarantee for post-war security, and he became increasingly indifferent to what that authority might be or do. The Belgian stage became too small for him and the acting talent he had inherited from his mother fed on international applause for performances whose integrity, although certainly not lacking, was not what it had been.

The vagueness at the heart of his thought made him an easy convert to Monnet's narrower, more specific organizational conceptions of European integration. His mind became fixed on the need for a central executive

[9] ibid., pp. 191 ff.

authority, like the High Authority of the Coal and Steel Community, and he seems to have wished it to be directed by Monnet. He could not see the underlying commercial trends which were pushing European states towards a customs union and looked, as he had earlier looked to Britain and then to the United States, for a central authority which would enforce integration from above, building on the method of the Coal and Steel Community.

Like Spaak, Robert Schuman appears to have been indifferent to the question of European unity before the Second World War and to have become convinced only in 1948 that the interests of his country would be best served by some form of European union. Yet within three years he was to become an apostle of a federal Europe and within five years venerated as the founding father of the Coal and Steel Community. For him, as for Spaak, the idea of European integration became dominant when he was called upon as foreign minister to grapple with the problem of national security.

Elements of a post-war French foreign policy in which national security might be found within French leadership of a western European bloc of nations, linked by a formal institutional commitment to some kind of authority higher than that of the national governments themselves, had already been adumbrated by some members of the wartime government in Algiers and there had been several post-war initiatives of that kind by the Quai d'Orsay before Schuman became foreign minister. Only in 1948 did plans within the Quai d'Orsay for integrating a reconstructed western Germany into a western European bloc go beyond speculation. It was Monnet who turned these plans, which had often embraced the idea of a common management of the French and Rhineland coal and steel industries, into the proposals for the Coal, Iron and Steel Community by grafting on to them the concept of the High Authority. It was Schuman who, even more decisively, took up Monnet's suggestions as an official foreign policy initiative. The decisiveness of his action at that moment sprang from the accord between these proposals and his own insight into past and future Franco–German relations.

He took the general ideas of his officials, the specific version of them suggested by Monnet, the increasing desperation of the Americans to find a way of binding Germany to the west, the extreme need of the first government of the Federal Republic to obtain a measure of equality of rights with the other nations, the wave of vague sentiment in favour of European unification, and from the combination of all these elements produced a foreign policy coup which turned out to be a major contribution to French national security.[10] He could not have done this without the clarity of his perceptions of the two countries and cultures with which his

[10] A.S. Milward, *The Reconstruction of Western Europe, 1945–1952* (London, 1984), pp. 380 ff.; R. Poidevin, 'Le facteur Europe dans la politique allemande de Robert Schuman (été 1948–printemps 1949)', in Poidevin (ed.), *Histoire des débuts de la construction européenne*

life had been so long and at times so sadly intertwined. Neither could he have grasped the force of Monnet's ideas, unless his own understanding of the post-war state had enabled him to do so.

He was consciously seeking a permanent reorientation of relationships, a change of hearts and minds, and not merely a victory of *Realpolitik*. Nevertheless this change of heart was not something he saw occurring in a sudden moment of conversion. Rather it was something that could only come on the basis of grappling over a long period with common, and all too real, difficulties. It was this conviction which gave him the tenacity to pursue his May 1950 proposals until they were a completed act of policy. And it was the strength and complexity of this same conviction that pushed him by 1951, before the Treaty of Paris had been ratified, into becoming the defender of its ultimate implications against the advocates of a narrower nationalism. The man who earlier had never spoken except as a national foreign minister pursuing a national interest began to write and speak as a visionary of a future federal Europe. He wished the work of the treaty to be defended, even before its ratification, not on its narrower conceptions, highly effective though they were, but on its implications for the security, and at times he seemed to say the redemption, of the whole of Europe.

By March 1951 he was insisting that the division of Europe into small states had become 'an anachronism, a nonsense, a heresy', the last being the strongest term of abuse.[11] The European states, he asserted, could no longer solve their domestic economic difficulties by their own efforts. But neither could an economic union by itself suffice to remedy the situation. A political union with a supranational political body was the precondition of success for any economic union. This was a surprising declaration from a man who, when faced with British objections, ten months earlier, to this precondition for entry into the negotiations for the Coal and Steel Community, had been on the point of altering his proposals until his resolve was stiffened by Monnet. Yet it is impossible to read any of his subsequent remarks on the subject without being impressed by the firmness with which he held this new conviction. He had done what is not uncommon for politicians, he had transmuted practical action based on personal political instinct into a justifying belief system.

Without political machinery of its own the new Europe could not, he believed, fill the psychological void left in Germany after the wild excesses of nationalism. But supranational political machinery without a democratic element responsible to public opinion would neither satisfy this objective in Germany nor prove in the long run acceptable in France. Merely economic arrangements would not be a sufficient guarantee of the durability of the Treaty of Paris as a peace settlement. During the discussions over the

mars 1949–mai 1950 (Brussels, 1986); Poidevin, *Robert Schuman; Homme d'état* (Paris, 1986), pp. 208 ff.
[11] R. Poidevin, *Robert Schuman . . .*, op. cit., p. 240.

European Political Community in 1952–3 he wanted to extract this essential point from the convoluted political arguments and establish a democratically elected European assembly from the outset as the indispensable basis of any further step to political unification. It was, for Schuman, the fulfilment of an essential psychological need that policy should be deliberated not by an assembly chosen by governments but by one directly elected.[12]

It was this understanding by the democratic politician of the need for democratic representation at the supranational level, which distinguished Schuman's preferences from those of Monnet for a more bureaucratic system. The effective political difference made by a representative assembly would at first have been very small, for the constitution of the European Political Community which Schuman approved would, had it come into force, have left all real political power firmly in the hands of national ministers and it is evident that he never intended anything else. Nevertheless, he understood, as Monnet for some time did not, that in the post-war state the decisive and unavoidable forum for all political brokerage was the directly elected parliamentary assembly. It had been his lifetime's belief. Sectarian and regional politician though he had been in the inter-war period, his speeches and writings were steeped in the rhetoric of the Jacobin republican tradition. Representation of the people was the only possible basis of modern politics, he believed, and that meant that the activities and policies of political parties, even catholic parties, had ultimately to be shaped by the will of the masses they must represent.

This was a conviction which he shared with Adenauer and de Gasperi. Three sectarian catholic politicians from the 1920s, when each was a dissident within his own party, each struggling to liberate catholic parliamentary politics from control from above by the catholic hierarchy and to attune it to a response to popular pressures from below; all three could come to the forefront only in the context of the post-war state. After 1945 there could no longer be any doubt that catholic parties had to descend into the same popular arena as their opponents and win elections by struggling for votes over the whole range of political issues, on many of which papal encyclicals provided no guidance likely to be given much credence even by the faithful. Submission to the new demands of the democratic state was a prerequisite for the exercise of political power and thus for the redemption of society.

It is a persistent cliché of those who write about the origins of the Community that Schuman, de Gasperi and Adenauer were less committed to the nation-state as an organizational framework because each came from disputed border territory. Schuman came from Luxembourg and then moved to Lorraine when it was in the German Empire as Reichsland Lothringen. He trained as a lawyer at Bonn university and was conscripted

---

[12] R. Schuman, *Pour l'Europe* (Paris, 1963), p. 145.

into the German army in the First World War. Only after the war did he find himself for the first time a citizen of France. De Gasperi's political career began by representing the Italian minority of the Alto Adige before 1914 in the Imperial Reichstag in Vienna; Adenauer's by flirting with Rheinland separatism from the pagan socialist republic in Berlin after 1918. The assumption that these accidents of birth gave them a more detached relationship to the nation-state, while it is in accordance with their subsequent political actions, is far too shallow an explanation of them. Rather, the accident of where they were born provided each with a common formative experience of a different kind. For all three their early involvement in the politics of regional rights provided a first powerful impulse for their adherence to the mass-democratic political model and for their rejection of hierarchical and authoritarian alternatives. Defenders of citizens' rights against aggrandized secular, centralizing republics after 1918 – de Gasperi of the rights originally accorded by the Habsburg Empire to the citizens of the Trentino, Schuman of the separate rights of the former Reichsland Lothringen, Adenauer of a catholic Rhineland against a heathen republic – they could more easily make the transition to belief in the necessity of the equality of human rights on which post-1945 politics in western Europe was predicated. In the intervening time two of them, de Gasperi and Schuman, had been imprisoned by authoritarian opponents and one, Adenauer, driven from political life.

Each of these devout men needed to summon democratic theory to the defence of religious liberty. Schuman went further. Christianity and democracy were, for him, indistinguishable. Democracy, he believed, had its origins in the christian religion and the rights of man was a christian idea. Reading Schuman's speeches and writings it is difficult to avoid a wry smile at the facility with which he coupled his vision of a christian Europe to the Jacobin republican tradition, an intellectual reconciliation of some philosophical difficulty. It is this intellectual reconciliation which also helps to explain the speed with which he became a believer in a supranational western Europe. He saw the political experience of Germany after 1933 as a deeply tragic one from which redemption and transformation were impossible without a full acceptance of democracy as the foundation of political society. For this reason there had to be a democratic framework at the supranational level, no matter how empty it might for a long time remain.

If democracy and integration were fundamental to security, he did not believe that they could be achieved and maintained solely by foreign policy and arms; it was also a matter of social cohesion. For Schuman this already meant in the 1920s the defence of a more organic vision of society against the atavistic and, as he judged them, exploitative tendencies of laissez-faire capitalism. It meant a greater measure of social equity. He was a firm supporter, during his electoral campaigns of the 1920s, of a state-financed system of unemployment insurance and of industrial injury insurance.

He was a militant supporter of the catholic trade union movement and of trade union rights. At the Ministry of Finance, while opposed to the methods by which the nationalized industries were run, he was a supporter of the concept of a nationalized sector as well as of the concept of the state-financed Modernization Plan. His economic conceptions were those of a liberal by principle who had accorded a particular, necessary and important role to the state as the instrument of social justice and the undertaker of certain national tasks beyond the scope of markets. This necessity for the state's intervention sprang from the need to maintain social cohesion in a just society, the only sure foundation of security. In all these respects he found himself more in accord with the political trends after 1945 than with those of the 1920s. It is not so hard to understand why he should have lived most of his political life in obscurity, apart from the eight years when his ideas, domestic and foreign, were in tune with the times.

Even when he became the apostle of supranationality the nation remained the basis of his political thought. 'Our European States are a historical reality; it would be psychologically impossible to make them disappear. Their diversity is in fact very fortunate and we do not want either to level them or to equalize them.'[13] National sovereignty should not, he argued, be progressively eroded by the wording of the Treaty of Paris. It should be reduced episodically by the same repeated process of national bargaining between national governments. 'The competence of these supranational institutions applies, then, to technical problems rather than to functions which involve the sovereignty of the state.'[14]

It was for the security of the nation-states that the new edifice was to be built, so that they in their turn could provide security to their citizens. No matter how long and determinedly Schuman fought with the Americans and the British over the details of the London Agreements, which set the terms for the creation of the Federal Republic, and then with the Federal Republic itself over the status of the Saarland, he never deviated from his conviction that the Germans must be offered a sovereign nation-state, nor that in all the areas covered by the Treaty of Paris that nation-state would be accorded fully equal rights, would in fact negotiate as a nation. In this, too, he shared a deep accord not only with Adenauer but with de Gasperi.

Adenauer's anxieties for the security of his fellow citizens were of a more pressing and immediate nature in 1946. He accepted unquestioningly the racial prejudice of mainstream German conservative thought, that Russia was a barbaric non-European country. The barbarians were camped on the river Elbe, the eastern territories were lost, and the political priority was to defend the rest of the German population against a further incursion. Only the Americans, he believed, were capable of doing this. But they would

[13] R. Schuman, *Pour l'Europe*, op. cit., p. 23.
[14] ibid., 'French Foreign Policy Towards Germany since the War', Stevenson Memorial Lecture no. 4, Royal Institute of International Affairs, London, 29 October 1953.

only do it in the context of the defence of a world of common values. The unity of western Europe became a precondition for the defence of the German people against a physical and spiritual assault to which they might now succumb. Within this context of western European unity, however, a German state still had to exist as the prime protector of its people.

That the Federal Republic's foreign policy could only progress towards equality of rights by accepting the terms of the Schuman Plan and that these terms, although severely constraining, were not menacing in the way that French foreign policy had been after the First World War, might seem in itself sufficient explanation for Adenauer's support for Schuman's concept of a supranational layer of government. The public appeal for France to pursue such a policy came in fact first from the German chancellor. He had already in 1924 considered favourably the idea that the best way to reconstruct Europe peacefully would be through a Franco–German agreement for some form of joint management of the coal, iron and steel industries of the Rhineland, eastern France and Luxembourg. He readily saw the Schuman proposals as a return to the ideas which had interested him then.[15] But his post-war interest in them, like Schuman's, was a much deeper one. He saw the proposals as a step towards the unified western defence of common spiritual and political values, because his greatest fear was that a German state might become a bridgehead of Soviet values and power in western Europe. For this reason a new German state could not be safely erected merely on the intellectual vacuum left by the defeat of national socialism.

This is where his thought exactly met that of Schuman (who was himself quite free of the cant that Russia was an 'Asiatic' Society). Something new was needed ideologically to build a state and to forge the western unity which alone would guarantee its security. 'One has to give the people an ideology', he told the cabinet, 'and that can only be a European one.'[16] Coming back from the Hague Congress which founded the European Unity Movement in May 1948, he told his party committee that they should be well content with the Congress's resolution on the need for a European federation: 'Therein lies the salvation of Europe and of Germany.'[17] He described the negotiations in 1953 for the European Political Community as 'by far the most important historical event for Europe for hundreds of years'.[18]

No more than Schuman did Adenauer believe that the nation-state would be dissolved in the process of achieving western European unity, unless in very slow stages. Because the politicians of the European states were legitimated only by democratic national politics, national parliamen-

---

[15] K. Adenauer, *Briefe, 1949–1951* (Berlin, 1985), Bd. 3, p. 435.
[16] H.-P. Schwarz, *Adenauer, Der Aufstieg 1876–1952* (Stuttgart, 1986), pp. 856 ff.
[17] K. Adenauer, *Briefe*, Bd. 3, p. 562.
[18] K. Adenauer, *Teegespräche* (Berlin, 1985), p. 257.

tary democracy was the only possible basis of western unity.[19] In the famous interview in March 1950 that he gave to the American journalist Kingsbury-Smith, in which he openly invited Schuman to make proposals for a Franco–German association, he was careful to say that both any Franco–German association, as well as any west European union of which it would become the core, would have to have a parliament. The sceptical reactions to this led him to give the further press interview on 21 March in which he specifically advocated replicating the process of the formation of the Zollverein. The Zollverein, he emphasized, had had a common economic parliament to which the organs of administration were responsible.

It followed logically from this line of thought that the Federal Republic had to replicate the nation-states of western Europe. It must become the German nation-state, with all the political machinery which that implied. In domestic politics he drove the Christian Democratic Union (CDU) towards a democratic response to popular needs, the lack of which, as he believed, had been in part responsible for the weakness of parliamentary parties in the Weimar Republic in the face of a populist authoritarian upsurge, and particularly for the weakness of the catholic Zentrum. Few things are more impressive in Adenauer's life than the way in which at the age of 72 he toured a bombed and disunited country, crossing zonal boundaries with difficulty and suffering the privations of ruined cities to insist that his party mobilize political support at the grassroots level. He had, of course, had much time in the 1930s to reflect on the nature of modern politics and in forbiddingly serious circumstances.

To the right of his party on many issues, Adenauer was nevertheless a supporter of the welfare elements of the social market economy, as well as of the comprehensive welfare legislation from 1955 onwards. He used his political weight earlier to push through the legislation on *Mitbestimmung* and had cordially sympathetic relations with several of the leading socialist trade unionists. These facts suggest no more than that he had a realistic grasp of where political power lay in the post-war state and that he was helped in this, up to a certain point, by an older-fashioned catholic concern with welfare. Much the same could be said about de Gasperi. Each of the three, Adenauer, de Gasperi and Schuman, combined in fact what seemed at the time a curiously old-fashioned style with a positive view of public welfare and a noticeably modern understanding of political power. The insistence on European unity as the spiritual salvation of western European civilization, a belief which de Gasperi appears to have held as strongly as Schuman and Adenauer, combined these archaic and modern elements.

De Gasperi's first thoughts on European unity appear in 1943. They resembled closely, for similar reasons, those of Spaak at the same time. They were a vague proposal for a more effective League of Nations, not

---

[19] H.-P. Schwarz, *Adenauer* . . ., op. cit., pp. 855 ff.

crippled by the necessity for unanimity in decision-making and having at its disposal an armed force which would provide for the security of the weaker states. Later he put forward very similar proposals in what came to be regarded as the first manifesto of the Italian Christian Democratic Party (DC). Reviewing in a speech to the first national congress of the party in April 1946 the progress towards achieving the objectives set out in this manifesto, de Gasperi had not gone beyond these ideas.[20] Yet by the onset of winter 1948 'European unity' had become for him 'the principal problem'.[21] The Marshall Plan and the changing Italian relationship with the United States had given shape to his vague earlier ideas about Italy's relationship to the new international order.

In summer 1946 he thought of Italy as in a situation of strategic and spiritual peril in which the fulfilment of his hopes for a secure, stable, democratic, catholic nation looked remote in the face of internal and external threats. The external threat from Yugoslavia, still maintaining its claim to Trieste and heavily armed, was matched internally by that from the Communist Party. Only the intervention of the United States, he believed, could save the republic from overthrow by one or the other. Only with Italian entry into OEEC and inclusion in the offer of Marshall Aid were the first steps towards security taken. Military security had to be the immediate priority, at least until there was firm commitment by the other western nations to the defence of Italy. So long as there was no guarantee that Italy would be included in the projected North Atlantic Treaty Organization that commitment was lacking.

But national security could not be defined as military security alone. The extent of the success of DC in the April 1948 election was attributable to the fact that it was the party which could promise economic security. This promise depended on, and had to be publicly reinforced by, American intervention in the elections, in the form of secretary of state Marshall's public declaration that if the Communist Party were returned Italy would be excluded from Marshall Aid. At the same time covert political funds and propaganda were used by the CIA to back DC. By presenting itself as the party of welfare, and the Communist Party as the party of future hardship, and in being encouraged to do so by the American administration, DC obtained a strong political leverage over the United States.[22] When American pressure for Western European integration was especially strong in the first two years of the Marshall Plan, de Gasperi was ready to use this leverage.

At first he tried to use it in a traditional diplomatic mode to secure the return of the colonies and Trieste. It seems to have been only the failure of this approach that convinced him finally to link the questions of Italy's

[20] A. de Gasperi, *Discorsi politici* (Rome, 1969), pp. 73–4.
[21] Speech to Nouvelles Equipes Internationales at Sorrento, December 1948. M.R. Catti de Gasperi, *La nostra patria europa* (Rome, 1969), p. 29.
[22] J. L. Harper, *America and the Reconstruction of Italy 1945–1948* (Cambridge, 1986).

military and economic security to the process of European integration, but always on condition that NATO would include Italy.[23] That condition remained unalterable; participation in the European Defence Community, for example, was always subject to the condition that the EDC would be subordinate to NATO.

There was thus a complicated interplay of *Realpolitik*, a determination to reassert the role of Italy in the European and world order, and a clear understanding that welfare and the promise of economic security were the vital steps to national reassertion and Christian Democratic power. It was some time before the integration of western Europe was seen as the policy which could combine all three of these lines of action. Yet it was a part of de Gasperi's *Realpolitik* that he also saw the defence of the nation as a struggle for the souls of men, in which a western European bloc would be the spiritual rampart against the ideological assault of communism. But this attitude was not merely defensive. He frequently insisted that the purpose of European union would have to be a positive act of political mobilization and spiritual reattachment of the population to democratic government, which for him meant also christian government. 'Someone', he told the Italian senate, 'has said that European federation is a myth. It is true, it is a myth in the Sorelian sense.'[24]

De Gasperi himself attempted to use the cause of European unification in precisely that mobilizatory sense. When he was trying to save the EDC and the EPC European integration became the most prominent theme in his discourse. It was he who insisted in the first place that the Defence Community should not exist without a Political Community.[25] No more than Schuman did he wish that Political Community to be based at first on a genuine transfer of power from the nation-state. Its parliament was to be virtually powerless. But it was, nevertheless, essential; a European league of democracies could not provide security without a European parliament as a mobilizing symbol.

Monnet was distinguished from the other founding fathers by the fact that he was not an elected democratic politician, a calling which he eschewed as leading to powerlessness. His power and influence were derived not from elections and votes but from close and carefully cultivated relationships, particularly with a small group of bankers and lawyers in Wall Street and Washington who became prominent politicians. This was a source of great strength in summer 1947, when the decision for the European Recovery Programme was made in Washington. It was from Monnet that French ministers could learn what the American policy-

---

[23] P. Pastorelli, *La politica estera italiana del dopoguerra* (Milan, 1987), pp. 153 ff.

[24] Speech to the Senate, 15 November 1950. M.R. Catti de Gasperi, *La nostra . . .*, op. cit., p. 44.

[25] S. Pistone, 'Il ruolo di Alcide de Gasperi e di Altiero Spinelli nella genesi dell'art. 38 della CED', paper delivered to the conference, 'La Construction de l'Europe du Plan Schuman aux Traités de Rome', Luxembourg, 1990.

making elite was thinking and doing. It was on Monnet that the Americans mainly relied to sustain the momentum towards European integration and he was the man whom they often chose as a privileged interlocutor and interpreter of their plans to other governments, particularly the French government. As American influence and leverage over Western Europe diminished, so too did Monnet's own power and influence in Paris.

Much of his life remains obscure. There has been no genuine attempt at biography. There are only chapbooks and his own memoirs.[26] The public portrait which these offer has been assiduously and repetitively burnished by a clique of publicist disciples, whom he appears to have chosen as carefully as he did his acquaintances in the United States. There is much still to be discovered about a man, who, when America ruled the world, had easy access to one secretary of state, Dean Acheson, and was a close friend of another, Foster Dulles, as well as of George Ball, who became under-secretary with special responsibility for Europe. Foster Dulles lent him money in the 1930s to found the Monnet-Murnane bank on Wall Street and the former's ill-judged persistence, when he became secretary of state, with the EDC treaty as a keystone of American foreign policy in Europe seems to have owed much to Monnet's influence over him. David Bruce, who became American ambassador successively to France, the Federal Republic and the United Kingdom thought of Monnet as the greatest statesman of the age, 'The Philosopher'.[27] John J. McCloy, the first American High Commissioner to the Federal Republic, treated him as a political intimate. These grandees of the American foreign policy establishment commended him to many lesser officials, some of whom served him with the curiously worshipful admiration which he seems to have inspired in so many men. It might transpire, when more is known, that he exercised on occasions almost as much influence over foreign policy in the Federal Republic as in France, for his ease of contact with Adenauer resembled his relationships with American politicians. This impressive roll-call of close political associates – it even included the most prominent judge of the US Supreme Court Felix Frankfurter – could never be matched in his own country, where elected politicians held him at arms length. Once he had gone in 1952 to Luxembourg as head of the High Authority, he became increasingly impotent politically.

That the father of European integration was a most effective begetter of the French nation-state's post-war resurgence has always been an obvious fact of political parenthood. The first post-war French five-year plan, the Plan for Modernization and Equipment, still is known as the Monnet Plan and it was he who personally shaped the small Planning Commissariat and partially inserted it into the traditional bureaucratic machinery of the French state. The goal of the original Monnet Plan was thoroughly

[26] J. Monnet, *Memoirs* (London, 1978).
[27] J. R. Gillingham, *Coal, Steel and the Rebirth of Europe, 1945–1955* (Cambridge, 1991).

national, to shift the pattern of comparative advantage towards France in certain key manufacturing sectors as part of national economic reconstruction. In the documentation relating to the establishment of the Plan the only theme is that of France's place in the world; Europe scarcely appears.[28] It begins to make its appearance only later and in the context of the disputes over the future of Germany. Until 1946 Monnet had believed that the United States would contribute to the resources needed for reconstruction. When the narrow limits of America's contribution became depressingly clear in 1946 Monnet began to consider captive German resources as a substitute, particularly the resources of coal on which French steelmaking had always depended, for a central plank of the Plan was an expansion of French steel output. Germany was still at that stage, in 1946 and 1947, merely instrumental in Monnet's thinking to the planned reconstruction of France. In spite of a wartime interest in some form of larger political association of western Europe, which he appears to have thought might also be used as a platform for economic recovery, Monnet remained entirely uninfluenced by the burgeoning of political groups between 1945 and 1948 in favour of European unity. He is not once directly mentioned in the exhaustive 500-page study by Lipgens of all the politicians who shared those aspirations.[29]

In his memoirs there is no hard evidence of his having taken up the cause of Western European integration before April 1948. That was the time when he realized that it was a central objective of the American administration. In that month, he wrote to Schuman, all his thoughts and all his observations led him to the conclusion, which had become a matter of 'deep conviction', that there must be a European effort to ward off 'the danger that threatened' and which would 'only be possible through the creation of a federation of the west'.[30] The suddenness, boldness, and timing of this declaration strongly suggest that the ideas had come from America. The Marshall Aid legislation had just passed through Congress and the Economic Cooperation Agency was optimistically preparing the way for OEEC to become the first step towards a Western European federation.

Indeed, Monnet's own memoirs imply that it was on a visit to the United States that he first understood the scope of American thinking. For him the central problem became how to fit a Franco–German reconciliation, which would offer long-term security to France, into the programme of French national reconstruction with which he was primarily concerned. Two years of effort culminated in the Schuman proposals. Out of the Monnet Plan, whose original objectives had been solely the pursuit of national security and welfare, came the Coal, Iron and Steel Community in a logical

[28] P. Mioche, *Le Plan Monnet. Genèse et élaboration 1941–1947* (Paris, 1987), pp. 94 ff.
[29] W. Lipgens, *A History . . .*, op. cit.
[30] W. Loth, *Der Weg nach Europa. Geschichte der europäischen Integration 1939–1957* (Göttingen, 1990), p. 69.

continuity of action whose guiding thread was the importance of access to German resources and German markets for French reconstruction. It proved to be the political and economic basis for Western European integration and for the attachment of the Federal Republic to the west which the Americans themselves had been unable to find. Its starting-point, nevertheless, was in the determination not to allow the recovery of West Germany under the Marshall Plan to prevent French resurgence.

This is in no way to suggest that a European federation did not become the lodestar of Monnet's political actions from that moment onwards. Like his fellow saints he had come to understand that integration could provide security in the fullest sense without impeding national aspirations. Like them too he was well aware of the way that the post-war state would need to adapt. He was a forceful advocate of strong organized labour represen-tation. He championed this view, as we have seen, against the more anachronistic view of Belgian steelmasters during the negotiations for the Coal and Steel Community. The economists he listened to and was impressed by were all advocates of a measure of state intervention, not afraid to promote growth and welfare by state financing. And as we have seen the Monnet Plan was readily altered to fit in another aspect of the post-war consensus by making room for agricultural protection and subsi-dization. If the language of the first drafts of the Monnet Plan is reminis-cent of inter-war Soviet planning, with its concentration on physical output targets, it soon changed into the language of national income accounting, reflationary economics, and economic growth.

It was, though, typical of the man that he could never wean himself away from the belief that the political machinery of the ECSC would be equally applicable to a later period. He continued to believe that further functional High Authorities were essential to a European federation, because they would prove the only effective guarantees of supranationality. He clung to the concept of the European Defence Community with its autocratic defence commissioners after it had forfeited all hope of success and misrepresented its chances of acceptance to his American associates. Throughout 1955 and much of 1956 he regarded the proposals for a customs union with little enthusiasm. They would be at the best, he thought, an inferior substitute for his project of Euratom, which would replicate the High Authority of the ECSC.

The parallels with Schuman, Adenauer and de Gasperi break down at this point. Monnet's attachment to functional administrative machinery, and above all to a small and powerful committee able to take far-reaching decisions, sprang from his lack of conviction that the politics of the nation-state were genuinely capable of evolving into those of supranationality except over too long a period of time to serve his purpose. Nor did he see the need for democratic assemblies as a representation of the west's spiritual superiority. They too for him were another kind of functional political machinery. He did not believe the western world to be under spiritual siege. His attitude to the Communist Party, at least before autumn 1948, was a wholly pragmatic one; like any good practitioner of the mixed economy he preferred to have them with him rather than against him. After all, he shared their beliefs in production and planning as the basis of welfare increases.

There is, in spite of these differences, a strong common identity of thought between Spaak, Schuman, Adenauer, de Gasperi and Monnet. It is to be found in their understanding of the search for security by the western European population after 1945 and in the very wide interpretation which they, like the population, gave to it. Going far beyond the problems of military defence and physical protection, they interpreted it to mean an economic security in daily life of a more comprehensive and assured kind than before the war. When the more devout trinity of Schuman, Adenauer and de Gasperi added to this a spiritual security, they were not being fanciful, but also understanding a real need. Adenauer was clearly not wrong in believing that the German population should be offered an alternative belief system to fill the void after the Nazi period, and Europeanism was a realistic alternative or supplement to Christianity. We are not dealing with social reformers, nor, except in the case of Monnet, economic innovators, but merely with statesmen well attuned to the themes of fear, of the need of reassurance, and of the fundamentally conservative yearning for a more certain personal and political order which shaped democratic politics in those years.

They also had one other thing in common, a strong conviction that the nation-state could be rescued and made to serve as the foundation of a successful post-war European order. Another conservative theme, despair, the idea that the west was in decay and collapse, was entirely lacking. The west, they held, was faced with danger, but a danger that could be brushed aside by an acceptance of national political change and by the construction of supranational buttresses which would support that change.

The accuracy of their understanding of the true nature of integration appears more clearly if it is contrasted with that of other eminent post-war politicians, also strong advocates of European integration but whose understanding of it was so defective that they were wholly ineffective.

There is one especially telling example, Count Carlo Sforza, Italian foreign minister from February 1947 to July 1951. After serving as foreign minister from June 1920 to June 1921, Sforza became a vociferous opponent of the fascist regime during eighteen years of exile. A prominent organizer of the Italian National Committee in the United States during the Second World War, even winning some support for it within the State Department, he seemed a perfect choice for foreign minister of the post-war republic. His ideas, unlike those of Spaak, however, had not been reshaped by exile. He stepped on to the post-war stage an unreformed Mazzinian federalist in the oldest tradition of nineteenth-century European nationalism. For Sforza the purpose of the European federation in which he wholeheartedly believed was the liberation of the human spirit in the world harmony of liberated nations which Mazzini had proclaimed.

Much of his prolific inter-war journalism was devoted to defending the small nation-states created by the Treaty of Versailles against the charge that their weakness was a cause of the failure of the peace settlement. For him the Baltic states represented the same liberation of the soul as United Italy, won in struggle against the same oppressors, the great nineteenth-century multinational empires which had blocked progress towards the inevitable oneness of ethnicity, nationhood and the liberation of man.[31] The most interesting of his books is an admiring study of Nicola Pasic, who in Yugoslav historiography more usually appears as a narrow Serbian nationalist, an obstacle to any wider Slav union.[32] Nor would it be unreasonable for Yugoslav historians to depict Sforza as a man of equally narrow nationalism stridently defending in 1920–1 Italy's ethnic claims to Istria, Rijeka, Zadar and the Dalmatian islands. But this of course was, as most commentators on Mazzini have pointed out, a much more likely consequence than a federation of Europe of belief in ethnicity as the basis of political liberation. Like Mazzini, Sforza was quite unable to explain in what precise historical circumstances the ethnic states would realize that the principle of national liberation had rendered all it could give to the cause of human progress, that a European ideality had emerged from triumphant liberation, and that the time had come for a federation. It was not on the strength of such beliefs, however fervent, that effective action in the post-war world was to be built. Sforza's ringing declarations made good propaganda for Italy in Washington, but de Gasperi's *Realpolitik* did much more to advance the cause of integration.

Let us take a second example from Italian politics, Luigi Einaudi, minister of finance in 1947–8 and president from 1948 to 1955. It was his belief that the European federation would come from the application of the principles of mid-nineteenth century liberalism. He had already strongly criticized the League of Nations in two letters written to the *Corriere della Sera* in 1918 because it had made no provision for this inevitable development, but had been constructed as a purely nationally based organization. He clung to the proposition that economic development would automatically generate, through technological advance and specialization of function, a society in which merely national government would come to be perceived as functionally inadequate and out-of-date. Like so many belief systems based on the premises of neo-classical economics this took the form of an irrefutable abstract deduction leading to the enunciation of a universally valid law. In 1918 he had argued that the true basis of universal peace was not national sovereignty but perfect markets.

---

[31] C. Sforza, *Europe and the Europeans: A Study in Historical Psychology and International Politics* (London, 1936).

[32] ibid., *Fifty Years of War and Diplomacy in the Balkans: Paschich and the Union of the Yugoslavs* (New York, 1940).

These ideas came to the forefront again after his contacts with the Italian federalists in 1944. National sovereignty had become for him, as he wrote, the 'enemy number one' of human culture, because it was an anachronism delaying the arrival of the perfect global market.[33]

The level of abstraction to which this led is nowhere better seen than in the constitution which he drafted in 1944 for the federalists of the Italian resistance movement and which he republished for the second congress of the European Union of Federalists in 1948.[34] It consists of an *a priori* demonstration that most taxes could be levied at federal level as effectively as at national level, together with a discussion of the extent of federal power, emphasizing particularly the need for federal control of commercial policy so that it would not again become protectionist. Considering the dramatic history in 1944 of Italy and Europe, the absence of reference to any real event is extraordinary. That the mind should have sought refuge in supposedly timeless verities from violence and turmoil can be understood. That anyone should persuade himself that this text had anything to do with real political life can not. The European Movement had few supporters of equal political prominence, but his support was without significance for integration.

The contrast between Einaudi's ringing denunciation of the principle of national sovereignty and his almost complete lack of involvement in the practical politics of European integration was repeated elsewhere in Europe. In France the Jacobin tradition encouraged similar tendencies. Léon Blum, who had first become prime minister in 1936 and filled the same post from December 1946 to January 1947, described a remarkably vapid version of a European federation as a step towards world government and was able to add,

> not without some pride, that this bringing into harmony of patriotism and humanism is more natural and more comfortable for a Frenchman than for any other citizen of the world, because the particular temperament of France as I have already recalled it, has always included and still understands the noble need to think and to act for universal tasks.[35]

Paul Reynaud, prime minister at the time of the German invasion in 1940, became a similarly ardent but equally irrelevant advocate of European integration after 1945, on the grounds that European culture was a unity which it was dangerous to fragment. It was in Europe, he wrote, 'that sensibilities were the finest and the bloom on the soul the most exquisite'.[36] He was to survive to denounce de Gaulle in the 1960s for endangering the

---

[33] L. Einaudi, *Il Buongoverno. Saggi di economia e politica (1897–1954)* (Bari, 1954), p. 628.
[34] L. Einaudi, *La Guerra e l'unità europea* (Milan, 1948).
[35] L. Blum, 'A l'échelle humaine', in *L'Oeuvre de Léon Blum*, vol. 7 (Paris, 1955), p. 484. As Charlemagne informs us in the play by Barnave, 'Every man has two countries, his own and France.'
[36] P. Reynaud, *S'Unir ou périr* (Paris, 1951), p. 33.

future of the European continent.[37] The sensibilities of a more practical politician like Schuman were perhaps not fine enough to allow him so low a regard, in 1951, for the memories of the rest of the world.

The political sterility to which such views as these led has rightly justified the exclusion of their holders from the ranks of the blessed. If, when Lipgens compiled his massive study of all the participants in the European Unity Movement before 1948, he had considered the relevance of their views to the realities of the post-war world, it might then have become clear why so few of them achieved anything of political significance. The lives and teachings of the European saints were by contrast free of such claims to philosophical universality. Their aspirations were practical and their ideas valid only for the time and place in which they formulated them.

But the contrast between their understanding of their own times and the abstractions of a Sforza, an Einaudi, or a Reynaud is perhaps too blatant to make the point. What distinguished them from a man like the Belgian foreign minister from 1949 to 1954, and pre-war prime minister, Paul van Zeeland, on whom many in the European Unity Movement placed their hopes before 1948, and who shared most of the qualities here attributed to the fathers of the Community, yet who finally forfeited all claims to sanctity and became a critical, unenthusiastic fellow-traveller on the road to integration?

Van Zeeland was an early Keynesian, a propagandist for increased welfare and for employment policies, and also a strong catholic advocate of the need to link spiritual to economic recovery. He was even an early advocate of the need to contemplate some restrictions on national sovereignty in a new economic order, and he played a prominent part in the preparation of statements for the 1948 Westminster Conference of the European Unity Movement. His economic ideas had their origins in the great crash of 1929–32, whose effects he observed from his vantage-point as a graduate student in economics at Princeton and then during a period of employment with the Federal Reserve. Like several other European economists who were to play a prominent role in the post-war reconstruction, he was deeply influenced by participating in the debate over the New Deal at close quarters. It moved him to write two complementary works in the 1930s, one a plea for a return to an internationally agreed and managed system of international payments, the other a plea for a spiritual reassessment of the nature of domestic and international economic policy.[38]

As he made clear, the two works were to be seen as a whole. In the first he delineated, somewhat vaguely, an international payments system which

---

[37] 'And what judgement will history bring to bear on this effort at dividing the white peoples living under the threat of a thousand million Chinese . . .?' P. Reynaud, *La Politique étrangère du Gaullisme* (Paris, 1964), p. 265.

[38] P. van Zeeland, *La Crise de l'étalon-or: confrontation de sa forme classique avec les méthodes et les buts de l'économie contemporaine* (Paris, 1935); van Zeeland, *Révision de valeurs: essai de synthèse sur certains problèmes fondamentaux de l'économie contemporaine et leurs réactions politiques* (Paris, 1937).

would bring the same monetary stability as the gold standard, while allowing for domestic reflationary policies akin to those of the New Deal. In the second he explained the importance of such policies for a spiritual revival. Neither work upholds the reputation for intellectual distinction which van Zeeland enjoyed among his contemporaries, but the interest of both is that they were an early representation of a significant shift of economic opinion. The political economy of the liberal capitalist state as it had existed before the crash, he argued, must be modified in order to develop, sustain and stabilize levels of purchasing power on domestic markets. This could be done only through positive action by the state itself which must become an active instrument of economic change. The fundamental problem for mankind, van Zeeland argued, was no longer the production of resources but their distribution and to solve this a greater degree of intervention in the economy by the capitalist state was required. This was not merely an economic need but a profound spiritual one, because only a change of this kind, as he argued, could save a European civilization with common spiritual roots from a cruel and dictatorial antichristian authoritarianism either of the Marxist left or the fascist/national socialist right.

It was at this point that van Zeeland joined views with Adenauer and de Gasperi. He feared that democracy and christianity could not be defended against the forces of darkness, and like Adenauer was of the opinion that Russia did not share in the common European spiritual heritage. Both Stalinist dictatorship and Nazi Germany he thought of as incursions of Asiatic politics into European practice. They would triumph over European ones unless the tide could be reversed by a joint economic and spiritual renewal of European capitalism.

In the interests of promoting this renewal he was prepared to contemplate an international order in which the smaller nation-states would retain their existence, but in which elements of their sovereignty might be surrendered if this produced a better guarantee of economic and spiritual security. At first he thought that the League of Nations and the Bank of International Settlements, both of which he called 'supranational' in his publications in the 1930s, could be strengthened sufficiently to become the basis of this new international economic order. The difficulty became increasingly apparent in the 1930s, because the effective common international management which he advocated required common domestic economic objectives. In early 1933 he had listed these desirable objectives as: increasing the living standard of the masses; planning a mutual reduction of working hours; organizing a common anti-cartel and anti-concentration policy; and organizing a greater measure of labour training and specialization.[39]

When it became apparent that there could be no agreement on such a

---

[39] P. van Zeeland, *Regards sur l'Europe 1932* (Brussels, 1933).

common response based on this programme he concentrated his efforts on urging the need for international institutions to reduce barriers to foreign trade. International economic management, he argued, anticipating much of what occurred in the 1950s, should be directed towards harmonized reductions of tariffs and quotas and of controls over the exchanges. These ideas formed the core of a report which he was jointly commissioned by the British and French governments to make as the face-saving aftermath of the failed London Economic Conference in 1936.[40] The report fell on stony ground, but during the war in exile in the United States he began to advocate schemes for a new international political order which would allow for the commercial policies he had recommended in his report.

As he explained in a resistance manifesto published under the auspices of the catholic church in 1942, removing the Nazis would still mean having to reconcile the 'liberty of people' and the need for 'interdependence'.[41] 'At the base of every international construction', he was to announce in 1945, 'the national state must rest like a keystone, no matter whether it is a question of a unitary or a federal state; what matters is that the national state should stay in place and keep its sovereignty.'[42] Some higher authority than the nation nevertheless was necessary.

Van Zeeland had become a firm supporter of a universal body to govern the international economic framework. Another layer of international organization underneath the United Nations was needed, he argued, to preserve the stability of the system. To 'vertical' functional bodies like the BIS and the International Court of Justice could be added, he suggested, 'horizontal' regional groupings. These however could only cohere, he argued, if they had spiritual affinities and common historical traditions, otherwise they would not serve the purpose for which they were intended. This was, firstly, 'to increase the production of wealth in all its forms, to create new goods by using all the resources which modern technique puts at our disposal', and, secondly, to free the exchanges.[43]

To these purposes national sovereignty should not be allowed to become a barrier. It was, he argued, only a twentieth-century invention appropriate to a particular stage of history and not to be confounded with the powers and authority which the state exercised as a legal right.

It is up to us to revise our superannuated conception of sovereignty. Certainly, I remain a partisan of the sovereignty of the nation state; it is

---

[40] *Report presented by M. van Zeeland to the Governments of the United Kingdom and France on the Possibility of Obtaining a General Reduction of the Obstacles to International Trade, 26 January 1938*, Cmd. 5648. The report, while envisaging the removal of quotas on trade in manufactures, argued that the removal of quotas on agricultural trade would be unrealistic.

[41] *Devant la crise mondiale: manifeste de catholiques européens séjournant en Amérique* (New York, 1942).

[42] P. van Zeeland, *Belgique et occident européen: conférence prononcé le 15 octobre 1945* (Paris, 1945), p. 20.

[43] ibid., p. 25.

a necessary notion; patriotism is a mighty lever, legitimate and precious. . . . In this conception the nation state remains live, autonomous, master of its destinies; but using its rights and accepting its obligations it delegates certain powers to organizations of which it is an integral part and which fulfil tasks from which it will itself benefit. . . . In this compromise between two profound tendencies I see the best defence of small countries; it is there that their real chance of remaining what they are is to be found, masters of their destiny, in so far as their destiny depends on their own actions – masters of their kind of life – free to choose the education that they will give to their children, the language they will speak, the way in which they will regulate their leisure and their workers, but at the same time linked on a basis of equality to higher organizations where they will make their actions felt, where they will have their role, their say, in such a way that, integrated in an organization based on law, their rights will be no longer threatened as they have so often been in the course of the last century.[44]

Up to this point there would seem little to distinguish van Zeeland's political position from that of the founding fathers. Yet on closer inspection there were two differences which proved to be crucial, for each prevented him from believing that the European machinery which they created would prove satisfactory.

One was his insistence that the first task of any European organization must be to regulate the international monetary order. Unless this was done first he believed European integration would lack the political strength to survive. Economic policies in Western Europe, he persistently argued, were too varied to allow a common market, which was not also based on a common monetary policy, much chance of success. Full convertibility of the currencies was therefore the necessary first step, followed by harmonization of monetary and fiscal policies. To start with the harmonization of commercial policies while ignoring these other areas was to court serious danger.

Secondly, he took a different view of the state from Adenauer or de Gasperi. The state was for van Zeeland a permanent juridical entity, not, as it was for Adenauer, the fluid representation of the political interests which formed it. Elements of national sovereignty could be ceded, but the juridical permanence of the state, which beyond a certain point could not be changed by the interplay of political interests, remained. This was a view which was not unusual in Belgium, where the state was expected to be the guarantor of the compromise between the opposed linguistic interests out of which it had been created. It was a salient issue in the Belgian parliament during the debate over the ratification of the Treaty of Paris and one which van Zeeland several times himself raised during the negotia-

---

[44] ibid., p. 38.

tions for the treaty. The state could, he insisted, only cede what it had the power to cede.

Together these two arguments were massive objections to the work of the Treaties of Paris and Rome. To wait for a supranational organization to manage a common monetary policy before anything else could be undertaken was to postpone the creation of an effective supranational organization perhaps indefinitely. We are still waiting for that common currency and common monetary policy which some ambitious American diplomats thought they might generate by 1952. To define an inviolable core of the state, which must be preserved against any future trend of integration, was to negate the post-war process of integration as a solution to the national problem, for it was inherent to that process that it be accepted as a support to any national policy wherever necessary. The British government in 1989 made several loud declarations which perfectly matched van Zeeland's conception of community and state, and from which they seem in 1991 to be trying to retreat invisibly. The areas in which surrenders of sovereignty would occur could not be defined in advance, because the need for them would emerge only in the course of the continued evolution of the nation-state.

It was in accepting that uncertain future that boldness was required. For no matter how meticulously lawyers laboured in the treaty articles to fix finite limits to the surrenders of sovereignty, the process of integration continued within the framework of the Treaties of Rome and it was implicit that there could be further surrenders. They could, though, only originate from the restitution of the nation-state to its position as the fundamental organizing principle, and it was on this point that there was no discord between the founding fathers. It is no paradox that the arch-saint of integrated Europe was also the founding father of French national planning, nor that Adenauer can now be seen as the father of German reunification.

7   Britain and western Europe

The history of the United Kingdom after 1945 at first sight appears to fit well the model of the revived nation-state which has been used here to explain the process of western European integration. The post-war consensus on which the western European state was reconstructed resembled in its general lines that which formed the basis of British politics after 1945. The ambitions and functions of the state were extended in a similar way, and in the policies which ensued Britain differed much less radically from western Europe than it did from its own past. There was a burst of welfare legislation between 1945 and 1951. The first post-war government consciously sought to bring organized labour into policy formulation. The commitment to agricultural protection, although it spared consumers from higher prices, was in substance also typical of western European developments. There has been much argument over whether British governments were in fact committed to Keynesian ideas on deficit financing after 1945.[1] But full-employment policies were not confined to rhetoric only. It was of great importance to the British side in the Bretton Woods negotiations that the agreement should not endanger post-war employment levels, intended to be much higher than in the 1930s. Demand-management became an integral aspect of government intervention in the economy. The increased and sustained level of government budgets had the same effect on demand as elsewhere. The degree of state control and guidance over industry, too, was far more extensive than earlier. Export-drives and the rhetoric of exports were also more evident, although the cult of exports was more orientated to the need to earn dollars than to change the structure of the economy.

Given the apparent similarity of political developments in the United Kingdom to those elsewhere in western Europe the question arises, why did the United Kingdom not share fully in the historical process analysed here?

Much British post-war historiography gives the impression that the United Kingdom was either hostile or completely indifferent to that process,

[1] N. Rollings, 'British Budgetary Policy, 1945–1954; a "Keynesian Revolution"?', *Economic History Review*, xli, 1988; G. Peden, *Keynes, The Treasury and British Economic Policy* (London, 1988).

but in fact it stood much closer to it than any other non-member-state of the European Communities. After rejecting membership of the ECSC it assiduously pursued a policy of 'association' with it. Treasury officials devoted much time in 1952–4 to devising plans to integrate either the steel industry or the coal industry into the ECSC common market regulations. If the essential element in this association was a foreign policy position, it was nevertheless also true that, particularly in the case of the steel industry, subjection to the ECSC's commercial rules was seen as a way of modernizing the industry by making it less protectionist. Unwillingness to face up to the industry's opposition meant that when a Treaty of Association with the ECSC was eventually concluded in December 1954 its contents were anodyne; neither industry was subjected to the High Authority. The United Kingdom rejected the idea of participation in a European common market when it was first mooted as a programme by the Dutch government. Although it participated in the pre-Venice meetings of the Spaak Committee, once that committee had decided to recommend a common market to the foreign ministers of the Six the United Kingdom did not change its policy and it ceased to participate in the discussion. The realization that the Treaty of Rome would be signed led, nevertheless, to major changes in British commercial policy: the attempt to embed the common market of the Six in a wider free trade area including the United Kingdom. Although between October 1950 and August 1954 British governments had no intention of joining either the European Defence Community or the European Political Community, the Defence Community was regarded as so essential to Britain's security that increasing efforts were made to save it from collapse, including an eventual commitment of British troops to it. With Euratom, too, a Treaty of Association was concluded. In 1961 the United Kingdom was the first non-member of the EEC to decide to apply for admission.

It can hardly be convincingly argued, therefore, that the United Kingdom's foreign policy forbade a European rescue of the British nation-state. Nor does the argument that, having emerged victorious from the world war the United Kingdom had no need of such a rescue, carry conviction. The successive strategies designed to rescue the British nation-state were not European, in the sense in which the word has been used in this book, but the possibility that they should be or would become European was always there. After 1961 they would have become so, had the United Kingdom not been excluded from such an arrangement by France.

There were other countries whose post-war development also closely fitted the model described, but where one foreign policy consideration may well have dictated for a long time a rejection of integration. Such was the case, for example, in the neutral countries Sweden and Switzerland. It played a part in the long absence of Austria from the Community. In the case of the United Kingdom the usual argument has been the inverse, that it sought to exercise world power and that membership of a supranational

Community was incompatible with this over-ambitious and anachronistic objective.

The simple outline of Britain's relationship with the emerging European Communities seems in itself to refute that argument. The conflict between supporting European integration and even seeking a close relationship with supranational organizations on the one hand and the underlying hope that they would go away on the other hand did not arise out of any predisposition to act like a world power or any dismissiveness about Europe's reconstruction. The record shows how energetic a role the United Kingdom played in the Marshall Plan. Were we to rely solely on the volume of government records as a measure of the importance of a subject it would appear beyond doubt that no subject was more important to British governments between 1945 and 1955 than the future of Germany. The conflicts and contradictions arose from the unsuccessful attempts to construct an international framework in which the United Kingdom could guarantee safety and a high living standard to its citizens in a post-1945 world where its politicians were only too aware that what they had inherited from the war was an almost empty simulacrum of world power.

What remained in that simulacrum of world power was an extensive set of immediate advantages, most of which would, it could be easily seen, rapidly deteriorate in value. Any effective strategy for the future, if it were to guarantee the objectives of safety and security, had to use those advantages for bargaining purposes before they slipped away. To construe this as mistakenly acting like a world power is to postulate an alternative policy of giving away advantages, for nothing.

Their durability and value were various. The goodwill which had been earned by the country's resolute resistance to Nazi Germany in 1940–1 was evanescent. The number and power of the armed forces were already being reduced from summer 1944, to encourage investment to flow back into export industries. To pay for forces of that size was far beyond the capacity of a peacetime economy the size of that of the United Kingdom. Their dispersion around the globe added to their cost. The imposingly large colonial empire, already starved of investment in the inter-war years, was beyond Britain's resources to develop, or to defend. Although it was not intended to, the granting of independence to India opened the way for nationalist movements elsewhere to gain a similar status for their territories. The conceding of that was politically and economically easier than the resisting of it and but little foresight was needed to see that this would be so. The Commonwealth members had made an influential contribution to the Allied victory in the Second World War. Their support was a great addition to British political and economic power at crucial moments. It was nevertheless predictable that in a world made less dangerous for them by the Allied victory the interest of these large countries in supporting the United Kingdom would become much reduced and that in an age of superpowers it was to the USA that, in some cases, they would look first for their defence. This became clearly evident only by 1955. For the first post-war decade the conferences of Commonwealth prime ministers were big affairs, still reflecting some common sentiments. It could be reasonably believed until then that the Commonwealth's existence strengthened Britain's position in Washington. Nevertheless, all these were short-term bargaining advantages.

Only two were longer-term and giving better bargaining leverage. One was the continued role of sterling as an international currency. The second was the huge value and volume of the United Kingdom's international trade; in the years before 1950 it was only a little less than that of the USA. The first was an advantage only when the balance of trade and capital flows was favourable. In the balance of payments crises of 1947, 1949 and 1951 the loss of confidence in sterling was greatly exaggerated by movements out of sterling balances held outside Britain. The year 1950 on the other hand showed how quickly those balances could be restored by high demand for British exports. In that year the Treasury debated whether to revalue the currency upwards against the US dollar, undoing some of the effects of the steep 1949 devaluation. Sterling's international role and the extent to which it could be made more freely transferable or convertible into other currencies for commercial purposes played a major part in all post-war strategies for the rescue of the British nation-state. Yet this was always an integral and subordinate part of strategies primarily based on the long past history and contemporary reality of the United Kingdom as a great trading power, which constituted the most durable and powerful of its advantages.

Simplifying the matter, the United Kingdom can be seen to have put together three successive strategies for prosperity and safety in the post-war world. By October 1958 they had successively failed. All were based on the pursuit of a multilateral framework of trade and settlements as worldwide as possible. All relied ultimately, albeit in different ways, on alliance with the USA to provide safety.

The first of these strategies was born during the war and at the height of the influence of the American alliance, but also under heavy American pressures. This was the acceptance in principle of the American proposals at the Bretton Woods Conference for an international multilateral trade and payments framework as the foundation of a peaceful post-war world order. This would be supported by new worldwide international organizations one of which, the International Monetary Fund (IMF), would manage an international settlements mechanism based on registered exchange rates with only very narrow margins of fluctuation. British acceptance of these proposals was in effect the price of the post-war American loan to Britain. Over the timing and details of the introduction of this new commercial and, as the Americans hoped, political order there was sharp dispute, in spite of Britain's agreement with its principles. Sterling would have to be made freely and automatically convertible for trade purposes into the US dollar at the registered IMF rate by August 1947.[2] For British officials, who were proved right by events, this did not leave enough time for their exports to grow to the point where there would be trade surpluses or other returns, especially in dollars, such that the sterling–dollar exchange rate could be maintained. The temptation nevertheless to go along with a scheme so in harmony with the historical experience and practice of the economy made it acceptable as a strategy, the more so as it would help to preserve in some form the alliance with the United States and so solve also, perhaps, the problem of future security.

After the failure of sterling–dollar convertibility in 1947, in a bipolar world, with protectionism on the same scale as in the 1930s still in place in inter-European as well as in transatlantic trade, and with the weakness of the international organizations devised to support Bretton Woods exposed, Bretton Woods had little worthwhile foundation as a strategy. American–European relations were dominated for four years by the Marshall Plan, in support of which the USA not only permitted but encouraged trade discrimination by western Europe against North America. The time between August 1947 and the end of 1951 was characterized by emergency, mostly protectionist, responses by the United Kingdom to short-term events. The desire to get back to the Bretton Woods framework of multilateral trade and payments nevertheless remained. Its feasibility as a strategy, however, faded as American support for European integration, even for political union, in western Europe came to the forefront under the Marshall Plan.

The second strategy emerged with the election of the Conservative government in 1951. It was devised partly as a response to the movement towards integration on the continent. Its main plank was the resumption of the pursuit of sterling–dollar convertibility, if necessary independently of agreements with the USA, which was now generally discouraging towards the concept. The objective was to establish a non-discriminatory, multilateral trading regime in western Europe and the Atlantic when European recovery was complete. It was British leadership of an eventual intergovernmental and cooperative, rather than supranational, Europe. It was accompanied by the Trade Liberalization Programme of OEEC, whose objective was to widen and eventually remove import quotas on trade between OEEC member-states.[3] This strategy, getting as near to the principles of Bretton Woods as seemed possible in the changed circumstances, dominated the period of this book. It collapsed when another balance of payments crisis in 1955 drove home the message that sterling

[2] The fullest history of these negotiations is L.S. Pressnell, *External Economic Policy since the War*, vol. 1, *The Post-War Financial Settlement* (London, 1986). There is also much of value in R.N. Gardner, *Sterling–Dollar Diplomacy. Anglo-American Collaboration in the Reconstruction of Multilateral Trade* (Oxford, 1956).

[3] A.S. Milward and G. Brennan, *Britain's Place in the World. A Historical Enquiry into Import Controls 1945–1960* (London, 1996) is a full investigation of this aspect of the strategy, which can be only briefly touched on here.

could not safely proceed unilaterally towards sterling–dollar convertibility. It would have to proceed in some form of common European action.

Scarcely had this been accepted when the Spaak Committee raised the spectre of a discriminatory European common market, with American support, dashing the hopes of intergovernmentalism which the rejection of the European Defence Community had aroused. After ten years of peace, with most of its inherited bargaining advantages whittled away by time and history, the United Kingdom had to devise a third strategy. This was the free trade area proposal; to accept the existence of the common market and its commercial rules but to embed it in a wider free trade area, in which the member-states, while practising free trade between themselves and also with the common market, would, unlike the common market states, have no common external tariff. It failed late in autumn 1958 when it was rejected by France.[4]

The centrality of commercial policy to each of those strategies is obvious. After 1949 security relied on the American alliance within NATO. It is not uncommon for writers to denounce British financial and commercial strategy as hostile to 'Europe', because it was not favourable to supranational integration, when the correct strategy should, they would argue, have been to accept the supranational integrationist programme from the outset as the way forward for Britain. Three failed strategies in thirteen and a half years is likely to be attributable to more than bad luck, but it hardly seems the case that these strategies, whatever their defects, were founded on any underestimation of the major importance of western Europe to Britain's post-war prosperity.

It is hard to see in 1944 what else was possible other than accepting the conditions for Bretton Woods multilateralism in spite of their onerous nature. The subsequent pursuit of unilateral convertibility, leaving other European countries to follow after if they could, certainly had elements of grandiosity towards Europe which contributed to its 1955 failure. The free trade area proposal, although historians may finally judge it to have had errors which, though small, were, like those in an e-mail address, fatal, seems on present historical evidence to have pointed a way forward also for France, where it was carefully considered as perhaps being safer than France's chosen supranational strategy, and for Germany, where it may well

---

[4] The history of the free trade area proposal is not described or analysed in detail because it happened beyond the time period of this volume. The one general history of it, M. Camps, *Britain and the European Community 1955–1963* (Princeton, 1964) is now inevitably being replaced by specialized research correcting its detail. See, E. Bloemen, 'A Problem to Every Solution. The Six and the Free Trade Area', in T. Olesen (ed.), *Interdependence versus Integration. Denmark, Scandinavia and Western Europe 1945–1960* (Odense, 1995); F.M.B. Lynch, 'De Gaulle's First Veto. France, the Rueff Plan and the Free Trade Area', *Contemporary European History*, vol. 9, Part 1, March 2000; M. Schaad, 'Plan G – a Counterblast? British Policy Towards the Messina Countries, 1956', *Contemporary European History*, vol. 7, Part 1, March 1998; C.R. Schenk, 'Decolonization and European Integration: The Free Trade Area Negotiations, 1956–58', *The Journal of Imperial and Commonwealth History*, vol. 24, no. 3, September 1996.

have led to even greater economic prosperity than that achieved in the next decade of the common market. If trade and its monetary sinews were a large part of the foundations of all strategies for Britain's future, the lack of harmony between these strategies and the idea of a supranational governance of Europe did not mean that western Europe occupied only a low position in British priorities.

The USA came first. It seemed after 1949 the most reliable provider of security and, to Britain, it was also the commercial partner that mattered most. In a multilateral, non-discriminatory, worldwide framework of trade and payments the most important bargaining objective for Britain was to bargain down the American tariff. To bargain with, it had an important, but diminishing, part of its post-war inheritance: the preferential agreements signed in the 1930s with some Commonwealth countries. These had been unremittingly opposed by the USA from their signature onwards. British policy was to get something for them at the bargaining table – a reduction in US tariffs – before the trends of Commonwealth industrial policies and British domestic agricultural policy eroded them as a bargaining asset. The grand commercial strategic bargain was to be with the United States and on that bargain Europe had to wait. As chapter four demonstrated, western Europe's own economic development and the commercial strategies that it gave rise to meant that it did not. The outcome was that when, belatedly, the Eisenhower and Kennedy Administrations resumed the trend of tariff reduction that had halted in 1950, the grand commercial bargain with the USA was struck, not by the United Kingdom, but by the more powerful bargainer, the common market of EEC, able to meet the USA on equal commercial terms.

To this outcome indecisiveness over what the commercial relationship with the Commonwealth should be contributed. From 1955 to 1962 all attempts to formulate a policy which would come to terms with an emerging common market, and then with an existing and prosperous common market, were dogged by the effort to preserve much of the discriminatory trade relationship with the Commonwealth. Only if those trading relations were preserved would the United Kingdom exercise a comparable weight to the Six in commercial bargaining in Washington. When it was decided in 1961 to apply for membership of EEC the same struggle to preserve elements of the imperial preference structure was carried on into summer 1962, because that structure would have given the United Kingdom more commercial weight within the common market's international bargaining stance and it was still, although in this case implausibly, argued, more political influence at Washington.

In all that long effort to preserve the imperial preference structure for bargaining purposes the Commonwealth was nevertheless subordinate to the consideration of Britain's place in Europe. 'Taking the lead in Europe', that slogan which British governments still automatically mouth to explain their attitudes towards the European Union, was a slogan first coined for internal policy use in 1950 to characterize the Trade Liberalization Programme inside OEEC. Territorial safety and security depended on a settlement in Europe. Prosperity, although there were still in 1955 ministers who believed it could be found in a closer relationship with the Commonwealth, was for the great majority of British politicians and officials more dependent on economic relations with Europe, always, however, provided these were embedded in a transatlantic framework.

If, because of its post-war international inheritance, its bargaining stance remained almost worldwide, the United Kingdom's real interests and position were seen after the war as what they had become, those of a medium-sized European power. The idea that Britain did not join the supranational Communities because it was not 'European' is a platitudinous and false explanatory myth developed in parallel by continental federalists and banal anti-Americans on the one side and conservative British scholars and populists on the other. To explain why the United Kingdom's rescue avoided the supranational solution for so long it is necessary to show the points at which its chosen strategies conflicted with that solution.

In doing that, what follows sticks to the time period of this volume, otherwise the book might sink under its already excessive weight. The United Kingdom only came to some internal agreement on the terms on which it would accept membership of the European Communities in 1962 and was kept out of that membership until 1973. This, the fourth strategy, membership of the European Communities, was not abandoned but was unimplemented all through the 1960s, a decade when the country paid dearly for its earlier failed strategies and when public acrimony increasingly characterized the debate over the choice of EEC membership, so that its implementation became doubtful. Hopefully, the preceding remarks together with the detail in what follows about British policy during the period when for Britain's neighbours supranationality provided a way to national rescue will exemplify the argument. If not, the reader may turn to an even heavier book with more detail.[5]

BRITISH MANUFACTURING AND INTERNATIONAL TRADE

Chapter four commented incidentally on the difference in the geographical distribution of British exports compared with those of the six countries which first entered the Common Market. Annual British exports to the Six made up usually only about 11 per cent by value of total exports in each year over the period 1950–5. Only in 1956 did that percentage begin what proved a rather faltering increasing trend; it rose to 13.3 per cent. Annual exports to Canada and the USA together usually made up over

---

[5] The author is currently writing a two-volume study, *The United Kingdom and the European Community, 1945–1986*, from UK official records.

the years 1950–5 about 10 per cent of the grand total. Their share rose in the late 1950s in the same proportion as did the share going to the Six. The increase in both cases was mainly at the expense of a decline in the share going to Australia. This was hardly surprising, indeed it has to be a matter for astonishment that in 1951 Australia, at the time a country of only 9.3 million people, took 12 per cent of British exports. By 1957 this had fallen to only 6.9 per cent. In the light of the argument of chapter four, however, this was still very high. The German Federal Republic, around which the trade of the rest of western Europe increasingly pivoted, still took only 3.1 per cent of British exports in 1957.

Table 7.1   United Kingdom exports to various destinations as a percentage of total exports, 1950–7

	To the Six	To German Federal Republic	To Australia and New Zealand	To USA and Canada
1950	11.0	1.9	12.5	8.7
1951	10.6	1.9	16.1	10.2
1952	10.7	1.9	12.4	10.2
1953	12.2	2.2	11.8	11.9
1954	10.6	2.6	14.7	10.3
1955	11.2	2.6	14.1	10.8
1956	13.3	2.8	11.2	12.8
1957	13.3	3.1	11.0	12.8

Source: OEEC, *Statistical Bulletins of Foreign Trade*, Series II and IV

It should not be deduced from that small percentage that the average rate of growth of British exports to Germany was abnormally low by western European standards. As table 4.4 shows, it was not. British exports responded to the spectacular growth of German demand in the same way as those of the continental countries, but the share of exports going to Germany was so much smaller that the effect on British output of German demand was also smaller. That the reverse also applied is shown in table 4.15, where the United Kingdom's contribution to the growth of German exports over the period 1954–7 appears as less than one-third that of Denmark, Norway and Sweden combined. The United Kingdom was a part of the symbiotic trade network whose economic benefits led to the Treaty of Rome, but a much smaller part of its total commercial economy was involved in it.

Because so high a proportion of the value of British exports was made up of manufactures, 79 per cent in 1955, this has raised the question whether their geographical distribution restricted their rate of growth compared with that of exports of other western European countries. Appended to that question is usually a further one; did a slower rate of growth of export expansion play a part in a slower overall rate of growth of GNP compared with continental western Europe?

Exports of manufactures and services were a higher proportion of GNP in Britain than in the Federal Republic throughout the 1950s and a much higher one than in France. They were 26.9 per cent of GNP in 1950 and 23.0 per cent in 1960, so these questions have much point. If exports to the most rapidly expanding market, Germany, were still less than 3 per cent of total British exports by value in 1956, whereas they were 10.5 per cent of total French exports and 13.3 per cent of those of Italy (table 4.5), must not this have affected the comparative growth rates of GNP, through the smaller share which was being directed to the most dynamic market and the most counter-cyclically stabilizing market?

It would be impossible in the space of a book about the nature of the European Community to enter into any lengthy discussion of the voluminous and complex literature about the decline of Britain's industrial economy.[6] This decline has been a relative one and the usual measure of comparison the continental European economies. In the late 1950s there was a general awareness that, in spite of rates of income growth and levels of employment and welfare higher than in any other equally long historical period, output and incomes in the British economy had in fact been growing much less than on the continent. The rate of growth of industrial output in the six EEC members over the period 1950–73 was twice that in the United Kingdom. This was accompanied by a consistently higher rate of growth of labour productivity in manufacturing, over the period as a whole almost twice as high. At the same time there was a fall in Britain's share of world markets for manufactures. In 1950 British manufactured exports were one-quarter of the value of world manufactured exports, by 1970 only 10.8 per cent. The comparatively slower growth of output and productivity in British manufacturing contributed to a slower rate of growth of national income and perhaps to loss of market share. Whereas GDP grew at an annual average of 2.7 per cent in the United Kingdom over the period 1950–60, in the Federal Republic it grew at 7.75 per cent, in Italy at 5.85 per cent, and in France at 4.6 per cent.

Increasingly, this wide disparity was reflected in a much greater rate of acquisition of consumer goods on the continent than in Britain, and it was at that point that these statistical abstractions were translated into real political pressures. When French and German households were seen to have more cars, refrigerators and other gadgets than British households, a trend which could first be observed from the mid-1950s, the long introspection into British society began, and the sentiment of moral superiority

---

[6] For a compact discussion of the literature, B.W.E. Alford, *British Economic Performance 1945–1975* (London, 1988).

prevalent in British political thinking before 1956 began to be replaced by a rising mood of national pessimism.

The most frequently identified culprit for this relative decline was manufacturing industry. For a long time the critique of its performance was based on a comparison with the most visibly successful of its competitors, German industry. That competitor of roughly equal size before 1939, crushingly defeated in war, appeared by the end of the 1960s to have outproduced and outsold British manufacturers around the world and in the United Kingdom itself. The obverse of the image of Britain's 'decline' was that of Germany's 'economic miracle'. In both cases it was manufacturing that was held responsible. It is this comparison in popular writing and in the media, as well as in academic studies, that strengthens curiosity that it may have been Britain's reduced role in the beneficial trade pattern around the Federal Republic that contributed to the comparative decline which dissipated even more quickly than had been anticipated the country's inherited bargaining advantages.

The causes of the relatively poor performance of the United Kingdom's manufacturing industry have been listed as: lack of investment; the failure of the banking system to provide investment; inefficient investment; low labour productivity; the inadequate development of human capital; a refractory labour force; poor management; an antiquated system of labour relations; poor business organization; feeble entrepreneurship; shoddy goods; an inattention to export markets; inadequate research; excessive attention to pure research and not enough to the actual process of manufacturing; lack of interest in labour training and technical education; high military spending; and government policy. Under this last heading are variously listed: arbitrary restrictions on the domestic market to limit consumption; high interest rates to limit consumption and defend the currency; too much interference; too little interference; the lack of coherent restructuring policies of the kind attempted in France and elsewhere; a taxation system that taxed away profits and encouraged capital gains; the diversion of research and investment to defence industries. There may be others. Failures in industry and in government are often explained by a cultural distaste for manufacturing and the identification of social success with other activities.

The yardstick of comparison in the 1950s became the so recently defeated enemy, Germany. Whereas the USA served in the abstract as a socio-economic model, in practice its rate of growth of productivity and GNP was no higher than that of the UK. West Germany began to be identified as the model of success and also as a commercial threat. The idea that German manufacturing is a threat to Britain's well-being is an old one in the United Kingdom. It was the subject of much public discussion in the twenty years before the First World War. Since 1880 British goods have had increasing difficulty in competing with German. With only brief interruptions the rate of growth of productivity in German manufacturing appears to have been higher than that in British until the 1990s.[7]

The attempt to weaken the German economy over a long period after 1918 through reparations was ill-conceived, unsuccessful and never supported with conviction except as an electioneering gesture. The policy that received firmer backing from business interests in Britain after 1933 was the economic appeasement of Germany. Germany's economic expansion in Europe was to be recognized by bilateral agreements between British and German firms to which the British government would extend its blessing.[8] The low level of priority given to foreign trade by the Nazi regime and the great difficulties caused by its battery of trade and exchange controls meant that most of Germany's commercial expansion in Europe in the 1930s was south-eastward, so that before the Munich agreements the concessions which Britain had to make in the interests of mutual accommodation were small. War marked the failure of that policy, although this was fully accepted only with the German invasion of Scandinavia. It was a war begun on the British side with a deep sense of apprehension for the economic future. Heroic though the victory was, it was achieved only with stronger allies, whose views about the economic future of Germany were certain to have more weight than those of the United Kingdom.

Any strategy for founding the future prosperity of the United Kingdom on a worldwide multilateral trade and payments framework had to cast a thoughtful eye backwards and forwards over the way that Britain and Germany could each fit into such a framework. Occupation policy in Germany and Britain's ideas on Germany's post-war reconstruction were heavily influenced by considerations of how both countries could coexist within the Bretton Woods framework without harm to Britain's future.

It was regarded as essential in 1945 in Britain that conquered Germany be treated as one country and one economic unit. The British zone of occupation was dependent on food imports to sustain the population and division into four economically separate zones of occupation would greatly increase the financial burden on Britain. Besides, a unitary German state was believed to be a necessity in central Europe as a bulwark against Soviet domination. Plans to divide Germany and permanently weaken it economically were rejected on the grounds that they would leave 90 million Germans as a dangerously unstable element in European politics. However, the failure to reach any satisfactory agreements in the Allied Control Council about administering Germany as an economic unity, and Soviet political actions in their zone, especially the founding of the

---

[7] S.J. Prais *et al.*, *Productivity and Industrial Structure* (Cambridge, 1981); S.N. Broadberry, *The Productivity Race: British Manufacturing in International Perspective 1850–1990* (Cambridge, 1997).

[8] B.J. Wendt, *Economic Appeasement. Handel und Finanzen in der Britischen Deutschlandpolitik, 1933–1939* (Düsseldorf, 1971).

Socialist Unity Party, brought to the forefront a new British view. This
was that the western zones together might have to look after themselves
economically without help from the east and do so better than the Russian
zone. The alternatives as seen in London were either to run the British
zone as a separate economic entity, an idea rejected on the grounds of
its high cost, or to accept any American offer, if it was made, of an
economic merger of the British and American zones. Either way, it meant
that British policy had changed by late 1946 to accepting and even
favouring a future partition of Germany.[9]

STRATEGIES FOR POST-WAR COMMERCIAL COMPETITION WITH GERMANY

Partition was not intended in any way to modify the original goal of
making Germany a bulwark against Soviet expansion. It meant that
Germany must become, in Churchill's words, 'fat but impotent', the two
conditions necessary for Britain's future safety.[10] Much consideration of
how this might be achieved had been given during the Second World
War by the Malkin Committee, which began its studies in 1942. The same
problem was discussed later with the Americans in the Allied Control
Council, through the British Military Government, through the Bizone
government, within the reparations negotiations, within the Committee of
European Economic Cooperation, in the London Conference on Germany
and even through the first two years of the existence of the Federal
Republic, until eventually all plans petered out into a recognition that
British influence on the future of Germany could not, after all, be strong
enough to guarantee success. There was in any case an intrinsic contra-
diction in this objective which could never be resolved: the threat from
Germany was not only a military one. How could Germany be made fat
without threatening Britain's own post-war prosperity?

The experience of reparations after the First World War had convinced
almost everyone that they could only be paid by exports and the same
problem arose in trying to recoup the costs of a military occupation.
Keynes thought these costs should be paid by a tax on German exports.
'If Germany is thereby discouraged from developing a large volume of
exports, we are relieved of a serious competitor. If she is not discouraged,
we receive a useful contribution towards meeting our adverse balance
of trade.'[11] Some ministers proposed suppressing specific sectors of
German manufacturing. But except for industries that could be defined

[9] J. Farquharson, 'The "Essential Division". Britain and the Partition of Germany 1945–9',
German History, vol. 9, no. 1, 1991.
[10] B. Pimlott (ed.), *The Second World War Diary of Hugh Dalton 1940–1945* (London, 1986),
p. 275.
[11] L. Kettenacker, *Krieg zur Friedenssicherung. Die Deutschlandplanung der Britischen
Regierung während des Zweiten Weltkrieges* (Göttingen, 1989), p. 402.

as 'armaments-related' such proposals never attained official acceptance, for if post-war Germany did not become a successful exporter, Britain, it was believed, would have to pay dearly for its occupation.

These were the grounds on which Churchill had been forced by his own ministers to give up his flirtation in September 1944 with the notorious Morgenthau Plan, devised by the then secretary of the US Treasury, for the future 'pastoralization' of Germany. What had briefly tempted Churchill, apart from talk of a loan, had been Morgenthau's suggestion that the whole-sale disindustrialization of Germany would leave the United Kingdom free to capture post-war export markets worth $1,600 million annually.[12]

Once the decision had been taken at Yalta to accede to the Russian request for reparations, the problem of Germany's post-war exports was posed even more acutely, especially as the United States' fear that reparations would once more be paid out of American capital exports to Germany grew. After the Potsdam meetings which set up machinery for deciding on reparations the United States insisted that reparations could be paid only out of current production and only when Germany was in balance of payments surplus. The Reparations Plan eventually drawn up laid down that they would be paid out of the surplus when production and exports had reached a level which would maintain the German population at the average standard of living in Europe in 1936.[13]

The original British and American proposals for the Reparations Plan were far apart. The American proposals foresaw a future level of German exports 50 per cent higher than that of the British proposals. When finally settled between the Allies in March 1946, the Levels of Industry Agreement, which was supposed to set the ceiling on output at which Germany would maintain Europe's 1936 standard of living, looked much closer to British ideas. However, the agreement was 'the outcome of a bargaining process in which each decision was unrelated to the others and the resulting jumble could not be assumed to make any sense whatever'.[14] It constituted a set of limits on the permitted level of capacity and output in most German industries, which the occupying powers were supposed to enforce. Anything surplus to that was liable to be scheduled for reparations. The limits on capacity appeared to leave room both for the expansion of British exports at the expense of pre-war German trade and also for the acquisition of German manufacturing plant as reparations.

There had already been some looting of German industrial equipment. The transfer of German machines patents, scientists, engineers, and some-

---

[12] A.P. Dobson, *U.S. Wartime Aid to Britain 1940–1946* (London, 1986), p. 195. Had there been no other alteration in the flow of British trade such a gain would still have left a deficit of almost $500 million on British commodity trade in 1951.

[13] There are full accounts of the inter-Allied negotiations over German reparations in Sir A. Cairncross, *The Price of War. British Policy on German Reparations 1941–1949* (Oxford, 1986) and B.U. Ratchford and W.D. Ross, *Berlin Reparations Assignment* (Chapel Hill, 1947).

[14] A. Cairncross, *The Price ...*, op. cit., p. 128.

times skilled workmen into British industry which took place between the surrender and the conclusion of the Levels of Industry Agreement was not a haphazard or an unofficial process. Underlying these activities was the concern of the Board of Trade to improve British competitive ability in certain sectors of manufacturing where Germany appeared to have previously had decisive technological advantages and also the concern of the armed forces to obtain access to German weapons development. There is no coherent, published account of these activities.[15] They testify, however, to the existence of other views in Whitehall than those we have so far considered about Britain's correct international priorities. In the Ministry of Supply and in parts of the Board of Trade the concern was to try to use Germany's defeat to improve the capacity of British manufacturing. With the conclusion of the Levels of Industry Agreement such policies had to meet stiff conditions if they were to continue to be pursued: not to increase the costs of occupation; not to worsen the United Kingdom's balance of payments position; not to fall too foul of American policy, which with the start of the Marshall Plan insisted on a rapid German industrial recovery; and not so to antagonize the German population as to attract international censure. Some reparations claims on German equipment under the Levels of Industry Agreement could nevertheless, for a while, pass all these barriers.

One example was the blast furnaces of the Salzgitter steelworks. These were the original blast furnaces of the Reichswerke Hermann Goering, created in 1936 to use the low-grade iron ores of the Brunswick region. This became the most valuable single item on the British list of desired reparations, because it was to be used in an industrial development plan to boost the development of steelmaking from low-grade Midland iron ores, pioneered in the 1930s in Corby by Stewart and Lloyd. Fixing the future German steel capacity and output limits had been a central symbol of Allied agreement at Potsdam, because steel output was seen as the key to the level of output in almost all other industries and especially to Germany's future capacity to make armaments. The American military governor, General Clay, more or less forced through an arbitrary limit of 7.5 million tonnes annual capacity and 5.8 million tonnes actual output. Even an output as high as 12 million tonnes of steel a year in Germany had been seen in London as ensuring a satisfactory defence of British export markets, so that the base calculation of the Level of Industry

---

[15] There is an anecdotal account of the employment of German engineers and scientists in Britain in T. Bower, *The Paperclip Conspiracy. The Battle for the Spoils and Secrets of Nazi Germany* (London, 1987). Studies of the British dismantling policy are mainly uninformative and quantitatively misleading, except for A. Kramer, 'British Dismantling Politics, 1945–9', in I.D. Turner (ed.), *Reconstruction in Post-War Germany. British Occupation Policy and the Western Zones 1945–1955* (London, 1989), and A. Kramer, *Die britische Demontagepolitik am Beispiel Hamburgs 1945–1950* (Hamburg, 1990). There is a general survey of the state of the question in I.D. Turner, 'British Policy towards German Industry, 1945–9: Reconstruction, Restriction or Exploitation?', in I.D. Turner (ed.) *Reconstruction*.

Agreements seemed to leave the United Kingdom full scope to acquire the Salzgitter plant and to increase its own steelmaking capacity and exports at Germany's expense.[16]

In other ways too the Levels of Industry Agreements were shaped to favour the future growth of British manufacturing and exports at German expense. British negotiators stuck firmly, for example, to their position that the manufacture of civil aircraft was an armaments-related industry and so did establish one major industry where British post-war exports would be free from any German competition. In shipbuilding, too, they insisted on drastic size limits on the ships that could be built in German shipyards, confining production of sea-going vessels until 1949 to coasters. How far these decisions were influenced by pressure at a lower level from British manufacturing industry is a matter still requiring elucidation. So, too, is the exact influence of British firms in determining which German plant was to be dismantled and made available for sale in Britain. Presumably it was the larger companies that had easier access to the Board of Trade or to the Ministry of Supply, where the details of these policies were worked out. Direct contact with the Military Government may of course sometimes have been a substitute. The Economic Divisions of the Control Commission were largely staffed by eminent businessmen. Even major companies, however, could find that their wishes fell foul of the diplomatic objective of an economically strong Germany. The chairman of Imperial Chemical Industries (ICI), Lord McGowan, tried to have the manufacture of all dyestuffs prohibited in Germany, but was rebuffed.[17] The well-organized and heavily protected clock and watch industry failed to have its much larger German equivalent banned on the grounds that it was armaments-related.

There were occasional protests within the British government about the extent to which foreign policy priorities seemed to override considerations of future economic welfare. Herbert Morrison the home secretary demanded a 'coordination' of British and German exports. 'Let us see', he wrote, 'that she exports to us the things we need and to others the things which we do not mind them getting from Germany.'[18] He was told that the choice of what exports to permit the Germans had in fact been coordinated in the Level of Industry Agreements and the Reparation Plan with the needs of the British export drive. As the cabinet was told in 1947, the policy of taking reparations from current production had been shaped

---

[16] G. Müller, 'Sicherheit durch wirtschaftliche Stabilität? Die Rolle der Briten bei der Auseinandersetzung der Allierten um die Stahlquote des ersten Industrieniveauplans vom 26 März 1946', in D. Petzina and W. Euchner (eds), *Wirtschaftspolitik im Britischen Besatzungsgebiet 1945–1949* (Düsseldorf, 1984).

[17] The most detailed and informative study of these policies is C. Glatt, 'Reparations and the Transfer of Scientific and Industrial Technology from Germany: A Case Study of the Roots of British Industrial Policy' (unpublished doctoral thesis, EUI, Florence, 1994).

[18] PRO, BT 211/82, Cabinet Memo by Morrison, 'Economic Planning: Coordination of the German Economy with the United Kingdom', October 1946.

in the reparations negotiations to be 'so designed as to interfere as little as possible with our export policy'.[19] The Board of Trade could argue that the outcome of the Level of Industry Agreements afforded 'valuable openings for a permanent expansion of British engineering exports', by virtue of imposing a one-third reduction on the output of German engineering.[20]

To compensate for a reduction in its future exports of capital goods, steel, and transport equipment, Germany was to be allowed under the Reparations Plan to increase its exports of textiles, paper, toys and some smaller consumer durables, such as cameras, above their pre-war level. British post-war exports of capital goods would thus, it was thought, meet much less competition, while in return Britain would cede part of its pre-war consumer goods market, especially in low value-added goods, to post-war Germany. As the interdepartmental committee that had established this policy began to understand as early as November 1946, however, the European demand for capital goods for reconstruction was far beyond what the United Kingdom could itself hope to supply, in spite of the expansion of the manufacturing base since 1939.[21]

Once the shortage of European capital goods had provoked the balance of payments crises of summer 1947 and the Marshall Plan had begun its operations, the chances of persisting in this attempted coordination of German and British exports were negligible. The Marshall Aid programme was accompanied by strong American pressure to reduce and then to end the dismantling of German industrial plant and to modify the restrictions on German output. The Humphrey Committee on dismantling, led by the man who was to become Eisenhower's treasury secretary, forced America's allies to accept sweeping reductions in the list of plant due for dismantling. The London Conference on Germany agreed, despite French resistance, to an increase in steel capacity and output. The Petersberg agreements in 1949 removed other limits on German manufacturing. A riot was to halt the dismantling of the Salzgitter works. The belief in Whitehall after the conclusion of the Levels of Industry Agreements had been that Britain would have ten years' grace before German exports returned once more to their pre-war levels. From spring 1948 it was increasingly obvious that this had been far too optimistic.

But it was not just the unexpectedly early return to the charge by German exporters which was responsible for the failure of the United Kingdom to make the predicted commercial conquests. Equally responsible was the failure by British exporters to do battle. Pollard's assertion that in 1946 'the problem that exercised the statesmen of the day was whether the rest of Europe, even its industrialized parts, would be able to come within reach of, let alone catch up with, Britain' is only a small exaggeration and

---

[19] A. Cairncross, *The Price* . . ., op. cit., p. 172.
[20] PRO, BT 11/2697, 'The Reparations Plan'.
[21] PRO, BT 211/82, Draft Report of the Interdepartmental Committee on Coordination of the German Economy with the United Kingdom, 1 November 1946.

nearly as true for 1948 as for 1946.[22] What is so astonishing, given that general picture, is the extraordinary defensiveness and pessimism of British business and government. Although advantages arising from low wages and unused capacity could be forecast for German exports, the difficulties facing the Federal Republic's manufacturers were formidably discouraging. Huge territorial losses; transport and trade disrupted; contacts defunct; 6 million of its pre-war citizens killed, in comparison with about half a million in Britain; another million young men still prisoner in the Soviet Union; reparations; shortages of capital; shortages of housing; a natural hostility to all things German: these were handicaps indeed compared with Britain. Yet British industrialists, offered the opportunities arising from the occupation, did not take them. Industry and government together, while launching a propaganda offensive in favour of the export drive, in fact evolved a strategy of retreat from those European markets where it was, correctly, foreseen that the first shock of battle would be felt.

As soon as the Reparations Plan proposed to allow a greater level of German consumer goods exports than before the war there were strenuous protests from those sectors of British manufacturing which felt threatened. They clamoured for controls over the marketing of German consumer goods and on the type and quality of products which Germany would be allowed to sell. They lobbied for tariffs and quotas to protect the British market against proposed increases in German exports of bicycles, cameras, paper and textiles. Courtaulds requested that if it was really necessary to increase German exports of artificial fibres the increase should all be to eastern Europe.[23]

Those firms whose exports were supposed to displace reduced German output were no less protectionist. After the Volkswagen plant had fallen into British hands the Levels of Industry Agreements meant that its potential output was surplus to stipulated German needs. Officials in the Ministry of Supply and in the Board of Trade wanted to claim the plant under reparations. It was, though, considered too large to be absorbed by any of the existing British car manufacturing firms. Nor was there certainty that enough steel could be provided for its output, unless at the expense of existing car manufacturers. The Advisory Committee of the Car Manufacturers' Association, although interested in acquiring some of the machinery, was even more interested in preventing the Volkswagen plant from being used to compete against them in the future, no matter whose hands it was in.[24] Its reaction was that of a threatened cartel. It argued for the dispersal of 'the machines throughout British industry as a pre-emptive measure against

---

[22] S. Pollard, *The Wasting of the British Economy: British Economic Policy 1945 to the Present* (London, 1982), p. 2.

[23] PRO, BT 211/84, passim.

[24] S. Reich, *The Fruits of Fascism. Postwar Prosperity in Historical Perspective* (Ithaca, 1990), pp. 190 ff.

foreign competition'.[25] The issue was settled by the insistence of the Treasury that Volkswagen should be set to work as quickly as possible to produce cars for the occupation forces, thus saving money, and for exports from Germany, thus earning dollars to pay for Germany's food imports.

When the London Conference on Germany, which established the Federal Republic, agreed in 1948 that it would remove the restrictions imposed on the German scientific instrument industry, a similar reaction came from British firms. In spite of eight years of government subsidies, a large government market and freedom from German competition, they argued their complete inability to compete on equal terms. The Association of Manufacturers of Scientific Instruments claimed that they would at once lose exports worth 1 million pounds (4 million dollars) a month and that the industry would collapse.[26]

As the chairman of the Economic Planning Committee for the British zone wrote, when faced with ICI's demand to suppress dyestuffs production in Germany,

> The situation surely is that the British and other Allied producers have a splendid opportunity whilst Germany is prostrated of building up a competitive position. They ought to be told to concentrate on building up this competitive position and not to rely upon the elimination of competition by a perpetuation of control. . . . It strikes me as a defensive and indeed defeatist state of mind.[27]

The verdict was sustained by the Board of Trade official who conducted most of the negotiations with British manufacturers' associations on the various questions relating to the implementation of the Reparations Plan. He wrote: 'The general trend of the discussions at which I have been present has been defeatist, that is to say there is a presupposition that Germany will be successful in ousting British exports.'[28] In January 1949 the letter columns of *The Times* were filled with coordinated public appeals from industrial associations for protection against Germany. This was when German manufactured exports had scarcely begun.

In March 1949, after four years of uninterruptedly high demand and the absence of German competition, which had been supposed to lead to a permanent expansion of British engineering capacity, the Central Economic Planning Staff of the Treasury agreed with the Board of Trade that, although the margin between production and capacity in the engineering industry was still insufficient, there was now no reason to expect any overall increase in capacity. When Germany returned as a major exporter,

---

[25] PRO, BT 211/92, D. Wood to J.N.V. Duncan of the Control Office for Germany and Austria, September 1946.
[26] ibid., Memo on the Meeting of the Interdepartmental Committee on the Scientific Instrument Industry on 5 October 1948, 7 October 1948.
[27] PRO, BT 11/84, Memo by E. Seal, 24 July 1946.
[28] PRO, BT 11/4024, Memo by G. Bowen, 19 November 1948.

parts of the British engineering industry which had expanded capacity would, officials agreed, now have to shrink. There was a general agreement that re-equipment in western Europe was coming to an end and that the only way to make room for Germany was by a reduction in British capital goods exports by 1952–3.[29]

The irritation of civil servants with businessmen's attitudes, however, ill disguised their own defeatism and the pattern of thought which relegated Britain's trade with Europe to a lower priority. Whitehall's general sentiment, like that of industry, was that in the first battleground where Germany must be met, western Europe, direct competition would be a strategic mistake. One of the arguments which the Interdepartmental Committee on Coordination of the German Economy with the United Kingdom had adduced was that too rapid an expansion of British capital goods exports to western Europe would be an unwise commitment to markets which the United Kingdom could not permanently keep. What Britain did not take from Germany ought therefore to be exported to western Europe in order to divert German competition away from established British markets outside Europe.

> It is considered that where German essential goods compete with the United Kingdom, it will be better for Germany to supply Europe, and ourselves to concentrate on extra-European markets. German exports to European destinations now would relieve the pressure on the United Kingdom and assist us in increasing our supplies for home re-equipment and for those other markets where for overall balance of payments reasons we urgently require to increase our exports and where we think we stand the best chance of obtaining long-term goodwill.[30]

Clearly it did make immediate economic sense to try to increase British exports to North America. The dollar was the currency in short supply, the competition from other European exporters would, it was thought, be less, and there were long-standing business connections. This at least was a better-founded hope than the idea that British exports would encounter long-term goodwill in Australia, South Africa and other Commonwealth countries, whose import-substitution policies were to be one cause of the relative stagnation of British exports over the period 1951–4. The official view of the geopolitics of exports was that it would be in Britain's interest if the Federal Republic's exports were to mop up the surplus sterling earnings of other western European countries and the Federal Republic were to run a deficit with the sterling area from which it would import raw materials and agricultural products. If there was to be competition with Germany outside Europe, better in North America than in the sterling area: British exports to the sterling area would be purchased with the

[29] PRO, T 229/157, 'Exports of Capital Goods in the Long Term', 9 March 1949.
[30] PRO, BT 211/82, op. cit.

sterling area's earnings in German and other European currencies. In this way Germany was assigned its part in the multilateral system.[31]

Table 7.2   An index of the growth of British exports by value and by area, 1951–5 (1951 = 100)

	Total exports	To continental Europe	To sterling area	To USA
1951	100.0	100.0	100.0	100.0
1952	100.3	104.3	96.8	107.5
1953	100.3	112.6	95.6	116.7
1954	103.8	116.8	101.3	110.5
1955	112.8	122.6	109.1	134.6

Source: United Kingdom, *Accounts Relating to the Trade and Navigation of the United Kingdom*

It was with this view of the future geographical distribution of trade in mind that Britain began to shape its second post-war national strategy to replace Bretton Woods: the pursuit of sterling–dollar convertibility, if necessary without American support, as the first step towards general dollar convertibility for west European currencies and west European multilateralism.

The key to the system was that the United Kingdom should set about recreating its pre-war surpluses in what was to prove after the war the slowest growing market, the sterling area, in order to allow Germany to buy more sterling area raw materials with the proceeds of its exports to what was to prove the world's most rapidly growing market, western Europe. Western Europe would be ceded to German exporters and the danger of exporting to soft-currency sterling area markets would be recompensed by a successful competition against German exports in North America.

Global macroeconomic perspectives of this kind could not determine the ultimate direction of British exports, but they probably did influence the tempo of change. Not until the comparative sluggishness of sterling area markets became unmistakeable, dramatically so in 1956, did British exporters redirect their efforts towards Europe. Governmental juggling with perspectives for a world order was in harmony with the efforts of exporters themselves; it was in North America and the Commonwealth that they privately thought expansion would be easier. There had been less competition in Commonwealth markets since 1931 and it was towards large sheltered markets like Australia that their eyes first turned. Government's contribution was to exhort and cajole them to add Canada and the United States to the list, in order to earn dollars.

[31]   PRO, BT 11/4009, 'Note by the Board of Trade on the Scope and Effectiveness of German Competition', 1950.

Underlying this global macroeconomic perspective in which so little adjustment of the pre-war direction of British exports seemed to be required was also the economic reality that even when export markets were there for the taking British manufacturing did not expand sufficiently to take them. Long-run commercial strategy, as the experience of the German Federal Republic shows, may arise, not as a consciously thought-out programme, but as a set of individual firms' responses to economic circumstances. In so far as government in the Federal Republic had a long-term commercial strategy it was that announced by the minister for the economy, Ludwig Erhard, and his leading officials in their propagandistic publication of 1953: to promote German exports on worldwide markets.[32] Its illustrations of tropical-suited German businessmen sweltering under Brazilian palm trees, while beckoning turned out to have little or no contact with the reality of Germany's export growth in the 1950s. More than 60 per cent of the value of the Federal Republic's exports went to western European markets in 1960. Throughout the 1950s Germany was, in comparison with the United Kingdom and France, overwhelmingly a European trader. The force of European demand, as countries switched their manufactured imports from America to Germany, led to so rapid a growth in exports to Europe that any attempt to direct trade elsewhere towards particular currency markets became ineffective.

German manufacturers were like a man who had set one foot on a train which accelerated violently away from the platform, leaving him either to run at breakneck speed in order to hold on to it or to fall broken by the trackside. The choice was between sustained investment (which for the most part could only come out of profits) and sustained exports or loss of market share to their domestic rivals. In explaining the failure of British manufacturing, historians will need to compare the failure of firms to invest in good opportunities in 1946 with the often dangerous risks which German firms began to run only four years later. There were great rewards for those risks if successfully taken, as well as clear penalties for not taking them. British exporters believed themselves to have the choice of security on safe markets, although it was illusory. While British firms pursued this illusion the Federal Republic piled up a surplus on commodity exports of $10,605 million between 1951 and 1958, most of it earned in western Europe. This provided the base for the extension of manufacturing capacity in Germany and the permanent expansion of exports into extra-European markets. Britain's reluctance to compete in Europe in the long run only helped the spread of German manufactured exports outside Europe.

As state strategies might have little practical influence on the actual pattern of trade flows, so might that pattern itself have only a minor influence on the ability of firms to compete with foreign rivals. The Trade Liberalization Programme of OEEC removed, but only as late as 1955,

---

[32] L. Erhard, *Deutschlands Rückkehr zum Weltmarkt* (Düsseldorf, 1953).

a major instrument of direction from the state's hands, the import quota. Only on the French frontier did import quotas still exist after that year in sufficient variety and number on inter-west European trade to significantly alter its overall pattern and the Treaty of Rome was a promise that they, and the tariff surcharges which substituted for them, would go. Against North America OEEC members retained many import quotas. Only in the 1960s would they be enlarged or removed. The great range of purposes for which British governments deployed the weapon of the import quota before 1955, to say nothing of the wide variety of results obtained, show how exceptionally complicated it is to attribute accurately the weight of any state commercial strategy, even so direct and powerful a one as an import quota, within the complexity of influences that determine success or failure in international competition in any manufactured product.[33]

There is space in this book only to attempt such an assessment for one product. I have chosen cars, because they were in many respects the most typically growing export of the 1950s, because they are the consumer good for which it is easiest to obtain consistent and reliable data, because on them the weight of British government strategy fell heavily, and because the trade rivalry in western Europe in cars was first and foremost between the United Kingdom and West Germany.

COMPETITION IN CARS

Cars were the single commodity that contributed most during the period 1945–60 to the growth of manufacturing output in both Britain and Germany. They were the archetype of the mass-production process on moving assembly lines and of those economies of scale whose achievement meant higher productivity and higher rates of income growth. And they were the foremost symbol of that prosperous consumer society which politicians held up as one goal of the economy. Apart from shipbuilding, where special circumstances applied in both countries (the immediate post-war reconstruction boom in replacing vessels lost in wartime and the Allied restrictions on German output) the highest export ratio in any large sector of German manufacturing was in mechanical engineering. This is too diverse a sector to make effective direct comparisons across the whole range of German and British goods. It does, though, include car manufacture, where comparisons are easier.

Before the war, the German car industry had been smaller than the British and car ownership less widespread. The British industry, however, had been essentially confined to two large sheltered markets: the domestic market protected by high tariffs and the Commonwealth market, where it enjoyed the advantage of imperial preferences. The market for the German car industry by contrast had been western Europe, where its success gave

---

[33] A.S. Milward and G. Brennan, *Britain's Place* . . ., op. cit., pp. 240–89.

it in the last pre-war years about 10.4 per cent of the total of world car exports. This was in spite of a weak domestic market and a relatively low level of domestic car ownership. Planned Nazi investment in the motorization of the German economy was overtaken by rearmament and war before car ownership could expand to British levels, and the people's car, the Volkswagen, the core of the motorization project, made little impact on pre-war markets.

The Volkswagen manufacturing plant, designed to produce on a scale greater than that of any other car factory in Europe, was reactivated by the British administration earlier than other German car plants and was treated as a priority producer selling its products to the occupation forces. Nevertheless it still suffered from the same handicaps as the rest of German industry. Shortages of materials and the economic disruptions of occupation meant that for several years Volkswagen production was far below capacity. It was impossible for the Germans to take advantage of remarkably favourable market circumstances.

In the United States domestic demand for cars was high, steel controls limited their output, and manufacturers faced with long waiting lists of customers had little incentive to resume their pre-war exports to Europe, while American consumers turned to imported European models in order to obtain a car. In Europe countries other than Belgium and Switzerland refused to make dollars available for car imports, so that European exporters were free of any American challenge. But the German pre-war sales network in Europe had been broken by the war and the allocation of cars remained in any case under the control of the Military Governments. The British car industry, by contrast, was in an ideal position to supply as many cars as it could make to a sellers' market. It had, what is more, a very direct incentive. Car manufacturers were supposed to export half their output under the threat that they would not otherwise be provided with steel. By 1948 the proportion was set at 75 per cent, although the export ratios were again allowed to fall to one-half after 1951. In other ways too the post-war car industry was the subject of close government attention and of persistent political pressures to export.

In spite of this remarkable export opportunity, together with the large backlog of unsatisfied home demand, car output in Britain was overtaken by that in the Federal Republic in 1956 and the gap has widened ever since. In the same year the number of German cars exported overtook that from the United Kingdom (table 7.3). Despite the rapid growth of domestic demand an increasing share of output was exported and by 1960 the number of cars exported was more than 50 per cent greater than the British figure. By 1958 the Federal Republic had captured 34.8 per cent of the share of the world export market for cars and chassis, while the United Kingdom had only 25 per cent. Both industries had greatly expanded their share compared with pre-war at the expense of the United States, but the British share in 1950 had been about one-half and its subsequent decline could be attributed

Table 7.3 Output and exports of cars in the German Federal Republic and the United Kingdom, 1949–60

	United Kingdom			Federal Republic		
	Output	*Exports*	*Export ratio (completed vehicles) (%)*	*Output*	*Exports*	*Export ratio (completed vehicles) (%)*
1949	412,290	257,922	62.6	104,060	13,980	13.4
1950	522,516	398,302	76.2	219,110	69,033	31.5
1951	475,920	368,732	77.5	276,620	92,594	33.5
1952	448,008	309,822	69.1	317,660	102,689	32.3
1953	594,804	302,223	50.8	387,890	143,313	36.1
1954	769,164	366,084	47.6	561,170	246,437	43.9
1955	897,564	373,203	41.6	762,210	344,463	45.2
1956	707,592	337,052	47.6	911,000	413,352	45.4
1957	860,844	426,272	49.5	1,040,190	502,241	48.3
1958	1,051,548	486,816	46.3	1,306,850	630,515	48.2
1959	1,189,944	568,846	47.8	1,503,420	757,703	50.4
1960	1,352,724	569,916	42.1	1,816,780	865,341	47.6

Source: United Kingdom: Society of Motor Manufacturers and Traders, *Monthly Statistical Review*; Federal Republic: *Motor Business*, no. 29, January 1962

almost entirely to German competition. Because the motor industry was regarded as the flagship of the modern economy, because cars were the most dynamically growing single product in manufacturing industry to be produced on such a scale, because the multiplier effect of the industry on the rest of the economy was high, and because it was above all on the successful export of cars that government intervention in the British economy to force exports had concentrated, the British failure was more dramatic.

Supply to the motor vehicle industry together with the output of the industry itself amounted to 27 per cent of the growth in industrial production in Britain between 1954 and 1966.[34] On the basis of this figure, had the British car industry grown after 1954 at the same rate as its German equivalent and the rest of the industrial economy still performed as it did, the growth rate of British industrial output over that period would have been slightly more than 1 per cent a year higher than it actually was. The arithmetic is merely suggestive, but since there was little difference in the volume of domestic car sales in the two economies this hypothetical difference in national income growth could in theory be attributed to failure to compete with German exports. In the 1960s the industry began to lose ground faster. Today, cars and car parts are one of the biggest deficit items in the British balance of trade. They made up about one-sixth of the extremely large commodity trade deficit in 1988. More than

[34] A.C. Armstrong, 'The Motor Industry and the British Economy', *District Bank Review*, no. 164, September 1967.

one-third of the trade deficit of the United Kingdom with the Federal Republic, the biggest deficit with any single country, consisted in that year of cars and car parts. The failure to compete successfully in the 1950s heralded a long-term trend with large consequences.

The reasons for this particular industrial failure have been much discussed. Many of them are said to be the same as those for the weakness of British manufacturing in general. But some arguments have been seen as having particular force in the case of cars. These are: excess demand on the home market, excessive government interference, the absence of government interference, the impact of the Korean War, the 'stop-go' effect of demand management, and the inadequate design and technical quality of some car models. It is striking how often British writers on the subject ignore the extent to which some of these problems applied with equal force to the German industry.

'In some ways the German task was easier', Rhys writes, in the standard work on the subject, 'in that their car producers did not have to contend with the same high degree of domestic excess demand as the British.'[35] Such a judgement seems odd in the face of the more rapidly rising level of disposable income in the Federal Republic than in Britain, the lower pre-war level of car ownership, and the much greater destruction of the wartime stock. There is in fact no sign of any weakening in the growth of demand for cars on the German market until 1958. Before 1952, when growing incomes were still being spent on recouping other forms of consumption, it is conceivable that growth of demand on the German home market was weaker than in Britain. Yet in 1950 there were only 12.8 cars in use for each 1,000 inhabitants in the Federal Republic compared with 46 in the United Kingdom, so the potential backlog of demand to be released as personal income rose was much greater.

The propensity to buy a car in the 1950s was more closely correlated to increases in personal disposable income than were purchases of most other consumer durables.[36] From the start of 1952 to the end of 1956 there was a rise of about one-third in personal disposable incomes in Germany while the production costs of a car fell by about one-fifth. Compared with the level of car ownership in the United States the figures in both Britain and Germany were low throughout the 1950s and there was no reason to expect any contraction in demand for a long time in either economy other than general cyclical downturns. The total number of cars made in Britain between the start of 1951 and the end of 1957 was roughly 800,000 more than in Germany. But the increase registered as in use on the domestic road system was only 133,000 more, reflecting the initially higher export ratio of the British industry. Protection ensured that imports into both countries were very small, so that car ownership in the United Kingdom

[35] D.G. Rhys, *The Motor Industry. An Economic Survey* (London, 1972), p. 383.
[36] A. Maizels, 'Trends in World Trade in Durable Consumer Goods', *National Institute Economic Review*, November 1959.

still remained much higher in 1957 than in the Federal Republic, 83.3 per 1,000 inhabitants as opposed to 48.6.[37]

The increasing export ratio for German cars is partly explained by the wish to diversify markets, perhaps an acknowledgement of the earlier experience when pre-war export markets in western Europe had made a major contribution to profits. In some plant, Volkswagen for example, export sales were initially encouraged by Military Government as a way of earning dollars.[38] Under the Federal Republic, without controls, however, the export ratio of the German car industry after 1955 was slightly greater, at higher levels of output, than that of the British, with export controls. The sustained high level of German exports after the end of Military Government does not reflect any weakness in the growth of domestic demand. The reason officially given for the reductions in the German tariff on cars in April 1955 and July 1956, bringing it to only half the height of the British tariff for small cars and to two-thirds of it for larger models, was that the German industry could not itself meet the level of domestic demand. It may also have been an anti-inflationary measure, for that was a period of spectacular growth of income and output in Germany and the actual number of cars imported was still restricted by quotas.

The claim of British manufacturers that their exports were limited in the long run by excess domestic demand meant, presumably, that when markets were so segmented by quotas and tariffs, the same limited output could fetch a higher price on the home market than abroad, so that in spite of all honest efforts to meet the government's export targets the premium prices paid for cars on the domestic market were bound to weaken the impact of controls and incentives. The prices for comparable standard British and German car models, as we shall see below, are consistent with this argument, but also with the argument that in both countries manufacturers increased the price of domestic sales as a way of subsidizing more competitive export prices. The argument that the British car industry's failure to compete had its origins in excess domestic demand might seem more convincing had it always been operating at full capacity. Even in the boom year 1955 when the export ratio was at its lowest point and the government had to introduce credit curbs to cut back domestic consumption of consumer goods, if foreigners had placed orders at world prices there seems no reason to think the British car industry could not have satisfied them. In that same year the German industry was faced with shortages of labour and raw materials, and increases in the price of both, which led British observers to forecast severe difficulties for it in the immediate future.[39]

---

[37] Statistics on British car output, exports, ownership and use are from the Society of Motor Manufacturers and Traders, *Monthly Statistical Review*. German data on output and exports are from German Federal Republic, Statistisches Bundesamt, *Wirtschaft und Statistik*, and on ownership and use from UN, ECE, *Annual Bulletin of Transport Statistics for Europe*.

[38] A. Diekmann, *Die Automobilnachfrage als Konjunktur und Wachstumsfaktor* (Tübingen, 1975), pp. 28 ff.

[39] *Motor Business*, no. 4, September 1955.

When the British government required a high export ratio, the car industry complained about market distortions. When the requirement was reduced, it blamed its failure to compete in export markets on excess home demand. When home demand was curbed by credit restrictions, it complained that the drop in sales made an increase in investment and a reduction of costs through economies of scale impossible.

It is true that the car industry's salient position made it a field for experiment in demand management. Car tax, fuel tax and hire-purchase terms for cars were all used as regulators by government to influence domestic demand and even to influence the kind and size of cars produced.[40] The fall in output in 1956 was partly attributable, it was claimed, to the much greater stringency in hire-purchase terms introduced at the start of that year. There were certainly differences between this and German practice. The first restrictions on hire-purchase in Britain were introduced in February 1952 and lasted until July 1954. In February 1955 they were reintroduced, although in milder form, tightened further in July 1955 as sales increased, and then made more drastic than at any previous time in February 1956, when purchasers were required to lay down half the final price as the initial deposit. It was the February 1956 regulations that manufacturers blamed for the 20 per cent fall in sales on the home market which followed. In contrast the German tax reform of 1955 allowed income tax rebates for journeys by car to work and reduced car tax by 20 per cent.

The level at which a car could be priced depended on the economies of scale achieved through increasing the volume of output, so that the restrictions on hire-purchase terms, if they were responsible for the fall in domestic sales, would also have been responsible for a higher cost price of the finished car no matter what terms it was sold on. Yet it should not be overlooked that one purpose of trying to reduce domestic demand in Britain was to encourage the industry to export, which in 1956 it singularly failed to do and that at a time when the world demand for cars was rising so rapidly that every one of its European competitors had a big increase in exports. British car exports in 1956 in fact fell by 34,680 units.

This was in part blamed by British manufacturers on the general effect on prices of the reduction in the volume of output caused by domestic market restrictions. There were, however, four years in the 1950s (table 7.3, p. 369) when exports of British cars fell, while German output and exports expanded along a smooth upward curve and the increase in exports of French and Italian cars, although more erratic, was sustained.

The fall in car output and exports in 1951 and 1952 in Britain is usually attributed to controls which allocated steel to rearmament. It is interesting to note that steel production actually fell in the face of this alleged increased demand in the second half of 1951 and that imports at less than half a

[40] P. J. S. Dunnett, *The Decline of the British Motor Industry. The Effects of Government Policy, 1945–1979* (London, 1980).

million tonnes were insufficient to close the gap. By 1952 steel imports had increased threefold. Car output, though, continued to fall. To what extent a steel shortage due to rearmament was straightforwardly the cause of the fall in output of cars would be worth more attention than most studies have given it. The output of thin sheet steel, which was the main steel component of cars and for which cars were the main market, rose from 2,513,000 tonnes in 1951 to 2,703,000 tonnes in 1952, while car output continued to fall.[41] Furthermore in each year of this alleged shortage the United Kingdom exported more than 2.5 million tonnes of steel. These exports seem in part to have been commitments to Commonwealth countries which might otherwise have imported steel for dollars and so put greater strain on the sterling area reserves. The fulfilment of these commitments, if such they were, at a time when the export drive for cars was still also a high priority suggests that the reason for the fall in British car exports was a more complex one than the mere inability of manufacturers to lay their hands on enough steel.

Until 1953 allocations of steel to each manufacturer depended on successful compliance with the government's desired export ratio. For every model of which the requisite proportion could be exported, steel was theoretically available. When there were still very few post-war car models on sale this method of allocation encouraged producers to continue with the proliferation of pre-war models rather than to rationalize output into fewer and more modern models. Some of these pre-war models could not stand the competition from German models which began to appear on export markets in 1951–2 and there seems to be evidence, impressionistic though it is, that the fall in British car exports over those years was also due to their inferior quality.

Whatever the reason for the failure of British production and exports in 1951–2, it coincided with the first large surge of German exports and the period of most rapid productivity gains in Germany as spare capacity was taken fully into use. In spite of the hire-purchase restrictions introduced in 1952, British output and domestic sales recovered strongly in 1953. Exports still fell, whereas more than half the additional output of German cars in that year was exported. In 1956 British manufacturers were still offering for sale on the American market more than twice as many models as the German and French car industries combined, and it was evidently impossible to provide service and repair facilities for so wide a range. Yet it is also evident from the history of the car industry that any damage done to a firm's reputation and finances by a poor model, which most of them have turned out to be, can soon be repaired by a good model. The one Volkswagen model produced by the largest and most standardized car plant in Europe was the great exception in the post-war car industry; the rest of the German industry was not like that, yet

[41] UN, *Quarterly Bulletin of Steel Statistics*.

it too competed successfully against the British product. Poor British models might explain something of that success, but they were by no means all inferior to their German rivals.

It is usually implied that in the period before 1953 when the British car industry was being buffeted by government policies, German industry had lower costs which turned into a permanent advantage. Prices of cars are difficult to compare for obvious reasons. A comparison between domestic prices and export prices in the Belgian market, where there were no domestic producers and very active competition between British and German sellers, does suggest that German cars were cheaper. But so many factors other than price are involved in the decision to buy so relatively expensive a consumer item that the price difference would have to be wider than these figures suggest to conclude firmly that it was price differences that decided the issue in favour of German producers.

The higher domestic price of the Morris Minor compared with the Volkswagen and the smaller gap in export prices of the two models on a competitive market was partly the result of British fiscal policy. Of the 1952 domestic price of the Morris Minor 36 per cent was accounted for by tax. The fall in the domestic price of the Volkswagen between 1952 and 1957, which is repeated in the case of many other German car models, probably represents the reduction in costs from economies of scale as well as the price falls consequent on tax changes and tariff reductions. That, of course, would suggest a more marked potential increase in demand for car purchases on the domestic market in Germany than in Britain. On a competitive market, however, the price of the German product rose more steeply than that of the British product. This accords with the overall evidence in chapter four that the price of German manufactured exports in general rose more steeply in the 1950s than British.

Table 7.4   Comparison of the prices of the Volkswagen two-door saloon with the basic version of the Morris Minor, 1950–7 ($)

	Volkswagen		Morris Minor	
	Domestic market	Belgium	Domestic market	Belgium
1952	(1,298)[f]	1,085[b]	1,627[c]	1,237[b]
1957	1,095[a]	1,515[b]	1,764[d]	1,481[e]

Sources:
[a] *Motor Business*, prices are for September
[b] AN, F60ter469, Secrétaire Général du Comité Interministériel pour les Questions de Coopération Economique, 'Listes particulières et communes'
[c] *Motor Business*, October price
[d] Economist Intelligence Unit, *Britain and Europe* (London, 1957), p. 138, March price
[e] *Motor Business*, March price
[f] 1950 price, *Motor Business*

As a check on these prices, a much-exported larger German 'family' car, the Opel Olympia, sold on the domestic market in 1952 for $1,615 in 1950 and for $1,520 in September 1957.[42] Its price in Belgium in September 1952 was $1,237 and in March 1957 $1,481.[43] Its most plausible British rival in 1952, the Austin A40 saloon, sold in Belgium for $1,560. By 1957 the more plausible competitor was the Ford Anglia which sold there for $1,548.[44] In this medium range there does seem to be a small price advantage for the German car even in 1957. Across the general range of larger models in 1955 German cars were no cheaper on export markets than their British equivalents.[45] But the bulk market was the smaller models. These prices may be compared with the attempt by Gilbert and Kravis to establish comparable average prices for cars of comparable weights, with due allowance made for those differences in average per capita income which would make the typical British car larger than the typical German car. By their method of calculation, the typical German car in 1953–4 with a weight of 890 kg sold on the domestic market for the equivalent of $1,470 and the typical British car with a weight of 1070 kg for $1,419.[46] This is much less direct evidence, but the price advantage which German cars appear to have in the direct comparison of similar models is a small one. Even if we conclude that in the smallest cars, especially in the early 1950s, German exports did have a price advantage, we would also have to conclude that the advantage was only slight and the evidence for it is shaky. German pricing policy was to sell exports at first on very small margins in order to make a market and this perhaps gave them an initial impetus before export prices were forced upwards by increasing costs, seemingly more so than in Britain, although the difference between the domestic and export prices is exaggerated by the changes in 1955 in the tax laws which reduced domestic prices.

The purchase price of cars on the domestic market in Britain, because of taxation policy, was high in relation to most other western European countries. Before April 1953 domestic purchasers were charged a purchase tax of two-thirds, reduced after that date to one-half. In spite of the roughly equal level of money wages in Britain and Germany, in 1956 the price of a comparable small car was 114 per cent of the average annual wage in Britain but only 77 per cent of that in Germany.[47] If the evidence about relative export prices is weak, there is stronger evidence that government policy, by keeping up the retail prices of cars on the domestic

---

[42] *Motor Business*, no. 12, September 1957.
[43] 1952 price: AN, F60*ter*469, Secrétaire Général du Comité Interministériel pour les Questions de Coopération Economique, 'Listes particulières et communes'. 1957 price: *Motor Business*, no. 12, September 1957.
[44] ibid.
[45] *Motor Business*, no. 4, September 1955.
[46] M. Gilbert and I.B. Kravis, *An International Comparison of National Products and the Purchasing Power of Currencies* (OEEC, Paris, 1954).
[47] UN, ECE, *Economic Survey of Europe in 1958*, chapter V, p. 23.

market in Britain, limited domestic sales below their full potential. It was alleged that these limitations on the domestic market were responsible for the lack of the marginal increase in investment and a consequent reduction of costs through economies of scale and thus for the fall in exports in 1956. What validity did that argument have?

Costs per unit of output in the British car industry fell between 1950 and 1955 by about 20 per cent, about the same ratio as in the Federal Republic.[48] The investment plans of the British industry in 1954 in full expansion were as extensive and ambitious as those in the Federal Republic, in spite of the burden of taxation on domestic sales. Given the ambitious scope of investment plans and the fall in unit costs it seems implausible to attribute the comparatively slow growth of exports in 1955 and their decisive loss in 1956, both years when the world market was expanding rapidly, to limitations on domestic sales. If we take a crude productivity measure, the number of cars produced per employee, the British industry was still operating at a higher level of productivity than the German in 1956, and any loss in potential economies of scale which fiscal policy imposed might have been recouped by expanding exports, where this problem did not apply, and increasing the export ratio. Other reasons seem necessary to explain the export failures of 1955 and 1956.

When the British export drive began in 1945 it was directed towards the pre-war markets. Except for the six-week period of sterling–dollar convertibility in 1947 most larger Commonwealth countries practised discrimination against dollar goods and the surviving imperial preferences gave British exporters a small potential price advantage over other suppliers. The sterling area accounted for 48.6 per cent of British car exports by value in 1956; New Zealand alone for 10 per cent of them and Australia for 9.7 per cent. In earlier years the percentage going to Australia had often been higher. Europe took 23.9 per cent of British car exports in that year and North America 20.1 per cent. German exporters followed their pre-war pattern and concentrated their efforts on their immediate European neighbours. Before 1956 their main markets were Austria, Belgium, Sweden and Switzerland. In 1954 these four countries together accounted for 45 per cent of total German car exports by value. Except for Sweden, for British exporters these were individually marginal areas of activity with less investment on service networks than in America or Australasia. The most successful continental market for them was in Sweden, particularly for the smallest cars. Although a higher proportion of total car sales was made in Europe than in North America, the government's main interest remained the North American market. It altered the basis of the car tax in 1953 in conformity with its overall trade and payments strategy to encourage the production of larger models, which,

[48] G. Maxcy and A. Silberston, *The Motor Industry* (London, 1959), pp. 160 ff.

it was thought, would sell better there as well as in competition in sterling area markets against American models.

The import restrictions imposed by Australia in 1951 gave an early omen of the dangerous position of British exporters. The big recovery in car exports from 1953 to the end of 1955 was mainly due to the revival of sales in Australia and New Zealand when these restrictions were modified. The response of the Australian government to the increase in imports was to reimpose quota restrictions to support its policy of import substitution. As a result, in 1956 car sales to Australia and New Zealand fell by about one-half. This was, however, a collapse foreshadowed by the increasing failure to compete on European markets since 1950 and the collapse of sales to Australia was prefigured by a similar collapse in Europe earlier. In 1955, a year of record domestic car sales in which the export ratio fell, hire-purchase terms were tightened by government as a policy response to counteract this trend and to stimulate a higher proportion of exports.[49] However, in the second half of 1955, when domestic sales, responding to fiscal and credit policy, were falling by 10 per cent, export sales were falling by 15 per cent. This was almost wholly due to the loss of market share in Denmark and Sweden to German competition. Loss of share in such fast-growing markets, even though together they accounted for less than 5 per cent of total car exports, was a serious indicator of lack of competitive ability. The response to the restrictions on the Australian market in 1956 was a rapid one, 1956 being the best year in the decade for the growth of car exports to western Europe. But by this time British manufacturers were competing against well-established industries with large markets on the continent and were in the position of trying to regain rather than hold markets.

The greater strength of continental producers was shown by their ability to stand up to British competition in the USA. Although the number of British cars exported to the USA increased by more than fourfold between 1956 and the end of 1959 this was only marginally more than the increase in German cars going to the same market and no more than that of French. All European car makers had found a niche on the American market for small cars, which the American industry was not successfully filling. As soon as American producers reduced the sizes of their models the competition between European producers there became fiercer. It was won by Germany. From the start of 1955 German car exports to non-European destinations, although still very small, began to grow faster than exports to Europe. In 1956 the United States became Germany's biggest single car export market, by 1959 accounting for one-third of the value of total German car exports. In 1960 British car exports to the United States fell from the 310,000 units of the previous year to 135,000 and in

[49] PRO, BT 213/70, Cabinet Working Party on United Kingdom Export Trends, 'Exports to OEEC Markets in 1955', 13 February 1956.

1961 to 30,500. German car exports, mainly Volkswagens, continued to rise, so that from 1960 onwards the Federal Republic became the dominant exporter to both halves of the rich industrialized world and the British car industry on which such great hopes for international success had been pinned entered its long period of decline and fall.

An overall strategy for car exports in conformity with national trade strategy had ended, not in increased prosperity, but in relative decline. But government was certainly not solely to blame. Manufacturers, left entirely to their own devices, would have concentrated even more on sterling area markets. The taxation system did make cars dearer on the domestic market than they were in Germany, but this could have been counteracted by increasing exports. The 'stop–go' effects of credit policy on the domestic market likewise could have been counteracted by increasing exports, but at the crucial period, 1955–6, exports actually fell. It is plausible that the weakness of exports in 1951–2 was partly attributable to poor models, and that in turn attributable to government pressure to export pre-war models in 1945–50 when more effort might have gone into devising new ones. But after that date new models failed to compete. Mistakes in management, labour relations and company organization probably added their part.[50] Some of these failures at the production level seem like symptoms of an industry already in trouble, others may have been the cause of that trouble. But the overall problem was a general, worldwide inability, first seen in western Europe in the face of German competition, to compete successfully in export markets. Exports, in this case, were half the market. Underlying all the particular reasons for this was a rate of productivity improvement lower than in Germany which left British cars at a competitive disadvantage.

In the Federal Republic the car industry seemed the perfect example of the virtuous spiral in which an increase of exports, output and productivity, followed by yet more export increases, provided that continuous income growth which in the ideology of the day was to be the lasting basis of the new society. In Britain fluctuating output and exports generated relatively lower wages, worse labour relations, panicky management reactions and unsystematic and inconsistent government intervention. The causes of relatively slower productivity growth varied in their presence and in their relative weightings over time and between industries.[51] One of them, which seems to have carried more weight in the 1950s, was that output growth was less rapid. It is not easy to see any explanation for this phenomenon in the British car industry as strong as that of the geographical distribution of its exports.

Indications that this was not a story confined to the car industry can be gleaned from the sparse facts about manufacture and trade in the other mass-produced symbols of the newly affluent society of the 1950s.

---

[50] H.A. Turner *et al.*, *Labour Relations in the Motor Industry* (London, 1967); J. Wood, *Wheels of Misfortune; the Rise and Fall of the British Motor Industry* (London, 1988).
[51] S.N. Broadberry, *The Productivity Race . . .*, op. cit., passim.

The Federal Republic, in spite of its lower incomes in the early part of the decade, already had a relatively high level of ownership of certain consumer goods. Household ownership of refrigerators, for example, at 12 per cent of all households was already higher in 1955 in Germany than in Britain, where it stood at 10 per cent.[52] Nevertheless for most consumer durables, as with cars, ownership was more widespread in Britain until the end of the 1950s. Ownership of washing machines by households in Germany was still only half that in Britain in 1957.[53] These are all industries where economies of scale and gains associated with learning curves are suspected, and can sometimes be shown, to be of great importance. When disposable personal income was initially so far above that in the Federal Republic British manufacturers should have been able to capitalize on their favourable starting position in marketing these goods. In 1950 the United Kingdom had almost one-half of the world export market for electric washing machines, surpassing even the United States, and there were no German exports. Between 1955 and 1957 the Federal Republic overtook the British market share. For domestic refrigerators the United Kingdom had 22 per cent of the world market in 1950 and the Federal Republic only 4 per cent. By 1957 the German share was 24 per cent and that of the United Kingdom only 15 per cent.[54] In the same year the German share of the post-war market for gramophones and record players first equalled that of Britain. German exports of radios and radiograms had surpassed British exports even before 1955.

This was a reassertion of the pre-war pattern in which Germany and the United States had been the major exporters of consumer durables. But need the pre-war pattern have been inevitably re-established? Not only were German exports eliminated for four years but American consumer durables were excluded from many European markets.[55] One reason for the failure of British producers to change the pre-war pattern was that, as with cars, they saw western Europe at first as only a subsidiary market.

[52] F. Dewhurst *et al., Europe's Needs and Resources* (New York, 1961) p. 256.
[53] F. Knox, 'Some International Comparisons of Consumers' Durable Goods', *Bulletin of the Oxford University Institute of Statistics*, vol. 21, no. 1, 1959.
[54] A. Maizels, 'Trends in World Trade . . .' op. cit.
[55] All OEEC countries except Belgium and Switzerland used some form of licences, quotas and exchange controls to keep out American manufactures. Even Switzerland was careful to retain import licences on part of its machinery imports as an implicit bargaining counter against any threat of American protectionism against Swiss exports. The gradual relaxation of these restrictions before 1958 always affected consumer goods last. Some countries, such as Sweden, established an official annual quantity of dollar imports that could not be exceeded. In a less formal way Denmark, Italy and the Netherlands did the same thing by determining that licences could be issued only for dollar imports which were essential. The United Kingdom by agreement with the United States allowed in only a token quantity of dollar consumer goods. France and Norway virtually excluded them altogether. PRO, T 232/408, 'The Future of the EPU. Discrimination by OEEC Countries', Board of Trade Memorandum, 3 March 1954; EL, Records of the President's Commission on Foreign Economic Policy, 1953–1954, Box No. 11, 'Notes on the Quantitative Import and Export Restrictions Applied by Contracting Parties to the GATT', 17 December 1953.

This meant that the home market was often growing faster than the traditional markets, although no faster than the home market in the Federal Republic.[56] As with cars, deflationary policy, in the form of hire-purchase restrictions and the purchase tax, was used to reduce domestic sales and encourage exports. When sales of refrigerators on the domestic market showed a vigorous upward trend from early 1954, they were pulled down again for one year in 1956 by changes in hire-purchase regulations. A similar fall can be observed in that year across a wide range of consumer goods: television receivers, radios, washing machines, vacuum cleaners and electric irons. Only in the case of vacuum cleaners did reduced domestic sales accompany an increase of exports. Otherwise, as with cars, exports fell too.

Exports of refrigerators, radios and washing machines did not regain their 1955 level when domestic sales recovered from 1957 onwards, and this reduced the subsequent rate of growth of output, so that by 1960 British output was much smaller than that of Germany. The restrictions on the domestic market in Britain in 1956 were certainly imposed at an inopportune moment. Across the whole range of German consumer durables, 1956 saw a remarkably steep rise in exports, as high as 34 per cent in the case of washing machines. Before too much blame is laid at the door of government, however, a comparison has to be made with France, which also practised restrictions on hire-purchase as a demand regulator on the domestic market. There, the permitted terms of credit sales were varied eight times between 1954 and 1958. The minimum deposit required was at no point higher than 35 per cent, so the restrictions were never as drastic as they were in 1956 in the United Kingdom, and the total volume of credit sales in the French economy was only one-quarter that in the United Kingdom.[57] Even so, fluctuations in domestic sales of consumer goods followed changes in credit regulations. Yet by 1960, after starting the decade at much lower levels, the output of several categories of consumer durables – refrigerators and washing machines, for example – was much higher in France than in Britain. An important reason for this was that poor years for domestic sales in France did tend to be compensated by increased foreign sales, so that credit restrictions did not reduce total output as they did in Britain, where falls in domestic and export sales tended to coincide.

One explanation for this seemingly contrary behaviour of British sales is that the markets to which Britain exported were insufficiently buoyant to counteract a contraction on the domestic market. In the French case the countercyclical effect of German demand meant that restrictions on domestic sales were followed by export gains; in the British case export sales followed a similar pattern to sales at home, irrespective of taxation policy, because the North American economy suffered falls in demand

---

[56] As a proportion of total private consumption, expenditure on consumer durables in the United Kingdom was only above the average for western Europe over the period 1949/58 in three years. F. Dewhurst *et al., Europe's Needs* . . ., op. cit., pp. 143 ff. and Appendix 5–1.

[57] R. Harris *et al., Hire Purchase in a Free Society* (London, 1958), p. 214.

which were replicated elsewhere outside Europe. German exports themselves, going as they did in such large measure to western Europe, were less exposed to those effects. For refrigerators, for example, Austria, Belgium, Italy and the Netherlands were initially Germany's best markets, although exports to Italy fell away after 1954 as the Italian refrigerator industry developed and itself became Europe's most successful exporter. The other three remained the leading markets throughout the decade. Their share in the total of German refrigerator exports rose steadily to 1957 when, together with Switzerland, they accounted for half the total value.[58] The same group of countries accounted for 54 per cent of all German exports of washing machines in 1953 and for 77 per cent in 1957.[59]

Table 7.5 Output of domestic refrigerators in France, the Federal Republic, Italy and the United Kingdom, 1954–60 ($ million)

	1954	*1955*	*1956*	*1957*	*1960*
France	48.6	58.3	88.9	139.5	150.7
German Federal Republic	51.0	56.7	77.9	85.3	187.5
Italy	6.4	13.0	22.7	38.4	79.1
United Kingdom	46.0	46.3	41.4	48.9	106.9

Source: OECD, *The Engineering Industries in North America – Europe – Japan 1965* (Paris, 1965), table IV.58

The Board of Trade inquiry published in spring 1957 attributed between a quarter and a third of the loss of Britain's share of world export markets after 1951 to their pattern of geographical distribution and their commodity composition.[60] It was suggested in chapter four that this was probably an underestimate, because the competitive advantages which were determined by the method of inquiry to have accounted by definition for the rest of the gains of Britain's competitors, essentially Germany, were not in reality causally separate from the geographical distribution of exports. Exporting to western Europe generated competitive advantages which exporting to the rest of the world did not; because of the rapidity and persistence with which European demand grew, technological improvements leading to economies of scale were more likely to be the consequence of a high level of sales to Europe than elsewhere. It would be in cars and consumer durables that we would particularly expect to see this revealed; the evidence of the car trade, as well as that of trade in other consumer durables,

[58] German Federal Republic, Statistisches Bundesamt, *Der Aussenhandel der Bundesrepublik Deutschland*.
[59] ibid.
[60] *Board of Trade Journal*, 30 March 1957.

suggests that the geographical distribution of British exports before 1956 was a handicap.

Although consumer durables, including cars, still amounted to no more than 18 per cent of the value of world foreign trade in manufactures by the end of the 1950s, the increase in their ownership and consumption in the early 1950s was one of the principal reasons for the underlying economic dynamism of those years. These were goods at the crucial margin of expansion. Success in selling them abroad was the consequence of technological innovation, and also of adaptation to contemporary shifts in sensibility and the organization of human life which these goods themselves often brought about. Consumption at higher levels of personal income was, as popular writers of the decade perceived, altering the way in which demand for goods made itself felt on producers, as well as the way in which producers and advertisers could shape the pattern and rhythm of demand. The success of Volkswagen as well as of other German consumer goods producers was related to their ability to react to these modern trends. Their foreign trade was almost entirely to markets where these trends were developing most rapidly in the period, and these trends themselves were an aspect of the sustained buoyancy of the European market.

This buoyancy of demand for consumer goods led the upswings in production in France and Italy from 1953 and these were also the economies whose exports of consumer durables grew most rapidly over the decade as a whole. As a share of the value of total engineering output consumer durables rose in OEEC Europe from about 15 per cent in 1953 to about one-fifth in 1959. This figure probably understates the contribution they were making, for the relative price of most consumer durables fell in the 1950s while that of capital goods rose.[61] The yearly increase in the value of deliveries of consumer goods at current prices by European engineering industries between 1951 and 1955 was 16 per cent and between 1956 and 1960 11.6 per cent. Over the second period it was much greater than the comparable figure for increases in deliveries of capital goods, 7.4 per cent.[62] As with cars, any loss of output caused by a loss of potential exports, would have retarding repercussions on economic growth.

Across the whole range of British and German manufacturing it seems therefore probable that if a greater share of Britain's foreign trade had been directed towards western Europe this would have done something to mitigate the slow rate of productivity improvement which was the general cause of the inability of British manufacturers to compete. If this conclusion is acceptable, the national strategy on which the United Kingdom finally settled after the demotion of the Bretton Woods agreements, while it did make room for Britain and Germany in a multilateral world order, did so by impeding the growth of Britain's own prosperity.

---

[61] OEEC, *The Engineering Industries in Europe 1959–60* (Paris, 1960).
[62] OECD, *The Engineering Industries in North America – Europe – Japan 1965* (Paris, 1965).

STERLING, THE DOLLAR AND THE WORLD ORDER

If national strategy was so commercially unpropitious, at what was it really aimed? Were its commercial choices influenced by other, less purely commercial, considerations? It seems a curiously incomplete view to have concentrated so much effort on returning to a multilateral world while doing so little to ease western Europe's path in the same direction.

In part it can be attributed to bureaucratic compartmentalization within government. International settlements machinery was a matter for the Overseas Finance Section of the Treasury and for the Bank of England. Policy reached the chancellor through that route. The Foreign Office and the Economic Section of the Treasury could comment only from outside the chain of policy development. More damagingly, commerce belonged to the Board of Trade, so that commercial policy had little connection with that same chain of policy-making until the chancellor himself had accepted policy positions within his own more influential ministry. While R.A. Butler was chancellor he had little interest in and less enthusiasm for the insistence of smaller continental western European countries on tariff reduction in Europe, for such ideas cut athwart the British strategy of targeting American tariffs first, nor for the insistence of all other OEEC members on common trade rules as an essential aspect of an inter-European settlements mechanism, nor, most emphatically, for the idea of a much more highly formalized trade regime between the Six.

These administrative inefficiencies, however, could not easily have persisted had there not been a pervasive underestimation of the economic effects and political consequences of western Europe's great trade boom over the same years. In putting together a bold strategy to replace the Bretton Woods road to the one multilateral world, the first post-war Conservative government failed to take full enough account of the very rapid growth in inter-west-European trade and of the commodity structure of those trades that were growing. In so doing, they offered to western Europe an ever less satisfactory role in that strategy.

As far as Britain was concerned the Marshall Plan was at first merely a temporary interruption in the process of making the Bretton Woods agreements the foundation of a functioning worldwide economic order based on rules formulated jointly by Britain and the United States and in which Britain took second place only to the USA. But once the Marshall Plan had established the integration of western Europe as a priority of American foreign policy it was difficult to stop this concept taking on a very ambitious and, in its impact on Britain, an unwelcome definition. Several officials in the ECA and the State Department hoped entirely to remake the Old World in the image of the New, using the leverage of American aid to create a United States of Western Europe.[63] Perhaps

---

[63] M.J. Hogan, *The Marshall Plan. America, Britain, and the Reconstruction of Western Europe, 1947–1952* (Cambridge, 1987); A.S. Milward, *The Reconstruction of Western Europe, 1945–1952* (London, 1984).

because it appealed so strongly to an idealized image of America's own national history that served as an increasingly useful myth as the Cold War intensified, the idea persisted, even after the agenda for European integration had been captured by the Schuman Plan. American policy for western Europe became fixed. It was to be encouraged to become a politically and economically integrated area which would serve as a bulwark of capitalist society and prosperity, an outer defensive bastion of the United States. Although after 1949 attempts to force the United Kingdom into that arrangement came to an end for some time, American ambitions for western Europe nevertheless led the United States to a view of the future world order which was in several important respects incompatible with Britain's multilateral ambitions.

During the Marshall Plan American officials in the ECA made constant strenuous efforts to liberalize trade and foreign exchanges in Western Europe. These achieved a breakthrough in 1950 with the establishment of the European Payments Union (EPU), a central clearing mechanism for trade settlements between OEEC members in which they agreed within defined limits to make their currencies transferable for trade purposes. The EPU was a multilateral mechanism, replacing the network of bilateral agreements which had promoted and financed the growth of intra-western European foreign trade since 1945. National currencies had to be made freely transferable between central banks up to the limits set out in the agreement for the settlement of current account deficits and surpluses. The settlements were made not directly between central banks themselves, but through the medium of a multilateral clearing house, the Bank of International Settlements (BIS) in Basle. The limits within which currency transfers had to be automatically made in settlement were expressed by initial currency quotas, allotted to each member-state on the basis of the estimated value of its foreign trade.[64] These, together with $350 million allotted from Marshall Aid, made up the working capital of the EPU. Deficits were settled monthly by multilateral compensations between the various debts and surpluses, carried out by the BIS in terms of the EPU's own unit of account, the écu, equal in value to the American dollar.

The terms on which overall net deficits had to be settled were far more generous than under earlier international multilateral payments systems such as the gold exchange standard of the 1920s. An initial tranche of 20 per cent of each country's original quota had to be provided as credit to potential trade debtors. After that initial tranche, debtors paid on a sliding scale in which the proportion of gold or dollars that they were required to pay in settlement of their debt increased and the proportion of their national currency decreased with each successive tranche of the quota. When the debt was between 20 and 40 per cent of the original quota it was necessary to make 20 per cent of the settlement in

---

[64] There is a full account of the operations of the EPU in G.L. Rees, *Britain and the Postwar European Payments System* (Cardiff, 1963).

gold/dollars. When the debt reached more than 80 per cent of the original quota it was necessary to settle up to 80 per cent in gold or dollars, and only once the quotas were exhausted did settlement have to be made entirely in hard currency.

Although the aim of these rules was to provide a progressive disincentive to countries to run trade deficits, the volume of credit which they allowed was still much greater than that which IMF could make available to its members. Furthermore, it was a negotiating machinery. The Management Board of EPU reported to the Executive Committee of OEEC and it was supposed to follow the same cooperative methods. With agreement, a debtor could increase its import barriers without question of retaliation. The Federal Republic, which ran almost immediately into a debt that exceeded its quotas when the EPU began operations, was actively encouraged to raise barriers to imports under the supervision of the other members. Internal economic equilibrium could thus be more protected and adjustments to trade flows made more gradually than the Bretton Woods agreements had originally intended. Concerned though they had been by the question of post-war employment, the negotiators at Bretton Woods had not envisaged the range of other interventionist policies which made it more difficult for states to maintain their currencies in the strict alignment which Bretton Woods demanded. More credit in international settlements and tolerance of trade restrictions became the West European answer to this dilemma.

The Americans, especially the Treasury and the Federal Reserve, would have preferred harder settlement rules. Their first priority, however, was to bring bilateralism to an end and through the medium of multilateral settlements machinery promote a further stage in European integration. At the outset some ECA officials hoped that EPU would be the start of a rapid progress towards a common European currency and a European central bank. In the course of the negotiation the tenacity with which each economy defended its own national interest deprived the EPU agreement of virtually any commitment to the political integration which the United States had hoped it would promote.

Sterling was by far the most important currency in Western Europe in 1950 and the United Kingdom by far the biggest trader. It made no sense if sterling was not included in the EPU. The including of it meant that all the political implications which America had at first seen in the agreement had to be dropped, because Britain in particular was not prepared to accept them, although there was little sign that any other country was either. All that was left of those hopes was the symbolism of calling the common unit of account, which was the equivalent of an American dollar, the écu.

The outcome of the agreement gave rise to a long-running division of opinion in the US Administration. The Treasury and the Federal Reserve took the view that the United States had betrayed its post-war policy, proclaimed by the Bretton Woods agreements, of support for worldwide multilateralism by supporting and subsidizing a soft-currency trading area in Western Europe. By allowing countries like France with persistent large trade deficits to obtain international credit on relatively easy terms the United States had now become a party, the US Treasury argued, to postponing the achievement of a sound international economic order. For the State Department, on the other side, there was a more important immediate objective. 'We felt', the Department argued before the National Advisory Council on International Monetary and Financial Problems (NAC), 'that EPU combined with the trade liberalization program was a step towards the US objective of west European unification.'[65] This division of opinion was to persist. The State Department and the successor agencies of the ECA were to continue to support almost every manifestation of European integration, usually exaggerating its significance as a step towards political union. The Treasury was to continue to question whether this policy was fully in accord with America's own economic interest. But the State Department had the powerful support of the presidency. In retrospect the view of the US financial authorities looks mistaken. The Bretton Woods agreements, while they had devoted much effort to making an international system of trade and payments which was compatible with full-employment policies, had taken no account of how the system of fixed exchange rates which they introduced could be maintained when so many other policies and policy instruments were going to be employed at will by national governments.

From the British perspective, while the EPU provided shelter and currency transferability after the shock of convertibility's failure, it also meant membership of a settlements mechanism which was built on regional trade discrimination and not on the worldwide multilateralism which had so appealed as a strategy at Bretton Woods. Under the Labour governments this was seen as having temporary advantages. When in 1950 the chancellor of the exchequer Hugh Gaitskell modified Britain's strong initial objections to the ECA proposals for a payments union and agreed that Britain should join EPU, he did so on two grounds. One was the rapid improvement in that year in the size of the reserves. The other was his growing awareness that the settlement terms of EPU would in fact support a defence of the British balance of payments against external pressures.[66] In this, he showed a well-judged foresight. In return for a temporary liberalization of import controls against western European exports in 1950, as part of the OEEC programme of trade liberalization Britain was able in the 1951–2 balance of payments crisis to run a deficit with the EPU of £540 million ($192.8 million). Under the previous system

[65] US T, EUR/9/12/v.1, 'The Future of EPU and the OEEC Trade Liberalization Programme', National Advisory Council Staff Document no. 485, 26 December 1950.
[66] P.M. Williams (ed.), *The Diary of Hugh Gaitskell 1945–1956* (London, 1983), pp. 186 ff.

of bilateral trade the gold outflow would have been much higher. Nor could the IMF have provided help on this scale.

This did not stop the Conservative government which took power in the middle of the crisis from formulating plans which might mean leaving EPU. These plans went back to 1949 when a Treasury team led by Sir Leslie Rowan had had lengthy official talks with US Treasury officials about their mutual interest in the restoration of a multilateral payments system.[67] While ECA officials were putting together plans for the EPU, Rowan and the US Treasury were discussing the possibility of a currency union between Britain and the United States.[68] Their objective was the speediest possible restoration of sterling's convertibility into dollars. The ideas pursued on the United Kingdom Treasury side in these talks were developed into proposals which Rowan and the governor of the Bank of England put before the new chancellor of the exchequer, R.A. Butler, on the government's first day of office, ostensibly as a way of staunching the loss of reserves. The proposal was to make all sterling earned on current account transactions convertible into dollars for non-residents of the United Kingdom, but at the same time to abandon the Bretton Woods system of fixed exchange rates and allow the sterling rate to float. The proposals acquired the secret code name Operation Robot.[69]

The proposed break was to be made without warning. On the day when the new chancellor of the exchequer was to present his first budget to parliament he would also announce that all sterling earned on current account transactions and owned by foreign banks and individuals outside the sterling area could be converted without restriction into dollars. There was to be no prior consultation with the United States or with the IMF, let alone with other EPU member-states. The exchange rate would be allowed to float, which against the dollar at first could mean only to sink. In the initial discussion of the plan there was no indication that there would be any limits to this downward movement. But when Butler presented the secret

[67] Sir Leslie Rowan, 1908–72. Born in Ireland, the son of an Anglican clergyman. Brought up in India, and then at public school; civil servant in the Colonial Office and then principal private secretary to Churchill, 1943–5; to Attlee, 1945–7; permanent secretary and head of the Office of the Minister for Economic Affairs, 1947; senior Treasury official in Washington, 1949–51; head of the Treasury Overseas Finance Division, 1951–8; financial director, and then chairman, of the armaments firm Vickers, 1958–70; chairman of the British Council, 1971–2; captain of the England hockey team, 1938–47, playing his last match against the country in which he had been born.

[68] PRO, T 236/2400, 'Currency Union with the USA', November 1949.

[69] Sir A. Cairncross, *Years of Recovery. British Economic Policy 1945–1951* (London, 1985), pp. 234 ff. Sir Richard Austen Butler, 1909–82, later Lord Butler of Saffron Walden: son of a British civil servant in India; public school and Cambridge University. Through family connections he was elected in 1929 as one of the youngest MPs to sit in the House of Commons, in a Conservative pocket borough. Under-secretary of state for India, 1932–7; under-secretary at the Foreign Office, 1938–41; a supporter of the Munich agreements and, until the bitter end, of Neville Chamberlain; president of the Board of Education, then minister of education, 1941–45; chancellor of the exchequer, 1951–5; home secretary, 1957–62; foreign secretary, 1963–4. Married a millionairess. Described by Churchill's parliamentary private secretary as 'very, very smooth'.

plan to cabinet the proposals indicated an exchange rate floor of $2.40 below which the pound would not be allowed to fall, instead of the registered par rate existing since September 1949 of $2.80. As soon as the operation began all sterling balances held in London would be temporarily frozen. They would then be either reduced or funded into long-term debt.

The rationale of Operation Robot was a return to a long-term national strategy for Britain's future, in the face of the increasing difficulties being placed by the US government in the way of Bretton Woods. The inevitable devaluation would stimulate exports, and in particular, as one of its advocates, the Treasury official R.W. Clarke, argued, would encourage a greater quantity of exports to flow to America and Canada, where it was hoped they would successfully compete with American goods. It was, as Clarke argued, in North America that the export battle had to be fought if the decline in British economic power was to be reversed, and not in the soft-currency zones of western Europe.[70] The EPU, so the architects of the plan claimed, by creating a separate area where settlements could be made on easy terms in soft currencies diverted British exports away from hard currency markets. There would be a direct competition at the lower dollar exchange rate of the pound with American goods both in sterling area and dollar zone markets. Controls against imports from the dollar zone would be removed shortly after the introduction of dollar convertibility.

It is hard to see that proclamation of the convertibility of non-resident sterling earnings would have had much effect on dollar–sterling trade. American importers were not restrained by shortages of sterling from importing British goods. The removal of trade controls against imports priced in dollars, however, would certainly have increased their volume and, through the devaluation of the pound, their value. The commercial rationale for Robot was unconvincing. Underlying the scheme was a more general global objective, to restore sterling's reputation as an international currency. This had been the prime objective of the Bank of England in the Bretton Woods negotiations.[71] In alliance with the Treasury's Overseas Finance Division the Bank had formulated a new strategy to end the repeated balance of payments crises and restore sterling's status, and had attached to it a dubious commercial rationale.

Three balance of payments crises and three associated runs on the reserves coming so close together, in 1947, 1949 and 1951, had convinced some Treasury officials and the Bank that the policy of waiting for a position of reserve strength under existing economic policies before establishing convertibility would fail and that something bolder must be tried. If the pound could not be made convertible at the devalued par rate with the dollar set in September 1949, the basic principle of long-run fixed exchange rates established at Bretton Woods must be overturned in

[70] PRO, T 236/3240, Clarke to Rowan, 25 January 1952.
[71] L.S. Pressnell, *External Economic Policy* . . ., op. cit., pp. 262 ff.

order to retain the implicit principle of Bretton Woods that the dollar and the pound would be the two major international currencies of the post-war world. A floating exchange rate would be cheaper to support than a fixed one, for as it fell pounds would become cheaper to purchase. The rate would fall to its true level at which speculation would be a two-way bet and because pounds would be as good a reserve currency as dollars they would become worth holding at that rate.

What the real economic advantages, rather than the more general considerations of political power and prestige, of the international use of sterling in the post-war world actually were is a question about which there is little agreement. Its use in making international settlements was mainly confined to empire and Commonwealth countries, although some middle-eastern oil producers, whose output and earnings were growing rapidly, also used it. The value of the income accruing to the British economy from the use of sterling as an international currency has been estimated at widely varying levels, but the proportion which depended in the 1950s on sterling being readily convertible into dollars has generally been estimated at only about a third of the total.[72] The total value of the United Kingdom's invisible earnings in 1951 was about 40 per cent that of its commodity exports. Assuming that the international use of sterling was responsible for one-third of all invisible earnings from whatever source, it was contributing about £133.5 million ($374.1 million) in earnings. That sum was about 9.7 per cent of total earnings and 13.6 per cent of commodity earnings. As a rough guide to political choices therefore, it might have been said that to give the first priority to the financial advantage of removing restrictions on sterling would have been justified providing the commercial consequences did not entail a loss of more than 13.6 per cent of the value of exports. Of course, the strategy was long-run, so that judgement had to be based on less measurable quantities. Would it permit an increase in invisible earnings (and possibly also as its supporters implied an increase in exports) which would outweigh any loss in export earnings caused by its introduction?

A question of this kind could not be separated from questions of prestige. George Bolton, the Bank of England official with primary responsibility for the Overseas Division, who was Rowan's principal ally in the scheme and its chief advocate in the Bank, saw Robot almost wholly in terms of national prestige. To restore Britain to its role as the chief decision-making power in the international financial system after the United States was for him the only international policy which guaranteed the nation's survival in worthwhile form.[73] If reconstruction was reconstruction

---

[72] B.J. Cohen, *The Future of Sterling as an International Currency* (London, 1971), p. 201; A. Shonfield, *British Economic Policy since the War* (London, 1958), pp. 155 ff.

[73] Sir George Lewis French Bolton, 1900–82. Merchant banker and businessman with extensive interests in Latin America and Canada. Entered the Bank of England to help in the management of the Exchange Equalization Fund, 1933; executive director of IMF, 1946–52; director of the Bank of England, 1948–68; director of the BIS, 1949–57; chairman of the Bank of London and South America.

from the collapse of 1929–32, it had to mean for Britain, he believed, reconstruction of its worldwide economic role and an end to a long period since 1932 in which the City's international business activities had been at a low ebb. This was the Bank's version of the sentiment expressed by the Labour government's foreign secretary Ernest Bevin when he protested to the American under-secretary of state that Britain was 'not just another European country'.[74]

In a general sense foreign policy considerations argued in favour of re-establishing the international role of sterling as foreseen by Bretton Woods. To play a greater role than any other European country meant to have a stronger claim on advantages of cooperating closely with the United States and to hope that the Commonwealth and empire would give the extra weight and importance to British foreign policy which would mean that the relationship with the United States was not that of a mere satellite. Because the use of sterling was one of the few organic links between the whole of the Commonwealth and the United Kingdom, foreign policy interests suggested that the sterling area and its common financial arrangements should be maintained. This did not mean that there was any strong political support for extending the use of sterling in world trade and payments beyond the existing users, although on occasions ministers toyed with the idea of including France, Scandinavia and even the Netherlands in the sterling area settlements machinery. The fact remained that about a third of the value of world trade was still invoiced in sterling, and that gave workings of the international economy an immediate influence through external balances on domestic monetary policies if currency controls were weakened.

The main domestic issue on which the Conservatives had won the election was decontrol of the domestic economy. Many, like Butler, saw decontrol of the currency as the first, essential step in decontrol of the whole economy.[75] Without freedom of the money markets, derationing and the decontrol of commodities were, he thought, only a timid step forward. The chancellor and his colleagues had leanings towards the use of monetary instruments rather than fiscal measures, forecasts and plans to direct the economy. After nineteen years of an unchanging interest rate of 2 per cent, the bank rate was raised to 4 per cent in 1952. Even if the main reason for that increase was to reassure international financial circles as part of the attempt to reverse the outward flow of reserves, the subsequent further increase in 1955 was primarily intended to reduce demand. Policy was inconsistent, as also was to be the government's behaviour over Robot, but a tendency to let interest rates function as the main regulator of the domestic economy and to subjugate the domestic economy to the

---

[74] *FRUS*, 1947, III, p. 271, Meeting of under-secretary of state Clayton with members of the British cabinet, 24 June 1947.
[75] R.A. Butler, *The Art of the Possible: The Memoirs of Lord Butler* (London, 1971), pp. 160 ff.

movements of the external balance can be discerned. Dollar convertibility at a floating rate would have been a giant step in that direction.

It was precisely that which led to what appears to have been the most vigorously voiced argument against it, that of Churchill's close adviser Lord Cherwell. He argued that the deflation and unemployment that it would cause would lose the government, which had an extremely small majority, the next election. Essentially his argument was that the government could not govern without maintaining the post-war consensus of which full employment was an indispensable component. Whether that was the argument which led to the rejection of the plan in February 1952, in spite of Butler's support, is not known. Others argued against Robot on the grounds that a floating rate would constitute that very devaluation of sterling balances held by Commonwealth countries which Britain had refused to contemplate in the 1945 settlement with the Americans, and would be even worse received after the devaluation of 1949. It would, they argued, do more to weaken than strengthen Commonwealth ties. Others were alarmed that the plan was to go ahead in secret from the Americans, fearing that this would not contribute to a close association with the United States and fearing also that sterling reserves were too small to risk such an action unless they were financially supported by the United States from the outset. They were so supported inside the EPU.

The proposal was not finally rejected by the cabinet, but was postponed for further consideration. When it was again discussed in June 1952 the balance of payments crisis had been overcome by the use of import controls and the momentum had been lost. Butler later thought that its rejection was a turning-point in Britain's post-war history, committing the country to supporting a fixed exchange rate which it was able to support only at the expense of credit restrictions which slowed the rate of investment in British manufacturing by imposing periodic restrictions on the rate of growth of output, the much criticized 'stop–go' cycle. That too was the view of one of the best-known commentators on British economic policy in the period, Samuel Brittan. Even if, he argued, the floating rate was too risky in 1952, 'if the economic planners in the Treasury had come out wholeheartedly in favour of convertibility at a floating rate in, say, 1954, the whole course of subsequent British economic history might have been changed immeasurably for the better'.[76]

There was thus important argument over the impact of the convertibility strategy on domestic economic policy and welfare, but in the opposition to Robot few mentioned other than as a subsidiary matter the consequences for EPU, and through EPU for the growth of intra-west-European trade. A floating exchange rate was incompatible with the settlements mechanism in EPU. Without the participation of sterling EPU would have had much less attraction to its members, but the other members were for the most

[76] S. Brittan, *Steering the Economy* (London, 1964), p. 200.

part not in a position to establish the dollar convertibility of their currencies at a fixed rate and unwilling for political reasons to do so at a floating rate. Their chief concern was with inter-European trade and its facilitation. One probable overall consequence for British trade would be that if other EPU member-states had to treat imports from the United Kingdom as the equivalent of dollar imports, they were likely to discriminate against them, as they already did against imports from North America. Even if the consequences of a declaration of sterling convertibility could have been confined to its immediate effect on British exports to Europe these would probably have been too great to be compensated by a growth of exports to North America, even allowing for a fall in the sterling exchange rate to $2.40.

In 1952, 23 per cent of the value of British exports went to OEEC markets. North America accounted for 11 per cent. If we estimate that discriminatory trade controls over OEEC as a whole were applied against 40 per cent of manufactured exports from North America and that the same degree of discrimination would have been practised against British exports after a declaration of sterling–dollar convertibility, this would have meant a fall in the value of British exports to OEEC markets of $672 million. To recoup this by exports to North America would have required them to increase by 83 per cent. If we make a less drastic assumption, that every EPU country with a chance of establishing the convertibility of its currency into dollars would have done so and also lifted trade discrimination against dollar-good imports, that still would have left at least seven countries – Austria, Denmark, France, Greece, Italy, Norway and Turkey – which at that date had no chance of establishing convertibility. If only these countries had practised 40 per cent discrimination against British exports this would still have required an increase of 75.7 per cent ($613 million) in exports to North America to compensate. Was this really possible?

But this is to suppose that the danger to British trade would only have consisted in the possibility of exports excluded through trade discrimination by OEEC members. A greater danger surely lay in arresting the expansion of trade between the other west European countries and especially their trade with the Federal Republic. Assuming the same seven countries to have remained inconvertible and the Federal Republic to have made an attempt at Deutschmark–dollar convertibility, what then would have been the consequences? Those seven countries took 22.3 per cent of German exports in 1952. The collapse of the EPU would have meant a return to bilateral trade with a small degree of multilateral settlements where they involved merely neutral cancellations of debts as in 1948–9. Assuming that the Federal Republic lost, because of the return to bilateral settlements, 40 per cent of the value of those exports, and assuming it had tried to recoup that loss by sales to the USA and the sterling area, what would have then been the impact on British exports when Germany was trying to raise the value of its exports to dollar markets by $890 million? The question was not raised in London. But there was not room on the American market for such an expansion of sales by both countries so quickly.

In Bonn the Federal Ministry for the Economy complained frequently and strenuously in 1952 that EPU concentrated German exports too narrowly on western European markets. The generosity of its settlement terms to debtors meant that in return for these exports Germany received an excessive proportion of transferable soft European currencies and mostly in the form only of claims on exports of other EPU members. From the perspective of German businessmen, however, this was a machine for increasing the flow of their exports to expanding west European markets which might, in a stricter settlements mechanism, otherwise have had to restrict imports. France, for example, was a persistent large debtor in EPU. Exporters got their money from the government against the IOUs which government piled up in Basel, and French imports continued because IOUs could pile up.

In the United Kingdom, the Bank and the Treasury, while also interested in maximizing the inflow of hard currency and gold for British exports, were in a different position from the Federal Republic. The United Kingdom piled up a very large debt in EPU during 1951. This, of course, presented a serious obstacle to any proposal for sterling which might have led to the dissolution of EPU, if EPU without sterling would have been so unappealing to its other members as to make it no longer worthwhile. There would have been dynamic consequences from the dissolution of EPU which would have had inimical repercussions on British trade. British discrimination against continental exports was just as probable an emergency measure as continental discrimination against British exports. It was indeed included in the draft proposals for Robot that trade controls would be reimposed against any EPU countries which redirected exports to Britain in order to earn convertible sterling. This might have been a brief episode until the pound had reached a stable exchange rate, but the damage would have been done. EPU in 1951 was the settlements mechanism for more than half the total value of world trade, and also the biggest creditor to Britain in the world trading system. The effect of its dissolution would surely have been to slow the overall expansion of world and British trade, no matter what export successes British goods achieved in North American markets. The potential increase in invisible earnings could not have offset the unavoidable reality of a slower expansion of intra-west-European trade than that which occurred. Yet it was not until summer 1955 that British governments were to abandon the idea of a unilateral move to dollar convertibility.

When Robot was finally rejected in the summer, it had become clear from the discussion in the interval after its initial rejection that there was not sufficient confidence to establish convertibility without some form of international support. What followed was the Collective Approach, which was discussed with Commonwealth members in November and December 1952. It responded to the criticisms of Robot by envisaging a much more managed and restricted float, and thus a smaller potential devaluation. And it was no longer a plan for a sudden, unannounced move to sterling–dollar convertibility but an attempt to bring other currencies to convertibility at the same time as sterling. Nevertheless the idea of a unilateral move which some but by no means all OEEC members could follow was not renounced and any element of cooperation with western European countries was subordinate to cooperation with the USA and the Commonwealth.

In British eyes the United States was being offered a new start, a renegotiation of Bretton Woods which would avoid the weaknesses of the original agreement. The American government was to be asked to provide a line of credit, as with the 1945 dollar loan, to support a return to sterling–dollar convertibility of the same restricted kind as Operation Robot had intended. Convertibility would be offered only to non-residents of the sterling area and only for transactions on current account. The rate would be 'flexible'. The sterling–dollar exchange rate would be allowed to fluctuate within wider fixed limits on each side of the IMF par rate. These were sometimes indicated as likely to be as much as 5 per cent either side of par, but the proposals eventually settled on a 3 per cent permissible fluctuation in either direction. Such margins were still a big change from the Bretton Woods rule that rates must be kept within 1 per cent of par.

American financial support for these proposals, it was envisaged, could either be extended between the two governments directly in the form of help in funding the sterling balances held by other countries, or take the form of an increase in the capital of the IMF, part of which would be set aside specifically to guarantee sterling reserves against any rush to convert sterling into dollars. The proposed size of this 'exchange support fund', as the Bank of England called it when the proposals for the Collective Approach were put before the Commonwealth prime ministers and officials, was variable.[77] The assumption was that a credit of about $2,500 million was needed to ensure a safe transition to convertibility. If the second procedure were adopted this might mean an increase of the order of $3,000 million to $5,000 million in IMF funds, because it would also be necessary to back the convertibility of the other European currencies which would be made convertible at the same time.[78]

There were other proposals, some originating from Rowan's 1949 talks with the US Treasury, which tried to link the sterling area and the dollar zone more closely while providing dollar support for sterling. The most important was for some form of long-run institutionalization of American financial involvement in the empire and Commonwealth. One

[77] BOE, OV 44/52, 'Borrowing from the IMF etc', 11 November 1952.
[78] PRO, T 230/268, Note by Rowan, 'Note for Meeting with Humphrey', n.d.

of the strongest political objections to going ahead with Robot had been that the value of claims represented by the sterling balances was so much larger than the value of the sterling area gold and dollar reserves in London that the operation would have been too dangerous. One of the proposals put to the Commonwealth conference which accepted the Collective Approach was that in order to increase the dollar earnings of the sterling area the Americans would be asked to increase their raw material purchases from the empire and Commonwealth for strategic stockpiles. They would also be asked to lower their trade restrictions against sterling area and British exports. The British declaration of formal convertibility for non-resident sterling earned on current account would be eventually followed, although it was not clear exactly when, by the removal of the commercial barriers against dollar exports to the sterling area, both post-war dollar discrimination and the imperial tariff preferences of the 1930s. This was the grand commercial bargain with the USA put into somewhat more pragmatic terms.

A weaker alternative to this grand bargain had been actively considered by the foreign secretary, Ernest Bevin, and pushed on to his officials from 1947 onwards as the vision of Bretton Woods receded and the Marshall Plan began to demand increasing British participation in forms of European integration. A British–French imperial commercial union, involving perhaps a merger of their imperial preferences, might be a defence, Bevin thought, against these American pressures and might exercise, also, a sufficient commercial threat against the USA to bring it to the tariff bargaining table in a more concessionary mood. A formal military alliance with France had been an early step towards post-war safety and it was less than a decade since the offer of mutual citizenship had been made to try to keep France fighting in the Second World War. In the last throes of France's decision in 1956 to sign the Treaty of Rome the government of Guy Mollet would raise this alternative possibility, perhaps testing whether it might not be politically and economically a more prudent choice than entry into a common market with Germany. Diplomatic historians have had difficulty in determining how seriously this alternative was taken in London, although all agree that it rose and fell in importance as the terms of the USA's commitment to providing for British security rose and fell.

The Franco-British alternative was also an economic strategy for the future. Its economic appeal to France was the sharp reduction it would bring in the cost and difficulty of obtaining raw materials from the sterling area, France's largest source of supply. For Bevin, with his fits of exasperation at the USA's tergiversations and what he saw as its relegation of the United Kingdom's status as an ally, it was a return to ideas he had often publicized in the 1930s. It had the immediate advantage of dispelling the threat which European integration posed to any British unilateral, one-world strategy. It has to be said, however, that neither his ministerial colleagues nor his officials displayed anywhere near the same enthusiasm for this strategy as he did between 1947 and 1950. Ultimately it was for economic reasons, not for those of security, that they were proved right. Neither country was prepared to make the imperial economic concessions which could have brought the idea to fulfilment.[79]

The EPU had been created for two years in the first place. When the issue of its continuation and the renewal of the American capital contribution to it came before the National Advisory Council in Washington in 1952, the US Treasury's scepticism about the value of the agreement was matched by that of the Federal Reserve, the Export-Import Bank, and the Department of Commerce. But what carried the day was the State Department's argument that 'there may be a real move towards federation in the next fifteen months'.[80] The integration of Western Europe remained essential to the perceived national security of the United States; any attempt to establish an international trade and payments system which would be divisive in its effects on Western Europe would not be supported.

The change of Administration to the Eisenhower presidency raised British expectations that the days of the Marshall Plan were gone for good, but also meant that no meeting could be arranged between the two governments until March 1953. In spite of the orthodox financial rhetoric of the Republican election campaign and the denunciations of foreign aid, it was to transpire that the view of America's foreign policy interests had not altered. It would have been impossible for the new US Administration to have persuaded Congress to make as much money available to Britain, once more, or to the IMF as the Collective Approach requested. At the end of January 1953 this was already clear to the British ambassador.[81] At the annual IMF/World Bank meeting in September 1952 the American representatives had argued against any increase in the IMF's capital.[82] There was no sign that this would change. The official American position on the eve of the March 1953 meeting with the chancellor of the exchequer

---

[79] S. Greenwood in *Britain and European Cooperation since 1945* (Oxford, 1992) and *The Alternative Alliance: Anglo-French Relations Before the Coming of NATO 1944–1948* (London, 1996) argues that Bevin pursued the French alliance seriously, for defence and security purposes and that in that respect policy towards Europe before NATO was positive in its intent. There is much in J.W. Young, *Britain, France and the Unity of Europe 1945–1951* (Leicester, 1984), which lends support to this view. A. Bullock, *Ernest Bevin. Foreign Secretary 1945–1951* (London, 1983) takes a different view, implying that it was manoeuvring designed to bring pressure to bear on the USA to guarantee British security and thus America was always Britain's and Bevin's true love. None of them shows any interest in the choice as an element of economic strategy for Britain's future, as though such strategies were an entirely subordinate aspect of the life and death of nations.

[80] FRC, RG 56, National Advisory Council on International Monetary and Financial Problems, Meeting no. 190, 13 March 1952.

[81] PRO, T 236/3521, Makins to FO, 28 January 1953.

[82] *FRUS*, 1952–4, vol. 1, pt 1, p. 313, National Advisory Council on International Monetary and Financial Problems, Meeting no. 196.

and his team was that 'the proposal for additions to the present dollar resources of the Fund involves a number of serious difficulties'.[83]

Naturally, the staff of the IMF themselves had been pressing for a more important role for the Fund in the world economy and the Managing Director, the Swedish banker Ivar Rooth, thought that a standby loan to back sterling convertibility might be the way to achieve it. In scope and size, though, the backing requested looked more like the large stabilization loans of the 1920s than anything IMF had been set up to do. At the close of 1953 its capital was still only $3,300 million.

American objections to the Collective Approach went beyond its harmful effect on integration and the political difficulties of securing the money. They were based on the general view that the British economy was not ready to stand the strain even of the limited convertibility envisaged. The economist Frank Southard, who was primarily responsible for the Federal Reserve Board's attitude, was no friend of EPU, but even he believed the British proposals to be unsound.[84] Through their harmful impact on inter-west-European, and thus on world, trade, so the Federal Reserve concluded, the proposals if supported would only weaken the British economy still further. A brief episode in August 1952, of which the world of central bankers was well aware, suggests he was right. In that month European countries had been allowed to buy dollar commodities on London commodity markets with their own currencies. The rush to effect this kind of indirect convertibility through commodities had been so great it had had to be stopped almost at once.[85]

Before the official visit to the United States in March 1953 the Bank of England had put together a scheme which it hoped would meet American objections. An enlarged IMF, continuing to act directly elsewhere in the world as lender of last resort to other central banks, would act in Western Europe only through EPU as its intermediary.[86] But this still did not explain how EPU could survive if some of its currencies became convertible into dollars and others did not. The Bank thought that once talks with America were completed it would be possible to form a nuclear group of Western European currencies which would follow the example of sterling. In September 1952 Belgium, France and the Netherlands had been thought of as the probable members. It does not

---

[83] EL, White House Central Files 1953–61: Confidential File, Box 67, Office of the Secretary of State, Van Hollen to Hauge, 'U.S. Position for Conversation', 4 March 1953.

[84] Frank Southard, Jnr, 1907–. PhD in economics University of California, 1930; professor of economics, Cornell University, 1943–5; financial adviser to Allied Headquarters in Germany, 1948–9; associate director of research and statistics, International Section, Federal Reserve Board, 1949–62; US executive director of IMF, 1962–74. Author in 1931 of a work on American industry in Europe which has seemed more significant to scholars recently than when it was written, as well as of a little-known but very useful study of the financial policies of the liberation armies.

[85] J.C.R. Dow, *The Management of the British Economy, 1945–1960* (Cambridge, 1970), p. 85.

[86] BOE, OV 44/59, 'Note of a Meeting with Sir Leslie Rowan and others', 28 January 1953.

diminish the British presumption that they had developed plans for other people's currencies which would be divulged only after the USA had endorsed them. The head of the British delegation to OEEC, Hugh Ellis-Rees, though himself no supporter of European integration and an ardent advocate of a speedy return to sterling convertibility, poured scorn on this. It would not, he rightly predicted, be possible to interest any European country in joining the nuclear group.[87]

This advice from a friendly quarter was ignored. The Foreign Office spent some effort, unsuccessfully, in trying to get this attitude changed. It urged that there should be preliminary negotiations with intended European partners before the official talks in Washington.[88] So too did the two chief European representatives of the Mutual Security Agency (MSA), William Draper and Lincoln Gordon. Butler could not be moved.[89]

If the Americans accepted the British proposals at the March talks, the existing debt of the United Kingdom to EPU was to be converted on the dissolution of EPU into a series of bilateral debts, repayable over three years, not in gold or dollars but in the newly created convertible 'external' sterling. The moment when this would happen would be left to British choice, but the internal British discussion seems to have assumed that it would be at a time when the Federal Republic would be able to follow the lead and establish Deutschmark–dollar convertibility. The assumption seems to have been that France and Benelux would do the same, the Scandinavian countries would peg on sterling, and the United States would be left to look after the so-called structural debtors in EPU – Austria, Greece, Iceland and Turkey – by continuing to pay off their debts through military and other dollar aid transfers as it was already doing. The only area of doubt in this scenario was Italy, 'not a suitable candidate for inclusion in the Collective Approach'.[90] If the lira was not made convertible, trade between Italy and the other EPU members would, it was assumed, become more difficult, would perhaps even have to be carried out once more by bilateral agreements. In London, this future scenario did not perturb; in Washington it was probably sufficient by itself to make the talks pointless.

When the British delegation arrived in March in Washington it spent the first day exchanging formalities. On the second day Butler and his officials were simply told by secretary of state, Dulles, before any working talks with Treasury officials could begin, that British proposals ran directly counter to American foreign policy and 'that it might be more profitable to spend some time in trying to get the pattern of production and trade

[87] PRO, T 236/3368, Ellis-Rees to Sir H. Brittain, 19 September 1952.
[88] BOE, OV 44/59, 'Note of a Meeting with Sir Leslie Rowan and others at H. M. Treasury', 28 January 1953.
[89] PRO, T 230/268, Meeting of Butler with Draper and Gordon, 29 January 1953.
[90] BOE, OV 44/52, Memo by Copleston, 'The Collective Approach and EPU etc.', 7 November 1952.

better before embarking on convertibility'.[91] Butler was ready to break off talks even before the conference next morning with Treasury officials, although he must have expected kinder treatment from them than from State. In the event Treasury secretary George Humphrey was presented with a copy of a lengthy memorandum outlining British proposals, which he does not appear to have read with any great attention, and the talks descended at once to the merely technical level.[92] On the way back Butler and his officials stopped for talks in the Canadian Department of Finance. The Canadians, as disappointed as the British with what they saw as a lack of American leadership, said gloomily that 'some of the officials in the previous Administration had done some homework on the move towards multilateral trade. It was a depressing exercise merely concerned with the enlargement of regional blocs.'[93]

Had the United States provided the sums asked for, would Britain have actually taken the decision to declare sterling–dollar convertibility at that stage? That would surely have depended on a modification of the terms for dissolving EPU. The United Kingdom remained the greatest financial beneficiary of EPU. Its financial position there had improved rapidly from summer 1952, but not so much as to pay off the debts accumulated in the previous year (table 7.6). One reason for the large size of the financial support requested from the Americans was the overhanging sterling debt which would have been due to European creditors. The EPU had been renewed in summer 1952 for only one year, because the United Kingdom had refused to renew for longer. On the date for its next renewal in June 1953 the cumulative sterling debt to it was $1,105 million. The Bank of England, despite the rebuff in Washington, wanted to renew the EPU agreement for no longer than six months. But the UK Treasury could see no alternative to renewal for a full year, since the existing terms for dissolving EPU would mean immediate large gold payments, to which would be added the gold payments for imports currently purchased against EPU credits.

Even with a debt of that size the United Kingdom was still far from the point where the whole of the last tranche of its EPU debt need be settled in gold. If the size of this credit is compared with the possible extent of credit through the IMF the ambiguities in Britain's position can be understood. Members' purchases of currency from IMF were limited

[91] BOE, OV 44/60, Record of a meeting at the State Department on 5 March 1953. A fuller account of the talks is in J.J. Kaplan and G. Schleiminger, *The European Payments Union. Financial Diplomacy in the 1950s* (Oxford, 1989), pp. 175 ff.

[92] George Magoffin Humphrey, 1891–1970. Son of a lawyer. LLB, University of Michigan. Company lawyer. Became a hero of American industry by rescuing the company founded by the notorious Cleveland political boss Mark Hanna, 1929; chairman of the Industrial Advisory Committee on Germany, 1948; secretary to the Treasury, 1953; where he became famous for denouncing his own 1957 budget as immoral. A hunting and fishing crony of President Eisenhower.

[93] BOE, OV 44/60, Record of a meeting at the Canadian Department of Finance, 13 March 1953.

to 25 per cent of their initial quota, which for Britain was roughly the equivalent of the value of 2.5 per cent of total imports or about $340 million. After three years of trade surpluses with the EPU following the bad period of 1951–2 EPU credits to Britain were still more than twice the maximum possible borrowing from the IMF. The high-handed diplomatic attitude towards the other EPU members contrasted starkly with Britain's financial weakness. It was to no small extent the generous provision made for debtors in the EPU and its non-retaliatory behaviour which was still enabling Britain to finance the consequences of the 1951 balance of payments crisis.

Bolton and Rowan saw the debts in EPU as the outcome of the distortion of world trade flows caused by the regional settlements bloc and the inclusion of the whole sterling area in it. If the USA would not accept its duty to create a single worldwide system of payments, Britain, Bolton now argued, should create 'a second-best system'; two worlds, not one. There would have to be two separate currency zones, one of which would serve the sterling area and Western Europe, with sterling as its convertible unit of account and London as its financial centre.[94] He even consoled himself with the thought that with *détente* the Soviet Union and its satellites would soon re-enter the international economy and, like the rest of Europe, would transact their business in London. Better, he thought, that the City should be the leader in a regional bloc, than that it should remain as inactive as it had had to be in the 1930s.

By gradually eliminating the controls on its transfer between different kinds of account for use in different areas of the world, sterling could be made *de facto* a freely convertible currency, even if there was to be no major international support which would give it that status *de jure*. As the Bank governor Cameron Cobbold told the US deputy Treasury secretary Randolph Burgess a year later, it was

> our desire, on which we had already made much progress, to get to a position where there was *de facto* overseas convertibility and where there was no pressure behind the dam against sterling, without saying too much about it. We should be very happy if we could allow those things to happen and help to make them happen, leaving certain policy aspects and final arrangements to be completed between Governments at the appropriate time. This seemed to us greatly preferable to a hullabaloo at an International Conference about convertibility.[95]

Bolton and Rowan put together a programme of action which projected a series of gradual changes in the controls on sterling until the different

[94] ibid., Record of a meeting in the Treasury, 10 March 1953.
[95] BOE, OV 44/63, Governor's Note, 3 May 1954. William Randolph Burgess, b. 1889. PhD in Economics, Columbia University. Vice-president of the Federal Reserve Board, 1936–8; National City Bank of New York, 1938–52; under-secretary in the Treasury, 1953–7; permanent representative on NATO, 1957–61; author of several works on money.

Table 7.6 Net annual surpluses (+) or deficits (−) within EPU, 1951–8 (1 July–30 June) ($ million)

	1950–1	1951–2	1952–3	1953–4	1954–5	1955–6	1956–7	1957–8	1958*
Austria	−104	−38	+42	+106	−103	−6	+23	−4	+24
Belgium/Luxembourg	+236	+509	−33	−55	+80	+222	+14	+153	+66
Denmark	−68	+46	−17	−92	−94	+4	−43	+10	−1
France	+194	−602	−417	−149	+115	−180	−969	−576	−317
German Federal Republic	−281	+584	+260	+518	+296	+584	+1,336	+826	+350
Greece	−140	−83	−28	−40	−27	+40	+5	+7	−49
Iceland	−7	−6	−4	−5	−2	−4	−3	−3	−9
Italy	−30	+194	−223	−210	−225	−125	−94	+219	+73
Netherlands	−270	+477	+139	−42	+84	−62	−36	+86	+181
Norway	−80	+21	−59	−61	−70	−27	+41	−78	−30
Portugal	+59	+28	−23	−19	−59	−33	−38	−54	−37
Sweden	−59	+284	−44	−37	−104	+6	−38	−30	+11
Switzerland	+11	+158	+85	+73	+10	−66	+111	−189	+20
Turkey	−64	−96	−50	−94	−38	−27	−83	−50	−14
United Kingdom	+604	−1,476	+371	+107	+136	−327	−225	−317	−267

* 1 July to 27 December

Source: EPU, Management Board, *Final Report on the Operations of the European Payments Union* (1959), p. 36

kinds of accounts in which countries were allowed to hold it would have been reduced to two, dollar-account sterling for use in the dollar zone and transferable-account sterling for use elsewhere.[96] At that point the only restraint upon sterling's convertibility into dollars would be the controls on movement between these two kinds of accounts and the remaining trade controls against imports from the dollar zone. This programme would be linked to a programme of decontrol in the domestic economy, which would include the reopening of gold, foreign exchange and commodity markets in London. For the restoration of this *de facto* non-resident convertibility there was also a projected timetable; it was intended to be spread over two years. It should, though, be noted that nothing tangible was proposed for eliminating import quotas against dollar zone exports; it was finance and invisibles that mattered more than trade.

Although such a programme could be unilateral, in the sense that the timing of each particular step could be decided in London alone, where it involved the relaxation of trade controls against European exports this was clearly something that had to be undertaken with reference to the OEEC Trade Liberalization Programme. In fact an initiative of that kind, when France was in no position to match it, would put the United Kingdom in a favourable light in Washington compared with the Six. At the first OEEC ministerial meeting after the Washington talks Britain announced the removal of many of the quotas imposed in the 1951–2 balance of payments crisis and pressed for a general resumption of trade liberalization. Taking the lead in the resumption of trade liberalization was to be associated with taking the lead in steering EPU away from its role as a soft-currency zone. If the settlement terms in EPU could be made gradually harder until all debts were settled in gold/dollars, EPU would also have achieved *de facto* convertibility. In these new circumstances, with no hope of any immediate American action to try to recreate a multilateral one-world system, the United Kingdom's second strategy for future prosperity went forward.

STERLING AND WESTERN EUROPE

Only in June 1953 did Butler and Bolton finally accept that it would be impossible 'to continue the momentum of our proposals while continuing to keep the Europeans as ignorant as they had been so far'.[97] From this point onwards the difference between the view of international reconstruction in the continental countries and in Britain emerged at its simplest and also at its most unbridgeable. Every intended member of the proposed nuclear group articulated the opposite priority from Britain. Their priority was to guarantee the post-war institutional framework for the expansion

[96]   BOE, OV 44/60, 'Programme', 26 March 1953.
[97]   ibid., Memo by Sir G. Bolton, 'Commonwealth Economic Policy Next Stage', 6 June 1953.

of intra-western European trade as the precondition of any move towards dollar convertibility. For all the Western European countries any progress towards convertibility which might involve even a temporary loss of trade was to be rejected.

This emerged most dramatically in the case of Belgium, a relatively hard-money country of which the Bank of England had the highest hopes as an ally. In the early discussions on the nature of the post-war trade and payments system Belgium had advocated a return to the gold exchange standard. Over the first two years of EPU Belgium had been its most severe critic, demanding that the settlements be hardened so that Belgian trade surpluses with Western Europe would be repaid in gold which could be used to settle Belgium's deficits with the dollar zone, and even threatening not to renew the agreement. However, the Belgian delegation to the renewal meeting in summer 1952 received last minute instructions to support renewal for two years, although the British were insisting that it should be for only one.[98] The Bank of Belgium was silenced at the crucial moment. The Belgian government regarded as imperative the need to sustain the flow of exports, 62 per cent of the total value of which went to the EPU area. When the Managing Board of EPU, under British prompting, first discussed convertibility in the autumn and produced a draft report, Belgium argued strongly against any early move and pressed instead for a return to the Trade Liberalization Programme as the first priority.[99]

By the time of their official talks with Britain on the Collective Approach the Belgians had accepted, albeit with reservations, the Beyen Plan for a customs union as part of the EDC treaty. Enforceable commercial rules of the kind which existed in EPU and on which the Beyen Plan insisted much more strongly had, the Belgian delegation declared, to be an integral part of any post-war payments system.[100] That did not mean that they were any less eager for progress to global convertibility, but this had to be associated with trade rules which ensured the sustained growth of Western Europe's trade. To progress towards 'flexible' dollar convertibility before the customs union was established might make its achievement more uncertain. Ultimately, so foreign minister Van Zeeland thought, a guaranteed framework for foreign trade over the whole of Western Europe might develop. If it did, but only then, EPU could be encouraged to evolve into a monetary authority for the area akin to the Federal Reserve Board.[101]

Not surprisingly, the primacy of trade was made even more explicit by Beyen himself during the official talks with the Netherlands. 'The EPU', he was reported as telling Butler, 'though temporary, had been very successful

---

[98] PRO, T 230/210, OEEC Delegation to FO, 27 June 1952.
[99] PRO, T 230/213, Memo by Ellis-Rees, 'Convertibility: The European Attitude', 4 November 1952.
[100] PRO, T 236/35818, Ellis-Rees to Rowan, 13 May 1953; ibid., 'Record of conversation on 15/16 May 1953 with Belgian experts'.
[101] MAECE, 17.771/1, 'Entretien du 4 mai 1953, Van Zeeland, Meurice, Erhard'.

and whatever our [the British] plans were they should not involve any loss of the advantages of EPU.'[102] Suardus Posthuma, the Dutch representative on the EPU Management Board, published the same argument.[103] Butler's statement to Beyen that 'for the United Kingdom a flexible rate was inevitable', can be weighed against the remark in a book later published by the governor of the Dutch central bank that the Netherlands had 'never considered establishing a fluctuating exchange rate'. The reason was that 'a fluctuating rate would constitute a very severe obstacle for export industries'.[104]

When the Collective Approach was being drawn up in September 1952 the most important member of the proposed nuclear group had been France. As the French balance of payments deteriorated rapidly this idea disappeared and by spring 1953 there was no hope that the talks with France could produce any support for the British programme. There were strong supporters of convertibility there, even those who advocated a return to the gold standard as a check on inflationary domestic policies. When they presented their case in a debate in the Conseil Economique in 1952, the governor of the Bank of France Wilfried Baumgartner, apparently summarizing official policy, rejected any such step other than in the context of a joint agreement between all Western European countries to achieve convertibility by gradual alignment of their domestic policies. Mendès-France, who had led the French team to the 1952 IMF meetings, had argued there that IMF should support EPU as the soundest basis for restoring a wider multilateral system.[105] In the official talks on the Collective Approach 'a good deal of the preoccupation of the French officials appeared to be whether any wider system of trade rules could be made to operate in such a way that it did not degenerate into a process of disguised bilateral bargaining'.[106]

Official policy in France was in fact flatly opposed to the Collective Approach, even though in public it was appropriate to take a more conciliatory line.[107] Convertibility of sterling would have created a sterling payments problem for France of the same dimensions as its dollar payments problem, because of the large volume and essential nature of its raw material imports from the sterling area. France was at the time of the talks in April 1953 almost as big a debtor to EPU as the United Kingdom.

---

[102] BOE, OV 84/15, 'Meeting between chancellor of the exchequer and Beyen', 18 June 1953.
[103] S. Posthuma, 'Note on Convertibility', *Economia Internazionale*, vol. 6, no. 3, 1953.
[104] M.N. Holtrop, *Money in an Open Economy* (Leiden, 1972), p. 219. 'The fixed parity no doubt sets a limit to the effectiveness of a monetary policy that would prefer to aim at internal equilibrium only. This, however, is the price that has to be paid for enjoying the advantages of international integration.'
[105] J.K. Horsefield, *The International Monetary Fund 1945–1965*, 3 vols (Washington, 1969), vol. 1, p. 306.
[106] BOE, OV 44/60, Discussions with French officials, 24/25 April 1953.
[107] MAE, DE-CE, Service de coopération économique. Memorandum, 14 June 1953.

There remained the Federal Republic. In summer 1952 when the first ideas for the Collective Approach were formed it had barely emerged from a balance of payments crisis which had threatened to wreck EPU as soon as it had begun and in which it had been shored up only by EPU and American aid. By the end of 1952, however, German reserves were larger than those of France. They would continue to climb until in 1955 they overtook the value of sterling reserves and by the end of the decade were more than twice their value. Roughly one-third of the increase of $18,000 million in gold and dollars held outside the United States between 1950 and 1960, much of it gold flowing out from the USA itself, accrued to the Federal Republic. Nothing could have better demonstrated that commercial success was the basis of financial strength, for Germany's reserves grew through the growth of manufactured exports.

Erhard was eager even in autumn 1952 to cap his programme of internal decontrol with the decontrol of the currency. As soon as reserves began to increase he asked the central bank, the Bank Deutscher Länder (BDL), to consider setting a timetable for the establishment of a convertible Deutschmark and even for the removal of controls on capital movements. Although the Federal Republic had recorded a balance of payments surplus for 1951, this was only due to the inflow of American aid, and in the central bank's view capital inflows would still be needed to reach a positive balance for some time to come. There could be no running the risk of provoking any outward capital movement through public discussion of a convertible mark.[108] 'Recognition that the removal of exchange controls is an ultimate objective means the clear realization that the objective is unattainable now and in the foreseeable future', the bank told Erhard in August 1952.[109] If the goal was convertibility, so Erhard was advised within his own ministry, it should be reached not only by financial decontrol but by commercial agreements which would increase the flow of German trade.[110] The implication was that a programme to reach dollar–Deutschmark convertibility, while not necessarily depending on following the lead of sterling, could certainly not be unilateral.[111]

The issue was referred to an inter-ministerial committee. There, the British objective of currency convertibility for non-resident accounts only was criticized as being primarily intended to restore sterling's international role rather than to promote world commerce. The Germans had no ambition to make the Deutschmark an international reserve currency and the general trend of advice to the minister was that the first purpose

---

[108] O. Emminger, *D-Mark, Dollar, Währungskrisen: Erinnerungen eines ehemaligen Bundesbankpräsidenten* (Stuttgart, 1986), p. 22.

[109] BA, B102/12650/2, Homann to Erhard, 4 August 1952.

[110] ibid., Abschrift Schöne, 'Lockerung bzw. Beseitigung der Devisenzwangwirtschaft', 23 July 1952.

[111] The subsequent attitude of the Bundesbank to currency convertibility is studied in M. Dickhaus, *Die Bundesbank in Westeuropäischen Wiederaufbau: die internationale Währungspolitik der Bundesrepublik Deutschland 1948 bis 1958* (Munich, 1996).

of currency convertibility must be to facilitate commodity trade. This objective, the Council of Economic Advisers of the Ministry for the Economy argued, needed in turn an agreed set of commercial 'rules of the game'.[112] These rules should link the progress of exchange decontrol within Western Europe to the progress of the OEEC Trade Liberalization Programme, at first by forcing Britain and France to return to their level of trade liberalization of 1950. This meant retaining as the main forum for commercial and exchange rate policy OEEC and EPU.

In a country where even the central bank perceived the currency as primarily an instrument of commerce, it was unthinkable that the opinions of industrial exporters could be ignored. When consulted, the industrial association Deutscher Industrie-und Handelstag was even more insistent than the BDL that any division between convertible and inconvertible currencies within EPU was a threat to German exports.[113] This was to be a consistent position of German industrialists. Their collective organization, the Bundesverband der deutscher Industrie, made the same argument two years later. Anything, they argued, which broke up the EPU would hold back the rapidly growing exports to EPU members who would no longer be able to pay for them with the same ease.[114]

On leaving Washington in March 1953 Butler and his team had left behind a draft of their ideas. Their intention was to keep up the pressure on the Americans. At first they were encouraged by the nomination of Lewis Douglas, the US ambassador to Britain at the time of the Marshall Plan, to work with the NAC to study the question. Douglas, however, had no staff of his own and could work only within existing agencies. Rowan, visiting Washington again in April, had 'depressing' talks with US Treasury officials. Randolph Burgess, Humphrey's deputy as treasury secretary, explained that while he was personally in favour of expanding IMF's capital to support sterling–dollar convertibility when the opportune moment came, because of the balance of political power in Washington no support could yet be expected. 'Quite clearly', wrote Rowan, 'in his mind there is no question of our ideas materializing in the next year or so.'[115] When Bolton went to Washington a month later the Federal Reserve told him that majority opinion in the Federal Reserve and the Treasury was also against flexible rates.

In the event, Douglas's recommendations fell well short of what the United Kingdom hoped. He tried to reconcile progress towards convertibility with the more immediate international concerns of the Administration: saving the underdeveloped economies from communism by promoting their

---

[112] ibid., Memo Karl Albrecht, 'Aufzeichnung über den Stand der Diskussionen zur Frage der Reform der EZU . . .', 17 January 1953.
[113] BA, B102/12651/2, IFO, 'Zur Frage der Konvertierbarkeit der D-Mark', May 1953.
[114] BA, B102/12653/3, Bundesverband der deutscher Industrie, 'Die Handelspolitik in der Übergangsphase zur Konvertibilität', 7 June 1955.
[115] BOE, OV 44/60, Report on a visit to Washington by Rowan, 19–21 April 1953.

economic development (as cheaply as possible); encouraging European integration; and avoiding any increase in protectionism or a return to bilateral trade. He supported the idea that New York banking houses should participate in loans to underdeveloped sterling area economies. If the Export–Import Bank guaranteed the transferability of the loan proceeds into dollars and the British government guaranteed the exchange rate, this would be a further step towards *de facto* sterling–dollar convertibility. His other recommendations were also variations on British proposals. They were: that the USA should time its purchasing of sterling area commodities for stockpiling with a view to stabilizing the sterling–dollar rate; that it should be prepared at times to waive interest and amortization payments on the post-war loan to Britain for the same purpose; and that it should help financially to maintain British troops in other parts of the world, because they were cheaper than American troops. It effectively already did as much with French troops in Indo-China. He also supported the British requests for lower American tariffs and more simplified customs procedures.[116] But on the central point for the British side, whether these policies should be pursued independently of EPU or only in conjunction with it, Douglas refused to commit himself.

His hesitation was an indication of the continuing division of opinion in Washington about the future of the world economic order. In March it had been easy enough to take a consistent view of the Collective Approach. It had not offered the USA very much: an end to imperial preferences at a date not specified, a promise to enter, also at an unspecified date, into a programme to remove quotas worldwide, and an immediate abandonment of discrimination against imports of dollar goods by former holders of what would become 'external' sterling. In return the USA had been expected not only to raise yet another large loan to support sterling but to begin dismantling its own extensive protection. It was also expected to alter the main lines of its foreign policy in Europe since the start of the Marshall Plan. It was only necessary to think about the task of explaining this to Congress in order to unite and say no.

On the other hand, the basic argument of the British proposals, that EPU was not the way back to Bretton Woods and that American support for integration was strengthening a discriminatory trading bloc, did find supporters in Washington. Trade liberalization between OEEC members left their quotas still in place against the USA, while their intra-trade grew. What should be encouraged instead, Treasury Department officials insisted, was the individual removal by the stronger countries of their quotas and other import controls against American goods.

Continued emphasis on the EPU thesis of regional trading on a soft-currency basis represents an attempt to work toward the formation of

---

[116] ibid., Copy of a memorandum by Douglas, 'Memorandum of conversation at the White House on June 30 1953'; Douglas to Eisenhower, 6 July 1953.

an economic bloc, comprised of strong industrial countries, weak industrial countries, and non-dollar underdeveloped countries, which would
maximize their transactions with each other and minimize trading with
the dollar area. The stronger countries are now making efforts to
move out of this system and to build up their transactions with the
dollar area. The US should encourage these efforts, rather than coun-
tering them with pressure on political grounds for further expansion of
regional arrangements.[117]

To encourage OEEC countries to divert resources into a further stage of
mutual trade liberalization 'would be a serious and most unfortunate
mistake'.[118] Unfortunately for Bolton and Rowan these closet allies in
Washington would not commit themselves to anything more than quiet
administrative support.

In the battle of memoranda the State Department and MSA exalted the
EDC treaty as the culminating triumph of America's efforts to integrate
Europe. 'The proposed European Political Community, as it stands in
the draft treaty presented to the six governments in March 1953 by
the Ad Hoc Assembly, represents a step towards political unity that could
probably serve well the relevant US objectives', William H. Draper, the
MSA special representative in Europe, reported to Eisenhower.[119] Without
some vision of a world order which included an integrated Western Europe,
without a vision that would allow, even encourage, some possibility of a
closer political association there, the United Kingdom was in no position
to claim American support for its own international priorities.

Secretary of state Foster Dulles believed in European integration with
a fanatical evangelical fervour and spoke of it with all his formidable
reserves of religiosity. He believed it to be a duty of the Europeans to
improve themselves morally, and to prove by integration that they had
done so. He told Erhard, whom he blamed for opposing integration, 'that
the people of the US and Congress believed firmly that the division of
Europe was the cause of wars in the past'. 'The Europeans', he said, had
'an obligation to tie themselves together' so that they would not have to
call on the United States again.[120] He had already held similar views in
the inter-war period when he had been a business associate of Monnet's,
may even indeed have been one of the sources of Monnet's own convic-
tions.[121] With his mixture of Wilsonian internationalism and identification
of America's own interests with true morality there was no arguing.

---

[117] US T, EUR/3/12/v.1, Memo 'US Approach to EPU and Trade Liberalization', submitted
to a meeting at MSA on 17 June 1953.
[118] ibid., Wills to Bissell, 31 July 1953.
[119] EL, White House Files (Confidential Files), Office of the US Special Representative in
Europe, 'Strengthening the Political Basis of the Atlantic Community'.
[120] *FRUS*, 1955–7, vol. IV, p. 291, Memo of a conversation, 7 June 1955.
[121] F. Duchêne, 'Jean Monnet's Methods', in D. Brinkley and C. Hackett, *Jean Monnet and
the Path to European Unity* (London, 1991), p. 194. See also, F. Duchêne, *Jean Monnet:
The First Statesman of Interdependence* (New York, 1994).

On the question of European integration Eisenhower was not merely delegating to Dulles from the golf course. The President shared his secretary of state's hope that American forces would not be involved forever in Europe, that the New World could put the Old World back into moral order and then return to its own affairs. It was he who, when appointed the first NATO commander-in-chief in western Europe, had argued with the Administration in favour of EDC, when opinion in Washington had been sceptical. His first State of the Union message declared the political unity of western Europe to be a priority for his own Administration. He told the NAC, when it was considering the Spaak Committee's activities, that the unity of western Europe would solve the problem of the peace of the world and that 'it must be demonstrated to all the countries of western Europe individually that each and every one would profit by the union of them all and that none would lose'. He 'cited the development of the American historical pattern as an illustration of the point he was making'.[122] When the text of the Treaty of Rome was ready he told the French foreign minister Christian Pineau 'that the day this common market became a reality would be one of the finest days in the history of the free world, perhaps even more so than winning the war'.[123]

Eisenhower took the time-honoured route of governments everywhere. He appointed a Presidential Commission in August 1953 under the chairmanship of the steel industrialist Clarence Randall to report on the whole range of foreign economic issues. Mainly, the issues were the Administration's desire to reduce both the level of protection of the economy and the extent and size of foreign aid. The issue of what sort of international trade and payments system America should support was also a part of the Commission's brief, if a less salient political issue. There remained for British strategy the lingering hope that the Randall Commission might be influenced.

It did not report until January 1954. It seemed to the British delegation at the annual IMF meeting in September 1953 that US Treasury officials had scarcely read the British memoranda with which they had been fed. When Butler reminded Humphrey of their gist, the need for American backing of the sterling area reserves, Humphrey 'said with great emphasis that there was no prospect whatever of any action involving legislation in Congress being taken during 1954'.[124] Butler persisted. In December he told Humphrey that what was wanted was another historic American act of state comparable in scope to Lend-Lease. Humphrey showed 'some aversion from this idea', remarking that 'he had always

[122] *FRUS*, 1955–7, vol. IV, p. 348, Editorial Note on the 267th Meeting of the National Security Council, 21 November 1955.
[123] EL, Ann Whitman File, Box No. 12, Memo of Conversation Eisenhower–Pineau, 26 February 1957.
[124] PRO, T 230/268, 'Notes on the Washington meetings', September 1953.

been brought up on the basis that while he would put his name on the front of a bill he would certainly not put it on the back of one'.[125] 'Unless we can change our tactics to an attack in force with genuine and acceptable Allies (Germans and Dutch with Canada actively associated on our side)', Bolton wrote to the governor of the Bank, 'on specific objectives we are going to get nowhere.'[126]

A month later Rowan passed on to the chancellor of the exchequer an alleged German plan to establish convertibility at the same time as did Britain, with IMF backing.[127] There was, it seemed, a greater urgency to establish sterling–dollar convertibility in order to make sure that it was the pound that gave the lead to the Deutschmark.

Table 7.7   Level of official sterling reserves in London, 1945–58 (end of year) ($ million)

1945	2,476	1952	1,846
1946	2,696	1953	2,518
1947	2,079	1954	2,762
1948	1,856	1955	2,120
1949	1,688	1956	2,133
1950	3,300	1957	2,273
1951	2,335	1958	3,069

Source: UK, Central Statistical Office, *Economic Trends*, Annual Supplement, 1984

Table 7.8   Official reserves of the German Federal Republic, 1950–8 ($ million)

	Estimated value of gross reserves at end of year	Net EPU position at end of year
1950	274	−192
1951	518	n.a.
1952	1,190	+253
1953	1,956	+424
1954	2,636	+489
1955	3,076	+521
1956	4,291	+688
1957	5,644	+1,010
1958	6,321	+1,095

Sources: IMF, *International Financial Statistics*, August 1959

[125] BOE, OV 44/61, Note of discussions with the secretary to the US Treasury, 16 December 1953.
[126] ibid., Bolton to Cobbold, 15 September 1953.
[127] PRO, T 230/264, Rowan to Butler, 'Germany and Convertibility', 23 October 1953.

Various schemes for establishing Deutschmark–dollar convertibility were indeed devised in the Ministry of the Economy in Bonn after the appointment of the Randall Commission.[128] On a visit to Washington at the end of the year Erhard harangued American officials on the advantages of convertibility with a speech so long that there was time for only one question,

> and this led to another long speech which had little direct relation to the question. It was also in German so that most of his listeners did not understand. The Americans listened (apparently with a little impatience towards the end) to his interminable spate of words, but gave him no encouragement whatever to 'go it alone'.[129]

That was not what the German government was going to do. Policy became to move to full convertibility immediately after a British move. The gradual progress towards ending exchange controls which the Bank and Treasury made after their rebuff in Washington was always made with one eye on the similar trend in the Federal Republic and another on the timetable for achieving *de facto* convertibility by unifying the different kinds of sterling accounts. The lack of American support did not deter them.

With each step in the Bolton–Rowan programme towards the unification of sterling exchange rates there was usually a parallel step to liberalize the mark. The transfer of dividends on foreign-owned investments in the Federal Republic, as well as on the foreign debt covered by the London Debt agreement, was permitted in September 1953, where these had been owned on 15 July 1931 by a citizen of one of the other signatories of the agreement. In March 1954 transferable account status was given to all sterling except that on dollar account, thus leaving the Bank of England with only two official sterling exchange rates to manage and which it hoped to be allowed to bring together. This was at once followed by the German authorities giving permission for the multilateral use of non-resident mark accounts in two separate areas: the non-dollar area; and a miscellaneous area consisting of the Soviet Union, China and countries with which the Federal Republic had no payments agreement.[130] This was bound to keep alive the idea in the Bank of England that their unilateral policies would eventually force a rift between the Europeans; France remained wrapped in a cocoon of trade and currency controls.

The policy with a more obvious appeal to Germany, however, and which would still satisfy German demands for more gold in return for its European trade surpluses, was that a parallel gradual hardening of EPU settlements

---

[128] BA, B102 12651/2, Memo by Gocht, 'Arbeitsunterlage zur Vorbereitung einer Stellungnahme des BWM zum weiteren Vorgehen . . .', 3 August 1953; Memo by Gocht, 'Entwicklungstendenzen im Aussenhandel Westdeutschlands nach Einführung der Konvertierbarkeit', 2 October 1953.

[129] PRO, T 236/3519, Hall-Patch to Rowan, 15 December 1953.

[130] C. Buchheim, *Die Wiedereingliederung Westdeutschlands in die Weltwirtschaft 1945–1958* (Munich, 1990), pp. 148 ff.

and the removal of trade barriers by OEEC would enable France to share a move to convertibility initiated by a move to hard-currency settlements in EPU.[131] That way there would be no break with France.

The Randall report when published was indecisive. It seemed to accept that countries might proceed to convertibility at their own speed and in their own way. It recommended the continuation of EPU and the American financial contribution to its working capital. It accepted that floating rates might ease the removal of exchange controls; but it made no positive recommendation that the policy of fixed rates should be modified. The main report did not rule out US financial support for establishing the general convertibility of major currencies. A minority report objected strongly to any direct United States government credits to foreign central banks. On the central question, the relationship between currency convertibility and European integration, it was silent. The Department of State complained that there was still need for 'careful thought' about the relationship between currency convertibility and EPU, 'in view of the value of the European Payments Union as an instrument for promoting European unification'.[132] Dulles was said to be interpreting the Randall report to mean that EPU should continue for another three years before any move to convertibility.[133]

The MSA felt that the Randall report had cleared the decks for a positive attempt to link the British drive towards the one-world system and the EPU. 'EPU was essential if progress was to be made towards a Federated Europe', its director Harold Stassen told the British ambassador.[134] However, if that federated Europe could be tied into an Atlantic payments framework, within which EPU could gradually relax its discrimination against dollar imports, convertible sterling might play the role the British wished without disrupting the European institutions. Credits which had accumulated in EPU might, Stassen suggested, be discounted through the Federal Reserve, thus giving the United States an active participation in the settlements mechanism instead of the merely passive participation which its renewable loan of working capital offered. At the same time British and continental interests could be compromised by giving the Managing Board of EPU the authority to recommend exchange rate adjustments within EPU as a way of restoring equilibrium in the payment flows. It would then be legitimate to discriminate against countries which refused these adjustments.[135] Hope was thus kept faintly alive in Whitehall.

'This approach, frankly', the US Treasury minuted on the Stassen proposals, 'does not favor allowing sterling and the deutsche mark to move more rapidly than the French franc for political reasons.'[136] If the United

[131] BA, B102 12651/2, Memo by Gocht, 'Konvertibilität', 14 October 1953.
[132] *FRUS*, 1952–4, vol. 1, pt 1, p. 55, 'Department of State Comments on Recommendations of the Randall Commission'.
[133] PRO, T 232/408, Owen to Copleston, 30 March 1954.
[134] BOE, OV 44/62, Makins to FO, 30 April 1954.
[135] US T, EUR/2/12/v.2, 'Comments on the Memorandum of January 12, 1954'.
[136] US T, EUR/3/12/v.2, 'Stassen Proposal on European Payments', 21 January 1954.

Kingdom was in fact prepared, as Rowan and Bolton were demanding, to renew the EPU agreement only on the new condition that there should be an escape clause allowing Britain to leave at any time, then America, the US Treasury argued, should support this position.[137] It was not inevitable that this would break up EPU.

> If the British were to lead, however, it is quite clear that the Germans, the Swiss, the Belgians, the Dutch and the Scandinavians would quickly follow, and there is a good possibility that France and Italy could also go along. The French government has for some time been waiting for an external excuse to adjust its exchange rate.[138]

However much views of this kind encouraged the UK to persist, this was not the sort of pressure which the State Department was ready to exert on France.

If the increasing strength of US Treasury support for a loan to back sterling convertibility was not enough to sway State Department and President, it was enough to be an important factor in preventing any rapprochement between Britain and Germany in a commitment to joint action to harden the EPU settlements. As long as London thought it might get the money from Washington for unilateral action on convertibility it could postpone the awkward question of the heavy gold payments that any hardening of the EPU settlements would mean. In May 1954 Burgess and Southard came to London and initiated an attempt to draft the terms of a suitable agreement with IMF for expanding its funds to support convertibility operations. The IMF's managing director and research staff were, as Hall-Patch, the British executive director put it, 'all on our side'.[139]

'If it were not for the EPU difficulties and the difference of opinion about American/continental relations', Southard said, 'he believed that rapid progress could be made between London and Washington on all convertibility matters.'[140] Butler and Bolton set a timetable for 'really practical talks' to be held in September 1954, the date by which it was thought that IMF would be empowered to make a loan to support sterling convertibility.[141] Southard was given the task by Burgess of producing a scheme for agreement between London and Washington before the September IMF meeting and indicated that 'He saw little or no difficulty about a substantial Fund standby'.[142] Burgess was equally euphoric, remembering 'that he had participated in the 1924/5 stabilization loan for sterling. He would regard it as the supreme achievement if he were once again able to participate in the convertibility of sterling.'[143]

---

[137] ibid., Humphrey to Stassen, 26 January 1954.
[138] ibid., Treasury Paper, 'US Economic Policy Toward Europe', 13 April 1954.
[139] BOE, OV 44/61, Hall-Patch to Rowan, 1 May 1954.
[140] BOE, OV 114/62, 'Note of a Conversation with Southard etc.', 3 May 1954.
[141] PRO, T 230/268, 'Note of a Discussion at Lunch at No. 11 Downing St.', 3 May 1954.
[142] BOE, OV 44/63, 'Note of a Conversation with Mr. Southard etc.', 3 May 1954.
[143] PRO, T 230/268, 'Note of a Discussion at Lunch . . .', op. cit.

For the Bank this timetable was too slow. It would have preferred to aim at a declaration of sterling–dollar convertibility in September rather than begin substantive talks then. But Butler and the Treasury had become increasingly cautious about unilateral action. After most of the restrictions on the use of transferable account sterling for making current settlements had been lifted in March 1954 the Bank of England had asked permission to operate covertly on the Zürich black market in order to close the gap between the exchange rates for transferable and dollar-account sterling. This was to be the last stage in the unification of the sterling exchange rates. Butler had not expected he could get agreement from his cabinet colleagues and was now 'concerned that further significant moves towards convertibility should be timed with full regard to the need to maintain accord with our Commonwealth and European collaborators'.[144] Much of the advice he was receiving was pulling against that of the Bank and Rowan. The Economic Section of the Treasury, for example, was advising him to wait and act from greater strength when the reserves had grown still further.[145]

Despite the support of the US Treasury and Federal Reserve for a loan that would re-establish the convertibility of sterling, the increasingly expressed hostility of the Western European countries to these British attempts at leadership perhaps increased Butler's caution and convinced him that support from some quarter in Western Europe was indispensable if the last stages of the Bolton–Rowan programme were to be achieved.

When the British proposals to establish the general convertibility of all Western European currencies through a large IMF loan to Britain, associated with smaller ones to other countries, were discussed in OEEC in spring 1954 they were subjected by the Benelux countries to a 'slashing' attack.[146] In Paris it was thought that the proposals would be very dangerous for France: 'the competent international bodies in the economic and financial sphere would be reduced to two: GATT and IMF; the method of operation and the spirit of each of them matches neither our policy nor our interests.'[147] Ezio Vanoni the Italian minister for the economy telegraphed the American OEEC delegation that the lira could not be made convertible and that 'In event breakdown EPU, his view serious risk that Italy would have to reimpose immediately restrictions on imports from Germany and Britain in order to balance its trade with these countries'.[148]

This was re-emphasized in a memorandum from the Italian embassy in Washington in July, which made the most direct case for retaining EPU. 'Nothing should be done', the memorandum insisted, 'to jeopardize the

---

[144] BOE, OV 44/63, Rowan to Bolton, 11 May 1954.
[145] A. Cairncross and N. Watts, *The Economic Section 1939–1961. A Study in Economic Advising* (London, 1989), pp. 302 ff.
[146] FRC, RG 469, Box 52, Telegram to all ECA missions from ECA delegation to OEEC, 8 April 1954.
[147] MAE, DE-CE, Memo, Service de Coopération Economique, 4 May 1954.
[148] FRC, RG 469, Box 52, Telegram to OEEC Mission, 25 May 1954.

function of the European market as an outlet for products which are the fruit of the programs for economic expansion which are being developed by a number of European countries.' 'The Italian government', it concluded, 'is definitely of the opinion that the restoration of currency convertibility in western Europe at this time would in all probability push back Europe toward the conditions of the first half of this century, rather than press it forward along the new road.'[149] The last word on the British proposals was pronounced by Europe's foremost champion of hard international money. They were, said the leader of the Swiss delegation to OEEC on the eve of the meeting which decided renewal of the EPU, worthy of a good luck telegram from the late Josef Stalin.[150]

In the face of such opposition it seemed obvious that there must be some modification of the British stance if the American government was to approve the terms of an IMF credit in September 1954. In response there gradually emerged in London over the summer the concept of some kind of European Fund which would help the weaker currencies to establish convertibility if the pound and the mark, either as a result of separate decisions or jointly, were made convertible. As envisaged by the British, the European Fund would provide short-term financial help out of the existing working capital of EPU, which could be retained for a short period and supplemented by new contributions. It would therefore be small and the period of any loan would be short. The laggards would have one year before themselves establishing convertibility or making whatever other arrangements they thought appropriate.

At first it was unclear from the British proposals who would manage this European Fund and whether the existing trade rules in Western Europe would still be maintained and supervised by any European organization. This was a serious objection. The Germans were no more prepared than earlier to abandon the new European institutions and the smaller countries had no intention of losing such leverage as they had acquired in the post-war world over the commercial policies of the larger ones. They were determined to retain the importance of the OEEC and EPU as trade bargaining forums, not just as a floor for cooperative discussions. They refused to be left with even less guarantee of the commercial policies of their major customers. Debtors, like Norway, refused to be cast on the mercies of the IMF, where their credit lines would be shorter. Denmark came forward with a counter-proposal for a European Fund which would supply automatic credits on the same scale as EPU for as long as five years. France supported this, and both insisted that the European Fund should have a capital of at least $1,000 million. This figure had been originally proposed by Italy, which wanted to use the European

---

[149] FRC, Lot File 58 D 357, Memorandum from Italian Embassy, 'Convertibility', 8 July 1954.

[150] BA, B102/12652/1, Bericht über die Expertensitzung der OEEC, 15–17 June 1954.

Fund for specific investment and development needs in southern Italy.[151]
It was four times what the British had been considering.

In Washington the Treasury welcomed the idea of the European Fund
as proposed by Britain, but the National Advisory Council was more
cautious. It agreed as early as July 1954 to allow the American assets in
EPU to be transferred to a European Fund, but only to one whose powers
would be determined by the OEEC Council. If the American capital was
to be used, there could be no separate agreement by some EPU members
to terminate EPU and institute the Fund. Nevertheless Stassen emphasized to the OEEC Council that the European Fund's purpose would be
limited to the objectives which the British proposals had set for it:
supporting currencies which could not yet establish convertibility.[152] The
OEEC agreed, against strong British dissent, that the size of a European
Fund might actually have to be as large as $600 million, which is what it
finally was. This would therefore require a large European contribution,
for of the original American contribution of $150 million to the working
capital of EPU only $123.6 million remained on account in Washington.[153]

Taking stock of the situation in July 1954, one month before the French
national assembly voted down the EDC Treaty, two opinions about the
second British strategy for reaching sterling convertibility in a multilateral
trade and payments system are equally valid. One is that, considering the
opposition it had met from the White House and the Department of State
and considering the unwillingness of any major western European country
to support it at the expense of breaking up EPU and its common trade
rules, it had come a surprisingly long way towards achievement. The other
is that there was still no sign that anything other than a unilateral declaration of convertibility could be achieved.

This was in spite of the obscurity over where the Six were actually
going. There looked to be little chance of the European Defence
Community coming into existence and the idea of European unity might
not survive its rejection. What not only held them together but bound
them also to other OEEC member-states was the common determination
to abide by common trade rules, to which any movement towards convertibility would have to be subordinated.

This was unnecessary, the UK argued in OEEC, because inter-western
European trade would simply become part of the regime of world trade.
This put the United Kingdom in a minority of one in OEEC. It, alone,
refused to approve the draft report of the EPU Managing Board in April
1954 which read: 'Convertibility is pointless unless such a system could
be adopted on conditions which would make it possible for intra-European

[151] ibid., Minutes of the OEEC Ministerial Examination Group on Convertibility, 28 July 1954.
[152] *FRUS*, 1952–4, vol. 1, pt 1, p. 363, Minutes of the 212th Meeting of the National Advisory
Council on International Monetary and Financial Problems, 2 July 1954.
[153] J.J. Kaplan and G. Schleiminger, *The European Payments Union*, op. cit., p. 213.

trade and trade between member countries and the rest of the world to be maintained or increased. Convertibility is not an end in itself.'[154]

It was certainly not impossible that, even if no official American support through IMF arrived, had sterling reserves continued to grow as they did in 1954 a re-elected government might have opted for a unilateral declaration of convertibility and abandoned the idea of any common action with its EPU partners. The collapse of the EDC treaty, many thought, would wean the other Western European countries away from their attachment to the idea of any distinct European political and commercial framework and encourage them to follow the British lead.

In retrospect, however, 1954 looks like the last grand summer of illusion for the United Kingdom. Reserves were rising. The threat of a second stage of European integration was receding. The economy had been relatively stable since 1951 and was now beginning to expand. For Britain to lead Western Europe into the 'one-world system' was still within the bounds of belief. The collapse of EDC was followed by a British diplomatic triumph, Western European Union, which replaced it. Yet everything from summer 1954 onwards was retreat and disillusion. The failure of EDC only cleared the way for an intensification of the efforts by the Six to guarantee the existing pattern and distribution of European trade by a more formal institutional structure. From the debris of EDC emerged the Dutch proposal for a common market, a proposal that survived the collapse unscathed. The seeming failure of political integration only strengthened the urgency to secure the trade pattern which was bringing prosperity.

Between June and the end of 1954 British reserves declined by $255 million. By November the balance of payments for 1955 was forecast to be worse than that of 1954. By February 1955 it was being predicted as a current-account deficit. In late February, while *de facto* convertibility according to the Bolton–Rowan programme was being achieved, credit restrictions were imposed throughout the economy. The reserves did not improve during the spring and from June 1955 began to fall more steeply. The tendency at the time was to blame the downturn in the reserves on swings in payments caused by sterling area settlements. The size of sterling liabilities on capital account made for volatility, and gold and dollars no longer flowed as they had in the pre-war period from the Commonwealth to London in sufficient quantities to offset the United Kingdom's own dollar deficit. But it was the British economy itself that was not standing up well to the liberalization of the exchanges.

Giving transferable-account status in March 1954 to all sterling except that on dollar account was followed by an increase of 20 per cent in imports from outside the sterling area in 1955, whereas imports from the sterling area grew by only 5 per cent. Yet formal discrimination against dollar-zone goods had remained almost unreduced. The effect of currency

[154] Report by the Managing Board of the EPU to OEEC, 14 April 1954.

decontrol was not what Bolton and his supporters had predicted. The steps towards decontrolling the Deutschmark, by contrast, were safely accompanied by the removal of 80 per cent of quotas on Germany's dollar-zone imports by the end of 1954. This did not halt the growth either of the Federal Republic's trade surpluses or of its reserves. The increase in the British trade deficit was accompanied by capital outflows set in motion by a mixture of nervousness about the economy and the continued semi-public discussion of a possible proclamation of sterling convertibility at a flexible rate.[155]

The changes in the currency regulations in March 1954 mark the onset of the depressing pattern which was to dominate the British economy afterwards. Imports began, with some delay, a sudden surge in response to an increase in industrial output, while exports continued to grow at an unchanged, and by European standards sluggish, rate. As the payments surplus diminished, interest rates had to be moved upwards to attract more short-term capital to London to cover the payments gap. To the wry amusement of the German delegation to the September 1954 IMF meetings – the time and place where Bolton had earlier planned that the chancellor would unilaterally proclaim sterling–dollar convertibility – Butler instead made a speech about the virtues of full-employment policy and welfare legislation, even criticizing the lack of similar policies in the United States as one cause of the recession there. He remarked to Erhard that it would be a pity to force France to accept terms for a European Fund which it found repugnant.[156] Reginald Maudling, economic secretary to the Treasury, stated 'quite definitely' that there was no likelihood of a convertibility operation being considered before October 1955. The impression, Bolton wrote sadly to Cobbold the Bank governor, was 'that the Collective Approach, certainly in its present form, is dead'.[157]

The end of the EDC and the banishment of the spectre of a European federation was thus followed one month later by the general admission that the United Kingdom's own strategy had also failed. This did not deter the Bank from pursuing the original Bolton–Rowan programme of establishing *de facto* convertibility through administrative action. When the fall in the reserves was temporarily halted in early 1955 its efforts resumed. In February the Bank was finally permitted to deal covertly in Zürich to bring the rates of transferable-account sterling and dollar-account sterling into line. The gap between them was narrowed so that it never became wider than 1.5 per cent. As far as any official establishment of legal convertibility by international agreement was concerned, however, and on the question of maintaining the European institutions that would support it, Britain was no longer pursuing a line separate from its OEEC associates.

---

[155] OEEC, *Seventh Report of the OEEC. Economic Expansion and its Problems* (Paris, 1956), p. 264.
[156] BA, B102/12652/1, Unterrednung Erhard–Butler, 26 September 1954.
[157] BOE, OV 44/64, Bolton to Cobbold, 24 September 1954.

In summer 1954 the agreement to renew EPU for a further year contained a provision to reduce the value of the gold payments that would have to be made by debtors on dissolution. Between summer 1954 and March 1955 the EPU members discussed a transition by which EPU settlements would be gradually hardened until they were made 100 per cent in gold/dollars. Once this effective dollar convertibility, at least for trade settlements, had been achieved, the European Fund would come into operation to enable the weaker members to comply with the new settlement rules. Until March 1955 the British remained adamant that the European Fund could not last for longer than one year after a general establishment of dollar convertibility.[158] But at the March 1955 meeting of the EPU Managing Board there came further significant retreats. The United Kingdom gave up its opposition to a Fund as large as $600 million, with the large European contribution that this implied; and it no longer insisted on a one-year maximum duration. The Fund, it agreed, could be empowered to make loans of two years' duration, though only on strict banking conditions comparable with those of IMF credits. In March also the Treasury decided that it could now risk agreement with the German proposal that EPU settlements be made 75 per cent in gold/dollars. The Bank, still setting its watch by the Bolton–Rowan timetable, wanted to insist on 100 per cent gold settlements.[159] The Treasury argued against this on the grounds of Britain's commercial weakness; it would mean matching the Federal Republic in the removal of discrimination against dollar imports. Indeed the Board of Trade actually opposed moving even to 75 per cent gold settlements, because it might make compliance with the resumed OEEC Trade Liberalization Programme too dangerous.[160]

Before the official opening of the meeting which was to confirm the renewal and agree the terms of EPU for its next year of operations, Butler took the German representative, the vice-chancellor Blücher, on one side and assured him that the British government had in fact abandoned all idea of unilateral action and was now seeking full cooperation in all points at issue with the Federal Republic.[161] The way was open for a general agreement to proceed in common to legal convertibility with the institution of a European Fund to come into operation on an agreed date. The details of the $600 million European Fund and the terms for an eventual dissolution of EPU, including the disbursement of its capital and the disposition of remaining surpluses and credits, were then incorporated into the European Monetary Agreement of 5 August 1955. So nervous had everyone become by that time about the British government's intentions that it still needed an official statement by Butler at the IMF meeting in

[158] ibid., OEEC Ministerial Examination Group on Convertibility, 10 May 1955.
[159] BOE, OV 44/65, Memo by Thompson-McCausland, 1 March 1955.
[160] BOE, OV 46/18, 'EPU/European Fund'. Meeting with Board of Trade officials, 14 March 1955.
[161] BA, B102/12653/2, Blücher to Adenauer, 20 June 1955.

September in Istanbul that there would be no unilateral declaration of formal sterling convertibility and no flexible rates for sterling, before speculation against it calmed down.

THE UNITED KINGDOM AND THE COMMON MARKET

Abandoning the idea of unilateral convertibility and devising an agreement which might make it easier for the OEEC members to move together to convertibility against the dollar did not mean accepting the commercial regime envisaged by Beyen, a European common market with certain other common policies to sustain it. The Beyen plan for a common market first returned to life in April 1955 at a Benelux summit in the Hague, after the UK government had withdrawn its opposition to the larger European Fund. A meeting of the foreign ministers of the Six at Messina on 2–4 June 1955 set up the semi-official Spaak Committee to examine the proposal.

The appointment of the Spaak Committee is often treated as the first step in an inevitable progress towards the Treaty of Rome and the final triumph of the European supranationalism first proclaimed by the Treaty of Paris in 1952. While the commercial weaknesses of British international economic strategy between the two treaties are apparent, the Collective Approach to multilateralism was certainly not condemned to failure by those weaknesses from the outset. It could hope for no support from the smaller European economies, on which Britain nevertheless relied in OEEC against France. Benelux and Scandinavia wanted collective tariff reductions from western Europe's medium-sized powers. Britain was not going to reduce its tariffs, or even let OEEC deal with tariffs, in response to that pressure, because its tariffs were reserved for a much grander bargain. The pursuit of unilateral convertibility, dragging after sterling those currencies whose governments could take a similar risk, was divisive in Europe because France was so far from being able to take that risk. But France's alternative risk, membership of a common market with Germany, was equally difficult and fearful. The geographical distribution of French trade, even if its dynamic growth was within western Europe, was worldwide, like that of Britain. When legal dollar convertibility did eventually come in 1958 it came through cooperation between Britain and France. The teleological history of European integration should not be accepted even by enthusiasts for European Union to the point where the Collective Approach is seen as anti-French or anti-German because it was anti-integrationist. It offered much to both countries.

Its proponents argued that any additional barriers which it raised against Britain's trade with Europe would be only temporary; the grand global strategy would overcome by its larger possibilities the tactical problems of payments and trade controls which might return to inter-European trade with a dissolution of EPU. However, British exports to the Commonwealth were likely to stagnate whatever happened and if the USA retained its 1951 level of protectionism the increase in British exports there would not compensate for their fall, perhaps temporary, to Europe. It was a strategy which took great commercial risks.

Of those, the greatest was that there would arise on the continent a common market discriminating in favour of its members' exports and against those of the United Kingdom, unless the United Kingdom abandoned all the main lines of its first two post-war strategies and opted for membership of a discriminatory club. That would certainly lead to a change in the geographical distribution of trade, but it would have many other consequences, economic and political.

Invited to participate in the discussions of the Spaak Committee after the Messina meeting of the foreign ministers of the Six in June 1955, Britain sent the appropriate Board of Trade official, R.F. Bretherton.[162] His sending only followed much argument between ministers. The Treasury would have preferred no British presence there. Harold Macmillan, who had become foreign secretary, wanted a presence there in order to divert the various initiatives which might emerge in the direction of something that Britain could join. The Board of Trade, in nominating the appropriate person, had to saddle him with a brief in which he could do very little, because there was no longer any existing national strategy to follow. Furthermore, the president of the Board of Trade, Peter Thorneycroft, inclined towards multilateral free trade as he was a strong opponent of the common market proposals. At the same time, however, he was an ardent advocate of a positive alternative policy. The wide differences of opinion between ministers did not augur well for the emergence of any new coherent strategy.

Neither did the disputes which arose between the various bits of the Whitehall machine which had to cope with this problem. Foreign Office officials, many of whom did not think the Six would agree on the terms of a common market, were inclined to wait for the threat to blow itself out. At the end of 1955 when Macmillan was moved to the office of chancellor of the exchequer they were able to assert their view more strongly. On the other hand, that same move placed at the head of the Treasury a man who took the Six's plans for an eventual federation seriously and who thought that if it happened 'Europe would be handed over to the Germans, a state of affairs which we had fought two world wars to prevent'.[163] It was from his collaboration with Thorneycroft, bringing the two economic ministries behind one policy, that the new strategy of the free trade area proposal would arise.

Until then, the only effective critique of the existing policy, that the United Kingdom could not join a European common market because

---

[162] For a fuller account of the British decision not to join a common market and of the formulation of the free trade area strategy, A.S. Milward, *The United Kingdom and the European Community 1950–1963* (forthcoming).

[163] PRO, FO 371/116042, Record of a meeting between the Secretary of State and Officials, 29 June 1955.

economic and political strategy forbade, came from the estimate, made by the Treasury's Economic Section, of the relative costs and benefits of joining a European customs union, which, among its various hypothetical scenarios, had one very firm conclusion: that if a common market did come into existence without Britain, 'we would certainly lose by the establishment of a common market without our participation'.[164] The implication was, that if there were sound political reasons for not joining, they would have to be very weighty to counteract this economic judgement. The balance of opinion in the inter-ministerial Mutual Aid Committee was nevertheless against any change of policy.

Spaak made up his mind in August 1955 to draft a report in favour of a common market, but subsequent strong doubts about how such a report would be received in France left his committee treading water until late October. By that date a special working party on the question had obfuscated the decision even further in Whitehall by arguing that were the United Kingdom to encourage a common market to come into being it was far from sure that the benefits it would derive would be greater than those from existing policies. It was not evident that there were now any existing policies.

When on 22 October 1955 Spaak told his committee of his intentions to draft a report in favour of a common market by private consultation with the heads of delegations Bretherton was effectively excluded, both by Spaak's decision and by his own government's brief. On 27 October the Mutual Aid Committee recommended that Britain could not join a common market. Cabinet did not have to discuss this, for it was already existing policy.

What mattered was the choice of a new strategy. Given the balance of opinion it had both to confront a common market which might come into being but also to continue the general line of policy which had been adopted in 1955 of cooperation with the Six in order to bring them into a multilateral non-discriminatory world. Out of this double requirement came the free trade area proposal in which the Six's tariff cuts and import quota extensions would be matched by those of the outer free trade area which would envelop it. The worldwide principle of British strategy did not change, but it now incorporated a programme which would increase Britain's trade to Europe. Unfortunately, it ignored the political ambitions of the Six to remain as a clearly demarcated unit moving towards supranational governance. Unfortunately, too, when it was translated into detail it did not offer sufficient economic advantages to them. That it would not do so could perhaps be already discerned from the detail of British strategy after 1951, and even more so from the fact that there was no fallback position in the event that convertibility did have to be a

---

[164] PRO, CAB 134/1029, Note by the Treasury Economic Section, 'A European Common Market', 14 July 1955.

European decision and not an unilateral act of British leadership. There was no fallback position because the only possible one required accepting the continental position that trade came first and its existing pattern in western Europe had to be secured. While for the United Kingdom that might well have been of long-term benefit, its immediate advantages were counterbalanced by its immediate disadvantages.

There was no European rescue of the British nation-state except in very different circumstances from those prevailing in the 1950s. The United Kingdom entered the European Community in 1973 coincident with the deceleration of national income growth rates, the return of high levels of unemployment, and in a period of high inflation. By that time the strategy of membership, on the terms available in late 1962, had become a general panacea for the country's economic difficulties.

A full history of the free trade area proposals and their failure remains to be written. Their rejection by France did not lead to any immediate change in the British government's policy of maintaining imports of cheap Commonwealth foodstuffs for consumers while sustaining high prices for domestic farmers. The United Kingdom entered into negotiations for membership of EEC in 1961 with this policy still a fundamental plank of its strategy, although almost all officials who had to deal with the tactics of the application thought, correctly, from the outset that such a position would be unacceptable to the Six.

The tariff structure of imperial preference was bargained away, fruit-lessly, in the negotiations in return for vaguely worded commitments by the EEC to a worldwide tariff bargain with the USA. The Dillon and the Kennedy 'rounds' of bargaining in GATT did represent a shift in American tariff policy of the kind for which the United Kingdom had been waiting. Because of the French government's veto on UK member-ship of EEC in 1963, however, the central bargaining remained between the Six and the USA. Imperial preferences, which would have been ended by British entry into the EEC on the terms available in 1962, were eroded in the 1960s partly because the foreign trade of Australia and New Zealand shifted rapidly towards closer Asian markets as, concurrently, British trade shifted towards Europe, in spite of the Six's discrimination in favour of each other. Throughout the decade after the United Kingdom's exclusion the gap between the average rate of growth of GNP of EEC members and that of the United Kingdom was about as high as in the 1950s.

Avoiding the economic costs of non-membership had been, for the Economic Section of the Treasury, the largest certain gain from entry. The financial costs of entry in 1963 would, however, have been heavier than the Treasury foresaw in the 1950s, because the Europeanization of agricultural protection, completed by the agreement on the Common Agricultural Policy reached in January 1962 (or in December 1961 by the EEC's own peculiar calendar), heavily discriminated against food importers from outside the Six thanks to the system of frontier levies by which it financed the whole political structure. This price, accepted in 1962, had therefore to be accepted on later entry.

That a supranational political governance of Europe brought political advantages to the United Kingdom did grow in importance as an idea in national politics. It could hardly fail to do so given its very small number of adherents before 1961. The idea that the outcome of this should be a European federation remained inimical to a majority of British voters. 'Taking the lead in Europe' has remained, in spite of this, the favourite slogan of almost all leaders of British political parties. It has often, as in the 1950s, meant leading Europe in directions in which it did not want to go.

The economic and political benefits which membership of the European Community and the European Union did bring to the United Kingdom were reaped in the worldwide framework at which British national strategies aimed after 1945, even when the strategy became Community membership. Only in that sense was there a European rescue of the British member-state. The price for that delay does seem to have been a lower rate of growth of output and income and a rapidly weakening political position for two decades. Looking at the evidence for the 1950s it is difficult to see how it could have been otherwise.

Envoi

As I finished the text for the first edition of this book in summer 1992, one former British prime minister was appealing in New York before an audience of American business leaders for Britain permanently to renounce any policies which might lead to a federal Europe and was urging the United Kingdom and the United States to form a free trade area. Another former British prime minister, at the same time, was urging the country at once to enter into a commitment to form a federal union of western Europe. The background against which the book was concluded was so reminiscent of British arguments and views in the 1950s that it was tempting to think that nothing had changed. Yet the twelve governments of the EEC had signed an agreement that the European Community should have a single central bank and currency within ten years, providing that several stringent conditions relating to inflation rates, public debt ratios, and the convergence of exchange rates had been met, and also that for Britain the agreement was reversible by parliament before the due date. That these conditions would actually be met looked scarcely plausible.

Now, in 1999, as I revise this text, it looks likely that there will be a European Monetary Union, although its durability is uncertain. Whether or when the United Kingdom will join that Union is more uncertain. The policy of the main opposition party is to renegotiate the Treaty of Rome so that only its commercial clauses will be binding. Without Monetary Union the new political commitments entered into at Maastricht would not justify the change of name from European Community to European Union (EU). The dissent between the United Kingdom and the European Union remains the same as that described in chapter 7. There are other dissidents. The common foreign, defence, and immigration policies to which the Treaty of Maastricht is to lead the way are to be achieved only by international cooperation, not by supranational organizations. They escape any control by the European Commission, the Court of Justice, and the Parliament. Yet the Treaty was nevertheless voted down in a national referendum in Denmark and so many exceptions subsequently made for that country in order to make sure that the additional protocols were accepted in a second referendum that Denmark's allegiance to the Treaty is even more qualified than the United Kingdom's. The special treatment for the United Kingdom was acclaimed nationalistically in the press as the 'victory' which the prime minister declared it to be. It should be noted that, apart from the particular opposition of Denmark and the United Kingdom to some central aspects of the Treaty, the other states could not agree amongst themselves to an extension of majority voting in the Council of Ministers except on issues which the larger states regarded as relatively unimportant. France opposed an increase in the powers of the European Parliament more energetically than Britain. Should Monetary Union fail, the Treaty of Maastricht will have strengthened the institutionalized interdependence of western European states, but it will not be another step on the road to integration.

The United Kingdom has taken up the cause of a wider union embracing much of eastern Europe as well as Scandinavia, which would not be founded on common economic and social policies other than relative freedom of trade and markets. Such a union could take its place in that 'one world system' which was the goal of Britain's strategies in the 1950s. The long British struggle of 1955–60 to link the nascent European Economic Community with a European Free Trade Area by the common practice of non-discriminatory trade rules, but without the other common policies which created the need for the European Economic Community no longer has so strong a foundation in national domestic political consensus. As in other member-states support for the EU, with a strong foundation of common policies as well as the rules of the common market, has grown. Drowning the present European Union in a greater Europe with widely differing economic arrangements between its member-states, bound in a looser institutional framework, might well not command majority support in any of them, including the United Kingdom.

When the successive worldwide strategies of the United Kingdom in the 1950s were crossed by the creation and early success of the EEC the British initiatives to link the common market institutionally with a wider free trade area, and later to join the EEC, were strongly motivated by foreign policy considerations. The political foundation of similar economic and social policies which determined the nature of the EEC was, as the previous chapter argued, not lacking in the United Kingdom. In London however the EEC was often misunderstood as an organization held together essentially by its political objectives; that its political cohesiveness came from its economic basis was not understood. That this economic basis gave it a European character, identifying the rescue of the nation-state as a process founded on the development of the European states themselves, was also not understood. No matter how well-disposed much opinion in Germany might be to the wider free trade area, German governments were ultimately going to bow to de Gaulle's veto on British membership. Not to have done so would have weakened their domestic electoral power base economically and would have detracted from the European ideology which had stood CDU politicians in such good stead. This does not mean that after 1957 there may not have been a consonance of foreign policy objectives between French and German governments which the Treaties of Rome confirmed and strengthened. But the ability to strengthen that consonance by adherence to a common institutional framework of a new and solemn kind rested on the consonance of domestic policy choices for the rescue of the nation-state.

The national strategies of the original six core member-states appear to have remained in place and retained public support, although in France, as has been the case from 1950 and the Schuman proposals, that support often is but a narrow majority and the strategy is always under question. For the later entrants strategies cover a wide spectrum, from clinging to the EU with all its present rules as an instrument of development and modernization to changing it into a looser commercial union and denying its self-proclaimed destiny as an ever-closer political union. The fundamental change in the structure of nation-states and the character of their domestic economic and social policies has, by dividing national electorates, made the EU a more divisive issue than were the European Communities of the 1950s.

Does such a consonance now exist, and if not, will one return? Monetary Union will not be durable without it. If between 1953 and 1968 inflation rates touched 4 per cent, if unemployment in Britain or France climbed briefly to 400,000, governments became anxious for the political consensus they had built. Now, there are more than 11 million unemployed in Britain, France, Germany and Italy, but governments are still re-elected. Colonies of homeless beggars sleep in parks, under bridges and in the public transport systems. In Britain and France income distribution now is made steadily more unequal while in Italy the trend towards greater equality seems to have stopped. Welfare is, if as yet only marginally, being made once more into a private concern. Industrial labour is a shrinking part of the labour force everywhere. Organized labour shrinks even more and trade union membership has fallen steeply in most countries as part of the total labour force. Agriculture no longer employs enough voters to command the political support of the post-war decades. Farmers carry less weight in shaping policy than the rentiers who have been created by two generations of income and savings accumulation, so that rates of inflation acceptable before 1953 are now regarded as utterly unacceptable and public expenditure is seen as a danger to income.

If the motivation for the first common policies of the EEC has changed. or disappeared, the political objective has also been radically altered. The Berlin Wall and the DDR are no more. Germany is now of far greater size and weight in the Community than France and even more so than the United Kingdom. Even before unification its national product was on some measures more than 40 per cent greater than the British and the value of its foreign commodity trade more than 50 per cent greater. One of the Federal Republic's main reasons for adhering to the Community has also gone; a united Germany is free to shape its own policy in eastern Europe.

The historical evidence shows that the real argument has never been about whether it is desirable that a supranational Europe should supersede the nation-state, but about whether the state can find a political and economic base for survival. The surrenders of national sovereignty after 1950 were one aspect of the successful reassertion of the nation-state as the basic organizational entity of Europe. The Community was the European rescue of the nation-state. Since all history is change, that rescue could only be temporary and the process of economic development itself has eroded the political consensus which sustained both nation and supranation after the war.

Whereas the general theories of integration propounded during the 1950s and 1960s almost all predicted that integration would continue, because the nation-state would prove increasingly unable to cope with the trend of modern economic development, in this book the historical evidence has been used to derive a fundamentally different theory of integration. This theory is open-ended; it does not forecast any particular outcome. It runs as follows. European states were reborn as puny weaklings into the post-war world. They developed particular bundles of domestic policies to satisfy a coalition of political interests. To support those policies they had available an inherited international order which had accepted to a varying degree the traditional system and principles of interdependence. Some of the domestic policies which they chose could be advanced through this inherited interdependent international economic order. Others could not and required something different, integration, involving a limited surrender of areas of national sovereignty. The close similarity between the sets of domestic policies chosen by Western European countries meant that integration was a path which could be chosen with reasonable hopes of success on several occasions. The choice between interdependence and integration was made according to the capacity of either system of international order to best advance and support domestic policy choices.

For example, when Italian governments selected emigration as a priority policy choice, an interdependent international order advanced such policies better than an integrationist one; the Six narrowly restricted at first the free movement of labour within their area, while Italians followed their historical pattern of worldwide migration. By the time that integration did provide special advantages in welfare for migration within the Community emigration was already becoming less of a priority policy choice for Italian governments. Similarly, when countries such as Denmark, France or Norway wished to pursue domestic policies which entailed large deficits in their foreign balances for several years, they were able to construct in the EPU an accepted, manageable framework of interdependence, which allowed them to borrow internationally on a much greater scale than the IMF could allow. This was maintained even against strong British opposition by countries like the Federal Republic whose foreign balances were in surplus. But when Belgium wanted to advance its policy of a gradual, managed decline of its coal industry integration was a better choice, because accepting in this case the full implications of interdependence would have meant the speedy extinction of most of the industry. Most strikingly, when faced with the inappropriateness of tariffs as well as of quotas to the industrial and commercial policies they wished to advance, the Six were able to use an integrationist framework to develop a new and altogether more appropriate form of foreign commercial policy, and for them a very successful one. With much travail they were eventually able to use the same framework to advance their policies of agricultural income support.

It depends, however, entirely on the nature of national, domestic policy choices whether the international framework which is needed to support them will be integrationist or not. The theory developed here predicts therefore that anything may happen in the future, unless another theory able to predict the future choice of domestic policies could make it more specific. It allows for further stages of integration, even as far as full political union; it allows for the present level of integration to be maintained unchanged; and it allows for the abandonment of the integration that has taken place. The outcome will be decided by the choice of domestic policies.

The historical evidence also suggests, however, that the last outcome is less likely than the others. When states chose to advance policies by integration one of the advantages that resided in that choice was the greater irreversibility of the commitment. To construct a wholly new framework for foreign commercial policy would have been too risky an undertaking without a commitment from the Federal Republic, which was as near as it was possible to come in international relations to a permanent commitment that it would continue to function as the key piece in that framework. There were other advantages in integration too which could lead to its choice. It offered a central enforceable law in place of that international law which has never been enforced and whose weakness is also a prime weakness of most frameworks of interdependence. It also offered the possibility of reducing the number of international actors within the framework. We have seen how this possibility attracted the Netherlands to the idea of a Common Agricultural Policy; the CAP functioned like a cartel from which Holland's superior rival as an agricultural exporter, Denmark, could be excluded. For the integration which has taken place to be renounced might therefore require events of a cataclysmic order, because the costs of renouncing it would be so high.

To use either a framework of interdependence or an integrationist framework to advance national policies requires a similarity of national policy choices between a sufficient number of states. There is less latitude for policy differences within integration than within interdependence. Since either is chosen in order to advance the national interest, the likelihood is that within the European Union new common policies will only emerge if the circumstances of the period 1945–68 can be repeated and most of its member-states choose similar sets of domestic policies. And, to continue with the extrapolation from the historical evidence, they are only likely to do that if such policies sustain a fresh political consensus which itself will sustain the nation-state.

There has been a sea-change in national economic policies and the way in which the European nation-state is managed since the early 1980s. After 1973 the relationship between foreign trade and economic growth in Western Europe altered; the rate of growth of trade between Community member states declined proportionately to the rate of growth of their trade with the outside world. Worse from their point of view, they began to lose their share of the Community market in many industrial products. If the first trend could be construed by some as healthy, because it was an expansion of exports to a wider area, the second could not. Whereas among the trends analysed in chapter 4 one was the growing competitiveness of Western Europe's manufactures against American goods and the gradual reduction of the share of the Western European market taken by American industry, the trend between 1973 and 1982 was for Japanese and American manufacturing to take a growing share of the Community market. This appeared to be especially the case in the products of new electronic technologies, but also in cars. German manufacturing, while losing none of its lead in capital goods technology, remained fixed in the mould into which the patterns of supply and demand of Western Europe's high-growth years had set it. The manufacturing sectors of the other countries, shaped as they had been around the same pattern dominated by Germany, were even less able to respond to Japanese competition. In those high-technology sectors where economies of scale and the gains in productivity associated with learning-by-doing were supposed to be greatest, and which were supposed to have been especially encouraged by the common market, European manufacturing was now falling behind. One result was that non-tariff barriers, especially state subsidies and national monopolies over state and local authority purchasing, began again to proliferate in intra-West-European trade. The Community was commercially less integrated by 1981 than it had been in 1973. This was seen as reducing the international competitiveness of each of its member-states.

The change in economic ideologies which came with the return of unemployment accompanied by often high inflation rates led to experimentation with the privatization and deregulation of the mixed economy. Although this change came with a different timing in different member-states, it had at first a common objective, to return to the high growth rates of national income of the years before 1974. The concern with stimulating supply rather than demand led to the idea that a further liberalization of the Community market could support certain of these new aspects of national economic policy and on this one aspect a Community consensus did come to prevail. The shift in ideologies meant that the Community policy of standardizing national regulations on each manufactured product in order to minimize the number of surviving non-tariff barriers could be abandoned for a different procedure. The European Council at Milan in March 1985 took the decision to, in the Commission's language, 'complete the internal market' by the Single European Act. The possibility of doing so by a much simpler method than before lay to hand in earlier decisions of the Court of Justice, that there must be a mutual recognition inside the Community of products manufactured in any one member-state. The mutual acceptance by member-states that less regulation of the Community market would improve their international competitiveness led them to use this principle to remove regulations, rather than to continue on the previous basis of increasing their number, and this was embodied in the Single European Act. The programme of market 'completion' by removing restrictive regulations was, theoretically, due to be completed by December 1992. It is far from complete.

European economies made a particularly strong recovery in the economic upswing after 1983. This was of course attributed in many countries, most vociferously in Britain, to putting the new economic ideologies into practice. It appeared as though western Europe was moving towards a new policy consensus. In this new consensus national government was to have a much smaller role to play, although it was only in the late 1980s and only in some countries that the national budgets which had sustained demand in the earlier period began to diminish as a share of GDP and they are everywhere still a much larger share than they were in the 1950s. The smaller role for the machinery of national government in the new consensus allowed a greater relative role for the Community; the European Commission could appear as a more potent agent of deregulation of markets precisely because its supranationality gave it a greater scope and effectiveness. The clearest indication however that the reduced role of national government did not mean any diminution of nationalism was that its admired champion was Margaret Thatcher.

The Single European Act was imbued with nostalgia. While it was a serious attempt to revive the concept of integration as an extra stimulus to national income growth, it relied on the intellectual framework of the 1950s as a guide to what should be done in the new circumstances. The concept of economic growth still remained the one possible ideology that could span the widening gap in economic and political ideas between and within the member-states. This was so even in the United Kingdom where the post-war consensus was represented as a huge political error and the source of the country's present troubles, not surprisingly since it was to Britain that it had brought the least benefits at the time. Reliance on the same basic idea that national income growth could best be stimulated by eliminating the constraints which the narrow confines of European national markets impose led to a revival of the federalist initiative based on the assumption that one market must mean one money, one money mean one central bank, and one central bank mean political union.

Europe has been there before. This was the American argument in ECA in 1950 when some officials hoped that the European Payments Union would lead within two years to a Western European central bank. The same argument was made at the end of the 1960s when the Community adopted the Werner Report proclaiming the necessity of a common currency. After the adoption of the Werner Report the gaps between the Community currencies' exchange rates with each other widened. It is true that throughout the 1980s exchange rates between most Community currencies were kept within fixed margins by various devices such as the European Monetary System. But these were almost as wide for the strong currencies, and wider for the weaker ones, than the margins of fluctuation which the British wanted to introduce in the 1950s when one of their motives was to break up the EPU and eliminate all possibility of a Community currency which might rival sterling.

In 1988 the European Commission tried to bring the pressures of those business and financial groups who believe they would benefit from Monetary Union to bear on central bankers through the Committee for the Study of Economic and Monetary Union. It was a measure of the way the political system in the 1980s had swung more towards representing the interests of capital. The central bankers themselves wished to assert their independence from the politicians who subjected them to so subordinate a role during the heyday of the post-war political consensus, and there is now a much more powerful political constituency arguing that this would be advantageous. An independent European central bank, so ran the argument, could liberate monetary policy from the inflationary importuning of national politicians trying to win elections. This had a strong appeal to the much greater share of the population than in the 1950s living off inflexible sources of income, especially the much greater proportion of aged and retired people.

The once-and-for-all gain from reducing the uncertainties caused by exchange rate fluctuations and from the elimination of the transaction costs arising from having eleven separate currencies in the Union is calculated to be no greater than the small static gains to trade estimated in 1956 to result from the removal of tariffs by the Treaty of Rome. As in the earlier case of commodity trade, it is on the unquantifiable dynamic forces which would be released by the change to one money that the advocates of European Monetary Union rely for the force of their argument. But which policies would best release these dynamic forces, if they exist? It is perfectly possible in present political circumstances, even in the western European country which has consistently had the lowest rates of inflation, to have a tight monetary policy and a highly inflationary budget deficit if that is what political priorities demand, as the history of Germany since 1989 shows.

In spite of the hopes that an anti-inflationary consensus across western Europe would be strong enough to generate common anti-inflationary policies, it was not. The inter-governmental discussions on currency union would probably never have got as far as the Maastricht negotiations in December 1991 had not the Soviet Union withdrawn its protection from the German Democratic Republic. European Monetary Union, fading as the basis for a political consensus, became for France the gage that Germany would remain within the integrationist framework in which it had been earlier fixed. It was the gaps in the Berlin Wall that led the Strasbourg European Council in December 1990 to call for a treaty on Monetary Union. By that date Monetary Union had come to be seen by France as the renewal of Germany's commitment to, and control by, the 'West'.

This recalls the central political condition which has been required in the past from every act of integration. To succeed, every step in the creation of the Community had always to be at the intersection of two tensions; the advancement of national policies had to be combined with a guarantee that Germany would be more safely contained within the framework. Only when both objectives could be simultaneously achieved were countries ready to abandon elements of national sovereignty.

The advancement of national policies was easier within an integrationist framework when the number of nations was small. Even when it is possible to find the crucial point of intersection between the pursuit of national economic advantage and the retention of Germany within a common political structure the complexity of the deals required is now much greater. The difficulty was seen most clearly in the field of social policy in the Maastricht Treaty. Over most of the Community the element of the old consensus which has survived most strongly is a commitment to social welfare. Even the poorest member-states were ready at Maastricht to accept a general declaration about the need for Europeanization of legislation on the length of the working week, on minimum wages and on provision for maternity leave, a complex document which reasserted the importance of labour to the political consensus. The argument for 'harmonization' (upwards) of wages and welfare made so vigorously by Belgium in 1950–2 and France in 1956–7 against Germany is now made by Germany against the others. The same concessions as before were made, except by the United Kingdom. To howls of patriotic fervour from the daily press a British prime minister successfully insisted on Britain's right to keep lower wages, lower social security benefits, and to continue to discriminate legally against trade unions. If these truly constitute an advantage in intra-Union competition, it may be only because the lower-paid are less able than the better rewarded to take advantage of the opportunities offered by the EU for Joyce's 'silence, exile, and cunning'.

It was not merely an intellectual exercise to derive a new theory of integration which fits the historical facts. It will not be simply decided by accidental pragmatism whether the European states do move to a further stage of integration or whether they content themselves with further experiments in interdependence. The choice depends on the way national political consensuses are reformulated. If the new economic and social policies which began to take shape in western Europe in the mid-1980s establish a common pattern, some of them may be better advanced within an integrationist framework whereas strong differences in national policy choices will make the Maastricht agreements a marginal comment on the flow of Europe's history, like the 1953 proposals for a European Political Community.

There has not been before a major international currency without a government supporting it. Domestic politics in Europe will determine the Euro's fate, not central bankers. The conclusion is not just that political science need not relapse into pragmatism but that there is an explanation of integration, albeit of little predictive power by itself, which fits the historical facts and helps in understanding what choices can and should be made over the next decade.

For the rescued and reconstructed European nation-state the ultimate basis for its survival is the same as it always was, allegiance. The well-attested secondary allegiance paid to Community institutions in member-states shows that the supranation, like the nation, if it endures and provides a consistent and effective level of organization can count on the loyalty of its 'citizens'. Over the forty years of its existence the Community has been a remarkably benign institution in comparison with the nation-state. It has no police, no prisons, no soldiers. Its law intrudes only into a very small number of areas and in many of those it is seen as an improvement on national law. Most of the attacks in the name of 'freedom' on regulations from Brussels can be readily identified as a cover for vested interests. The freedom to swim in a tide of sewage, like the freedom to dine at the Ritz, is a somewhat abstract principle on which to ask people to condemn a political organization. Even a free labour market within the Union threatens the social status of only small numbers of people and is obviously not the threat from immigration which they most fear.

The expression, and perhaps even the sentiment, of prejudice against fellow Community citizens is an increasingly unusual occurrence. For the citizens of member-states to denounce each other in the language commonly used by one alleged nationality in eastern Europe about another in general provokes only satirical ridicule. This makes a humane contrast with forty years of communist nationalist government as it does with western Europe's earlier history. It is admittedly an alliance of sentiment between the rich and mostly white. None the less, the sense of a common allegiance to something beyond the nation has developed with the sense that the supranation may in certain respects open channels for political action which would remain blocked within the nation itself. This, and the weakening of prejudice, suggest that the present European Parliament could function with the same democratic ease as national parliamentary assemblies, providing it had something to do.

What little it has so far had to do has been defined by the instrumentality of the Community as an integrationist solution to national problems.

The evolution of the Community's political machinery has had little to do with European federalism or with abstract demands for a European constitution as a desirable thing in itself, because the programme of the European federalists was irrelevant to immediate political needs. Many of them in any case, perhaps the majority, were opposed to the domestic policies of the nation-states. Attempts to mobilize political support for surrenders of sovereignty by evoking the idea of one federal democratic Europe were by no means always helpful to integration. Opposition to the Community, as well as support for it, could be mobilized around the same idea. The absolute defenders of national sovereignty, those for whom no solution to the problem of governance is acceptable other than a national one, can easily misrepresent the process of integration as the end of the nation. The truth is that whenever the Community member-states had to implement their surrenders of sovereignty they produced an arrangement which left almost all political power with the nation-state. This was still the case after 1989 with the French proposals for a closer political union. It is not through a federalizing of the state's remaining powers that Paris sees a guarantee of Germany's fidelity to the present framework, nor through granting greater powers to the European Parliament.

This is not surprising, when in the past to equip the European Communities with a parliament which replicated national democracy would have been needlessly to curb the states' powers to manage what was a restricted political device to provide additional support for policies already determined by national political parties. If parties have organized themselves only in a superficial way in the European Parliament, that is because no more has been needed. The political machinery of the Union resembles the court of the eighteenth-century German Empire. There is a numerous and deferential attendance around the President of the Commission. A hierarchical bureaucracy attends to the myriad small facets of relationships with the surrounding greater powers, the member-states, for every decision has to be finely attuned to the wishes of the real political power to which the Union's continued existence is useful. The struggles to appoint to its offices are like those within the Imperial Diet.

The history of national parliaments suggests that important popular demands will only focus on the European Parliament if the power of raising taxation is shifted to the Union level; 'No taxation without representation' appears as the one political slogan to keep its validity for more than two centuries. Until then it is within the nation that political parties have to fulfil their task of organizing a democratic consensus. It seems beside the point to denounce the European Community for an undemocratic and bureaucratic pursuit of policies which were themselves the choice of national democracies. If that however is construed as evidence that the nation-states themselves are not truly democratic, or that in internationalizing policies they are seeking to restrict the force of postwar democratic pressures, there is little in the argument of this book to refute those conclusions. Indeed there is much to suggest that the post-war role of more democratic political parties in formulating the immediate post-war domestic policy choices on which consensus depended was only a temporary phase and that these parties, especially since 1968, have become increasingly part of the executive.

Federalism is only a bogeyman; denouncing it a way of avoiding the real issues. National sovereignty is another bogeyman; preserving it is another way of avoiding the real issues. Elevating national sovereignty into an absolute irreducible entity, giving to it a mystical attribution, is to deny the historical record of the development of the European state. The evidence is that in the recent past sovereignty has been only a legal and administrative convenience, like the state itself. The argument that the Europeanization of policy necessarily usurps national democratic control treats the abstract concept of national sovereignty as though it were a real form of political machinery. The states will make further surrenders of sovereignty if, but only if, they have to in the attempt to survive.

Appealing though the idea of a united Europe is, the strength of the European Community does not lie in that abstract appeal. It lies in the uncertainty of the nation-state's destination. The European rescue of the nation-state, a positive and beneficent experience for the majority of people, marked some limits of the state's capacity to satisfy by its own powers and within its own frontiers the demands of its citizens. Equally positive national policy responses may demonstrate other limits to the state's capacity. In this sense, there may at any time emerge a force within the developed nation-state which may propel it towards integration. But whether the states make that choice still depends absolutely on the nature of domestic policy choices and thus on national politics. In whose interests will the brutal power of the state continue to exist? Who will run it? And for whom? It is the answers to these questions which will determine the future of the European Union.

Bibliography

The bibliography is confined to the works referred to in the text, except that a very small number of other general works which will be of particular value to the reader has been added.

LIST OF OFFICIAL PUBLICATIONS CITED

Belgium, Administration des Mines, *Annales des Mines de Belgique*.

Belgium, Banque de Belgique, *L'économie belge*.

Belgium, Fédération des Associations Charbonnières, *La Belgique devant le problème charbonnier* (Brussels, 1945).

Belgium Ministère des Affaires Economiques, Institut National de la Statistique, *Annuaire Statistique de la Belgique et du Congo Belge*.

Belgium, Ministère de l'Economie, *L'économie belge*.

Belgium, Ministère de l'Intérieur et de l'Hygiène, Statistique Générale, *Annuaire Statistique de la Belgique et du Congo Belge*.

Denmark, Danmarks Statistik *Vareomsætningen med Udlandet*.

European Coal, Iron and Steel Community, *General Reports on the Activities of the Community*.

——, *Recueil statistique*, 1953.

——, *Etude du développement économique des Régions de Charleroi, du Centre et du Borinage*, Collection d'économie et politique régionale no. 2. Programmes de développement et de conversion (Luxembourg, 1962).

——, *CECA 1952–1962. Résultats. Limites. Perspectives* (Luxembourg, 1963).

——, *Etude sur les perspectives énergétiques à long terme de la Communauté Européenne* (Luxembourg, 1964).

European Payments Union, Management Board, *Final Report on the Operations of the European Payments Union* (1959).

France, Commissariat Général au Plan. *Rapport général sur le premier plan de modernisation* (Paris, 1946).

——, *Quatre ans d'exécution du plan de modernisation* (1951).

——, *Cinq ans d'exécution du plan de modernisation* (1952).

——, *Rapport sur la réalisation du plan de modernisation et d'équipement de l'Union Française, Année 1952* (1953).

——, *Deuxième Plan de modernisation et d'équipement. Projet de loi portant approbation* (1954).

——, *Deuxième Plan de modernisation et d'équipement (1954–57)*, Loi no. 56–342, 27 March 1956.

——, *Troisième Plan de modernisation et d'équipement (1958–61)*, Decret no. 59–443, 19 March 1959.

France, Conseil Economique, *Incidences du Pool Vert sur la production agricole dans les territoires extra-métropolitains de l'Union Française, Rapport présenté au nom de la Commission de l'Economie de l'Union Française*, February 1954.

France, Direction Générale des Douanes et Droits Indirects, *Tableaux du commerce extérieur de la France*.

France, Institut National de la Statistique et des Etudes Economiques, *Etudes et Conjoncture*.

——, *Notes et études documentaires*, no. 1040, 'Situation et perspectives de l'agriculture française en 1948', December 1948.

France, Ministère des Affaires Etrangères, *Documents Diplomatiques Français*.

France, Ministère de l'Agriculture, *Notes et études documentaires, no. 1314, Le plan quadriennal (1948–1952)*.

——, *Commissions de la production agricole et de l'équipement rural, Résumé du Rapport Général* (1953).

France, Ministère des Finances et des Affaires Economiques, *Rapport général présenté par la Commission créée le 6 janvier 1954 pour l'étude des disparités entre les prix français et étrangers* (Paris, 1954).

——, Institut National de la Statistique et des Etudes Economiques, *Annuaire Statistique de la France*.

General Agreement on Trade and Tariffs (GATT), *International Trade*.

German Federal Republic, Auswärtiges Amt, *Gutachten zur Fragen eines Europäischen Agrargemeinschaft* (Bonn, 1953).

German Federal Republic, Bundesarchiv, *Die Kabinettprotokolle der Bundeseregierung*.

German Federal Republic, Bundesministerium für Ernährung, Landwirtschaft und Forsten, *Sicherheit und Landwirtschaft, Vertragsfolge der internationalen öffentlichen landwirtschaftlichen Tagung am 9 und 10 Mai 1951* (Hiltrop, 1951).

German Federal Republic, Bundesministerium für Ernährung und Landwirtschaft, *Grüne Berichte*.

German Federal Republic, Deutsche Kohlenbergbau-Leitung, *Die Kohlenwirtschaft der Welt in Zahlen. Statistische Ubersichten über die Kohlenwirtschaft Deutschlands und des Auslandes* (Essen, 1952).

German Federal Republic, Statistisches Bundesamt, *Der Aussenhandel der Bundesrepublik Deutschland*.

——, *Statistische Jahrbucher der Bundesrepublik Deutschland*.

——, *Wirtschaft und Statistik*.

International Monetary Fund, *Balance of Payments Yearbook*.

——, *International Financial Statistics* (August 1959).

International Sugar Council, *The World Sugar Economy: Structure and Policies* (London, 1963).

Italy, Istituto Centrale de Statistica, *Annuario Statistico Italiano*.

Netherlands, Centraal Bureau voor de Statistiek, *Maandstatistiek van den In–Uit–En Doorvoer van Nederland*.

——, *Tachtig Jaren Statistiek in Tijdreeksen, 1899–1979* (The Hague, 1979).

Netherlands, Centraal Planbureau, Monografie Nr. 10, *Voorspelling en realisatie. De Voorspellingen van het Centraal Planbureau in de jaren 1953–1963* (The Hague, 1965).

Netherlands, *Stichting voor de Landbouw, Jaarverslag* (1948, 1949).

Organization for Economic Cooperation and Development (OECD), *General Statistics*.

——, *Agriculture and Economic Growth* (Paris, 1965).

——, *The Engineering Industries in North America – Europe – Japan 1965* (Paris, 1965).

——, *Low Incomes in Agriculture. Problems and Policies* (Paris, 1965).

Organization for European Economic Cooperation (OEEC), *National Accounts Statistics 1950–1968*.
——, *Statistical Bulletins of Foreign Trade* (Series II, Series IV).
——, *Interim Report on the European Recovery Programme* (Paris, 1948).
——, *The Coal Position in Europe in 1953 and 1954. Report of the Coal Committee,* 20 November 1953.
——, *Intra-European Economic Cooperation in the Production and Distribution of Power* (Paris, May 1955).
——, *Seventh Report of the OEEC. Economic Expansion and its Problems* (Paris, 1956).
——, *First Report on Agricultural Policies in Europe and North America* (1956).
——, *Price and Income Policies. Second Report on Agricultural Policies in Europe and North America* (Paris, 1957).
——, *The Engineering Industries in Europe 1959–60* (Paris, 1960).
——, *Trends in Agricultural Policies since 1955, Fifth Report on Agricultural Policies,* (Paris, 1961).
Stockholm International Peace Research Institute (SIPRI), *Yearbook of World Armaments and Disarmament.*
Sweden, Sveriges Officiella Statistik, *Handel.*
United Kingdom, Board of Trade, *Board of Trade Journal.*
——, *Accounts Relating to the Trade and Navigation of the United Kingdom.* United Kingdom, Central Statistical Office, *Economic Trends.*
——, *Monthly Digest of Statistics.*
United Kingdom, Parliamentary Papers, Cmd. 5648. *Report Presented by M. van Zeeland to the Governments of the United Kingdom and France on the Possibility of Obtaining a General Reduction of the Obstacles to International Trade,* 26 January 1938.
——, Cmd. 6404. *Social Insurance and Allied Services* (1942).
United Kingdom, Society of Motor Manufacturers and Traders, *Monthly Statistical Review.*
United Nations, Economic Commission for Europe, *Some Factors in Economic Growth in Europe during the 1950s* (Geneva, 1964).
——, *Annual Bulletin of Transport Statistics for Europe.*
——, *Economic Bulletin for Europe.*
——, *Economic Survey of Europe.*
——, Coal Division, *Monthly Bulletin of Coal Statistics.*
——, Coal Division, *Bulletin of Statistics.*
——, Committee on Agricultural Problems, *Review of the Agricultural Situation in Europe at the End of 1958* (Geneva, 1958).
United Nations, Food and Agriculture Organization, *Commerce Yearbooks.*
——, *Production Yearbooks.*
United Nations, Statistical Division, *Commodity Trade Statistics,* Series D.
——, *Quarterly Bulletin of Coal Statistics.*
——, *Quarterly Bulletin of Steel Statistics.*
United States of America, Department of State. *Foreign Relations of the United States.*
World Tourism Organization, *Yearbook of International Travel Statistics.*

LIST OF PUBLISHED SOURCES

Abel, W., *et al.,* *Probleme einer europäischen Agrarintegration* (Vienna, 1953).
Abelshauser, W., *Wirtschaft in Westdeutschland 1945–1948. Rekonstruktion und Wachstumsbedingungen in der amerikanischen und britischen Zone* (Stuttgart, 1975).

——, 'Wiederaufbau vor dem Marshall-Plan. Westeuropas Wachstumschancen und die Wirtschaftsordnungspolitik in der zweiten Hälfte der vierziger Jahre', *Vierteljahrshefte für Zeitgeschichte*, Bd. 29, Heft iv, 1981.

Abramovitz, M., *Thinking about Growth and Other Essays on Economic Growth and Welfare* (Cambridge, 1989).

Adenauer, K., *Briefe, 1945–1947, 1947–1949, 1949–1951*, 3 vols (ed. R. Morsey and H.-P. Schwarz) (Berlin, 1983, 1984, 1985).

——, *Teegespräche* (ed. R. Morsey and H.-P. Schwarz) (Berlin, 1985).

Alford, B. W. E., *British Economic Performance 1945–1975* (London, 1988).

Andrieu, C., 'La politique du crédit, frein ou moteur de la modernisation (1945–1950)?', in P. Fridenson and A. Strauss (eds) (1987).

Armengaud, A., 'L'Europe, probleme économique et social', *Politique étrangère*, numéro spécial, *L'Union Française*, 1954.

Armstrong, A. C., 'The Motor Industry and the British Economy', *District Bank Review*, no. 164, September 1967.

Aron, R. and Lerner, D. (eds), *La querelle de la C.E.D.* (Paris, 1956).

Asbeek Brusse, W., *Tariffs, Trade and European Integration, 1947–1957. From Study Group to Common Market* (New York, 1997).

——, 'The Stikker Plan', in R. T. Griffiths (ed.) (1990).

——, and Griffiths, R. T., 'The Dutch Cabinet and the Rome Treaties', in E. Serra (ed.) (1989).

Von Bandemer, J. D., and Ilgen, A. P., *Probleme des Steinkohlenbergbaus. Die Arbeiter-und Förderverlagerung in den Revieren der Borinage und Ruhr* (Basel, 1963).

Barbadoro, I., *La Federconsorzi nella politica agraria italiana* (Rome, 1963).

Barmeyer, H., *Andreas Hermes und die Organisation der deutsche Landwirtschaft. Christliche Bauernvereine, Reichslandbund, Grüne Front, Reichsnährstand 1928–1933* (Stuttgart, 1971).

Barnett, C., *The Audit of War; The Illusion and Reality of Britain as a Great Nation* (London, 1986).

Barral, P., *Les Agrariens français de Méline à Pisani* (Paris, 1968).

Baudhuin, F., 'Le Plan Schuman prend forme', *Revue Générale Belge*, April 1951.

Baum, W. C., *The French Economy and the State* (Princeton, 1958).

Becker, J., and Knipping, F. (eds), *Power in Europe? Great Britain, France, Italy and Germany in a Post-War World, 1945–1950* (Berlin, 1986).

Von Beckerath, E., *et al.*, *Wirtschaftragen der freien Welt. Festgabe zum 60. Geburtstag von Bundeswirtschaftsminister Ludwig Erhard* (Frankfurt-am-Main, 1957).

Benoit, E., *Europe at Sixes and Sevens. The Common Market, the Free Trade Association and the United States* (New York, 1961).

Bertini, F., 'La DC e la politica agricola dal 1947 al 1955', *Il Ponte*, vol. xxxvi, no. 2–3.

Beyen, J.-W., *Het Spel en de Knikkers. Een kroniek van vijftig jaren* (Rotterdam, 1968).

Bienaymé, A., 'La réorientation de la croissance planifiée française et les risques de freinage par le commerce extérieur', *Cahiers de l'I.S.E.A.*, Série P. no. 4, August 1960.

Binder, A., *Internationale Regulierungen auf dem Weltweizenmarkt*, Kieler Studien, no. 23 (Kiel, 1952).

Bloemen, E., 'A Problem to Every Solution. The Six and the Free Trade Area', in T. Olesen (ed.), *Interdependence versus Integration. Denmark, Scandinavia and Western Europe 1945–1960* (Odense, 1995).

Blum, L., 'A l'échelle humaine', in *L'Oeuvre de Léon Blum*, vol. 7 (Paris, 1955).

Boarman, P. M., *Germany's Economic Dilemma* (New Haven, 1964).

Boerckel, W., *Einfuhr-und Vorratsstellen als Mittel der Agrarpolitik* (Mainz, 1959).

Bolton, Sir G., *A Banker's World. The Revival of the City 1957–1970* (ed. G. R. Fry)(London, 1970).

Bonato, C., 'Il piano dodecennale per lo sviluppo dell'agricoltura: 1952–1960', in *I Piani di Sviluppo in Italia dal 1945 al 1960. Studi in Memoria del Jacopo Mazzei* (Milan, 1960).

Bonelli, F. (ed.), *Acciaio per l'industrializzazione: Contributi allo studio del problema siderurgico italiano* (Turin, 1982).

Booth, A., 'The "Keynesian Revolution", in Economic Policy-Making', *Economic History Review*, vol. xxxvi, 1983.

—, *British Economic Policy, 1931–1949: Was There a Keynesian Revolution?* (Brighton, 1989).

Bourneuf, A., *Norway, The Planned Revival* (Cambridge, Mass., 1958).

Boussard, I., *Vichy et la corporation paysanne* (Paris, 1980).

Bower, T., *The Paperclip Conspiracy. The Battle for the Spoils and Secrets of Nazi Germany* (London, 1987).

Boyries, L., 'La repartition d'après les modes de financement des investissements réalisées dans l'agriculture française au cours des plans de modernisation et d'équipement', *Economie rurale*, January 1957.

Brinkley, D., and Hackett, C., *Jean Monnet and the Path to European Unity* (London, 1991).

Brittan, S., *Steering the Economy* (London, 1964).

Broadberry, S. N., *The Productivity Race: British Manufacturing in International Perspective 1850–1990* (Cambridge, 1997).

Brugmans, H., *L'Idée européenne, 1918–1965* (Bruges, 1965).

—, *Prophètes et fondateurs de l'Europe* (Bruges, 1974).

Buchheim, C., *Die Wiedereingliederung Westdeutschlands in die Weltwirtschaft 1945–1958* (Munich, 1990).

Bullen, R., 'The British Government and the Schuman Plan, May 1950–March 1951', in K. Schwabe (ed.) (1988).

—, 'Britain and "Europe", 1950–1957', in E. Serra (ed.) (1989).

Bullock, A., *Ernest Bevin. Foreign Secretary, 1945–1951* (London, 1983).

Burgess, S., and Edwards, G., 'The Six Plus One: British Policy-Making and the Question of European Economic Integration, 1955,' *International Affairs*, vol. lxiv, no. 3, 1988.

Butler, R. A. (Lord Butler of Saffron Walden), *The Art of the Possible; The Memoirs of Lord Butler* (London, 1971).

Cairncross, Sir A., 'The Postwar Years, 1945–77', in R. Floud and D. McCloskey (eds) (1981).

—, *Years of Recovery. British Economic Policy 1945–1951* (London, 1985).

—, *The Price of War. British Policy on German Reparations 1941–1949* (Oxford, 1986).

—, and Watts, N., *The Economic Section 1939–1961. A Study in Economic Advising* (London, 1989).

Camps, M., *Britain and the European Community 1955–1963* (Princeton and London, 1964).

Cao-Pinna, V. (ed.), *Le esportazioni italiane* (Turin, 1965).

Carew, A., *Labour under the Marshall Plan: The Politics of Productivity and the Marketing of Management Science* (Manchester, 1987).

Carli, G., 'Die Konvertierbarkeit der italienischen Lira', in G. Haberler *et al.* (1954).

Carré, J.-J., Dubois, P. and Malinvaud, E., *French Economic Growth* (Stanford, 1975).

Catti de Gasperi, M. R., *La nostra patria europa* (Rome, 1969).

Caves, R. E., *et al.*, *Britain's Economic Prospects* (Washington DC, 1968).

Cayre, H., *Vingt ans d'économie betterave sucre en Europe* (Strasbourg, 1966).

Cépède, M., *Agriculture et alimentation en France durant la deuxième guerre mondiale* (Paris, 1961).

Chapelle-Julière, J., 'La mobilité des mineurs du Charbonnage du Bois-du-Cazier (1900–1945), *Revue du Nord*, vol. lxxii, January–March 1990.

Chombart de Lauwe, J., 'Avons-nous une politique agricole aujourd'hui?', *Revue française d'économie et de sociologie rurales*, nos. 79 and 80, 1969 (numéro spécial, *Vingt ans d'agriculture française 1948–1968*).

Clarke, W. M., *The City in the World Economy* (London, 1965).

Cleary M. C., *Peasants, Politicians and Producers. The Organisation of Agriculture in France Since 1918* (Cambridge, 1989).

Clerx, J. M. M. J., *Nederland en de liberalisatie van het handels-en betalingsverkeer (1945–1958)* (Groningen, 1986).

Cohen, B. J., *The Future of Sterling as an International Currency* (London, 1971).

Coninx, A., 'L'agriculture belge et le protocol de Luxembourg', *Etudes Economiques*, no. 79, 1950.

Coppé, A., *Problèmes d'économie charbonnière. Essai d'orientation économique* (Bruges, 1939).

Crotty, R. D., *Irish Agricultural Production; Its Volume and Structure* (Cork, 1960).

Curzon, G., *Multilateral Commercial Diplomacy. The General Agreement on Tariffs and Trade and its Impact on National Commercial Policies and Techniques* (London, 1965).

Dassetto, F., and Dumoulin, M., *Mémoires d'une catastrophe. Marcinelle, 8 août 1956* (Brussels, 1986).

Day, A. C. L., *The Future of Sterling* (London, 1954).

Debuyst, F., *La Fonction parlementaire en Belgique: méchanismes d'accès et images* (Brussels, 1966).

Degryse, W., *et al.*, *Le Borinage* (Brussels, 1958).

Delarge, G., 'Le Plan Schuman et l'industrie houillère du Borinage', *Etudes Economiques*, no. 81/82, November 1951.

de Liagre Böhl, H., Nekkers, J., and Slot, L., *Nederland industrialiseert! Politieke en ideologische strijd rondom het naoorlogse industrialisatiebeleid, 1945–1955* (Nijmegen, 1981).

Delorme, H., and Tavernier, Y., *Les paysans français et l'Europe* (Paris, 1969).

Delville, P., 'L'Industrie charbonnière devant le plan Schuman', *Etudes Economiques*, no. 81/82, November 1951.

Demeure de Lespaul, C., 'L'industrie charbonnière belge devant la menace des importations', *Bulletin de l'Institut de Recherches Economiques et Sociales de Louvain*, vol. xv, no. 1, 1949.

Denison, E. F., *Why Growth Rates Differ* (Washington DC, 1967).

Deutsch, K., *et al.*, *Political Community and the North Atlantic Area* (Princeton, 1957).

Devos, E., *Le Patronat belge face au Plan Schuman (9 mai 1950–5 février 1952)* (Brussels, 1989).

Dewhurst, F., *et al.*, *Europe's Needs and Resources* (New York, 1961).

Dickhaus, M., *Die Bundesbank in Westeuropäischen Wiederaufbau: die internationale Währungspolitik der Bundesrepublik Deutschland 1948 bis 1958* (Munich, 1966).

Diebold W. J., Jnr, *Trade and Payments in Western Europe: A Study in Economic Cooperation 1947–1951* (New York, 1952).

——, *The Schuman Plan. A Study in International Cooperation* (New York, 1959).

Diekmann, A., *Die Automobilnachfrage als Konjunktur und Wachstumsfaktor* (Tübingen, 1975).

Dobson, A. P., *US Wartime Aid to Britain 1940–1946* (London, 1986).

Doria, M., *Ansaldo: L'impresa e lo stato* (Milan, 1989).

Dow, J. C. R., *The Management of the British Economy, 1945–1960* (Cambridge, 1970).

Duchêne, F., *Jean Monnet: The First Statesman of Interdependence* (New York, 1994).

——, 'Jean Monnet's Methods', in D. Brinkley and C. Hackett (1991).

——, Szczepanik, E. and Legg, W., *New Limits on European Agriculture* (Totowa, 1985).

Dumoulin, M. (ed.), *La Belgique et les débuts de la construction européenne. De la guerre aux traités de Rome* (Louvain-la-Neuve, 1987).

Dumoulin, M., 'La Belgique et les débuts du Plan Schuman (mai 1950–février 1952)', in K. Schwabe (ed.) (1988).

Dunnett, P. J. S., *The Decline of the British Motor Industry. The Effects of Government Policy, 1945–1979* (London, 1980).

Duroselle, J. B., and Serra, E. (eds), *Italia e Francia 1946–1954* (Milan, 1988).

Economist Intelligence Unit, *Britain and Europe. A Study of the Effects on British Manufacturing Industry of a Free Trade Area and the Common Market* (London, 1957).

Ehrmann, H. W., 'The French Trade Associations and the Ratification of the Schuman Plan', *World Politics*, vol. 6, no. 4, 1954.

Einaudi, L., *La Guerra e l'unità europea* (Milan, 1948).

——, *Il Buongoverno. Saggi d'economia e politica (1897–1954)* (Bari, 1954).

Emminger, O., *D-Mark, Dollar, Währungskrisen: Erinnerungen eines ehemaligen Bundesbankpräsidenten* (Stuttgart, 1986).

Van der Eng, P., *De Marshall-Hulp: een perspectief voor Nederland 1947–1953* (Houten, 1987).

English, J.-L., and Riot, D., *Entretiens avec Pierre Pflimlin* (Strasbourg, 1989).

Erhard, L., *Deutschland Rückkehr zum Weltmarkt* (Düsseldorf, 1953).

Esping-Andersen, G., *The Three Worlds of Welfare Capitalism* (Cambridge, 1990).

Farquharson, J., *The Plough and the Sword; the NSDAP and Agriculture in Germany 1928–1945* (London, 1976).

——, *The Western Allies and the Politics of Food. Agrarian Management in Post War Germany* (Leamington Spa, 1985).

——, 'The "Essential Division". Britain and the Partition of Germany 1945–9', *German History*, vol. ix, no. 1, 1991.

Fauvet, J., and Mendras, H., *Les Paysans et la politique dans la France contemporaine* (Paris, 1958).

Feldman, G. D., and Tenfelde, K. (eds), *Workers, Owners and Politics in Coal Mining. An International Comparison of Industrial Relations* (New York, 1990).

Flora, P., *et al.*, *State, Economy and Society in Western Europe 1815–1975* (Frankfurt-am-Main, 1983).

——, *Growth to Limits. The Western European Welfare States since World War Two*, 4 vols (Berlin, 1986–).

——, and Alber, J., 'Modernization, Democratization, and the Development of Welfare States in Western Europe', in P. Flora and A. Heidenheimer (eds), *The Development of Welfare States in Europe and America* (New Brunswick, 1981).

Floud, R., and McCloskey, D. (eds), *The Economic History of Britain since 1700*, 2 vols (Cambridge, 1981).

Forget, J., 'De Belgische landbouw tegenover de internationale vraagstukken', *Landbouwtijdschrift*, iv, April 1951.

Frank, I., *The European Common Market. An Analysis of Commercial Policy* (New York, 1961).

Freisberg, E., *Die Grüne Hurde Europas. Deutsche Agrarpolitik und EWG* (Cologne, 1965).

Fridenson, P., and Strauss, A., (eds), *Le Capitalisme français: 19ᵉ–20ᵉ siècle, Blocages et dynamismes d'une croissance* (Paris, 1987).

Fromont, P., 'Les équivoques du pool vert et les projets d'expansion agricole européenne', *Revue économique*, no. 5, 1953.

Fursdon, E., *The European Defence Community, a History* (London, 1980).

Gardner, R. N., *Sterling–Dollar Diplomacy. Anglo-American Collaboration in the Reconstruction of Multilateral Trade* (Oxford, 1956).

de Gasperi, A., *Discorsi politici* (Rome, 1969).

Gerbet, P., *La Construction de l'Europe* (Paris, 1983).

—— *et al.*, *Le Relèvement 1944–1949* (Paris, 1991).

Gilbert, M., and Kravis, I. B., *An International Comparison of National Products and the Purchasing Power of Currencies* (OEEC, Paris, 1954).

—— *et al.*, *Comparative National Products and Price Levels* (OEEC, Paris, 1958).

Gillingham, J. R., *Belgian Business in the Nazi New Order* (Ghent, 1977).

——, *Coal, Steel and the Rebirth of Europe, 1945–1955* (Cambridge, 1991).

Gilpin, R., *The Political Economy of International Relations* (Princeton, 1987).

Greenwood, S., *Britain and European Cooperation since 1945* (Oxford, 1992).

——, *The Alternative Alliance: Anglo-French Relations before the Coming of NATO, 1944–48* (London, 1996).

Griffiths, R. T., 'The Abortive Dutch Assault on European Tariffs 1950–1952', in M. Wintle (ed.) (1988).

——, 'The Schuman Plan Negotiations: The Economic Clauses', in K. Schwabe (ed.) (1988).

—— (ed.), *The Netherlands and the Integration of Europe 1945–1957* (Amsterdam, 1990).

Griffiths, R. T., and Lynch, F. M. B., 'L'échec de la "Petite Europe": les négociations Fritalux/Finebel, 1949–1950', *Revue historique*, vol. cclxxiv, no. 1, 1985.

——, 'L'échec de la "Petite Europe": Le Conseil Tripartite, 1944–1948', *Guerres mondiales et conflits contemporains*, no. 252, 1988.

——, and Milward, A. S., 'The Beyen Plan and The European Political Community', in W. Maihofer (ed.), *Noi si mura. Selected Working Papers of the European University Institute* (Florence, 1986).

Griliches, Z., and Ringstad, V., *Economies of Scale and the Form of the Production Function: An Econometric Study of Norwegian Manufacturing Establishment Data* (Amsterdam, 1971).

Groot, K. G., *De Financiering van de industrialisatie in Nederland* (Leiden, 1957).

le Guennec, J., *L'Agriculture dans le C.E.E.*, vol. 1, *24 ans de production*, Collections de l'INSEE, no. 528 (Série E, no. 104), 1987.

Guillen, P., 'La France et la négociation du traité d'Euratom', *Relations internationales*, no. 44, 1985.

——, 'Les vicissitudes des rapports franco–italiens de la recontre de Cannes (décembre 1948) a celle de Santa Margherita (février, 1951)', in J. B. Duroselle and E. Serra (eds) (1988).

Gutt, C., *La Belgique au carrefour, 1940–1944* (Paris, 1971).

Haas, E., *The Uniting of Europe. Political, Social and Economic Forces, 1950–1957* (Stanford, 1958).

Haberler, G., *et al.*, *Die Konvertierbarkeit der europäischen Währungen* (Zürich, 1954).

Hallstein, W., *Die europäische Gemeinschaft* (Düsseldorf, 1975).

Hansen, B., *Fiscal Policy in Seven Countries 1955–1965* (OECD, Paris, 1969).

Harper, J. L., *America and the Reconstruction of Italy 1945–1948* (Cambridge, 1986).

Harris, R., and Seldon, A., *Hire Purchase in a Free Society* (London, 1958).

Harrod, Sir R., 'Convertibility Problems', *The Bankers' Magazine*, vol. clxxviii, 1954.

——, *Topical Comment* (London, 1961).

Harryvan, A. G., and Kersten, A. E., 'The Netherlands, Benelux and the Relance Européenne 1954–1955', in E. Serra (ed.) (1989).

van der Harst, J., 'European Union and Atlantic partnership: political, military and economic aspects of Dutch defence, 1948–1954, and the impact of the European Defence Community' (Ph.D. dissertation, European University Institute, 1988).

Häuser, K., 'West Germany', in National Bureau of Economic Research and Brookings Institution, *Foreign Tax Policies and Economic Growth* (New York, 1966).

Heitzer, H., *Die CDU in der britischen Zone 1945–1949. Gründung, Organisation, Program und Politik* (Düsseldorf, 1988).

de Hen, P. E., *Actieve en re-actieve industriepolitiek in Nederland. De overheid en de ontwikkeling van de Nederlands industrie in de jaren dortig en tussen 1945 en 1950* (Amsterdam, 1980).

Herbst, L., *Der Totale Krieg und die Ordnung der Wirtschaft. Die Kriegswirtschaft im Spannungsfeld von Politik, Ideologie und Propaganda 1939–1945* (Stuttgart, 1982).

Hewstone, M., *Understanding Attitudes to the European Community: a Socio-Psychological Study in Four Member States* (Cambridge, 1986).

Hill, B. E., *The Common Agricultural Policy; Past, Present and Future* (London, 1984).

Hirsch, E., *Ainsi va la vie* (Lausanne, 1988).

Hoffmann, S., 'Reflections on the Nation State in Western Europe Today', *Journal of Common Market Studies*, vol. xxxi, no. 1, 1982.

Hogan, M. J., *The Marshall Plan. America, Britain, and the Reconstruction of Western Europe, 1947–1952* (Cambridge, 1987).

Hogg, R. L., *Structural Rigidities and Policy Inertia in Inter-War Belgium*, Verhandelingen van de Koninklijke Academie voor Wetenschappen, Letteren en Schone Kunsten van België, Klasse der Letteren, Jaargang 48, Nr. 118 (Brussels, 1986).

Holtfrerich, C. L. (ed.), *Interactions in the World Economy. Perspectives from International Economic History* (London, 1989).

Holtrop, M. N., *Money in an Open Economy* (Leiden, 1972).

Horsefield, J. K., *The International Monetary Fund 1945–1965*, 3 vols (Washington DC, 1969).

Howald, O., 'Agrarwirtschaftliche Zusammenarbeit in Europa', in W. Abel *et al.* (1953).

John, A., *Andreas Hermes und der Deutschen Bauernverband* (Hennef, 1978).

Johnson, H. G., 'The Gains from Freer Trade with Europe: an Estimate', *The Manchester School of Economic and Social Studies*, vol. xxvi, no. 3, 1958.

Joye, P., *Les Trusts en Belgique. La concentration capitaliste* (Brussels, 1964).

Jung, H. J., *Die Exportförderung im wirtschaftlichen Wiederaufbau der deutschen Bundesrepublik* (Cologne, 1957).

Kaiser, W., *Using Europe, Abusing the Europeans. Britain and European integration, 1945–1963* (London, 1996).

Kaldor, N., 'Conflicts in National Economic Objectives', *Economic Journal*, vol. lxxxi, no. 321, 1971.

Kaplan, J. J., and Schleiminger, G., *The European Payments Union. Financial Diplomacy in the 1950s* (Oxford, 1989).

Katzenstein, P. (ed.), *Between Power and Plenty: the Foreign Economic Policies of Advanced Industrial States* (Madison, 1978).

Kaufman, B. I., *Trade and Aid. Eisenhower's Foreign Economic Policy, 1953–1961* (Baltimore, 1982).

Keeler, J. T. S., *The Politics of Neocorporatism in France. Farmers, the State, and Agricultural Policy-Making in the Fifth Republic* (New York, 1987).

Keohane, R. O., and Hoffmann, S., 'Conclusions: Community Politics and Institutional Change', in W. Wallace (ed.), *The Dynamics of European Integration* (London, 1990).

—, and Nye, J. S., *Power and Interdependence; World Politics in Transition* (Boston, 1977).

Kettenacker, L., *Krieg zur Friedenssicherung. Die Deutschlandplanung der Britischen Regierung während des Zweiten Weltkrieges* (Göttingen, 1989).

Kindleberger, C. P., 'Germany's Persistent Balance of Payments Disequilibrium', in G. Haberler, *Trade Growth and the Balance of Payments: Essays in Honor of Gottfried Haberler* (Chicago, 1965).

—, *Europe's Postwar Growth. The Role of Labor Supply* (Cambridge, Mass., 1967).

Kitzinger, U. W., *The Politics and Economics of European Integration. Britain, Europe and the United States* (New York, 1961).

Klatzmann, J., 'La modernisation de l'agriculture', *Revue économique*, no. 5, 1953.

Kluge, U., ' "Du Pool Noir au Pool Vert", Wirtschafts-und Sozialprobleme des "Marché Commun Agricole de l'Europe" 1949–1957 aus deutscher Sicht', in E. Serra (ed.) (1989).

Knox, F., 'Some International Comparisons of Consumers' Durable Goods', *Bulletin of the Oxford University Institute of Statistics*, vol. 21, no. i, 1959.

Koch, H., *Histoire de la Banque de France et de la monnaie sous la IVième République* (Paris, 1983).

Kock, K., *International Trade Policy and the GATT, 1947–1967* (Stockholm, 1969).

Kramer, A., 'British Dismantling Politics, 1945–9', in I. D. Turner (ed.) (1989).

—, *Die britische Demontagepolitik am Beispiel Hamburgs 1945–1950* (Hamburg, 1990).

Krause, L. B., *European Economic Integration and the United States* (Washington DC, 1968).

—, 'Britain's Trade Performance', in R. E. Caves *et al.* (1968).

Kurgan-van Hentenryk, G., and Puissant, J., 'Industrial Relations in the Belgian Coal Industry since the End of the Nineteenth Century', in G. D. Feldman and K. Tenfelde (eds) (1990).

Kusters, H.-J., *Die Gründung der europäischen Wirtschaftsgemeinschaft* (Baden-Baden, 1982).

Lamfalussy, A., *Investment and Growth in Mature Economies. The Case of Belgium* (London, 1961).

—, *The United Kingdom and the Six. An Essay on Economic Growth in Western Europe* (London, 1963).

Latil, M., *L'Evolution du revenu agricole* (Paris, 1956).

van Leynseele, J., *La Politique de la betterave* (Paris, 1967).

L'Eplattenier, M., *Die Träger der internationalen Zusammenarbeit auf dem Gebiete der Landwirtschaft* (Winterthur, 1961).

Liebrücks, M., *Die technische und wirtschaftliche Entwicklung der amerikanischen Steinkohlenförderung* (Berlin, 1961).

Liesner, H. H., *The Import Dependence of Britain and Western Germany: A Comparative Study*, Princeton Studies in International Finance No. 7 (Princeton, 1957).

Lindberg, L. N., *The Political Dynamics of European Economic Integration* (Stanford, 1963).

Linthorst Homan, J., *Europese landbouwpolitiek, 2^e Rapport ingiedend bij de Europese Beweging* (Assen, 1951).

Lipgens, W., *Europa-Föderationspläne der Widerstandsbewegungen, 1940–45* (Munich, 1968).

—, *A History of European Integration, 1945–1947*, vol. 1, *The Formation of the European Unity Movement* (Oxford, 1982).

—— (ed.), *Documents on the History of European Integration*, vol. 2, *Plans for European Union in Great Britain and in Exile, 1939–45*, European University Institute Series B1.2 (Berlin, 1986).

——, and Loth, W. (eds), *Documents on the History of European Integration*, vol. 3, *The Struggle for European Union by Political Parties and Pressure Groups in Western European Countries, 1945–1950*, European University Institute Series B1.3 (Berlin, 1988).

Loth, W., *Die Teilung der Welt. Geschichte des Kalten Krieges 1941–1955* (Munich, 1980, 1989).

——, *Der Weg nach Europa. Geschichte der europäischen Integration 1939–1957* (Göttingen, 1990).

Lutz, V., *Central Planning for the Market Economy. An Analysis of the French Theory and Experience* (London, 1969).

Lynch, F. M. B., *France and the International Economy: from Vichy to the Treaty of Rome* (London, 1997).

——, 'De Gaulle's First Veto. France, the Rueff Plan and the Free Trade Area', *Contemporary European History*, vol. 9, part 1, March 2000.

McArthur, J. H., and Scott, B. R., *Industrial Planning in France* (Boston, 1969).

McCrone, G., *The Economics of Subsidizing Agriculture. A Study of British Policy* (London, 1962).

MacLennan, M. C., 'The Common Market and French Planning', *Journal of Common Market Studies*, vol. 3, 1964–5.

Maddison, A., *Economic Growth in the West. Comparative Experience in Europe and North America* (New York, 1964).

——, 'Economic Policy and Performance in Europe', in C. M. Cipolla (ed.), *The Fontana Economic History of Europe*, vol. 5 (London, 1976).

——, 'Origins and Impact of the Welfare State, 1883–1983', *Banca Nazionale del Lavoro Quarterly Review*, vol. 37, no. 184, 1984.

——, *Dynamic Forces in Capitalist Development. A Long-Run Comparative View* (Oxford, 1991).

Maier, C. S., 'The Politics of Productivity: Foundations of American International Economic Policy after World War II', in P. Katzenstein (ed.) (1978).

——, *In Search of Stability. Explorations in Historical Political Economy* (Cambridge, Mass., 1987).

Maizels, A., 'Trends in World Trade in Durable Consumer Goods', *National Institute Economic Review*, November 1959.

——, *Industrial Growth and World Trade* (Cambridge, 1963).

Malgren. H. B., and Scheckty, D. L., 'Technology and Neo-Mercantilism in International Agricultural Trade', *American Journal of Agricultural Economics*, no. 1326, 1969.

Marchal, G., 'Bilan énergétique de la Belgique. Année 1950', *Annales des Mines de Belgique*, 6, 1952.

Marciani, G. E., *Andamenti e linee evolutive delle produzione agricole 1951–1981* (Milan, 1972).

Marcy, G., 'Libération progressive des échanges et aide a l'exportation en France depuis 1949,' in *Cahiers de l'Institut de Science Economique Appliquée*, série P, no. 2, no. 81, May 1959.

Marjolin, R., *Le Travail d'une vie; Mémoires 1911–1986* (Paris, 1986).

Markus, J., 'Some Observations on the West German Trade Surplus', *Oxford Economic Papers*, vol. xvii, no. 1, 1965.

Martens, J., 'Evolution du droit minier et certains aspects de l'industrie charbonnière belge', *Annales des Mines de Belgique*, December 1950, September 1951.

Martin, B., and Milward, A. S. (eds), *Agriculture and Food Supply in the Second World War* (Ostfildern, 1985).

Massigli, R., *Une Comédie des erreurs 1943–1956* (Paris, 1978).

Matthews, R. C. O., 'Why Has Britain Had Full Employment since the War?', *Economic Journal*, no. 78, 1968.

Maurer, P., *Anbauschlacht. Landwirtschaftspolitik, Plan Wahlen, Anbauwerk 1937–1945* (Zürich, 1985).

Maxcy, G., and Silberston, A., *The Motor Industry* (London, 1959).

Meade, J. E., Liesner, H. H., and Wells, S. J., *Case Studies in European Economic Union. The Mechanics of Integration* (London, 1962).

Melandri, P., *Les Etats-Unis et le 'défi' européen, 1955–1958* (Paris, 1975).

Meyers, A., 'Aspects techniques de l'exploitation charbonnière belge en 1954', *Annales des Mines de Belgique*, no. 1, January, 1956.

Meynaud, J., Ladrière, J., and Pepin. F., *La Décision politique en Belgique* (Paris, 1965).

Michalski, W., *Export–und Wirtschaftswachstum. Schlussfolgerungen aus der Nachkriegsentwicklung in der Bundesrepublik Deutschland* (Hamburg, 1972).

Miller, M., and Spencer, J., 'The Static Economic Effect of the UK Joining the EEC: a General Equilibrium Approach', *Review of Economic Studies*, vol. xliv (1), 1977.

Milward, A. S., 'Tariffs as Constitutions', in S. Strange and R. Tooze (eds), *The Management of Surplus Capacity* (London, 1981).

——, *The Reconstruction of Western Europe, 1945–1952* (London, 1984).

——, 'The Belgian Coal and Steel Industries and the Schuman Plan', in K. Schwabe (ed.) (1988).

——, 'Motives for Currency Convertibility: the Pound and the Deutschmark, 1950–5', in C. L. Holtfrerich (ed.) (1989).

——, 'A Comparison of Spanish and Italian Trade with Western Europe in the 1950s', in L. Prados de la Escosura (ed.) (1991).

——, 'The Marshall Plan and German Foreign Trade', in C. Maier (ed.), *The Marshall Plan and Germany. West German Development within the Framework of the European Recovery Program* (Oxford, 1991).

——, and Brennan, G., *Britain's Place in the World. A Historical Enquiry into Import Controls 1945–60* (London, 1996).

Mioche, P., 'Aux origines du Plan Monnet: les discours et les contenus dans les premiers plans français (1941–1947)', *Revue historique*, no. 265, 1981.

——, *Le Plan Monnet. Genèse et élaboration 1941–1947* (Paris, 1987).

——, 'Le Patronat de la sidérurgie française et le Plan Schuman en 1950–1952: les apparences d'un combat et la réalité d'une mutation', in K. Schwabe (ed.) (1988).

Mitchell, B. R., *European Historical Statistics 1950–1970* (London, 1975).

van Molle, L., 'Le milieu agricole belge face à la "concurrence européenne" 1944–1958', in M. Dumoulin (ed.) (1987).

Mommens, T., 'Agricultural Integration in the Benelux', in R. T. Griffiths (ed.) (1990).

Monnet, J., *Memoirs* (London, 1978).

Müller, G., 'Sicherheit durch wirtschaftliche Stabilität? Die Rolle der Briten bei der Auseinandersetzung der Allierten um die Stahlquote des ersten Industrieniveauplans vom 26 März 1946', in D. Petzina and W. Euchner (eds) (1984).

Müller-Armack, A., 'Fragen der europäischen Integration', in E. von Beckerath *et al.* (1957).

——, *Wirtschaftsordnung und Wirtschaftspolitik* (Freiburg im Breisgau, 1966).

——, *Auf dem Wege nach Europa. Erinnerungen und Ausblicke* (Tübingen, 1971).

Murray, K. A. H., *Agriculture*, Official History of the British Economy in the Second World War (London, 1955).

Myrdal, A., and Myrdal, G., *Kris i befolkningsfrågan* (Stockholm, 1934).
Nash, E. F., 'The Competitive Position of British Agriculture', *Journal of Agricultural Economics*, vol. xi, no. 3, 1955.
——, and Attwood, E. A., *The Agricultural Policies of Britain and Denmark; A Study in Reciprocal Trade* (London, 1961).
Newton, S., and Porter, D., *Modernization Frustrated. The Politics of Industrial Decline in Britain Since 1900* (London, 1988).
Niehaus, H., and Priebe, H., *Agrarpolitik in der sozialen Marktwirtschaft* (Ludwigsburg, 1956).
Noel, G., 'Les tentatives de communauté agricole européenne entre 1945 et 1955' (Thèse de doctorat, Faculté de droit et des Sciences économiques, université de Nancy-II, 1982).
——, *Du Pool Vert à la politique Agricole Commune. Les tentatives de communauté agricole européenne entre 1945 et 1955* (Paris, 1988).
——, 'Le Congrès d'Agriculture de Munich 1949: échec d'une initiative "européenne" ', *Revue historique*, no. 266, 1981.
Olsson, U., 'Planning in the Swedish Welfare State', *Studies in Political Economy*, vol. 34, 1991.
Oury, B., *L'Agriculture au seuil du marché commun* (Paris, 1959).
Owen, N., *Economies of Scale, Competitiveness, and Trade Patterns within the European Community* (Oxford, 1983).
la Palombara, J., *Interest Groups in Italian Politics* (Princeton, 1964).
Pastorelli, P., *La politica estera italiana del dopoguerra* (Milan, 1987).
Patterson, G., *Discrimination in International Trade. The Policy Issues 1945–1965* (Princeton, 1960).
Peden, G., *Keynes, The Treasury and British Economic Policy* (London, 1988).
Petzina, D., and Euchner, W. (eds), *Wirtschaftspolitik im Britischen Besatzungsgebiet 1945–1949* (Düsseldorf, 1984).
Pflimlin, P., and Legrand-Lane, R., *L'Europe Communautaire* (Paris, 1966).
Pimlott, B. (ed.), *The Second World War Diary of Hugh Dalton 1940–1945* (London, 1986).
Pistone, S., 'Il ruolo di Alcide de Gasperi e di Altiero Spinelli nella genesi dell'art. 38 della CED', paper delivered to the conference, 'La Construction de l'Europe du Plan Schuman aux Traités de Rome' (Luxembourg, 1990).
Poidevin, R., *Robert Schuman; Homme d'état* (Paris, 1986).
—— (ed.), *Histoire des débuts de la construction européenne mars 1949–mai 1950* (Brussels, 1986).
Polk, J., *Sterling: Its Meaning in World Finance* (New York, 1956).
Pollard, S., *The Integration of the European Economy since 1815* (London, 1981).
——, *The Wasting of the British Economy: British Economic Policy 1945 to the Present* (London, 1982).
Posthuma, S., 'Note on Convertibility', *Economia Internazionale*, vol. 6, no. 3, 1953.
Prados de la Escosura, L., and Zamagni, V. (eds), *El desarrollo económico en la Europa del Sur: España e Italia en perspectiva histórica* (Madrid, 1992).
Prais, S. J., *et al.*, *Productivity and Industrial Structure; a Statistical Study of Manufacturing Industry in Britain, Germany and the United States* (Cambridge, 1981).
Pressnell, L. S., *External Economic Policy since the War*, vol. 1, *The Post-War Financial Settlement* (London, 1986).
Ranieri, R., 'La siderurgica italiana e gli inizi dell'integrazione europeo', *Passato e presente*, no. 7, 1985.
Ratchford, B. U., and Ross, W. D., *Berlin Reparations Assignment* (Chapel Hill, 1947).
Rees, G. L., *Britain and the Postwar European Payments System* (Cardiff, 1963).

Reich, S., *The Fruits of Fascism. Postwar Prosperity in Historical Perspective* (Ithaca, 1990).

Reichardt, F., *Andreas Hermes* (Neuwied-am-Rhein, 1953).

Reynaud, P., *S'Unir ou périr* (Paris, 1951).

——, *La Politique étrangère du Gaullisme* (Paris, 1964).

Rhys, D. G., *The Motor Industry. An Economic Survey* (London, 1972).

Riley, R. C., 'Recent Developments in the Belgian Borinage. An Area of Declining Coal Production in the European Coal and Steel Community', *Geography*, vol. 50, part 3, 1965.

Ritschl, A., 'Die Währungsreform und der Wiederaufstieg der deutschen Industrie', in *Vierteljahrshefte für Zeitgeschichte*, Bd. 33, Heft i, 1975.

Robertson, A. D., *Dutch Organized Agriculture in International Politics 1945–1960* (The Hague, 1981).

Robinson, A., 'The Economic Problems of the Transition from War to Peace: 1945–49', *Cambridge Journal of Economics*, vol. 10, 1986.

Roeper, H., *Die D-Mark* (Frankfurt-am-Main, 1978).

Rogge, K., Jnr. and Schubert, W., *Die Zuckerwirtschaft der Benelux*, Marktforschungsstelle Zucker, Bd. 31–2, September 1959.

Rollings, N., 'British Budgetary Policy, 1945–1954, a "Keynesian Revolution"?', *Economic History Review*, vol. xli, 1988.

Romero, F., *Gli Stati Uniti e il sindicalismo europeo, 1944–1951* (Rome, 1989).

Rosecrance, R., *et al.*, 'Whither Interdependence?', *International Organization*, vol. 31, 1977.

Rossi, E., *Viaggio nel feudo di Bonomi* (Rome, 1965).

Schaad, M., 'Plan G – a Counterblast? British Policy towards the Messina Countries, 1956', *Contemporary European History*, vol. 7, part 1, March 1998.

Schenk, C. R., *Britain and the Sterling Area. From Devaluation to Convertibility in the 1950s* (London, 1994).

——, 'Decolonization and European Integration: the Free Trade Area Negotiations 1956–58', *Journal of Imperial and Commonwealth History*, vol. 24, no. 3, September 1996.

Schmidt, H. G., *Food and Agricultural Programs in West Germany 1949–1951*, Historical Division, Office of the Executive Secretary, US High Commissioner for Germany (Bonn, 1952).

Schmitt, M., *Das deutsche Dollarproblem* (Frankfurt-am-Main, 1953).

Schuman, R., 'French Foreign Policy Towards Germany since the War', Stevenson Memorial Lecture no. 4, Royal Institute of International Affairs, London, October 1953.

——, *Pour l'Europe* (Paris, 1963).

Schwabe, K., (ed.), *Die Anfänge des Schuman Plans 1950/51* (Baden-Baden, 1988).

Schwarz, H.-P., *Adenauer, Der Aufstieg 1876–1952* (Stuttgart, 1986).

Scitovsky, T., *Economic Theory and Western European Integration* (London, 1958).

Seers, D., *Changes in the Cost of Living and the Distribution of Income since 1938* (Oxford, 1949).

Segré, C., 'Medium-Term Export Finance. European Problems and Experiences', *Banca Nazionale del Lavoro Quarterly Review*, no. 11, 1958.

Self, P., and Storing, H. J., *The State and the Farmer* (London, 1962).

Serra, E., 'L'unione doganale italo–francese e la Conferenza di Santa Margherita (1947–1951)', in J. B. Duroselle and E. Serra (eds) (1988).

——, (ed.), *Il Rilancio dell'Europa e i Trattati di Roma* (Brussels, 1989).

Sexter, D. A., 'The Belgian coal mines in the European Coal and Steel Community' (Ph.D. Dissertation, University of California, Davis, 1969).

Sforza, C., *Europe and the Europeans: A Study in Historical Psychology and International Politics* (London, 1936).

——, *Fifty Years of War and Diplomacy in the Balkans: Paschich and the Union of the Yugoslavs* (New York, 1940).

Shonfield, A., *British Economic Policy since the War* (London, 1958).

——, *Modern Capitalism. The Changing Balance of Public and Private Power* (London, 1965).

Smets, P.-F. (ed.), *La Pensée européenne et atlantique de Paul-Henri Spaak* (Brussels, 1981).

Snoy et d'Oppuers, J. C., 'Le rôle du Bénélux dans la relance européenne en 1955', in *Belgische buitenlands beleid en internationale betrekkingen. Liber Amicorum Prof. Omer de Roeymaker* (Leuven, 1978).

Spaak, P.-H., *Combats inachevés*, 2 vols (Paris, 1969).

Stikker, D. U., *Memoires. Herinneringen uit de lange jaren waarin ik betrokken was bij de voortdurende wereldcrisis* (The Hague, 1966).

Sunou, P., *Les Prisonniers de guerre allemands en Belgique et la bataille du charbon, 1945–1947* (Brussels, 1980).

Tholl, G., *Die Luxemburger Agrarpolitik in der Nachkriegszeit (1945–1959) und ihre ordnungspolitische Problematik* (Dissertation, Diplom-Volkswirt, Bonn, 1963).

Thorbecke, E., *The Tendency Towards Regionalization in International Trade* (The Hague, 1960).

Tollison, D., and Willett, T. D., 'International Integration and the Interdependence of Economic Variables', *International Organization*, vol. 27, 1973.

Tomlinson, J., 'Why was there never a Keynesian Revolution in Economic Policy?', *Economy and Society*, vol. 10, 1981.

Tracy, M., *Agriculture in Western Europe. Challenge and Response 1880–1980* (2nd edn, London, 1982).

Tremelloni, R., 'The Italian Long-Term Program Submitted to the OEEC', *Banca Nazionale del Lavoro Quarterly Review*, vol. ii, no. 8, 1949.

Triffin, R., *Europe and the Money Muddle* (New Haven, 1957).

Turner, H. A., Clack, G., and Roberts, G. *Labour Relations in the Motor Industry* (London, 1967).

Turner, I. D. (ed.), *Reconstruction in Post-war Germany. British Occupation Policy and the Western Zones 1945–1955* (London, 1989).

Tyszynski, H., 'World Trade in Manufactured Commodities, 1899–1950', *The Manchester School of Economic and Social Studies*, vol. 19, 1951.

Unga, N., *Socialdemokratin och arbetslöshetsfrågan 1912–1934. Framväxten av den 'nya' arbetslöshetspolitiken* (Stockholm, 1976).

Université Libre de Bruxelles, Institut de Sociologie, *Les Régions du Borinage et du Centre a l'heure de la réconversion* (Brussels, 1962).

Verdoorn, P. J., 'Welke zijn de achtergronden en vooruitzichten van de economische integratie in Europa, en welke gevolgen zal deze integratie hebben, met name voor de welvaart in Nederland?', in Netherlands, Vereeniging voor de Staathuishoudkunde, *Prae-Adviezen*, 1952.

——, and Meyer zu Schlochten, F. J. M., 'Trade Diversion and Trade Creation in the Common Market', in Netherlands, Central Planning Bureau, *Reprint Series*, no. 93 (The Hague, 1965).

Vernant, J., 'L'économie française devant la C.E.D.', in R. Aron and D. Lerner (eds) (1956).

Vinck, F., 'Le Problème charbonnier', in Université Libre de Bruxelles, Institut de Sociologie (1962).

Viner, J., *The Customs Union Issue* (New York, 1950).

Wallace, W. (ed.), *The Dynamics of European Integration* (London, 1990).

Wallich, H. C., *Mainsprings of the German Revival* (New Haven, 1955).

Walter, I., *The European Common Market. Growth and Patterns of Trade and Production* (New York, 1967).

Warner, I., 'Allied–German Negotiations on the Deconcentration of the West German Steel Industry', in I. D. Turner (ed.) (1989).

van der Wee, H., *Prosperity and Upheaval. The World Economy 1945–1980* (London, 1986).

Weilemann, P., *Die Anfänge der Europäischen Atomgemeinschaft. Zur Gründungsgeschichte von Euratom 1955–1957* (Baden-Baden, 1983).

——, 'Die deutsche Haltung während der Euratom-Verhandlungen', in E. Serra (ed.) (1989).

Weiller, J., 'Relations commerciales et financières de la France au cours de la reprise des années 1952 à 1956', *Cahiers de l'I.S.E.A.*, P9, no. 145, January 1964.

Wemelsfelder, J., 'The Short-Term Effect of the Lowering of Import Duties in Germany', *Economic Journal*, vol. lxx, no. 277, 1960.

Wendt, B. J., *Economic Appeasement. Handel und Finanzen in der Britischen Deutschlandpolitik, 1933–1939* (Düsseldorf, 1971).

Whetham, E., *British Farming 1939–1945* (London, 1952).

Wiel, P., *Untersuchungen zu den Kosten-und Marktproblemen der westeuropäischen Kohlenwirtschaft* (Essen, 1953).

Wielenga, F., *West-Duitsland, Partner uit Noodzak. Nederland en de Bondsrepubliek 1949–1955* (Utrecht, 1989).

Williams, P. M. (ed.), *The Diary of Hugh Gaitskell 1945–1956* (London, 1983).

Williamson, J., and Bottrill, A., 'The Impact of Customs Unions on Trade in Manufactures', *Oxford Economic Papers*, vol. xxiii, no. 3, 1971.

Wintle, M. (ed.), *Modern Dutch Studies. Essays in Honour of Professor P. King* (London, 1988).

Wood, J., *Wheels of Misfortune; The Rise and Fall of the British Motor Industry* (London, 1988).

Wright, G., 'Agrarian Syndicalism in Postwar France', *American Political Science Review*, vol. xlvii, no. 2, 1953.

——, *Rural Revolution in France* (Stanford, 1964).

Young, J. W., *Britain, France and the Unity of Europe 1945–1951* (Leicester, 1984).

——, ' "The Parting of the Ways"? Britain, the Messina Conference and the Spaak Committee, June-December 1955', in M. Dockrill and J. W. Young, *British Foreign Policy 1945–56* (London, 1989).

Zamagni, V., 'Betting on the Future. The Reconstruction of Italian Industry, 1946–1952', in J. Becker and F. Knipping (eds) (1986).

van Zanden, J. L., and Griffiths, R. T., *Economische geschiedenis van Nederland in de 20ᵉ eeuw* (The Hague, 1989).

Zassenhaus, H. K., 'Direct Effects of a United States Recession on Imports', *Review of Economics and Statistics*, vol. xxxvii, no. 3, 1955.

van Zeeland, P., *Regards sur l'Europe 1932* (Brussels, 1933).

——, *La Crise de l'étalon-or: confrontation de sa forme classique avec les méthodes et les buts de l'économie contemporaine* (Paris, 1935).

——, *Revision de valeurs: essai de synthèse sur certains problèmes fondamentaux de l'économie contemporaine et leurs réactions politiques* (Paris, 1937).

——, *Devant la crise mondiale: manifeste de catholiques européens séjournant en Amérique* (New York, 1942).

——, *Belgique et occident européen: conférence prononcé le 15 octobre 1945* (Paris, 1945).

Index